STUDIES IN
AMERICAN SOCIOLOGY
UNDER
THE GENERAL EDITORSHIP OF
STANFORD M. LYMAN

VOLUME V

Postmodernism and a Sociology of the Absurd And Other Essays on the "Nouvelle Vague" in American Social Science

Stanford M. Lyman

The University of Arkansas Press

Fayetteville 1997

HM
73
.L95
1997

Library of Congress Cataloging-in-Publication Data

Lyman, Stanford M.
    Postmodernism and a sociology of the absurd and other essays on the "nouvelle
vague" in American social science / Stanford M. Lyman.
        p.   cm. — (Studies in American sociology ; v. 5)
    Includes bibliographical references and index.
    ISBN 1-55728-453-9 (alk. paper)
        1. Postmodernism—Social aspects. 2. Sociology—Philosophy. 3. Structuralism.
I. Title II. Series
HM73.L95   1997
301'.01—dc21   96-50984
                                                                              CIP

To Marvin B. Scott
colleague, critic, friend,
fellow sociologist of the absurd

ACKNOWLEDGMENTS

Portions of the argument of this book were presented at the following roundtables, academic conventions, convocation lectures, colloquia, and meetings of professional associations:

"Postmodernism and a Sociology of the Absurd," paper presented at the annual meeting of the Society for the Study of Symbolic Interaction, Washington, D.C., August 20–21, 1995, to be published in Jonathon S. Epstein, ed., *Wilderness of Mirrors: Symbolic Interaction and the Postmodern Terrain* (New York: Garland Publishing Co., 1996). Reprinted by permission of Garland Publishing Company.

"History and Sociology: Some Unresolved Epistemological Issues," plenary address presented to the Southwest Sociological Association Annual Meeting, Dallas, Texas, March 1995, published in the *International Journal of Politics, Culture, and Society,* 9:1 (fall 1995): pp. 29–55. Reprinted by permission of Human Sciences Press, Plenum Publishing Corporation.

"Interstate Relations and the Sociological Imagination Revisited: From Social Distance to Territoriality." Inaugural Alpha Kappa Delta Distinguished Lecture, presented at the American Sociological Association Annual Meeting, Los Angeles, California, August 8, 1994, published in *Sociological Inquiry* 65:2 (May 1995): pp. 125–42. Reprinted by permission of the University of Texas Press.

"Postmodernism and the Race Question: The Problem of Alterity," paper presented at the annual meeting of the Southern Sociological Society, Atlanta, Georgia, April 1995.

"The Race Question and Liberalism: Casuistries in American Constitutional Law," *International Journal of Politics, Culture, and Society* 5:2 (winter 1991): pp. 183–247. Reprinted by permission of Human Sciences Press, Plenum Publishing Corporation.

"The Chinese before the Courts: A Prolegomenon to a Study of Ethnoracial Construction and Marginalization," revised version of a paper presented at the American Sociological Association Annual Meeting, Pittsburgh, Pennsylvania, August 20–24, 1992, and published in slightly different form in Munson A. Kwok et al., eds., *Origins and Destinations: Forty-one Essays on Chinese America* (Los Angeles: Chinese Historical Society of Southern California and UCLA Asian American Studies Center, 1994), pp. 41–70. Reprinted by permission of the UCLA Asian American Studies Center.

"The Assimilation-Pluralism Debate: Toward a Postmodern Resolution of the American Ethnoracial Dilemma," *International Journal of Politics, Culture, and Society* 6:2 (winter 1992): pp. 181–210. Reprinted by permission of Human Sciences Press, Plenum Publishing Corporation.

"Anhedonia: Gender and the Decline of Emotions in American Film, 1930–1988," paper presented at the Eighty-third Annual Meeting of the American Sociological Association, Atlanta, Georgia, August 24–28, 1988, and published in abridged form in *Sociological Inquiry* 60:1 (February 1990): pp. 1–19. Reprinted by permission of the University of Texas Press.

"Without Morals or Mores: Deviance in Postmodern Social Theory," revised version of a paper entitled "Postmodernism, Deviance, and a Sociology of the Absurd," presented at the annual meeting of the Mid-South Sociological Association, Mobile, Alabama, October 1995, and published in *International Journal of Politics, Culture, and Society* 9.2 (winter 1995): pp. 197–236. Reprinted by permission of Human Sciences Press, Plenum Publishing Corporation.

"The Bequests of the Twentieth-Century Sociology to the Twenty-first Century," presidential address, presented at the Mid-South Sociological Association Annual Meeting, Lafayette, Louisiana, October 26–29, 1994, published in *Sociological Spectrum* 15:3 (1995): pp. 209–25. Reprinted by permission of Taylor and Francis, © 1995.

"Animal Faith, Puritanism, and the Schutz-Gurwitsch Debate," revised version of a commentary on Steven Vaitkus, "Multiple Realities in Santayana's *Last Puritan*" and on Elizabeth Suzanne Kassab, "'Paramount Reality' in Schutz and Gurwitsch," presented at the Alfred Schutz Memorial Symposium in commemoration of Alfred Schutz's ninetieth birthday and the publication of the Schutz-Gurwitsch Letters, New School for Social Research, New York City, November 30–December 1, 1989. Published in *Human Studies: A Journal for Philosophy and the Social Sciences* 14:2–3 (July 1991): pp. 199–206. Reprinted by permission of Kluwer Academic Publishers.

"The Drama in the Routine: A Prolegomenon to a Praxiological Sociology," paper presented at the conference on "Writing the Social Text," University of Maryland at College Park, November 18–19, 1989, published in *Social Theory*, 8:2 (fall 1990): pp. 217–23. Reprinted by permission of the publishers.

* * *

Without the sustained, critical, and constructive advice of Marvin B. Scott, as well as his warm support for the project, this book would not have been completed. I am also indebted for how much I learned from the many conversations on this and related topics over the years with Patti Adler, Peter Adler, David Altheide, Valerie Malhotra Bentz, Joel Best, Richard Harvey Brown, Patricia Clough, Randall Collins, the late Carl Couch, Donna K. Darden, the late Fred Davis, Norman K. Denzin, Carolyn Ellis, Lester Embree, Jonathon Epstein, Arthur Evans, Franco Ferrarotti, Gary Alan Fine, Andrea Fontana, David Franks, the late Erving Goffman, Cecil Greek, Mark Gottdiener, Rom Harrè, Herbert Hill, Roscoe Hinkle, Gisela Hinkle, Michael Hughey, Robert Jackall, Gary Jaworski, John M. Johnson, Tetsuden Kashima, Joseph Kotarba, Paul Leslie, James Liu, Helena Lopata, Mary Lydon, David Maines, Peter K. Manning, George J. McCall, E. Doyle McCarthy, Mari J. Molseed, Guy Oakes, Virginia Olesen, C. Eddie Palmer, Robert Prus, Laurel Richardson, Adam Seligman, Dmitri Shalin, Stephen Park Turner, Arthur J. Vidich, Andrew J. Weigert, Jacqueline Wiseman, and Charlotte Wolf. A special word of thanks is owed to my sister, Sylvia, for presenting me with a copy of *The Zen Teaching of Huang Po,* a work that enlightens all who read it seriously.

Funded in part by the Florida Atlantic University Foundation and the work-study program, my research assistants, Stanley Tang, Connie Tang, Eiji Murai, and Jamie McCluskie, have searched out hundreds of items central to the project reported in this book. The word processing of the manuscript has been carried out by Joan Schilling and Charlotte Steinberg, to each of whom I owe much for putting up with, and deciphering the scribblings of, my premodern word processor, a pencil. The index has been prepared by Mr. John J. Huckle. Once again, the editors and staff of the University of Arkansas Press have served the series of which this volume is a part with excellence in manuscript styling, proofreading, artistic design, and marketing. For all errors, I take full responsibility.

Horizons are the absolute presupposition within which individuals and indeed whole civilizations do their living . . . But what a burden falls upon the will when the horizons of definition are gone.
  George Grant, Time as History

And so we come to the end, barbarism replaces culture . . . The life of the mind has quietly moved out of the way, making room for the terrible and pathetic encounter of the fanatic and the zombie.
  Alain Finkielkraut, The Defeat of the Mind

If it is a myth to believe that life is meaningful and valuable, then it is a myth that we cannot afford not to have.
  Shu-hsien Liu "Toward a New Relation between Humanity and Nature: Reconstructing t'ien-jen-ho-i"

CONTENTS

Part I

Introduction

Introduction

Enlightenment springs from Mind . . . You cannot place a head upon your head, or lips upon your lips; rather, you should just refrain from every kind of dualistic distinction. Hills are hills. Water is water. Monks are monks. Laymen are laymen. But these mountains, these rivers, the whole world itself, together with sun, moon and stars—not one of them exists outside your minds! The vast chiliocosm exists only within you, so where else can the various categories of phenomena possibly be found?
The Zen Teaching of Huang Po

Recently, a storm of protest and a tidal wave of thought have blown across the Atlantic and struck the shores of American social science. The flood threatens to crash through the latter's epistemological dikes and, in a deluge of de[con]struction, drown the established traditions of Western thought, overwhelm its legacy of social and political praxes, and send its foundational values to the bottom of a newly created Occidental sea of dross.[1] Like the hurricanes that annually threaten the eastern coast of the United States, this *tsunami* has a name.[2] It is called *postmodernism*. And just as storms have their beginnings in meteorological changes in the weather system, so postmodernism has its immediate beginnings in the sudden shifts in the political and social weather of the 1960s, changes, however, that might have been brewing in the Western world's cultural atmosphere for centuries.

In its boldest presentation of itself, postmodernism proposes that social scientists discard both the intellectual foundations of knowledge and the political theory of freedom. Each is regarded as a weathered but no longer sustainable strand of an allegedly "obsolete theory of science and . . . a decrepit theory of power"[3] that derives from the Enlightenment. Whereas Peter Gay, a modernist historian of the Enlightenment, insists that the French "*philosophes* . . . believed in the cultivation of the classics, . . . were active in humanitarian causes, and in the widest philosophical sense, . . .

placed man in the center of their moral universe"[4] and that, as a movement, the Enlightenment's precepts of reasonableness, humanity, and secularism spread across eighteenth-century Europe and into the American colonies, becoming embedded in thought and praxis, uniting an otherwise disparate body of cosmopolitan intellectuals "in their single-minded praise of criticism,"[5] Jean-Francois Lyotard, a leading postmodernist, holds that the emancipatory thrust of the Enlightenment commitment to critique has exhausted itself. He observes that "The oldest and most all-encompassing Western grand narrative, Christianity, stopped shaping the social, political, economic, and cultural institutions of Western communities long ago," while "Marxism, the last shoot stemming from both the Enlightenment and Christianity, seems to have lost all of its critical power."[6]

Absent a foundation for critique, the function of the Enlightenment's *manceps*—that is, the one who takes hold, the emancipator, the bringer of critical light—has eroded.[7] "The 'intellectuals' who made up the *Aufklärer* and their nineteenth-century heirs thought that propagating education would strengthen the freedom of the citizen, would get rid of political sectarianism, would hinder wars," Lyotard writes in a lamentation for what he regards as a grand illusion. "Today," he goes on, "no one expects teaching, which is discredited everywhere, to train more enlightened citizens—only professionals who perform better."[8] Hence, the argument runs, evil has been liberated from its erstwhile restraints and runs rampant. "We can no longer speak Evil," observes Jean Baudrillard,[9] another of the quartet of French postmodernists—the other two are Jacques Derrida and Michel Foucault, about whom more infra—who deny the efficacy or denounce the effects of the Enlightenment. "All we can do," Baudrillard complains, "is discourse on the rights of man—a discourse which is pious, weak, useless and hypocritical, its supposed value deriving from the Enlightenment belief in a natural attraction to the Good ... What is more, even this Good *qua* ideal value is invariably deployed in a self-defensive, austerity-loving, negative and reactive mode."[10] In sum, in the words of Barry Smart, the postmodernists believe that "Our explanations, assumptions and values, along with the grand narratives of liberalism and socialism which derive from that complex eighteenth-century configuration known as 'The Enlightenment,' are found wanting when we try to make sense of contemporary conditions."[11]

In America, some sociologists have set sail on the flood tide of postmodernism, seeking to navigate its treacherous waters and to steer a course toward a new kind of humanism, one devoid of the "terror" that both Lyotard and Baudrillard claim is the legacy of the last two centuries' degradation of the moral but illusory message of the Enlightenment. "Kant . . . knew," Lyotard has written, "that the price to pay for such an illusion is terror." And, he goes on to assert, "The nineteenth and twentieth centuries have given us as much terror as we can take."[12] Baudrillard, moreover, goes even further, linking a ubiquitous terror to the Occident's distorted uses of power. "Terrorism in all its forms is the transpolitical mirror of evil . . . The force of anathema and the power of speaking Evil are no longer ours . . . For power exists solely by virtue of its symbolic ability to designate the Other, the Enemy, what is at stake, what threatens us, what is Evil."[13] But, while Baudrillard offers up a "necrospective" on the coming *fin de siècle*,[14] Lyotard turns his critique into an epistemological *casus belli*: "Let us," he proposes, "wage a war on totality; let us be witnesses to the unpresentable; let us activate the differences and save the honor of the name."[15] American postmodernists have, for the most part, accepted all too uncritically the critique of the Enlightenment spelled out in the writings of Lyotard[16] and Baudrillard,[17] adding to it both the Enlightenment-undermining, post-Saussurean linguistic theses of Derrida that disconnect signifiers from that which is signified and relate language to power and power to hegemony,[18] and the archaeological-political critique of Occidental discursive practices with respect to madness, imprisonment, and sexuality offered by Foucault, who treats them as rationales of subjugation and sources for an epistemological tyranny over intellect.[19] In effect, the postmodern sociologists—as well as some existential, phenomenological, and symbolic interactionist sociologists who, like the author of this volume, have chosen to surveil the roiling epistemological waters—treat modernity, or, at any rate, the postmodern conception of it, to borrow an apt term from Perry Anderson, as a zone of engagement.[20] It is also the case that positivists,[21] Marxists,[22] and functionalists[23] have entered the maelstrom that has so recently appeared. But, for the most part, they seek to defend positions that have been attacked by both modernists and postmodernists, and sometimes lump their opponents into a single category associated with a hostility to science, for example, as antinaturalists.[24]

Postmodern sociologists are participants in and critics of their own discipline. Of course, they are not the first insiders to take up this role. But, unlike their predecessors, most take their point of departure from the critique of the Enlightenment and modernity offered by Lyotard and Baudrillard, or in relation to a post facto claim that the postmodern flood has already inundated the epistemological, moral, cultural, social, political, and intellectual landscapes, requiring recognition and empathic response.[25]

Although postmodern sociologists in America perceive themselves as an embattled minority,[26] they also arrogate to themselves a higher morality, one derived, though this often goes unacknowledged, from the *carpe diem* politics of intellectual engagement put forward by Walter Benjamin.[27] Hence, present-day postmodernists seek to inaugurate a new form (or, perhaps, an antiform) for social science, one that will correlate to their claim that there has already taken place "an epochal shift or break from modernity involving the emergence of a new social totality with its own distinct organizing principles."[28] That (anti) form, so some of its advocates claim, could have an effect on sociological discourse like that of Arnold Schönberg's breaking of the Occidental scale in music, that is, it could open its representational practices to the rhetorics of hitherto unheard voices.[29]

Despite, or, perhaps, because the voicing of a polyphonic dissatisfaction with the central paradigms of sociology—that is, the domination of the discipline by functionalist and positivist perspectives—had reached what sounded like a cacophonic crescendo in the 1970s,[30] the later American postmodernist sociologists contextualized and sought to distinguish their position from what they took to be "the erosion of the triple dogma modernism/modernity/avantgardism" by focusing on the problem of "Otherness" and the continuing marginalization of those groups and individuals designated as members of the "Other."[31] That the "Other" had remained an "Other" was often seen as an outcome of the processes whereby the Age of Reason had been reduced to and vulgarized as the modern era of instrumental rationality and virtually limitless rationalization.[32] Indeed, for this and related reasons, the writings of Max Weber on this topic have been reconceived;[33] no longer seen as the principal prophet of the West's "iron cage," Weber's life as well as his *oeuvre* have become a catalog of the doleful effects of rationalization and a basis for the postmodern call to resist them.[34]

The groups perceived as constituting the "Other" are women; ethnoracial minorities; non-white, non-Anglo members of post-colonial societies and states; and homosexuals. Each is treated as a social and sociological entity that has been the victim of the Occident's subject/subjugation paradox. The *Shoah* is perhaps the paradigmatic foreshadowing case. For, as Julian Pefanis, drawing on the work of Pierre Clastres,[35] reminds us, "The genocide of the European Jews . . . was the logical result of a racism which was allowed to develop freely. That the ends or the goals of this enterprise were irrational or paranoiac should not prevent the recognition of such a system as the quintessence of rationality, defined in terms of the organization and administration of state power."[36] In this formulation of the matter, the destruction of the European Jews embodied the dark side of rationality, the Enlightenment's teleological endpoint: "Instrumental reason at the service of humanity, authorized by the people (Volk), is crossed, double-crossed by the signs of its historical failure: Dachau and Auschwitz."[37] The same might be said—indeed, has been said—about the decision to drop the atomic bombs on Hiroshima and Nagasaki.[38]

Postmodernists tend to focus on three interrelated topics for investigation and critique:[39] (1) the necessity of giving a privileged voice to women as well as to other marginalized peoples;[40] (2) a humanistic social science that will decolonize both the imagination and the subject;[41] and (3) a tripartite sociology that will overcome the methodological primitivism that still limits the use and contributes to the abuse of participant-observation,[42] will destigmatize the "deviant,"[43] and will provide for an ethic of humane justice.[44] A number of studies have been carried out in each of these areas. A few examples will illustrate the character and direction of these investigations. Dorothy Smith has formulated a feminist sociology that gives voice to "woman" by locating "a subject outside the textually mediated discourse of sociology; . . . in her own life, in her self as a unitary being, as a body active, imagining, thinking, as a *subject situated in her local and particular actualities.*"[45] Homi K. Bhabha's own migratory wanderings over the earth, coupled with his appropriation of some of Derrida's "wit and wisdom," have allowed him to propose a multidisciplinary social science that reconceives marginality—"For," as he concludes, "it is by living on the borderline of history and language, on the limits of race and gender, that we are in a position to translate the differences between them into a kind of solidarity."[46] Outlining a perspective on democracy that will conform to the new conditions of postmodern diversity, Chantal Mouffe points out that "The creation of political identities as radical democratic citizens depends . . . on a collective form of identification among the democratic demands found in a variety of movements: women, workers, black, gay, ecological, as well as in several other 'new social movements' . . . , a conception of citizenship which . . . aims at constructing a 'we,' a chain of equivalence . . ."[47] But, he goes on, "Such an approach can only be adequately formulated within a problematic that conceives of the social agent not as a unitary subject but as the articulation of an ensemble of subject positions, constructed within specific discourses and always precariously and temporarily sutured at the intersection of those subject positions."[48] Ultimately, within the demands for recognition of a multicultural pluralism, there is the postmodernists' quest for a formless form, the oxymoronic structure that uniquely suits the postmodern situation: "Might we not," asks Baudrillard, "transpose language games on to social and historical phenomena: anagrams, acrostics, spoonerisms, rhyme, strophe and catastrophe?" And this would reverse modernity's disenchantment of the world: "Such would be the enchanted alternative to the linearity of history, the poetic alternative to the disenchanted confusion, the chaotic profusion of present events."[49]

* * *

"Postmodernism," Joseph Kotarba has observed, "may . . . turn out to be the single most influential new theoretical development in our discipline since ethnomethodology . . ."[50] In the present volume I offer commentaries on and critiques of the postmodernist perspective.[51] The argument of the volume is fivefold: First, that many of the themes and issues posed by contemporary postmodernism have been addressed in Marvin B. Scott's and my own works on a sociology of the absurd[52] and the drama of social reality.[53] Second, that the latter approaches, while speaking to and criticizing the several dimensions of modernity's default on the promise of the Enlightenment, do not require, indeed actively oppose, postmodernism's abandonment of Reason and the quest for rational bases for knowledge and action.[54] Third, that the problems of historical knowledge and a sociologically sound historiography are better informed not by rejecting metanarratives and macrosociological outlooks altogether, but by subjecting any or all of them to critiques already extant in modernist discourse.[55] Fourth, that the issues deemed significant in elementary modes of the "social problems" discourse—that is, ethnonational movements,[56] racial myths and divisions,[57] gendered hierarchies, sexual preference, and all the practices categorized as deviance[58] in America, as well as in many other parts of the globe—are features of an already multivalent societal order[59] that needs to find not only a medium of representational adequacy,[60] but also an applicable theory of justice[61] and a new noncontractual basis for its social contract.[62] And, fifth, following from the previous points, that a sociology of this absurd world would focus on it as Giordano Bruno (1548–1600) looked on his—as an acentric labyrinth.[63] As Wardell and Zajicek have observed, "[L]etting the content of society organize sociological knowledge, where politics, economics, history, and sociality, or, race, class, gender, and sexuality are not neatly separated, and where personal troubles and public issues become entangled in a social labyrinth, we might well restore [what C. Wright Mills called] 'an essential tool of the sociological imagination . . .'"[64] The foundational bases for such an approach are territoriality, temporal structures, and exculpatory accounts. Each, as well as all, separately or jointly, express the drama of a social reality that is necessarily non-teleological and always contingent.[65] But, such a world is filled with subjects of all kinds and with every sort of capacity and incapacity; they constitute and cannot escape from constituting its dramatis personae. Such subjects are neither dead, diminished, nor abandoned by dint of their condition in the postmodern world.[66] Rather, they should be regarded as possessors of protean selves;[67] victims or heroes of the copings necessary to live, love, and work within the shifting standards by means of which aesthetic elites construct and deconstruct gendered and racialized versions of the perfect body type;[68] and dwellers in multiethnic, multicultural, and problematically gendered societies wherein—despite the pessimism that currently seems to chill even hope for the future,[69] and the belief in some postmodern and symbolic interactionist circles that a humane resolution of the "Social Question" is to be found only at the local level[70]—justice must be sought after at the highest (societal) as well as the lowest (communal and individual) levels of praxis and policy, and in the discourses of sociology itself.[71]

Part II

Theoretical and Epistemological Issues

CHAPTER ONE

Postmodernism and a Sociology of the Absurd

And what if reality dissolved before our very eyes?
Jean Baudrillard, The Ecstasy of Communication

Introduction

In 1970, together with Marvin B. Scott, I published a small volume entitled *A Sociology of the Absurd.*[1] Nineteen years later, a revised and expanded
version of this work was issued.[2] During those decades a wave of new
thought crossed the Atlantic and affected—perhaps permanently—first the
humanities and then the social sciences. *Postmodernism* is the designation
associated with a set of themes, variations, and arguments in the writings of
poststructuralists Michel Foucault and Jacques Derrida, and postmodernists proper Jean Baudrillard and Jean-Francois Lyotard (to name but the
leading figures who have contributed to the development and diffusion of
this *nouvelle vague.*) Although more recent French social and political
philosophy has treated postmodernism as part of the "long stream of French
antiliberalism,"[3] once out of its national home, postmodernism transcended
its political *habitus* and insinuated its epistemological and substantive
perspective into the realms of philosophy, literature, and sociology. The
coincidental arrival of postmodernism from France and a sociology of the
absurd in the United States poses the question of their possible relationship. In this chapter, I shall present a thesis that holds, first, that whatever
the understandings about postmodernism entertained by the advocates of
positivism, Marxism, and functionalism, its basic position is parallel to that
advanced in *A Sociology of the Absurd;* and, second, that the potential for a
new nihilism or, as in the instances of some of the feminist and racialist adap-
tations of certain selective aspects of postmodernism, of a neoessentialism,
is avoided in *A Sociology of the Absurd* by the "Absurd's" designation of the

anchor points by which both understanding and study of the postmodern condition may proceed.

That postmodernism has aroused considerable apprehension among Marxists as well as other adherents of the more conventionalized paradigms is clear from their sometimes angry, sometimes petulant outcries against it. Steven Best and Douglas Kellner assert, "It is our view that postmodern theorists like Foucault, Baudrillard, and Lyotard have made a serious theoretical mistake in severing their work from the Marxian critique of political economy and capitalism precisely at a point when the logic of capital accumulation has been playing an increasingly important role in structuring the new stage of society which can be conceptualized as a new economic and technical restructuring of capitalist society."[4] E. Ann Kaplan has observed that "[Jürgen] Habermas's well-known call for a continuing of the Enlightenment project and his appealing, if Utopian, model for a democratic cultural community, may be read as a desperate reaction against postmodern culture."[5] Christopher Norris, reflecting on what he regards as right-wing tendencies in the writings of postmodernist historian J. C. D. Clark, worries over the effects on that discipline of the latter's argument that, in his paraphrase of it, "historians can only be deluded if they try to make sense of the past on the assumptions that derive from an outworn mythology of reason, progress and enlightened secular critique."[6] In the face of a rising postmodernism in sociology, Jonathan Turner, a leading protagonist of the positivist orientation, treats advocacy of his own perspective as but a futile fight for an already lost cause. "I think that the prospects for general and positivistic theory in sociology are not very bright . . . [W]ith the invasion of so many new intellectual stances from Europe, as well as the fostering of those initiated in the United States, theoretical activity is partitioned into too many 'camps,' 'orientatons,' 'perspectives,' or 'paradigms' for any general theory . . . to ever be possible . . . [M]ost 'theorists' in sociology do not believe that sociology can be a natural science."[7] Mike Featherstone goes even further than Turner, suggesting that the postmodern perspective is sufficiently revolutionary to threaten the very foundation and future existence of sociology as a discipline.[8] In light of these and many other fearful commentaries, one can readily agree with Charles Lemert that "postmodernism, whether 'good' or 'bad,' must at least be considered a real event in world history—not just idle, obscure writing and talking."[9]

Those sociologists who have fallen under the sway of one or another variant of postmodernism perceive its critique of foundational and other conventionalized schools of social scientific thought as nothing less than a liberation from moribund and already discredited paradigms. Thus, Steven Seidman, whose critique of Marxism is nothing less than a reproof of Best's and Kellner's thesis, holds that "Much sociological theory is unconnected to current research programs, divorced from current social movements and political struggles and either ignorant of major political and moral public debates or unable to address them in ways that are compelling or even understandable by nontheorists."[10] By contrast, Seidman proclaims, the new postmodernism restores theory by centering on its proper form as narrative, a narrative suffused with praxiological and moral intent. Laurel Richardson conceives of "postmodernism as an opportunity to save sociology from itself," but broadens the gulf between discipline and practitioner when she proclaims, "If sociological theory is to be a viable human resource in the postmodern world, individual and group stories need to be told sociologically, although not necessarily by sociologists and not necessarily in sociological prose."[11] The allegation that postmodernist thought is at best amoral and bids fair to justify immorality has been challenged effectively by Zygmunt Bauman whose pathbreaking essay on postmodern ethics not only criticizes the moral pretensions of modernity, but emancipates moral responsibility from its conventionalized iron cages and elevates it to "the most personal and inalienable of human possessions, and the most precious of human rights."[12]

A Sociology of the Absurd: Parallels to Postmodernism

Fundamental to the arguments advanced in both *A Sociology of the Absurd* and postmodern social theory are two theses: (1) the world makes no ultimate ontological sense and yet is (almost) everywhere and always regarded as having a meaning; and (2) the self and society are social constructions. The two theses are intimately related. The point can be illuminated by comparing and contrasting the rhetorics describing self and society in the works of George Herbert Mead and Erving Goffman. Whereas Mead, who adapted part of his social psychology from modernist evolutionary and Wundtian theories, conceives of the self arising in patterned stages and seems—in some formal sense—to say that it is constituted out of the results of orderly passage through "play" and "game" phases, Goffman treats the self as never existing in an ontological sense; rather, it is that which is *presented* to the other in order to achieve some objective. The Goffmanic self, insofar as it appears in the context of social action, manifests itself as a particular but changeable representation of the social ideas about that phenomenon. Mead is more a postmodernist in his discussion of society. He speaks of society as constituted within the individual as "the generalized other," that is, a representation of norms and ideas that appear to the individual to guide or reprove his or her actions. For Goffman, society is even more elusive, ever capable of escaping the bonds and boundaries that circumscribe it—a point perhaps best made in Goffman's confession that he could not locate the locus of his own pronouncements about behavior and social relations.[13] The larger point, however, is that interactionist thought centers on the inherency of social construction. To put it bluntly, it is not the social construction *of* reality—suggesting another ontological reality that is out there and independent of the social—rather, it is that the social construction *is* reality.

However, as Epstein and Epstein have pointed out in their discussion of a Simmelian postmodern but still formal sociology, "The social manifests itself in multiple forms, that ultimately can place itself in 'violent conflict' between the 'individual' human and the 'social' human, as the continuing conflict between 'artistic freedom' and 'community standards' demonstrates."[14] The latter conflict, incidentally, was perceived by Mead, who once observed, "The value of an ordered society is essential to our existence, but there also has to be room for an expression of the individual himself if there is to be a satisfactorily developed society,"[15] and in a more critical context by Herbert Blumer who pointed out that while Mead had "recognized that there could be a gap between the larger social act in which a person was participating and the person's picture of this social act as given by his generalized other," and, hence, had urged "that the participants have to develop an understanding of their larger social acts through the medium of a more accurate generalized other," he had left unanswered "how the generalized other is formed and how its formation may be improved . . ." In the end, Blumer contends, Mead has given us "no aid in tracing how people construct their 'generalized others' [nor any description of] a set of techniques which would enable people and scholars alike to improve their ability to take group roles."[16] The problematics of the social construction of self and society are topics for the sociology of the absurd, but they form the horizon of the critique of modernism developed by postmodernists.

In effect, one of the contributions of postmodernism is its elaboration of the sociology of the absurd's critique of ontological meaning. When, for example, Derrida[17] proves, in the words of Madan Sarup, that "the signifier does not yield us up a signified directly, as a mirror yields up an image," and goes on to point out, again quoting Sarup, that "There is no harmonious one-to-one set of correspondences between the level of the signifieds in language," he shows us that "meaning is not immediately present in a sign."[18] One sign leads only to another. Ontological meaning will always remain elusive. We shall have to make sense—and see how others make sense—by a different approach to signs and signifiers.

Derrida has also helped in two ways to understand what Lyman and Scott were referring to when they wrote that "all systems of belief, including that of the conventional sociologists, are arbitrary."[19] By developing a devastating critique of what he calls the "metaphysics of presence," Derrida has undermined the grounding of certainty about the favored situs for sociological investigations, that is, the "here and now." Hence, when either Husserlian phenomenologists or Lundbergian positivist sociologists rest their researches on a taken-for-granted assumption that the "present is the province of the known,"[20] they are treading on quicksand. "By challenging access to the present," Sarup has pointed out, "Derrida poses a threat to both positivism and phenomenology."[21] However, as we shall see presently, this challenge is met, at least in part, by the principles governing research in accord with the perspective taken by *A Sociology of the Absurd*.

Derrida's other contribution to the issues under discussion arises out of his resolution of the problem presented by his own metaphysics—the privileging of speech over writing, of phonocentrism over logocentrism.[22] Much of conventional sociology has been *presentist* in its orientation. The "here and now," place and time held immobile, is the stuff of such commonplace sociological enterprises as the survey and the ethnography. However, in each, the present is presented in logocentric rhetorics—either as written prose or prose reduced to, or derived from, numerical practices. When sociologists interrogate their respondents by means of a questionnaire, the very speech process is treated epiphenomenally, as data having value only in relation to the preestablished purposes of the interrogation. Derrida, on the other hand, concerned to overcome the problematics inherent in logocentric approaches to presentism, urges recognition of the literal priority and, indeed, the privileged place which he would give to the voice, to that which is spoken rather than written. In *A Sociology of the Absurd*, Lyman and Scott have given special place—indeed, a place that holds in check the Hobbesian chaos—to one aspect of speech—*accounts*. Accounts are closer to the present because, in most cases of everyday experience, they are uttered in response to an accusation. In presenting an account, an actor excuses or justifies the alleged infraction in the instant (usually) of its invocation.[23] And this act is a speech act, conforming, because of its special relation to the problem of order, to Derrida's elevation of such speech acts to a privileged place.

The constructionist thesis has been further developed in several of the works of Baudrillard,[24] but despite the delight and consternation that his ironic description of the American hologram has given to its readers, it should be pointed out that the constructionist thesis put forward in *A Sociology of the Absurd,* incorporating the basic theme of Harold Garfinkel's early ethnomethodological studies, resolves the problem of nothingness, of ontology, that so many adherents and opponents of postmodernism claim is both its epistemological dead-end as well as its inevitable consequence. Baudrillard's pronouncements are sometimes caught between accusations of overdetermined and inauthentic representations (i.e., simulations) that appear, so he has argued, in democratic political elections,[25] and the presumptive truth value of his own descriptions of society-wide representations as occur, for example, in his picture of a wholly holographic United States.[26] Unlike Derrida, who has challenged the very idea of history, Baudrillard is certain that he is living in an end-time, that of "the end of the social." To his question, "Do modern societies correspond to a process of socialisation or to one of progressive desocialisation?," he answers that the latter is the case: "Our 'society' is perhaps putting an end to the social, of burying the social beneath a simulation of the social."[27]

In fact, Baudrillard—despite the postmodernists' reluctance to introduce new grand historical metanarratives—has done just that in his linear history of the four phases of the image.[28] These four phases, however, coexist, so to speak, in the several epistemes of modernity that Baudrillard and other postmodernists wish to bury. The first is that which conceives of thought as holding a *mirror* up to the world, the episteme of positive science; the second is that of the *mask,* that is, the contention that humans, at best, see the world darkly, its reality shrouded by deceit, false consciousness, or counterfeit appearances, the episteme of sciences aimed at demystification and disenchantment; the third, a late twentieth-century phenomenon according to Baudrillard, is that of the *simulacrum,* a move beyond mere masking, that substitutes signs of the real for a reality that is lost, stolen, or strayed, or that never existed at all, the episteme that gives birth to the postmodern era; and the fourth phase, that he calls hologrammatic and that might be called *simulacra-for-themselves,* arises when all images are representations of themselves, having no other reality than that which manifests itself in them.[29] This is the holographic world which Baudrillard purported to see in his (real? imaginary?) road trip across America. For Baudrillard this episteme sounds the death knell of the world:

"It might seem a terrific idea to talk about this in New York of all places since this is the world's epicentre, but on reflection, there is no sense reflecting on this in miniature in a scenario which is necessarily inferior to its model." "Except"—and this is a big "Rortyan" exception—"the very requirement that we should rescue the *idea* of the end of the world from its real occurrence—which is the habitual labour of intellectuals."[30]

This issue is approached in a transpositional manner by sociologies of the absurd. Neither taking the world for granted nor imposing any a priori categories of understanding and image decoding upon it, a sociologist working out of the Absurdist position would move Baudrillard's thesis about "the end of the social," as well as his epistemes of representation, out from the mind of the observer-researcher and into the *Umwelt* of the social actor. The kind of alienation that speaks to Baudrillard's conception of the end of the social might or might not, in whole or in part, be constituted in the outlook of the social actor. The epistemes of mirror, mask, simulacrum, and hologram constitute the problematic for persons engaged in the task of everyday living. They must find their way through what might be a funhouse-like structure of representations that reveal, conceal, simulate, or appear to be a reality that is always and simultaneously constructed, constructable, deconstructed, deconstructable. The epigram that thematizes *The X-Files,* a 1990s televised postmodern serial drama about an FBI agent's investigation of the possibility that his own agency is concealing the presence of extraterrestrials, states the matter succinctly: "The truth is out there."

Just as Derrida has provided the critique of linguistic philosophy that aids us in seeing just what is meant by the Absurdist claims about meaninglessness, and Baudrillard's emphasis on representations reveals, in spite of his own pessimism, that the social is alive and well, as well as being protean in the ethnomethods[31] of everyday actors, so Lyotard's turn to Wittgenstein's treatment of language games as a solution to the crisis of modernity brings postmodernism into synchronicity with the Absurdist emphasis on game frameworks.[32] In his opposition to totalization and metanarratives—he once wrote, "Simplifying to the extreme, I define *postmodern* as incredulity toward metanarratives"[33]—Lyotard opposes his own version of the new wave of thought to what he sees as the crumbling but by no means impotent authority of existent Occidental culture, social organization, and political economy. Yet, secreted within this seemingly monolithic modernist structure are interstices wherein a certain amount of freedom, of "give" in the "system," permits not only resistance, but also creativity, not only liberty, but also terror.[34] In such social spaces, language games may not only be played out, but these same games may be rewritten with respect to rules, roles, and relationships. These interstices—for example, in the colloquy of friends—"allow and encourage the greatest possible flexibility of utterance."[35]

Both Lyotard and the writers of *A Sociology of the Absurd* have drawn upon the work of Erving Goffman. Goffman's influence on the former has been regarded as so important by one commentator on the late sociologist's place in the social scientific canon as to cause him to place Goffman's name in nomination for the honor of being a precursor of postmodernism;[36] while another sees the later writings of Goffman, especially his essay "Felicity's Condition,"[37] as nearer to Derridean deconstruction, including a deconstruction of the conclusion he had reached in an earlier work, *Frame Analysis*.[38] Combining Goffman's emphasis on dramaturgy with Wittgenstein's and other analysts' descriptions of gaming and game rules, Lyman and Scott had developed, as early as 1970, an enlarged outlook on the process which they designated as "game frameworks."[39] After further thinking over the matter, Lyotard had come to reconsider, as well as debate[40] the scope of the gaming perspective, noting, *inter alia,* that it is available for research into macro- as well as microproblems. In 1983 he had focused attention on "Wages, profits, funds for payment and credit, investment, growth and recession, the money market: it would indeed be interesting to analyze these objects as moves or rules proceeding from various language games." And then, he had queried, "what if capital were a multiform way of dominating time, of linking?"[41] Lyman and Scott had anticipated such a move. Commenting in 1989 on the uses of their own game framework, they wrote: "our essay on game frameworks outlines the strategies and tactics appropriate to keeping or breaking a relationship; maintaining or spoiling an identity; hiding or fathoming a secret; and obtaining or resisting hegemony."[42] In effect, the coincidental recognition of the role of language games, gaming, and game frameworks by Lyotardean and Absurdist sociologists virtually brings the only seemingly parallel lines of these independently developed schools of thought to a meeting point.

However, three problems have yet to be addressed: (1) the problem of history, best explored through a discussion of postmodernist and Absurdist thought on the subject; (2) the problem of research strategy, best explored through the Absurd's provision of anchor points for a postmodern sociology; and (3) the question of whether the subject and the self can survive postmodernist and Absurdist scrutiny.

The Problem of History and Social Change

The poststructuralist orientation toward history—in the writings of Foucault and Derrida, for example—consists, in the words of Sarup, in their "antipathy to the notion that there is an overall pattern in history."[43] Foucault's "historical" studies[44] are animated by his denial of both the Hegelian dialectic and any thesis holding that there is a trajectory of progress; Derrida's critique opposes the modernist belief that there is a *telos* or an end-point to history. Foucault's approach draws on Friedrich Nietzsche's "On the Genealogy of Morals,"[45] and. as Sarup reports, like Nietzsche, "breaks off the past from the present and, by demonstrating the foreignness of the past, relativizes and undercuts the legitimacy of the present."[46] To Foucault and others who adhere to this variant of the poststructuralist critique, grand historical sociologies of systemic development—Talcott Parsons's monograph on the evolution of modern society would be a good example[47]—are discredited in favor of a close reading of singular events, especially those affecting the poor, the voiceless, the deviant, the demoralized, and, in general, the losers in the historical struggles depicted in grand historical narratives.[48] "According to Foucault," Sarup observes, "there has been an insurrection of subjugated knowledges, of a whole set of knowledges that have been discredited as inadequate—naive knowledges located low down on the hierarchy, beneath the required level of scientificity."[49]

The genealogical approach, however, is more than another critique of historicism. In the hands of some of its most articulate spokespersons it becomes a discursive weapon in the epistemological arsenal of those who would emancipate from canonical history, and also privilege, the downtrodden elements of contemporary society. As such, its ultimate aim is not merely the enunciation of an alternative truth, but a reversal of hegemony—it seeks empowerment for those whom the historicist episteme has degraded. "In his later work," Sarup points out, "Foucault . . . shifted from linguistic determination to the view that individuals are constituted by power relations, power being the ultimate principle of social reality."[50] For those who would be beneficiaries of Foucault's emancipatory attitude toward the victims of metanarrative history, resisting hegemony and obtaining power are desiderata. Although *A Sociology of the Absurd* does not take history, historicism, or historiography as one of its central problems,[51] it draws on the idiographic ideas of Simmel, Schutz, Natanson, and Burke[52] to forge an implicit attitude toward history that matches some of the ideas of Derrida and Foucault but differs profoundly with others. With Derrida and

Foucault—in Lyman's case, by adapting the Teggart school's critique of the Comtean tradition;[53] in Scott's case, by moving on from his own critique of functionalist foibles in sociology[54]—there is agreement that grand teleological narratives have lost their credibility on both empirical and methodological grounds. However, neither Lyman nor Scott believes that empowerment of the abused and neglected victims of any long-prevailing episteme is the proper object of a sociologically informed conceptualization of the past, or of a critique of historicism. Such a project might well be the proper task of true believers, members of social movements, and advocates and supporters of one or another kind of sociocultural change.[55] But it is not a sound basis for a sociology, modern or postmodern.

To the Absurdist sociologist, history consists of a sense of and a sensibility toward the past that is brought to bear on an interaction or in an encounter. That sense and sensibility might resonate with what Natanson calls "big histories," that is, those that bear the stamp of legitimacy, or it might derive from what he refers to as "little histories," that is, those that enjoy a truth value insinuated into beliefs and praxes that are located in one or another of the interstices of a pluralistic social order.[56] Or, a protagonist of a "big history" might be confronted by the representatives of a "little" one in what amounts to a challenge to the former's authority. A state society whose "big history" is constituted by and through an authoritative metanarrative that is under severe assault from a host of "little histories" is a society suffering from and through a legitimation crisis.[57] Natanson also recognizes the reason that a proponent of a "little history" might wish to move it into a higher place: "In 'little history' the individual is the self-acknowledged master of his [or her] plans and projects; in 'big history' he [or she] is the instrument of others."[58] Such thoughts appear to adumbrate the insurgencies that Foucault has described. But just as a class revolution is not the inexorable consequence of class consciousness, so "little history" insurgency is not the necessary sequel to feelings of inadequate representation by the prevailing idiographic discourse. As Natanson points out, "the decisive point here is that the [hero-victim] of 'little history' is completely aware of this very situation: The common-sense individual acts within a world he knows is dominated by others; but he lives within a world defined by his attitudes toward domination."[59]

The "meaning of history, without which we would not find it worthwhile to produce a construct of history," Simmel once observed, "is determined by presuppositions that establish a qualitative distinction between history and 'the brute facts.'"[60] Such is also the case with "little history." Each employs typifications and concepts to "fix the real event" and establishes "syntheses of sequence events" in its "construction of a world of knowledge."[61] For Natanson, and for the Absurdist sociologist, "History as a finite province of meaning is the microcosm created by the subjective interpretation of actors in daily life who place the accent of reality upon their own interpretations of the 'big history' which remains transcendent to the world of 'little history' in which they live."[62] The point here, in contrast to that of those followers of Foucault who seek to establish a regime for one or another episteme of a hitherto unauthorized voice, is that the latter project is a *topic* for a postmodern and Absurdist investigation, not a *resource* to fire and fuel the investigation.

Both the conventional narrative historian and the commonsense actor share an attitude toward history that can be designated as naive realism. For both, as Michael Oakeshott has characterized (or, to be charitable, we might say, caricatured) their point of view, "fact is the material of experience; it is the solid datum which experience must accept and may come to understand."[63] Whereas the everyday actor brings a particular version of past reality into practical usage when it suits his or her purposes in an encounter, the professional naive-realist historian is engaged in a presentation of "the furthest reach of experience [that] is the collection and reflective consideration of unalterable facts."[64] To which such a critic of naive realism as Oakeshott replies—and on this point the Absurdist and the poststructuralist would also grant their respective assents—"Facts are never merely observed, remembered or combined; they are always made. We cannot 'take' facts, because there are none to take until we have constructed them. And, until a fact is established, that is, until it has achieved a place in a coherent world, it is not more than a hypothesis or a fiction."[65] All facts, thence, whether they have achieved a place in the coherent world of "big history" or found their home within one or another "little history," partake of and are constituted by the social construction of historical realities.

Disagreement arises among historians and sociologists who have accepted the critique of naive realism over its consequences for epistemology and praxiology.[66] Some who identify with Foucault[67] see their own project as, in effect, an idiographic and very serious version of the old children's game "king of the mountain." They enter the game in order not only to dislodge (e.g., deconstruct, disprivilege, decenter) the reigning "monarch" (e.g., "the grand narrative," "the dominant paradigm," "the ruling idea"), but also to replace that figure with one or perhaps several that has been silenced, muted, impoverished, or neglected. The form of such an insurgent activity, despite its claims to the contrary, is that of a rebellion, not a revolution.[68] The hierarchical structure of the hegemonic disciplinary discourse remains in place; only the incumbents at the top of the hierarchy have been replaced by allegedly more-deserving others. "Revolutionary movements are against principles; rebellions against men."[69] The post-structuralist revolt against metanarrative and history may have begun as a principle-driven revolution; all too often in its everyday praxis it has descended to a person- or paradigm-driven contest for disciplinary power or a more privileged place in the commonwealth of letters and science.

However, in some cases the "mountain" upon which the old "monarch" sat with such impunity is to be, or already has been, utterly deconstructed. In its place, the once and future victors in the game have proposed a vast and supposedly level, but uncultivated, playing field—the space their insurgency has opened, one on which the successor regime can settle and develop further. However, that regime is not a kingdom, but a loosely, if at all, integrated communitarian republic. "Instead of [metanar-rative] Truth," observes Robert Jackall, "there exist only 'local narratives,' stories, constructions, points of view, or perspectives, each with their [*sic*] own valence."[70] And the new or soon-to-be elites of the burgeoning commu-nitarian republic are those persons hitherto defined by the social categories that both Marxist and non-Marxist metanarrativists had marginalized—that is, those whose peripheralization has been based on race, ethnicity, gender, sexual preference, or age.[71] In such a neo-Foucaultian communal republic, the critical stance against both history and science—for, as Lyotard has shown, the principles behind the critique of metanarrative are equally appli-cable to science,[72] creating, to borrow from Natanson's lexicon, a "big science" and what might be called a "little *Wissenschaft*"—is vulnerable to reductionism or essentialism. Some recent examples: for the history of Western civilization, there is substituted "the Afrocentric idea";[73] for the structure of Anglo-Hispanic relations, there is "Chicanismo" and the inter-ests of "la Raza";[74] for the white, patriarchal hegemony over both human-ities and the social sciences, there is feminist discourse;[75] for a heterosexual hegemony over culture and social organization there is "Queer Theory."[76] While such reductionisms and essentialisms[77] are often identified with both poststructuralism and postmodernism, neither is a necessary feature of these new waves of thought, and both are avoided in the Absurdist tradition's provision of anchor points for a postmodern sociology.

Anchor Points I: Time Tracks and the Problem of Duration

Although the poststructuralist critique of the metanarrative claims originality, it in fact is not the first critique of that kind against such perspectives. More than seven decades ago, a critique of the ruling metanarrative
of anthropology and sociology, that is, of those disciplines' developmentalist Comtean heritage, had been put forward by Frederick J. Teggart in
the United States[78] and, in a wholly separate form, by Max Weber in
Germany.[79] Just as the poststructuralists point to the hegemonic role of a
particular metaphor with respect to Occidental historiography, so Kenneth
Bock, a disciple of what might be called the subterranean Teggart school,
took note of how the organicist imagery had become the difficult-to-move-
around, indeed, virtually impossible to dislodge, familiar furniture of the
Western social scientific mind.[80] However, this school's critique was largely
(but not entirely)[81] couched within a historicism that sought a neopositive
science of history. That science would substitute a veritable high school
chemistry set approach—that is, "if-then" propositions tested against a naive
realist notion of the happenings that made up the "if" part of the
formulation[82]—for both the cyclical or stage-phased metaphors[83] and associated methodologies that prevailed in the grand paradigms of anthropology and sociology, as well as for the ethnonational narratives and other
entelechic trajectories that had been inspired by Rankean historiography.[84]
The limitation of this approach—the reason that its critique must be designated prepostmodern—is embedded in its a priori epistemological assumption, namely, that there is an inherent comparability of happenings and
occurrences that makes a positivist social science of history possible. Thus,
Bock approvingly quotes Gaetano Salvemini on treating the study of revolutions in terms of their exemplification of regularities in social experience:
"We must compare one with the other the greatest possible number of revolutions . . . and we must see whether between these phenomena so far apart
in space and time there can be discovered similarities or dissimilarities
which are constant."[85] Indeed, absent this assumption, or, worse, in the face
of its Foucaultian opposite—that among happenings there is an inherent
incommensurability—and a positivist science of history would be either
impossible altogether or left to the metaphoric and conjectural approaches
adopted by those historicist scholars who opted for the "biological anal-
ogy, the idea of progress, the [Comtean variant of the] comparative method,
evolutionism, the doctrine of survivals, and theories of diffusion or independent invention . . ."[86] The postmodern turn, as we have already seen,
entails rejection of both the modernist nonpositivistic metanarratives Bock

lists and the positivistic science of history that the Teggart school championed.[87] For the postmodernists, any and every metanarrative of history exemplifies arbitrary hegemony. What then, is left?

On this point, the Absurdists and the postmodernists agree on the existential condition but disagree on its consequences for a social science. Absurdists and postmodernists share in the critique of linearity and of the extant metanarratives. The Absurdists, however, do not reject the very possibility of metanarratives. The issue that divides them is their respective attitudes toward both the concept of time and *durée*.

The clearest vision of the postmodern thesis on the subject has been presented by Fredric Jameson.[88] Drawing on the writings of the postmodern psychoanalyst Jacques Lacan, Jameson conceives the impossibility of a science of history or of its minimalistic representation, biography, as arising out of a fundamental disjuncture in language and language games—a disjuncture that makes problematic any identification with past, present, or future and any linkage of them to biography or history. Building on Lacan's conception of schizophrenia as a malfunction in language-gaming, Jameson in effect sees the existent postmodern condition as pathological. With meaning now located in moves from one signifier to another, the signified is but a meaning-effect, that is, "that objective mirage of signification generated and projected by the relationship of signifiers among themselves."[89] But the postmodern condition is even more dire, for, as Jameson sees the matter, it is characterized by a malfunction in that relationship. For a Lacanian psychoanalyst, such a condition is defined as schizophrenia. Jameson agrees with the terminology but asserts that the schizophrenia about which he is concerned has been widely diffused and has become generalized. Hence, he observes, precisely because "personal identity is itself the effect of a certain temporal unification of past and future with one's present; and . . . that such active temporal unification is a function of language, . . . we are . . . unable to unify the past, present, and future of our own biographical experience or psychic life."[90] In the face of such a chaos, neither a consensually validatable history nor an internally consistent biography is possible.

In the Absurdist tradition, the matter is perceived differently. The language of pathology is abjured in favor of a closer reading of the putatively "schizophrenic" condition. Like the schizophrenic—and the inhabitant of Jameson's postmodern world—the dweller in the land of the Absurd experiences, or is capable of experiencing, a fragmentation of time, a sense of the perpetuity of disparate presents, a varying of coexistent durations. He or she possesses a sensibility that there are a multiplicity of "pasts," both hegemonic "big histories" and a plethora of sequestered "little" ones, and a feeling that identity, however it is linked to past, present and future—that is, to predecessors, contemporaries, and successors[91] (in any one of those, presents are problematic) is a challenge or a task. For such a subject—for as we shall soon see, the inhabitant of the Absurd world is the subject of any sociology of the Absurd—time and its problems are a fundamental feature of that more-or-less-than-obdurate reality with which he or she must engage. The situation is not one in which language itself has become the most demonic of the incomprehensible alien forces that make life impossible; rather, for most, it is in effect empowering—a situation that brings to the fore the belief in, and the praxes associated with, human dignity, especially as that term has been defined by Bock: "a belief that we can control our lives."[92] For such a belief does not entail a corollary that humans will control their lives, or manage their affairs effectively, or succeed in their endeavors. Rather, as Bock points out, "we must recognize that people can use, and have used, this capacity to serve both rational and nonrational ends, to produce and to destroy, to do both good and evil things . . . Leading a human life is a difficult matter."[93]

With respect to history, biography, and its own presentist position, *A Sociology of the Absurd* eschews any postmodern sense of nothingness; rather, it supplies a metaconcept for understanding the various senses of *durée* that play such an essential part in scholarly disciplines and everyday life: the *time-track*.[94] "Time tracks," observe Lyman and Scott, "are temporal periods employed by individuals, groups, and whole cultures to designate the beginnings or the termination of things."[95] Time tracks are products of social constructions set against the humanistic horizon that conceives "of life as divided into temporally specific, qualitatively different event activities."[96] Among the trajectories of such tracks are those that follow either a humanistic or fatalistic direction and those that either move continuously or are punctuated by episodes. The metanarratives of history, whether of "big history" or of the "little" variety, follow along one or another of these tracks. From the Absurdist position it is an empirical question, that is, one through which the investigator seeks to determine which type of time track and which version of that track becomes authenticated among the members of a society or group. For subscribers to the Marxist variant of historical dialectics, for example, the passage of happenings over time is said to conform to a trajectory of thesis-antithesis-synthesis as various modes of the ownership and relations of the means of production develop, create the conditions of their own destruction, and construct a new form. This particular track is fatalistic and possesses its own entelechy; that is, its defining events are said not only to arise outside the arena of mastery in which the ordinary social actor lives, but also to reach an end-point, one at which History (with a capital H) comes to an end. Moreover, although commanding respect among a number of scholars and persons active in social movements designed to hasten its inevitable fulfillment, this historical track did not achieve official recognition in the Occident, serving instead as a challenge to the officially recognized one until the horrors of its representative regimes became public knowledge, or until the disintegration of the Soviet Union caused it to lose ground in the struggle to achieve legitimacy. Indeed, much of the postmodern thrust is a response to the failure of Marxist history to fulfill its promise, some of its advocates holding that if Marxist historiography is not valid then history itself is impossible, a god that failed.

Protagonists of teleological and fatalistic time tracks are subject to profound disillusion when their particular historical prophecy fails. A fine example is found in the responses certain social scientists gave when the promissory outcome of Robert E. Park's race relations cycle[97]—namely, the final assimilation of all peoples and the end of race relations as such—failed to occur within what they regarded as a reasonable amount of time. Although the duration of the race relations' time track—that is, the chronological time necessary for the several races to pass through the four stages of race relations that Park had said were "progressive and irreversible"[98]—had not been specified, and, in fact, the time allotted was meant to apply to races that, at the moment of the cycle theory's enunciation, were at different moments in the cycle, most of its adherents supposed that the desired end would have been reached in America at the midpoint of the twentieth century. Anticipating from the beginning that some malfunction might affect the pace of the sociotemporal process, Park had acknowledged that "Customs regulations, immigration restrictions and racial barriers may slacken the tempo of the movement; may perhaps halt it altogether for a time"; but, he had held fast to his belief that these "cannot change its direction; cannot at any rate reverse it."[99] Moreover, in his original formulation, Park had evaluated the forces arrayed against the cycle's reaching of its outcome and dismissed them on account of their weaknesses: "It does not follow that because the tendencies to the assimilation and eventual amalgamation of races exist, they should not be resisted and, if possible, altogether inhibited. On the other hand, it is vain to underestimate the character and force of the tendencies that are drawing the races and peoples about the Pacific into the ever narrowing circle of a common life."[100] Twenty-four years later, Park would evince considerable pessimism about what he had originally supposed would be the singular final outcome of his cycle, trifurcating the latter into separate time tracks ending in either assimilation, caste structure, or a people's permanent status as a minority group.[101] But his followers had become too enamored of the original version of the cycle. When, by the 1950s, it still showed no sign of having reached fulfillment, they became disappointed, disconsolate, and despairing. Their responses—not consciously postmodern in their presentation—are nevertheless indicative of what was to come and showed signs of cognitive dissonance.[102] Chagrined over her discovery that Chinatown's Chinese had been outstripped in the race to assimilation by the Japanese, whose settlement in America had been only half as long, Rose Hum Lee accused her ethnic compatriots of a failure of nerve.[103] Perceiving even earlier the possibility that some races might need more time than others to assimilate, Emory Bogardus had begun the construction of different and uneven cycles for each of the races.[104] Supposing that Park's cycle might survive only if it was removed from the demands of positive verification, three disciples of Park's orientation—E. Franklin Frazier[105] and, in a separate monograph, Tamotsu Shibutani and Kian Moon Kwan[106]—transposed the cycle into a logico-temporal ordering of the race relations process. James A. Geschwender, in effect torn between the Popperian test of validity that Park's cycle has not yet passed and an unwillingness to eject the theory altogether from empirical science, hit upon a resolution that might have satisfied its purely academic adherents but would certainly receive a cynical smile from all those who saw its irrelevance to the peoples eagerly awaiting emancipation from the unfair competition, cruel conflict, and grudging accommodation that characterized America's race relations. He conducted "an integral reading of all of Park's works," and on that basis he claimed to have discovered that Park had envisioned a duration for the race relations cycle that would greatly exceed the period of time allotted to it by both its adherents and critics. Park, Geschwender claimed, "believed that in the long run (perhaps over several centuries) the development of the modern world would bring about complete assimilation . . ."[107] However, neither Lee's reprimand of its subjects, Bogardus's reconstructions; Frazier's, Shibutani's and Kwan's shift of it from a theory to a model; nor Geschwender's stretching out of the temporal dimensions of the race relations cycle could save it.[108] It had provided the historico-temporal metanarrative that defined the race problem and predicted its solution during the first half of the twentieth century.

Once its discreditation had been complete, it induced a veritable post-modern despair over the very possibility of theorizing on this topic. The skeptical anthropologist Brewton Berry stated the issue plainly and in a manner that could be recognized by any postmodernist who took an interest in the matter. Having shown that neither Park's nor any of the other sociologists' race relations cycles could pass evidentiary muster, Berry expressed his doubt over whether any "universal pattern" could ever be found in the processes affecting race relations. Like a Foucaultian postmodernist—which, incidentally, he is not—Berry inclined "to the belief that so numerous and so various are the components that enter into race relations that each situation is unique . . ." In a protopostmodern vein he warns, "the making of generalizations is a hazardous procedure."[109] Absent Park's metanarrative, so the argument seems to run, theorizing itself is impossible.

The Absurdist perspective on time tracks approaches this impasse in quite a different manner. Neither sanguine nor despairing, the Absurdist holds that the question has been wrongly put by both the modernists and the postmodernists. The specific error of each is to mistake the *topic* for the *resource*. For all interpretive sociologies the methodological issue has been stated succinctly by Thomas P. Wilson: "[C]onceiving of social interaction as an interpretive process opens up the possibility of treating the interpretive process itself as a phenomenon for investigation. In such inquiries, the documentary method of interpretation is not taken for granted as a resource in the study of patterns of action but is viewed as a topic for investigation in its own right."[110] The conceptualization of time in terms of time tracks partakes of the methodology to which Wilson refers and permits a critique of both modernist and postmodernist perspectives. Put plainly, the issue is not which historico-temporal metanarrative is valid according to the tenets of positive science, but rather which if any enjoys authority over others, and how and where, if at all, the less than authoritatively-consensual and historico-temporal narratives find expression.

For purposes of beginning a sociological inquiry, the Absurdist accepts much of what Lyotard, Baudrillard, and Derrida have to say about the postmodern condition. The great metanarratives have indeed lost much of their force among those who can no longer afford to take them for granted. But note that Absurdism provides for a presentist-oriented sociology of everyday life. As such, it recognizes the possibility of numerous conceptions of time—including both authoritative and discredited temporal narratives—operating simultaneously in society. These operant conceptions are the topics *of* such a sociology, not the resource *for* it. Such a sociology recognizes and takes empirical note of the possibility that individuals and groups might be living within a society where a long-accredited temporal narrative is under assault, but where an unknown number continue to treat it as the historico-temporal horizon against which they carry out routine activities; another unknown number actively resist its impositions on their interests; and still others are ignorant of or indifferent to it. Absurdist sociological inquiry investigates human activity with respect to whether it is situated on, or in opposition or indifference to, episodic or continuous time tracks; whether individuals or groups engage in "sidetracking" or "track-switching" as part of a strategy of coping with the plurality of durational trajectories that present themselves; and the conditions under which individuals or groups experience "time panic" with respect to their goals, identities, actions, and interactions.

Dissenting from Baudrillard, the Absurdist sociologist does not take as his or her own outlook that the temporally social has disappeared to be replaced only by a nostalgic simulacrum of it, but rather looks into the world to see whether anyone is in fact experiencing such. The Absurdist sociologist might agree with the critics of historico-temporal entelechy that neither Marx's historical dialectic nor Park's race relations cycle has been validated by or as normative social science. But for the Absurdist the matter does not end there; it is, to repeat the point, shifted from that of a *resource* to that of a *topic.* Does the communist cell member believe that the party must undertake actions to overthrow the government by force and violence now, before the word about the death of the Marxist discourse becomes public knowledge? Or does he or she believe that all is lost and the party should cease and desist from any and all insurrectionary activity? Or do its members believe that the deconstruction of the Soviet Union opens up a new era for Marx's dialectic to realize itself, perhaps one permitting the emergence of socialism with a human face? By the same token, does the erstwhile "Negro," who in the space of forty years has moved from that term of self-reference to being first "black" and then "African American," sense that his or her integration into society is being held at a standstill by these biocultural-historical-temporal shifts? Or does he or she perceive "progress" to have been made, and the full measure of emancipation to be nearly realized? Or does he or she sense a "time panic" over the fact that the rewards and opportunities opened by government-supported affirmative action programs are likely to be short-lived because a newly elected legislature and a conservative court are now opposed to them? Such questions are grist for the mill of an Absurdist sociology—one that focuses on time and *durée* as a horizon against which its researches can be directed and with which social actors must contend.

Anchor Points II: Territoriality and the Problem of Spatialization

Postmodernism has coined the neologism "hyperspace." This linguistic innovation is brought forth, however, not only to indicate that all hitherto accepted conceptions of space are meaningless, but also to jar awareness of a geographical revolution that has occurred: "Space doesn't act according to modern assumptions," observes Pauline Marie Rosenau, a friendly critic of postmodernism. Rather, she continues, "It has been annihilated, and spatial barriers have disappeared. Everything is in geographical flux, constantly and unpredictably shifting in space."[111] The term "space" itself has been deconstructed—or, perhaps, fragmented beyond restoration by its own implosion—so that it and such correlative concepts as "site" or "situs" no longer refer to fixed spatio-temporal locations, but rather to "places that cannot be definitely determined."[112] However, the implications of this point are themselves disaggregated among the several postmodernist thinkers, dividing neatly those that Rosenau calls "skeptical post-modernists" from those she designates "affirmative post-modernists."[113] The former—for example, Jameson—hold that spatial conditions are so much in flux that, in Jameson's words, "the capacities of the individual human body to locate itself, to organize its immediate surroundings perceptually, and cognitively to map its position in a mappable external world"[114] have been transcended. The latter, on the other hand, employ the postmodern critique as a rallying cry for reinvigorating the modernist qualities and virtues said to prevail in local areas;[115] restarting the once prominent modernist quest for community that prevailed among sociologists and planners;[116] and restoring the sense of fellow feeling that earlier advocates of a *Volksgemeinschaft*[117] felt ought to give succor to the urbanized, the ethnoracially marginalized, and the sexually stigmatized denizens of modern metropolitan society;[118]—indeed, to all those whom Robert E. Park had once called the "human junk of civilization."[119] "The affirmative's concern," Rosenau points out, "is that modern assumptions about space and time are manipulated so as to confine and enclose, [to be used] as tools of discipline."[120] They take such demoralizing and self-destroying total institutions as slave plantations,[121] asylums,[122] and prisons[123] as examples of such tools. They look to the spontaneous and participatory democracy of small groups who carve out a local place for themselves as emancipatory activities appropriate to the postmodern condition, and they reject both fictive and factitious metanarratives of conquest, settlement, nation-building,[124] and state-making as both hegemonic and evil.[125]

A more specific approach to spatialization has been taken by the postmodernist scholar-planner Edward Soja.[126] His critique is aimed at displacing what he regards as academic modernism's privileging of time and history over space and geography. Calling for a postmodernized reinvigoration of a "geographical and spatial imagination," Soja proposes that the postmodern mind be vitalized by and through "a practical theoretical consciousness." Such a consciousness, he asserts, "sees the lifeworld of being creatively located not only in the making of history but also in the construction of human geographies, the social production of space and the restless formation and reformation of geographical landscapes: social being actively emplaced in space *and* time in an explicitly historical *and* geographical contextualization."[127] For Soja, space is a veritable Lazarus, waiting to be resuscitated, released from modernism's death grip upon it—a death grip that Foucault had contrasted to the nineteenth-century's granting of a living and vital status to time and history: "Space [Foucault observed] was treated as the dead, the fixed, the undialectical, the immobile. Time on the contrary was richness, fecundity, life, dialectic."[128] Soja, unlike the more radical postmodernists who seek to do away with history and the temporal altogether—that is, those who, in Soja's words, "overstate their case, creating the unproductive aura of an anti-history, inflexibly exaggerating the critical privilege of contemporary spatiality in isolation from an increasingly silenced embrace of time"[129]—more modestly proposes a greater equalization for space in the spatio-temporal epistemologies that he perceives are already rising to replace the moribund modernist metanarratives: "Geography," he points out, "may not yet have displaced history at the heart of contemporary theory and criticism, but there is a new animating polemic on the theoretical and political agenda, one which rings with significantly different ways of seeing time and space together, the interplay of history and geography, the 'vertical' and 'horizontal' dimensions of being in the world freed from the imposition of inherent categorical privilege."[130] Soja holds that the precedents for such an innovative perspective can be gleaned from the writings of Nietzsche, Hegel, Heidegger, Sartre, Baudrillard, Foucault, Simmel, and Walter Benjamin, and he credits the last-named with a call for "'blasting' the embedded historical object out of its temporal matrix and into a more visual, imagistic, and spatial contextualization."[131] As we shall see presently, the Absurd's employment of the concept "territoriality"[132] adumbrated Soja's call and, together with the already discussed conceptualization of *durée* via "time tracks," provides for a postmodernistic approach to the kinds of substantive problems that interest Jameson and Soja—and at both the macro- and microlevels.

However, before proceeding to the discussion of territoriality, it is useful to the present project to take note of a prepostmodernist critique of the evolutionary historical metanarrative as that master-narrative affected epistemological construction of a conjectural space-time continuum in ethnology and sociology. It is Foucault who once remarked, "For all those who confuse history with the old schemas of evolution, living continuity, organic development, the progress of consciousness or the project of existence, the use of spatial terms seems to have the air of an anti-history."[133] Yet one subterranean modernist school of thought—that associated with Teggart and his epigoni—not only did not succumb to that confusion to which Foucault refers,[134] but also proposed a humanistic historical geography to replace linear developmentalism[135] and engaged in a telling critique of the Comtean methodology adapted by ethnologists and sociologists from the latter.[136] In relation to the issue of spatialization, the Teggartian school's critique may be said to have called attention to how the ethnologists' and sociologists' employment of Comte's so-called "comparative method" privileged a conjectural linear time sequence over contemporary space, converting the latter in effect into a representation of stages on an evolutionary time track. The effect of such usages has been not only to marginalize the minority inhabitants of present-day state societies or colonies—for example, in the Goldenweiser thesis about the Eskimo, Tlingit, Haida, and Iroquois members of the Native American people, as well as the Baganda and the dark-skinned denizens of the Australian interior, each of whom is declared to be "primitive" and all of whose ways of life are said to be living simulacra of "*early* civilization"[137]—but also—as in the thesis advanced by Robert Park's associate in the Pacific Coast survey of immigrant Asian Americans and their progeny, Winifred Raushenbush,[138] who transposed two geographically copresent Japanese American communities into representations of a temporal sequence by invoking her own ad hoc variant of the Aristotelian doctrine of accidents to account for the "anachronism"—to put the temporal imperatives of the metanarrative above what on-the-spot investigation shows to be the case. Convinced that a positivist conception of happenings in time and space is a "given" that is to be the incontestable resource for a science of history, the Teggartian school remains resolutely modernist.[139] Nevertheless, its critical examination of the nonempirical basis of the spatio-temporal perspective in the major metanarratives of modernity earns it an as yet unheralded acknowledgment as precursor to one aspect of the postmodernist credo.

The Absurdist perspective accepts much of the thesis about spatialization advanced by Soja, but it holds that its own conceptualizations on the matter provide it with a useful roadmap. Following that map will facilitate a social science that meets the exigencies of the postmodern condition, makes both macro- and microinvestigations possible, encourages empirical approaches, and, avoiding the imposition of suspect metanarratives, moves space and time within whatever frameworks the actors on the scene are able to give to them or to resist. The central concept introduced by *A Sociology of the Absurd* is territoriality.[140] Territoriality is a concept that sensitizes the investigator to the modes and processes humans employ in their many and varied constructions of spatial reality. The topos is regarded as "raw"; it is the material substance out from which humans "cook"—I am here appropriating the language of Lévi-Strauss for my own uses[141]—in order to make it serve their own purposes.

In *A Sociology of the Absurd,* Lyman and Scott develop four types of territory—public, home, interactional, and body. *Public territories* are those to which access, egress, and activity turn on official designations, legislation, and authoritative laws and their interpretations by those charged with their enforcement. *Home territories* are arenas appropriated by a specific group or aggregate for purposes of indicating, celebrating, and gathering together in behalf of its interests, concerns, creed, or course of action. *Interactional territories* set the boundaries wherein interpersonal communication and conduct may take place. *Body territories* include the epidermal area of a human being and all that can be done to affect its imagery and definition. None of these territories is invulnerable to encroachment in terms of such actions as invasion, violation, or contamination. The not uncommon conflicts over territories evoke various modes of resistance to these encroachments. From such examples as citizen militias or state-sponsored armies rising to resist the move of foreign troops onto their lands to a delinquent gang's arming of itself to thwart a turf invasion by one of its rivals, we can see that the range of such defenses runs from macrogeographic to microecological areas.[142] However, there are less violent defenses against territorial trespass. These include the placement of barriers insulating the endangered arena, and linguistic collusion, a complex process whereby the intruder is labeled as an outsider while the integrity of the group is reaffirmed. With territoriality as a fundamental concept, the postmodern investigator may take every question—whether of history conceived as the spatio-temporal construction of the terraqueous globe, or of interaction carried out at the microecological level—into the new social science.

Because Park's race relations cycle has been used here to illustrate the sociological modernist's commitment to grand spatio-temporal theorizing, it is illuminating to apply the Absurdist's conception of time and space not merely to its deconstruction but to its reconstruction in a postmodern idiom. In terms of its inexorable temporal trajectory of stages, both the Absurdists and the postmodernists are agreed on its rejection. Indeed, the emancipatory element animating each of these perspectives would likely take comfort from an observation made long ago by Amitai Etzioni: "While [racial and ethnic] groups are often forced into contact by the process of technological, economic, and social change, and perhaps this is an unavoidable process," he wrote, "the remaining stages [of Park's cycle] should be seen as alternative situations rather than links in an evolutionary process culminating in assimilation. Groups are either in conflict or accommodation or assimilation."[143] Employing the Absurdist perspective on territorialization, Park's stages can be transposed into spatial representations of the socioeconomic situation that an ethnoracial group experiences.

For example, Park's two final stages—accommodation and assimilation—might be reconceptualized in terms of a dramaturgic territoriality. Here any one of the cyclical "stages" exchanges its determinative temporal locus for one that designates one or another of the arenas on which the dramas of America's racial reality are played out. Accommodation for an unacculturated ethnoracial group might have its field of free expression—that is, a freedom to live out one's "alien" ways without the imposing surveillance of the minions of the host society—in a place of territorial sequestration. The ghetto, the racial slum, and the ethnic neighborhood are examples, each being a home territory carved out of the public space of the cosmopolitan city. Behind the invisible wall of a Chinatown, Harlem, Little Italy, Germantown, or Polonia, ethnics might realize and reaffirm their respective identities. Isolated from the uncomprehending stares and clucks of disapproval of the assimilation-oriented members of the host society, immigrants could obtain the kind of recognition and response that linked their personal individuality to their cultural heritage. They could decorate homes, stores, streets, and sidewalks with the emblems of their particular peoplehood; they could measure their conduct by the tape of their own traditional norms.

In terms of the linkage of the body to home as a territory, especially in those societies where race is indicated by visual inspection of epidermal pigmentation, eye shape, and hair texture, and where the ideology of race has become *a* if not *the* prominent element in self and group identification, the spatial segregation of races may make not only for subordination and isolation, but also for the subordinated group's active participation in the construction and maintenance of a racially exclusive home territory—as well as for its defense against encroachment from racially different outsiders. However, the isolation created thereby modifies the character and quality of the space made available for social interaction. As Park and Burgess point out, "Of themselves, differences in skin color between races would not prevent intercommunication of ideas. But the physical marks of racial differences have invariably become the symbols of racial solidarity and racial exclusiveness."[144] And, as they go on to note, "Membership in a group makes for increasing contacts within the circle of participants, but decreasing contacts with persons without."[145] The fact—or to be more precise, the socially constructed and long-established valences—of race has become not only the basis for body typing and community building, but also the foundation for the visual representation of America's creedal dilemma.[146] "The problems of humanity," Park and Burgess concluded, "are altogether different from what they would have been were all races of one complexion as they are of one blood."[147]

Assimilation conceived in terms of its spatial expression is realized in the agora. There the greatest degree of racially unmodified freedom of individual action, interaction, and communication takes place—or so the advocates of assimilation claim. As a socially constructed space, this territory of and for assimilation is in the public domain. It is the locus of civil society and, in Park's and Burgess's understanding, of civilization itself. To be excluded from that territory, as are "the mountain whites in the southern states," is to be deprived of "contacts and competition, participation in the progressive currents of civilization."[148] The "progressive currents" of modern civilization flow into and in accord with the money market. Park, like Marx, Mill, and Simmel before him,[149] believed that money was the universal solvent.[150] As he and Burgess put it, "In a free society competition tends to destroy classes and castes."[151] And, they add, "Competition . . . had its origins in the market place."[152]

Park's theory of the racial cycle envisioned a spatial locus on which, as well as a temporal moment at which, the termination of race relations would occur. Not only would this cycle's entelechy be realized in the final period of the chronologically indeterminate time trajectory, but also it would materialize on and through a historically established economic situs—the agora, the space associated with the rise of modern competitive society. Such a spatial arrangement, however, while it would, in Park's and Burgess's estimation, facilitate the emancipation of the individual and hasten the decline of the hereditary ethnoracial caste group, would also engender alienation, atomization, and anxiety. It is this effect of assimilation that has fueled radical dissent and social movements. "The anarchistic, socialistic, and communistic doctrines . . . ," they pointed out, "are based on ecological and economic conceptions of society in which competition is the fundamental fact, and from the point of view of these doctrines, the fundamental evil of society."[153]

Assimilation, for Park, ultimately meant the absorption of all peoples currently dwelling on the periphery of society into its civilly organized center. He conceived of the process as one that is inherently spatio-temporal in character. Thus together with Burgess—who had espoused a theory of the city that conceived of its growth as occurring in the form of a movement in time and space dominated by the interests of the central business district, one that composed its human topography in and as a series of concentric zones, each representing a spatio-temporal stage in the civic adjustments of immigrants, minorities, and newcomers[154]—he observed that "The ecological conception of society is that of a society created by competitive cooperation."[155] However, the character of the competition associated with centralization, civilization, and assimilation was profoundly different from that which occurred among the immigrant and minority peoples living on the margins of society. The latter had transplanted the "precivilized" folk cultures of their homelands or home territories to the ghettos and ethnic enclaves of the cities, where they experienced group conflicts and competition with other folk groups and, more significantly, with the individual members and corporate collectivities of the surrounding and hegemonic civil society. The outcome of the long and arduous struggles between the peoples of the periphery and the people of the center, Park predicted, would be the victory of the latter and the sociocultural annihilation of the former. "Races and cultures die," he wrote, "it has always been so—but civilization lives on."[156]

The space allotted to free-market civilization is a public territory, marked by its centrality, if not in geographical terms, certainly in terms of its centricentric symbology. "Society has a center," Edward Shils pointed out. "There is a central zone in the structure of society." And, in the

Absurdist outlook on territorialization, this center of society is a public zone insofar as access to and exclusion from it are defined in terms of one's formal status in the civic association, an association that in large measure is determined by public laws, settled customs, and traditional practices. "Membership in the society," Shils goes on to point out, "in more than the ecological sense of being located in a bounded territory and of adapting to an environment affected or made up by other persons located in the same territory, is constituted by relationship to this central zone."[157] The assimilated, then, are best understood as those who have the least social, cultural, economic, and political distance—that is, no distance at all—from this zone. Indeed, they are the human occupants and representatives of this zone and the gatekeepers at its points of entry. For the center, or the central zone, to modify a statement made by Shils,[158] is the realm of their values and beliefs—"the center of the order of symbols . . . which govern the society."[159]

The postmodern project begins with the deconstruction of the linear, cyclical metanarrative that culminates in the universal institutionalization of the Western tradition; in that metanarrative society moves from that enclosing a congeries of spatially circumscribed folk communities to one that is unified by and through its central zone—that is, from a multiform of peripheries to a uniform center, from pluralism to assimilation. Much of the postmodern effort is taken up with dismantling what, borrowing terminology from Natanson, might be called "big spaces" and describing and encouraging more formations of "little enclaves." One need not adopt the stance of the postmodernists on this matter to undertake an investigation within the framework of *A Sociology of the Absurd*. Recognizing that both pluralism and assimilation partake of an ideologically driven dichotomous imagery—e.g., mosaic-melting pot—the issue can be transposed from that of social science resource to one of sociological topic. In effect, the concepts of territoriality and time track, speaking to the social construction thesis, tell us to look into the world to see how people organize their lives around the fundamental anchor points of time and place.

A recent study by historian Barry S. Strauss, although neither explicitly postmodernist nor carried out in accordance with the perspective of the *Absurd*, illustrates how a particular reconstruction of ancient Athenian ethnoracial reality resolved that city-state's anxious debate over whether a pluralist or a unitary social organization was best.[160] Countering the oft-made claim that the Athenian polis was in fact composed solely and exclusively of those whom Aristophanes called "the true noble autochthonous people of Attica,"[161] Strauss uncovers the "noble lie" told and authenticated by Cleisthenes. The Athenian rulers had permitted foreign suppliants, refugees from other states' floods and famines, exiles from other lands, and alien skilled workers to resettle in the city-state's domain. Moreover, by the time of the classical period (fifth and fourth centuries B.C.E.), a significant minority among its citizens had descended from foreigners, some becoming part of the ruling elite. In brief, then, Athens's much-vaunted "Autochthony . . . was a myth." Yet, by coercively reorganizing the plural structure of Athenian society—"The traditional units into which Athenians were divided were abolished and replaced by 139 local 'peoples' (demes) and ten newly constitued tribes named for Athenian heroes"[162]— Cleisthenes was able to place a unitary civic shibboleth over a demographically multiethnic polis: "Faced with diversity, the Athenians embraced an artificial unity . . . [I]mmigrants and their descendants were guaranteed equality in the form of a new 'all Athenian' identity . . . The Cleisthenic solution . . . demanded that immigrants completely renounce their various ancestral traditions . . . Yet the Cleisthenic solution also demanded a degree of renunciation from Athenians of native descent, for they had to renounce their traditional tribes and patronymics and to accept people of immigrant ancestry as equals."[163]

In effect, Strauss's analysis of the Cleisthenic reforms illustrates how the elites of a society may reshape public space and establish and legitimate a new sense of group position[164]—a unitary, assimilation-oriented civic agora is erected in the face of great cultural diversity and a quarrel over multicultural versus monocultural social organization.

The technique employed by Cleisthenes was that of the spatiogenerative "noble lie." "By making citizens the figurative sons not of human fathers but of the localities of Attica, by promoting a civic rather than a biologic identity, Cleisthenes averted civil war."[165] Strauss offers two observations at the conclusion of his study—one directed at historians, another at the makers of policy in a postmodernized but racially conflicted America. To historians, who consciously or unwittingly have been guided by adherence to the unitary-society, civic-myth metanarrative, he suggests what in effect is a Goffmanic outlook—namely, "start from the skeptical position that societies *present themselves* as unitary even though they are in reality highly diverse."[166] To makers of public policy in the United States, he suggests that conscious social construction of a civic myth similar to that advanced by Cleisthenes might do much to relieve the stresses of those caught between the constraints of peripheral home territories and the demands of the public center: "A 'noble lie' of common identity, artificial civic myths, and institutions in which to make 'mixing' (dare one say integration?) a reality are three principles that could go far toward building a new society out of America's great ethnic and racial diversity."[167]

The Absurdist concept of territoriality unites the kind of concerns about spatialization and identity exhibited in Strauss's investigation with the postmodern conceptualization of hyperspace. Among other things, it permits understanding how the pluralized periphery may be moved into the center, and the center masked to present its denizens with a consciously distorted mirror image of their ideologically proclaimed unity. It permits a spatio-temporal construction of what the Italian philologist Gian Biagio Conte calls an allusion: "a poetic dimension . . . created by the simultaneous presence of two different realities whose competition with one another produces a single more complex reality."[158]

The Self and the Subject: Postmodernism vs. the Absurd

Among that element of the postmodernists whom Rosenau labels "the skeptics," the subject is dead.[169] Or, if not dead, banished to the nether world of modernist metanarratives and therefore dead to the postmodern world. Absent a subject, and social science—certainly the kind of social science associated with modernist metanarratives and their methods— becomes not merely impossible but ridiculous.[170] However, as Rosenau's careful study of postmodern texts reveals, the subject to whom the skeptical postmodernists put finis is but their own metonymic construct—a designation that masks the actual historically specific actor which these critics must eliminate in order to justify the postmodern antiproject. In addition, on their part, it is at one and the same time a synecdochical metanoia—a reduction of the generalized subject, whose total emancipation has been the aim of Enlightenment social thought and its praxes, to a simulacrum of one of its types—specifically, to that of an agent of the Protestant ethic[171] as that personality type appears, idealized, in the twentieth-century Occident. Rosenau provides a summary description of the skeptic's image of the subject that is worth quoting:

> [T]he modern subject is a hardworking, personally disciplined, and responsible personality. S/he is constrained by "effort" and has a self-image of "trying hard" and doing his/her "best." S/he has no personal idiosyncrasies, or at least s/he does not dwell on such issues. S/he plans ahead, is organized, and defers gratification. The modern subject may become committed to political projects and work for goals of an ideological character. S/he may believe in free will and personal autonomy,

but s/he will follow majority opinion (or the party line) once the vote has been taken and a decision is made. The modern subject is, in other words, willing to subordinate her/his own interests for the good of the collective. S/he respects rational rules, the general will, social conventions, fixed standards that seem fair. S/he searches, in good faith, for truth and expects that ultimately such a quest will not be fruitless ... [T]he modern subject has confidence in reason, rationality, and science and puts all these ahead of emotion. S/he is optimistic about the future of mankind and the possibility of progress. S/he claims to be a knowledgeable human agent, and s/he has a distinct, set personal identity.[172]

By consigning this "subject" to the postmodern necropolis, the postmodernists bury the object of their dislike and facilitate the uplift of their favored subjects—the subjugated. Their method here entails both a critique of humanism and a bit of epistemological legerdemain. Because they "object to the philosophy, the knowledge claims, the action orientation of this particular subject-form,"[173] the skeptical postmodernists not only kill the agent of it, but also treat the very idea of a subject as beyond the possibility of resuscitation in the present and future age. In so doing they sharpen their attack on humanism, holding not only that the subject is a product of modernist humanism, but also charging the latter with having unwarrantedly essentialized "man," empowering this unworthy creature with the capacity to reason effectively, dominate others, and be naively sanguine about his capacity to ameliorate the human condition. The humanistic subject is said to exert his (and only rarely her) powers via instrumental rationality. That modernist limitation leads him—or her—to solve the problem of poverty by such means as the welfare state and the incentive system, to employ the "technical fix" to improve the efficiency as well as the relations of production, and to justify Occidental imperialism as the realization of Western rationality.[174] As for privileging the assimilated subject who occupies the spatio-temporal terminus in Park's race relations cycle, the skeptical postmodernist treats such a humanistic approach to race relations as one that disrespects blue-collar and agricultural work relations but "unwittingly reproduces existing power relations."[175]

However, neither skeptical nor optimistic postmodernists can dispense altogether with the idea or the realization of the subject. Their critical dichotomy, that of the subject/subjugated, causes them to smuggle into the postmodern commonwealth two alternative versions of what might be called a quasi-subject: the postmodern individual and one or another version of a reconstituted, open-ended nonpossessive person. The former avoids any taint of humanism by in effect acting as if she or he is guided by the norms of egoistic narcissism.[176] The latter—as (in Anthony Gidden's "structurationist" portrait of him or her) one who, although embedded in the topos of a relational language that shackles every agent to the social structure, nevertheless seeks a freedom of action;[177] or who (as in Pierre Bourdieu's conceptualization of life against habitus,) is living in accordance with an individually unique configuration of speech, mannerisms, life-style, table etiquette, posture, and body shape[178]—is repositioned and constitutes a new figure, the postmodern citizen.

The Absurd approaches this topic from a different point of departure. *A Sociology of the Absurd* derives its perspective from radical pragmatism. It begins with James, Dewey, and Mead, draws on the early work of C. Wright Mills, employs concepts derived from the phenomenology of Alfred Schutz, the existentialism of Maurice Merleau-Ponty, the linguistic philosophy of Ludwig Wittgenstein, and the dramaturgical approach of Erving Goffman. It also receives guidance from the ethnomethodology of Harold Garfinkel. Radical pragmatism culminates in Richard Rorty's *Philosophy and The Mirror of Nature,*[179] a work asserting that the search for a universal epistemology of and for science is and always has been a bootless quest. What is left once we realize this is what Rorty calls edifying philosophy, a practice "having sense only as a protest against attempts to close off conversation by proposals for universal commensuration through the hypostatization of some privileged set of descriptions."[180]

The endless conversation that Rorty hopes to privilege finds expression in *A Sociology of the Absurd*'s adoption of Kenneth Burke's dramaturgical pentad, as well as its postulation of the anchor points of time tracks, territoriality, and such strategic interactional language games as are presented in exculpatory accounts, or in quests for information, face, relation-building-or-destroying outcomes, and for exploitative hegemony. For a postmodern sociology to be possible in the world after Rorty, narrative becomes the order of the day. Burke's formulation of the elementary basis of dramatistics, especially his suggestion that the act be perceived in terms of scene, agent, agency, and purpose, provides a horizon against which the stagecraft of ordinary actors can be depicted. For it is the ordinary actor who must come to terms with the multiplicity of time tracks that coexist in his or her life-space; who must choose how and when to traverse or avoid the roadways of public, home, interactional, and body territories; and who must enter into the conversational play of information, power, status, inter- or impersonal relations, and who seeks exculpatory escapes from accusations.

And is there a subject?[181] Of course. The postmodernists' dichotomy of subject/subjugated is transposed from a resource of postmodern thought to a topic for Absurdist investigation. Humans are sometimes the subjects who master their own and others' lives; other times they are the subjugated who must bow to the hegemonic power of persons or corporate bodies; and still other times—like Rosencrantz and Guildenstern in Shakespeare's *Hamlet* and in Tom Stoppard's necromantic drama about them—they flounder in a world where their own *virtu* is helpless against forces which they neither perceive nor understand.[182] The subject of Absurdist sociology is Goffman's social actor, who engages in a daily round of impression management, presenting his or her self to advantage when able, rescuing what can be salvaged after a bad performance, knowing the forms of talk suitable to the occasion, keeping care of his or her footing, and moving in and among frames of reference. Everyday life poses to the subject the challenges of carrying off interaction rituals, employing proper deference and appropriate demeanor, resisting the attempts of others to stigmatize him or her or be made the object of a degradation ceremony,[183] being intimate when occasion demands, distant when social proximity would be unwise, and in general being alive to the dangers and opportunities associated with behavior in both public and private places.

And what of the self?[184] The Absurdist sociologist accepts the principle behind Goffman's *Presentation of Self in Everyday Life.* The self is that which is presented to others and that which is sought after in the surveillance of others' presentations. Is there a single stable self guiding each actor? That, as both a postmodernist and an Absurdist might say, is a problem for the actor to solve.

CHAPTER TWO

History and Sociology: Some Unresolved Epistemological Issues

If turning away from the life-world is the problem, returning to it is the obvious solution.
  A. T. Nuyen, "Truth, Method, and Objectivity: Husserl and Gadamer on Scientific Method"

Conceivably, there are four different angles from which the history of this outlying province of Spain and Mexico might be presented. Ordinarily, the historical student will be disposed to follow the activities and the development of the political power . . . On the other hand, the story may be told by the missionary . . . Again, there is the point of view of the Mexican-Spanish settlers . . . Lastly, one might imagine an instructive account written from the standpoint of the unfortunate Indians. . .
  Frederick J. Teggart, "Englehardt: Missions of California"

For any particular study one can choose a particular variety of time. But any attempt at a global explanation—like the history of civilizations—needs a more eclectic approach. One must consult many different snapshots of the past, each with its own exposure time, then fuse times and images together, rather as the colours of the solar spectrum, focused together, combine at last into pure white light.
  Fernand Braudel, A History of Civilizations

Introduction: The Everpresent Crisis

The disciplines—the very idea of scholarly disciplines—are under assault! W. B. Yeats's querulous question—put forward in his poem, "The Second Coming"—seems to be before us on the eve of the millenium:[1]

> The blood-dimmed tide is loosed, and everywhere
> The ceremony of innocence is drowned;
> The best lack all conviction, while the worst
> Are full of passionate intensity.
>
> Surely some revelation is at hand;
>
> . . . . . .
>
> And what rough beast, its hour come round at last,
> Slouches toward Bethlehem to be born?[2]

I speak here of the rough beast of postmodernism, moving across land and water, trampling down the vintage of the metanarrative, devouring in its androgynous jaws the patriarchates of literature, history, and the social sciences, and spitting up the shreds and pieces of a modernity, crumpled into a hyperspatial chaos. Who and what can repel this beast? Can the creature even be described before it is sighted crashing through the gates of modernist knowledge? Among us, is there no Jael—the bold heroine of the *Tanakh* (Judges 4, 5)—to pretend to offer it food and rest and then drive the tentstake of a revived modernity through the skull of this incarnation of Sisera?[3] Or shall we succumb?

Critiques of Modernity I: Before the Present Crisis

Once again, history and sociology are facing a crisis in their very foundations and purposes for existence.[4] Perhaps it is a characteristic of this century that they experience crises, for, as the Italian historian Franco Venturi has said in response to being asked a question about the meaning of the twentieth century: "Historians can't answer this question. For me the twentieth century is only the ever renewed effort to understand it."[5] At the beginning of the century, the matter seemed more amenable to social scientific scholars. The example of Albion W. Small's foray into comparative historical sociology is instructive. In 1910, Small, who had founded the department of sociology at the University of Chicago in 1892,[6] published a volume of his lectures entitled *The Meaning of Social Science*. Small called for a reunification of the social sciences around the a priori claim of sociologists—namely, that a functional interdependence prevails in all matters involved in the relations of humankind to nature and to one another: "[S]ociologists declare," he observed, "that the experience bounded by the reactions between men and physical nature on the one hand and the reactions of men with one another on the other, is an interconnected experience, and that we shall have a science of it only in the proportion of our insight into the way and degree in which each item of this experience is affected by every other item of it."[7] Sociology, however, would not be crowned as queen of the sciences. Rather, Small argued, "sociologists have something to say which is bound to be one of the factors in organizing [the proposed] unified science."[8]

Recognizing that the once and future domain of a unified social science had been fractured—indeed, that it had been splintered, divided into discrete disciplinary specializations, as well as broken up into administrative units through departmentalization[9]—Small outlined what in fact it would take to carry out a synthetic social scientific research project. He chose, for purposes of illustration, the investigation of a complex problem: "The meaning of the process by which the old Germano-Roman imperialism first resolved itself into the four hundredfold particularism of Germany beginning with the Reformation, and the further process by which, after the breakdown of particularism in the Napoleonic era, decadent particularism transformed itself into the new imperialism of the modern empire."[10] The temporal period of the project was set at four hundred years, 1510–1910;[11] its spatial arena was all of Central Europe. No single-factor hypothesis could satisfy the imperatives of Small's grand conception of a unified social science, for, as he put it, the "part that one of these factors plays at a given moment is a function of the operation of all the other factors at the same time."[12]

To Small, the factors that culminated in this particular historical skein are threads sewn into the very fabric of human existence, from the topographical to the psychological. Hence, to even begin the project that he proposed, "Twenty-four or more of the philosophers, and psychologists, and cultural and political and church historians, and lawyers, economists, sociologists, etc., would [have to] become responsible for running down the evidence, each for one of [the] twenty-four strands woven into the web of the experience, and each would try to learn from the others how his particular strand was woven with the other strands so as to make up the complete experience."[13] Small envisioned the project taking five or ten years of sustained work, but he insisted that such an expenditure of time and effort would have been worth the cost: "After five years or ten," he wrote, "the results would not be either of the academically disjointed sciences represented by individuals in the co-operating group. The synthesized result would be an organized body of social science; a knowledge of a section of the experience of men in association."[14] Moreover, Small concluded, he would have no objection if the discipline and method that he advocated would be called *historical science*—so long as the definition of the latter corresponded to that which he quoted in English translation from Ernst Bernheim's 1908 work entitled *Historische Methode*: "Historical science is the science which investigates and exhibits the temporally and spatially bounded facts of the evolution of men in their singular as well as in their collective activities as social beings, in the correlation of psychophysical causation."[15] Small insisted that both historians and social scientists had an obligation to construct the kind of historical science that he proposed, but he pointed out that the burden of carrying forth this mission had yet to be assumed, either by historians or sociologists. Those who would take it up would have to treat social science not as a career but as a vocation—one that "calls for combinations of large numbers of the best equipped men to carry on the tasks of social science in co-operation."[16] In the decades that followed, however, no body of scholars answered the religiously minded sociologist's plea for historical science to become such a vocation.

The epistemological question that lay hidden behind Small's proposal had already emerged before he had put it forth. It stood sentinel over the very possibility of the latter kind of historical science to enter, much less to unite, the established nobility of the scholarly realm. That question, put in its boldest form, inquired whether a study of particulars was compatible with a science demanding generalizations. In a recent monograph, Harry Bash stated the issue directly: "Dictated by its quest for general, rather than particular, explanation, science must proceed in terms of a formal abstractedness, through categories that transcend the particularity and immediacy of any narrowly specific subject matter."[17] Known to philosophers of science as the division between idiographic and nomothetic conceptualizations, this problem had pitted, and continues to pit, the idiographically oriented particularists, that is, historians, against the nomothetically minded generalists, that is, the sociologists and other social scientists.

For those who hoped to classify and compare, as well as for those who regarded such an enterprise as bootless, the aforementioned matter took form as a debate over the following question: Which unit of human activity, if any, might be subjected to such treatment, and which unit might be forever beyond the pale of commensurability? For anthropologists, to take one example, the issue of units for comparison emerged in a quarrel over whether traits (either a biologic, material, or nonmaterial aspect of a culture), or institutions (conceived as organized, intentional, standardized, and purposive social behavior), or various empiric aggregates (e.g., totemism, culture complexes), or any or all of these are the proper and scientifically grounded unit categories for an ethnological science that also seeks a place among the historical disciplines.[18]

For the sociologists concerned to establish a historical science of society, the unit of investigation and the methods and outlook appropriate to such an investigation were first enunciated by Georg Wilhelm Friedrich Hegel (1770–1831), and developed further by his disciple, Lorenz von Stein (1815–1890).[19] In this largely European sociological tradition, there was established the privileging of a putatively empirical aggregate, "class," in effect making it at once both fact and concept, and treating it as both a generalized and an inevitable form of human social organization, as well as the social unit that acts or is acted upon by and through the course of history. Class, in turn, was signified by and through an individual's occupation. "According to the laws of the economy," Stein had observed, "the various occupations are organic parts of a whole . . . the individual enters irrevocably into the economic order at a specific point; he cannot leave it at will. Thus the organization of economic life becomes the order of the human community."[20]

Stein carried off a significant intellectual feat by conceptually distinguishing society from the state. However, he went even further, noting each's implications in the fate of the other and setting forth a generalized developmentalist metanarrative that would supervene the process. That metanarrative would, in turn, guide the next century's social scientists in their selection of unit-categories for comparison, classification, and exposition: "[T]he principle of the state is in direct contradiction to the principle of society . . . ," he wrote. "[T]hese two poles—state and society—determine the life of the human community precisely because they are opposed to each other. It follows that social life can only be understood by comprehending the *nature* and the *strength* of these two elements . . . [Moreover, the] struggle between them produces a movement *regulated by definite and intelligible laws*."[21]

A sociological science of history and social change, therefore, would begin by investigating the precise nature and exact strength of the social aggregates engaged in the struggle between state and society; then the investigator would locate the participants on the temporal trajectory indicated in the predetermined definite and intelligible law of societal motion; and, having done all this, the investigator could predict the likely outcome of the struggle, if it was still ongoing, or, if an instance from the already closed past, place it on the hypostatized time line where other instances of the same struggle were to be found.

Stein envisioned the social changes that had already happened or that would happen as occurring in a nonrandom fashion, slowly, orderly, and with a definite and predetermined outcome: "It is not by chance that a dominant class develops suitable privileges," he pointed out, going on to show "that the class thus privileged becomes an estate, and . . . the estate tends to become a caste . . ."[22] The orderly movement thus projected, he insisted, "is a general law of social development within the state . . ." It occurs as it does "because this development is inherent in the nature of class relations." The social scientist could respond to the practical interest that arises over any immediate instance of such a struggle by observing "its operation under the specific conditions of any one society." However, Stein warns, the "definite and intelligible" law that he had designated "encompasses the whole of history," and because of that spatio-temporal fact, "it never exhausts itself suddenly in a single generation." Rather, he continues, "the life of society moves towards its irrevocable goal in a grandiose, quiet pace of thousands of small, untiringly repeated attempts, formations, repetitions, deviations—but always with unshakable consistency." Because the happenings that historians usually take to be unique and incomparable are, in Stein's pronouncement of the law of social development, mere instances of the inexorable unfolding of the sociohistorical process, their alleged incommensurability is overthrown a priori: "[T]he individual experiences only a small part of the process taking place . . . And for this reason the thought, the will and the action of the individual [i.e., the very elements that historians insist make for a happening's uniqueness] are powerless against this movement." In their place is a new role for the social investigator: "[I]f this law is known," Stein asserts, "[a] new field of investigation opens up . . . for the science of society, which includes the history of society." That new field would "detect [the law of development's] traces in individual events."

Happenings, occurrences, and events are thus epiphenomenal illustrations of the law of development that underpins them. That law is itself not a matter for investigation as to its validity; rather, it is to be taken on faith (or perhaps on the grounding of Reason with a capital R), for as Stein insisted, "The immaturity of our science still conceals how much there is to learn, to describe, and to analyze." He wanted to contribute his law to its maturation: "In spite of their endless variety, the lives of the people can be comprehended on the basis of the law that we have established: the movement of every social order is a development towards social dependency in different stages . . ." What Stein accomplished in his scientific application of Hegelian philosophy was a twofold breakthrough: the data of narrative history had been subordinated to the lawlike processes depictable by social science; and the laws of social development had been relieved of the onerous requirement that they be empirically validated.

Historians of the nineteenth century had also been seeking a baseline from which to continue their development of a form of idiographic presentation that, while respectful of objectivity and skeptical about sources of reliable data, would provide their studies with both meaning and purpose. A major epistemological move in that direction was made when leading members of the discipline adopted the historiographical approach enunciated by Leopold von Ranke (1795–1886).[23] The objectivity appropriate to particulars conceived idiographically was preserved through each historian's application of Ranke's promise that the past would be reported "*wie es eigentlich gewesen* (literally, "as it actually was"). But, Ranke's more formidable contribution was—in contrast to Stein's basic thesis that "society has a history of its own"[24]—to provide a new grounding for the privileging of the state, and more particularly the nation-state, as the *telos* as well as the triumph of divinely-guided Reason. In effect, Ranke's innovation was built on a variant of Herodotus's method—namely, to narrate the details of a recent event (in Herodotus's case, the Persian invasion and its outcome), including a prefatory account of the circumstances preceding it, but with the main focus on its denouement.[25] For Ranke, the coming-to-be of the national state, and more especially that of the Prussian imperial hegemony of his own time, was a denouement not only devoutly to be desired, but also a determination of the Divine will on humans—whose actions in its behalf were the objective materials for both a new historiography and a new narrative.[26]

That narrative, however, did not meet all of the criteria of science then being put forth. It certainly did not conform to the approach to the same problem that Small would lay out a quarter century after Ranke's death. In particular, it failed one of Small's tests of description, but passed another, more controversial Hegelian test of teleology. Ranke's elevation of the national-state to history's end point seemed, in the light of later evaluations, to require what in 1909 W. M. Urban would call "appreciative description." That mode of description would be carried out "in order to pass judgment on the intellectual, moral, and aesthetic worth of the objects in question in the light of transcendental ideal standards of value." [27] On the other hand, Ranke's claim that states were spiritual entities (*Gedanken Gottes*) whose raison d'être was to civilize mankind, and his assertion that they had emerged out from a fusion of Germanic and Roman peoples,[28] seemed to bespeak his discovery of what Scottish historian John Caird regarded as the sine qua non of scientific history, namely, "a secret order of reason in the life of nations and of the world."[29] Thus an issue was joined that has continued to plague any rapprochement between history and sociology: Rankean historians and positivist sociologists hold respectively opposed positions on the question of whether the cunning of Reason should hold sway over, or be subordinated to, the mundane contemplation of facts.[30]

Historians are still concerned with particulars, and their unit-categories are, usually, individuals—except that the individuated datum of a history might be an organized collectivity, for example, a state, a nation, an empire, or a city. Sociologists, following in the tradition handed down to them from Comte,[31] abjured mere chronological sequencing, preferring instead to project stages of development and to classify unit-categories on the basis of structural or functional similarities and differences.[32] However, both historians and sociologists engaged in practices against which they often preached: Some historians—for example, Arnold J. Toynbee, until Teggart warned him off the practice[33]—analogized macrohistorical developments to the human life cycle; some sociologists—for example, Robert E. Park and his associates in presenting the findings of their Pacific Coast survey of 1926,[34] and among his epigoni for years thereafter—treated data disconsonant with the postulated progressive and irreversible four-stage race relations cycle as inconsequential with respect to the latter's validity.[35] The central issue evoking both modernist and postmodernist critiques of history and historiography remained unresolved—the problem of commensurability.

Critiques of Modernity II: The Teggart School and Commensurability

Frederick J. Teggart (1870–1946)[36] founded a school of thought that sought nothing less than to solve the problem of commensurability by refuting the dual science thesis. That thesis had been proclaimed in 1894 by Wilhelm Windelband (1848–1915). In his rectorial address at Strasbourg, Windelband had isolated two distinctive kinds of science: "One kind of science is an inquiry into general laws. The other kind of science is an inquiry into specific historical facts . . . [T]he objective of the first kind is the general, apodictic judgment; the objective of the other kind of science is the singular, assertoric proposition."[37] Sociology and the other social sciences seem to belong to the first kind; history, to the second. As Windelband saw the matter, a great and unbridgeable gulf separated the two kinds of science, the one associated with "laws," the other with "events." "The law and the event," he concluded, "remain as the ultimate, incommensurable entities of our world view."[38] As Guy Oakes has pointed out, "Windelband's lecture outlines the problematic within which Dilthey, Simmel, Rickert, and Weber attempted to develop a philosophy of the historical or sociocultural sciences."[39] Windelband's own position on the matter was pessimistic. The epistemological division of the two kinds of sciences had set up "the boundary conditions where scientific inquiry can only define problems and only pose questions in the clear awareness that it will never be able to solve them."[40] Teggart—who had begun his career as a heterodoxical historian and gone on to found and chair the Department of Social Institutions at the University of California at Berkeley, the forerunner to that university's Department of Sociology and Social Institutions[41]—was, on the other hand, sanguine about the possibility of constructing a historical social science.

Elsewhere I have outlined the principal features of the Teggart school's project—in brief, its proposal to establish a neopositivist science of history to which would be appended a phenomenological theory of social change.[42] Here it suffices to show that the problem of commensurability—the issue that adumbrated Windelband's pronouncement of a permanent epistemological divide—has not yet been solved to the satisfaction of those sociologists who have sought to throw a bridge across the Windelbandian gulf.[43] On one side is the thesis offered by Kenneth E. Bock, a disciple of Teggart, to the effect that "The conviction, fostered by some historians and philosophers and accepted by many social scientists, that the record of men's [and, we might add, women's] experiences is something that can be comprehended only in a quivering ecstasy of subjective and intuitive interpretation, is something that we must get out of our systems."[44] On the other side is an argument about certain foundational differences between sociology and history that has been recently reiterated by Franco Ferrarotti: "The elaboration of general concepts," he observes, "is . . . a logico-instrumental question that concerns both disciplines. Sociology gives us the 'homogeneous,' the 'typical,' while historiography provides the 'individual.' . . . Both sciences . . . have a common subject matter—social action and human initiative—in their specific historical determination. However, these basic common characteristics cannot justify any summary reduction of one to the other."[45] The irresolution of the issue is illustrated by two commentaries made sixty years apart, one by a historian, the other by a sociologist, on whether the actions contributing to revolutions constituted a unique "individual" unit-category or a type of activity subject to comparison and the making of generalizations. Ironically, it was the historian, Gaetano Salvemini (1873–1957), who took up the latter position: "To determine whether revolutions are governed by constant laws, there is only one method: we must compare one with the other the greatest possible number of revolutions . . . [A]nd we must see whether between these phenomena so far apart in time and space there can be discovered similarities or dissimilarities which are constant."[46]

The sociologist Piotr Sztompka holds that the individual factors involved insured a condition of unpredictable ungeneralizability: "Because revolutionary events depend on actions taken by multitudes of individuals, they occur as aggregated effects of myriads of individual decisions. Each of these decisions is taken by individuals placed in unique biographical and social situations, and each human individual happens to be at least marginally erratic, capricious, underdetermined in what he/she decides to do. Thus on the aggregated macro-scale, the condition described in the natural sciences as 'chaos' seems to prevail, preventing any specific prediction."[47] The mainstream of sociology had sought a way around the impasse created by the "chaos" of unique happenings by distinguishing generalizations made without regard to spatio-temporal specificity from those made by historians. Thus in 1921 Park and Burgess noted "As soon as historians seek to take events out of their historical setting, that is to say, out of their time and space relations, in order to compare them and classify them; as soon as historians begin to emphasize the typical and representative rather than the unique character of events, history ceases to be history and becomes sociology."[48]

For a true historical social science to come to the fore of scholarship, the members of the Teggart school held, there would have to be an acceptance of its very possibility in the epistemologies of both historians and sociologists. Such a conviction, however, flew in the face of the heritage of

assumption that had come down, in Bock's conception of the matter, to
debilitate the scholarly praxes of both disciplines. For, as he put the matter
in 1956, there exists a "widespread agreement among social scientists, historians, and philosophers that historical happenings are unique, that the accidental and the historical are almost synonymous, and that the specific
time-place data of history must, as a consequence, be grasped more in artistic than in scientific fashion."[49] The effects of one's acquiescence to this
covenant of epistemological faith are twofold: For the historian, it has
entailed a resort to artful constructions of narrative and an individually varying discursive orientation. The latter is usually accounted for by reference
either to the individual historian's genius, or to his or her adherence to a
particular philosophy of history, or school of historical thought. Such
philosophies or schools guide the selection of happenings so that they
compose themselves into a particular spatio-temporal sequence. For the
sociologist, on the other hand, the science of society has taken up the task
of tracing a course around history, first by adding on to the charge that
historical occurrences are unique and incomparable, that they are "subjective" products of the individual mind of the actor, and, hence, relativistic,
irrational and useless to science.[50] In their place, sociologists have sought
to build up a science of society that speaks to the organic relationships (i.e.,
functions)[51] that must prevail among their spatio-temporally coexistent
elements (e.g., social institutions) in order for the motion of society to
remain stable (i.e., the thesis of dynamic equilibrium,[52] or, in the felicitous
phrase of Seymour Martin Lipset, "stability in the midst of change")[53].
However, in abstracting from the human experiences that which one would
think to be the inescapable data for such a science, sociologists "shift from
the view that the abstract can be elicited from an analysis of experiences to
the view that the abstract has an existence in experience independent of
and apart from the concrete, and, therefore, that the general can or must
be sought by avoiding attention to detail."[54] A parade of ahistorical
procedures—all too familiar to the conventional sociologist—follows. As
Bock summarizes them: "Hence the effort to seek the nature or functioning of society outside of social histories; hence the postulation of 'forces' or
'factors' in experience that produce or are responsible for observed happenings; hence the belief that process can be discovered in the essential nature
of the entity undergoing process."[55] Holding that both modern history and
modern social science have gotten off on the wrong foot, Bock advocates
recognition of the actual character of science, namely, its probabilistic character, as its most distinctive feature: "The precision of absolute truth may

be sought in theology or in philosophy of history; but science thrives on inexactitude. Its propositions must be continually refuted or the enterprise is finished. Scientists make statements of probability, and although they use these as working hypotheses, a constant proviso is that they are improbable."[56]

In Bock's perspective, a neopositivistic, and probabilistic, historical social science, however it might be labeled (e.g., as "history," "sociology," "comparative history," "comparative sociology," etc.) has been too long awaited. However, such a science could only come into its own after certain deeply embedded but debilitating assumptions about both history and science had been set aside. These assumptions included (1) the belief that happenings and events are unique and therefore incapable of being compared for purposes of arriving at probabilistic generalizations; (2) the belief that social change occurs in slow, orderly, continuous, and teleological stages; (3) the belief that given the incommensurability of happenings, historians should be content with presenting chronologically linear narratives of what had happened; (4) the belief that given the same assumption about the facts of history, both social scientists and historians are free to construct conjectural metanarratives that produce one or another variant of a Hegelian grand History; and, (5) the belief that for purposes of study, if not for other purposes, a society, or any unit thereof, may be analogized to an organism.[57] From the fact that the perspective offered by Bock and the other members of this school of thought has not yet been fully accepted either by the discipline of history or in the various fields of the social sciences, the coming of the rough beast of postmodernism entails an epistemological manifestation of one more obstacle to the completion of the Teggart school's mission.[58]

Confronting the Beast: The Claims of Postmodernism

"Postmodernism seems doomed to be an intermission," Todd Gitlin had concluded in 1989.[59] A sociologist attuned to, and a student of, the excitement that had attended the student revolt in the sixties,[60] Gitlin, while able to discern the outlines of what I have called a secular variant of Yeats's rough beast, is not sure to what it is a transition, or, for that matter, how long the transition will last: "[H]istorical time is treacherous to assess," he notes. "Intermissions can last a very long time . . ."[61] As Gitlin sees the matter, postmodernism "refers to a certain constellation of styles and tones in cultural works: pastiche; blankness; a sense of exhaustion; . . . a relish for copies and repetition; a knowingness that dissolves commitment into irony; acute self-consciousness about the formal, constructed nature of the work; . . . *a rejection of history*."[62] Here, we will be concerned with the last-named item.

Fundamental to the postmodern vision is the shattering of what once was science's and history's mirror held up to nature. According to Gitlin, the breakup of the mirror has occurred recently and in three phases, each of which corresponds to an era characterized by a master imagery of social, cultural, and historical reality: The first era, the *premodern,* is one in which there prevails a unity of vision, a single narrative voice, linear sequential continuity, high culture, Renaissance-rooted aesthetic judgments and either supportive or oppositional individualism. The period of the *modern* reverses this: the unity aspired for is constructed from fragments or shocks or out of the various juxtapositions of things; the order of the world is called into question, and the established sociopolitical, cultural, and economic order is critiqued. In addition, the modern subject is estranged; beauty arises out of discord; and there is a longing for the return to, or the coming of, an apocalyptic age. The time of the *postmodern* is that in which the trends and forces of the modern reach their apotheosis; in which those who once quested for unity abandon all hope in the face of endless incommensurable texts; in which there is a "cultivation of surfaces endlessly referring to, ricocheting from, reverberating onto other surfaces,"[63] and, hence, evoking the triumph of arbitrariness. In the time of the postmodern, "Anything can be juxtaposed to anything else. Everything takes place in the present, 'here,' that is, nowhere in particular . . . The implied subject is fragmented, unstable, even decomposed; it is finally nothing more than a crosshatch of discourses . . . there is . . . a collapse of feeling, a blankness . . . Genres are spliced, so are gradations."[64] Postmodernist discourse exhibits, in the language of its own discourse, a *trace* of the modern even as it seeks simultaneously to disown and succeed it.

It is beyond the scope of the present work either to summarize or to evaluate the entire set of beliefs, notions, and praxes that make up the discursive text of postmodernism. Our task, rather, is to see its consequences for the already troubled relations between the disciplines of history and sociology. It is an unusually complex relationship, for the postmodern critique of both history and sociology cuts across the modernist critique of conventionalized history and sociology that Bock—and, before him, Teggart—had given. Postmodernist thinkers, unmindful of that critique, restate some of its elements but take no notice of the profundity of its double-barreled assault on *both* conjectural metanarratives *and* fact-privileged artistic narratives. In the event, those postmodernists who bother with history at all reject all metanarratives, whether historical or sociological in character. But because they believe they are entering an era that, while demarcated in time from its predecessor, still occupies a portion of its epistemological space, they seek to privilege a localized, microecological, and emancipatory representation of what Teggart,[65] Bock and their followers had sought to admit into a deromanticized science of history—romantically resuscitated, racial, sexual, and gendered minorities. To the extent that narrativity constitutes the postmodernists' methodological stance—that is, that despite its inherent defects it is the only approach scholars can take to write the historical or the social text[66]—they have become witting or unwitting followers of Richard Rorty.[67] In 1979, Rorty had held the historical and scientific mirror up to nature and perceived that he could not see its reflection.[68] However, at the same time, postmodernists are seekers after a judgmental ethics, one that is freed from the iron cages imprisoning both scientific and historical, and hence discredited, discourses.[69]

Holding the Mirror of History Up to Postmodernism

"If postmodern theories are taken seriously," observe Joyce Appleby, Lynn Hunt, and Margaret Jacob, "there is no transhistorical or transcendent grounds for interpretation, and human beings have no immediate access to the world of things or events."[70] And, although they are not the only theories taken seriously today, these theories *are* taken seriously. According to their principal spokespersons, the late Michel Foucault (1926–1984) and Jacques Derrida (1930–), knowledge is driven by language, language cannot escape from its own prison-house of signifiers, and the development of any discourse is motivated by the will to power. Hence, the quest for a reliable and valid scientific history is both a sham and a shibboleth—a mask covering both a chaos of signs and a hidden hegemonic desire. Because of the limitations imposed by the actual nature of language—namely, its incapability of representing reality objectively—the hitherto legitimated logocentric genres of language, for example, history and science, are impossible of realization. Each is a mode of discourse, or, worse, mere information. Where Nietzsche had insisted that man is the inventor rather than the discoverer of truth, Foucault tells us that disciplinary discourses and metanarratives, as well as the institutions that are expressed and manifested through them, invent both individuals and truth. What was once considered the foundation of Western rationalism, the autonomous subject, is decentered, that is, removed from having a primary role in, or being the active agent of, history.[71] In his or her place are institutions of domination legitimated by the discourses that create and grant them their hegemony. In a commentary on Foucault's *Discipline and Punish: The Birth of the Prison*,[72] Peter Burke has claimed that "after [Foucault's] corrosive criticisms of the conventional wisdom, the history of incarceration, sexuality, and so on will never be the same again."[73] To the extent that Burke's assertion obtains widespread assent, Foucault's *oeuvre*, as well as that of the other leading postmodernists, bids fair to become an instance of what Teggart called an "intrusion"[74]—that is, a special kind of "event," one that triggers a "crisis"[75] that in turn establishes the conditions[76] under which a true sociocultural change might occur.[77]

The Prospects for History and Sociology

"The world of learning," Folke Dovring observed in 1960, on the eve of the postmodern invasion, "is no quiet place, and many scientific contests tragically resemble the *odium theologicum* of the dark centuries of the religious wars."[78] The coming of postmodernism, however, has not caused this conflict to descend to the level of a *bellum omnium in omnes*. The disciplines, in contrast to nation-states, are organized something like the Catholic church, that is, they have in their several disparate schools of thought the functional equivalents of denominations, orders, and sects, but, unlike the church, there is no clearly established Holy See. The character of postmodernity might well be recognized as Agnes Heller and Ferenc Feher envisioned it. To them postmodernity "is neither a historical period nor a trend with well-defined characteristics." Rather, it is "the private, collective time and space, within the wider time and space of modernity, delineated by those who have problems with or queries addressed to modernity . . . , by those who want to take it to task, and by those who make an inventory of modernity's achievements as well as its unresolved dilemmas."[79] And precisely because postmodernity, its rough beasthood untamed, has begun to penetrate the gates of the scholarly commonwealth, to add its growl to those already being heard, its status and citizenship are yet to be determined.

"Those who have chosen to dwell in postmodernity nevertheless live among moderns and among premoderns."[80] And hence it is the case that despite their claims to have discredited all metanarratives, decentered the subject, and deconstructed the texts of Occidental racial patriarchy, their situation is that of suppliants. Thus, to take one illuminating example, Steven Seidman, a leading protagonist of an *engagé* variant of postmodernism—he charges that "the hegemony of sociological theory within sociology has contributed to rendering sociological theorists insular and [to] making their products—theories—socially and intellectually obscure and irrelevant to virtually everyone except other theorists"[81]—treats his own position as a "postmodern hope."[82] As Heller and Feher point out, the postmodernists are dwellers on a presentist time track whose temporal-based syntax coerces them to adopt the future-perfect tense. "Thus," they write, "the primary concern of the present when it is being lived as postmodern is that we are not living in the present, we are not where we are but we are 'after.'"[83]

This coexistence of different spatio-temporal life experiences, however, is paralleled by an even greater multiplicity of attitudes toward history, some embedded in the official canon, others part of the several peoples' histories; some representing continuing adherence to older metanarratives, others new attempts to ground modernist sequential theories in a linear or multi-linear narrative; some continuing to privilege the rise of the Occident, others seeking to elevate the neglected or marginalized voices of those who have been the Occident's victims. Even if Seidman insists "general stories are still needed" after "we . . . abandon the great modernist narratives,"[84] his own attitude toward history and social science will, I believe, be forced to recognize its limited place in the larger epistemological impasse that Rortyan postmodernism has exposed. With language, selfhood, and the ideal of the liberal community reduced to matters of fundamental contingency,[85] Rorty concedes that there is left only narrative, and the only concern is finding ways to continue the multivocal conversation.[86] A plurality of histories and of arts and sciences of history is thus assured, perhaps in perpetuity.[87]

Now I should like to focus on two epistemological issues brought to the fore by both the modernist critique made by the Teggart school and the postmodern challenge to all received historical and sociological theories: (1) the problem of the grand theory or metanarrative; and (2) the problem of alterity, or the privileging of the subjugated. Then I shall suggest a "phenomenological" resolution of the entire matter, treating the issues raised as features of human consciousness in a world that is forever ontologically unknowable but always interrogated for its meaning.[88]

Metanarratives and Grand Theories

A fundamental difference between the critique of metanarratives made by the Teggart school and that offered by the postmodernists is that the former couches its assault on the several grand developmentalist theses in terms of their inadequacy as theories within the frame of Western rules of evidence and proof; while the postmodernists reject the very possibility of metanarratives primarily because neither they nor their makers can overcome the logocentric limitations that affect all humans living within the prison-house of language,[89] and secondarily because these metanarratives work to degrade, demean, and delegitimate the lives and actions of such subjugated aggregates as the nonwhite, non-European peoples; women; the sexually different; and the physically challenged. The Teggart school does not rule out the possibility of a properly scientific historian producing a grand narrative, while the postmodernists would banish all such from the scholarly scene. Thus, the late Teggartian school sociologist-historian Robert A. Nisbet, while deploring the universalistic and holistic thinking that continues to make "capitalism," "kinship," or "social system" into objects for a sociohistorical investigation of their origins and development and attributing the latter to such immanent metaphorical constructs as "evolution," "growth," or "development," nevertheless insisted that what the evidence delivers is "simply the behaviour of human beings in their varied procreative, wealth-getting, comfort-seeking, status-aspiring, order-making activities," and he argued, in effect, that this evidence, scientifically gathered, classified, and compared, could become the grounding of more than one grand narrative showing "how human beings actually behave within finite space and time."[90]

In contrast to the position of the Teggartians, Lyotard, Baudrillard, and Jameson and their postmodern followers) argue from the vantage point of a post-Saussurean linguistic philosophy that neither social scientists nor historians will ever be able to find their way out of the forest of signifiers, none of which refers to anything signified. They conclude from this that the making of metanarratives is impossible.[91] Equally critical, Seidman rejects the quest for a foundationalist sociological theory as productive of nothing but a cacophony of metaphysical discourses, "a virtual babble of different vocabularies addressing a cluster of changing disputes."[92] In place of such a debilitating discursive proliferation, he calls for "a concentrated, productive discourse focused on a limited set of problems . . ." But, suspecting that "science is tied to the project of Western modernity and to a multiplicity of more local, more specific struggles around class, status, gender, sexuality, race, and so on . . . , [and further supposing that the victims of this science include] African Americans, gay men and lesbians, Latinos, Asians, the differently abled, and so on," Seidman holds that "no social discourse can escape the doubt that its claims to truth are tied to and yet mask an ongoing social interest to shape the course of history," and to gain and sustain its own position of power. "Once the veil of epistemic privilege is torn away," he concludes, "science appears as a social force enmeshed in particular cultural and power struggles."

The metanarratives are to be ruled out of court in postmodern sociology because of their inappropriate and unjust earlier legitimation as authoritative discourses. "Social discourses," Seidman writes, "especially the broad social narratives of development produced by sociological theorists, but also the specialized discourses produced by demographers, criminologists, organizational sociologists, and so on, shape the social world by creating normative frameworks of racial, gender, sexual, national, and other types of identity, social order, and institutional functioning . . . [and such discourses] carry the intellectual and social authority of science." More particularly, Seidman not only charges the already well-known Occidental metanarratives with providing a scientific veneer for a theory of Eurocentric entelechy, but also taxes those who would continue to adhere to them with failing to see "that behind the aggrandizing intellectualism of the modernists were the expansionist politics of the age of colonialism." However, Marx's metanarrative fares no better in Seidman's perspective, for here he seems to be definitely pre-Teggartian, calling for separate national histories of events that are allegedly not comparable: "I believe," Seidman writes, "that the immense sociohistorical differences among European and Anglo-American societies and between them and non-Western societies would affect seriously the form and functioning of industrializing dynamics. Individual societies evolve their own unique configurations and historical trajectories, which are best analyzed historically, not from the heights of general theory." Moreover, but in a move that puts him closer to the Teggartian camp, Seidman's evaluation of general theories claims that not only are they, in their broad conceptualizations of matters, repressive of subjugated minorities, but also, "when [their] conceptions are stretched to cover all times and places or to be socially inclusive, . . . [that they are] so contentless as to lose whatever explanatory value they have." Unable to accept the possibility of a postmodern comparative historical science of society and unwilling to abandon a belief in unit-categories that are unique, Seidman's approach to postmodernism flirts briefly with Mertonian middle-range theories, but believing "that they remain tied too closely to scientism and to the modernist ideology of enlightenment and progress that have been suspect for decades," moves away from them and toward a special variant of alterity that he has developed since his original essay and which he calls "queer theory."[93]

However, although such an astute observer of the intellectual scene as Fred Dallmayr believes, on the one hand, that "postmodernity signifies indeed a farewell to the grand 'metanarratives' of metaphysics," but, on the other, that "the abandonment of all fixed foundations ... [will] lead to chaos or a general 'war of all against all' ...,"[94] at least one contemporary social scientist, Robert Heilbroner, concerned about the mood of pessimism in the West, has turned his by no means inconsiderable talents toward grand developmentalist theorizing and to offering a statement about the prospects, that is, the future, of the present era.[95] In the event, the product of his efforts demonstrates that neither the Teggartian school's modernist critique of modernism nor the postmodernist challenge to metanarratives has displaced the older historico-sociological tradition altogether. Justifying a preliminary foray into futurology by quoting a paradoxical statement made by the medievalist historian Vassily Kliuchesky—namely, "History teaches nothing but only punishes for not learning its lessons"[96]—Heilbroner, at first, confined himself to examining disparate predictions about the future of capitalism in the writings of Adam Smith, Karl Marx, Alfred Marshall, John Maynard Keynes, and Joseph Schumpeter. He concluded that study by emphatically predicting that "Participatory economics will not become the social order in the twenty-first century, no matter what, catastrophes included,"[97] but, he added, more cautiously, that "twenty-first century capitalism will be dominated by a spectrum of capitalisms, some successful, some not."[98]

In a more recent work, *Visions of the Future*, Heilbroner assumed the mantle of Comte, delineating the successive epochs of humankind's sociocultural evolution and offering his readers some observations on what tomorrow's era would bring. It is beyond the scope of the present study to evaluate the whole of the thesis that Heilbroner presents. Suffice it to say that his quadripartite periodization of all of human history—(1) "the distant past," that had begun "with primitive societies dependent for at least a hundred thousand years on stone and flint implements, followed by ten to twenty thousand years during which the gradient of material change slowly tilts upward with the use of copper and bronze, to be followed, in turn, starting perhaps in the sixth millennium B.C., by the scaling of a great escarpment of social change—atop which were established the first completely stratified societies of history, the Mesopotamian, Egyptian, Indian, and

Chinese kingdoms and empires," and goes on to embrace "the glory that was Greece and the grandeur that was Rome, the political confusion of the Middle Ages, and finally the appearance of the modern nation-state in Europe in the seventeenth century . . .";[99] (2) "yesterday, . . . the period in which our forebears grew up and most of us have come of age," that had commenced "in the time of our great-great grandparents' great-great grandparents, and [had lasted] until . . . perhaps . . . the end of World War II and the collapse of the Soviet Union";[100] (3) "today," which seems to have begun with the ending of the Cold War and is continuing until the advent of (4) "tomorrow," some time in the unforeseeable future[101]—commits every error pointed out years ago by Teggart and his school. There is the presentation of an unfalsifiable hypothesis; the employment of a variant of the Comtean comparative method; an absence of historical evidence to support the very existence of the hypostatized stages of human advance—and all of the thesis is put forward with the disclaimer that "In a work of this scope, substantiation becomes a hopeless problem. A volume twice this size would be needed to provide scholarly evidence to underpin what I have written . . ."[102] Like earlier variants, Heilbroner's "grand narrative recounts the story with an overtly causal, covertly teleological self-confidence."[103]

The point of mentioning Heilbroner's entry in the contest of competing metanarratives as well as the contestation of all of them is less to engage in another Teggartian critique[104] than to point to a phenomenon given little notice by either proponents or critics—namely, that the several attitudes toward history and historiography that are under discussion have a "geologic" character about them. They are so deeply and profoundly "sedimented" within the academic discourses that even Foucault's "archaeological" approach, while able to uncover them, will not prove capable of dislodging them altogether.[105] Like the radioactive junk deposited underground at a hazardous waste site, even the discredited and discreditable philosophies and metanarratives of history have an ever-long half-life; those decentered as well as those not yet decentered must still be contended with. When Heller and Feher remind us that postmodernists are living in the era of modernity,[106] they call attention to the fact that the era is characterized not so much by acceptance of a single uniform idea of "History" as by a grudging toleration of and a disquieting annoyance over the temporal copresence of a plethora of histories, each seeking recognition and response for itself. Such is also the case with some postmodernists' epistemic turn to alterity as a proposed new form for sociological history.

Alterity: From Subjugated to Subject

The theme of alterity takes its point of departure from Walter Benjamin's (1892–1940) thematization of "the tradition of the oppressed" in opposition to Ranke's proffered mandate to present history *wie ist eigentlich gewesen*.[107] "It means," Benjamin observed, "to seize hold of a memory as it flashes up at a moment of danger."[108] However, for those who are the subjects and victims of oppression, "the 'state of emergency' in which we live is not the exception but the rule," and the mission of the historian is to turn away from historicism's tendency to tell the story of that struggle from the point of view of the documented victor. For "[w]hoever has emerged victorious participates to this day in the triumphal procession in which the present rulers step over those who are lying prostrate." For Benjamin, the true historian "approaches a historical subject only where he encounters it as a monad," that is, as a configuration "pregnant with tensions." Moreover, the historian is *engagé*, recognizing in his or her consideration of the subject "a revolutionary chance in the fight for the oppressed past . . . , blasting a specific life out of the era or a specific work out of the lifework." Benjamin's conception of the present time as the occasion for his "blast[ing] a specific era out of the homogeneous course of history" in turn set the terms for a new nomothetic-idiographic of the despised, degraded, and declassed. The subjugated would become subjects.

When Benjamin's plea for the tradition of the oppressed is seen also to intersect with his own as well as Foucault's and Lyotard's critique of the grand metanarratives, there is produced a claim for decentering the latter and privileging the discourses of the latter's victims. At present, the epistemological debate centers on whether there is a modernist (or even premodernist) essentialism entailed in the epistemes proposed for the allegedly subjugated members of racial, gender, sexual, and physically challenged peoplehoods, or whether, as Seidman has insisted with respect to the debate over gender essentialism, the responses given to this question have been misunderstood. The "postmodern feminists," he claims, "have criticized the esentialist discourse of gender—both androcentric and gynocentric—that posits a bipolar gender order composed of a fixed, universal 'man' and 'woman.'"[109] And he gives particularist emphasis to his point by asserting that "There is no reason to believe that a middle-class southern heterosexual Methodist woman will share a common experience or even common gender interests with a northern working-class Jewish lesbian."[110]

However, his claim of incommensurability with respect to singular elements of human identity seems to lend itself to a Benjamin-like claim for an epistemic essentialism, especially when, in a more recent essay, Seidman calls for a separate "queer theory" to be developed when homosexuality and homoerotic desire become simultaneously resources for and topics of a social scientific discourse.[111] At the same time, his more general proposal— namely, that "Our social narratives should be attentive to [the] concept of multiple identities; our stories should replace the flat, unidimensional language of domination and liberation with a multivocal notion of multiple, local, heterogeneous struggles and a many-sided experience of empowerment and disempowerment"[112]—seems to move his version of alteritic social science some distance from the *carpe diem* demanded by Benjamin. How and whether the subjugated will move, or will be moved, to become empowered subjects of their own discourses, and whether those discourses will embrace a recognizable sociology or history are matters yet to be investigated.

Conclusion

From a postmodern sociological point of view, history as well as the several contending epistemes of history should be regarded as finite provinces of meaning within an ever-presentist condition.[113] Many years ago, an eminent historian, Carl Becker, pointed out that, "History . . . cannot be reduced to a verifiable set of statistics or formulated in terms of universally valid mathematical formulas."[114] For Becker, and for the author of this work, history "is rather an imaginative creation, a personal possession which each one of us, Mr. Everyman [and Ms. Everywoman], fashions out of his [or her] individual experience, adapts to his [or her] practical or emotional needs, and adorns as well as may be to suit his [or her] aesthetic tastes."[115] Moreover, these finite provinces of meaning are divisible into those that enjoy the legitimation that is indicated when a particular narrative is inscribed on stone tablets, printed in school texts, or celebrated on public holidays, and those that reside in the interstices of a society, are passed down from generation to generation as folk tales rather than being read in books, or are part of a secret or hidden history whose adherents are unable or unwilling to bring it into the light of public scrutiny or to subject it to the exacting standards of official authenticating devices. Whether metanarratives or folk sagas, whether documented theses or localized antiquarianisms, whether public knowledge or clandestine tales of the past, these histories exist in and through human consciousness and the institutions of history-presenting and history-preserving that such consciousness constructs. The attitudes toward history of the professional historian are but one set of this complex structure of idiographic consciousness.

For the kind of sociology that I am here proposing—and of course, what I have just said about the plurality of histories applies as well to the many kinds of sociologies—the basic questions are ones related to what should be called the political sociology of historical knowledge. That is, its inquiries should seek to find out: How does a particular version of history become authoritative? What are the processes and procedures whereby and wherein a sense of the past is said to be official? How is it that the histories of, let us say, African Americans, Asian and Pacific Island Americans, Hispanics or Latin Americans, Native Americans, women or sexual-preference groups, have only recently become candidates for admission into the canons of academic history? These and many other queries like them are grist for a historical sociological mill that will grind down the teeth of postmodernism's rough beast but not kill it. They also will serve to reorder the old issues—about metanarratives, methods, truth values, and the alleged incommensurability of happenings or persons—by moving them from the backstage of endless and unresolved academic epistemic debates to the front stage of people's senses of the past, present, and future, and how they construct and authenticate them.

CHAPTER THREE

Interstate Relations and the Sociological Imagination Revisited: From Social Distance to Territoriality

As with every map, however, a certain ambiguity always remains.
Cultural maps are capable of multiple readings. But . . . dominant
readings never go completely unchallenged; resistance is always
possible.
      Peter Jackson, Maps of Meaning

Conceiving of space as a concept, as able to mark out a domain,[1] as a metaphor for indicating aesthetic, cognitive, or moral proximity or distance,[2] as a feature of both human embodiment[3] and sociocultural interaction,[4] and, when united with history-as-memory,[5] as a way to reinvent one's legacy of identity and assert claims to what was once, perhaps, only an imaginary community,[6] is the comprehensive legacy that comes down to us from the seminal work of Emory Bogardus. Bogardus, no doubt influenced by Simmel, introduced the concept of social distance to American sociology.[7] It was, he said, a "measuring stick" for gauging ethnic and "racial antipathies." Space served as both metaphor and marker for this measurement, for, as Bogardus pointed out, "If there be newcomers, especially from another race as immigrants, status and distance are everywhere coexistent." Although Bogardus confined his researches on the topic to the American scene—and generated two generations of surveillance over the vicissitudes of social distance in the United States—he conceded that it was very likely a universal phenomenon, and one that contributes to misunderstandings and conflicts as well as to intimacies and solidarities. As such, it deserves study as a basic building block for a global sociology—one attuned to the shifting grounds of association and dissociation that are occurring in the new and yet-to-be-charted world order.

The terraqueous globe is made up of spaces on which peoples, ethnic groups, races, and nations have carved out territories over which they form themselves into sovereign bodies politic, on which they can interact, through and across which they can pass with ease or difficulty, at the borders of which they can erect barriers or open the area to migrants and trade. Hence, I propose territoriality as the successor concept to social distance and as both a basic concept and a fundamental process in all of human life.

Territoriality

All forms of social organization find either symbolic or substantive expression via spatialization. Because the dynamic characteristics of this process had been developed by the early pioneers of human ecology[3] and reintroduced into current sociological thought through an eponymous essay by Lyman and Scott,[9] as well as by Ericksen's,[10] Hall's,[11] Sommer's,[12] and Bakker and Bakker-Rabdau's[13] conceptual elaborations, and the findings in a number of subsequent empirical studies,[14] it is sufficient here to expand the analysis to the global macroecological level. As Lyman and Scott pointed out in 1967, "[M]icro sociological studies of territoriality . . . may be extrapolated [and applied in] an analysis of macro-sociological inquiries, especially in the realm of international affairs."[15] Their suggestion had been anticipated one year earlier, when Raymond Aron took note of the fact that "Every international order, down to our own day, has been essentially territorial . . . , an agreement among sovereignties, the compartmentalization of space."[16]

Territoriality is not "natural" in a biodeterministic sense. Some years ago, Herbert Blumer criticized such a perspective and showed that it had permitted the early human ecologists to suppose that territoriality had "its own inherent organization, moving along in fixed and regularized ways, strictly repetitive in a given class of cases, and functioning as a whole in definite patterned ways."[17] Rather, as Blumer observes, the ecological process is always to be understood as an application of human agency: "Human beings," he notes, "in locating themselves and their institutions on land surfaces, are . . . acting on the basis of their ideas and their feelings."[18] Moreover, "Human beings are involved in the ecological process not as mere implementers of that process but as [exerters of] direction on that process."[19] The various scenarios given life by these ecological processes have been enacted and reenacted on the global stage throughout human history. Migrations, invasions, conquests, and successions are the principal but not the only forms of this human activity. They permit settlers, conquerors, and rulers to draw boundaries around portions of the earth's surface, to give names to these ecological niches, to mark them with their special seals and memorials, establish one or another form of political authority over them, define the sense of and qualifications for recognized peoplehood within them, to defend the now-established area of dominance against invaders from without and subversives within, and, often enough, to utilize the space so organized as a base from which to launch attacks on other pieces of the earth's surface.

The apportioning and reapportioning of the earth's domain among peoples constitutes an action whereby unoccupied lands or weakly defended settlements come under the domination of an organized peoplehood. Hence, the designations "national" and "supranational" are perceivable as merely two possible outcomes of the many modes by which one or more peoplehoods becomes attached to a land surface. Not only are there intra- as well as international kinds of ecological organization, there are other, perhaps less-well-conceptualized, forms of domination over, or collaboration with, bodies of land and water that operate below, beyond, and sometimes in opposition to the statist or suprastatist forms of domination that happen to prevail at any one time.[20]

In the event, it seems appropriate to focus attention on three of the territorial subprocesses: domestication, boundaried communication, and territorialization of the body politic.

Domestication

"In the beginning," John Locke (1632–1704) once observed, "all the world was America."[21] Locke seemed to be suggesting that the then-ongoing European migration to, domination of, and settlement in the Americas constituted an instance wherein geopolitical ontogeny was recapitulating global-historical phylogeny.[22] Although it would violate Blumer's strictures in behalf of the indeterminate character of human agency to apply such a biotic thesis uncritically to human affairs, Locke's statement sensitizes us to the need to extract from any particular case, including that of America, a process whereby uninhabited or undefended portions of the earth's surface are transformed into a particular and circumscribed geopolitical domain. The process entails conversion of a piece of land into a "home territory."[23] Conversion practices include enunciating and legitimating a new toponym, one that simultaneously justifies sovereignty over the territory so denominated, authorizes and empowers those who are in a position to enforce the new name on others, and subordinates the rights of, or excludes from the area altogether, those who will not accept or cannot be accommodated by it. The case of America in the centuries after Locke made his famous statement provides a complex example of the workings of the domestication and toponymic processes.

Although the twin processes of domestication and toponymic domination are observable as a virtual leitmotif of America's development as both a continental nation-state and a world power, these modes of territorialism are to be found everywhere. Hence, to give a few examples, promulgating a new name for an old land and then selectively enforcing on its indigenes, settlers, immigrants, and successor generations all that the name entails are to be found: in the debates over what to call and where to draw the boundaries of the successor states to the land mass until recently overseen by the Union of Soviet Socialist Republics; in map-makers' discussions of how cartographically to recognize the postcolonial state that has long been known as Burma but now wishes to be designated as Myanmar; in whether and how to distinguish the natives of the Czech Republic from those of newly seceded Slovakia; in what geopolitical entities the world powers should permit to emerge out of the dismemberment of Yugoslavia; and in the centuries-long conflict over what geopolity is to enclose the Irish people inhabiting the uneasily United Kingdom.

A number of strategic research sites for investigating the toponymic features of the land domestication process have been revealed by the disputes dividing members of the NATO alliance in the aftermath of the Cold War. Two stand out because they clearly illuminate the basic forms by which attempts are made to achieve home territorialization. In what since 1991 has come to be known as the "Macedonian question," a region of the former federated republic of Yugoslavia, which in the interwar era had been designated as "South Serbia," seceded from the crumbling federated multi-ethnic polity that once held sway over it and redesignated itself as "Macedonia," a new sovereign state. Although the new state of Macedonia received recognition by most members of the Western alliance and by the United Nations, its very existence, and, more important, its name, evoked an outcry from leaders of both the ruling and opposition parties of Greece. To the Greek leaders, "Macedonia" is not only the name of a region of the

Greek state that borders on the new republic, but also is the proper term of reference for the realm of Alexander the Great, (356–323 B.C.E.), king of Macedonia, conqueror of the Greek city-states and of the Persian Empire, and an iconic figure from whom the Greeks claim at least a symbolic descent reinforcing their exclusive claim to a glorious Attic heritage.

The basic practices of toponymic domestication are liable to evoke opposition and resistance. Those revealed in the Macedonian situation include (1) competition over ownership or control of the material symbols of a legitimating geocultural identity, (2) toponymic protests, (3) disputes over ethnonational heritage and collective anthroponymy, and (4) utilization of trade embargoes, international juridical institutions, and propaganda to establish or discredit a particular domestication of territory. In the case of the new republic of Macedonia, home territorialization is at the present writing still in process and by no means assured.

A different aspect of home territorialization is illustrated in the issues arising over Kaliningrad (formerly Königsberg), a city whose protean status as a national home territory is thematized in the famous "Königsberg bridge problem"—an arithmetic graph puzzle solved by the appropriately Swiss mathematician Leonhard Euler (1707–1783), who proved that one cannot cross in a continuous path all seven bridges of this erstwhile capital of East Prussia without recrossing any bridge. Birthplace of Kant, Königsberg, for over 700 years the major cultural as well as political center of East Prussia, was captured by the Soviet army in 1945, has been renamed Kaliningrad, and has been held as a prize of war ever since.[24] With the emancipation of Lithuania and Belarus and the disintegration of the Soviet Union in the 1990s, six hundred land miles and two new states separate Kaliningrad from its still-enforced membership in Russia, the successor state to the U.S.S.R. At the same time, its once-proud German heritage is being reasserted not only by a migration of Russian Germans to the city and by new trade relations opened up with a reunified Germany, but also by the claims of those Germans who intermarried with Russians and now seek a place where some representation of both of the maritally espoused cultures can be realized and passed on to their offspring. "Here," said "Sergei," a Russian army officer who moved from Kazakhstan to Kaliningrad with his ethnic German wife, "there is a chance to have both cultures." However, these claims of biculturalism and a relationship to a former homeland are resisted by the Russian authorities in the city, who in 1945 went so far as to remove from the city streets all manhole covers bearing German emblems. In 1994, according to Raimar Neufeldt, director of the city's Russian-German House and Germany's official representative there, the older Russian inhabitants behave in a manner that indicates "a kind of . . . allergy to any German presence," while the authorities in Moscow have dispatched approximately 200,000 of their own troops to the area to ensure against what it regards as an increase in German cultural and economic hegemonism. "There is no Germanization of Kaliningrad," insists the city's Russian mayor, despite the fact that, as one of Russia's newly created "free economic zones," the city is attracting German investors, visitors, and increasing numbers of those who are seeking or who hope to place the escutcheon of German culture on the city.

Whether symbols become substance and what effects this will have on geopolitics in Europe are examples of the kinds of problems which a sociology attuned to the dynamics of home territorialization could address. Such a sociology requires a reactivation and global application of the now nearly forgotten science of *sphragistics,* that is, the discipline that took as its topic of investigation both the ideas and the praxes related to the use of seals and signet rings, and its synthesis with *ekistics*, the scientific study of human settlements. These and related phenomena are the stuff of home territorialization, the ways on which humans establish domiciliary claims on pieces of land carved out of the earth's surface.

Boundaried Communication: The Bridge, the Door, and the Theater of Strategic War

Raymond Aron once observed that the earth's surface might be characterized either as a natural environment, a stake, or a theater of international relations.[25] The latter conceptualization in an epistemological sense embraces the other two, for these relations are each instances of the drama of social reality[26] in which all players are engaged in one or another kind of interaction, much of which is strategic,[27] and all of which are bounded by interaction territories. "Surrounding any interaction," Lyman and Scott observe, "is an invisible boundary, a kind of social membrane."[28] At the macroecological level such membranes might appear as borders surrounding a homeland territory, and indeed be the markers that indicate that turf domestication has been, at least for the historical moment, secured. However, precisely because the borders of this aspect of territorialization are both porous and movable, such senses of security as are gained from them are for the most part inadequate. "The world," wrote the Swiss international jurisprudent Johann Caspar Bluntschli (1808–1881) in 1870, "should be split into as many states as humanity is divided into nations."[29] And, though the researches of Walker Connor have shown that Bluntschli's global ideal has not yet been attained, and indeed is highly unlikely,[30] "The predominant principle in establishing these boundaries and [their attendant] identities," Philippe C. Schmitter has observed, "is that of 'nationality.'"[31]

But even—or perhaps, we should say, especially—in these cases, a breakthrough of these interactional border defenses is possible, because, as Schmitter and so many others before him have noted, the very idea of nationality is fraught with definitional and praxeological difficulties.[32] Advancing "nationality" as the basis for an enclosure of interaction is carried forward by means of a concatenation of appeals—to the unity that is supposed to be occasioned by the mystery of blood, to common linguistic symbols, to historical memories, and to future-oriented hopes—as well as by "residual elements of opportunistic choice and collective enthusiasm."[33] Encroachment on these fragile membranes is not only facilitated by advanced means of telecommunication, but also by the counter concatenation of appeals—to the values of diversity, to the efficiency obtainable by the employment of supranational linguistic signs and symbols, to a future-oriented multicultural harmony, and, as pointed out in the writings of William Graham Sumner, against the pernicious effects of ethnocentrism. Networks of interaction need not and often do not form themselves along the lines drawn to mark nation-state borders on geopolitical maps. Such networks range from the personal to the professional and indicate elements of a burgeoning international civil society that transcends the boundaries and circumvents the defenses against interaction across state lines. Thus, on the basis of her careful study of a century of demographic changes in Europe, Susan Cotts Watkins has recently observed how "[b]etween 1870 and 1960, the scale of these interactions expanded [as the] expansion of markets from local to national extended personal networks" and, incidentally, led to "an increase in the proportion of marriages in which one spouse was born in another province."[34]

Any advance in the sociological study of interactional territorialism on a global level must build upon the dynamic elaboration of this phenomenon presented in Simmel's writings on the subject.[35] Here, however, it will be sufficient to emphasize the relationship to a transcendent geopolitical sociology of three of his observations: First, that "The boundary . . . is our means for finding direction in the infinite space of our worlds";[36] second, that boundaries are both exclusive and inclusive; and third, that the fixing and unfixing of boundaries occur by no "natural" means; rather, such activities are attempts to limit social proximity or expand human sociation, and, thus understood, are parts of a pure sociology of conduct with respect to spatialization. Hence, at the global level, interactional territories might be spatial but not necessarily cartographied on a geopolitical map. They are situses on which there occur specifications of the right to participate and encroachments on this right by migrants, invaders, emergent groups, minorities, and other kinds of "outsiders." The borders and border-guard practices established by states are more or less effective defenses of exclusive interactional turfs, but the defenders of a beleaguered interactionally exclusive territory sometimes resort to even stronger measures: restrictions on egress or ingress, linguistic collusion, or insulation[37] in the form of fortified and thus seemingly impenetrable barriers—such as the Berlin wall, which for twenty-seven years stood sentinel against any but life-risking escapes from the German Democratic Republic, but which, as Nigerian Nobel Laureate Wole Soyinka would recall,[38] could not prevent communication by voice and gesture across the fence. Whatever their intent, hence, such barriers might become either "doors" or "bridges"—to use Simmel's felicitous terms[39]—enclosing behind them or opening up beyond them such interactions as are made possible by the ingenuity of humans determined to restrict or to expand their territories of interaction, to lengthen or decrease the social distance separating one human group from another.

However, interactional territorialism takes on a special character when the interactants are players in the drama of diplomacy or playwrights of the scenarios that take place in a theater of such military operations as war. The practice of diplomacy, according to Henry Kissinger, took to a new interactional style after the conclusion of the First World War, when Europe's statesmen, realizing that "there was no geopolitical basis for the Versailles order, . . . were driven to invoking their personal relationships as a means of maintaining it—a step none of their predecessors had ever taken."[40] However, since that era the new style, that is, "the trend toward personalizing [diplomatic] relations has accelerated,"[41] and no doubt this contributed considerably to the style as well as the substance of negotiations bringing an end to the Cold War, and seeking resolution in such ongoing disputes as that in the Middle East.

When diplomacy fails—or, when it is not given an opportunity to prove its worth—one likely outcome is war. Warfare, as a violent form of both symbolic and substantive interaction, is also limited in its territorialization. The advent of the nuclear age has had a paradoxically limiting effect on war, one, incidentally, that had been predicted by Lester F. Ward's disciple, James Quayle Dealey, in 1909: "Science and human ingenuity," he wrote, "if properly stimulated, could probably develop destructive implements of such power as to banish henceforth the possibility for war, for wars will more likely cease because of their destructiveness and cost than because of an altruistic objection to human slaughter."[42] In fact, "the balance of terror" that prevailed during most of the Cold War era, while it restrained any decisive move toward total war by either the United States or the Soviet Union, tended not only to enhance the value of direct interactive diplomacy, but also to permit "surrogate" regional wars to be fought in several areas.

The Clausewitzian and post-Clausewitzian scenarios of war as a form of strategic interaction took on an even greater significance as diplomacy assumed a style associated with interpersonal relations but always with an eye to the bipolarized territorial factors affecting both the "Cold" peace and war. The era beginning in the 1990s is as yet unclear with respect both to its appropriate mode of interaction and to the boundaries of its emerging interaction territories. However, one thing seems to be clear. Unlike the Cold War era, the emerging period is and will likely remain multipolar in terms of its interacting units.[43] Although the territorialized state is likely to remain a basic form of polity, other modes of sociation—religion, race, peoplehood, and nationality[44]—while bidding for or claiming territorial expression, will also participate in whatever complex interactional configurations that develop. Of these, the peoplehood that seeks to form an ethnonational state is perhaps most striking in that its claim usually involves a rearrangement of spatio-temporal priorities and interactions.

What one journalist calls a manifestation of "Balkan ghosts"[45] provides a pertinent example of a spatio-temporal reconfiguration that is the occasion for the building of new nations, polities, and bodies politic on the ruins of the short-lived state known as Yugoslavia. What is involved is the mobilization of collective memory emphasizing a present meaning that is to be given to specific events drawn from the annals of Balkan history. The events chosen—for example, the Ustasha-ordered killings of Jews, Serbs, Gypsies, and Muslims during World War II; or the Turkish massacre of the Serbian knights at Kossovo Polje on June 28, 1389—are not treated as history as that discipline is conceived by professional historians. Rather, they are dredged up and separated out from the welter of happenings that also occurred and made to speak to the contemporary collective consciousness—indeed to be the *ding an sich* of that consciousness. An interactional membrane is drawn around the eventful memory and the people who regard it as such. That membrane shuts out alternative interpretations of the event and in so doing enhances the action program that the memorialistic demagogue—for it is he or she who is the charismatic agent of these developments—has proposed. Thus, to give one pertinent illustration: On June 28, 1987, five hundred ninety-eight years to the day after Serbian prince Knez Lazar was martyred at Kossovo Polje, the Serbian communist party leader Slobodan Milosevic addressed a crowd gathered to memorialize the event. Pointing his finger into the distance, he made a promise: "They'll never do this to you again. Never again will anyone defeat you."[46] Thus was the revolt in behalf of an independent and "Greater Serbia" begun. Memory of a momentous event had been rendered as the referent incident out of which a peoplehood would be reborn in vengeance and in what came to be known as "ethnic cleansing." An interactional territory that overjumped 600 years of history had become the basis for establishing—or, to the Serbians, reconstituting—a homeland.

Territorialization of the Body Politic

There is, in effect, a territorialization of the collective body.[47] It is exemplified in one of the several forms of world building now taking place in the post–Cold War era. Like the epidermis of the human body, the surfaces of the body politic are subjectable to symbolic "anatomic" markings. Creative artistry, nostalgic portraits, degrading graffiti, and other innovative identity tags may be inscribed with consent or by force, figuratively or literally, onto human collectivities as much as onto individuals. At the global level, such tattooings are fundamental features of group assertion and the claim for legitimation and recognition.

The process whereby a body politic becomes territorialized entails a pressing of the claims of a single peoplehood for sovereignty over a particular piece of the earth's surface. When completed, it signifies the merger of anthroponymy with toponymy—thus, for example, "the German people" and "Germany," or, more ominously, "the Aryan nation," the "German *Volk*," and a territorialized *Volksgemeinschaft*. Whether the peoplehood is marked in one or another of the usable fictions—for example, "blood," heritage, tradition, history, or religion, or some combination thereof—is less significant for the formation of a modern (but not necessarily pre- or post-modern) body politic than the fact (or desire) that it is claimed as justification for establishing sovereignty over and on terra firma. Hence, Johann Gottfried Herder's (1744–1803) conception of an ontological *Volk* whose sovereignty might be territorialized, and Friedrich Schleiermacher's (1768–1834) linkage of knowledge to linguistic practices and of both to a common spatial location were moves adumbrating the constitutive construction of a specific geographically bounded body politic.[48] By the same token, Talcott Parsons's conceptualization of four ideal-typical social systems—namely, the universalist achievement, universalist ascriptive, particularist achievement, and particularist ascriptive are—as Jean L. Cohen and Andrew Arato have recently pointed out[49]—each couched in reference to an already established body politic that has as its habitus a territorial unit. That unit both circumscribes a societal community and defines and prescribes the mode of sovereignty over the peoplehood within it, that is, the "nation."

"What is the sociology of the body?" asks Anthony Synnott. He answers, "It is the study of the self as embodied, and of the various attributes, organs, processes and senses that constitute our being embodied . . . ; it is the study of the body as a symbolic system and a semiotic process . . ."[50] Analogously, we inquire here, what is the sociology of the body politic? And, like Synnott, we propose that it is the study of a peoplehood as an embodied collective self, and of the characteristics and processes whereby such a body comes to recognize itself as such, sovereignizes itself, and makes claims to recognition and territory to epitomize itself. Such a body, to paraphrase Synnott, is at the heart of collective life and social and intercultural interaction and provides one possible source for personal identity as well.[51] In the post–Cold War world, a number of new and revived bodies politic are emerging.[52] These bid fair not only to define the international structure, but also to defy moves toward a supranational order.[53] In some cases, notably in that area of the globe that, until the disintegration of the Soviet Union, had been called the "Third World,"[54] the bodies politic that are nascent seem more like tribes with flags than nationalities;[55] in other areas, old "blood"-based ethnonationalities are seeking territorialized national self-determination;[56] while in still others, localized ethnoracial collectivities agonize over choosing between the pull of acculturation, assimilation, and amalgamation or the push of independent existence, group autonomy, and endogamy.[57]

What Goffman tells us about the territories of the self is applicable to the territories of the body politic.[58] Like the self, the body politic has its "central markers" that make claim to a territory; its "boundary markers" that determine where the former claim begins and ends and who may proceed across or into it and with what rights, duties, and privileges; and its "system of reference" indicating what ideographic and nomothetic understandings are to be associated with it. And, to continue with Goffman's terms, a body politic may be violated by profanation of its symbols, encroachments on its territory, invasion of its lands, and forced surrender of its identity and sovereignty. Long ago, Lester Ward coined the term *social karyokinesis*[59] to refer to the more volatile dynamics of this process—a process that, often violent in character and sometimes destructive of whole peoplehoods in result, provided for an irregular reconstruction of territorialized regimes in the world; a process, despite Ward's assertion to the contrary, that had no definite nor determining *telos*.[60]

The postmodern liberation of human agency from its imprisonment in positivist, deterministic, and teleological paradigms—and the freeing of contingency to assume a central place in human action—are simultaneously causes for celebrating the emancipation of the human spirit and sounding the alarm over how that spirit might wittingly or accidentally express itself. At present, statesmen and soldiers are contributing to the shape of things to come, but neither has a clearly pictured template of that shape. Scholars are either seeking to refurbish the shabby paradigms of yesterday or announcing the death of any possibility of knowledge in the postmodern age. The situation of the 1990s and beyond seems not unlike that presented in 1906 by William Graham Sumner. He had stared into the political, social, and cultural abyss created by the failure of Americans to have constructed a just and coherent set of mores—on the basis of which they might have developed a new social order in the decades immediately following the Civil War: "We are like spectators at a great natural convulsion. The results will be such as the facts and forces call for. We cannot foresee them . . . The mores which once were are a memory. Those which anyone thinks ought to be are a dream."[61] However, such a moment need not give rise only to reaction or despair. Rather, the momentous political and epistemological events of our time ought to remind us that the prospects for a scientific breakthrough are greatest at moments when the windows out of which we look at the *Lebenswelt* seem about to be shattered.

In the present work, the focus has been on a sociology that would take the entire globe as its topos and seek to organize a systematic approach to its processes of formation and reformation. The conceptual center of the thesis presented here is territoriality and its role in human group expression.

A synthetic sociology that emphasizes the interplay of ekistics with *sphragistics*, that is, of human settlements with the emblematic markings on persons and lands, will illuminate the manifold ways the terraqueous globe has become an object of and for human realization.

Here, I wish to subjoin the discourse of modernity to that of post-modernity in behalf of a social-territorial perspective on a global sociology. Postmodernity has much to say about "texts" and their "disprivileged" status. However, the praxeological texts of global reconstruction are being "written" performatively by those who seek and sometimes succeed in maintaining, establishing, or replacing a partial or total sovereignty of a population segment over a portion of the earth's surface, or in carving out a niche of free interactional territory within a sovereignized area, or in recalling and reviving moments of a claimed past in order to advance a claim to a long lost-home territory. The processes and projects whereby such activities occur tell us that these texts are not disprivilegeable merely by being so labeled, but rather are the basic stuff from which a postmodern global sociology could discover how some texts become legitimated and others marginalized.

Conclusion

In conclusion, then, I propose a supranational sociology built around a transcendent application of the concept "territoriality."[62] The concept is enlarged to embrace the social processes entailed in peoples' efforts to create, sustain, and in some cases expand a habitus on the terraqueous globe. The forms taken by these territorializations go beyond the geopolitical. They include patterns of migration, dispersal, diasporic, and imperialist domain-establishing settlements;[63] inclusive and exclusive interactional territories—embracing among other things the yet-to-be-created techno-communicative "superhighway"—whereon people may readily communicate with one another; and territorialization of the many and varied bodies politic that exist in some degree of unacculturated formations within an established state, or that live in voluntary, enforced, or unrecognized diasporic distance from a "homeland."

A sociologist who takes territorialization as a global sociological concept takes as his or her task the politico-sociocultural mapping of the earth's surface. He or she must heed Roland Robertson's admonition that any "attempt to theorize the general field of globalization must lay the grounds for relatively patterned discussion of the politics of the global human condition, by attempting to indicate the structure of any viable discourse about the shape and 'meaning' of the world-as-a-whole."[64] Territorialization as a dynamic sociological concept must also acknowledge that the forms which any human habitus takes are subject to Simmel's observations about fixation and fluidity: "These forms are frameworks for the creative life which, however soon transcends them . . . The bounded forms acquire fixed identities, a logic and lawfulness of their own; this new rigidity inevitably places them at a distance from the spiritual dynamic which created them and which makes them independent."[65] Of all these forms, the state, and its self-proclaimed identity as the sovereignized habitat of the nation, has been most prominent in the study and praxis of international relations. However, a postmodernized sociology must take account of both supra- and infrastate formations and of the relations among each and countenance the possibility of the exhaustion of geopolitical form in the policies and ideologies of the actors involved.[66]

Territorialized everyday life consists in the *Lebenswelt*[67] that surrounds a human habitat. It, in turn, can become the object of an "intrusion"[68] so great as to generate a "crisis"[69] in its very raison d'être. A series of such occurrences can undo an established territorial order and open up thought and action pursuant to the formulation of yet another one.[70] The dynamics of ordering and reordering the world occur as territorial effects that incursions on a *Lebenswelt* have on any particular life-world.

Such incursions as well as the responses to them are products of human agency. Hence, a new sociological worldview[71] will have to recognize both the actuality and the constraints on human endeavor, the realities as well as the praxiologies of social distance and social proximity. And the ethic of a new epistemology will have to be applied to all those who have hitherto been treated as the "other." As Zygmunt Bauman observes, "In a postmodern ethics, the "other" would be no more he who, at best, is the prey on which the self can feed to replenish its life-juices, and—at worst—thwarts and sabotages the self's constitution. Instead, he will be the gatekeeper of moral life."[72] A golden rule is here reconstituted. The self, the group, and the proximate and distant spaces—their interactions on earth, in the air, on or under water, with or without fire—are elements of a global sociology that, like Yeats's indescribable rough beast, is slouching toward Bethlehem, waiting to be born.

Part III

Postmodern Arenas: Race, Law, Cinema, Deviance

CHAPTER FOUR

Postmodernism and the Race Question: The Problem of Alterity

> *The fate of our times is characterized by rationalization and intellectualization and, above all, by the "disenchantment of the world." Precisely the ultimate and most sublime values have retreated from public life either into the transcendental realm of mystic life or into the brotherliness of direct and personal human relations . . . [A]cademic prophecy, finally, will create only fanatical sects but never a genuine community.*
> *Max Weber, "Science as Vocation"*

> *[W]e had better disregard entirely the mystic effects of a community of blood, in the sense in which the racial fanaticists use the phrase. The differences among anthropological types are but one factor of closure, social attraction, and repulsion. They stand with equal right beside differences acquired through tradition.*
> *Max Weber, "The Nation"*

> *The road from clan comradeship to universal society is beset with hazards . . . It is a tragedy of moral history that the expansion of the area of the moral community has ordinarily been gained through the sacrifice of the intensity of the moral bond, or, . . . that all men have been becoming brothers by becoming equally others.*
> *Benjamin Nelson,* The Idea of Usury: From Tribal Brotherhood to Universal Otherhood

> *For the self, the world of the biologically human split into two*

*sections kept strictly apart and rarely confused: that of the neigh-
bours and that of the aliens. An alien could enter the radius of physical proximity only in one of three capacities: either as an enemy to
be fought and expelled, or as an admittedly temporary guest to be
confined to special quarters and rendered harmless by strict obser-
vance of the isolating ritual, or as a neighbour-to-be, in which case
he had to be made like [a] neighbour, that is made to behave like
the neighbours do.*
  Zygmunt Bauman, Postmodern Ethics

Introduction

The "race question"—that has always been central to American sociology, but that has not always been recognized as such—has been respecified
with the advent of postmodernism. Where once the issue was defined in the
respectively different but compatible vocabularies of Josiah Royce
(1855–1916),[1] Nathaniel Shaler (1841–1906)[2] and Robert E. Park (1864–1944)[3]
as a struggle between the forces favoring incorporative egalitarian neigh-
borliness at either an individualistic or a group level, and those seeking absolute expulsion of, or permanent separation from, peoples designated as
"alien" or "other," it is now coming to be perceived as a distinctive feature
of a praxiological discourse in service to the Occident's internal domination
and global hegemony over non-Western peoples and their practices.[4]

This shift in perspective is significant, for it calls into question not only
the epistemological basis of all received variations of a sociology of race and
ethnic relations, or of ethnoracial minorities, but also, precisely because it
rejects general theory and metanarratives, it entails in the writings of some
of its adherents a veritable revolt against the discipline itself, or even against
all modes of social scientific discipline.[5] Thus, Linda Nicholson asserts that
"a tendency of general theory is to move between triviality and ethnocentric projection";[6] while Mas'ud Zavarzadeh and Donald Morton argue that
the effect of the postmodernists' relegation of the concept "individual" to
the graveyard of the "historically obsolete" has "been so far-reaching that
the very function of the humanities curriculum itself has been displaced."[7]
By respecifying sociological theory as being both a creature as well as a
creator of both a debased Enlightenment[8] and a hegemonic colonialist
discourse[9]—as, among others, Steven Seidman did when he flung down
the postmodern gauntlet in order to challenge the very foundation of the
discipline[10]—the postmodern critic discerns a less than honorable purpose

for it. As Homi K. Bhabha puts the matter: "The objective of colonial discourse is to construe the colonized as a population of degenerate types on the basis of racial origin, in order to justify conquest and to establish systems of administration and instruction."[11] Putting Bhabha's thesis together with an earlier one formulated by Robert Blauner on how America's sequestration of its several racial minorities constitutes an instance of "internal colonialism" that had engendered a "ghetto revolt,"[12] the conventional sociological discourse on race and ethnic relations in the United States—with its main emphasis on Anglo-conformity and assimilation as providing the solution to problems of prejudice and discrimination[13]—is all too easily interpretable as a rhetoric that justifies ideological as well as administrative controls over those regarded as "others." Nor is the modernist sociological approach to the other's "marginality,"—namely, as a transitional spatio-temporal state of collective being that an ethnoracial group occupies on its road to full-fledged incorporation in or pluralistic recognition within a state society[14]—acceptable to postmodernists.[15] As George Yudice has pointed out, whereas "There was a time when to be 'marginal' meant to be excluded, forgotten, overlooked . . . , [t]oday, . . . the 'marginal' is no longer peripheral but central to all thought."[16] Indeed, according to Julian Pefanis, "postmodern aesthetics, in their positive (Lyotard) and negative (Baudrillard) forms . . . are examples of thought aiming to preserve the difference of otherness, resisting the totalizing and totally compromised tendency of civilization."[17] In sum, postmodernism has placed the question of "otherness," of alterity, on an entirely new plane.

Alterity and a Sociology of the Absurd

In 1970 (and in a revised and expanded edition published in 1989), Marvin B. Scott and I formulated an approach to our common discipline that we called *A Sociology of the Absurd*.[18] Much of the argument of that book anticipated and complements the postmodern perspective without suffering from the latter's potential for encouraging either a debilitating nihilism[19] or a reductive essentialism.[20] The complementarity of postmodernism and a sociology of the absurd has been developed elsewhere.[21] Suffice it to say here that the Absurdist position holds that the world makes no ontological sense but nearly always is socially constructed to make sense; that the anchor points for comprehending the always constructed and reconstructed social reality are space, time, and character; and that sociological investigations may proceed by finding out how and to what extent human agents are able to transform space into various kinds of territories; convert *durée* into the disparate time tracks onto which they have entered, fallen, or been thrust; and how they render accounts,[22] employ disclaimers,[23] or develop aligning actions[24] in the course of securing, maintaining, or shoring up the sometimes stable, sometimes fragile, and sometimes fractured sociations in which they find themselves.[25] Like any other sociological phenomenon, the problem of alterity may be approached from this perspective and with these concepts.

The Problem of the "Other"

A postmodern approach to the problem of the "Other" arises out of that perspective's decentering of the "subject" and of the relation of that deconstructive exercise to the emancipation of the "subjugated." The ambiguity of the term "subject"—that is, its capability of being oxymoronically defined as the agent of self-chosen human action and the object over which hegemonic authority is exercised—is thematized by postmodern investigators of the vocabularies as well as the institutions that foster various conceptions of "race," "ethnicity," "nationality," and "gender," each perceived as an aspect of the patriarchal colonizer's model of a Eurocentric world.[26] The "subject" that such postmodern leaders as Foucault have displaced from its putative autonomy is that which is a paragon of the Protestant ethic,[27] the victor, as Walter Benjamin once noted,[28] despite Weber's mordant warnings about this agent's imprisonment in modernism's iron cage,[29] of the last four centuries' march of "progress."[30]

In place of that only apparently triumphant figure, some postmodernists wish to subjectify, others to elevate, those humans who have been the latter's victims of "progress": the dark-skinned "Other" who has not been fully accepted as a "brother" by his historically connected white Anglo sibling; the non-Anglo female "other" who has been subordinated on the basis of both her "race" and her "sex"; the homoerotically inclined of either gender, who have been degraded and exiled from civil society by reason of their sexual preference; the physically challenged, who because of the prominence given to their alleged "disability," have been stigmatized and denied a dignified place in both political economy and history. Because of the exigencies of time and space, our concern in the balance of this work will be confined to categorizations of human groups as ethnoracial aggregations and with their "Otherhoodedness."

The negative status of both premodernist and modernist forms of "Otherhood" is redolent with the apprehensions that Herbert Blumer ascribed to holders of race prejudice. Blumer defined the latter as a "sense of group position."[31] As in the prejudices held against the several ethnoracial peoples whom he had in mind,[32] the "Other," conceived either as a representative individual or as an entire group, is regarded as (1) naturally, culturally, socially, or morally inferior to whatever people or configuration of peoples holds societal or intersocietal sway; (2) as intrinsically different and alien to the dominant group; (3) as inherently undeserving of the latter group's proprietary claim on areas of privilege or advantage; and (4) as desirous of unwarrantedly securing the prerogatives that the dominant group has won through its own legitimate efforts.[33] Nor has the "racism" of "Otherhood" prejudices been eliminated, or even reduced very much in its inherency quotient,[34] when, as has occurred in twentieth-century social scientific thought, the determinative factor in designating a people as "Other" has shifted from the biological onto the cultural plane;[35] or when, as in the recent work of Herrnstein and Murray, it has been reconceived as an emergent, arising out of the intermingling of endowments from nature and class;[36] or, finally, when, as in the work of Thomas Sowell, "culture" has been reconceived as a form of "human capital" that has been unevenly distributed among the peoples of the world.[37]

Paul Gilroy has recently reminded us of a "new racism" that has been perceived as a surrogate for the now discredited ideas about collective genetic inheritance and that appears as "manifestations of irreducible cultural difference." "This new racism," he goes on to point out, has been "produced, in part, by the move towards a political discourse which aligns 'race' closely with the idea of national belonging and stresses cultural difference rather than biological hierarchy."[38] In the place of this or any other form of racialist hierarchy, Donna Haraway has set aside the modernist's consideration of what kind of racial order is likely to arise under what conditions—that is, whether and under what circumstances a dominant elite would decide either to acculturate an "Other" so comprehensively as to drive out altogether its separate sociocultural existence; or to sequester the "Other" in some form of benevolent tutelage; or to expel the "Other" from its domain; or to commit genocide on it—in favor of a conceptualization that simultaneously celebrates the "Other's" autonomous actions and casts doubt about modernist social science's claims to represent the "Other" as he or she actually is. Haraway writes: "I stress actants as collective entities doing things in a structural and structuring field of action; I have framed the issue in terms of articulation rather than representation. . . . Other actors are more like tricksters . . . Boundaries take provisional, never-finished shape in articulatory practices . . . It is the empty space, the undecidability, the wiliness of other actors, the 'negativity,' that give me confidence in the *reality* and therefore *unrepresentability* of social nature and that makes me suspect doctrines of representation and objectivity."[39]

Haraway's thesis points toward the development of a different approach to a sociology of race and ethnicity. That sociology is capable of being both *of* and *for* the "Other," making him or her not only a newly empowered subject, but also the principal (but not the only) participant in the making of his or her own past, present, and future. That sociology emanates from the social constructionist point of departure and treats the categories of "Otherness" as arising out of the elementary forms of the classificatory act itself. Classification, while in general necessary for everyday life to go on, takes on a special character when it formulates images of individuals and groups in terms of an invidious and value-laden hierarchy. The classification, whether it takes form as a mentally imagined abstraction, or as a hierarchically oriented attitude toward the latter or its representation in statistical aggregations, cultural stereotypes, or concrete individuals, constitutes a foundational element in the formation of "Otherhoods." How the social construction of such categories occurs, how they become legitimated, and how and to whom they are applied are the old questions to which this new sociology might be put to answer.

It is unlikely that we shall ever overcome classification itself, or, for that matter, that we would want to, given its necessity in the face of the everpresent buzz of words about things. Nor does it seem too likely that the drawing of invidious distinctions among humans will be altogether eliminated from the public or private spheres of life. Thus, although Van Langenhove and Harrè believe that it is possible to "chart the history of [such] a transformed discursive convention [as an ethnoracial stereotype] from its moment of birth in some idiosyncratic use of discursive device by an individual to its entrenchment as a public conversational mode," they claim that "this appears [to occur] . . . as a quasi-Darwinian process over which we have little control."[40] Given their thesis, it behooves a postmodern sociologist to search out not only whether or how deconstruction of the old metanarratives could be accomplished, but also, and more directly, to apply what conceptualizations are left to us by the postmodern critique to a reconceptualization of the race question—one that might well be moved to its formulation by the postmodernist's demand for a moral intent,[41] but also, while seeking assiduously to steer its line of inquiry between the Scylla of an overdetermined essentialism and the Charybdis of an untestable metatheory, one that focuses on the spatio-temporal positioning of ethnics and its discontents. Such an approach, I would suggest, recalls to a new application the concepts Marvin B. Scott and I developed a quarter century ago: territoriality, time tracks, and manner, that is, the qualities, as well as the dilemmas and contradictions, that arise in the presentation of what is often taken to be a protean, if not inauthentic, self.

Territoriality: Toward a Sociological Geography of Race and Ethnicity in Hyperspace

Postmodernist thought has introduced the term *hyperspace* to refer to what it alleges is a new geographical condition, namely, that the order of the geographic *topos* has disintegrated and in its place is a "field of clashes" arising out of the "play of power among plural elements."[42] Some postmodernists contend that this situation is one not only of chaotic flux, but also of a kind such that "hyper-space can be invented and with equal ease commanded to vanish, or it can be expanded with the aid of mental gymnastics by pure intellectual construction."[43] Hyperspace, according to this conception, "speaks to the 'dissolution of things' and the unexpected is the order of the day."[44]

Public Territories and the Race Question

An activated concept of hyperspace is positively applicable to the everyday world of ethnoracial groups, and to the individuals so inscribed, only insofar as they are able freely to carve their own parameters of existence out of the space that is under their feet or before their eyes; or, negatively, insofar as it is imposed upon them as part of a display of dominating authority over them. In either event, and whether in kind or degree, there exists the construction and reconstruction of free space either as public territories, sequestration or home territories, interaction territories, and territories of sociosomatic expression. Insofar as a people are "subaltern"[45]—are, that is, the kind of "subject" that postmodernists indicate by the term "subjugated"—their rights to move onto or traverse public territories is restrictable; their sequestration or congregation on and within officially or customarily circumscribed areas permits establishment of a home territory, but in the very same process limits the spaces wherein their place in history is represented as well as on which their interactions and intimacies are likely to occur;[46] and their situation is made to highlight the bodily indicators of their subordinated status.[47] Although postmodernists speak of a widespread and expanding hyperspatial chaos, ethnics are for the most part migrants in or residents of a modernist world wherein the spatial order is secured through the unequal exercise of authority and control.[48]

Precisely because topographical chaos speaks to what Zygmunt Bauman calls "the observers' inability to control the flow of events, to obtain the desired response from the environment, to prevent or eliminate happenings they did not plan and did not wish to occur,"[49] it is not likely to be more than an incident in the reconfiguration of territories. Nevertheless, that spatio-temporal moment is pregnant with the possibility of becoming an "intrusion,"[50] that is, an interruption of the social order that permits the social equivalent of the epoche[51] to emerge around the old order of space. Such intrusions onto the spatial order—the sit-ins in segregated restaurants and the "freedom rides" during the civil rights movement of the 1960s provide telling examples[52]—encourage crises of thought and conscience and direct attention to actions that might rectify and will surely change the sociospatial situation.[53]

Whereas the older metanarratives of race and ethnic relations entered into the topicality of the situation not by merely predicting that the end of such relations and of "Otherhood" would occur when the process of assimilation had been completed, but also by lending social scientific support to the desirability of such a denouement,[54] critical modernists, while still employing metanarrativity, treat both assimilation and pluralism as alternative outcomes deserving only objective description and, perhaps, factor analyses.[55] Thus, before presenting his remarkable elaboration of a developmentalist model of ethnicity in America as a multistep process moving what we are here calling an "Other" from first contact to eventual assimilation, Elliott R. Barkan prefaces his thesis with a disclaimer: "no value judgment is implied here with respect to the desirability or inevitability of assimilation."[56] Yet there are still those modernists who are unable to sever their connections with inexorability and entelechy; for them, the urge to document the inevitable spurs ever greater efforts in service to its validation. Thus, to take one recent example, Christopher A. Reichl begins his study of "Stages in the Historical Process of Ethnicity: The Japanese in Brazil, 1908–1988" with the assertion that "All immigrant populations probably share a developmental sequence of ethnic history."[57] Postmodern analysts, many of whom take their point of departure from the critique of Eurocentric colonialist discourse,[58] not only reject all metanarratives of eventual assimilation, whether of a determinative or contingent variety, but invert the question, negating such narratives because, *inter alia,* they establish a horizon against which the social scientist, as at least one postmodernist sees the matter, presents, either explicitly or implicitly, an authoritative prose of counterinsurgency.[59] In more general terms, for the postmodern sociologist, "one critical task has been representing a more successful means of coming to terms with nonhegemonic group thinking and identity, especially notions of groups not anchored in hierarchies."[60] A reconfiguration of epistemological as well as geocultural space is the new imperative.

From both the Absurdist sociologists' conception of the several domains of territoriality and the postmodernist human geographers' ideas about the processes attendant upon toponymy, it is now clear that "Space . . . is, like the text, both produced by and constitutive of society and embedded in a system of social practices."[61] Such practices include placing boundaries around peoples and values, such that the *ethnos*, among other human aggregations, becomes both creature and agent of its "Otherhood" within a protean spatial situation.[62] For instance, if assimilation "most accurately represents the point at which *individual* members of ethnic groups have shed the cultural, linguistic, behavioral, and identificational characteristics of their original group as well as disengaged from the associational, or structural, activities that have set them apart from others,"[63] then its spatial domain is the "public territory," that is, that portion of the civic arena that is open to all full-fledged members of a society. Moreover, that space is also the assimilated person's "home territory"—for on its escutcheon are carved the cultural emblems and social symbols of the dominant society of which such a person is an ethnically undifferentiated member—and his or hers "interactional territory" as well, the arena, that is, where public as well as private speech acts may take place with all the impunity that the law allows. Moreover, the assimilate's "body territory" is colored by the hue that corresponds to the dominant group's understanding of the epidermal pigmentation that corresponds to that of the citizenry that makes up the "body politic."[64]

Home and Sequestered Territories

By contrast, the unacculturated "Other" occupies a domain set aside— sometimes in time as well as space—for his or her "kind," either by choice or constraint or some combination of the two. Such a boundaried arena becomes a socially organized "home territory" of inclusion and exclusion. For the old school of American ethnology, one of these territories for sequestering a non-Occidental "Other" had been created by the Bureau of Indian Affairs.[65] But, for an even earlier ethnological science, "Others" were to be found on the islands of Oceania,[66] or inside landlocked enclaves of peoples who had fallen under the hegemonic but often indirect rule of colonial imperialism[67] or,—and here the postmodern anticolonial discourse is pertinent (though not original)[68] in its critique—at outposts whereupon the ethnologist could fix his or her gaze on a theoretically inscribed living representative of premodern history[69] This anthropology made it possible for the ethnologists to engage in nothing less than the "observation of savages,"[70] a central outcome of which, according to Adam Kuper, was the ethnologists' "invention of primitive society."[71]

If for the imperial British, Dutch, Spanish, Portuguese, German or French ethnologist the "Other" existed in a geographically and culturally distant domain from which few could depart, for the American sociologist the same human phenomenon in the form of nonwhite, non-Anglo ethnoracial minorities dwelt closer to home. Indeed—although Native American aborigines had been forcibly resettled on "reservations," Mexican Americans confined to "barrios," Asian immigrants and their children sequestered for a long time in "Chinatowns" and "Little Tokyos,"[72] the coercively recruited laborers from Africa first held as human chattel on slave plantations, and, after that institution had been abolished, forced into rural peonage and urban segregation[73]—in the 1950s and 1960s, advances in civil rights and toward what Talcott Parsons called "full citizenship"[74] seemed to portend the onset of a new social order, one that would abolish America's system of apartheid[75] and make each of these peoples, if not into "neighbors," then into a physically proximate but still socioculturally distant different kind of "Other"—what Robin M. Williams Jr. called "strangers next door."[76] But more than a quarter century after the passage of the first modern-day civil rights act, Andrew Hacker, while taking note of the demographic fact that "Hispanics, Asians, Native Americans, and Hawaiians are now the nation's fastest growing groups," pointed out that "blacks are [currently] separated more severely than any other group," and concluded that "A huge racial chasm remains, and there are few signs that the coming century will see it closed."[77] A postmodern variant of hyperspace, in the form of the several ethnoracial domains of the nation and of its fragments,[78] seems to define the present and future order in America and elsewhere. Such being the case, there is renewed reason to give sociological attention to the ethnoracially circumscribed home, interactional, and body territories. Here we can only suggest a sketch of the emerging reconfiguration of this field of study.

Of the variety of forms taken by ethnic enclaves, the ghetto constitutes the paradigm case. Associated with the medieval isolation of the Jews in Europe,[79] the term has been expanded and elaborated upon to embrace such spatially constituted congregative ethnic communities as "Polonia,"[80] "Little Italy,"[81] "Little Brazil,"[82] et cetera, as well as such intraurban segregative areas, sealing off many of the major elements of the African American population, as Chicago's "Bronzeville,"[83] New York City's "Harlem,"[84] and the District of Columbia's "Soulside."[85] For the purpose of this work, *ghetto* will stand as a synecdoche for every configuration of space constituting an ethnoracial enclave. Such enclaves give topographical expression to such groups' "home territory."

Ethnoracial ghettos can and do occur in hyperspace—as well as in geographical—space. There is, in fact, not only a ghetto of the city with its markers indicating both boundaries and emoluments, but also—and increasingly as class and mobility factors engender group migrations out of, and individual escapes from, ethnoracial enclosures—a ghetto of the mind; that is, a consciousness that one or the entire group is bound together by invisible but strong ties of time, heritage, and collective identity.[86] For some, however—the working-class, underclass, or unemployed, inner-city-dwelling African American provides a telling example—the situation has not changed appreciably from that described by Robert C. Weaver in 1948: "The modern American ghetto is a Black Belt from which the occupants can escape only if they move into another well-defined Negro community."[87] For the latter peoples, the ghetto proves all too often to be a harsh haven in a heartless world.

As Steven Castles and Mark J. Miller have recently pointed out, "Residential segregation is a contradictory phenomenon . . . [I]t contains elements of both other-definition and self-definition."[88] Where racism is a prevalent value, it may force ethnoracial newcomers, as the new object of "Otherhoodedness," to live together out of fear and for their own protection; yet, such ghettoization, reinforced by segregative real-estate practices and customary prejudices, gives rise to the apprehension that the clustering group will not give up its own sociocultural habits and that it will seek to spread itself and its ways of life beyond the confines of its sequestered space. On the other hand, ethnoracial newcomers, or long-established ethnics overtaken by a resurgence of ethnoracial consciousness, might want to dwell and work together, making the territorial area that they occupy into a place where memory of a former or even ancestral way of life may be preserved, and whereon a few of its most valued traditions may be continued.[89] Or, they might seek these in hyperspace. Thus, in the United States, even when the "cultural and political focus on the individual rather than the group . . . worked over time to erode primary identifications with ethnic symbols . . . ; [or when] the promise of America . . . represented economic opportunity and personal and political freedom . . . , [making] an Old World ethnicity [stand] in the way of their acceptance as full-fledged Americans . . . , not only have some groups successfully resisted assimilation, but they have maintained an almost undiluted ethnicity as the basis of their community life."[90] In this sense, and to the extent that they can succeed in their endeavors, such peoples have carved a home territory out of hyper- or material space that overcomes the stigma visited upon their "Otherhood" without becoming socioculturally indistinguishable members of the dominant society's "brother- and sisterhood." The detailed sociology of this phenomenon is a worthy task for the postmodern social scientific investigator to undertake.

Interaction in Home and Public Territories

Bounded spaces create places where social interaction can occur but across which such interactions are restricted. Where residential ghettoization occurs without an accompanying total enclosure of a people—where, for example, a member of an ethnic "Otherhood" is permitted to work but not to sleep or play on the public domain—a dual system of interaction is likely to arise. Whereas Robert E. Park had supposed that primary interpersonal intimacies would arise unnoticed among those only seemingly locked into the limited state of impersonal and secondary relations dictated by the interethnic etiquette appropriate to "accommodation," the penultimate stage of his race relations cycle—and perhaps this did occasionally occur—empirical studies suggested that the interactants would more likely remain imprisoned in their respective modes of articulation, ethnic strangers to the full-fledged citizens of the civic arena, kith and kin with their fellow ethnics in the ghetto. Paul C. P. Siu's close study of the Chinese laundryman who plied his trade in white neighborhoods but ate, slept, and enjoyed whatever leisure time he could spare in the Chinatown ghetto shows how his public "Otherhood" has the effect of transfiguring his basic identity as a human being. In the eyes of whites, he becomes a nonhuman, a mechanism:

> The neighborhood grocer may have primary-group contacts, but not the Chinese laundryman. The difficulties which the laundryman has which are different from most of the people in these other services is the

fact that his cultural heritage is so vastly divergent from [that of] the dominant group. This, together with his language handicap, racial visibility, and, perhaps, his un-American standard of living, makes him an undesirable individual for anyone [in the dominant group] to have as a personal friend.... Using the Chinese laundryman as a subject of discussion, a group of [white] college girls concluded that he is a sort of public utility ... [T]he laundryman is simply a thing.[91]

Orientations toward, as well as interactions within, a ghetto that has arisen primarily in service to a dominant group's interest in sequestering a people, especially if that people has become acculturated, may not have the same valences that they would have among peoples who are unacculturated or who retain positive "Old World" outlooks. Thus, the American Chinatowns that provided personal recognition and social response to the otherwise isolated Chinese laundryman were not harmonious communities, but the basis of their internal conflicts was not only intramural, but inextricably connected to those prerevolutionary Chinese traditions and institutions that survived among the overseas migrants and were adapted for use by their descendants.[92] These communities persist not simply because the social distancing techniques of the discriminatory elements are still effective—though less so than they used to be—but, more importantly, because there are interests working to retain these vestiges of a non-American culture.[93]

On the other hand, although there has been a resurgence of interest in Africa's heritage among contemporary black Americans,[94] and although there is a renewed interest in taking seriously the argot of the black ghetto,[95] few African Americans seek to build up the kind of segregated community that has existed in America since slavery was abolished. As long ago as 1948, Robert C. Weaver pointed out that "The Negro ghetto of today is made up of people who are American to the core, who are part of the national culture and who share a common language with the majority of Americans. This ghetto has all income and social classes."[96] But, by 1993, Massey and Denton would assert that the black "ghetto is part and parcel of modern American society ... Indeed, as conditions in the ghetto have worsened and as poor blacks have adapted socially and culturally to this deteriorating environment, the ghetto has assumed even greater importance as an institutional tool for isolating the by-products of racial oppression; crime, drugs, violence, illiteracy, poverty, despair, and their growing social and economic costs."[97]

Roger D. Abrahams captured the difference between these two

orientations when he compared the actions and attitudes toward "place" of two groups, one of Mexicans, the other of blacks in the 1960s: "While Negroes were rioting to demonstrate the degradations of their mode of existence, destroying the very places—the ghetto—with which they are identified, Reies Tijerina was organizing a guerrilla band and 'recapturing' Kit Carson National Forest from the Gringo Forest Rangers, and proclaiming their sovereignty over the land under the provisions of the Treaty of Guadalupe-Hidalgo."[98] As Abrahams went on to point out, "Both riots and revolutions are aggressive acts, directed at 'the enemy' whites, but one chose to act in the spirit of rebuilding a world once lost, . . . while the other, reacting to restrictive policing, struck out blindly, destroying and looting."[99] The black ghetto is the kind of home territory away from which some of its denizens would like to run, if they could. But, as Mitchell Duneier observes on the basis of his ethnographic study of a group of Washington, D.C., black ghetto dwellers who regularly meet at a "soul-food" cafeteria: "Although the black regulars find contact with white society fulfilling, one should not infer that what they discover in the wider white society is in any way superior because it is white . . . [Rather, the] wider society . . . is a vehicle for them to express their own civility."[100] How and whether the wider society will welcome the people, whose "cool pose"[101] continues to mark its "Otherhood" as well as its civility, to the interactional territory in its public domain remains a matter to be strategized by African Americans and studied by a postmodern sociology.

The Ethnoracial Body as a Territory

The postmodern approach to race calls for a recognition that the praxiological construction of the latter is manifested in, through, and as an inscription on the human body. To *inscribe*, in the sense intended here, is conspicuously to mark the surface of the human body, and by extension, of all bodies similarly perceived, with enduring, imagistic, identifying, and classifying words and characters. The modern praxes associated with Occidental inscription appear to have begun in the eleventh century on the European frontier[102] and in the late fifteenth and early sixteenth centuries[103] coincident with the beginnings of the Spanish, Dutch, English, Portuguese, and French seaborne empires.[104] The leaders of these enterprises, through their ethnologically minded spokesmen, exercised their anthroponymic imaginations by designating, classifying, and morally evaluating the color of the epidermis, the morphology of the eye, and the texture of the hair.[105]

Inscriptions of "race" are implicated in both touch and sight. "Otherhood" with respect to the body is, as Sander L. Gilman has pointed out,[106] established through bringing together in a single comprehensive stereotype what Immanuel Kant, (1724-1804), had conceived as the inherent antithesis of these two faculties. For the German philosopher, each represented a radically different way of obtaining knowledge about the world, the one through sensual, that is, irrational, experience, the other through reflection and ideas. But, as Gilman is at pains to reveal, it was Johann Wolfgang von Goethe, (1749-1832) who undermined Kant's epistemological dichotomy at the same moment that, haunted by the homoerotic aesthetics of Johann Joachim Winckelmann (1717-1768), he inverted the gender-based aestheticism that had restricted beauty to being a unique characteristic of the female body.

According to Gilman, late nineteenth-century German thought extended the aesthetic compound of sight and touch beyond the gender groups, which it once again inverted, to embrace persons of color groups.[107] Thus, Gilman asserts, Friedrich Nietzsche's outlook "places the black, the 'Skin-man' in a position of insensitivity, for *sensitivity* . . . is an aesthetic term, and the nineteenth century knew that blacks had no aesthetic sensibility."[108] Furthermore, given Nietzsche's valorization of the white female intellectual, there resulted what Gilman calls "an ironic reversal." "The spectrum 'Hottentot-European', which marks the movement toward 'civilization' for the European intellectual of the nineteenth-century, is replaced with the spectrum 'Black-Female Intellectual' to measure the distance 'civilization' has created between the human being and his or her body." And, within the same rhetorical process, Nietzsche had not only found a new way to locate the African on the lowest, that is, the precivilized, rung of the great chain of being-civilization, but also he had feminized the Jew, placing the latter people on the highest rung of that chain but, because of their gender confusion, subjecting them to inherent mental illness. For our purposes, Gilman's original analysis, whatever value we grant it as theory, sensitizes us to a new understanding: A postmodern sociology of race and ethnic relations would focus on the conditions under which discourses linking touch of the body of another person to race, color, and gender either legitimate this sensual practice of social interaction or convert it into a tabooed act, forbidden with respect to an "Other" conceived as an "untouchable."

A history of forced ghettoization functions as both cause and consequence of the untouchability attached to an "Other's" body. When regarded as untouchable, the body acts as a medium of personal somatic degradation in service to the ceremonies and in support of the prevailing racial hierarchy; and this can be the case even after desegregation has ended the exclusion of the "Other" from interethnic social contacts. In an incident that could serve to recall W. E. B. DuBois's first experience of racial untouchability, when a white girl refused to exchange visiting cards with him,[109] Barry Glassner reports what happened to "Charlie," a thirty-seven-year-old African American, who spent a portion of his childhood in Pennsylvania: "In seventh grade," Charlie reminisces, "I had a crush on a white girl in my class. We were talking back and forth, and one day I said something, and she jokingly hit me on the top of my head. But once she had touched me—she'd done it impulsively—she took her hand back and looked at it. Then she wiped it on her skirt."[110] In "Charlie's" response to her reaction to touching him, there is illustrated a race-based variant of what Richard Zaner has called "the third ontological dimension of the body."[111] That dimension is realized when, as in fact was exhibited in "Charlie's" response, "he apprehends *himself* as an 'outside,' as *looked-at* in a way which is impossible for him to adopt."[112] Recalling that experience, Charlie tells Professor Glassner, "I think that must be the worst feeling a person can have . . . Knowing that your body is different, and that it's repulsive to another human being, and not even being able to understand why you're different."[113]

Nor is such epidermal "Otherhood" merely skin deep, nor capable of being overcome by a stereotyped reversal from aversive repulsion to erotic attractiveness. As Samuel Thomas von Soemmering, author of *Über die korperliche Verschiedenheit des Negers vom Europäer* (1785), a seminal tract of the eighteenth-century literature stigmatizing the black person on the basis of skin color, observed: "If skin is the only difference then the Negro might be considered a black European. The Negro is, however, so noticeably different from the European that one must look beyond skin color."[114] In "Charlie's" case, the "noticeable difference" manifested itself as a revisioning of his touchability as it could be expressed through his color-valorized body. And it had lasting effects. After an injury-foreshortened career as a high school football player, followed by a period in which he drifted into a drug- and crime-related street life, "Charlie" obtained a civil service job where he "met a lot of women, most of them white, many of whom were intrigued by the possibility of sleeping with a handsome and successful black man."[115] "And so," Glassner ends his narrative about "Charlie's" physique and its fatefulness, "he became something of a sex object."[116] The Eurocentric social construction of a racially embodied

"Other," as Gilman has suggested and as Phil Cohen has argued directly, has as its "surface structure of conscious reasoning . . . a phantasy system in which . . . [p]ositions of racial superiority are associated with an ideal desexualized image of the [white] body . . . , whilst racial inferiority is associated with a degenerate or monstrous [black] body, in which the power of sexuality, repressed at the other pole, returns as a purely negative principle."[117]

Spatio-temporality: The Acceptance, Rejection, and Reconstruction of Histories

One purpose to which the postmodernists' critique of "totalizing" metanarratives[118] has been put is to grant legitimation to the narratives of the hitherto voiceless,[119] the victims of "progress,"[120] and to all those whom logocentric epistemologies have condemned to exclusion from history.[121] The nonwhite races and non-Anglo peoples, subjugated by colonial practices have, it is argued, also been oppressed by the only seemingly objective colonialist discourses that, as conventionalized histories, rationalize their subjection. Although among postmodernists there is a generalized opposition to foreshadowing metanarratives[122]—such as Park's race relations cycle, a sociohistory that promised to eliminate ethnoracial problems altogether by sentencing African Americans, Asian Americans, Hispanic and Latin Americans, and aboriginal Native Americans to an eventual assimilation-induced oblivion[123]—there is a special kind of claim put on those who would engage in a postmodern reconstruction of ethnoracial history.[124] That claim seeks to incorporate territorialization into the temporal construction of a people's past. It has been given its most generalized thematization in the epistemology put forward by Edward Soja,[125] but its specifics are still in process. Here, precisely because it is still in the early stages of its development, we can only sketch the anchoring points of this excursion into idiographics and, in the next section of this work, point to one of its still-to-be-resolved problems. The postmodern human geographer Edward Soja has set the terms for this new development with his attempt "not to replace historicism with an equally subsumptive spatialism, but to achieve a more appropriate trialectical balance in which neither spatiality, historicity, nor sociality is intepretively privileged a priori."[126]

Any project that seeks to combine Soja's postmodern geography with Lyman's and Scott's conceptualization of territoriality, forming a postmodern sociology of race and ethnic relations, will find such problems for investigation as: (l) how and to what extent ethnic domains have been constructed over time and in space such that public, home, interactional, and body territories have been ethnoracially circumscribed;[127] (2) how and to what extent and with what consequences what Franklin Henry Giddings referred to as a "consciousness of kind"[128] became a feature in the historical phenomenology of both the hegemonic policies of group positioning[129] and the subaltern modes of resistance to or accommodation with such policies;[130] (3) how and to what extent and with what consequences spatiotemporal conceptions of one or several people's pasts, presents, and futures, came to be discreditable and deconstructible, or were secretly insinuated within the cracks and contradictions that existed in a society's official attitude toward its favored discursive history;[131] and (4) how, when, and to what extent, and with what consequences an Enlightenment conception of the individualized self related to the hegemonic construction of group consciousness, the emancipatory struggle against that hegemony, and the ambiguities of individual or ethnoracial symbolic and somatic embodiments.[132] Central to all of these issues is the necessity of converting postmodern theses on race and ethnicity into *topics* for investigation, that is, refusing to accept these and cognate themes as a priori *resources* used to explain social, economic, or political occurrences.

Manner: The Presentation of Ethnoracial Selves in Hyperspace

One specter that haunts the postmodern domain is the character, the qualities—indeed the very existence—of the ethnoracial self. Postmodern perspectives beg this question by assuming that a stable, consistent, mastering self is a figment of the delusions about language that make modernist narratives possible. In its place they posit the postmodern individual, a creature rafting in a sea of hyperspace without a compass to guide him or her.[133] Here the postmodern challenge to ethnoracial self-identity is fundamental. For if the postmodern project with respect to the hitherto subjugated "Other" is to restore him or her to the estate of an autonomous subject, and if that project requires the establishment, authentication, and, perhaps, the privileging of the ethnoracial self, then the postmodern condition, with its assumption of "a crisis of the subject," that is, of a permanently cracked, divided, and inchoate self,[134] stands in the way of that project's completion.

The ethnoracial self is conceived as one that emerges out of, or is presented as the calculated representation of, the interplay of the ethnoracially social mind with the ethnoracial member's experiences. In the words of George Henry Lewes (1817–1878)—who was, according to Giddings, "the first writer to formulate a scientific conception of the social mind"[135]—"A nation, a tribe, a sect is the medium of the individual mind, as a sea, a river, or a pond is the medium of a fish: through this it touches the outlying world, and is touched by it; but the direct motions of its activity are within this circle. The nation affects the sect, the sect the individual."[136] Lewes did allow for a limited activation of independent agency to operate within the domain of the social mind. Thus he observed that while, on the one hand, "this social medium . . . makes a man accept what he cannot understand, and obey what he does not believe . . . , [making his] thoughts only partly his own . . . [and his] actions . . . guided by the will of others . . . ," still what he called the *"consensus gentium"* did not make "the individual . . . passive." Rather, Lewes concluded, "he is only directed; he, too, reacts *on* the sect and nation, helping to *create* the social life of which he partakes."[137] Elaborating further on Lewes's thesis, it may be suggested that the formation of the ethnoracial self partakes of a general but often overlooked aspect of the process of human socialization, one that has recently been called to social psychologists' attention by Herbert Blumer: "Self-interaction," Blumer observed, "has the potential of placing an individual in opposition to his associates and to his society."[138]

By conflating the term "subject" with the term "self" and claiming that the "decentering" of each constitutes a fundamental feature of the postmodern condition, postmodernism appears to suggest that a basic element in the self-formation process has been damaged, perhaps beyond repair. George Herbert Mead, as Blumer explains, had argued that the self emerges out of an interactional process whereby the individual is able to become "an object" to him- or herself, and, Blumer went on to assert, the "scholarly task becomes that of explaining how the young child comes to be an object to itself."[139] But, as Zavarzadeh and Morton have pointed out, "In contrast to the dominant notion, (post)modern critical theory does not conceptualize the subject as a stable entity but argues that the parameters of the subject vary according to the discursive practices that are current at a given historical moment."[140] The ethnoracial self is caught up in and will be defined through the praxes and discourses that contend with this instability.

The ethnoracial self faces an existential problem of immense and agonizing proportions.[141] It is not one readily understood in terms of pathology, however. How individual ethnics and persons of mixed or unknown ethnic heritage,[142] as well as the several ethnoracial groups, respond to their particular situation[143] is properly a topic for *sociological* postmodernist investigations. The sociological problem may be stated as follows: On the one hand, the residue of the Enlightenment's promise to emancipate the individual from all ascribed statuses encourages each member of an "Otherhood" to seek to overcome and to transcend every vestige of the ethnoracial group's claim upon his or her mind, self, and social action.[144] On the other hand, the resurgent ethnoracial critique of that transcendence respecifies the representation of the hitherto idealized "universal" group as a shibboleth covering the hegemonic aim of the European white tribe.[145] The long and varied peripheralizations of the ethnoracial "Others," however, have led not only to a painful and not usually equally weighted choice between acculturation or resistance, but more often to a spatio-temporally limited selection of strategic interactions on the part of those so marginalized. Ethnicities themselves are multifarious in content, permitting the tactical employment of their several "saliencies," as Douglass and Lyman have termed them.[146] Such saliencies might be presented, obscured, deferred, or deemphasized as the occasion and situation demand. It is not the case that ethnoracial individuals either assimilate or dissimilate;[147] rather, and always in accordance with the power element that prevails—that is, given what controls they have, what strengths they can muster, and what skills they can put into play—they adapt their repertory of traditional knowledge or subcultural roles to the immediate situation. Thus, to give one example, African Americans, while in bondage and regarded as ignorant, superstitious, and less than fully evolved humans, that is, as "Sambos,"[148] could and did revolt,[149] run away,[150] or, in many more instances than have been counted, secrete the cultural origins of elements of their African ways,[151] and also engage in the plantation-economy-subverting practice that came to be known amongst themselves as "puttin' on ole Massa."[152] The self that developed out of these and related practices was that of a more than double-consciousness, each element of which had its own status markers and presentational strategies,[153] but the maintenance of which ought not to be regarded as pathological. The mistake of such postmodernists as Lacan and Jameson,[154] who employ such terms as "schizophrenic" to describe the condition of the postmodern self, is to regard the protean dynamics of self-presentation that actually prevail, especially among marginalized or subjugated peoples, as abnormal.

One strategic research site for a postmodern investigation of how ethnoracial identity and the ethnoracial self develop and operate is to be found in the thoughts and practices of those of mixed racial descent.[155] American law exercised its hegemonic controls over "race" by making it into an identity peg on which could be hung civic rights and opportunities. During one period (1870–1952), the courts employed one or another variant of the principle of "preponderance of blood" to insist on monoracial classifications in relation to citizenship and segregation.[156] Persons of mixed racial descent were usually classified as belonging to whichever race had the lower status.[157] Recognition of the fact that monoracial status hierarchies affected one's life-chances led those who could to "pass" as "whites";[158] while the over two hundred communities of mixed-race peoples who could not be fitted into any of the "black," "white," "red," or "yellow" categories that constituted America's color caste system were shunned, given local appellations, or, seeking a way out of their anomalous condition, sought through various artifices to be reclassified as "white" or "red."[159] Although the postmodern critique of "colonialist discourse has called for a deconstruction of the term 'race,'"[160] and given greater voice to the demand that "whites . . . learn to see themselves—their 'me'—in black selves, the hardly acknowledged 'thee' of the extreme other,"[161] the postcolonial quest for an authentic "blackness" has not only sparked a great interest in recovering and identifying African and other ethnoracial histories,[162] but also discouraged those of mixed racial descent from remaining perched precariously on the color line that divides one race from another.[163] Moreover, as illustrated in the case of Henry Louis Gates's critique of the claim of the multiracial Jean Toomer to be representative of "the new American," the postmodernists have sought to deconstruct such an argument and uncover beneath it a true "blackness."[164]

Conclusion

In investigating such practices as territorialization, temporal reconfigurations, and self-identity movements, a postmodern sociologist will be able to discern the social, cultural, political, and legal constructions of ethnoracial reality that work to effect the plurality of "Otherhoods," each of which seeks recognition, response, and justice in America and the world.[165] It is to the credit of Hans-Georg Gadamer (1900–) that a remarkable proposal to overcome alterity has entered into the postmodern discourse on the idiographic and interactional aspects of the topic. Gadamer's proposal employs the Husserlian term "horizon" as a spatiotemporal and perceptual concept. A horizon, he observes, "is not a rigid frontier;"[166] rather, it constitutes "the boundary marking seen from a particular vantage point."[167] For Gadamer, a horizon exists in a perpetually potential hyperspace and time; for a "horizon . . . moves with one and invites one to advance further."[168] From the perspective of the horizon of each vantage point, let us say the vantage point of a particular ethnoracial consciousness of its own history and culture, another such point is necessarily an "Other's" viewpoint. Moreover, horizons partake of temporal as well as spatial vantage points. The expression of its temporality is to be found in its sense of and attitude toward history. Hence, Gadamer posits the existence of a plurality of spatio-temporal "horizons" coexisting at any one time and on many spaces. For this world of interfacing "Others," each looking at the other from its own point of view, there would appear to be a plethora of irresolvable conflicts, a human geography of chaos like that imagined by Jameson. However, Gadamer puts forward a solution: the "fusion of horizons"[169] that he believes is made possible by the capacity for transcendent hermeneutic empathy that he locates in humanity itself. Hence, "it seems a legitimate hermeneutical requirement to place ourselves in the other situation in order to understand it."[170] However, Gadamer does not call for a single transcendent horizon to arise out of his projected "fusion." He asserts "The standpoint that is beyond any standpoint, a standpoint from which we could conceive its true identity, is a pure illusion."[171] What is possible—and, in terms of the problem of alterity, necessary, if that problem is to be resolved—is first, a realization that "Every encounter with tradition that takes place within historical consciousness involves the experience of the tension between the text and the present,[172] and, second, a recognition that the hermeneutic task consists in not covering up this tension by attempting a naive assimilation but consciously bringing it out."[173] For the fusion of horizons to be completed there must also be cognizance of the condition that "Historical consciousness is aware of its own otherness and hence distinguishes the horizon of tradition from its own," as a result of which the "projecting of the historical horizon . . . is overtaken by our own present horizon of understanding," the total process leading to "a real fusing of horizons." That is, "as the historical horizon is projected, it is simultaneously removed." Gadamer designates "the conscious act of this fusion as the task of the effective-historical consciousness."

If Gadamer's effective-historical consciousness is to inform a postmodern sociology of the ethnoracial "Other," that is, overthrow the debilitating effects of an essentialist "Otherness" that both Harvey and Lambropoulos have criticized,[173] there must be a setting aside of the scholastic debate over his proposed hermeneutic—for example, the critique offered by Marina Vitkin to the effect that "In radical interpretation, 'fusion' of horizons is impossible without violence to the alien one, and hence 'fusion,' 'synthesis' and 'integration' are euphemisms for, and so inadvertent invitations to, yoking others by force into a frame of reference alien to them"[174]—in favor of empirical investigation. To undertake such an investigation the sociologist will have to see just how much of the understanding of horizons exists in the society; how and in what degrees of power dimensions the interface of these horizons occurs; how and in what way the hyper space and time are reorganized as an outcome of their contact, collision with, or isolation from one another; and how and in what manner the ethnoracial self enters into and survives this process. As Gadamer has said in relating how his project has been obscured up to now "by aesthetic historical positivism in the train of romantic hermeneutics," this "task . . . is, in fact, the central problem of hermeneutics. It is the problem of application that exists in all understanding."[175] Moreover, Gadamer reminds us that carrying out that task "requires particular finesse of mind"[176] on the part of the investigator. It also requires, we may add, a sensibility of and a sensitivity to the postmodern ethic of the "Other" as presented by Bauman: "In a postmodern ethics, the Other would be no more he [or she] who, at best, is the prey on which the self can feed to replenish its life-juices, and—at worst—thwarts and sabotages the self's constitution."[177] A postmodern sociology would overturn the gothic ethic that,—as Bauman here suggests and Robert E. Park's early writings on modernist forms of imperialism in the Congo illuminated[178]—characterized the epistemologies and praxes of an era that is, at last, coming to a close. With the fusion of horizons it might be the case that, as Bauman seems to hope, the "Other" becomes "the gatekeeper of moral life,"[179] but, under any circumstance, the "Other" will be a "subject."

CHAPTER FIVE

The Race Question and Liberalism: Casuistries in American Constitutional Law

Any cultural trait, no matter now superficial, can serve as a starting point for the familiar tendency to monopolistic closure . . . Almost any kind of similarity or contrast of physical type and of habits can induce the belief that affinity or disaffinity exists between groups that attract or repel each other . . . The belief in group affinity, regardless of whether it has any objective foundation, can have important consequences, especially for the formation of a political community.
Max Weber, "Ethnic Groups"

Introduction

In 1989, a highly placed figure in the United States Department of State put forward the thesis that history (in the Hegelian sense of that term) had come to an end. To Francis Fukuyama, deputy director of the State Department's policy planning staff and a former analyst for the RAND Corporation, the tide of recent events—for example, the proclaimed end of the Cold War, a burgeoning economic union in Western Europe, the pending reunification of Germany and the latter's incorporation into NATO, the deconstruction of communist states in Eastern Europe, President Gorbachev's proposals in behalf of *glasnost* and *perestroika* in the Soviet Union, a potential collapse of the U.S.S.R.'s political economy, and the possibility that that state's republican structure would disintegrate—served as incontrovertible evidence of the "triumph of the West, of the Western idea." Fukuyama not only proclaimed Clio's imminent apotheosis, but also reinterpreted the Hegelian perspective on history to buttress his argument.[1] One part of that argument focused on the current conditions affecting the status and opportunities of blacks and other minorities in the United States and their relation to Fukuyama's general, and generally sanguine, thesis. It is this aspect—admittedly a minor part of his presentation but an important issue in its own right—that is the subject of the present discussion.

According to Fukuyama, "the century that began full of self-confidence in the ultimate triumph of Western liberal democracy seems at its close to be returning full circle to where it started: . . . to an unabashed victory of economic and political liberalism."[2] Although Fukuyama readily concedes that this victory has not been accompanied by an equitable distribution of the material goods, social status, or political power among the several peoples making up the population of the United States, he remains generally sanguine about liberalism's beneficence. In particular, he admits that one minority group has been especially deprived: the African Americans. However, Fukuyama holds that this people suffers from an especially debilitating psychosocial heritage, and that that heritage derives from the ethos of a nonliberal, precapitalist era. Hence, he concludes, the plight of America's blacks is not chargeable either to liberalism's fundamental idea or to its present-day praxis. Whether the triumph of liberalism will eventually reward blacks is more or less a moot point for Fukuyama.

Liberalism: As Economy and as State Formation

"The state that emerges at the end of history," Fukuyama observes, "is liberal insofar as it recognizes and protects through a system of law man's universal right to freedom, and democratic insofar as it exists only with the consent of the governed."[3] Fukuyama derives both his interpretation of Hegelian historicism and his identification of liberal political economy as the ultimate form of the polis from the writings and life of the Russian emigré philosopher turned European Economic Community bureaucrat, Alexandre Kojeve (1902–1968).[4] In a footnote to his essay, Fukuyama points out that Kojeve at first had claimed that the "universal homogeneous state," that is, the liberal state formation that is supposed to emerge in Hegel's vision of history's cessation, had arisen in postwar Western Europe. But, as a dedicated American Hegelian, Fukuyama dismisses these countries as little more than "flabby, prosperous, self-satisfied, inward-looking, weak-willed states whose grandest project was nothing more heroic than the creation of the Common Market."[5] Fortunately, for Fukuyama's thesis,

Kojeve, in a later addendum to his study of Hegel, had "identified the end of history with the postwar 'American way of life' toward which he thought the Soviet Union was moving as well."[6] In these pithy remarks are buried some of the pressing dilemmas and internal contradictions that accompany the alleged once and future triumph of liberalism in world history and in the United States.

Insofar as liberalism entails a concomitant economic system, that system is capitalism. In the Hegelian phenomenological tradition, Fukuyama notes, that system, like any other, is driven by ideas, or, to be more precise, by a single complex of ideas that has become so engrained as not only to undergird it, but also to make correlative and coordinate acts in support of it into unreflected-upon habits.[7] Other students of liberalism have made a similar argument. "Common to all contemporary classical liberals," writes John Gray, the Oxford Fellow and Tutor in Politics at Jesus College, is a vision of an ideal political economy: Its "goal [is] a form of limited government under the rule of law in which (aside from narrowly demarcated emergency provisions), the central economic powers—powers of taxation, spending and the issuance of money—are subject to rules no less stringent than those which protect personal liberties."[8] That goal, in turn, derives from liberalism's core idea, namely, that "the individual is held to be the seat of moral worth."[9] However, it would seem that, if liberalism is to be fully secure in its triumph, the personal security and chances for advancement for each individual—irrespective of race, color, or previous condition of servitude—ought to be ensured. Failure in this aspect of its praxis would invite counter ideological claims of conservatism or of socialism, liberalism's chief competitors, or of some other anti-individualist ideology (e.g., nationalism, chauvinism, irredentism, or secessionism). These dissident ideologies might attract the allegiance—or arouse the passions— of the dissatisfied.

Fukuyama does not consider the potential attractiveness of conservatism, socialism, or racial nationalism for those who are currently consensually (or grudgingly) governed in accordance with his proclaimed liberalism triumphant. Indeed, insofar as non- or antiliberal claimants couch their critiques of the new global *pax liberalis* in materialist terms, Fukuyama dismisses them out of hand: they are among those who fail "to understand that the roots of economic behavior lie in the realm of consciousness and culture . . . [and that failure, in turn,] leads to the common mistake of attributing material causes to phenomena that are essentially ideal in nature."[10] One need not quarrel with this phenomenological essentialism—

to which, incidentally, the present author subscribes—to point out that there are structures of consciousness moving both the conservative and socialist alternatives to liberalism, and to take note of the fact that the other ideologies, for example, nationalism, racism, and ethnochauvinism, that stand opposed to liberal capitalism's self-proclaimed triumph are rooted in what is probably the ultimate nonmaterial secular idea—what Max Weber once referred to as the "mystic effects of a community of blood."[11] For more than three hundred years, black American intellectuals formulated alternative liberationist ideologies. These systems of thought and action fluctuated in popularity in direct relation to the degree of hope (or futility) felt among the African American masses.

Although Fukuyama believes that the "two major challenges to liberalism" in the twentieth century have been fascism and communism, it is in fact the case that in the United States institutionalized racism has been far more pervasive than either of these essentially European ideologies. Moreover, racism, in both preachment and practice, opposes liberalism's promise of a universal individualism and an equal opportunity for all; indeed, it works to undermine the latter. Kojeve, Fukuyama's mentor on the matter of the end of history, treated the American situation in a typically European—that is, class-oriented, rather than race-ridden—manner: "One can say," he wrote, "that, from a certain point of view, the United States has already attained the final stage of Marxist 'communism,' seeing that practically, all the members of a 'classless society' can from now on appropriate for themselves everything that seems good to them, without thereby working any more than their heart dictates."[12] Fukuyama shares much of Kojeve's sanguine perception about America. He goes so far as to assert that "the class issue has actually been successfully resolved in the West."[13] Ultimately, he denies that the social and economic inequities that do continue to cause concern in the United States are fundamental challenges to either the liberal idea or to America's political economy. As Fukuyama sees the matter, "the root causes of economic inequality do not have to do with the underlying legal and social structure of our society, which remains fundamentally egalitarian and moderately redistributionist, so much as with the cultural and social characteristics of the groups that make it up, which are in turn, the historical legacy of pre-modern conditions." Although he does not tell us precisely what social and cultural characteristics are inimical to the achievement of equality, or how they have managed both to insinuate themselves into the hearts and minds of several generations of one group of Americans and to resist the liberal idea's tendency to overwhelm those counterliberal elements that seek to halt its inevitable triumph, he does single out one racial group for notice in this regard: "black poverty in the United States is not the inherent product of liberalism, but is rather the 'legacy of slavery and racism' which persisted long after the formal abolition of slavery."[14]

Fukuyama's separation of the race question from both liberalism and the class struggle, his consignment of it to a resilient premodern heritage, and his inference that the legacy of slavery consists of certain dysfunctional social and cultural characteristics that cling to generation after generation of African Americans constitute a triple line of defense against any challenge to his central claim: that liberalism has triumphed over all its ideological opponents and that that triumph signals an end to history. Gertrude Himmelfarb, one of the critics of the Fukuyama thesis, took notice of this aspect of his argument, pointing out that even if the current forms of the race problem owe their origins to some ideational complex other than liberalism, they "continue to plague us and the solutions continue to evade us." Moreover, she goes on to observe that it is possible to argue that "black poverty, and the poverty of the underclass in general, is not the relic of an old problem but an entirely new problem . . ." Nevertheless, Himmelfarb observes, "it may be . . . subversive of liberal democracy; perhaps even more so because liberal democracy does not understand it, let alone know how to cope with it." And on this aspect of Fukuyama's argument, she concludes, "History has a habit of bequeathing to us disastrous legacies, bombs that can explode at any time and any place."[15]

However, valuable as it is, Himmelfarb's critique does not address certain larger aspects of Fukuyama's discussion of what once was called the "social question." In this respect, it is worth observing that the race problem might indeed be related to the class struggle, but that relationship manifests itself in a form and moves according to a dynamic not imagined by conventional students of the subject. It was Friedrich Engels (1820–1895) who observed in 1893 that no socialist revolution was likely to arise in America until and unless the race and nationality divisions within the working class could be overcome, permitting an interracial and interethnic class consciousness to develop.[16] And, nearly fifty years later, it was the American sociologist Robert E. Park (1864–1944) who argued that the class struggle in America would only begin after the race relations cycle—consecutive stages of which would occur as contact, competition, accommodation, and eventual assimilation—had completed itself.[17] However, as the researches of Herbert Hill and others have shown, racial and ethnic divisions were exacerbated and escalated by most of the elements of the labor movement. This resulted in the aggregate job eviction of blacks from their hard-won niches in the American occupational structure; their racially based exclusion from craft and some industrial unions; and their racial segregation within the few unions that would admit them. Taken as a whole, these events had the general effect of splitting off blacks, as well as Asians, Hispanics, and Native Americans, from the supposedly emerging class-based interracial coalition.[18]

The claim from the Left that the class struggle would inevitably absorb and neutralize the racial conflict in America[19] has proved to be as evanescent as the assertion of nineteenth-century liberals and their twentieth-century sociological epigoni that the introduction of a money economy would dissolve ethnic and racial sodalities in its rationalist-utilitarian flux.[20] America's often-proclaimed "exceptionalism" with respect to the Europe-originated class struggle might well have been purchased at the price of racial justice.

Racial Character and American Social Structure

Fukuyama's vague but powerful inference about how certain groups' dysfunctional social and cultural characteristics interfere with liberalism's tendency to effect economic justice speaks to a one-sided analysis of the long-lasting vestiges of slavery and race discrimination. It suggests—or, to be fair, could be used to suggest—that the poverty so widespread in contemporary black America is a victim-precipitated phenomenon. Accordingly, the poverty found in today's black American communities could be explained by reference to a collective character defect that had insinuated itself within the mentality of enslaved African Americans and had been passed down through succeeding generations. This peculiar temperament, so it might be alleged, is antithetical to the individual effort required for success in a capitalist economy. Such a thesis has been enunciated by the neoconservative black American economist Thomas Sowell, who observes, "The slaves were kept dependent on the slave owners for rations of food or clothing and for the organization of their daily lives and living conditions . . . With many generations of discouragement of initiative and with little incentive to work any more than necessary to escape punishment, slaves developed foot-dragging, work-evading patterns that were to remain as a cultural legacy long after slavery itself disappeared." Sowell adds, "Duplicity and theft were also pervasive patterns among antebellum slaves, and these too remained long after slavery ended."[21] Presumably, indolence, deceitfulness, delinquency, and dependence are the character traits that have had a debilitating effect on black economic success.

A related point has been made more recently by an African American professor of English, Shelby Steele. Steele insists that the angst that he claims is so prevalent in the psyches of black Americans is rooted in "an inferiority anxiety that makes the seizing of opportunity more risky for us, since setbacks and failures may seem to confirm inferiority."[22] Like Sowell—but without introducing the latter's implicit neo-Lamarckian argument in behalf of the intergenerational inheritance of an acquired character—Steele holds that the "most obvious and unarguable source" of the blacks' claim to their own innocence with respect to the racist crimes of America "is the victimization that blacks endured for centuries at the hands of a race that insisted on black inferiority as a means to its own innocence and power."[23] It is clear, though unstated, that Steele is referring to slavery when he speaks of victimization. However, like Fukuyama and Sowell, Steele associates slavery and its victimization of blacks with a preliberal political economy that quite properly could have been, ought to have been, and was challenged by the collective efforts of the advocates of liberalism and the Enlightenment. Moreover, he holds that in the current age of liberal democratic American capitalism, the politics of racially based challenge and the encouragement of an active collective identity are no longer effective tools in the struggle to achieve individual mobility and social change. In their place, Steele, a true scion of Protestant ethic liberalism, offers the strategy of bargaining and proposes a revival of individualistic self-assertion among African Americans.[24] "From this point on," he confidently asserts, "the race's advancement will come from the efforts of its individuals."[25]

There is, however, another legacy of the more than two and one-quarter centuries of African American bondage, one that challenges Fukuyama's (and, even more, Sowell's and Steele's) sanguine image of liberal triumph and respecifies the purpose of egalitarian policy in a modern liberal capitalist regime. That legacy, it is argued, has been sedimented over many generations within the majority (i.e., white) element of the American population as racism. That legacy, moreover, was recognized by the leading members of both the Civil War and the postwar Congresses, who even before that bloody conflict had ended, sought to prevent racism from continuing to work its wicked will once institutionalized slavery had been abolished. Designated as the "badges," "indicia," and "incidents" of slavery,[26] this heritage of the era of bondage had been summed up by one dissenting Supreme Court justice—in the *Civil Rights Cases* [109 U.S. 3 (1883)]—as consisting in part in precisely the discriminatory practices that the Thirteenth Amendment to the United States Constitution had been devised to eradicate: "I hold that since slavery . . . was the principal cause of the adoption of that amendment, and since it rested wholly upon the inferiority, as a race, of those held in bondage, their freedom necessarily involved immunity from, and protection against, all discrimination against them, because of their race, in respect of such civil rights as belong to freemen of other races."

Justice John M. Harlan went on to urge that in the Civil Rights Act of 1875—which forbade racial segregation in transportation, inns, and theaters; required racial equality in the selection of juries; and directed enforcement of its provisions at the prohibited actions of both private individuals and corporations (and which the majority of the Court had just declared to be an unconstitutional extension of the states' authority over a "private wrong")—Congress had ordered "in effect, that since the nation has established universal freedom in this country, for all time, there shall be no discrimination, based merely upon race or color, in respect of the accommodations and advantages of public conveyances, inns, and places of public amusement." From Harlan's perspective—which appears to have been the point of view of both the post-1838 abolitionists as well as the more prominent framers of both the Civil War amendments and subsequent supportive civil rights legislation[27]—the legacy of slavery consisted *not* (as Sowell, Steele, and, perhaps, Fukuyama would have it) in some characterological syndrome deposited in the hearts and minds of the freedmen and women, but rather in the "burdens and disabilities" that a slavery-supportive racist ideology had inflicted and was still inflicting upon them. These burdens and difficulties, moreover, had not only not been removed by the Thirteenth Amendment's prohibition on slavery as an institution, but had been given nurturance by the newly established practices of racial segregation and color discrimination in public and business, as well as in private, arenas of American life. "I am of the opinion," Harlan concluded, "that such discrimination practiced by corporations and individuals in the exercise of their public or quasi-public functions is a badge of servitude the imposition of which Congress may prevent, under its power, by appropriate legislation, to enforce the Thirteenth Amendment . . ."[28] Harlan's opinion was by way of a dissent from the Court's majority. Race discrimination by leave of law would continue for another seventy years in the United States.

In this brief discussion of the Harlan dissent in the *Civil Rights Cases,* there are three points that serve to cast doubt upon Fukuyama's argument about the irrelevance of the race question for liberal capitalism's triumph. First, consistent with his Hegelian phenomenology, the legacy of slavery and racism to which Fukuyama refers all too obliquely might be reconceptualized as an engrained idea. Indeed, as Justice Harlan seemed to be predicting, it is the lingering badge of servitude that public law, corporate policy, labor union practices, and individual conduct in America would fasten onto generations of descendants of the slave population—as well as onto their racial surrogates, Asians, Hispanics, and Native Americans[29]— in the form of hundreds of discriminatory procedures and practices, overt and covert, and in accordance with an ideology that serves the interests of white supremacy. As such, and as an institutionalized and activated ideology, racism would curtail, and in fact has restricted, the realization of the ideals of liberal capitalism, subverting (but not altogether obliterating) their universalist and egalitarian advancement.

Second, insofar as liberal capitalist ideology encourages support for a laissez-faire orientation toward rectifying economic or social inequities, Harlan's dissent in the *Civil Rights Cases* (as well as his ringing dissent in *Plessy* v. *Ferguson*, 163 U.S. 537 [1896]) offers a challenging corrective: Governmental intervention, in the form of civil rights statutes and concomitant legislation that will enforce the desired universal freedoms, would appear to be necessary in order that a democratic and egalitarian society might put its much-vaunted ideals into practice. Removing the badges of slavery would seem to require laws, programs, and public policies that secure freedom and equality for all those peoples who are still suffering under the yoke of this allegedly premodern and antiliberal legacy. A truly civil society might require more, not less, governmental intervention in behalf of its least-favored minorities.

Third, it is worth noting that even if one accepts Fukuyama's claim that a premodern or antiliberal heritage from America's slave era affects contemporary black Americans' abilities to participate effectively (i.e., successfully in a material sense) in a modern capitalist economy, there still remains the question of whether the extant economic system of the United States is to be equated uncritically with productive efficiency, a positive work ethic, a democratic polity, and moral progress. From their statements on the matter alluded to in the previous discussion—and from Sowell's extensive writings on race and economics[30]—it would appear that Fukuyama, Steele, and Sowell subscribe to the functionalist thesis that links an undesirable political economy with an inefficient labor system and ties both to a degradation of human worth. Thus, Sowell makes much of the fact that the classical economists opposed slavery on both moral and economic grounds, noting that its most noticeable feature was the "absence of the incentives of self-interest by the worker."[31] Sowell insists that slavery was not only debilitating to the slave population's sense of individual self-worth, but also conducive to the development of profligate and unproductive habits, even when—especially when—masters offered economic rewards that threatened to raise efficiency or productivity norms.[32] It is this claim—about the relationship of work norms to efficiency and morality—that links liberal capitalism to the unresolved race problem.

The claim that slavery was both morally reprehensible and economically unprofitable is directly put forward by Sowell,[33] and it is implied in Fukuyama's attempt to detach the causes of black poverty from both the ideology and the operations of free-market capitalism. However, the entire question of such a linkage has been reopened by the debate over whether and what kind of relationship exists between black personality, the slave heritage, various systems of political economy, individual incentive, and moral worth. The debate had begun earlier[34] but was enlivened and given even greater emphasis by the publication in 1974 of a study that threatened to undermine the established beliefs connecting slavery to inefficiency and to contemporary black attitudes toward work. In *Time on the Cross*, their remarkable reanalysis of the economics of slave labor, Robert W. Fogel and Stanley L. Engerman sought to show that the efficient and productive efforts of the enslaved blacks have been obscured from the attention they deserve by a paternalistic but racist mythology that continues to stigmatize them to the present day: "For they were held on the cross not just by the chains of slavery but also by the spikes of racism . . . The spikes are fashioned of myths that turned diligent and efficient workers into lazy loafers and bunglers, . . . that turned those who struggled for self-improvement in the only way they could into 'Uncle Toms.'"[35]

The claim that there existed an African American equivalent of the Protestant work ethic among the slaves, an ethic that would resonate both with precapitalist bondage and with a liberal capitalist conception of America's eventual abolition of enforced labor, is not without both conservative and liberal critics. Indeed, it has been widely challenged: by advocates of the thesis that the South's form of black bondage was the centerpiece of a system of seigneurial socialism,[36] administered by a plantation magistracy and justified by a claim of warrantable obligation[37] owed by recalcitrant heathens to their masters;[38] by revisionist historian Kenneth

M. Stampp's claim that the whip, rather than any internalized attitude (except, perhaps, that of fear and dependency) made up the more likely explanation of the slaves' expenditure of effort;[39] and by a multidisciplinary critique of the methodology employed in Fogel's and Engerman's cliometric analysis.[40] Much of the conclusion on this issue depends on still unresolved debates over what legacy, if any, comes down to today's blacks as a heritage of master-slave relations; of what effects manumission policies and practices had on Afro-American mores; of the extent and kind of familism among the slaves and its later effects; of the extent and degree to which African and American sociocultural values, attitudes, and religious outlooks interpenetrated one another; and whether resistance orientations that developed among slaves affected their descendants and helped shape a unique and intergenerational African American personality and outlook.[41]

Of particular importance with regard to the latter point is Stanley Elkins's assertion that the "Sambo" characterology so commonly attributed to black slaves in the nineteenth century—an epithet that described slaves as typically lazy, shiftless, mischievous, and superstitious—was not a stereotype but an institutionally introduced collective character disorder of a kind similar to that induced among inmates of Nazi Germany's concentration camps.[42] Critics of Elkins's thesis, on the other hand, hold that slaves were neither efficient or good laborers nor victims of a personality disorder, but rather that their tomfoolery at work, their breakage and misuse of tools, their resistance to master-and-overseer authority, their runaways, and their outward appearances of abjection, sleepy-eyed indolence, superstitious fearfulness, as well as their more than two hundred armed revolts, constituted a calculated, multifaceted, but less than perfectly coordinated campaign of opposition to the slave system.[43]

In replying to his host of critics, Fogel may not have satisfied all of their complaints, but for our purposes it is significant that he raised the question of functional linkage that has so long been taken for granted in western social science and which is central to both the substance and the epistemology of Sowell's, Steele's, and Fukuyama's arguments.[44]

It is as a part of the Occident's transvalued Protestant heritage, Fogel has recently observed, that a myth about slavery, ethics, personality, and political economy had emerged—first, to assuage the disappointment among certain overly sanguine abolitionists, and, later, to become sedimented in the latent morality underlying conventional theories of Western socioeconomic development. Fogel writes: "The tenacity with which abolitionists clung to the contention that emancipation was bringing prosperity

. . . strongly suggests that they were swayed by a theory which told them that their expectation of prosperity had to be correct . . ." According to this theory, or, as Fogel corrects himself, to the theological proposition that served as its a priori starting point, "divine Providence rewarded virtue and punished evil." That proposition, he goes on to observe, is not only still prominent in the belief system of contemporary Protestant evangelicals, but also is more significantly employed in a secularized version by twentieth-century philosophers, historians, and social scientists. This "optimistic theory implies that immoral economic systems cannot be productive, for that would reward evil, and moral systems cannot be unproductive, for that would punish virtue." Hence, subscribers to either the religious or the secular variants of this Protestant thesis must insist on both the inefficiency of slavery's system of labor and the unprofitability of a slavocratic economy. By the same token, the free-market political economy that emerged after slavery must be seen to be simultaneously productive, prosperous, and just, a sign that divine Providence, or its secular surrogate, the moral cunning of history, rewards the triumph of Good over Evil in human affairs.

A corollary of this myth requires that evidence that would contradict its promise of a providential outcome be explained as epiphenomenal or accidental, or that it be attributable to extrasystemic or extratheoretical causes. In the years immediately following Emancipation and the abolition of slavery, Fogel asserts, the failure of prosperity to follow upon such good deeds evoked accounts blaming the southern planter class, whose unreconstructed members, it was urged, were unable or unwilling to adjust to the emerging free-market economy. Later, when both economic success and social mobility continued to elude the freedmen and women and their descendants, the causes of their plight were sought not in some basic defect in either the principles or the actual operations of America's free-market capitalism, but rather in a degradation of character, or will, or incentive, or sense of self-worth that was alleged to have undermined the black psyche. Conceived as a product of either an unfortunate legacy of slave mentality, or as a sign of constitutional inferiority, the low caste position of African Americans was regarded as an exception, and, in some cases, an obstacle to liberal free-market capitalism's march toward an ever enlarging triumph over all other competing economic philosophies. From this perspective, it is not difficult to discern how Fukuyama's thesis, excepting black poverty from its potential of being charged against the liberal triumph, is but the latest variant of this species of argument.

Fogel holds that the "time has come to . . . cut the tie between economic success (or failure) and moral virtue (or evil)." Not only does he assert that a "quarter century of research on the economics of slavery . . . [demonstrates] that no such connection exists," but also he insists that the very idea that "systems that fail must be evil," while those that succeed must be virtuous must be set aside. In effect, in what might be seen as an American historian's introduction of the postmodern epistemology of deconstruction to that discipline, Fogel has veritably called for recognition of the separation of the Protestant ethic from the spirit of capitalism. "Slavery," he notes, "deserved to die despite its profitability and efficiency because it served an immoral end." Nevertheless, Fogel insists, it does not follow that "such technological advances [under free-market capitalism] as the blast furnace, electricity, and medical surgery . . . are intrinsically good . . . [E]ach has been used at various times for demonic ends." And, carrying Fogel's argument forward, we may observe—in criticism of Sowell, Steele, and Fukuyama— that the much-vaunted triumph of liberal capitalism does not carry with it any assurance of either continued prosperity or the inevitable furtherance of social justice. Indeed, the very fact that Fukuyama finds it necessary to blame black Americans for continuing to wear, however unwillingly, the badges of slavery indicates his own attempt to separate them and their problems from the liberal triumph.

Affirmative Action: A Mandate of the Thirteenth Amendment

Whether valid or not, Fukuyama's assertion that the current socioeconomic condition of blacks and other minorities is neither chargeable to nor any disconfirmation of the triumph of liberal capitalism in America does not disoblige American policymakers from their responsibility for ameliorating it. Indeed, as long ago as 1963, Seymour Martin Lipset urged, "Unless whites are willing to take up their cause in order to force politicians, businessmen, labor organizations, and other relevant groups to support the necessary measures, Negro inequality will remain a blot on the American claim to be democratic and will prevent foreigners from recognizing how real and significant is the national commitment to equalitarianism . . ."[45] Lipset attributed what he called "the low emphasis on achievement" in the measured accomplishments of African Americans to "their past, their weak family structure, and their segregated public schools, all adversely affect[ing] their capacity to gain from education."[46] To break what he called "this vicious cycle," Lipset called for a multifaceted program that differed sharply from the laissez-faire attitude toward the problem evinced in more recent years by such critics as Sowell and Steele. As Lipset saw the matter, what was required was a policy that recognized the necessity of "treat[ing] the Negro *more than equally*, . . . spend[ing] more money rather than equal amounts for Negro education, . . . hav[ing] smaller classes with better teachers in predominantly Negro schools, . . . enlarg[ing] the scope of counseling and recreation facilities available for Negro youth, and the like."[47] For far too long, Lipset asserted, "Americans have been under pressure either to deny the Negro's right to participate in the society, because he is an inferior, or to ignore his existence, to make him an 'invisible man.'"[48] Lipset abjured the notion of black inferiority and proposed making African Americans beneficiaries of a new and melioristic visibility.

Lipset seemed to be saying that the race and inequality question was sufficiently urgent to call for an unusual response—a concerted programmatic effort that would be so one-sided as to threaten the delicate balance of liberty and equality that had for so long prevailed in America's social institutions. That balance, he claimed, had been the basis for stability in the midst of the many social and economic changes that had taken place in the United States since the time of the American Revolution.[49] But, though he acknowledged the truth of Gunnar Myrdal's thesis that "even men who have strong prejudices against Negroes must assent publicly to their rights," Lipset insisted that the "pace is all too slow; the poison of anti-Negro prejudice is a part of American culture, and almost all white Americans have it, to a greater or lesser degree."[50] Undoing the process of dynamic equilibrium to resolve the inequities in American society seemed worth the risk. Indeed, Lipset then held to the position that assuring equal opportunity to blacks was both a "moral responsibility" of the white community and a matter that would require like-minded whites and blacks to use "[e]qualitarian values . . . as political weapons."[51] However, as he went on to observe, "The forces making for elitism, for inequality, will seek, often successfully, to strengthen themselves." Although not without hope for its survival, Lipset in 1963 warned that "The American experiment might fail," and that its "fostering [of] economic growth and democracy under the aegis of equalitarian values," would not be likely to hold "out hope for the rest of the world" if its "prosperity, freedom, and equality . . . [continued to exist] for white men only."[52]

Lipset's suggestion about treating blacks "more than equally" did not receive widespread support from other sociologists, nor did it resonate with an apparently growing public disapproval[53] that by 1991 had made "special treatment" and the fear of "quotas" in hiring a basis for both a conservative backlash and a race-baiting electoral weapon.[54] By 1979, Lipset had come to the conclusion that, while "White Americans look favorably upon 'compensatory action,' since compensation for past discrimination is consistent with the egalitarian creed and essentially makes the conditions of competition 'fairer' without violating the notion of a competitive system . . . , most Americans, including many blacks, oppose the notion of 'preferential treatment,' since such treatment precisely violates the notion of open and fair individual competition."[55] In great part, however, comprehension of this issue, like so many others affecting a resolution of the race question in America, is clouded by the confusions entailed in what Lipset rightly terms "notions" about the actual meaning of the concept "equality" and about the judiciary's original understanding of the intent and appropriate policies designed to abolish all vestiges of slavery in America and assure to all persons under the jurisdiction of the United States the equal protections of the law. That confusion is so widespread and pervasive as to distort virtually all discussions of the further extension of civil rights and to render controversies over those programs designed to effect racial justice in education and in the job market for select minorities beyond possibility of resolution.

A first step toward overcoming this confusion, a proper analysis of the real issues in this matter, requires acceptance of the United States Supreme Court's long-recognized thesis that a legislature's imposition of burdens, requirements, or benefits on a particular group, or aggregate of persons or things, that is, the lawmakers' irrevocable duty to take notice of the different kinds and aspects of elements in the social order that require their legislative attention, does not of itself violate the Fourteenth Amendment's command to the states that they make no law denying to any person under their jurisdiction the equal protections of the law. Although the matter is not without numerous problems of interpretation—for which, incidentally, the holdings of the Supreme Court in the 128 years since the amendment was adopted constitute a virtually untapped treasure trove of sociological data for analysis—the general principle is that a classification that is made in a law in order to accomplish a legitimate public purpose and that treats all persons similarly situated with respect to that purpose in a like manner is, unless held to be otherwise unreasonable or for some other reason *ultra vires*, worthy of constitutional respect and judicial approval.[56] Employing this principle as an intellectual resource and a methodological tool, it is possible not only to show that Lipset's proposed program is not a request to treat the Negro more than equally, but also to overcome most of the objections to current proposals seeking to implement affirmative action. Once they have become recognized as a legitimate means for accomplishing a goal of America's public philosophy, programs and policies of affirmative action could be recommended as one legitimate way to begin to obey the Thirteenth Amendment's command that America remove once and for all the ignominious badges of slavery that still stigmatize a portion of its people. Legitimation of such programs would go far to make Lipset's vision of America as the first nation to synthesize liberty and equality commensurate with Fukuyama's claim that Enlightenment liberalism has at last triumphed over all of its enemies.

In the past, selective legislation has not been held to be inconsistent with either the Fourteenth Amendment or the development of a civic-minded American industrial and corporate capitalism.[57] In this light, it should be recalled that Justice Oliver Wendell Holmes's oft-quoted dictum—"The Fourteenth Amendment does not enact Mr. Herbert Spencer's Social Statics"[58]—was delivered in a rare dissent, one of only two cases out of seven hundred ninety similar disputes adjudicated between 1889 and 1918, in which the Supreme Court's majority failed to uphold state-enacted regulatory statutes over particular kinds of businesses and various types of corporations.[59] In fact, recognition of much of the general principle we are here enunciating was made by the Court in 1884 in a case reviewing a San Francisco laundryman's challenge to the constitutionality of a municipal ordinance establishing a district within which laundries and washhouses might be operated, requiring licensing after inspection of such places of business by public health authorities and firewardens, and setting the hours during which the washing and ironing of clothes would be prohibited. The Court first took notice of the city supervisors' claim that the ordinance in question had been enacted to protect against the outbreak of fire, but also considered the petitioner's assertion that his equal rights under the Constitution had been violated because no other type of business had been burdened by the law's hours-of-work requirements. On the latter point the Court observed: "It may be a necessary measure of precaution in a city composed largely of wooden buildings like San Francisco, that occupations, in which fires are constantly required, should cease after certain hours at night until the following morning . . ." The court went on to enunciate a more general principle under which it would declare that this regulation did not deprive the petitioner of his equal rights under the law:

> From the very necessities of society, legislation of a special character, having these objects in view, must often be had in certain districts, such

as for draining marshes and irrigating arid plains. Special burdens are often necessary for general benefits—for supplying water, preventing fires, lighting districts, cleaning streets, opening parks, and many other objects. Regulations for these purposes may press with more or less weight upon one than upon another, but they are designed . . . to promote . . . the general good. Though in many respects special in their character, they do not furnish just ground of complaint if they operate alike upon all persons and property under the same circumstances and conditions.[60]

However, as Joseph Tussman and Jacobus tenBroek point out in their elaboration on the logic entailed in this thesis, the Court's reasoning here is incomplete; the test of a law's constitutionality with respect to equal protections requirements must turn on whether the classification made by the ordinance in question is one "which includes all persons who are similarly situated with respect to the purpose of the law."[61] A law's purpose, then, determines the classification to be made by it, that is, the particular variant of the public good to be accomplished by the law evokes, or, to be more exact, should evoke, a classification that will burden or benefit precisely that particular group or entity the regulation of whose conduct is related to the accomplishment of that good.

It is just this question, the one in which the demands for the equal protections of the law confront the necessity to determine the constitutionality of particularistic legislative classifications, that confounds the debate over affirmative action. Opponents of such programs decry the benefits that various affirmative action agreements would confer on African Americans, Asian Americans, Hispanic Americans, Native Americans, and women, treating these classifications in the same manner as late nineteenth-century progressive opponents of what was then called laissez-faire constitutionalism treated allegedly beneficial class legislation, that is, those laws and ordinances that supposedly gave undue support to the property rights and to the entrepreneurial classes at the expense of the working men and women and the poor. Calling programs that confer certain benefits on racial minorities and women instances of "racism in reverse," "reverse discrimination," or "affirmative discrimination," these critics seem to suggest that the very legislative act of singling out one group, or a cluster of groups, for special—and, in these instances, beneficial treatment—ought to be unconstitutional *ab initio*.[62] To this point, however, the Supreme Court has never assented. Indeed, it has often moved in quite a different direction. Justice Holmes's reasoning with respect to a lumber company's challenge to the state of South Dakota's antimonopoly law, an ordinance that regulated the prices that might be fixed in the sale of commodities by a seller who operates in two places, but exempting one who sells in one establishment, goes far to establish the constitutional right of a legislature to enact special legislation: "The 14th Amendment does not prohibit legislation special in character . . . If a class is deemed to present a conspicuous example of what the legislature seeks to prevent, the 14th amendment allows it to be dealt with, although otherwise and merely logically not distinguishable from others not embraced in the law."[63] It could follow from an acceptance of this reasoning that if the economic, occupational, and educational conditions affecting blacks, Asians, Hispanics, Native Americans, and women constitute a conspicuous example of what the legislature wishes to ameliorate in service to the general welfare of society, their receipt of special treatment would not of itself be fatal to a law's constitutionality or to the true understanding of equality.

However, in recognizing that the special class of entities singled out by a piece of legislation must be selected with an eye to accomplishing a legitimate public purpose, the Court has often warned against purposes unrelated to the public good and made clear its opposition to arbitrary, unreasonable, or capricious classifications. Classifications that impose a burden on racial minorities have been held to be especially suspect.[64] A fine example of such reasoning was presented in 1911, in an advisory opinion by the Supreme Judicial Court of Massachusetts, answering the legislature's query whether a statute proposed under the general police powers of the state to regulate health, morals, safety, and welfare, and "making it a criminal offense for any woman under the age of 21 years to enter a hotel or restaurant conducted by Chinese, . . . [etc.]" would be consistent with the equal protections clause of the Fourteenth Amendment. The Massachusetts justices pointed out that:

> The enactment of such legislation is not a proper exercise of the police power. It has no direct relation to the evil to be remedied. It forbids the entry of a young woman into the hotel or restaurant of a Chinese proprietor, even if it is a model of orderly and moral management, and it permits the entry of young women into a hotel or restaurant kept by an American, when it is known to be maintained in part for the promotion of immoral or criminal practices. The classification of hotels and restaurants into those that are open to young women and those that are closed to young women is not founded upon a difference that has any just or proper relation to the professed purpose of the classification . . . The

fact that a man is white, or black, or yellow is not a just and constitutional ground for making certain conduct a crime in him, when it is
treated as permissible and innocent in a person of a different color.[65]

With these principles of a public philosophy for equality in mind, let
us examine the question of whether programs and plans, undertaken
through state action, or by private corporations seeking to implement a civic
interest—for example, agreements or contracts that provide for the award-
ing of contracts to minority entrepreneurs; that create set-aside seats in
professional schools, postgraduate education, or job-training programs;
that ensure the employment of hitherto un- or underrepresented elements
in a particular labor force; that assure the entrance of hitherto disadvantaged members of the minority population into racially exclusive labor
unions; or that guard against the inequities that unmodified seniority agreements ensure with respect to the laying off of newly hired members of the
minority labor force during a period of job retrenchment—are within the
limits of the Fourteenth Amendment to the Constitution. Such programs
as those just enumerated are not mere hypotheticals, but rather the reality
of a variety of programs established in behalf of affirmative action and tested
in the Supreme Court. Thus far, the Court's rulings on these matters have
been inconclusive with respect to the general principles being questioned,
on the one hand offering its belief in a vaguely defined idea of affirmative
action as a policy, but, on the other, approving some and denying other of
the various attempts by municipal authorities, state universities, business
corporations, and minority public-interest groups to implement particular
forms of such a policy. What seems to be required is a firmer understanding of just what public purpose is being served by affirmative action
programs and whether and to what extent the classifications of types of
persons such programs make are reasonably related to that purpose.

It would not be inappropriate to justify affirmative action programs on
the ground of fulfilling the mandate issued by the Congress that enacted
the Thirteenth Amendment[66] and affirmed by Justice Harlan in his dissent
in the *Civil Rights Cases*, that is, to remove the badges of slavery from all
those to whom they are still affixed. The forms of race discrimination that
derive their authority from the more than two centuries of involuntary servitude are the evil manifestation of such badges and are, hence, the proper
objects of legislative attention with respect to effecting the public interest.
Moreover, insofar as such legislation may be seen to be unwarranted interferences in free enterprise, namely, to restrict employers in the manner in
which they use their property and laborers—and, thus, to be regarded as

unwarranted interferences in the legitimate rights of entrepreneurs, employers, or other paragons of Enlightenment capitalism—it should be remembered that the Supreme Court long ago announced that "Rights of property, like all other social and conventional rights, are subject to such reasonable limitations in their enjoyment as will prevent them from being injurious, and to such reasonable restraints and regulations established by law as the legislature, under the governing and controlling power vested in them by the Constitution, may think necessary and expedient."[67] Moreover, because much affirmative action legislation affects the right of hitherto disadvantaged or deprived persons to be hired and promoted precisely because in the past their rights of this kind had been abridged on account of their race, color, creed, gender, or previous conditions of servitude, it is pertinent to take note of the fact that in 1880 a federal district court, in invalidating a California statute that prohibited the employment of any Chinese person in any corporation then existent or in future formed under the laws of that state, asserted: "The right to labor is, of all others, after the right to live, the fundamental, inalienable right of man, wherever he may be permitted to be, of which he cannot be deprived, either under the guise of law or otherwise, except by usurpation and force."[68] But there is accumulating more and more evidence to the effect that it is precisely in the deprivation of the right to work—as well as in the ancillary and auxiliary right to an education,[69] and to the opportunity to prepare oneself for the higher callings of expert jobs and professional careers[70]—that the post–Civil War local, state, and national governments engaged. After 1876, there was a retreat from the Reconstruction era's promise[71] to lift once and for all time the bar of race discrimination from all persons of color to whom it had and might in the future be applied. As a preeminent historian of that era, Kenneth Stampp has pointed out, after 1876, "The federal government had renounced responsibility for reconstruction, abandoned the Negro, and, in effect, invited southern white men to formulate their own program of political, social, and economic readjustment."[72]

That blacks—despite the post–Civil War granting of birthright citizenship to them if born in the United States and of the right to naturalization if not so born but of African nativity or African descent[73]—were still long denied most of the privileges and immunities that so many believed were attendant upon that citizenship is a matter of such well-known record that it need not detain us very long here.[74] The lasting import of the relevant section of Justice Taney's opinion in the *Dred Scott* case,[75] in the pithy summation of Professor Dudley O. McGovney, was that the slaves were not citizens at all and "that the free negroes were citizens, though without full rights."[76] In 1866, as if to reinforce *Dred Scott,* the Supreme Court observed that the conferral of citizenship on a person does not necessarily nor automatically confer upon him or her the full panoply of rights, privileges and immunities that some suppose are thereunto pertaining. "Citizenship," the Court announced, "has no necessary connection with the franchise of voting, eligibility to office, or indeed with any other rights, civil or political."[77]

For blacks, the era immediately following the Civil War seemed at first to portend the removal of all those burdens of life that had been their lot as slaves or as free Negroes without full rights. But, as the historian John Hope Franklin summed up the matter, even "the Reconstruction years were marked by half-hearted, light-hearted, inconclusive steps taken by the state and federal governments to introduce a semblance of racial equality in America. The feeble effort was an abject failure . . ." With the end of Reconstruction, "An uneasy peace settled over the South and North, as the old order of racial degradation, now buttressed by Supreme Court decisions and executive and legislative indifference and inactivity, continued to prevail."[78] Rather than being removed, the badges of slavery had been pinned ever more tightly onto the bodies of the Freedmen and women and their descendants, and, despite protests against them, they would remain in place for nearly a century after emancipation. Their newly-acquired citizenship was undermined by a veritable extension of the Taney doctrine of their status as less-than equal citizens and by a growing use of color as a criterion of rights.

Citizenship, properly understood, should have entailed making the freedmen and women and their descendants an equal part of the American national community. "Nationality," in turn, observed the legal scholar Dudley O. McGovney in 1911, "is the characteristic or status of a person by virtue of which he [or she] belongs to a particular state." McGovney went on to point out that the antonym of citizenship is "alienage," and that "Alienage is regarded as a disability, an incapacity."[79] Insofar as the state and federal laws, court decisions, and local ordinances disabused blacks of their civic and national rights, privileges, and immunities as citizens of the United States, while still recognizing them as de jure members of the body politic, they established them de facto in an oxymoronic status as, in effect, alien citizens. That status arose, in turn, from their having been reclassified in law as "colored persons." Nowhere was this ignominious status more fully realized than in the juridical support given to statutes establishing segregation and other limitations on civil rights for persons designated as persons of color.

In the majority decision delivered in *Plessy v. Ferguson* (1896), the Court had left the matter of determining what characteristics constituted the basis for a person's racial status up to the several states—the plaintiff Homer Adolphus Plessy having complained that Louisiana's railroad segregation statute had been inappropriately applied to him, a person of one-eighth Negro blood.[80] In 1910, after reviewing extensively the matter of race and color status in the law,[81] the District Court of Appeals of the District of Columbia upheld a refusal by the superintendent of the Brookland School, a public school reserved for white pupils, to admit a young girl of one-sixteenth Negro blood, a girl who manifested no "ocular" sign of being black and who claimed to have always been treated and recognized as white by her neighbors and friends. The Court ruled that the popular meaning of the term "colored," as might be gleaned from consulting ordinary usages and dictionaries, must prevail in all such disputes over the matter, and that the term "as applied to persons or races is commonly understood to mean persons wholly or in part of negro blood or having any appreciable admixture thereof."[82]

But the Court went further in its quest to establish a permanent legal definition for the terms "Negro," "mulatto" and "colored," not only substituting a criterion of "blood" descent for one of visible epidermal pigmentation, but also insisting that the term "colored" was codeterminative with and limited to the term "negro." In behalf of the latter thesis, Chief Justice Shepard quoted approvingly from the trial judge's opinion as to the meaning and scope of the term "colored":

> That the common use of the word throughout the United States is in nowise significant of mere complexion is quite definitely established by considering the universal habit of the people in their unalterable failure to apply it to the Indian, who is red, to the Mongolian, who is yellow, or to the Malay, who is brown; its application to one of these unfair complexions is not anytime to be heard; to those of negro blood alone it is ever found to be suited; and then, not depending for the propriety of its application upon a shade of particular blackness, but rather upon an admixture of a particular racial blood, the negro.[83]

What Justice Harlan had warned against in his dissents in the *Civil Rights Cases*, in *Plessy*, and, once again in 1908 in *Berea College v. Kentucky*[84]—that the command of the Thirteenth Amendment to protect the former slaves and their descendants from race discrimination, the badge of servitude, was being disobeyed and defied by acts of the legislatures, rulings of the lower courts, and by the majority votes of his brethren on the Supreme Court—seemed all too obvious.[85]

W. E. B. DuBois had predicted that the major problem of the twentieth century would be that of "the color line."[86] A few years later, Ray Stannard Baker traced out the contours of that color line as it meandered through the institutions of the United States.[87] In the midst of the Second World War, St. Clair Drake and Horace Cayton followed that line as it had developed in the environs of Chicago.[88] Later still, Herbert Blumer likened that demarcation to a bastion "like the Maginot Line," but one whose inner battlements would be more difficult to break than those of its military counterpart had proved to be.[89] A condition amounting to alienage—in McGovney's sense of the term—had become the law and praxis of the land as far as African Americans were concerned. So constrained was their situation that, in 1965—eleven years after the Supreme Court had ruled that separate-but-equal school facilities were a violation of the Fourteenth Amendment—when he first took notice of their plight, Talcott Parsons sought to discover how "full citizenship for the Negro" might at last be effected.[90]

Citizenship, Color, and Equal Opportunity

Contrary to the claims of either color-blind or class-oriented scholars, prejudices of race and culture have gone hand-in-hand with the development of America's modern industrial society. The light of Enlightenment Reason has not been so bright as to obliterate the less-rational claims of "blood" and heritage, especially as they impinge on citizenship in the United States. The essentials of citizenship were denied to blacks for many years after their emancipation from slavery. Less obvious was how the establishment of a condition of permanent alienage for all those persons who were held to be neither "white" nor of "African nativity or descent" would bring together under a virtually common legal distinction persons whose ancestors had never been enslaved in America with those whose forebears had.

CHINESE

That the alienating form of race discrimination that arose out of their historic condition as erstwhile enslaved persons would not be confined to the freedmen and women and their descendants, or to the descendants of those Africans and African Americans who had always been free in America,[91] was, perhaps, first indicated in the vain attempt of an immigrant from China to become naturalized as a citizen of the United States in 1878. Nearly a half century later, this extension was elaborated upon in the Supreme Court's sustaining of a Mississippi court's ruling that the American-born citizen daughter of a Chinese alien was to be considered a "colored person" and, like Negroes, to be denied entrance to the public school set aside for white children in a county of that state.

In 1870, during the congressional debate over revising the 1802 naturalization act that had limited United States citizenship to "Free white persons," Senator Charles Sumner had attempted to strike the word "white" from the new statute. He was unsuccessful. Opposition to his proposal turned on the assumption that if the term "white" were to be removed, the door would be open for Chinese immigrants to become citizens of the United States. The language of 16 Stat. 256, sec. 7 was changed to extend the right of naturalization to "aliens of African nativity and to persons of African descent," but the term "white" was retained to define all other eligibles.

Eight years later, Ah Yup, "a native and citizen of the empire of China, of the Mongolian race, presented a petition . . . praying that he be . . . admitted as a citizen of the United States." He was refused. The argument rejecting his petition was said to be consistent with anthropological science. According to the several admittedly disparate classifications of races that the federal district court was willing to accept—that of Buffon as modified by Blumenbach, who claimed there were five of such; or that of Linnaeus, who allowed for the existence of four; or Cuvier, who only permitted three— only white persons belonged to the "Caucasian" or "European" race, while Chinese were of the "Mongolian" or "Asiatic" race. As neither "in popular language, in literature, nor in scientific nomenclature, do we ordinarily, if ever, find the words 'white person' used in a sense so comprehensive as to include an individual of the Mongolian race," and because it appeared to the court that Congress had intended to exclude "Mongolians" from the right to naturalization, the court concluded that "a native of China, of the Mongolian race, is not a white person within the meaning of the act of Congress."[92] This decision provided juridical legitimation to the burgeoning anti-Chinese movements in western America;[93] it also gave a judicial imprimatur to those municipal ordinances, state statutes, amendments to the California state constitution, and to earlier lower court decisions discriminating against Chinese. These decisions had already stripped California Chinese of the right to testify in court in cases involving white people,[94] at first expelled and then segregated Chinese children in the public schools,[95] limited their occupations,[96] and, with less success, attempted to inflict cruel and unusual punishments upon them.[97] In addition, anti-Chinese immigration legislation, similar to the pass laws that troubled the comings and goings of black slaves and the freedmen and women subjected to the post-Emancipation "black codes,"[98] required Chinese aliens to obtain and keep on their persons at all times a special certificate entitling them to enter, reside, and travel in the United States. Failure to have such a certificate would subject the person so found to deportation.[99] From 1882 to 1943, laborers and their wives and children from China were not only included in the category of those ineligible for naturalization,[100] but also were excluded from entry to the United States,[101] the prohibitions extending to their legitimate or illegitimate offspring, to persons only half-Chinese, and to Chinese aliens who had served in the United States armed forces.[102] As a result, the only other way by which persons of Chinese descent could acquire citizenship in the United States—birth on American soil—was narrowed considerably.[103]

As early as 1876—that is, before passage of the Chinese Exclusion Act which, *inter alia,* specifically denied citizenship to subjects of the emperor of China—one Toy Long was dispossessed of his and his fellow Chinese workers' mining claim in Oregon in part because of a federal court's interpretation of his legal status as a "dreaded Chinaman."[104] Once denial of their right to naturalization had become part of the nation's law and of a revised treaty with China, Chinese who had somehow acquired United States citizenship in one of the several states discovered that their new status could be voided by a higher court; that their license to become an attorney-at-law could be withheld despite their qualification for it on the merits; that their U.S. passport could be revoked; and that their reentry to the United States could be denied after but a brief trip to their native land.[105] Years later, a federal district court ruled that not even the foreign-born though illegitimate son of a Chinese who was a lawful citizen of the United States could be admitted into the United States.[106] Until 1943, when a special act of Congress granted the subjects of America's ally in the war against Japan the right to become naturalized, Chinese aliens in the United States could not become United States citizens.[107]

Although the court's opinion in *Wall v. Oyster* had stated that the term "colored" applied exclusively to Negroes, the noticeable presence of

Chinese in the southern states[108]—and the desire on the part of many southern states to segregate the peoples of unknown racial origin from both whites
and blacks[109]—prompted a reconsideration of the scope of that term. In
1925, the China-born mother of Martha Lum, "a minor of school age, of
pure Chinese and Mongolian race, and . . . a native born citizen of the United
States," filed a suit demanding that her daughter be admitted to
Mississippi's Rosedale consolidated school, a public institution reserved
for white children. Because Martha had been excluded from that school on
the basis of her Chinese descent, her mother's suit argued *inter alia* that
since the term "colored" had been restricted to Negroes and to persons of
some measure of Negro "blood," her American-born daughter could not
be considered to be "colored" nor compelled to attend a school set aside
for "colored" children. However, the Mississippi Supreme Court, drawing
upon an early California Supreme Court decision that barred black,
mulatto, Indian, and Chinese testimony from admissibility in criminal
trials,[110] as well as the decision in *Ah Yup* and in subsequent cases extending the denial of naturalization to immigrants from Japan[111]—and avoiding
any mention of *Wall v. Oyster*—held "that the term 'colored persons' was
not necessarily limited to negroes and those having an admixture of negro
blood in their veins." The court went on to observe, that, because people
classified as "Mongolian" could not be included among those considered
"white" but could, in accordance with Mississippi's miscegenation statute,
maintain intimate social relations and intermarry with blacks, a person of
Chinese descent would not be improperly treated when excluded from a
white-only school and assigned to a school for "colored" children. As the
court was careful to point out, "the dominant purpose of . . . the
Constitution of our state was to preserve the integrity and purity of the white
race . . . [and] the segregation laws have been so shaped as to show by their
terms that it was the white race that was intended to be separated from the
other races."[112] Chinese had, in effect, been added to the peoples bearing
the badges of a bygone slavery.[113]

JAPANESE

The denial of "white" status was extended to immigrants from Japan as
well as from other parts of Asia and the Pacific Islands. With that denial there
ensued further restrictions—on their right to naturalization, to acquire land,
to form corporations, to attend the school of one's choice, to marry across
the color line, et cetera. These limitations on their life-chances constituted

a veritable consignment of them to the status then being visited upon the descendants of black slaves. The common feature defining their condition was "color," as that term was legally constructed by legislative enactments and court interpretations.

In 1891, the United States Supreme Court upheld the actions taken to prevent the entry to the United States of Ms. Nishimura Ekiu, a young woman from Japan whose claim to be immigrating in order to join her already domiciled husband was disbelieved. Ms. Nishimura was designated as a member of a class of persons ineligible to land under an amendment to the immigration act—"persons likely to become a public charge"—but was not excluded on account of her race or color.[114] Three years later, however, a federal district court turned down Shebata Saito's application to become a United States citizen on the ground that "The Japanese, like the Chinese, belong to the Mongolian race . . ." and that "difference in color, conformation of skull, structure and arrangement of hair, and the general contour of the face are the marks which distinguish the various types." Unlike later court decisions, this one held that "the color of the skin is considered the most important criterion for the distinction of race." In the *Saito* case, the court distinguished human groups as either "chocolate brown" (Australoid), "brown black" (Negroid), "yellow" (Mongoloid), "fair whites" (Xanthochroic), or "dark whites" (Melanchroic). However, the court added that these differences "do not exist in the case of each individual . . . but . . . are sufficiently distinct to form the basis of well-recognized classification."[115] It was a classification, the court seemed to say, that could be used to distinguish those ineligible to United States citizenship from those eligible.

After California and ten other states had passed laws prohibiting aliens ineligible to citizenship in the United States from acquiring any legal interest in agricultural land,[116] the question of how to determine membership in the excluded and included categories became even more significant. With naturalization open only to free white persons and persons of African descent or nativity, peoples from Japan, Southeast Asia, South Asia, and Southwest Asia, as well as from some other parts of the globe, became objects of juridical scrutiny. A key statement on the matter was issued in a Supreme Court decision of 1922, when the Court ruled that Takao Ozawa— a lawfully admitted immigrant from Japan who, the Court readily conceded, had resided for two decades in the United States, had graduated from an American high school, attended the University of California, had been, together with his family, a regular churchgoer, and who regularly used the

English language in his home as well as elsewhere—was ineligible to be naturalized.[117] Ozawa's lawyers argued that the term "white" should be read in the first instance solely to exclude Negroes and Indians. But, regardless, they urged that Japanese be considered "Caucasians," since there was ethnological evidence to indicate that they are descended from the Ainu[118] and thereby are racially distinguishable from the Chinese who are not.[119] The Court disagreed on every point, denying that the original intent of the first naturalization act had been to exclude only blacks and Native Americans; insisting "that the words 'white person' were meant to indicate only a person of what is popularly known as the Caucasian race"; disposing of Ozawa's claim to be "Caucasian" by a flat denial ("The appellant . . . is clearly of a race which is not Caucasian"); and introducing a new approach to determining the racial assignment of persons seeking naturalization in the United States:

> The effect of the conclusion that the words "white person" mean a Caucasian is not to establish a sharp line of demarcation between those who are entitled and those who are not entitled to naturalization, but rather a zone of more or less debatable ground outside of which, upon the one hand, are those clearly eligible, and, outside of which upon the other hand, are those clearly ineligible for citizenship. Individual cases falling within this zone must be determined as they arise from time to time by what this court has called, in another connection, . . . "the gradual process of judicial inclusion and exclusion."

When, in the *Dred Scott* case, Chief Justice Taney had excluded both free Negroes and black slaves from citizenship in the United States, he had made it clear that they had been excluded from "the people" that constituted the sovereign element in the republic.[120] Excluding those who were neither white nor of African nativity or descent—and forbidding them to intermarry with whites[121]—accomplished a similar objective. For example, Chinese and Japanese alien residents of California, and of the other states that imposed burdens on all those who were ineligible to naturalization, could not vote, serve on juries, acquire land, form corporations, or work at those professions that required United States citizenship as a prerequisite.[122] As a result, both peoples came to be confined to the residential areas and occupational niches that their alien status and the widespread color prejudice in America against Asiatics consigned them. Their children born on United States soil were United States citizens but all too often were made to bear the stigma attached to their racial ancestry and to their legally defined "color."[123] Japanese aliens did not receive the right to naturalization until 1952.[124]

BURMESE, KOREANS, HAWAIIANS

The "zone of more or less debatable ground" created by the *Ozawa* decision had, even before the Court's ruling, become a contested area on which peoples from East Asia, India, Southwest Asia, the Pacific Islands, and certain elements of the population derived from lands south of the Rio Grande would fight for decades for the right to become American citizens. Nothing better reveals the embeddedness of race and color prejudice—as well as the triumph of ethnonational racism over Enlightenment liberal and meritocratic individualism—within the institutions of American peoplehood than the casuistries employed by the courts to deny various immigrant peoples the opportunities, privileges, and immunities that are a concomitant of United States citizenship.[125] Individuals representing at least sixteen different peoples repaired to the courts seeking naturalization by reason of their asserted membership in either the "white" race or, less often, as among those of "African nativity or African descent." Most would be disappointed in their quest.[126]

Among the peoples coming to the United States from parts of East Asia other than China or Japan, those from Burma[127] and Korea[128]—the latter applicant being a man who had been drafted into and served honorably in the United States army in 1918—were also declared ineligible to naturalization on account of their membership in the "Mongolian," that is, nonwhite and nonAfrican, race. And, as Messrs. Kumagai, Bessho, Narasaki, and Toyota were each to discover, United States military service did not serve to lift the stigma of color from Japanese aliens either.[129] When in 1889, Kanaka Nian, an immigrant to the United States from the kingdom of Hawaii, applied for naturalization after residing in the state of Utah for six years, his petition was rejected by that state's supreme court. As in *Ah Yup,* the court chose to review the findings of various scientific authorities on the classification of races—that is, Blumenbach, who, the Court said, had divided "the human family into five varieties, viz., the Caucasian, Mongolian, Ethiopian, Malay, and American"; Cuvier, as well as Jacquinot, who had "reduced the five classes of Blumenbach to three, viz., the Caucasian, Mongolian, and Ethiopian, treating the Malay and American as subdivisions of the Mongolian"; E. B. Tylor and Huxley, who had proposed a different division of humanity, namely, into "Australians, Negroes, Mongols, and Whites, dividing the whites into the fair whites and the dark whites . . . [and including among] the Mongols . . . the Chinese, the Dyak Malays, and the Polynesians"; Van Rhyn, who, within the "Malayo-Polynesian Races and Languages, includes . . . the inhabitants of the Hawaiian islands"; Rev. J. F. Whitmee, who subdivided the "Polynesians into Nguto-Polynesians and Malayo-Polynesians, and among the latter places the Sandwich islanders"; and "the highest authorities . . . [who] class the Hawaiians among the Malay tribes"—and, without deciding definitively whether Mr. Kanaka Nian or his countrymen were "Mongolians," "Mongols," "Polynesians," "Malayo-Polynesians," or merely among the peoples who made up the "Malay tribes," declared that since "No authority on such subjects classifies them with either the Caucasian or white races, or the Ethiopian or black races," neither he nor any other of "the Hawaiians" were entitled to citizenship in the United States.[130] Full and comprehensive citizenship was to be granted to those who could qualify as true members of what historian Alexander Saxton has recently designated as "the white republic."[131]

ARMENIANS

If the courts of the United States were going to deny Burmese, Chinese, Japanese, Koreans, and Hawaiian Islanders the right to naturalization in the United States on account of the legal construction of their "color" status, there still remained the petitions for citizenship sent to them by the peoples of Southwest Asia, South-central Asia, Mexico, Puerto Rico, and the Philippines, as well as those put forward by Amerindians and mixed-bloods. In treating these, the courts further complicated the claims of law upon unfettered reason, unalloyed individualism, and true meritocracy. In what should have been taken as an instructive ruling of 1909, the Federal Circuit Court for the District of Massachusetts admitted four Armenians, Messrs. Halladjian, Ekmakjian, Mouradian, and Bayentz, subjects of Ottoman Turkey, to citizenship in the United States over the objections of the United States attorney.[132] The latter had insisted that Armenians were not white and had gone on to assert, "Without being able to define a white person, the average man in the street understands distinctly what it means, and would find no difficulty in assigning to the yellow race a Turk or Syrian with as much ease as he would bestow that designation on a Chinaman or a Korean."[133] However, indicating his keen distaste for the whole matter, Circuit Judge Lowell would not accept the construction put by the U.S. attorney on the terms "white," "European," or "race." In an exhaustive analysis of the etymology, ethnology, and history related to these terms,

Judge Lowell found all of them to be ambiguous and unclear. With respect to the color term "white," the judge found it to have "been used in the federal and in the state statutes, in the publications of the United States, and in the classification of its inhabitants, to include all persons not otherwise classified; . . . [and he took note of the fact that though] the word 'white' . . . has been narrowed so as to exclude Chinese and Japanese in some instances, yet [it] still includes Armenians."[134]

However, even after this decision, not all would assent to the idea that Armenians were "white" and could, thence, be naturalized in the United States. In 1925, suit was brought in the District Court of Oregon to deny Mr. Cartozian, "a native of that part of the Turkish Empire known as Turkey in Asia, or Asia Minor, . . . [a man] born in Sivas, which is located in Western Armenia, towards Anatolia, and . . . of Armenian blood and race" the issuance of his certificate of naturalization in the United States.[135] Once again, the Oregon court examined the question of "whiteness" in American law. The court's decision reminded the U.S. attorney that skin pigmentation could not be the definitive test of "color," and then undertook a summary of the ethnological evidence on Armenians, including in its hasty review, comments from Herodotus, Strabo, D. C. Brinton, H. F. B. Lynch, W. Z. Ripley, R. B. Dixon, A. C. Haddon, and the testimony presented in behalf of the petitioner by Franz Boas. The court also took note of the arguments set forth by the foreign secretary of the American Board of Foreign Missions, an already naturalized Armenian American attorney, an Armenian-born, Berlin-educated woman who had married an American citizen, and a sociologist who had studied intermarriage in New York City. All of these statements tended toward the court's conclusion that "Armenians in Asia Minor are of the Alpine stock, of European persuasion; . . . that they are white persons, as commonly recognized in speech of common usage, and as popularly understood and interpreted by our forefathers, and by the community at large, . . . and . . . that they amalgamate readily with the white races, including the white people of the United States."[136] However, although Armenians had received the judiciary's imprimatur of "white," and had thus been declared naturalizable, other groups would not be so fortunate.

SYRIANS

Syrians, also at that time subjects of Turkey, presented a more difficult challenge to the courts' construction of ethnoracial identity. In 1909, the federal district judge for the northern district of Georgia allowed Costa George Najour—who hailed "from Mt. Lebanon, near Beirut" and was "not particularly dark, and has none of the characteristics or appearance of the Mongolian race," and who had "the appearance and characteristics of the Caucasian race"—to become a citizen of the United States.[137] But where other judges had occasionally acknowledged the ambiguities that arose when seeking to apply the race-color classification system that had descended from Blumenbach and subsequent ethnologists, Judge Newman relied on a "Quite . . . recent work . . . 'The World's People,' by Dr. A. H. Keane" to inform his decision that, following Keane, divided "the world's people into four classes, the 'Negro or black, in the Sudan, South Africa, and Oceania (Australasia); Mongol or yellow, in Central, North, and East Asia; Amerinds (red or brown), in the New World; and Caucasians (white and also dark), in North Africa, Europe, Irania, India, Western Asia, and Polynesia.'" Because Keane "unhesitatingly places the Syrians in the Caucasian or white division," Judge Newman followed suit, only adding that the U.S. attorney's objection that Najour had been born "within the dominions of Turkey and was heretofore a subject of the Sultan of Turkey" could not overcome the petitioner's claim to be white, lest "the extension of the Turkish Empire over people unquestionably of the white race would deprive them of the privilege of naturalization."[138]

One year later, one Mudarri (no first name is in the record), born in Damascus, appeared before the same Massachusetts judge who had admitted the petitioners in the Halladjian case to American citizenship. He too was granted citizenship, but Judge Lowell observed that "Those who call themselves Syrians by race are probably of a blood more mixed than those who describe themselves as Armenians. However this may be, the older writers on ethnology are substantially agreed that Syrians are to be classed as of the Caucasian or white race. Modern writers on ethnology, who have departed from the ancient classification, are not agreed in substituting any other . . ."[139] In the face of these anomalies, Judge Lowell utilized the occasion of Mudarri's case to challenge the basic racial dichotomy that excluded Mongolians from citizenship and, in effect, he urged the federal government either to clarify or to abandon altogether the use of its constricted and confusing race and color classifications for naturalization: "What may be called for want of a better name the Caucasian-Mongolian classification is not now held to be valid by any considerable body of ethnologists. To make naturalization depend upon this classification is to make an important result depend upon the application of an abandoned scientific theory, a course of

proceeding which surely brings the law and its administration into disre-
pute . . . The court greatly hopes that an amendment of the statutes will
make quite clear the meaning of the word 'white' . . ."[140] In fact, however,
abandonment of the race-color classification for naturalization would not
occur until 1952.[141]

In the same year that Judge Lowell penned his critique of the terms of
the naturalization statute, a federal district court in Oregon, while admitting a Syrian Maronite from the environs of Beirut to citizenship, found that
the applicable "words 'free white persons' are devoid of ambiguity." Judge
Wolverton saw no difficulty in rejecting the contention of the United States
attorneys that those words should be defined to include "only those peoples
of the white race who, at the time of the formation of the government, lived
in Europe and were inured to European governmental institutions, or upon
the American continent, and comprehended such only of the white races
who, from tradition, teaching, and environment, would be predisposed
toward our form of government, and thus readily assimilate with the people
of the United States."[142] But, in a matter of three years, the issue was thrown
open once more when in two cases involving Syrian petitioners before a
federal district court in South Carolina, a judge denied their eligibility, ruling
that the applicable definition of the words "free white persons" was that
understanding which prevailed at the time of the adoption of the
Naturalization Act of 1790, and that at that time they referred only to the
peoples of Europe and their descendants considered to be white.[143]

In his rehearing of one of these matters involving Syrians, the *Dow* case,
Judge Smith carried out one of the most elaborate disputations about the
term "white persons": He inquired whether that term could refer to persons
of the "Caucasian race" independent of their color; whether the term
"Caucasian" included members of the "Semitic nation"; whether European
Jews, having long been recognized as eligible for citizenship in the United
States, were to be considered "Semites" in the same sense as Syrians; and
whether the history and position of Syrians, and especially "their connection through all time with the peoples to whom the Jewish and Christian
peoples owe their religion, makes it inconceivable that the [naturalization]
statute could have intended to exclude them."[144] To each of these queries,
Judge Smith provided an answer that would lead him to exclude the Syrians
from naturalization. Blumenbach's designation of the Caucasian race as
encompassing the peoples of Europe, the Caucasus, Asia Minor, Western
Asia (including Syria) and North Africa was held to be without either philol-
ogical or ethnological foundation; the ethnolinguistic terms "Aryan" and

"Indo-European" were not to be regarded as synonymous with "white persons"—lest the latter be forced to expel from their family the Magyars, the Finns, and the Turks, that is, speakers of Ugric and Turanian tongues, or the Basques, whose language was said to be unique unto itself; Syrians were not "Semites," but more likely the mixed-blood descendants of the ancient Hittites, "a Mongolic race," and, thus, "Asiatics in the sense that they are of Asian nativity and descent and are not Europeans"; European Jews are not "Semites" either, but "a professing Jew from Syria who was not of European nativity or descent would be as equally an Asiatic as the present [Syrian] applicant, and as such not within the terms of the statute"; a "dark complexioned present inhabitant of what formerly was ancient Phoenicia is not entitled to the inference that he must be of the race commonly known as the white race in 1790, merely because 2,000 years ago Judaea, a country whose inhabitants have since entirely changed, was the scene of the labor of one who proclaimed that He had come to save from spiritual destruction all mankind." In fine, Judge Smith declared that, "The broad fact remains that the European peoples taken as a whole are the fair skinned or light complexioned races of the world, and form the peoples generally referred to as 'white' and so classed since classification based on complexion was adopted."[145] Although Judge Smith was overruled—on the ground that the naturalization statute of 1873, revised in 1875, could not be interpreted in terms of the definitions understood in 1790—the circuit court of appeals declared Syrians among the group designated "white persons" because "the consensus of opinion at the time of the enactment of the statute now in force was that they were so closely related to their neighbors on the European side of the Mediterranean that they should be classed as white . . ."[146] In addition, it is worth noting that Circuit Judge Woods complimented Judge Smith on his opinion in the matter, referring to it as "supported with remarkable force and learning."[147]

ARABS

That a conflation of color, race, language, religion, and ethnohistory had come to confound the determination of what peoples might be included within the classes eligible for naturalization is illustrated by the outcomes and arguments in two cases before the district courts of Massachusetts and Michigan in 1944. In the Massachusetts case, petitioner Mohamed Mohriez, "an Arab born in Sanhy, Badan, Arabia," a speaker of "Arabian [sic] as his native language" who had arrived in the United States in 1921, sought naturalization in the United States but was opposed by the local representative of the Immigration and Naturalization Service on the ground that he was not a "white person."[148] District Judge Schoonmaker rejected the argument of the INS, pointing out that in accordance with previous court rulings and the Nationality Act of 1940, "the question of whether one is a 'free white person' . . . has now . . . to be settled 'in accordance with the understanding of the common man' and turns on whether the petitioner is a member of one of the 'races . . . inhabiting Europe or . . . living along the shores of the Mediterranean' or . . . , perhaps, is a member of a race of 'Asiatics whose long contiguity to European nations and assimilation with their culture has caused them to be thought of as of the same general characteristics.'"[149] Mohriez should be placed with the population groups defined in the latter two categories, according to Judge Schoonmaker. Philologically, and in common understanding, he asserted, "the Arab people belong to that division of the white race speaking the Semitic languages . . . [so that both] the learned and the unlearned would compare the Arabs with the Jews towards whose naturalization every American Congress since the first has been avowedly sympathetic." Further, he pointed to what "every schoolboy knows," that "the Arabs have at various times inhabited parts of Europe, lived along the Mediterranean, been contiguous to European nations and been assimilated culturally and otherwise, by them." Moreover, noting the examples set by Avicenna and Averroes, as well as "the sciences of algebra and medicine, the population and the architecture of Spain and of Sicily, [and] the very words of the English language," Judge Schoonmaker urged how all of these "remind us as they would have reminded the Founding Fathers of the action and interaction of Arabic and non-Arabic elements of our culture," and he concluded "that even by the narrow criteria which were adopted in the opinions of Mr. Justice Sutherland [in the *Ozawa* case and in *United States v. Thind,* discussed infra] the Arab passes muster as a white person."

Judge Schoonmaker added a dictum that persons lawfully admissible to the United States ought to be naturalizable, arguing that "It is contrary to our American creed to create a superior and inferior brand of permanent residents."[150] However, the fact was that such a hierarchy had already been created by the immigration and naturalization laws affecting persons deemed to be alien Asiatics—they could not be naturalized and, after 1923, could no longer be admitted to the United States, but their children born on American soil were United States citizens according to the principle of *jus soli*. It was this distinction that in some small measure had led Chief

Justice Fuller, together with Justice Harlan, to dissent from the majority's ruling in *United States v. Wong Kim Ark,* opposing a decision that granted automatic citizenship to American-born children of alien Chinese in part because it fostered just such a division within the Chinese population in America, but more because the two justices inferred that parents ineligible to United States citizenship would not be likely to bring up their children to be proper citizens of a country to which they themselves were permanently denied naturalization.[151] Judge Schoonmaker, who made no reference to *United States v. Wong Kim Ark* in his decision in the *Mohriez* case, seemed to have its anomalies in mind when he concluded his obiter dicta in the latter proceeding by remarking favorably on the recent changes in the immigration and naturalization laws affecting Chinese, that is, the setting of a national quota of admissions and the granting to Chinese aliens of the right to apply for United States citizenship: "[W]e as a country have learned that policies of rigid exclusion are not only false to our professions of democratic liberalism but repugnant to our vital interests as a world power."[152]

However, if Judge Schoonmaker's liberal interpretation of the "free white persons" phrase and his stated belief that "it is highly desirable that . . . [the Nationality Act of 1940] should be interpreted so as to promote friendlier relations between the United States and other nations so as to fulfill the promise that we shall treat all men as created equal"[153] seemed to indicate a fundamental change pending in the outlook on race and color in citizenship matters, the decision of Federal Judge Tuttle of the Eastern District Court of Michigan, in a case decided in the same year involving the petition for naturalization of a Yemeni Arab, illustrates how old, if confused, racialistic ideas had remained as a thread running through the institutional fabric of America. In the Michigan case, Mr. Ahmed Hassan's petition for naturalization was challenged, as in that of *Mohriez,* on the ground that, as an Arab whose "skin was undisputedly dark brown in color" and one who hailed from a region wherein "the extremely dark complexion of petitioner's skin is typical of a majority of the Arabians . . . which in fact is attributed to the intense heat and the blazing sun of that area," he was not a "white person."[154] Judge Tuttle fell back on earlier decisions to remind Mr. Hassan that although skin pigmentation was not to be regarded as decisive in determining his legal status, "when an individual applying for citizenship has a skin of a different color than is usual for the members of the group from which he claims to come, a strong burden of proof then rests upon him to show by the usual measures of proving genealogy that he is in fact a member of that group." Further, Judge Tuttle also held to the earlier ruling, rejected in the final proceeding of the *Dow* case, that the understanding of the lawmakers and people of America in 1790 should prevail in determining the definition and scope of the term "free white persons." In that regard, he then found that "petitioner is an Arab and that Arabs are not white persons within the meaning of the [Nationality] act."

Moreover, Judge Tuttle combined this restrictive understanding with his view of how the religion and culture found among the inhabitants of the Arabian peninsula would relate to that of Euro-America: "Apart from the dark skin of the Arabs, it is well known that they are a part of the Mohammedan world and that a wide gulf separates their culture from that of the predominantly Christian peoples of Europe." Distinguishing the Hassan situation from that in the *Cartozian* case, he noted that the latter involved Armenians, "a Christian people living in an area close to the European border, who have intermingled and intermarried with Europeans over a period of centuries." Pointing to the evidence offered in *Cartozian* on the extent of intermarriage among Armenian immigrants to America, Judge Tuttle predicted that "It cannot be expected that as a class ... [Arabs] would readily intermarry with our population and be assimilated into our civilization."[155] For doubtful cases, then, religious compatibility and assimilation, the latter to be defined in accordance with a judge's view of the likelihood and amount of amalgamation that would occur, would be crucial aspects of the test of whether an immigrant people were "white persons."[156]

EAST INDIANS

Armenians, Syrians, and Arabs were not the only peoples whose classification along the "white"-"Mongolian" dichotomy would become a matter of contradictory interpretations. Several representatives of the distinctive peoples of India who had migrated to and settled in various states of the United States also petitioned the courts for the right to become citizens. In some of these cases the matter was complicated by California's desire that no "Oriental" acquire agricultural land in the state[157] and by the American government's wish to offer no asylum to anticolonial nationalists from India, who, it feared, might exploit their freedom and security in the first nation to throw off English colonial rule to mount a campaign to liberate what the British Empire considered the jewel in its imperial crown.[158] In the year 1909, in which *In re Balsara*, an important case involving East Indians, was begun, only 337 "Asiatic" Indians were admitted to the United States, an enormous drop from the 1,710 who had been admitted the previous year, or the 1,782 who would be admitted in 1910. But the number excluded kept up a steady pace—417 in 1907; 438 in 1908; 331 in 1909; 411 in 1910; and 862 in 1911. The number deported—9 in 1908; 1 in 1909; 4 in 1910; 36 in 1911; 20 in 1912; and 32 in 1913—speaks to a growing apprehension on the part of the American authorities.[159] In 1917, Congress enacted a new immigration law that prohibited the entry of laborers from any country behind the line of a newly demarcated "barred zone"; India was among the Asian countries behind that line.[160]

On May 28, 1909, Circuit Judge Lacombe of the Southern District of New York reluctantly conferred American citizenship on Bhicaji Franyi Balsara, a merchant from India, a Parsee who "appears to be a gentleman of high character and exceptional intelligence."[161] Judge Lacombe's reluctance stemmed from his belief that there "was much force in the argument that the Congress which framed the original act for naturalization of aliens ... intended it to include only white persons belonging to those races whose emigrants had contributed to the building up on this continent of the community of people which declared itself a new nation ..."; and from his worry that if the phrase "free white persons" were to be broadened so as to include "all branches of the great race or family known to ethnologists as the Aryan, Indo-European, or Caucasian ... it ... [would] bring in, not only the Parsees, ... which is probably the purest Aryan type, but also Afghans, Hindoos, Arabs, and Berbers."[162] Judge Lacombe granted Balsara's petition only on the publicly given assurance that the United States attorney would appeal his decision, and in the hope that the proceeding in a higher court would lead to "an authoritative interpretation" of the meaning of the terms indicating eligibility and ineligibility in the naturalization statute. The U.S. attorney kept his promise, and the matter was carried to the circuit court of appeals in 1910.

Both the district and circuit court decisions would exert a confusing hold on later cases. (Afghans presented a similar problem to the courts. A case involving one Abdullah Dolla—an Afghan born in Calcutta who had arrived in New York in 1894, resided in Savannah, Georgia, for twelve years, and had been awarded "white" status after a local court judge, noting Dolla's dark facial complexion and dark eyes, decided to examine the color of his shirt-covered arms and chest and determined that he was sufficiently fair to meet a "white" color standard—had been thrown out on appeal because of a technicality.[163] Eighteen years later, the petition of Feroz Din, described as a "typical Afghan and a native of Afghanistan," was rejected by the District Court of the Northern District of California on the grounds that he "is not a white person, nor of African nativity or descent," Judge Bourquin adding, "What ethnologists, anthropologists, and other so-called scientists may speculate and conjecture in respect to races and origins may interest the curious and convince the credulous, but is of no moment in arriving at the intent of Congress in the statute aforesaid."[164]) In the *Balsara* case, the circuit court of appeals decided the matter in behalf of the Parsee petitioner on five separate but related arguments. The court held that "The Parsees emigrated some 1,200 years ago from Persia into India and now live in the neighborhood of Bombay . . . constitut[ing] a settlement by themselves of intelligent and well-to-do persons, principally engaged in commerce, and are as distinct from the Hindus as are the English who dwell in India"; that a strict and literal construction of what the Congress of 1790 meant by the terms "free white persons" would require the court to exclude from citizenship Russians, Poles, Italians, Greeks and other Europeans who had not formed the basis of the original colonial populace; that Congress "probably had [had] principally in mind the exclusion of Africans, whether slave or free, and [Native American] Indians"; that those early "Congressmen certainly knew that there were white, yellow, black, red, and brown races"; and that "Whether there is any pure white race and what peoples belong to it may involve nice discriminations, . . . for practical purposes there is no difficulty in saying that the Chinese, Japanese, and Malays and the American Indians do not belong to the white race . . . , [while] in our opinion the Parsees do belong to the white race and the Circuit Court properly admitted Balsara to citizenship."[165]

However, neither the admission of Balsara to citizenship nor the distinction offered by the circuit court of appeals to Parsees as opposed to Hindus secured for all time the naturalization of the former group. Twenty-nine years after Balsara had been granted his citizenship in the United States, the same circuit court of appeals that had affirmed his naturalization rejected the petition of Rustom Dadabhoy Wadia, reversing the finding of the *Balsara* court and insisting that the understanding of the "common man," and the racial conceptions of the Congress of 1790 were to prevail in such matters.[166] Wadia had been born to Parsee parents in Bombay, India, in 1899, emigrated to the United States in 1923, married Gladys Voorhees in 1928, and fathered two children with her. At the time of his application for citizenship, he and his family were living on the Lower East Side of New York City; "his occupation was that of a life insurance agent and substitute teacher and in religion he was a follower of Zoroaster."

Judge Hand interpreted the *Balsara* decision to have held "that the words 'free white persons' conferred the privilege of naturalization upon members of the Caucasian race." Such a conferral could no longer be sustained, he ruled, because the United States Supreme Court had in 1923 denied the petition for citizenship of a Hindu while conceding that he was a "Caucasian."[167] The terms "free white persons" were to be interpreted as "common speech" and in accordance with the understandings of the "common man." So interpreted, Judge Hand went on, "A Parsee of a race which immigrated from Persia to India some 1,200 years ago, even though retaining, as is claimed, blood differing little, if any, from that of its original ancestors, can hardly be differentiated in the mind of the common man from that of the Hindus beside whom the Parsees have lived for 1,200 years." "Each stock is Caucasian," he admitted. "The language of each is of Aryan origin, but neither can properly be classed as 'white persons.'"

Judge Hand put a different construction on the historical understandings that should be accepted regarding the Congress of 1790. Conceding that "at that time there was little or no thought of the admission of immigrants who did not come from Great Britain, Germany, Sweden, Norway, France or Holland," he slid over the potentiality for limiting "free white persons" to emigrants from those countries, adding, simply, "naturally, persons indigenous to Spain, Italy, Russia and other European nations were regarded as within the meaning of the words as soon as they sought to immigrate . . ." But then he quickly added that this enlargement of the white group had occurred "although some of their inhabitants were of dark complexions and even in the case of certain Russians of a Mongolian caste of countenance." Ultimately, admitting that "it is not altogether safe to generalize," Judge Hand opined that "it may fairly be said that members of races inhabiting Europe or living along the shores of the Mediterranean are ordinarily to be classed as 'white persons' [and that the] same thing may be true of some Asiatics whose long contiguity to European nations and assimilation with their culture has caused them to be thought of as of the same general characteristics."[168] "Parsees" and "Hindus," however, were not to be counted among those "Asiatics."

The citizenship of "Hindus" remained a matter of considerable contention until 1946, when the bar to their immigration, naturalization, and right to acquire property was lifted by congressional passage of the Luce-Celler Bill.[169] Although a Washington court had granted citizenship to Akhay Kumar Mozumdar in 1913[170] and a California court had done the same to another East Indian in 1914—and although by 1922 at least sixty-nine East Indians had been admitted to United States citizenship in eighteen of the United States—the denial of "white person" status to East Indian "Caucasians" in the case *United States v. Bhagat Singh Thind* led to largely successful attempts to strip those already naturalized of their citizenship and to enforce such statutes as California's alien land law against them.[171] The *Thind* case, following one year after that of *Ozawa*, provided the United States Supreme Court with another opportunity to respond to the requests of more than one federal district judge that it clarify the meaning of such terms as "free white persons," "Caucasian," "Mongolian," and "Hindu" insofar as these words and phrases pertained to the enforcement of the immigration and naturalization laws and the rights obtaining to alien persons under the Constitution of the United States.

In a 1917 decision, a district judge of the Federal Court of Eastern Pennsylvania had presented a remarkably ambivalent and confused tour through these terms before denying the petition for U.S. citizenship of another "Hindu," Mr. Sadar Bhagwag Singh, an "applicant [who] belongs to the race of people commonly known as Hindus,"[172] and one of the leaders of the anticolonial Ghadar Party whom the U.S. government had been seeking to deport.[173] Three years later, Judge Wolverton of the Federal District Court of Oregon granted the petition of Mr. Bhagat Singh Thind, a "high caste Hindu born in Armitsar, Punjab, in the northwestern part of India," who had served six months in the United States Army and had been given an honorable discharge.[174] The district court judge passed lightly over Thind's possible involvement in the Ghadar movement and turned to questions of whether the Immigration Act of 1917, that is, the act creating a "barred zone," required either the deportation of East Indians who had entered the United States lawfully before its enactment or the denial of their right to naturalization. Judge Wolverton decided that it did not require either of these measures and went on to suggest that "it may well be that Congress designed thenceforth to exclude Hindus from entry into the United States, and still permit such as were domiciled here the privilege of being naturalized."[175] As to the government's assertion that Thind was ineligible because he was not a "white person," the judge declared, "I am not disposed to discuss the question . . . [but] am content to rest my decision . . . upon a line of cases of which *In re Mohan Singh* . . . , *In re Halladjian* . . . , and *United States v. Balsara* . . . are illustrative." Other decisions contrary to these three, stated Judge Wolverton, "are not in line with the greater weight of authority."[176] The government immediately appealed this decision to the United States Supreme Court.

For the matter of race, color, and citizenship, the U.S. Supreme Court's decision in the *Ozawa* and *Thind* cases—although riddled with contradictions—would prove definitive. In *Ozawa*, the Court had stated that the terms "Caucasian" and "white persons" were synonymous, giving Thind and other East Indians the hope that, unlike Ozawa, their court-conceded identification as "Caucasians" would assure their right to naturalization. However, Justice Sutherland, who had only one year earlier written the *Ozawa* decision, did not agree. The "conclusion that the phrase 'white persons' and the word 'Caucasian' are synonymous does not end the matter," he began in his opinion in the *Thind* case. "'Caucasian,'" he observed, "is a conventional word of much flexibility, . . . and while it and the words 'white person' are treated as synonymous for the purposes of that [i.e., the *Ozawa*] case, they are not of identical meaning . . ." Although Thind and other "Hindus" had relied on their membership in the "Caucasian" race to secure their legal classification as "white persons," Justice Sutherland, pointing to the fact that the word "Caucasian" was not to be found in the naturalization statutes, and that "as used in the science of ethnology, the connotation of the word is by no means clear," declared that in matters affecting United States citizenship the popular as opposed to the scientific meaning of the fateful term was to be followed by the courts. That popular understanding of the term is "sufficiently [well known] so as to enable us to say that its . . . application is of appreciably narrower scope" than that employed by the ethnologists. The term "white persons" imposed a racial test, the justice went on, "but the term 'race' is one which . . . must be applied to a group of living persons now possessing in common the requisite traits." In a burst of his own contribution to ethnological reasoning on the matter, Justice Sutherland set forth limits on the claims of common racial descent that a petitioner might make: "It may be true that the blond Scandinavian and the brown Hindu have a common ancestor in the dim reaches of antiquity," he allowed, "but the average man knows perfectly well that there are unmistakable and profound differences between them today; and it is not impossible, if that common ancestor could be materialized in the flesh, we should discover that he was himself sufficiently differentiated from both of his descendants to preclude his racial classification with either." Moreover, the understandings of the "common" or "average" man were imputed by Justice Sutherland to the legislators of the Naturalization Act of 1790, who were also said to subscribe to the "Adamite theory of creation—which gave a common ancestor to all mankind—[but, he added,] . . . it is not at all probable that it was intended by the legislators of that day to submit the question of the application of the words 'white persons' to the mere test of an indefinitely remote common ancestry, without regard to the extent of the subsequent divergence of the various branches from such common ancestry or from one another." Noting that it might even be the case "that a given group cannot be properly assigned to any of the enumerated grand racial divisions," the justice held, together with his brethren on the Court, that "We are unable to agree with the district court, or with other lower Federal courts, in the conclusion that a native Hindu is eligible for naturalization." The words "white persons" were to be seen as "inclusive" rather than merely exclusive of Negroes and Native Americans, as Thind and his attorneys had contended, and its terms of inclusion were to be those of the original framers of the statute of 1790—peoples from "the British isles and northwestern Europe" to which were later added "immigrants from eastern, southern, and middle Europe, among them the Slavs and the dark-eyed, swarthy people of Alpine stock," because the latter groups had been "received as unquestionably akin to those already here, and readily amalgamated with them."[177]

Justice Sutherland's decision was to have proactive effects long after the date of its announcement, and it would modify America's relations with its allies during World War II. Two decades after the *Thind* decision, at a time when the United States was allied with the British Empire and others in a war against Germany, Japan and their other Axis allies, when Judge Haney, of the ninth circuit court of appeals, rejected Kharaiti Ram Samras's petition that his naturalization be granted—as well as his plea that the section restricting United States citizenship to free white persons and persons of African nativity and African descent be declared unconstitutional because, among other things, the statute was "manifestly and grossly unreasonable, irrational, illogical, arbitrary, capricious and [set into law a] discriminatory classification based on race or color"[178]—he felt constrained to follow the directives of the *Thind* decision, but he observed, pointedly, that the "power over naturalization is political," and that aliens had no Constitutional right to citizenship in the United States.[179]

PUERTO RICANS AND FILIPINOS

Not all persons subjected to naturalization proceedings by the United States were aliens in the legal sense of that term. Another category of noncitizens had been created by America's acquisition, as a spoil of the Spanish-American War, of territories once part of the Spanish seaborne empire. The anti-imperialist sociologist, William Graham Sumner, bitter over the

American takeover of Cuba, Puerto Rico, and the Philippines as part of the treaty that settled that war, detailed a parade of horrors that connected the then current treatment of blacks to the likely outcome of the introduction of other nonwhites into the racially prejudiced American body politic: "Worse still, Americans cannot assure life, liberty, and the pursuit of happiness to negroes inside of the United States. When the [South Carolina] negro postmaster's house was set on fire . . . and not only he, but his wife and children, were murdered . . . and when . . . this incident passed without legal investigation or punishment, it was a bad omen for the extension of liberty, etc., to Malays and Tagals . . ."[180]

In fact, full citizenship was not immediately extended to the nonwhite former subjects of the king of Spain. Promising eventual independence to the Philippines, Congress enacted a law in 1916 that enlarged the local powers of what Dudley O. McGovney called "this inchoate independent nation," and three years later that entity enacted its own exclusive naturalization law.[181] The matter of United States citizenship for brown-skinned Filipinos and Puerto Ricans became enormously complicated by the decades-long debate over whether the nonracial citizenship provisions of the Fourteenth Amendment were applicable to the Philippines or to Puerto Rico.[182] Professor McGovney, perhaps the outstanding legal authority on the matter, supposed that fear of the possible eligibility of the islands' Chinese and Japanese residents to U.S. citizenship had fueled the faction that disputed the thesis that the entire Constitution followed the flag.[183] In fact, however, the fears about Chinese immigrants would find their own way into the law of the Philippines. In 1928, the Supreme Court of the Philippines held that a Chinese man born in China and domiciled in the Philippines from 1881 to 1925, the date of his application for citizenship, was ineligible to naturalization because of his race.[184]

However, the race and "color" of the "brown-skinned" Filipinos and "dark-skinned" Puerto Ricans seemed to matter as much to the Congress and the courts of the United States as that of the Chinese. In a series of cases beginning in 1912, with two subsequent court proceedings in 1916, two in 1917, one in 1921, one in 1927, one in 1931, and another in 1935, Filipinos sought, for the most part unsuccessfully, to change their status from that of noncitizen nationals to that of citizens of the United States. In some of these cases, the petitioners had served honorably in the United States military forces and hoped to take advantage of an earlier law that permitted alien enlistees in the United States Navy or Marine Corps to apply for naturalization. Puerto Ricans fared better in these cases than Filipinos, perhaps because as persons of Spanish descent they were regarded as "white," and if dark-skinned, as persons of "African" or mixed African and white descent.[185] However, in many of these cases, the Filipino petitioner was denied on the grounds of "color." Thus, in 1912, Eugenio Alverto, the grandson of a Spaniard and a "Philippino woman," who had served seven years in the United States Navy, was refused citizenship in the United States on the grounds that he was not a "free white person," the latter category defined to embrace only "members of the white, or Caucasian race, as distinct from the black, red, yellow, and brown races."[186] Four years later, another U.S. Navy veteran, "one Lampitoe," described as "the son of a Filipino mother and a father whose mother was a Filipino and whose father was a full-blooded Spaniard, resident in Manila," was rejected on the same grounds as Alverto.[187] In the same year, and again in 1921, two more veterans of the U.S. Navy were disallowed not on account of their race or color—for, in the first case, the district judge for Massachusetts interpreted the relevant section of the Naturalization Act of 1906 to have had no intended restriction with respect to Filipinos or Puerto Ricans—but on a nonracial technicality.[188] But one year after the *Mallari* decision, a navy veteran and "Philippino," Penaro Rallos, was denied naturalization, the federal district judge for the eastern district of New York observing that were he to rule otherwise, it "would mean that Chinese, Japanese, and Malays could become [United States] citizens."[189] In 1921, however, a more thorough hearing was given to the legal status of Filipino veterans in the case of Engracio Bautista, "a Mestizo . . . born in the province of Bulacan on the Island of Luzon . . . on the 14th of March, 1888," for many years a resident of the United States, and a United States serviceman who was then serving his third four-year hitch in the navy. Referring to the debates over adoption of the Foraker Amendment to the Naturalization Act of 1906, Circuit Judge Morrow ruled that the act, as amended, intended "to admit to citizenship all persons, not citizens, who, owing 'permanent allegiance to the United States' and possessing the other qualifications provided by the statute, became residents of any state or organized territory of the United States . . . [and that this] was done by Congress with full knowledge that the Filipino belonged to the Malay or brown race."[190] However, the judge was quick to point out that Chinese, Japanese, and other aliens ineligible to citizenship in the United States, though residents in the Philippine Islands, were not in permanent allegiance to the crown of Spain at the time of the Philippine cession and, hence, were still ineligible by the amended Naturalization Act of 1906.[191]

However, a decade later, and two years after a district court had granted citizenship to a Mr. Javier, "a native-born Filipino ... [who had not] served in the United States Navy, Marine Corps, or Naval Auxiliary Service," the Court of Appeals of the District of Columbia denaturalized him on the grounds that he "was not a free white person, nor a person of African nativity or descent," that he was not exempted from this prohibition on his naturalization by reason of military service, and that "his certificate was illegally obtained."[192] Even after 1929, when the provisions of the naturalization act covering the citizenship petitions of Filipinos and Puerto Ricans who had served in the military forces of the United States were broadened, U.S. government attorneys sought—unsuccessfully, as it turned out—to prevent Filipino veterans from becoming U.S citizens. In 1931, District Judge Byers rejected an attempt by the Department of Commerce to deny naturalization to Mariano Villamin Rena, a native-born Filipino who had honorably served out two enlistments in the U.S. Navy, on the grounds that he had not filed his application within six months of his last honorable discharge, a construction the department put on a proviso of the amended statute.[193] But the exemption of Filipino veterans of certain branches of the American armed forces from the "color" provisions of the naturalization acts was not extended to those Filipino noncitizen nationals who had not enlisted; hence, in 1935, the ninth circuit court of appeals found no difficulty in refusing the petition for naturalization of Roque Espiritu De La Ysla, "born in Manila on August 16, 1902, ... of the Filipino race, ... a citizen of the Philippine Islands ... [who] has not served in the United States Navy or Marine Corps or the Naval Auxiliary Service," and who was neither a "free white person" nor a "person of African nativity or African descent."[194]

The anomalous citizenship status of Filipinos did not end until 1946 when Congress enacted special legislation that made it possible for all Filipinos, regardless of race or color, to apply for U.S. citizenship.[195] On July 4, 1946, the Philippines became an independent republic, and emigration from the former U.S. possession became subject to the various kinds of restrictions contained in the several immigration acts passed since that date.[196] In the final years of their status as noncitizen nationals, an unsuccessful attempt was made to enforce California's alien land law against them, the Supreme Court of California ruling that they were not "aliens" ineligible to citizenship in the United States, as had the Chinese been until 1943 and as would the Japanese be until 1952, but rather non-naturalized "nationals," who, therefore, could not be subjected to a law applying solely to a class of "aliens."[197] In the two years immediately preceding Philippine independence, Emory Bogardus, a sociologist who had devoted much of his life to measuring and working to reduce the "social distance" that separated one people of America from another, published an eloquent plea that Congress enact legislation granting Filipinos eligibility for United States citizenship.[198] Linking his exhortation to the events of the time, Bogardus asserted that the "proposed naturalization law would constitute another step toward changing the national policy of the United States from a provincial one to one consistent with the Four Freedoms and with the spirit of the Constitution of the United States."[199]

NATIVE AMERICANS

Aside from the various classes of "aliens" declared ineligible to citizenship in the United States and the noncitizen nationals also so declared, there remained two other categories: "Indians," that is, Amerinds or Native American aborigines, and noncitizen descendants of more than one "racial" or "color" stock. In treating these, again color, culture, and conduct were intertwined to form a barrier against naturalization. That barrier gave the lie to the claim that "assimilation" or "assimilability" would provide a sure ticket of admissibility to American citizenship.[200] Emory Bogardus, an analyst as well as an advocate of assimilation, once pointed out that "Assimilation processes are easily halted and turned back upon themselves."[201] Definitive examples of Bogardus's thesis are to be found in the court struggles over the citizenship status of Native Americans and the restrictions on the naturalization of those of mixed Indian-white-African descent.[202] With respect to the former people, John Collier, who served as commissioner of Indian affairs from 1933 to 1945, observed, "The longest 'colonial' record of the modern world is that of the governments [of Europe and the Americas] toward their Red Indians."[203] Red men and women would test both the color and culture bars to full-fledged peoplehood in the United States.

The court proceeding that in its majority decision subverted the hope that Amerindian acquiescence to mainstream American folkways would be followed by the granting of full-fledged citizenship occurred in 1884.[204] John Elk, born a member of an Indian tribe inhabiting the central plains of the United States, had severed all relations with his tribe, and, according to his uncontradicted testimony, "fully and completely surrendered himself to the jurisdiction of the United States." Having moved into Omaha, Nebraska, acquired property in his own name, become a domiciled resident thereon, and become eligible to serve in the militia, Elk sought to vote in a municipal election in 1880. His application for registration as a voter was turned back on the grounds that he was an Indian and therefore neither a citizen, nor a person eligible to become a citizen of the United States through his own efforts. Elk, however, claimed that his right to vote devolved from his United States citizenship, and that the latter, in turn, derived from that provision of the Fourteenth Amendment that declared that "all persons born or naturalized in the United States, and subject to the jurisdiction thereof, are citizens of the United States and of the state wherein they reside." The majority of the Supreme Court, speaking through Justice Gray, disagreed with his contention, however, holding that Elk's averments did not "allege that the United States [had] accepted his surrender [of tribal jurisdiction], or that he has ever been naturalized, or taxed, or in any way recognized or treated as a citizen by the state or by the United States." Justice Gray went on to insist that "The Indian tribes, being within the territorial limits of the United States, were not, strictly speaking, foreign states; but they were alien nations, distinct political communities, with whom the United States might . . . deal, as they thought fit, either through treaties . . . or through acts of congress." Moreover, he continued, echoing both the definitive Georgia cases, wherein Chief Justice John Marshall had decided the categorical identity and future status of the Amerinds,[205] and the *Dred Scott* decision, "The members of those tribes owed immediate allegiance to their several tribes and were not part of the people of the United States. They were in a dependent condition, a state of pupilage, resembling that of a ward to his guardian." Elk was informed that as such a "ward" he could not become a citizen of the United States merely by voluntarily placing himself outside the jurisdiction of his tribe and, equally voluntarily, defining his own status as that of a member of the people of the United States: "an Indian cannot make himself a citizen of the United States without the consent and cooperation of the government."[206]

Although the Court did not bring up the matter of Elk's "color" as a bar to his becoming a registered voter, and although that issue had seemingly been settled in the *Dred Scott* case—wherein Chief Justice Taney had declared that Indians "may, without doubt, like the subjects of any other foreign government, be naturalized by the authority of Congress, and become citizens of a State, and of the United States; and if [such] an individual should leave his nation or tribe, and take up his abode among the white population, he would be entitled to all the rights and privileges which would belong to an emigrant from any other foreign people"—it would surface again when Indian emigrants from Canada and from the other Americas sought citizenship in the United States. For example, in 1900, a long-time Alaskan resident, Samuel Burton, applied for United States citizenship.[207] Burton had been born in British Columbia. His application was denied on several grounds: that he was neither a free white person nor a person of African descent; that Indians in Alaska had, according to the territory's criminal code, a special status akin to that of a "minor or intoxicated person"; and that Alaska's land laws treated Indians "as a race or peculiar people, and in no way [treated] them . . . as persons having the rights of citizens of the United States."

The court conceded that "under some circumstances an Indian may acquire the rights of citizenship." But the circumstances of Burton's birth and color disqualified him. "By the act of February 8, 1887, . . . an Indian born within the United States, to whom land has been allotted, and who has severed his tribal relations, and adopted the habits of civilized life, thereby becomes a citizen of the United States . . ." However, the court went on to observe, "This seems to be the only method provided by law whereby an Indian may become a citizen . . . [for no other] provision has been made by Congress for the naturalization of Indians or other peoples of color or their descendants, except Africans." As for Mr. Burton: "Mr. Burton is an Indian . . . If he was not born within the territorial limits of the United States, . . . then there is no law of the United States, of which this court is advised, whereby he may be admitted to citizenship by the court." In effect, Burton and others like him had been assigned the same status as Chinese and Japanese aliens, that of aliens ineligible to citizenship in the United States.

Although alien Indians seem to have remained ineligible to citizenship in the United States until race and color qualifications were dropped from the law,[208] Indian nationals received a blanket naturalization from the provisions of an act of Congress passed in 1924.[209] However, because this law had been enacted without any prior, accompanying, or subsequent treaty revisions, and because some states, notably Arizona, refused for many years to extend the vote to citizen Indians,[210] some tribes—especially those that felt deprived of a measure of their sovereignty by a section of the 1871 law stating that "no Indian nation or tribe within the territory of the United States shall be acknowledged or recognized as an independent nation, tribe, or power, with whom the United States may contract by treaty"[211]—refused to acknowledge it. The issue became important when the likelihood of an American involvement in the war against the Axis powers resulted in the passage of the Selective Service Act of 1940. The Native American responses to the military draft were many and varied. In one unsuccessful court proceeding, the mother of Warren Green, an Onandaga youth who was a member of the Six Nations Confederacy and a resident of Syracuse, New York, sought to have her son's induction into the armed services set aside on the grounds that he was not a United States citizen, the Iroquois having never been conquered or subjugated by the United States, and his people, therefore, having never ceased to be a separate nation subject to the treaties between the United States and the Six Nations Confederacy of 1784, 1789, and 1794.[212] Other tribes resisted induction through selective service and insisted on their rights as separate nations to decide on a policy with respect to the Axis threat. In 1942 the Cheyenne tribe of Oklahoma formally declared itself in a state of war with Germany, Japan, and their allies;[213] "the Tunica, among other Louisiana Indians, objected to the military draft . . ., claiming that only the tribe held sovereignty over its manpower and refusing to let Tunica youths be inducted into segregated units . . . [nevertheless,] virtually all the young men of that tribe went to war as volunteers";[214] the "Zunis of western New Mexico resisted by declaring all of their young men were priests and should receive religious deferments . . . [and as a result] only 213 of the populous Zuni were taken into military service";[215] after three largely unsuccessful attempts to enforce voluntary but universal registration for the draft among the Florida Seminoles, a special investigation by an army officer determined that they "possessed little knowledge of English and were somewhat unsanitary, and [that] it would not be worthwhile to use force against them . . ."[216]

Although a considerable number of Native Americans did serve in the armed forces during World War II, as well as in later American wars in Korea, Vietnam, and the Persian Gulf, the issue of their "color" and culture rankled. When, in the Second World War, they proved to be able and efficient soldiers, the *American Legion Magazine* treated their performance in commando fighting as natural: "Why not? his ancestors invented it . . . Some can smell a snake yards away and hear the faintest movement; all endure thirst and lack of food better than average."[217] When, on the other hand, those enlisting or drafted into army units in the South discovered that they would be classed as "colored" and placed in the same units as African Americans, they resisted such designation, demanded to be treated as "whites," and, in some instances, went to prison rather than accept what they considered to be an ignominious status.[218] Indians would also serve, the government seemed to be saying, but they would be made to stand and wait for a long time before being granted the full measure of their citizenship and civil rights.

MIXED-BLOODS

Despite the claims put forward at least since the Reconstruction era ended,[219] and reiterated as recently as 1963 by Norman Podhoretz,[220] that racial intermarriage would eventually eliminate America's race problem by eliminating the separate races as distinctive units, neither the seventeenth- and eighteenth-century American colonies,[221] nor the majority of states of the United States,[222] nor the courts[223] until the period 1948–1967, when, one by one, the state laws forbidding miscegenation were declared unconstitutional,[224] would sanction such marriages.[225] Indeed, there has long been a hiatus in sociological thought separating those who regarded amalgamation as both the final solution to the race problem and the ultimate stage of assimilation[226] from those who perceived marriage across the color-culture line in American society as so anomalous that it required separate classification, as "intermarriage," and as a phenomenon that would have to be explained by special theories.[227] As for those who were American citizens by birth or naturalization, what little intermarriage that did take place— with the notable exception of American citizens of Chinese and Japanese descent in the third and fourth generations[228]—occurred across the line of nationality rather than color. Hence, black Americans find themselves still debating the worthwhileness of interracial marriage in terms not too different from those put forth by Edward Byron Reuter in 1931;[229] while one recent student of the subject projected whatever sanguine effects intermarriage might provide for resolving America's race problem into the next century.[230] Until 1952, however, for aliens of mixed racial or "color" stocks seeking naturalization in the United States, their parents' transgression against America's mores about miscegenation could and often did bring about a denial of admission to citizenship.

Mixed-blood aliens challenged the "color" test of the naturalization laws because of the latter's dependence on every individual's membership in but a single race.[231] Because until 1952—except for the provisions made in 1919 for those Native Americans and Filipinos who served in United States military services, for all Native Americans in 1924, for Chinese in 1943, and for Filipinos in 1946—naturalization in the United States was limited to "free white persons" and "persons of African nativity and African descent," questions arose about the eligibility of those whose immediate forebears included white and "red" or "yellow" persons who had intermarried. Twenty-five years before the adoption of the Fourteenth Amendment, the Supreme Court of Ohio had ruled that a person of "more than one-half white blood" should be counted as "white" for purposes of racial assignment in a segregated public school system.[232] "Percentage" of "blood" would later become the basis for determining the eligibility of mixed-bloods for United States citizenship.

That the fundamental issues defining the race question in America determined both domestic regulations and naturalization laws is revealed in the first and most often cited court proceeding concerning a mixed-blood petitioner for United States citizenship. In 1880, the Circuit Court of the Oregon District passed judgment on the petition of Frank Camille, born in 1847 in Kamloops, British Columbia, to a "white Canadian" father and "an Indian woman," and a resident of Oregon since 1864.[233] District Justice Deady, noting that no less an authority than Chancellor Kent had expressed doubt about whether "the copper-colored natives of America, or the yellow or tawny races of the Asiatic . . . are 'white persons' within the purview of the law," and that the naturalization laws had not extended citizenship rights to the "copper-colored natives," stated that in the matter before the court the question was "what is the *status* in this respect of the petitioner, who is a person of one-half Indian blood?" Citing as authority the Ohio court's rulings in four earlier cases involving mixed-bloods. Deady ruled that "where the colored blood was equal to or preponderated over the white blood, the person was not white." Camille, hence, was not a white man, and his petition was rejected. But, to what race did he belong? Justice Deady's answer provides as precise a definition as the courts would offer of what later sociologists would call the racial hybrid, a "marginal man":[234] "As a matter of fact, he is as much an Indian as a white person, and might be classed with the one race as properly as the other. Strictly speaking, he belongs to neither."And how did it come to pass that a man who is neither wholly Indian nor wholly white is by that fact also ineligible to citizenship in the United States? Justice Deady treats these matters in his summary of the legislative history of naturalization in the United States, an obiter dicta that related in less than approbative language how the Civil War amendments extending citizenship to Negroes had been so worded that they implicitly denied naturalization to red and yellow persons and to all those who are not at least 51 percent white. In effect, his commentary illustrates how race prejudice, once the badge of slavery, has spread out from its original object to separate other nonwhites from the white claimants to an exclusive status:

> From the first our naturalization laws only applied to the people who had settled the country—the Europeans or white race—and so they remained until 1870, . . . when, under the pro-negro feeling, generated and inflamed by the war with the southern states, and its political

consequences, congress was driven at once to the other extreme, and
opened the door, not only to persons of African descent, but to all those
of African nativity—thereby proffering the boon of American citizenship to the comparatively savage and strange inhabitants of the "dark
continent," while withholding it from the intermediate and much-better-
qualified red and yellow races.

However, . . . the negroes of Africa were not likely to emigrate to
this country, and . . . the provision concerning them was merely a harmless piece of legislative buncombe, while the Indian and the Chinaman
were in our midst, and at our doors and only too willing to assume the
mantle of American sovereignty . . .

Indians, Asians, and mixed-bloods were to be denied citizenship so that
they could not share in the form of sovereignty that prevailed in a democratic republic, namely, that, as Chief Justice Taney had said in *Dred Scott,*
vested that all important element of rule in "We the people."

Subsequent rulings followed the precedent set in the *Camille* case.
That the matter of a "color" test would be put to persons of African nativity and African descent in terms of a preponderant percentage of the eligible "blood" was indicated in a federal district court proceeding of 1938.[235]
Bernedito Cruz, who testified that "My mother is half African and half
Indian and my father is a full blooded Indian . . . I believe my father's ancestors were all full blooded Indians," petitioned for United States citizenship
as a person of African descent. The court rejected the petition, rephrasing
the issue before it as an inquiry into "whether a person who is one-quarter
Negro is of 'African descent'" within the meaning of the naturalization
statute. In reaching his decision in this matter, District Judge Byers relied
on an important dictum enunciated by Justice Cardozo in a 1933 case involving an alleged conspiracy to evade California's alien land law. Citing the
Thind case as precedent, Cardozo had observed that, "The privilege of
naturalization is denied to all who are not white (unless the applicants are
of African nativity or African descent); and men are not white if the strain
of colored blood in them is a half or a quarter, or, not improbably, even less,
the governing test always . . . being that of common understanding."[236]
However, the *Cruz* case involved a claim of African descent, from a person
of part Indian parentage, not one of membership in the exclusive white race.
Indeed, that Cardozo was uneasy about the citizenship rights of persons of
mixed eligible and ineligible blood is indicated in the same opinion in his
footnote about the citizenship rights of part-Indian Mexicans: "There is a

strain of Indian blood in many of the inhabitants of Mexico as well as in the peoples of Central and South America ... Whether persons of such descent may be naturalized in the United States is still an unsettled question."[237] Judge Byers made no mention of Justice Cardozo's concern, referring instead to a 1909 law review article that had described the widely varying definitions of "Negro," "mulatto," and "person of color" in the several states and adding that "if this petitioner were of one-quarter white blood and three quarters Indian, he could not be admitted to citizenship." Byers then concluded that "in order for a petitioner to qualify [for naturalization] under the statute, his African descent must be shown to be at least an affirmative quantity, and not a neutral thing as in the case of the half blood, or a negative one as in the case of the quarter blood."[238] Hence, although some of the states classified a person as a "Negro" if he or she had but one-sixteenth Negro blood,[239] and a legislator of the state of Louisiana had in 1908 unsuccessfully attempted to extend the term to embrace a person of one thirty-second part Negro blood,[240] for purposes of naturalization a person of mixed African and other non-white descent would have to have 51 or more percent of the former blood to qualify.

Conclusion

When Francis Fukuyama raised—if only briefly and in order to set the matter outside the purview of his analysis—the status of the race question in relation to the end of the Cold War, he was following in a little-explored tradition of discussion and policy on the matter. America's treatment of its racial minorities has been an element in the nation's foreign relations and in the maintenance of its image abroad as the first modern state society to throw off the yoke of European colonial domination. The basic problem has always been how the values enunciated in the Declaration of Independence might be squared with those practices of racial subordination permitted in the unamended version of the Constitution of 1787—and how this resolution would be featured in America's picture of itself to other countries. Chattel slavery had been virtually confined to Africans and persons of African descent during the colonial era, but the "peculiar institution" continued until the Civil War ended it. However, the "badge of slavery"—race prejudice and discrimination—not only continued to be pressed onto African Americans after emancipation, but also reached out from its original institutional base to engulf those persons of non-white color and non-Occidental culture who had come to the United States in search of political freedom, economic opportunity, and social advancement. Although the methods of total institutionalization—plantation slavery and government reservation—were not applied to Chinese, Japanese, Koreans, East Indians, and the peoples of Southwest Asia (as they had been to enslaved African Americans and corralled Native Americans, respectively), other burdens, including the denial of naturalization; restrictions on jobs, occupations, union membership, and the professions; prohibitions on land ownership, corporation formation, licensing, and intermarriage; segregation and ghettoization; and the myriad of hurts that arise from racist slurs and the popular usage of ethnophaulisms—and, in the case of the Pacific coast Japanese Americans, wholesale incarceration during World War II— pinned that ignominious badge upon them as firmly as had the enslavement of blacks. America had—despite its protestations to the contrary—become a *Herrenvolk* democracy and a white republic.[241]

The Second World War proved to be the first major challenge to America's domestic praxis of white supremacy. Such important social scientists as sociologist Robert Park (1864–1944)[242] and his anthropologist son-in-law, Robert Redfield (1897–1958),[243] pointed out the inconsistencies entailed in America's championing of freedom and equality abroad while enforcing white supremacy at home. At the end of the war, a research analyst for the Immigration and Naturalization Service pointed out, on the basis of a careful analysis of the laws governing aliens in thirty-five nations, that no country other than the United States utilized racial criteria for naturalization.[244] Moreover, this agent of the Justice Department took especial note of the fact that "The Nazi Nuremburg laws appear to be the only modern instance where a nation, other than the United States, has imposed a racial disqualification restricting eligibility for naturalization to members of designated racial groups."[245] Seven years later the color qualification for naturalization was eliminated from American naturalization law. Even more significant, perhaps, is the fact that desegregation and the extension of civil rights became not only the single most important domestic event in post-war America, but also an important feature of American international impression management during the entire era of the Cold War—the struggle against communism requiring the escutcheon of America to be cleansed of any racist blemishes.[246]

As the Cold War comes to an end, there appears to be less a rising of capitalist market economies or of newly invigorated Enlightenment than of angry ethnonationalism and parochial chauvinism. Marxism and Soviet communism seem in retrospect to have merely covered over the seething senses of ethnocentrism that had been so prominent before the First World War. In America, the toppling of the outer bastion of the white republic's institutionalized racism—legislatively established segregation, "Jim Crow" laws, and juridically enforced race discrimination—has made its second line of defense—the walls built against job opportunities and occupational advancement—both more visible and less vulnerable to assault.[247] Currently, the issue is popularly and politically defined in terms of "quotas" and the alleged need to resist "reverse discrimination." It should be seen in quite another way, namely, in terms of the desire to enlarge upon a more humane enlightenment and a more comprehensive civil rights policy—in effect, to extend the principles of the Declaration of Independence to the performances required by the Constitution of the United States, and to remove from all who still wear them the badges of slavery.

One aspect of such an extension and elaboration would be a renewed understanding of the principle of equality as expressed through the Thirteenth and Fourteenth Amendments to the Constitution. The late Justice Thurgood Marshall once remarked: "While the Union survived the civil war, the Constitution did not. In its place arose a new, more promising basis for justice and equality, the fourteenth amendment, ensuring protection of the life, liberty, and property of *all* persons against deprivations without due process, and guaranteeing equal protection of the laws."[248] Much of the present difficulty can be credited to the failure of so many to see that the protection of the life, liberty, and property of *all* persons sometimes requires the enactment of laws that benefit *some* of those persons—the minority whose rights have been violated, neglected, abrogated, or never before recognized.[249] Those who still bear the burden of the badge of slavery—and in this work, we suggest that the evidence presented supports the claim of an aggregation of peoples that includes African Americans, Asian Americans, Hispanic Americans, and Native Americans and—though not discussed in this essay—women[250]—belong among the beneficiaries of laws, programs, and policies that seek to provide affirmative action in behalf of jobs, education, training, and professionalization. Such laws, programs, and policies are not rightly considered to be instances of reverse discrimination; rather, they apply precisely to those to whom they ought to apply and work in behalf of a legitimate public purpose—the mandate of the Thirteenth Amendment.

However, even if it should be agreed that the cluster of peoples designated *supra* are appropriately classified with respect to the fulfillment of the aims of the Civil War amendments, there still would remain the question of how to determine whether an individual, if challenged as to his or her ancestry, is in fact a member of the ethnoracial group that is benefited. Here, the review of the naturalization cases discussed earlier provides a preview of what might occur and a warning about the difficulties yet to be overcome.

CHAPTER SIX

The Chinese before the Courts: A Prolegomenon to a Study of Ethnoracial Construction and Marginalization

The spectacle now presented by the Government of this country, in its attitude toward the Chinese, even leaving Christianity entirely out of the question, ought to bring the blush of shame to the face of every honorable fair-minded man.
      Mrs. S. L. Baldwin, Must the Chinese Go? *(1890)*

Introduction

On May 25, 1992, an editorial in a prominent Canadian newspaper proposed that the parliament of that country see fit to "make amends for ...[the] racist actions of the state ...[by voting a] formal apology and [granting a] financial compensation to the families of those [Chinese] who [had] paid the [head] tax," first enacted in 1885. That head tax had provided $23 million in revenue during its thirty-eight years of operation.[1] The editorial writer went on to observe that Canada's less-than-just treatment of its Chinese immigrants had included not only the onerous head tax, but also unwarranted wage discrimination (in the building of the Canadian National Railway, their pay had been set at one-half of that given to white railroad laborers); wholesale exclusion from 1923 to 1946; and denial of citizenship rights and the franchise until 1947.[2]

In the United States, no such proposal for redress has been put forward either for its Chinese immigrants or for their descendants, though its record of ethnoracial prejudice and discrimination against this people is at least the equal of Canada's,[3] and, despite advances in civil rights in recent years, bids fair to continue in various forms into the future. In this respect, it is worthy of note that in February 1992, the United States Commission on Civil Rights, in a report entitled "Civil Rights Issues Facing Asian Americans in the 1990s," in addition to recalling the long history of America's anti-Chinese and anti-Asian legislation, took care to point out the continuing effects of ethnoracial prejudice on the life-chances of these peoples, among many of which was one that echoed their earlier marginalization in both Canada's and the United States' labor forces—and suggested its persistence in the latter country: "The Commission has received allegations that Asian Americans are virtually shut out of construction unions in New York City and as a result are forced to take lower paying jobs restoring or repairing buildings."[4]

The construction of a marginalizing ethnoracial identity for America's Chinese is the topic to be investigated in the present chapter. I use the term "ethnoracial" throughout my discussion in keeping with the issue as defined by Floya Anthias: "that race can only be considered as an analytically valid category if it is incorporated within the more inclusive, albeit highly heterogeneous, category of ethnos. The hallmark of this set of phenomena is inclusion and exclusion, difference and identity; the construction of entities, on the one hand, by way of some notion of a historical point of origin or essence and, on the other, the construction of a collective difference from an 'other.'"[5] Here it shall be argued that the agency that in America took as its charge the construction of the Chinese as an ethnoracial entity was the higher judiciary. Proceeding on the necessity of having to declare who belonged to the ethnoracial groups designated by the law as eligible for inclusion in the citizenry of the United States, the courts were led to classify individuals according to the ethnoracial groups to which they "belonged," and then to locate that categorization within or outside of the limited legislative classes of eligibles for naturalization in the United States. The categories of eligibility and ineligibility for naturalization, in turn, established the basis for a subsequent legislation of inclusion and exclusion with respect to property rights, the franchise, occupational opportunity, and primary and secondary human associations. The Chinese were the first people declared to be "aliens ineligible for citizenship in the United States." They were so designated as a resolution of the premier issue affecting the opening phase of post–Civil War America's judicial and civic discourse on the relationship of race and ethnicity to naturalization, a discourse that would subsequently stigmatize all those who could be categorized in the same way. That discourse is unilaterally hegemonic in character and in general works to privilege white males over all other kinds of human individuals or aggregates.

In an illuminating discussion of Asian American literature, Elaine H. Kim observes: "Familiar representations of Asians—always unalterably alien—as helpless heathens, comical servants, loyal allies, and, only in the case of women, exotic sex objects imbued with an innate understanding of how to please, serve, and titillate, extend directly to Asian Americans and exist in all cases to define as their dialectical opposite the Anglo man as heroic, courageous, and physically superior, whether as soldier, missionary, master, or lover."[6] Although Kim[7] and others[8] have pointed out that racist and culturally demeaning images of Asians are to be found in the works of such formerly popular white Anglo authors as Bret Harte (1836-1902),[9] Jack London (1876-1916),[10] Earl Derr Biggers (1884-1933, who foisted "Charlie Chan" on America),[11] and Arthur Henry Sarsfield Ward (1883-1959, who, under the nom de plume Sax Rohmer, gave the Occident its archenemy, "Dr. Fu Manchu"),[12] as well as in the writings of earlier now-forgotten writers,[13] the civic stigmatization of Chinese and, later, other Asian and Pacific Island peoples, was juridically established by and legitimated in the judicial casuistries of the courts of the United States.

That appellate judges and U.S. Supreme Court justices are mindful of the twin facts that in their rulings they are constructing as well as construing a civic discourse and in the process giving legitimating voice to the basic definition of the sociocorporeal entity that is before them is doubtful. As long ago as 1913, Roscoe Pound, the father of sociological jurisprudence, pointed out that "the judge is hampered at every turn by the theory that he can only discover, that the principles of the unwritten law are invariable, and that application of a rule which has at least a potential logical preexistence in the received system is his sole function."[14] In treating with the laws governing eligibility for United States citizenship from 1870 to 1952, however, the courts discovered, occasionally to their openly stated consternation, that the principles underpinning the written law were ambiguous and that the application of a rule of that law evoked the possibility that it had no logical preexistence, even no rational basis whatsoever. Nevertheless, their interpretations of the law—for they could not evade their responsibility to interpret the law and rule on its relation to the statutory code or to the Constitution of the United States—lent the imprimatur of "The Law" to an exclusionary division of humankind, privileging certain ethnoracial peoples, disparaging and disempowering others. Once having been excluded from citizenship, the hapless aliens could be made to bear additional burdens—all of the latter being justified by the rhetoric that defined and disenfranchised them in the first place.

The label "alien ineligible for citizenship in the United States" could be—and, in fact, was—employed to strip away economic, educational, social, and personal opportunities from those on whose ethnoracial escutcheon it could be pinned. The significance of the Chinese in the social history of America's attempt to establish itself as a white republic is that—together with the Native Americans, who in 1831 were made into noncitizen, domestic, dependent nations;[15] the African American slaves, who were deemed unworthy of citizenship altogether before their emancipation;[16] and the free men and women of color of the antebellum era, whose official civic status remained at best anomalous until the Thirteenth, Fourteenth, and Fifteenth Amendments to the Constitution had been adopted;[17]—they became the collective human situs on which post-Emancipation citizenship in the United States would be worked out.[18] The result was a multifaceted marginalization of this people and, subsequently, of all others similarly labeled.

The concept and process of marginalization are the topics of a critique by Janice E. Perlman.[19] According to her, the term has been applied virtually exclusively to the psychological state as well as to the sociocultural status of the urban poor, who have been unfairly and unwarrantedly stigmatized thereby. She goes on to offer a threefold complaint: that the concept is embedded in an unanalyzed ideological context; that it is employed all too uncritically by social scientists who bring to bear on their studies of it as a phenomenon diverse methodologies and divergent and even contradictory theoretical perspectives; and that it owes its origins and persistence to the seminal, double-sided—and often misread—psychosociological formulations of Robert E. Park[20] and Everett Stonequist.[21] It is not necessary for the present work that I answer each of Perlman's objections, for I am using the term in a special and limited sense that draws not only on the *sociological* aspects of the Park-Stonequist perspective, but combines that orientation with both the hierarchical-hegemonic corollary introduced by Dickie-Clark[22] and the phenomenological[23] and postmodernist[24] outlooks that have revivified the concept and enhanced its usage for social critique.

Citizenship and Marginalization

From the moment of their first arrival in the United States, the Chinese have experienced and have been subjected to an ambiguous welcome. Their merchant leaders were—for a brief moment—regarded as astute business-men who might someday vote and serve in the legislature alongside other new immigrant entrepreneurs;[25] however, their laboring classes were spurned by virtually all parties to the debate over the "Chinese question." Exploited for their labor power by capitalist developers and refused entrance into the burgeoning workingmen's associations that had begun to spring up among the Irish and other European newcomers, the Chinese workers were defended for a time by a few Protestant missionaries in search of new fields for soul-harvesting[26] and, more altruistically, by a small coterie of civic-conscious attorneys seeking to advance the progress of American democracy. Even before the issue of their citizenship arose, immigrants from China had been made the objects of what would become nearly four decades of state laws seeking to restrict or halt altogether their entrance to America. These statutes were opposed in the courts and struck down, one by one, as state intrusions on the federal government's sole jurisdiction over immigration.[27] In 1882, Congress enacted a law that forbade the coming of Chinese laborers for ten years. That law, despite care taken not to abuse their rights by certain federal court judges in California and the Northwest,[28] laid the basis for subsequent statutes establishing permanent exclusion, and its penumbra shadowed the establishment of a quota system in 1943,[29] and a "needs" and family reunification modification in 1965.[30]

What proved most effective for marginalizing the Chinese in America were statutes and judicial rulings that excluded them from participation in the body politic. It is true, of course, that, as Jonathan D. Spence has recently observed, "The restrictive immigration laws levied against the Chinese—and at no other foreign nationals at the time—form a melancholy theme in late-nineteenth-century American history."[31] Even more tragic, however, was their formal exclusion from the benefits, rights, and opportunities of U.S. civil society that, at least in the casuistry of law and the rhetoric of public policy, were then accorded to all other newcomer Americans and, in theory but not practice, to the recently emancipated African Americans. For, if it is valid to hold—as Constitutional scholar Robert A. Goldwin asserts—that "The Constitution of the United States is unusual, and perhaps unique among the constitutions of the world, . . . [in] that rights are inherent in individuals, not in the groups they belong to; that we are all equal as human beings in the sense that no matter what our color, sex, national origin, or religion, we are equal in the possession of the rights that governments are instituted to protect . . ."[32] then it is necessary to point out that the Chinese were a people singled out by both the federal and various state legislatures and municipal councils, as well as the judiciary, for exclusion from this individuating process. In the attempt to construct a new social order in the thirty-five-year era after the Civil War had ended black slavery in America—when the need for settlers and workers had brought peoples from the farther reaches of the Eurasian continent to America, and while the aboriginal peoples were being conquered and sequestered on unpopulated wastelands—neither Congress nor the courts seemed ready to accept the full implication, the radical meaning, of President Lincoln's Gettysburg Address—that the war had been midwife to a rebirth of an America dedicated to the principles of equality that had been laid down in the Declaration of Independence.[33] The search for order in that era, as Robert H. Wiebe has shown, led to a reconstructed hierarchicalization of the peoples in and coming to America, and to a limitation on their civil rights—both justified by an emergent ideology "compound[ed] of biology, pseudo-science, and hyperactive imagination."[34] That hierarchy not only assured that those "alternately called Anglo-Saxon or Teutonic or Nordic always rested at the top" of its scale of deservedly privileged peoples, but also designated "all people of yellow, brown, or black skin as innately inferior."[35] Seven years before the outbreak of the war to preserve the Union, the California Supreme Court had begun the degradation of the Chinese immigrants in that state by denying to them a basic right and protection of that civil association—the chance to testify in a judicial proceeding involving whites.

The First Phase: Exclusion of Chinese Testimony—*People v. Hall* (1854)

When, in 1992, Americans, Spaniards, and Italians observed the quincentenary of Columbus's voyages to the Americas, scholars and supporters of civil rights should have reflected on how, in 1854, the California Supreme Court had invalidated the testimony of Chinese witnesses in judicial proceedings, by invoking, *inter alia*, the Genoese "discoverer's" intentions and conflating the ethnoracial physiognomy and cultural heritage of California's aborigines with those of the Aleuts, "Esquimaux," and the immigrants from the empire of China.[36] The matter before the court concerned a homicide allegedly committed by "a free white citizen of this State" in the city of San Francisco. The only eyewitnesses to the killing were immigrant Chinese whose testimony provided the jury with information leading to the accused's conviction of a capital crime. Lawyers for the convicted man appealed the trial procedure, the verdict, and the sentence, charging that the Chinese witnesses' testimony should have been excluded on the ground that, State law having already provided that "No Black or Mulatto person, or Indian, shall be allowed to give evidence in favor of, or against a white man," that prohibition should have been understood to extend to Chinese, since the latter are either descendants of the racial stock that in prehistoric times had provided California with its aborigines, or, alternatively, are to be understood as the judical equivalent of blacks, that is, a portion of that congeries of persons held to be nonwhite.

Chief Justice Murray of the California Supreme Court agreed with the petitioner. In its decision, the court put forth a tentative and much qualified juridical casuistry that combined a homage to Columbus with a conjectural history, and added to these a pseudoscientific ethnology of Sino-Amerindian relations. It also designated the Chinese as judicially functional "blacks," thus ensuring their inadmissibility to the civic community. At the outset, the court took notice of the fact that "When Columbus first landed upon the shores of this continent, in his attempt to discover a western passage to the Indies, he imagined that he had accomplished the object of his expedition . . . Acting upon this hypothesis, and also perhaps from the similarity of features and physical conformation, he gave to the [San Salvadorean] Islanders the name of Indians, which appellation was universally adopted, and extended to the aboriginals of the New World, as well as of Asia." Next, the court observed that the understanding of California's law would in part be based on the recognition that it had been adapted from those of other states admitted to the Union much before California's accession in 1850. The adumbrating statutes had been enacted, so Chief Justice Murray claimed, when "Ethnology . . . was unknown as a distinct science, or, if known, had not reached that high point of perfection which it has since attained by the scientific inquiries and discoveries of the master minds of the last half-century." Murray announced the Court's willingness to accept the classificatory schema that had been developed by Baron Georges Leopold Chretien Frederic Dagobert Cuvier (1769–1832), "one of the most eminent naturalists of modern times," to the effect "that there were but three distinct types of the human species, which in their turn, were subdivided into varieties of tribes." Cuvier had not only presented the tripartite division of humankind as "Caucasian," "Mongolian," and "Ethiopian," but also he had arrayed them in a descending order of physique and culture: Caucasians at the apex, the Mongolians less advanced, and the Ethiopians at the bottom.[37]

It fell to Chief Justice Murray to commit the analytical error of confusing race as lineage with race as type,[38] for the aim of the first section of his judicial opinion was to place the Chinese within the category "Indian," making the latter term "generic," that is, broad enough to embrace both the immigrants from Asia and the aborigines of America under the same classificatory heading, and to deny to both "Indians" and "Chinese" the right to testify in court proceedings involving whites. To accomplish these goals, he proposed that a probable assent should be given to the "ingenious speculations" about the human settling of pre-Columbian America. "It has been supposed," he pointed out, "and not without plausibility, that this continent was first peopled by Asiatics, who crossed Behring's Straits, and from thence found their way down to the more fruitful climates of Mexico and South America." To lend even more plausibility to this hypothesis, Murray called attention to the geographical situation of the Aleutian Islands, that, he said, "From the eastern portions of Kamtschatka . . . form a long and continuous group, extending eastward to that portion of the North American Continent inhabited by the Esquimaux." Murray now could assert that the existence of an island chain connecting eastern Asia to western North America made it at least possible for peoples from the former area to have crossed over to the landmass of the latter. But he had already designated at least four distinct "tribes" along that route: Asiatics, Aleuts, Eskimos, and California's aborigines. Were they related? If so, how?

Murray's tendentious ethnocultural conjectures gave him answers that were helpful but not judicially sufficient. First, he noted that the Aleutian Islands "are inhabited by a race who resemble, in a remarkable degree, in language and appearance, both the inhabitants of Kamtschatka (who are admitted to be of the Mongolian type), and the Esquimaux, who again, in turn, resemble other tribes of American Indians." These resemblances form the basis for his imputation of greater credibility to the proponents of the Bering Straits hypothesis. ("The similarity of the skull and pelvis, and the general configuration of the two races; the remarkable resemblance in eyes, beard, hair, and other peculiarities, together with the contiguity of the two continents, might well have led to the belief that this country was first peopled by Asiatics, and that the differences between the different tribes and the parent stock was such as would necessarily arise from the circumstances of climate, pursuits, and other physical causes . . .") However, such probablistic reasoning, valuable as it was for promoting his thesis, did not satisfy Justice Murray's more exacting judicial mind. After all, he observed, it was always possible that "the light of modern science" would someday demonstrate that the Americas had not been "peopled by the inhabitants of Asia,"[39] or "that the Aborigines are a distinct type, and as such claim a distinct origin."[40] If Chinese were to be placed under the legal rubric of "Indian," a sounder argument would have to be presented.

Murray approached the question anew, armed with his knowledge of juridical hermeneutics and legal semiotics. "[T]he words of the Act," he announced, "must be construed in *pari materia*." That is, the prohibitory statute under investigation would have to be read as a whole, giving equal weight and dignity to such other terms of racial reference in it as "white" and "Negro." The latter terms were indisputably to be regarded as "generic," Justice Murray observed, lest "the most anomalous consequences ... ensue." In the event that the readers of this decision would not intuitively grasp precisely what those anomalous consequences were, the chief justice offered up a parade of horribles: "The European white man who comes here would not be shielded from the testimony of the degraded and demoralized caste, while the Negro, fresh from the coast of Africa, or the Indian of Patagonia, the Kanaka, South Sea Islander, or New Hollander, would be admitted, upon their arrival, to testify against white citizens in our courts of law."

A generic designation for the terms "white" and "Negro" would go far toward accomplishing the "evident intention of the Act," Murray argued; for its purpose "was to throw around the [white] citizen a protection for life and property," a situation that "could only be secured by removing him above the corrupting influences of degraded castes." Moreover, generic designation was further indicated by the testimony statute's usage of the term "black" rather than "Negro"; for, as Chief Justice Murray took care to point out, "The word 'black' may include all negroes, but the term 'negro' does not include all black persons." Then, having laid the interpretive groundwork, the chief justice enlarged on his thesis, expanding its scope so as to embrace the exclusion of the testimony of Chinese, as well as that of Indians and Africans, in all proceedings involving whites. "The legislature," he ruled, "if any intention can be ascribed to it, adopted the most comprehensive terms to embrace every known class or shade of color, as the apparent design was to protect the white person from the influence of all testimony other than that of persons of the same caste."

Aware of the vulnerability of ethnological theories, Chief Justice Murray had found an additional and more secure way to deny Chinese any opportunity to give evidence in a court proceeding where whites were parties to the action. Not only did he rule that the generic term "black" was to be understood as inclusive of all persons not white, regardless of color, but also he held that the "word 'white' has a distinct signification, which ... excludes black, yellow, and all other colors." Thus, he had forestalled any judicial consequences that might arise should his speculations about the ethnohistorical and physical-anthropological origins of America's aborigines be invalidated by future scientific investigations. "[E]ven admitting the Indian of this continent is not of the Mongolian type," he concluded on this issue, "... the words 'black person'... must be taken as contradistinguished from white, and necessarily excludes [*sic*] all races other than the Caucasian."

In *People v. Hall* black and white had been rendered mutually exclusive judicial categories, with the former term enlarged to embrace Chinese, Indians, and all other nonwhites, while the latter term had been constricted to embrace only Caucasians. Chief Justice Murray indicated his antipathy toward the immigrant Chinese in his extraordinarily heated closing remarks, pouring forth an indictment of their culture, social organization, personality, and style of life, and virtually inviting their further persecution:

> The anomalous spectacle of a distinct people, living in our community, recognizing no laws of this State, except through necessity, bringing with them their prejudices and national feuds, in which they indulge in open violation of law; whose mendacity is proverbial; a race of people whom nature has marked as inferior, and who are incapable of progress or intellectual development beyond a certain point, as their history has shown; differing in language, opinions, color, and physical conformation; between whom and ourselves nature has placed an impassable difference, is now presented, and for them is claimed, not only the right to swear away the life of a citizen, but the further privilege of participating with us in administering the affairs of our government.

In declaring Chinese ineligible to participate in any meaningful way in the judicial system of the state, Chief Justice Murray knowingly and intentionally drove the first nail in the coffin of their exclusion from America's civil society. As he stated, it was in the interests of "public policy", for the "same rule which would admit them to testify, would admit them to all the equal rights of citizenship, and we might soon see them at the polls, in the jury box, upon the bench, and in our legislative halls." For the next two decades, other courts upheld his ruling, which remained in force until 1873, when the adoption of a superseding code of civil procedures for the state of California revoked its authority.[41]

Denial of Citizenship: The Race-Naturalization Question after Emancipation

Classification of Chinese and all other nonwhites as blacks did in fact deny them the rights, duties, and privileges associated with United States citizenship before the adoption of the Thirteenth, Fourteenth, and Fifteenth Amendments. In 1857, U.S. Supreme Court Chief Justice Taney's decision in the *Dred Scott* case, without raising the Chinese issue, had, in effect, given a national imprimatur to the California Supreme Court's dictum about the civic status of blacks in *People v. Hall.*[42] After the Union victory in the Civil War, however, the Constitution was amended to prohibit slavery or involuntary servitude; to require that states not deny the equal protections of the law to all persons; and to assure birthright United States citizenship and the franchise to the former slaves and their American-born descendants. More significantly, in relation to the Chinese question, the naturalization statute was revised in 1870; however, Senator Charles Sumner's attempt to strike the word "white" from its classificatory terminology of eligibles—admittedly an attempt to assure to Chinese immigrants the same right to seek United States citizenship as was then about to be granted to any dark-skinned newcomers from Africa—failed. Instead, the statute of 1870 added two common descent groups, "aliens of African nativity or persons of African descent," to the class of eligibles that since 1790 had only allowed naturalization to "free white persons."[43]

The Constitutional elevation of aliens of African nativity or persons of African descent to United States citizenship, together with a granting of the former slaves' right to the franchise, to jury service, witness competence, and property rights—although all too often dishonored in practice for the ensuing eighty years[44]—bid possible fair to undermine the intended effect of Justice Murray's "generic" application of the term "black" to all who were nonwhite. Indeed, in 1869, a mulatto defendant accused of robbing one of California's resident Chinese aliens successfully defended his newly acquired rights under the Civil Rights Act of 1866 and the Thirteenth Amendment to behave exactly as a white defendant was permitted, that is, to disallow the testimony of the Chinese witnesses to his misdeed.[45] Justice Murray had asserted that while all Negroes were blacks, not all blacks were Negroes. Ergo, he had included Chinese under the rubric "black," while limiting the applicability of the term "white" to all persons not held to be black. The Thirteenth, Fourteenth, and Fifteenth Amendments had freed the slaves and elevated them, arguably in some jurists' minds,[46] to a civil equality with whites. But naturalization had been newly granted only to "aliens of African nativity and persons of African descent," not to "Negroes" or to "blacks" (and, of course, it continued in force for "free white persons"). Were Chinese—who had been ethnologically linked to Indians (not taxed and, under the Constitution, ineligible to citizenship), or, alternatively, generically to blacks (as slaves ineligible to citizenship, or as nonwhite alien "persons of African nativity or descent," ineligible to naturalization before 1870)—"Indians," "blacks," "whites," or of "African nativity or descent"? Or did they belong to some other class of humankind?

The available genealogical, ethnological, and juridical casuistries make any of these possible, but, at the same time, each is problematic. For example, Chinese in America might be descended from the same original stock that had also produced the Amerindians, but unlike the latter, the Chinese had been taxed. (Indeed, their virtually unprotested acquiescence[47] to the foreign miner's tax imposed unsuccessfully on all other non-Americans in California had had the effect of providing the new state with its sole source of revenue for several years.)[48] The Chinese might be generically "black," that is, among those not declared to be "white," but as one federal justice had implied,[49] they and some others might be "white" in that the latter term might be interpreted so as to encompass all those who are not "black." It is even possible—although no court case on the matter arose after the time that this thesis was advanced by some paleontologists—that Chinese are among the wide variety of persons who are of African descent, especially if one accepts one or another of the subsequently announced claims, namely, that all humankind descend from the paleolithic Australopithecus of South Africa;[50] or from the erstwhile inhabitants of Olduvai Gorge;[51] or, from "Lucy" or "Lucy's child," two more recent fossil finds from East Africa.[52] Still another possibility is that all humans are descended from an autochthonous "Peking Man";[53] or, alternatively, as a recent hypothesis has it, that "Peking Man" had no surviving descendants, and that all humankind originated in Africa.[54]

In light of the changed civic status of America's ex-slaves after 1865, it would become necessary for courts to revisit ethnological theory more than once as part of their quest for a scientific grounding for United States citizenship.[55]

As reported in chapter 5, *supra,* the issue was first joined in 1878, when a federal district court chose to adjudicate the ethnolegal dispute over whether "Ah Yup, a native and citizen of the empire of China, of the Mongolian race, ... [could] be admitted as a citizen of the United States."[56] From the very beginning, the court treated as undisputed fact that natives of China were members of the "Mongolian" race. That race, however, had not received legislative recognition in either the original or the revised statutes relating to the naturalization of aliens. Hence, the court took as its duty the answering of two questions: (1) Is a person of the Mongolian race a "white person" within the meaning of the revised naturalization statute of

1870? (2) Do the provisions of that statute forbid the naturalization of all but white persons and persons of African nativity or African descent? It is of some significance to note that Circuit Judge Lorenzo Sawyer did not even think to raise the possibility that "Mongolians" might be "persons of African nativity or African descent," or, in keeping with the decision in *People v. Hall*, to consider the possibility that Chinese might be "black." However, Judge Sawyer did echo Justice Murray's opinion in ruling that, "As ordinarily used everywhere in the United States, one would scarcely fail to understand that the party employing the words 'white person' would intend a person of the Caucasian race." Like Justice Murray, Judge Sawyer did not question the etymology, validity, or epistemological provenance of the term "Caucasian"—a designation that in fact Johann Friedrich Blumenbach had introduced into the technical language of anthropology little more than a century earlier in order that he might be able to distinguish the unique craniology of the peoples of Western and Central Europe. Blumenbach had been struck by the resemblances of a skull found in the Caucasus mountain region of Russia to those of the Germans and speculated that that region might have been the original homeland of the Europeans.[57]

Judge Sawyer did take judicial notice of the fact that among three of the most prominent of the original group of European authorities on ethnology there had been no agreement on the precise number of human races making up the varieties of humankind. Blumenbach had listed five, a taxonomy of which Judge Sawyer quoted from *Webster's Dictionary:* "1. The Caucasian, or white race, to which belong the greater part of the European nations and those of Western Asia; 2. The Mongolian, or yellow race, occupying Tartary, China, Japan, etc.; 3. The Ethiopian, or Negro (black) race, occupying all Africa, except the north; 4. The American, or red race, containing the Indians of North and South America; and 5. the Malay, or Brown race, occupying the island of the Indian Archipelago." However, Carolus Linnaeus had designated one less in his epidermal-pigmentary division of humanity ("1. European, whitish; 2. American, coppery; 3. Asiatic, tawny; and 4. African, black"); while the aforementioned Cuvier had named only three: "Caucasian, Mongol, and Negro." Judge Sawyer acknowledged that "Others make many more," but the classificatory schemas of Blumenbach, Linnaeus, and Cuvier served his adjudicative purpose, for as he pointed out, the *New American Cyclopedia*'s entry under "Ethnology" included the assertion that "no one of those classifications recognizing color as one of the distinguishing characteristics includes the Mongolian in the white or whitish race."

However, one issue in *Ah Yup* and *People v. Hall* was whether color was to be used as the index of eligibility for race and, therefore, for the extension of civil rights and citizenship. Moreover, if color was to be so used, how was it to be defined and determined? These questions would confound jurists until 1952, when the color issue was obviated from naturalization law.

In *People v. Hall*, such color terms as "white" and "black" had been used in a nonpigmentary sense—the former term to refer to members of the Caucasian race; the latter to refer to all persons—including Chinese—who were not white. The fact that prominent ethnologists employed what appeared to be terms referring to the hues of complexion to differentiate the varieties of humankind raised doubts about their applicability to a judicial proceeding where a different definition and usage of color terminology might be required. For example, a person with a "yellowish" shade of skin might be "black" because he or she is not white; "red" or "coppery," "American" because he or she is said to descend from a prehistoric common original stock; or "white" because he or she is neither "African" nor "American." Judge Sawyer's determination that Ah Yup was not white depended on how well he could articulate a color dictum that did not depend on a literally pigmentary usage of "white."

Judge Sawyer's approach took advantage of, and, in fact, derived its basic argument from, Senator Sumner's foiled attempt to have the word "white" struck from the revised naturalization statute. Ah Yup, Judge Sawyer averred, could not claim that "white" was meant to include persons of his race in the first instance because "I am not aware that the term . . . , as used in the statutes as they have stood from 1802 till the late revision, was ever supposed to include a Mongolian." Moreover, even more significantly, the judge pointed to the Congressional debates over the statute's revision "to show that it was universally understood in that body . . . that it excluded Mongolians." After quoting extensively from the remarks of those who favored and those who opposed Sumner's amendment, Judge Sawyer concluded that "Congress retained the word 'white' in the naturalization laws for the sole purpose of excluding the Chinese from the right of naturalization." That inferred and uncriticized purpose—derived by Judge Sawyer from his own reading of the Congressional debates—was in effect deemed to be an acceptable motive for ethnoracially exclusive legislation by a democratically elected legislature.

Civil Rights and Hostile Intent: *Ho Ah Kow v. Nunan*

Precisely because this judicial proceeding established the precedent of excluding Chinese—as well as others who could be tarred either with the brush of "Mongolian" status or stigmatized with the negation of their claim to be white or of African nativity or descent[58]—it is worth inquiring into one of the issues that the learned judge did not address. Having determined that the legislative intent of the revised naturalization statute was "to exclude the Chinese"—"as all white aliens and those of the African race are entitled to naturalization under other words, it is difficult to perceive whom it could exclude unless it be the Chinese"—Judge Sawyer did not inquire into whether such a purpose was *ultra vires*.

It has been noted by some legal scholars that naturalization statutes have rarely been subjected to challenges with respect to their constitutionality.[59] *Ah Yup* was decided ten years after the adoption of the Fourteenth Amendment to the Constitution. That amendment provided all persons, regardless of their citizenship status, with the equal protection of the laws; however, the amendment's wording allowed for its applicability to be limited to state rather than federal legislation.[60] Had Judge Sawyer seen fit to extend the provisions and prohibitions of the Fourteenth Amendment to the national government—for example, by boldly[61] declaring that such Congressionally enacted civil rights acts as those of 1866, 1870, and 1875 were not only appropriate measures of enforcement of the postwar amendments but also laws that superseded those federal statutes that treated selectively and arbitrarily certain "persons" differently[62]—he might have deemed it appropriate to inquire into the constitutionality of the naturalization statute's intent.

To accomplish what *legitimate public* purpose had the naturalization statute been revised?, he might have asked. The asking of such a question is a sine qua non of judicial inquiry, especially when issues of arbitrariness, prejudice, and unlawful interest are alleged to be the intendment of a law.[63] That inquiry, in turn, entails a threefold process: (1) the discovery of the legislative intent; (2) the determination of the extent to which the operation of the law realizes that intent; and (3) the judgment as to whether that intent is within the scope of public law or of the powers granted to the legislative body that enacted it. A judicial ruling in 1879 by United States Supreme Court Justice Stephen J. Field, sitting, together with Judge Sawyer, as a justice in the United States Circuit Court for the District of California, nicely illustrates this mode of reasoning, often utilized effectively with respect to state legislation and municipal ordinances but rarely if at all applied to federal naturalization statutes.

The matter before the circuit court was a suit for the recovery of damages incurred by an alien Chinese plaintiff through the sheriff's enforcement of a San Francisco ordinance, enacted in June 1876, and requiring that "every male person imprisoned in the county jail . . . shall immediately upon his arrival at the jail have the hair of his head 'cut or clipped to an uniform length of one inch from the scalp thereof.'"[64] The ordinance had been passed in response to the plaintiff's and hundreds of his countrymen's refusal to pay a fine for violating the city's nine-year-old and only occasionally and selectively administered ordinance requiring five hundred cubic feet of air space for each person found sleeping or lodging in a rented room or apartment. The lodging house law, in fact, had been enforced only in San Francisco's Chinatown, and the Chinese convicted for violating it had refused to pay the fine, in effect staging a sit-in in the jail and making the latter institution potentially liable for violating the very same statute.[65] The haircutting ordinance, however, threatened the Chinese alien immigrant convict with the severing of his queue, the mandatory badge of subjection to the Manchu Empire, the loss of which could result in execution for a remigrant to Qing China.[66] The plaintiff, Ho Ah Kow, petitioned the court for redress, but the defendant, San Francisco Sheriff Nunan opposed his claim. Justice Field decided the matter in behalf of the plaintiff.

Relevant here is the manner and method of his decision and the contrast it presents with *Ah Yup* and other naturalization cases. Unlike Judge Sawyer's uncritical acknowledgment of Congress's intent in revising the naturalization statute, Justice Field's interrogation of San Francisco's assertion that its haircutting ordinance was merely one more instance of the city's lawful exercise of its police powers illustrates one method by which institutionalized racism can be uncovered by a detailed reading of the relevant facts and circumstances surrounding a particular legislative enactment. In reply to Sheriff Nunan's argument that the ordinance in question served the general purposes of securing improved sanitation and establishing appropriate discipline at the jail, Field, invoking the language of the Fourteenth Amendment, pointed out that in fact the evidence indicated that it "is special legislation on the part of the [board of] supervisors against a class of persons who, under the constitution and laws of the United States, are entitled to the equal protection of the laws." Field (1816–1899), who had resided in California for many years and served for six years (1857–1863) as its supreme court's chief justice,[67] but who was no firm friend of the Chinese immigrant,[68] found it juridically impossible to acquiesce before the defendant's claim that San Francisco's board of supervisors had acted out of racially neutral and benevolent motives: "When we take our seats on the bench, [he observed], we are not struck with blindness, and forbidden to know as judges what we see as men; and where an ordinance, though general in its terms, only operates upon a special race, sect, or class, it being universally understood that it is to be enforced only against that race, sect or class, we may justly conclude that it was the intention of the body adopting it that it should only have such operation, and treat it accordingly."

Field probed even more directly into the aim of San Francisco's law. Exploring the city council's debate over the adoption of the ordinance, he was able to show that the supervisors openly avowed the selective character of their proposed piece of legislation; to observe that "the ordinance is known in the community as the 'Queue Ordinance'"; and to conclude with certainty that "it is not enforced against any other persons [but the Chinese]."

As to the board of supervisors' claim that the reserved police powers gave it the right to regulate sanitary conditions at the county jail, Justice Field made two objections: The first—necessarily outside the sociological scope of the present study—was that "the board of supervisors had no authority to . . . determine what special sanitary regulations should be enforced . . . [for that] is a matter which the [state] legislature had . . . seen fit to intrust . . . to the board of health of the city and county . . ." The second, applying to each of the city's claims, namely, that its haircutting ordinance was both a sanitary regulation and a disciplinary measure, illustrates a method appropriate to effecting a sociological jurisprudence of minorities in the United States: how the classification made by a law may be examined to determine what relation, if any, it has to the officially proffered legislative intent and, if found to be unreasonably so related, the finding utilized to suggest a hidden and suspect purpose—in this instance, a purpose that violated two amendments to the United States Constitution.

Justice Field's employment of the purpose-classification methodology is exemplary and deserves direct quotation because of its unusual usage here, that is, in cases involving a legislative body's invocation of a particular aspect of its police powers to justify regulations aimed at an ethnoracial minority: "The cutting off of the hair of every male person within an inch of his scalp, on his arrival at the jail, was not intended and cannot be maintained as a measure of discipline or as a sanitary regulation. The act by itself has no tendency to promote discipline, and can only be a measure of health in exceptional cases. Had the ordinance contemplated a mere sanitary regulation it would have been limited to such cases and made applicable to females as well as to males, and to persons awaiting trial as well as to persons under conviction . . ." In other words, the classification made by the ordinance was *underinclusive*, that is, it encompassed too few, with respect to the elimination of, or control over, the unlawful mischief or unsanitary condition which the board of supervisors alleged to be its objective. However, it was also *overinclusive*, that is, it included too many in its embracement, since, as Justice Field pointed out, "The ordinance was intended only for the Chinese in San Francisco" and only applied to the convicted members of that group who elected a jail sentence in lieu of payment of a fine. Although he did not write out the rest of the logic of his argument, Justice Field's reasoning seems to infer that, in the absence of any evidence to the contrary, it cannot be assumed a priori that Chinese males convicted of violating the lodging house ordinance are the sole wearers of unsanitary coiffures, or that they are the unique carriers of a compulsion to undisciplinary conduct, either of which trait might require a prophylactic haircut to within one inch of the scalp. As Tussman and tenBroek seem to suggest in their seminal essay on the methods appropriate to determining whether an official statute or governmental order meets the requirements of the equal protections provision of the Fourteenth Amendment, the discovery of a classification that is both under- and over-inclusive might set off a warning bell to the judge or justice adjudicating the matter and send him or her in quest of a legislative intent that is ultra vires.[69] In *Ho Ah Kow v. Nunan*, Justice Field rose to the occasion in no uncertain terms: "The claim . . . put forth that the measure was prescribed as one of health is notoriously a mere pretense. A treatment to which disgrace is attached, and which is not adopted as a means of security against the escape of the prisoner, but merely to aggravate the severity of his confinement, can only be regarded as a punishment additional to that fixed by his sentence." And what hidden purpose might have moved San Francisco's board of supervisors to enact such a law? Justice Field's inquiry into that body's debate over the adoption of the ordinance led him to assert: "The reason advanced for its adoption . . . is, that only the dread loss of his queue will induce a Chinaman to pay his fine. That is to say, in order to enforce the payment of a fine imposed on him, it is necessary that torture should be superadded to imprisonment."

However, there is implicit in this designation of the actual purpose of the ordinance a further set of questions: (1) Is the newly discovered purpose for the statute one that is forbidden to lawmakers? (2) If so, what provision of state law, or, more significantly, of the Constitution does this ordinance violate? (3) Can a regulatory ordinance that is general in its terms and that does not designate a particular class to be the object of its provisions nevertheless be deemed to be of the same type of legislation as that doomed by its open-faced and hostile class character?

Justice Field answered the first and second questions by declaring his
assent to Ho Ah Kow's claim that the ordinance in question "is special legislation imposing a degrading and cruel punishment upon a class of persons
who are entitled, alike with all other persons within the jurisdiction of the
United States, to the equal protection of the laws." That particular ordinance, he went on to observe, had been enacted with no other objective than
"to add to the severity of his punishment." It was, he continued, *inter alia*,
an act of "wanton cruelty." Field compared queue-cutting, when carried out
as a means to punish those who chose a stay in jail over payment of a fine,
to the infliction "of the bastinado, or the knout, or the thumbscrew, or the
rack, [which, he acidly observed,] would accomplish the same end." Yet,
his comparative statement implied, none of these modes of regulation with
respect to choosing between a fine or incarceration would be permitted.

In quotation marks, but otherwise uncited with respect to its source,
Field invoked the language of the Eighth Amendment to the Constitution,
which prohibits "cruel and unusual punishments." However, he rested his
argument on the provisions of the Fourteenth Amendment, (making this
decision, perhaps, a unique adumbration of the "incorporation" thesis that
would be recognized more than seven decades later), and on the inherent
repugnance of the statute itself. It was, he wrote, a piece of "legislation which
is unworthy of a brave and manly people"; worse, "It is not creditable to
the humanity and civilization of our people, much less to their Christianity,
that an ordinance of this character was possible."

That queue-cutting by force of law was wanton cruelty did not make
such an act *ipso facto* a violation of the Fourteenth Amendment. To bring
the statute into conflict with the equal protection clause of that amendment,
Justice Field chose not only to show it to be a form of selective class legislation, but, more importantly, to assert that that amendment prohibits legislation that is both discriminatory and *hostile*. Tussman and tenBroek have
taken note of the cases in which "Laws are invalidated by the [United States
Supreme] Court as discriminatory because they are expressions of hostility or antagonism to certain groups of individuals."[70] Although they do not
cite the district court's ruling in *Ho Ah Kow v. Nunan* as a lower court
instance of this basis for a decision, examination of Justice Field's reasoning on this point reveals it to be an early forerunner of it. Having noted the
more than unfriendly attitude toward the Chinese that prevailed in
California—and, indeed, in a later part of the decision, indicating his own
and other "thoughtful" persons' "hope that some way may be devised to
prevent their further immigration"—Justice Field pointed out that "in our
country hostile and discriminating legislation by a state against persons of

any class, sect, creed or nation, in whatever form it may be expressed, is forbidden by the fourteenth amendment of the constitution." And he went on to observe that the protections established by that amendment are "assured to every one whilst within the United States, from whatever country he may have come, or of whatever race or color he may be . . ." In his discussion of hostile and discriminatory legislation, Field took particular care to point out that the prohibitions on every state's deprivation of any person's life, liberty, or property without due process of law, or denial to any person of the equal protection of the laws "applies to all the instrumentalities and agencies employed in the administration of . . . [state] government, to its executive, legislative, and judicial departments, and to the subordinate legislative bodies of counties and cities." Moreover, perhaps recalling the restrictions on Chinese testimony effected in *People v. Hall*, Field ruled that the Fourteenth Amendment had ensured that, regardless of a person's race or color, "the courts of the country shall be open to him on the same terms as to all others for the security of his person or property, . . . [and] that no charges or burdens shall be laid upon him which are not equally borne by others, and that in the administration of criminal justice he shall suffer for his offenses no greater or different punishment." Field, later, seemed to imply that, to a Chinese, loss of his queue was a deprivation of his liberty to practice his religion. However the deprivation be interpreted, so long as it was of the kind protected by the Fourteenth Amendment, Field pointed out, the Civil Rights Act of 1870 had established the liability of anyone who subjects "any . . . person within the jurisdiction [of the United States] . . . to the deprivation of any rights, privileges, or immunities secured by the constitution and laws, [to a] suit in equity or other proper proceeding for redress."

The question of the ordinance's hostility to the Chinese was at the heart of the third question; for, on its face, San Francisco's haircutting statute appeared both broadly general and racially neutral. Tussman and tenBroek have called attention to the difficulties entailed in establishing the hostile purpose of a piece of constitutionally challenged legislation that seems to bear neither a class character nor a written trace of animus toward those to whom it applies—difficulties that, no matter how great, they argue, must be surmounted if a logically and empirically sound adjudication of the matter is to be effected.[71] Justice Field approached this issue by first claiming that "the class character of this legislation is none the less manifest because of the general terms in which it is expressed," and then going on to assert the court's obligation "to take notice of the limitation given to the general terms of an ordinance by its practical construction as a fact of its history . . ." That history included not only an account of the Sinophobic antipathy that went into the making of the statute, but also what Field emphasized, the fact that "the ordinance acts with special severity upon Chinese prisoners, inflicting upon them suffering altogether disproportionate to what would be endured by other prisoners if enforced against them." Field, having already reported on Ho Ah Kow's averment that "it is the custom of Chinamen to shave the hair from the front of the head and to wear the remainder of it braided into a queue; that the deprivation of the queue is regarded by them as a mark of disgrace, and is attended, according to their religious faith, with misfortune and suffering after death . . . ," as well as having noted the plaintiff's claim that Sheriff Nunan "knew of this custom and religious faith of the Chinese, and knew also that the plaintiff venerated the custom and held the faith," could not but conclude about the law that "Upon the Chinese prisoners its enforcement operates as 'a cruel and unusual punishment.' " As such, both its purpose and its usage indicated unwarranted hostility toward those to whom it applied.

Field pointed out that a court's failure to conduct the kind of investigation he had made into the prepossessing origins and selective application of San Francisco's seemingly general and apparently unprejudiced statute would allow "the most important provisions of the constitution, intended for the security of personal rights, . . . [to] be evaded and practically annulled." And, lest the hostile disregard of the sacred customs of the Chinese indicated in the enforcement (but not the wording) of the municipal ordinance be regarded lightly, Field illustrated how a very similar law, though general and unprepossessing on its face, could be used against a perhaps better-favored minority group in the United States, a people some of whose customs, however, also make them stand apart from the majority population:

> We have, [he observed] . . . in our community a large number of Jews. They are a highly intellectual race, and are generally obedient to the laws of the country. But, as is well known, they have peculiar opinions with respect to the use of certain articles of food, which they cannot be forced to disregard without extreme pain and suffering. They look, for example, upon the eating of pork with loathing. It is an offense against their religion, and is associated in their minds with uncleanness and impurity. Now, if they should in some quarter of the city overcrowd their dwellings and thus become amenable, like the Chinese, to the act concerning lodging-houses and sleeping apartments, an ordinance of

the supervisors requiring that all prisoners confined in the county jail should be fed on pork would be seen by every one to be leveled [*sic*] at them; and, notwithstanding its general terms, would be regarded as a special law in its purpose and operation.

Conclusion

Justice Field's decision in *Ho Ah Kow v. Nunan*, like the Supreme Court's decision seven years later in *Yick Wo v. Hopkins*,[72] stands out in the otherwise dreary history of Chinese litigants seeking equitable justice in the courts of the United States.[73] Although the addition of "person" to the due process and equal protection clauses of the Constitution's Fourteenth Amendment provided the basis for a great many Chinese aliens to seek redress for the violation of their personal and property rights,[74] the denial of citizenship, affirmed in *Ah Yup* and remaining in force until 1943, stood as a bar to their integration into the American political community and civil society. Until 1943, when the right to naturalization was granted to Chinese aliens as part of a gesture to America's Kuomintang ally in the war against Japan, immigrant Chinese were officially marginalized in America's invidious hierarchy of races. They all too often were made to bear the burden of a juridical interpretation that had originated in the joint and separate employment of a conjectural ethnohistory, a dubious and contradictory ethnology, and, with rare and occasional exception, the judiciary's failure to discover and evaluate the real intent of the classificatory schemas that had begun to stigmatize them when they were first designated as generic "Indians" or as equally generic "blacks." Like blacks, Chinese had been tarred with the badge of slavery: race discrimination; unlike blacks, they had not been emancipated in 1865.[75]

CHAPTER SEVEN

The Assimilation-Pluralism Debate: Toward a Postmodern Resolution of the American Ethnoracial Dilemma

As a matter of fact, the ease and rapidity with which aliens, under existing conditions in the United States, have been able to assimilate themselves to the customs and manners of American life have enabled this country to swallow and digest every sort of normal human difference, except the purely external ones, like the color of the skin.

> Robert E. Park, "Racial Assimilation in Secondary Groups" (1914)

Indeed, . . . the challenge that we are facing today is precisely that of developing a view of citizenship which is adequate for multi-ethnic and multi-cultural societies. We have to accept that national homogeneity can no longer be the basis of citizenship, and that pluralism must allow for a range of different ethnic and cultural identities.

> Chantal Mouffe, "Democratic Politics Today" (1992)

Divisions in the Interests of Racial Justice

Broadly speaking, the camps of those fighting for racial justice have long been divided over whether America will have fulfilled its promise as the "first new nation"[1] of the Enlightenment by establishing an unalloyed, universal, and personal achievement-oriented society, or by institutionalizing a pluralistic social order rooted in peaceful particularism and a noninvidious but culturally preservationist ascription. The former seeks the emancipation of the individual from all forms of hereditary claim;[2] its validation of acculturation will have occurred when an individual can honestly credit and be credited with his or her successes or failures in accordance with that which he or she has been able or unable to *do* rather than *be*.[3] The latter seeks collective emancipation and social as well as personal well-being in accordance with the sense of necessary self-esteem and rightful entitlement that derive from ethnocultural perpetuation, recognition, and response; its validation of acculturation will have occurred when each and every one of the peoples of America are corporately constituted as a heritage group with an equal right to persevere and to seek after all the material and moral benefits that the society has promised to each individual. The former finds its ideal typification and root metaphor in the "melting pot;" the latter in the "mosaic," or, more prosaically, the "salad bowl."[4] The former emphasizes the benefits that will accrue from assimilation, acculturation, and amalgamation; the latter encourages multiculturalism, multiracial accommodation, and ethnoracial endogamy. Each regards its table of desiderata as the exemplification of racial justice. Each has its eminent scholar antecedents—J. Hector St. John de Crevecoeur (1735–1813)[5] and Israel Zangwill (1864–1926)[6] for the assimilationists; Horace Kallen (1882–1974)[7] and Randolph Bourne (1886–1918)[8] for the pluralists.

The Jewish Question: Assimilation versus Pluralism in Europe and America

It is relevant to our discussion to observe that both positions owe their philosophical development in twentieth-century America to intellectual responses to the "Jewish Question." Although the matter had arisen in policy considerations in Eastern Europe in the late eighteenth century,[9] the question of whether and how diasporic Jews could be accommodated in industrializing nineteenth-century nation-states came to haunt the socio-cultural theories of such classical European social thinkers as Karl Marx, Max Weber, and Theodor Mommsen, and the resolution of that issue would become a point of departure for the American sociologists' approach to their own country's response to its rapidly enlarging ethnoracial mix. Karl Marx (1818–1883) had treated the question in his pithy, scathing, but endlessly ambiguous statement: "The social emancipation of the Jew implies the emancipation of society from Judaism."[10] In this and other statements on the issue, Marx, according to one of his most astute critics, was asserting "that Jews had a right to emancipation in spite of their 'anti-social' role in society, because the whole of society was adopting their 'anti-social,' i.e., commercial, practices."[11]

However, even if one were to accept Marx's extraordinarily tendentious equation of the socioreligious tenets of Judaism with the spirit and practice of capitalism, one would still want to know whether he envisioned Jewish emancipation as utterly de-Judaizing; as dependent on the rise of a new yet-to-be-realized noncapitalist societal form into which both Jews and Christians would be equally secularized and assimilated; or whether he somehow envisioned the survival of an "ethnic" Jewishness that would become attenuated from its religious origin but associated with one or another of the disparate conceptions of Jews as a people either united by a commonality of beliefs, culture, or traditions; sharing a community of interests; forming a nation; comprising a race; or existing merely as an aggregate, for example, an economic category.[12]

Marx, baptized at the age of six (August 24, 1824), had been born into a family whose paternal ancestry included several generations of rabbis. His father had undergone baptism a year or more before Karl's birth. He had accepted a nominal Christianity in order to enter into the legal profession, wherein he defended the rights of Jews. Karl Marx did not maintain either a Protestant or a Jewish identification during the course of his life.[13] Rudolf Bienenfeld has described a philosophy of Jewishness that is sometimes ascribed to Marx, its precepts derived neither from nationality, race, nor religion, but rather from a commitment to four Jewish tenets: *equality* as a matter of right rather than grace; *justice* as a matter of principle and not convenience; *reason* as a duty associated with continuous learning; and an *inner-worldliness* that requires the establishment of human and institutional perfection in the here and now rather than in the afterlife.[14] Whether Marx subscribed to these principles is, however, less important than the fact that they refer to a belief in the good society as one grounded in a civil association of law rather than in one dependent upon a communion of faith, that is, that they form the basis for a fundamental division between Jewish and Protestant social thought and give one pause when a "Judaeo-Christian" tradition is invoked.

Most of the early American sociologists who came to espouse an assimilationist orientation received their higher education in Wilhelmine Germany.[15] There, they came in contact with the *Methodenstreit* scholars' orientation toward Bismarck's "blood-and-iron" approach to imperial, cultural, and national hegemony. But, upon returning to the United States, and in the spirit of Sarah E. Simon's careful distinctions among the several forms of assimilation,[16] they tended to transpose the phenomenon of social adjustment in a multiethnic society from a coercive Prussian public policy into either a gradual karyokinetic process or a merely acculturative American *telos*.

However, the Jewish Question had challenged both program and process in Germany—and would do so again in America. For Max Weber (1864–1920), the Jews were a "pariah people" because of their religion.[17] In contrast to both Marx's and Sombart's (1863–1941) claims[18] about their originating role in the construction of modern capitalism, although they had had a definite role in premodern capitalistic economic formations, Weber insisted that Jews had done very little with respect to establishing two of the major institutions of production of modern capitalism: domestic industry and the factory.[19] Weber's position on the Jewish Question ultimately was in keeping with that of other *fin-de-siècle* German scholars, that is, that of progressive Gentiles whose political-economic ideology was national liberalism. To these, as Gary A. Abraham has summed up the matter, "emancipation was . . . seen . . . as a means to the end of normalizing minority-majority relations under the new conditions of open and 'civil' societies." In return for their admission into civil society, Jews were expected to acculturate, that is, to "cease to organize their attentions around an ancient subculture and social group and [to] turn toward the center along with all other citizens."[20] In the end, Weber's solution to *die Judenfrage* in Germany was similar to that enunciated by the Chicago sociologist Ellsworth Faris for America in 1937[21]—a group commitment to radical assimilation that would ultimately extinguish altogether their existence in and as a religious or cultural peoplehood.

The society to which Jews (and, later, all other ethnoracially distinctive peoples) were advised to assimilate was modern, industrial, civilized—and *Christian*. Indeed, such a society was said to be not exclusive to a particular European or American nation-state but to modern civilization itself. This is the civilization that lauds the Protestant ethic as the spirit of capitalism, the civilization whose mainline Protestant denominations illuminate "a picture of what it might mean to live a biblical life in America,"[22] a civilization whose most eminent theologians "held America under the judgment of God."[23] Theodor Mommsen (1817–1903), a scholar who had considerable influence on Max Weber, treated the Jewish Question in such civilizational terms and observed in 1880, "The word *Christianity* in our day no longer means what it used to mean; nevertheless it is the only word which still defines the entire international civilization of our day and which numerous millions of people of our highly populated globe accept as their intrinsic link."[24] For neither Weber nor Mommsen could the Jews escape from their destiny: absorption into this expanding world civilization. Weber warned Jews against tarrying in unacculturated exile, in the hope of deliverance by a messiah.[25] Mommsen agreed, prophesying in relation to the new Zionist movement that had startled the Gentile peoples of Europe and America,[26] "The Jews . . . will not be led by another Moses into the Promised Land"; and admonishing them in what should be recognized as lingering vestiges of his generalized anti-Jewish attitude, "whether they sell trousers or write books, it is their duty to do away with their particularities wherever they can do so without offending their conscience."[27] But even offenses to their Jewish conscience did not seem to matter ultimately to Mommsen. He concluded his essay on the subject with a command: Jews "must make up their minds and tear down all barriers between themselves and their German compatriots."[28]

An American Kulturkampf: Zangwill versus Kallen

The German discourse on assimilation became one basis for America's second great *Kulturkampf*. It entered the fray in the form of a multifaceted debate over whether not only the Jew, but also the immigrant, the Asiatic, the Indian, and the Negro could be made full-fledged members of the rapidly industrializing, urbanizing nation. In its earlier version—that of the letters from the eighteenth-century "American farmer," Crevecoeur—the Jewish question had not arisen. Rather, Crevecoeur had focused on the role that intermarriage and an emergent Christian ecumenism would have on Americanizing the denizens of the newly decolonized nation in embryo. The "American farmer" had supposed that inter-national matrimony and its socioculturally melding effects on the ways of life of subsequent generations would not only dissolve the bonds of nationality and culture that isolated the peoples of Europe from one another, but also would fuse the European settlers with America's red aborigines. However, Crevecoeur, who opposed slavery, did not include the African American in his delineation of the "American . . . [a] new man, who acts upon new principles . . ." Black-white relations did not loom large in Crevecoeur's sociological imagination. For this first proponent of amalgamative assimilationism, however, the religious divisions that had led to so much conflict in Europe would be ended in America: "[T]he various Christian sects," he prophesied, ". . . [will] wear out, and . . . this mixed [American] neighborhood will exhibit a strange religious medley, that will be neither pure Catholicism nor pure Calvinism."[29] Noticeably, he did not mention Judaism.

The second debate over how America might construct its cultural configuration began in the latter part of the nineteenth century. It compounded Crevecoeur's imagery by adding to its beneficent message a number of agonizing questions about the place of color, race, ethnicity, and non-Christian religions in a modernizing democratic republic—and by posing a pluralist alternative to assimilation.

The Jewish Question figured significantly in this reopening of the cultural debate about America. Israel Zangwill led off with his melodramatic promise that Christian-Jewish intermarriage would be but one forerunner of America's "great Melting Pot." Interethnic intimacies would make for a bubbling cauldron that would fuse the bloodlines and combine the cultural heritages of "Celt and Latin, Slav and Teuton, Greek and Syrian,—black and yellow—Jew and Gentile."[30] Zangwill was motivated in great part by his concern over the revival of the Jewish Question in Europe and America. He had served as president of the Emigration Regulation Department of the Jewish Territorial Organization, a body that undertook to settle thousands of victims of Russia's anti-Semitic pogroms in the United States.[31] However, widely publicized apprehensions about Jewish "anarchists,"[32] fears about the type, number, and spread of crimes that New York City's Jewish gangs might commit,[33] a concern over the ambiguous American response to the Dreyfus affair,[34] and worry over the effect the revival of the notorious "blood libel" might have on American-Jewish relations[35] led some Jewish intellectuals, including Zangwill, to espouse Zionism for Europe's Jews and to issue a promissory note of Jewish disappearance in America, a virtual dissolution of one people's ethnocultural identity that would in the process also help to relieve the United States of all of its non-WASP ethnic groups.[36]

Horace Kallen's and Randolph Bourne's versions of pluralism were developed in part to oppose Zangwill's advocacy of Jewish ethnocultural extinction. Kallen, as John Higham observes, "argued for the indestructibility of ethnic cultures in an effort to resist the disintegration of his own."[37] An active cultural Zionist who had been brought to Boston from his birthplace, Silesia, when he was five years old, Kallen had founded the Harvard Menorah Society in 1906 while serving simultaneously as William James's protégé at that university and discovering through the teachings of Barrett Wendell that the assimilationists' model of the ideal culture for America, that of genteel, Puritan, New England, owed its origins to the values and credos enunciated by the ancient Hebrew prophets.[38] Applying James's idea that the universe is "more like a federal republic than like an empire or a kingdom"[39] to the ethnocultural structure of the United States, Kallen began to formulate a thesis that found its most powerful statement in the claim that a true democracy would oppose a melting pot.[40] Granting a sphere of public policy and economic life to the modern equivalent of an assimilationist-oriented and democratically elected Caesar, Kallen nevertheless hoped to preserve an inner, private, but unghettoized sphere of Jewish communal existence against the siren song of Protestant, Anglo-Saxon, cultural conformity.[41] In formulating his thesis as a general proposition, however, Kallen perceived that Jewish ways of life could not be preserved and protected unless those of every other ethnic group could be made equally secure. Hence, he abjured adherence to Zangwill's melting pot of merely once-proud nations, envisioning in its stead a democratic republic of English-speaking but culturally distinctive nationalities and dialects—"a multiplicity in a unity, an orchestration of mankind."[42]

Bourne, destined by the accidents attending his birth to go through his short life a hunchback and a dwarf, and by his uncompromising individuality and shrewd intelligence, as well as the example of his father's own business failures, to revolt against his aristocratic, Presbyterian, and Puritan New England heritage, adapted Kallen's ideas to his own formulation of an emergent United States that he called "trans-national America."[43] Convinced that the "allure of fresh and true ideas, of free speculation, of artistic vigor, of cultural styles, of intelligence fused with feeling, and feeling given fibre and outline by intelligence"[44] could never arise from the reigning American philosophy of technocentric instrumentalism, and that the Anglo-conformity that characterized the official program of Americanization had been both a failure and a mistake, Bourne pointed out that, in fact, the actual processes of "Assimilation . . . , instead of washing out the memories of Europe, [had] made them more and more intensely real,"[45] and, he insisted, this counter-Zangwillian process had been truly beneficial for the nation.

For the Gentile Bourne, as for the Jewish Kallen, American Zionism provided the ideational model for what he believed was a burgeoning American cultural pluralism. Bourne understood the American variant of Zionism to have proclaimed that a nonmilitarized and antichauvinist "Palestine is to be built as a Jewish centre on purely religious and cultural foundations . . . [and] is not to be the home of all the Jewish people."[46] Hence, for Bourne, Zionism instantiated the best example of his own proposal for a fundamental separation of state citizenship from ethnonational group identity. Zionist Jews in America might send their cultural and even financial support to a reconstituted religious and cultural center in Israel, but they would remain loyal citizens of the United States. "Cultural allegiance," he prophesied, "will not necessarily coincide with political allegiance."[47] Under such a political and cultural praxis, true internationalism would flower *within* America, itself to become a culturally conscious state-societal mosaic of nationalities. Bourne believed that his philosophy of diversity might be institutionalized, finding its best expression in a cosmopolitan celebration of ethnic distinctiveness that had even broader implications for global unity: "America is already the world federation in miniature," he observed, "the continent where for the first time in history has been achieved that miracle of hope, the peaceful living side by side, with character substantially preserved, of the most heterogeneous peoples under the sun."[48]

In addition to their common foundation in alternative responses to the Jewish Question, the advocates of assimilation and pluralism each developed different orientations toward the white Anglo-Saxon peoples dominating the culture of America. Central to the assimilationist position is a public denial (coupled all too often with a private assurance to the contrary) that the several races and cultures of America are permanently arrayed along a more or less fixed, vertical and invidious line of rights, opportunities, privileges, and status. The proclamation of that line speaks to what Herbert Blumer reminds us is the basic characteristic of race prejudice—a hierarchicalized sense of group position;[49] the denial of its fixity, to the Jeffersonian ideal of the eighteenth-century American Enlightenment—that all men are created equal. Taken together, this fundamental contradiction constitutes what Gunnar Myrdal in 1944 called the "American Dilemma."[50] Treated analytically, however, the easily demonstrated thesis that the vertical ethnic order continues to exist undermines both the assurances of equalitarian ethnoracial assimilation and the promises of egalitarian ethnocultural pluralism.

In their critiques of assimilation, Bourne and Kallen exposed the privileged place of the white Anglo-Saxon and Protestant elite in America, but neither quite perceived how the latter group's securely entrenched position in society—which they harshly criticized—might not only subvert their respective programmatic philosophies of a federated multicultural America, but also cool the fires of Crevecoeur's and Zangwill's melting pot. Two issues contributed to this potentiality for a double-sided subversion—intermarriage and the conflation of the color-culture question.

Crossing the Color Line: The Question of Amalgamation

Marriage across religious and Old World national lines was central to Zangwill's theatricalized picture of the melting pot, and crossing the color as well as the culture line was certainly indicated in the rhetoric of his play's denouement. Yet by 1922, when he published a "new and revised edition" of his drama, Zangwill provided an afterword that reveals an extraordinary confusion of biosocial ideas as well as an increased ambivalence about Negro-white marriages. Insisting that "it is as much social prejudice as racial antipathy that today divides black and white in the New World,"[51] he nevertheless tells his readers that "No doubt there is an instinctive antipathy which tends to keep the white man free from black blood;" that "the [African's] prognathous face is an ugly and undesirable type of countenance . . . that . . . connotes a lower average of intellect and ethics"; that "Melanophobia, or fear of the black, may be pragmatically as valuable a racial defence for the white as the counter-instinct of philoleucosis, or love of the white, is a force of racial uplifting for the black"; and that "white and black are as yet too far apart for profitable fusion." Holding that such African American painters as the expatriate Henry Ossawa Tanner or such black poets as Paul Lawrence Dunbar "show the potentialities of the race even without white admixture," Zangwill preferred that persons of this class and status intermarry rather than having miscegenation occur among "the dregs of both races." Yet, even in these cases, he hesitated. "Blacks of this temper," he suggested, referring to those "heroic souls . . . [who] dare the adventure of intermarriage . . . would serve their race better by making Liberia a success or building up an American negro State, . . . or at least asserting their rights as American citizens in that sub-tropical South which without their labour could never have been opened up."

Although he allowed that the "African negro has . . . not a few valuable ethnic elements—joy of life, love of colour, keen senses, beautiful voice, and [an] ear for music—" and that these might come to fruition through inter-marriage as "contributions that might somewhat compensate for the dragging-down of the white and, in small doses at least, might one day prove [to be] a tonic to an anaemic and art-less America," Zangwill now put the full force of his assimilationist faith behind "the spiritual [rather than physical] miscegenation which, while clothing, commercialising, and Christianising the ex-African, has given 'rag-time' and the sex-dances that go to it, first to white America and thence to the whole white world." Ultimately, Zangwill perceived his cautiousness about black-white marriages as also providing a way for Jewish endogamy to continue in melting-pot

America: "The Jew may be Americanised and the American Judaised without any gamic interaction."[51] In effect, he seemed to disavow the necessity and advantage of intermarriage that had been the core argument of his melodrama *The Melting-Pot*. Assimilation could occur without amalgamation.

Intermarriage was neither an issue nor a desideratum in Kallen's or Bourne's conception of cultural pluralism. Their outlook (and especially that of Kallen) took equality to be centered in the right to be racially, ethnically, and culturally different: "The men who wrote and signed the Declaration [of Independence] and the men and women who fought and suffered and died for it," he wrote in 1948, "did not intend by that proposition either to abolish or to penalize differences. They intended to vindicate differences, to acknowledge, and to defend their equal right to life, liberty, and the pursuit of happiness."[52] Among the differences to be kept both free and equal were those of race, ethnicity, and nationality. For Kallen, the invidious distinctions among races, nations, and ethnic groups in the various "Americanization" programs of his day exemplified a fundamental misunderstanding of the Jeffersonian ideal of democracy. To Kallen, the "full practical meaning of the democratic faith as a program of conduct is exemplified by nothing so much as its repudiation of slavery."[53] And, as the central theme of his philosophy implied, this repudiation did not entail the genocidal, cultural, or social extermination of blacks. Rather, as one people of the American ethnoracial multiverse, their color as well as their cultural and ethnic integrity were to be protected and cherished. Endogamy certainly seemed to be implied—but not required—in Kallen's conception of pluralism. Intermarriage seems not to be ruled out altogether; for the whole of his philosophy emphasized the freedom of the individual to realize him- or herself through making courageous, if risky, choices.[54]

However, pluralism has often foundered on the question of color and its relation to culture. Bourne's and Kallen's perspectives on pluralism emphasized the equality of cultures and envisioned American society as providing (in Bourne's words) for "a cosmopolitan federation of national colonies, of foreign cultures, from whom the sting of devastating competition has been removed,"[55] or, (in Kallen's) for "orchestration, . . . modes of the free association of the different . . ."[56] Much of their efforts was expended in extolling the benefits that would accrue to America from the energizing of the transplanted cultures of the peoples from Europe. But a burning question in their own day as well as the present era is whether and to what extent the cultures of the enslaved peoples from Africa had survived the Middle Passage, the "seasoning" in the West Indies, and the 225 years of bondage in America, and, if they had, what place they deserved in an American cultural mosaic.

Bourne insisted that all races and nations could contribute to the "cultural progress" of America and observed that "the Southern white man's policy of keeping down a race . . . is the least defensible thing in the world."[57] Later, he went on to denigrate life in the states of the white South as "culturally sterile because it has had no advantage of cross-fertilization like . . . Wisconsin and Minnesota . . . [where] strong foreign cultures have struck root . . . , [and where] German and Scandinavian political ideas and social energies have expanded to a new potency."[58] But, he made no mention of any African political ideas and social energies that might be liberated to work their wonders on the states of the former slavocracy. Kallen was even more cautious, postponing analysis of African cultures in America and the designation of their value to a special investigation that in fact he never carried out: "I do not discuss the influence of the negro upon the esthetic material and cultural character of the South and the rest of the United States," he wrote in 1924. "This is at once too considerable and too recondite in its processes for casual mention. It requires a separate analysis."[59]

The perspectives of Zangwill on the one side and Bourne and Kallen on the other were largely philosophical and broadly programmatic in character.[60] None of these men had carried out detailed sociological analyses of the actual situations of the several racial and ethnic groups then contending for recognition and response in the United States. The social and cultural adjustment—as well as the civic status and economic opportunity—of the European and Asian immigrants and the freedmen and women and their offspring had from 1880 to 1920 been left largely to the ministrations of the newly aroused Social Gospel movement and its urban settlement-house missionaries. In these newly established settlement houses, the "race question"[61] came together with the "Jewish question,"[62] each having to contend in its own way with the "immigrant" and "urban" questions of which it had become an unresolved part.[63] By 1913, Robert Park—who had formulated a thesis relating racial oppression to European expansion while serving as an investigative reporter for and international secretary of the Congo Reform Association; who had studied the situation affecting African American life-chances in the rural and urban South during an eight-year stint as private secretary, ghost writer, and amanuensis to Booker T. Washington;[64] who together with the Tuskegean leader had journeyed through Europe to find "the man farthest down";[65] and had taken an interest in the emerging "Japanese problem"[66] that had arisen on the Pacific coast,—put forward a pessimistic thesis on the resolution of the race issue: "the chief obstacle[s] to the assimilation of the Negro and the Oriental are not mental but physical traits ... The Japanese, like the Negro is condemned to remain among us an abstraction, a symbol not merely of his own race, but of the Orient and of that vague, ill-defined menace we sometimes refer to as the 'yellow peril.'"[67]

During the 1920s and 1930s, as the living conditions and economic opportunities for blacks, Asians, Amerindians, and Hispanics seemed not to improve appreciably, Park, who had become a leading theorist of assimilation, grew less and less sanguine about the likelihood that America would accomplish its officially proclaimed mission of becoming the modern world's first fully integrated melting-pot democracy.[68] The assimilation-oriented Social Gospel movement began to wane after the First World War. Its surviving settlement houses "did not recognize race relations as a major problem during the 1930's."[69] For the most part the movement's leaders continued to segregate blacks in separate settlement houses and to accommodate their philanthropic programs at the state and local levels to prevailing Jim Crow sentiments. As Judith Trolander observes, "They still thought of their movement primarily in terms of white middle class workers living in poor white neighborhoods."[70] "Their greatest successes," she concludes, "had been in helping immigrants to assimilate, and by the 1930's they had not totally adjusted to the decline in immigration."[71]

Nor did the Social Gospel-inspired aid to European immigrants to America do much to resolve the Jewish Question. Many of the settlements were strictly religious in character and aimed their "Americanization" programs toward the fulfillment of a proselytizing mission—to make the society into a Christian republic.[72] Yet, for "world Jewry," as Aaron Berman has pointed out, "the decade and a half between 1933 and 1948 was traumatic and cataclysmic."[73] Even after Hitler had been defeated and the Holocaust brought to a halt, there remained the unresolved status of the thousands of homeless and stateless Jewish survivors, a people whose horrifying experiences challenged theodicy itself,[74] and whose immediate needs accelerated the pressure to establish a Jewish homeland. This situation, in turn, reopened the debate over whether the meaning given to Zionism by Kallen and Bourne would in fact prevail against the tide of events[75] and the undercurrent of suspicion[76] and ambivalence that had shadowed it—from within and without[77]—from the beginning.

Zionism, Racism, and the American Dilemma

The Jewish ambivalence over whether to opt for assimilation or plural-ism is no better personified than in the life-choices made by Israel Zangwill. Zangwill had explained the larger message of his play *The Melting-Pot* to an enthusiastic Theodore Roosevelt, then President of the United States: The play "dramatises your own idea of America as a crucible in which the races are fusing into a future America . . . combining as it does, the American and the American-Jewish problem."[78] Despite this apparent capitulation to assimilationism, Zangwill, who had married a Gentile in 1903, announced his unswerving support for Zionism, that is, he became a Jewish national-ist, thereby opposing the very fusion his melodrama had celebrated. As his most recent biographer observes, "Precisely at the time he decided to cast his lot in with the apparent historical destiny of Western Jewry to have its identity absorbed ineluctably into the majority population, he joined actively with those determined to rescue and preserve the Jewish people from just such absorption."[79] The paradox is resolved, perhaps, by imput-ing to Zangwill and other ethnoculturally concerned Jews a belief in America's exceptional promise with respect to the race issue in general and the Jewish Question in particular. After 1919, some American Jewish lead-ers hoped that such promulgations as the Bolshevik Declaration of the Rights of Peoples and the several minority treaties agreed to by the postwar conferences would protect their coreligionists from the worst features of prewar anti-semitism,[80] while Britain's Balfour Declaration held out the promise of a future Jewish homeland in Palestine.[81] America, they hoped, would solve its Jewish problem either by assimilation or by a muted Kallen-Bourne style of ethnoracial pluralism, separating the cultural elements of Jewishness from the political sphere of an increasingly secular civil society.

Despite his own paradoxical response to it, Zangwill's philosophy persisted for five decades as a societal desideratum for America's ethno-cultural minorities. At the level of social action and institutional change the years following World War II witnessed the dismantling of judicially and legislatively supported racial segregation, the virtual elimination of avowedly "Jim Crow" practices, and, at the national, state, and local levels, the passage of laws aiming to ensure the civil rights of racial as well as some other minor-ities. In effect, what Herbert Blumer had designated as the outer bastion of America's color-line fortress had been breached, but its inner walls remained more or less intact. Whereas Myrdal's vision of the "American dilemma,"—the contradiction between the "higher" values of freedom and equality on the one side and the sense of racial invidiousness on the other—

was that of a problem that could be resolved by the reaffirmation of the former at the levels of law, politics, and, to a lesser extent, economic opportunity, the assimilation-pluralism debate, that is, the questions of the place of racially based color consciousness and of ethnic culture, as well as of their relation to each other and to the emerging national and world orders, remain unanswered to the present day.[82] These questions arise anew—old wine in new bottles—as American thought and institutions cross the postmodern divide.

Pluralism and Assimilation in Postmodern Thought: Derrida, Gates, and the Problematic of Jean Toomer's "Blackness"

Jacques Derrida offers up a world wherein all the metanarratives of the late nineteenth century have lost their efficacy. This includes that of assimilation versus pluralism. Introducing the term "deconstruction" to the discourse on postmodernity, Derrida, born into a Jewish family residing in Algeria, regards culture and cultural life as a series of "texts" weaving in and out of one another, yet, as David Harvey points out, each having "a life of its own." "Whatever we write conveys meanings we do not or could not possibly intend, and our words cannot say what we mean."[83] Hence, the deconstructive project aims to examine a text to see how it contains, covers up, or superimposes itself over another, indeed, over many others. However, the ultimate project of postmodernism is to document the end of all privileged texts and all hegemonic narratives—and with that documentation, to put an end not only to the established canons of thought and praxis, but also, as its Marxist critics bitterly complain, to the hopes of all current and future disprivileged but aspiring texts of emancipation.[84] Every established, that is, privileged, text—and, although Derrida does not refer to these terms specifically, this would include every authorialized text defining such signifiers as, or purporting to delineate a discourse on, "Negro," "black," and "African-American"; "Chinese," "Japanese," "Oriental," and "Asian American"; "Mexican," "Chicano," and "Hispanic"; and "Indian," "Amerindian," and "Native American"—is now discreditable, an appropriate topic for a "deconstructive" analysis that would both deny the privileged validity of the author's own definition and expose the many meanings upon which the author's has been superimposed.

There is both an assimilation and a pluralism to be derived from Derrida's version of postmodernism and to be found in postmodern society. Both the "assimilation" and the "pluralism" are Lyotardean: its version of assimilation in effect contains the plurality of elements—the shards and shibboleths of color, culture, and ethnicity that form the seemingly chaotic mosaic of an over-commercialized civilization. Precisely because these elementary forms of postmodern life are shards and shibboleths, Derrida's concept of *écriture* is fundamental to the emerging structure of human group differentiation, of, as we shall show, a pluralistic assimilation that is caught up in an open-ended time warp.

Color, Culture, and "Erasure": A Postmodern Assault on Assimilation

Écriture, in its special Derridean sense, arises as a part of the process whereby every term of a discursive text becomes eligible for a deconstruction that places it, as it were, under erasure, that is, the term is still there, visible beneath the "x" that stands for its placement *sous rature*. Such placement acts as a warning to the reader to be sceptical about the word, especially about its privileged authorial meaning. In the spirit of this aspect of Derrida's approach, America's leading African American culture critic, Henry Louis Gates Jr. has written the following about the term "race": "Scores of people are killed every day in the name of differences ascribed only to race. This slaughter demands the gesture . . . to deconstruct, if you will, the ideas of difference inscribed in the trope of race, to explicate discourse itself in order to reveal the hidden relations of power and knowledge inherent in popular and academic usages of 'race.'"[85]

In one sense the project of poststructuralism denies at the very moment that it encourages the aims of both assimilationists and pluralists. On the one hand, by deconstructing the oppressive rhetorics of race at work in the Occident since at least the sixteenth century,[86] postmodernism might encourage an integration of the races that permitted equality in the presence of acknowledged anatomical difference. Such a cultural as well as politico-economic cosmopolis, Lester F. Ward prophesied shortly after the turn of the nineteenth century, would arise when the harsh but amalgamative process of social karyokinesis had so blended the peoples of America and the world that whatever epidermal pigmentary distinctiveness still remained would form but an aesthetic relief on the cartography of a fully acculturated technocentric civilization.[87] More recently Charles Johnson, author of novels described as philosophical fictions, director of the creative writing program at the University of Washington, and a literary critic of African American writing, has predicted a new "species of black American fiction . . . taking form on the horizon of contemporary practice." This species, he asserts, will herald the end of a discourse of "narrow complaint" in black writing and the beginning of a "broad celebration": "When we have finally crossed this great distance, the prehistory of Afro-American literature will [have come to an] end. We will not have 'black' writers or books long out of print and collecting dust in Black Studies libraries . . . Rather, we will see a fiction by Americans who happen to be black, feel at ease both in their ethnicity and in their Yankeeness, and find it the most natural thing, as Merleau-Ponty was fond of saying, to go about 'singing the world.'"[88]

However, such feeling at ease in one's ethnicity as well as one's Yankeeness is precisely the kind of bland assimilation that must be overthrown, according to such pluralistically oriented culture critics of canonical literature and African American letters and life as Henry Louis Gates Jr.[89] Gates has criticized the earlier and assimilative uses of Negro literature, holding them to be motivated by the desire to give evidence for a thesis that only a racist culture would demand—namely, that blacks were indeed a part of the "humanity" that an Enlightenment-oriented, Eurocentric America might recognize.[90] In its place, Gates puts forward a black cultural aesthetic that seeks "to valorize (and demonstrate in what ways literature can contribute to) a larger political and economic analysis of the position of the black person living in the United States . . ." Moreover, Gates claims that "The Black Aesthetic should repudiate the received terms of academic, or white, literary critical methods and theories."[91] Gates goes even further, appropriating the tools of Derridean deconstruction in order to assault both the Western canon and those African American writers, critics, and activists who have acquiesced to it, but, at the same time, dissociating his own emerging black aesthetic from the full implications of the project of the French postmodernists. "Our pressing question now," he stated when speaking to a conference of black scholars called to debate and to formulate *The Study of Afro-American Literature: An Agenda for the 1990s*, "becomes this: in what languages shall we choose to speak, and write, our own criticisms?"[92]

Gates's complex answer to that question is that of a Lyotardean guerrilla fighter secreted within the oppressor's camp: "Learning the master's tongue, for our generation of critics, has been an act of empowerment, whether that critical language be New Criticism, so-called humanism, structuralism, Marxism, poststructuralism, feminism, new historicism, or any other 'ism' that I have forgotten."[93] However, this learning will be ineffective, Gates asserts, if it is not accompanied by the kind of praxis enunciated by Wole Soyinka, the Nigerian Nobel laureate: "And when we borrow an alien

language to sculpt or paint in, we must begin by co-opting the entire properties of that language as correspondences to properties in our matrix of
thought and expression."[94] Failure to adopt Soyinka's epistemological
perspective will result in continued abjection. "To assume we can wear the
masks, and speak the languages, of Western literary theory without accepting Soyinka's challenge," Gates concludes, "is to accept, willingly, the intellectual equivalent of neocolonialism, placing ourselves in a relationship of
discursive indenture."[95]

This issue is more precisely met when we turn to one of Gates's finest
applications of Derrida's concept of *rature*—his deconstruction of the
identity-genealogy of Jean Toomer (1894–1967), the author of *Cane*,[96] a
major work associated with the Harlem Renaissance era in African
American culture. Toomer, a grandson on his mother's side of the mulatto
P. B. S. Pinchback (1837–1921) who had served for forty-three days as a
Reconstruction-era governor of Louisiana,[97] is a significant figure for analysis of the problematic of "blackness" because of his lifelong ambivalence
over his own racial identity, his respected but ambiguous place in the canon
of African American letters, his discipleship with the Armenian mystic
Georges Gurdjieff, and his decision a decade after the publication of his
seminal book, to "pass" as a white man.[98] At one point in his life, sometime
between 1920 and 1922, Toomer had come to a conclusion about his own
ethnonational identity as well as that of all other Americans—one that is
strikingly consonant with that of Crevecoeur:

> I had observed [he wrote] that . . . very few . . . United States citizens
> were aware of being *Americans*. On the contrary, they were aware of, and
> put value upon, their hearsay descents, their groupistic affiliations . . .
> Yet, underlying what they were aware of, underlying all of the divisions,
> I had observed what seemed to me to be authentic—namely that a new
> type of man was arising in this country—not European, not African, not
> Asiatic—but American. And in this American I saw the divisions
> mended, the differences reconciled—saw that (1) we would in truth be
> a united people existing in the *United* States, saw that (2) we would in
> truth be once again members of a united human race.[99]

When Toomer shared this bit of reasoning with a friend whom he described
as "a colored fellow of more than ordinary mental grasp," his companion
dismissed it with a single phrase, "You're white," adding to Toomer's plain-
tive inquiry about his own identity, "[I'm] colored." Toomer saw his friend's
perspective as the product of a misleading, pervasive, and pernicious "racial

conditioning" that he alone could not "unfix."[100] Gates, however, seizes upon this colloquy as a singular but exemplary piece of discourse worthy of a Derridean deconstruction.

Toomer had earlier claimed about his own discovery of the Americanness of himself and his contemporaries: "I began feeling that I had in my hands the tools for my own creation."[101] From this statement and from Toomer's autobiographical American credo, Gates uncovers a subtending *rature*: "Toomer's 'tools for my own creation,' paradoxically, were 'but words,' yet words with which he put his Negro ancestry under erasure: his grandfather, P. B. S. Pinchback, Toomer rewrites, 'passed' or crossed over to being a Negro only to seek and gain political office during the Reconstruction; Toomer simply reversed the chiasmus. If Grandfather Pinchback was white, then Grandson Jean was Negro." Having proceeded this far, Gates asserts that "To be a human being, . . . Toomer felt that he had to efface his mask of blackness, the cultural or racial trace of difference, and embrace the utter invisibility of being an American." And, recalling Derrida's observation that "The 'matinal trace' of difference is lost in an irretrievable invisibility, and yet even its loss is covered, preserved, regarded, and retarded," Gates resurrects Toomer's "tell-tale trace of blackness"—no matter what the author claims about his identity or ancestry—from the discourse in his novel *Cane*.

Although Gates can now claim to have restored the supposedly complete erasure of blackness that Toomer might have been attempting in his autobiography and in the rest of his life, it is to be noted that another major African American critic of black letters regards *Cane* as "an artistic fusion . . . of Christian myth and elements of the African and Afro-American experience," and goes on to treat this *fusion* of cultural forms as that which, together with its usage of black music, "establishes the book as a unique contribution to the tradition of the Afro-American novel."[102] Is "blackness" a separate and independent element that must be resurrected from its hiddenness under an erasure, or is it the emergent product of an intercultural chiaroscuro fusion?

Fusion, it is to be noted, a term usually associated with assimilation, acculturation, and amalgamation, has figured occasionally—and always significantly—in anthropological as well as cultural approaches to African American life. Thus, in one of his early researches in physical anthropology, Melville Herskovitz, the ethnologist most well known for his lifelong insistence—over the vigorous objections of black sociologist E. Franklin Frazier[103]—that features of African culture survived both slavery and emancipation and continued, sometimes in syncretic form, to play a part in the everyday lives of ordinary black Americans,[104] also claimed that the people he wished to designate as "the American Negro" were a uniquely interbred descent group, having been procreated over several generations marked by a significant amount of black and white amalgamation.[105] Indeed, it was just such a fusion that Jean Toomer invoked as justification for his own claim to be an "American": "Racially, [he observed in 1922], I seem to have (who knows for sure) seven blood mixtures: French, Dutch, Welsh, Negro, German, Jewish, and Indian. Because of these my position in America has been a curious one. I have lived equally amid the two race groups. Now white, now colored. From my own point of view I am naturally and inevitably an American. I have strived for a spiritual fusion analogous to the fact of racial intermingling."[106] However, Toomer discovered that his attempt to let the several bloods that flowed through his spiritual veins "function as complements . . . [and] live in harmony" was difficult if not impossible to accomplish as a way of life. His visit to Georgia and his decision to give vent to his artistic expression while living and working among the black peasantry of that area "pulled me deeper and deeper into the Negro group . . . And a deep part of my nature, a part that I had repressed, sprang suddenly to life and responded to them."[107] It is this deep part—what, perhaps, Robert E. Park would have assigned to "temperament," a biosocial element which he designated as the source for the distinctiveness that made for each race's expressive uniqueness[108]—that it seems Gates would have us resurrect as the basis of Toomer's "blackness," and that others (including myself) might designate as the ineffable psychocultural basis of the symbolic estate of an acculturated ethnicity.[109]

Black "Absence" and White "Presence": The Postmodern Thesis of Toni Morrison

There is, however, another way to read Toomer's and Crevecoeur's Americanist credo, one that bids fair to collapse the polarity of pluralism and assimilation in a dialectical fusion wherein blackness becomes the trace as well as the resource for whiteness. The possibility that blackness might be the color-culture element of whiteness *sous rature*—the thing "absent" that defines the "thingness" of the white "present"—has been suggested recently by the African American novelist and critic Toni Morrison.[110] In Morrison's trenchant deconstruction of the writings of such canonical white American writers as Edgar Allan Poe, she uncovers the trace, or "shadow," as she calls it, of blackness that allows figures with "skin 'the perfect whiteness of snow'" to appear. "Because [such figures] . . . appear almost always in conjunction with representations of black or Africanist people who are dead, impotent, or under complete control," Morrison observes, "these images of blinding whiteness seem to function as both antidote for and meditation on the shadow that is companion to this whiteness—a dark and abiding presence that moves the hearts and texts of American literature with fear and longing."[111]

Morrison, drawing upon Bernard Bailyn's historical researches on the origins of the American people,[112] in effect, and without any acknowledgment that she is engaged in this kind of deconstructionism, takes up one of the two meanings contained in Derrida's major concept, *différance*, that is, "to defer."[113] In her study, she emphasizes how, for the original white Anglo-Saxon settlers of America, the new society they were forging seemed to promise them the opportunity to realize four desiderata unavailable to them in the Old World—"autonomy, authority, newness and difference, [and] absolute power." To the extent that these promises were realizable, each was "shaped by, activated by a complex awareness and employment of a constituted Africanism . . . that provided the staging ground and arena for the elaboration of the quintessential American identity."[114] Nevertheless, these promises form the not fully requited "romance" of both white American life and literature, an anguishing affair that on the one hand requires the permanent abjection of blacks—the group without whose subjection the promises could not be fulfilled—but, on the other, denies the reality of its embedded racism. "Eventually," Morrison observes, the sullied ideal of American "individualism fuses with the prototype of Americans as solitary, alienated, and malcontent."

There are, in fact, two separate deferrals implicit in Morrison's deconstructive project: The first, having to do with the unmeasured and uncalculable *durée* that marks the epoch during which the promise of autonomy, authority, novelty, and absolute power to whites in America is not yet consummated, is characterized by the haunting shadow of blackness that serves as a subliminal trace upon the otherwise bright white cultural escutcheon: "For the settlers and for American writers generally, this Africanist other became the means of thinking about body, mind, chaos, kindness, and love; provided the occasion for exercises in the absence of restraint, the presence of restraint, the contemplation of freedom and of aggression; permitted opportunities for the exploration of ethics and morality, for meeting the obligations of the social contract, for bearing the cross of religion and following out the ramifications of power." The African trace—the absence that makes the American whiteness possible as a presence—constitutes the essence of what distinguished America from Europe, the New World from the Old: "What was distinctive in the New was, first of all, its claim to freedom and, second, the presence of the unfree within the heart of the democratic experiment."

However, although Morrison does not make as much of it as she might, there is a second deferral, one that not only elaborates upon and confounds the first, but also permits us to return to Gates's deconstruction of Toomer's life and work and to perform upon it a deferential deconstruction of our own making.

To Differ or to Defer? That Is the Question

Let us first, however, proceed to unpack Derrida's second meaning of *différance*. That term incorporates two significations—"to differ" and "to defer." Here we are concerned with the latter signification—the one that, according to Derrida, "makes the movement of signification possible only if each element that is said to be 'present,' appearing on the stage of presence, is related to something other than itself *but retains the mark of a past element and already lets itself be hollowed out by the mark of its relation to a future element.*"[115] This sense of *différance*, then, evokes the dynamic tension of any present element as it stops, as it were, while still in motion along a time track.[116] It is this temporal but potentially protean sense that Morrison attaches to the term "American." "Deep within the word 'American,' [she writes], is its association with race. To identify someone as a South African is to say very little; we need the adjective 'white' or 'black' or 'colored' to make our meaning clear. In this country it is quite the reverse. American means white, and Africanist people struggle to make the term applicable to themselves with ethnicity and hyphen after hyphen after hyphen."[117] If, to overcome this exclusionary sense of "American," we take note of and attach to the term American, the hope, or in this sense, the deferral, expressed by Charles Johnson that the prehistory of Afro-American literature will evolve into a future history in which neither black nor white but only American writers and literature is recognized; or the wish made recently by the African American historian Joel Williamson that in the twenty-first century the offspring of racially mixed marriages will cease to be designated as mulattos or assigned to the racial status of the lower-caste parent and instead become "the first fully evolved, smoothly functioning model of a people who have transcended both an exclusive whiteness and an exclusive blackness and [have] moved into a world in which they accept and value themselves for themselves alone . . . ,"[118] we shall have completed the project of a fully realized *différance* only to find that our efforts place the discovery of a true difference in blackness as a moment of deferral of its ultimate *telos*—the forging of a newly integrated people in a newly emergent nonracial society and culture.

Thus, if we perform a deconstruction on top of Gates's deconstruction of Jean Toomer's belief that though he could not "fix" the matter for others, he, like Crevecoeur 138 years earlier, could sense and see the emergence of a new raceless humankind in America, his recognition of the blackness in his ancestry and his agonizingly qualified erasure of the blackness in himself was not merely an attempt to notice and cover up a difference, but also a promissory deferral, a putting off until a later time what would be the deracinated telos of America. Our second deconstruction of the blackness in Toomer's life and work yields the exposure of but a moment in a long unfolding but unidirectional history of white and black Americans, a moment between the past assertion of Pinchback's Negro identity and the future coming to be of Toomer's and others' nonracial sensibility of being American. Unreserved assimilation, acculturation, and amalgamation thence become the final outcome of America's pluralistic dynamic.

Conclusion: Assimilation-Pluralism—From *"Différance"* to *"Allusion"*

The discourse on assimilation and pluralism takes a new turn in postmodernist thought. In conventional and modernist discourses—which, it should be noted, are discourses of the sociological discipline, and therefore like other discourses, are worthy candidates for deconstructive analysis[119]—the concepts are typically treated as polarities pointing up two dichotomous metaphors of social structure—respectively, "the melting pot" and the "mosaic." Moreover, each metaphor stands for an ideal toward which a modern society might move at a pace determined by the motility of its norm-engaging institutions. Hence each idealized outcome is regarded as uncompleted in every presentist analysis of the issue.

The metaphoric language in which these ideals are usually expressed tends to conflate ethnic with racial aspects of the problem, confound attempts at exact depiction of the societal structure toward which each is directed, and cover over the forms of coercion and power that make each effective. Hence, the claim that blacks, Hispanics, Asians, and other persons are assimilating in American society, or that they ought to be, must confront the twin issues of the well-established ethnoracial pluralism that exists "beyond the melting pot,"[120] and the hidden hand of white Anglo-Saxon Protestant power that informs and modifies the assimilative process.

The "crucial thing about the melting pot," observed Charles Silberman in 1964, "was that it did not happen."[121] Although a number of sociocultural changes transformed the several peoples living in America so much that their immigrant forebears would not recognize them as dedicated conservers of a mummified Old World culture, Silberman insisted that "the ethnic groups are not just a political anachronism . . . The WASPs . . . , the Irish Americans, the Italian Americans, the Jewish Americans . . . differ from each other in essential ways." Regarding each of these ethnically distinct peoples as equally serviceable models of emulation for would-be assimilators, Silberman poses a question: "[I]f Negroes are to assimilate, if they are to integrate with the white American, . . . with *which* white American [people are they to accomplish this feat]?" The racial epithet "white" breaks down into its diverse ethnic constituencies. "For in truth," Silberman concludes, "there is no 'white American'; there are only white Americans."

However, Silberman's conventional critique of assimilation does not reach the political dimension of the issue. It is a cardinal point of postmodernist criticism to perceive culture and the discourses and debates on culture as mediations of power relations. In this sense, it is necessary to see how the assimilationist discourse both privileges WASP culture and hides the process whereby that privilege is hegemonically encoded.[122] A fine elucidation, a virtual deconstruction of the latter process, has been presented by Roxana Robinson in an essay reviewing a book of Louis Auchincloss's short stories:

> White Anglo-Saxon Protestants [Robinson writes], have created an insular and powerful world, and have maintained it by means of an ingenious sociological mechanism. Ethnic outsiders could succeed as themselves in politics and finance, but to succeed in society they had to abandon ethnic outsiderness. Society was tightly and exclusively controlled by WASPs, who permitted little cultural deviation. This meant these newcomers did not assert their ethnic individuality but instead tried for assimilation. Conformity to the prevailing social ethic and marriage into Protestant families meant that other ethnic identities dissipated within a generation or so.[123]

The postmodern project undertaken by such black critics as Henry Louis Gates Jr. and his followers does much to expose the privileged status of the WASP text on assimilation, but it does not identify nor does it locate the source of social justice in the society to come, that is, the postmodern society. How societal coordination will occur in a society in which all texts are disprivileged, and no particular ethnoracial group exercises ethnoracial control, is unanswered. Paradoxically, however, an answer is provided by the ideal society projected in modernist assimilation theory—Should unreserved assimilation, acculturation, and amalgamation take place in a market-oriented, industrial society, the normative order would reside in racially integrated classes, and in the policies that accorded with the interests of the oligarchy of power and privilege that the dominant classes had organized. For Marxists, and even for those like Robert E. Park who did not adhere either to the Marxist agenda or to its theory of history, the outcome of ethnoracial assimilation would inaugurate a new conflict, the class struggle.[124]

However, the essential elements of postmodern cultural analysis go beyond these issues, transcending the modernist discourses on both power and culture as they are deconstructing them. Postmodernism overcomes the dichotomies central to Western modernism by imposing *différance* as an intrusion upon them. For the discourse on assimilation-pluralism, this promises not only an effort at extracting ethnoracial diversity from its stigmatizing and disvaluing hierarchicalization under the modernist regime of particularistically valorized and selectively privileged WASPishness, but also, and only seemingly paradoxically, a refiguration of the metaphorized ideals of both Crevecoeur's and Toomer's assimilationism and Kallen's and Bourne's pluralism as *deferrals*, that is, as desiderata put off to a future not yet realized.

However, postmodernism does even more. Its critique is epistemologically ecumenical but distributed over the geo-intellectual map according to the particular ideational locus of each privileged perspective. Thus, Kwame Anthony Appiah observes: "In philosophy, postmodernism is the rejection of the mainstream consensus from Descartes through Kant to logical positivism ... The modernity that is opposed here can thus be Cartesian (in France), Kantian (in Germany), and logical positivist (in America) ... In political theory, ... postmodernism is the rejection of the monism of Big-M Marxist (though not of the newer little-m marxist) and liberal conceptions of justice ... [E]very perspective [is] essentially contestable from other perspectives."[125] If we take seriously the utter contestability of perspectives, we may see how the dichotomy of assimilation-pluralism—and of each's respective deferrals—may be dis- and then reintegrated in the acidic solvent of what the classical Italian philologist Gian Biagio Conte calls an *allusion.* An allusion is "a poetic dimension . . . created by the simultaneous presence of two different realities whose competition with one another produces a single more complex reality."[126] That single more complex reality is America's not yet fully realized civil society, a society perhaps already beyond the modernist's liberal conception of ethnoracial justice, but, still, a society whose ultimate ethnoracial dimensions are in a problematic state of conflicted deferral.

CHAPTER EIGHT

Anhedonia: Gender and the Decline of Emotions in American Film, 1930–1988

"What does a dame like you want with a guy like me?"
Burt Lancaster to Barbara Stanwyck, Sorry, Wrong Number

Introduction

Movies provide a situs for depicting all five of the concerns that Martin J. Malone holds are necessary for a theory of emotional communication.[1] Moreover, movies—especially American movies—are ideally suited to the cinematic presentation of emotional life because so often they concern themselves with primary relationships, the intimate aspects of life, and with the feelings and sentiments that are said to be appropriate to the vicissitudes of that life. Yet over the last half century, movies have set ideological, moral, and religious limits to emotional expression. Hollywood's films have treated the display and inhibition of emotions as part of an unfolding disenchantment of the idealization of gender, and, in the process, have exposed the sentiments supposed to surround the relations of men to women as affective frauds and cathectic systems of bad faith.

Religious Ethics and Emotional Expression

Anhedonia is a technical term among psychoanalysts that refers to a supposedly pathological condition wherein an individual is unable to experience pleasure. However, it is in fact the case that the writer-director-actor Woody Allen had considered entitling his film *Annie Hall* (1977) anhedonia,[2] and that he meant the rejected title to indicate modern, urban humankind's helplessness in the face of unsatisfied love. unstoppable aging, and the undeniability of death. Woody Allen's self-portrait as Everyman, derived from the Jewish "schlemiel" tradition,[3] is a creature of feeling—indeed, so much feeling as to give a semblance of truth to American Freudian A. A. Brill's remarkable statement in 1918: "From a very large clinical experience I can state unequivocally that . . . the Jew is disproportionately neurotic . . . [A]lthough the Jew is not disproportionately predisposed to insanity in the strict sense, he is more nervous than the non-Jew."[4] Maurice Yacowar, a biographer-critic of Allen, seems to concur with the thrust of Brill's estimate, holding that the self that remains after Woody Allen has stripped away "the inapt and inept images" presented in the latter's 1972 comedy, *Everything You Always Wanted to Know about Sex* (*but were afraid to ask)*, "is the core of the Allen persona—a nervous Everyman terrified by the prospect of life."[5] Brill had concluded that the "Jew is of a more sensitive makeup and hence adjustment to the environment is more difficult for him."[6] But Allen, who in several films has contrasted Jewish with Gentile life in America—and, who, in *Hannah and Her Sisters* (1986), comically permitted his character to attempt conversion to Christianity by switching to Wonder Bread and mayonnaise—knows differently. Although the WASPs of Woody Allen's films exhibit coolness and pride themselves on self-possession, there is, underneath these shibboleths of adjustment and command, a dark and pathological romance with death—a theme Allen directly presented in the terrifying suicidal admissions of Annie Hall's seemingly sound and self-assured brother—Christopher Walken, who would go on to play a supremely psychotic master sergeant to Neil Simon's autobiographical Jewish recruit in *Biloxi Blues* (1987)*—as he and Allen drive back to New York.

---

*Author's note to this edition: Walken went on to essay the role of "Max Shreck," a corrupt businessman-villain in Tim Burton's film *Batman Returns* (1992). "Max Shreck" seems to have been derived from Max Schreck (1879–1936), the actor whose portrayal of *Nosferatu* in F. W. Murnau's eponymous film (1922) is said to betray anti-Jewish sentiments and to personify an identification of the Jew with the vampire. The possibility of latent anti-Semitism in *Batman Returns* was sufficiently great to evoke publication of an op-ed piece in the *New York Times* (Rebecca Roiphe and Daniel Cooper, "Batman and the Jewish Question," *The New York Times*, July 2, 1992, p. A13 and further correspondence a few weeks later, *The New York Times*, July 20, 1992, p. A10.) In terms of the theses presented in the present study, Batman personifies the character of a postmodern Theseus suffering from acute anhedonia. In the three eponymous films (*Batman* [1989], *Batman Returns* [1992], and *Batman Forever* [1995]), he is a neurotic, obsessed with a self-imposed mission

Brill's thesis about the disproportionate amount of Jewish neurosis in America rests ultimately upon his belief that Jews "suffer from too many attachments of the past; . . . are victims of circumstances, and . . . are neurotic as a result of the conflicts between the taboos of the past and the demands of the present."[7] However, Christians, especially Protestants, can also be shown to be, at the very least, potential sufferers from their religion's Calvinistic impositions on the free play of feeling, the restrictions on the expression of eros, and the anxieties arising from limiting displays of lust, anger, envy, and pride. Indeed, in the repression and reallocation of sentiments reflecting these four of the seven deadly sins are to be found the cultural foundations of anhedonia that Woody Allen had perceived and that a half century of Hollywood cinema has revealed.

Although Brill and subsequent commentators on Jewish neuroses seemed not to notice, Protestantism has provided its practitioners, as well

---

of ridding a large city of its psychotic predators. Unable to commit to heterosexual love, romance, or marriage, he is, in the comic book version that predated the films, involved "in a permanent relation to his [adolescent] male counterpart, Robin, but never forms an abiding liaison with a woman." (Robert Jewett and John Shelton Lawrence, *The American Monomyth* [Garden City, N.Y.: Anchor Press/Doubleday, 1977], p. 63.) The man-boy relationship of Batman and Robin resulted in a charge of illicit idealized homosexuality being lodged against them (Frederic Wertham, *The Seduction of the Innocent* [New York: Holt, Rinehart, and Winston, 1953], p. 191) as well as a fierce and angry denial by comic historian and political cartoonist, Jules Feiffer (*The Great Comic Book Heroes* [New York: Dial Press, 1965], pp. 43-44): "Batman and Robin were no more or less queer than were their youngish readers . . . In our society it is not only homosexuals who don't like women. Almost no one does . . . Mass entertainment being engineered by men, it was natural that a primary target be women: who were fighting harder for their rights, evening the score, unsettling the traditional balance between the sexes . . . They were clearly the enemy." In the overtly anhedonic representations of Batman and his enemies in current films and comics, both represent the response to postmodern chaos that afflicts white men who feel they have lost their once unchallenged hegemonic powers: "Two Face is identical to Batman in that he's controlled by savage urges, which he keeps in check, in his case, with the flip of a coin. He's very much like Batman. The Joker is not so much a Doppelgänger as an antithesis, a force for chaos. Batman imposes his order on the world; he is an absolute control freak. The Joker is Batman's most maddening opponent. He represents the chaos Batman despises, the chaos that killed his parents . . . The Joker actually wears lipstick. He calls Batman 'Darling' . . . Batman isn't gay. His sexual urges are so drastically sublimated into crime-fighting that there's no *room* for any other emotional activity . . . He'd be *much* healthier if he were gay." (Christopher Sharrett, "Batman and the Twilight of the Idols: An Interview with Frank Miller," in *The Many Lives of Batman: Critical Approaches to a Superhero and His Media,* ed. Roberta E. Pearson and William Uricchio [New York: Routledge, 1991], pp. 36-38. See also James B. Twitchell, *Preposterous Violence: Fables of Aggression in Modern Culture* [New York: Oxford University Press, 1989], pp. 129-220).

as those who seek a worldly transvaluation of Protestant values, with a set of severe restrictions on emotional expression. Max Weber pointed to the inhibiting effects that the spread of ascetic Protestantism would have on both the value and expression of pleasure. In Christian thought, Weber observed, pleasure had come to be associated with worldly activities. The truly faithful Protestants would have to become inner-worldly ascetics, to flee from the bodily joys that would come from unalloyed surrender to sensuality and hedonism, and to engage unceasingly in a self-monitoring surveillance of their own affectivity. Saintliness would have to become the constant catechism of everyday life. Eudaemonic gratifications, ever-present temptations and threats to virtue, would be respecified as every person's evil companions: those that must be resisted. As Weber summed up the matter: "From the point of view of the basic values of asceticism, the world as a whole continues to constitute a *massa perditionis*." And, as Weber went on to emphasize, "[A]ny excess of emotional feeling for one's fellow man is prohibited [by Protestant moral guidance] as being a deification of the creaturely, which denies the unique value of the divine gift of grace . . ." Weber concluded that the "person who lives as a worldly ascetic is a rationalist, not only in the sense that he rationally systematizes his own personal patterning of life, but also in his rejection of everything that is ethically irrational, esthetic, or dependent on his own emotional reactions to the world and its institutions."[8] From the Protestant perspective described by Weber, giving way to sensual pleasures and the feelings associated with them becomes in effect a willing activation of sin, while anhedonia is emancipated from its locus in pathology and enhanced as an expression of a divine calling—the pious inner state that ought to accompany upright conduct and invisible secular sainthood.

American filmmakers, at first grudgingly, later actively, incorporated these aspects of the Protestant ethic into the content of their movies. From the beginning suspected of being subversive of American middle-class morality—with which Protestantism's value system came to be associated—movies were subjected to police surveillance, censorious religious and civil attacks, and legal challenges. Although the early leaders of the American film industry were parvenu outsiders, largely immigrant and Jewish in background, they soon came to see the patriotic, cultural, and commercial advantages of keeping films in line with the norms of what passed for public—that is, Protestant and Catholic, white and Anglo-Saxon—decency.[9] First in the National Board of Review (1908), then with the Hays Office (1920), next the Motion Pictures Production Code (1930), and most recently the age-graded Code of Self-Regulation (1968), the film industry sought not only to stave off external censorship and public regulation, but also to ingratiate itself with the movie-consuming public. The Motion Pictures Production Code, which was operative for thirty-six years, virtually enacted the hostility to the dramatic presentation of eudaemonist passions that were called for by both Protestantism and Catholicism. As Mortimer J. Adler observed in 1937, "This charge [that the movies are inescapably immoral] is the ancient Christian objection to the theatre as essentially obscene: it intensifies the carnal concupiscence which is a heavy burden of potential sin in man's corrupt nature."[10] The makers of movies could not count on any widespread agreement with the perspective on the matter offered one year earlier by the distinguished stage and screen actor Edward G. Robinson: "In my opinion, neither the movies nor the press can be held responsible for the widespread of lawlessness and the laxity of morals." Robinson wished that "our would-be censors were better sociologists . . . [so that they would become] more concerned with truth than with morals . . . [and could give] us a correct diagnosis of the symptoms . . ."[11]

The Motion Pictures Production Code[12] treated the supposed stimuli to immorality and vice that movies presented: it restricted the expression of sensuality and extolled the virtues of "pure love," lawful marriage, and the harmonious and loving family. It forbade positive dramatizations of evil; crime; illicit, homosexual, or pornographic sex; and the pictorializing of methods appropriate to the effective accomplishment of murder, theft, robbery, arson, and smuggling. It prohibited altogether any presentation of the illegal traffic in drugs. However, it was sex, sensuality, passion, and eros that most aroused the censoriousness of the Production Code. "*Pure love*, the love of a man for a woman permitted by the law of God and man is the rightful subject of plots," the Code admonished; but, it warned, "the passion arising from this love is not the subject for plots." Moreover, "*impure love*, the love of man and woman forbidden by human and divine law, must be presented in such a way that (a) It is clearly known by the audience to be wrong; (b) Its presentation does not excite sexual reactions, mental or physical, in an ordinary audience; (c) It is not treated as a matter for comedy." The makers of the Production Code were worried most about the cinematic excitation of sensuous affectivity: "Many scenes," they concluded, "cannot be presented without arousing dangerous emotions on the part of the immature, the young or the criminal classes." Among the prohibited scenes were "Dances with movements of the breasts, excessive body movement while the feet remain stationary . . . [and] so-called 'belly dances'. . . [all of which] are immoral, obscene, and hence altogether wrong." In addition, filmmakers were warned not to depict "Brothels and houses of ill-fame ... [that] suggest to the average person at once sex, sin, or ... excite an unwholesome and morbid curiosity in the minds of youth" or "Excessive and lustful kissing, lustful embraces, suggestive postures and gestures ...". "Seduction or rape ... should never be more than suggested, ... and [when allowed is] ... never [to be] the proper subject for comedy." Moreover, "Sex perversion or any inference to it is forbidden"; "White slavery shall not be treated"; and "Miscegenation (sex relationship between the white and black races) is forbidden." By adhering to the code, the moviemakers in effect promised to ensure that audiences would not become too emotionally aroused by filmic presentations of feelings, to extoll the virtues of instrumental rationalism, and to restrict severely, if not banish, altogether evocations of the passions that were religiously proscribed. Anhedonia had been made into a filmic ideal.

Gender Myths and the Discipline of the Emotions

Restricted by the limitations of the production code, Hollywood films nevertheless presented a subtext of culturally defined emotional expression. In effect, the passions associated with eros and sensuality were sublimated to facilitate cinematic support for instrumental rationality, individual achievement, and patriotic endeavor. The basic theme around which thousands of plots might be conceived was that later celebrated by Talcott Parsons as the norm appropriate to the American social system.[13] Parsons's sociology, as I have argued elsewhere,[14] is a secularized iconography of Protestant ideals, holding that the United States is a dynamically equilibrating system organized around the interplay of universalism, achievement, diffuseness, and affective neutrality. With respect to what Weber called the *Affektual*, the American social system calls for restriction and sublimation—specifically, eros is to be channeled, facilitating a romantic heterosexual quest for a homogamous mate, the formation of a nuclear household within a bilineal, neolocal kinship complex, and the linkage of the husband-father to the economy as a devoted family breadwinner. Emotions are to be harnessed to the achievement orientation, and affect is to be placed in service to the higher ideals of instrumental rationality. Although the "most *direct* path to gratification in an organized action system is through expressive orientations ...," Parsons observes, "relative to the expressive, both the instrumental and the moral modes of orientation impose renunciations or discipline."[15]

The cinematic translation of the normative pattern associated with the universalistic-achievement system is best perceived structurally—that is, in terms of the foundation myth from which it proceeds. In this sense, the mythos is, first and foremost, gender-specific. For women, Hollywood cinema has explored and exploited the mythopoetic Ariadne; for men, Theseus. In the hermeneutic entailed in Hollywood's unfolding of these intertwined myths will be found the disenchantment of their ideals, the devolution of their virtues, and the devaluation of their interrelated disciplinings of affectivity. Ultimately the basis for anhedonia as an ubiquitous gnawing anxiety will be made clear.

The Female Principle: Ariadne

In their most prominent portrayals, Hollywood's women are armed with Ariadne's purpose: to chasten adventurous, misanthropic, anxiety-ridden, or marginal men; to channel their promiscuous hedonism toward monogamy; to cheer them out of their misogyny; and to check their men's flights from their twin responsibilities: family support and civilizational progress. Cinematic heroines accomplish these purposes by employing the compelling power of their love to wind their men into his socially proper place—to repair their men's social, psychic, self- or war-inflicted wounds. Moreover, they exploit the pressures of heterosexual passion to both undermine all-male camaraderie and subvert any latent homoerotic feelings that bind the male hero to his buddy. The movies' men, who in emotional but antagonistic cooperation with these women personify many of the mythopoetic elements of the Attic adventurer Theseus, are at first apprehensive about these heroines, point to their dangerous, even magical powers to overwhelm their resistance, and seek escape into what the films show to be unfulfilling arenas of eudaemonic action or dionysian pleasure, but ultimately (in most cases) they succumb to the domesticated alternative to the womanly siren song: marriage, home, family, and a steady job.

The War Film

America's entrance into World War II posed a new problem for the protectors of the nation: how men, socially and economically dislocated by the Great Depression, distrustful of their government's war aims, and deprived for a decade of the advantages promised to those who strive in behalf of occupational achievement and status advancement, might eagerly

take up arms against the enemy. After war had been declared, Talcott
Parsons worried over his belief that the solid foundations for such patriotic
endeavor had not been sunk deeply enough in the national consciousness
and passed on his suggestions for morale-building to the government.[16]
The Roosevelt administration, already concerned on the matter, did not
wait for the Harvard sociologist; it established an advisory censor over
Hollywood's films, seeking to ensure that public morale would remain high
and that the sacrifices called for at home and abroad would be accepted
with grace and efficacy.[17] Hollywood responded to the exigencies of war.
Wartime films presented women not as a force compelling dyadic withdrawal,[18] blissful romance, or the immediate domestication of unmarried
men, but rather as secret agents of national purpose. In these movies the
male hero is all too often introduced as a disillusioned misanthrope (e.g.,
Humphrey Bogart in *Casablanca* [1941]; Alan Ladd in *China* [1943]); a self-
centered and greedy criminal (e.g., Cary Grant in *Mr. Lucky* [1943]) or a
weak, effete, and immature boy (Robert Walker in *Since You Went Away*
[1944]). Whatever the matter, these men are all patriotically reborn and
propelled into combat by a woman's love.

The heroic women of wartime movies sublimate their personal needs
and suppress the anxieties that trouble their interior lives—all in the name
of the war effort. They perform their patriotic duties not only by working
in shipyards, (Ginger Rogers in *Tender Comrade* [1943]); rolling bandages
in Red Cross hospitals (Jennifer Jones in *Since You Went Away*); directing
charities devoted to war relief (Laraine Day in *Mr. Lucky*); leading Chinese
war orphans to a safe haven in the heartless world of Japanese aggression
(Loretta Young in *China*); serving in the women's auxiliary armed forces
(Joan Leslie in *This is the Army* [1943]), but also and more significantly by
utilizing their patient and virtuous love to rekindle their men's flagging love
of country (*China*), send their men off to what turns out to be their untimely
deaths (*Since You Went Away*), or sacrifice a sensuous affair of the heart to
the larger demands of the war (*Casablanca*).

Such heroines of World War II films do not foresee any anhedonic
consequences to their patriotic endeavors. Indeed, in those prewar didactic films, (e.g., *Only Angels Have Wings* [1939]) where such sensuous women
as could be portrayed by Jean Arthur and Rita Hayworth learn through
harsh experience that they must not employ their charms to interrupt the
serious efforts and all-male bondings that are necessary for effective team-
work and combat solidarity, noninstrumental passion is treated as an unwarranted intrusion, virtually a sabotage of what the national security demands.

By the end of the war, Hollywood makes clear, these women have learned their lesson: In *Tender Comrade,* Ginger Rogers takes "the news of her husband's death with a soldierly stoicism . . . [and understands that] his death, however painful to her, was necessary for a better world."[19]

The Postwar Film

In wartime films, women have a moral and patriotic duty to send men off to war. But with war's end, it becomes clear that the final scene of farewell between the virtuous "girl" and her now combat-inspired lover was penultimate. When the war is over, these films implied, she will be waiting for him to return, expecting him to marry her, raise a family, and work at a useful and promising job; or, if they have married before he went into combat, to resume his husbandly and fatherly duties and return wholeheartedly to the demands and obligations of civilian life. Implicit in the films made between 1941 and 1945 is the idea that patriotic fervor is only temporary, "for the duration" of the war but not beyond it. However, as the post–World War II films only hinted, but post-Korean and post-Vietnam films made clear, for women to encourage bored, disillusioned, cynical, or frightened men to become personally committed and ideologically attuned to the war and to give them the incentive to march excitedly off to fight are potentially dangerous to postwar domesticity and peacetime society. Ariadne's thread might break before it can wind her lover home, where the heart is. In films made after the Korean War (e.g., *War Hunt* [1962]) and the Vietnam War (e.g., *Apocalypse Now* [1979]; *First Blood* [1982]), it is suggested that at least some men might refuse to come back to ordinary life, reject the blandishments of home, wife, and family, and resist the summons to adjust to the routines of a workaday world. Having exchanged the boring but anxious imperatives of the civilian achievement syndrome for the thrilling adventures of life-and-death combat; having renounced the inauthentic collegiality that substitutes for friendship in the career world for the real comradeship of the all-male society of soldiers; or having felt the atavistic arousal that military atrocities and the bloody scenes of battle evoke; some cinematically battle-scarred veterans seem to have been utterly and fundamentally transformed. The war and its homefront female supporters have inadvertently rekindled a primitive but powerful wanderlust in men (Marlon Brando in *Apocalypse Now*; Sylvester Stallone in *First Blood*), a wish to be free from both entangling alliances with women and the social compact (John Saxon in *War Hunt*). For some men, the post-Vietnam *Rambo* films seem to argue, war has resuscitated the very same irresponsible adventurousness that led the mythic slayer of the Minotaur, Theseus, first to abandon the cloyingly lovesick Ariadne at the island of Naxos and then to take up a lifetime of rash and male-bonded daredeviltry.

To reestablish the efficaciousness of the original pull of Ariadne's thread toward domesticity, post–World War II films respecified the instrumental usages and aims of female affection and womanly sensuality. It again fell to women to serve surreptitiously as agents of national, cultural, and socioeconomic purpose. The postwar Ariadne, acquiescing to those revived norms of peacetime America that had been shelved for the duration, would relegate herself to the seemingly insignificant role of fiancée, housewife, or mother. But while masquerading as persons who would be less able than men to manage the postwar economy and polity, and, in the process inspiring recently demobilized servicemen to become strong husbands, willing fathers, and ambitious members of the blue- or white-collar workforce, these new heroines benevolently exploit their sexual power and ever-patient influence to obtain uxoricentric authority over their menfolk. In effect, the first decade of postwar films argued that good women might *need* love in order to be fulfilled, but they could and would *use* love to ensure that their family in particular and American society in general got competent and responsible male support.

Both wartime films depicting working women and postwar films of the late 1940s and early 1950s accomplished their reconstruction of the proper use of emotions related to heterosexuality by showing that women who insisted on pursuing professional careers rather than matrifocal homemaking were either hurting their husbands' chances in the same or a related line of work (Doris Day in *I'll See You in My Dreams* [1951]); suffering from a latent lesbian or male-castrating pathology that could only ruin their own and their children's lives (Joan Crawford in *Mildred Pierce* [1945]; Rosalind Russell in *Take a Letter, Darling* [1942]; Ginger Rogers in *Lady in the Dark* [1944]); or were well-intentioned but affectively misguided holders of important positions that would be better tended by those men whom they had rescued from self-destructive neuroses, (Ingrid Bergman in Alfred Hitchcock's thriller *Spellbound* [1945]). Women were warned against open displays of economic and social independence. Fredric March put it succinctly in *The Best Years of Our Lives* (1946). After hearing how much his bright and cheerful wife, Milly (Myrna Loy), enjoyed being both breadwinner and homemaker and listening to his happy and untroubled teenage daughter, Peggy (Teresa Wright), add, "You don't have to worry about us Dad, we can handle the problems," he tells his wartime buddy (Dana Andrews) that coming home "feels like I was going in to hit a beach."

If the heroic Ariadne of the postwar era had to surrender her career ambitions in order to "make room for daddy," she also had to weave a skein of therapeutic help and loving support around those men who resisted readjustment to the workaday world of peacetime, were too wounded to cooperate, or too alienated to be of much service to economy, society, or family. In the screenplays of seven films released in 1945 and 1946—*Love Letters, State Fair, Those Endearing Young Charms, Adventure, Lost Weekend, Spellbound,* and *Pride of the Marines*—the male hero resists the ethically sanctioned enticements of marriage, love, and family, or the financial rewards of remunerative work, or both, because at bottom he suspects that the sociocultural promise that intertwines a happy marriage with a good job and a lifelong career is a powerful institutionalization of bad faith. In each film, however, love of a patient and understanding woman leads the man away from his feelings of normative estrangement and back into the conventional world of work and family. As late as 1959, in *Gidget,* Sandra Dee's mother explains that the family slogan is "To be a real woman is to bring out the best in a man," and the eponymous heroine, outwardly a pigtailed, nubile, naive nymphet, unworldly and uneducated, and seemingly interested only in a round of fun with the beach boys, proves herself to be a true chip off the family block, guiding her disillusioned older boyfriend (Cliff Robertson) away from an aimless life of surfing and back to his former profession as an airline pilot.

In some of these films, the man's resistance to his woman and his prospects are related to diagnosed infirmities—John Garfield's blindness in *Pride of the Marines;* Ray Milland's alcohol-related delirium tremens in *Lost Weekend*; Gregory Peck's guilt-ridden neurosis in *Spellbound*—and in others to unconscious apprehensions about his own masculinity or mental soundness—Robert Young in *Those Endearing Young Charms;* Dana Andrews in *State Fair;* Joseph Cotten in *Love Letters;* Clark Gable in *Adventure.* But in the course of his cinematic "growth," each learns that his resistance to settling down with a good woman and a worthwhile job arises out of an unacceptable-because-unmasculine evasion—doubt about whether he can measure up to what America expects of every man worthy of that appellation. The patient and loving woman almost always triumphs over her man's deep-seated troubles.

The Male Principle: Theseus

Theseus, the Attic hero, rejected both the responsibilities of marriage and the solace of settling down. In their place he chose a life of danger, wanderings, lustful encounters, and the society of equally daring male adventurers. Even when, after many years of adventure, he was rescued from a ten-year imprisonment in Hades, where he had been chained to a rock from which he could watch helplessly as his dearest comrade-in-arms, Pirithous, turned forever on the constantly revolving wheel of Ixion, Theseus continued a lustful, rash, and trouble-filled life. Ultimately, his own people turned against him, exiling him to the lonely island of Scyros, from which, having angered King Lycomedes, Theseus was hurled to his death. Years later, his heroics having been recalled, his body was brought back to Athens where the Acropolis was built in his honor, and he was worshiped as a demigod.

More openly in the 1920s and 1930s, but less obviously in the 1940s, Hollywood films lauded a Theseusian role model for heroic men. Over and over films suggested that the true traits of masculinity are expressed, forged, and tested when men essay the roles of wanderers, adventurers, or marginal misfits. As lumpen proletarians, agents of imperial advance, less than filial sons, disillusioned lovers, or deracinated emigrants from civilization, these makers of masculinity act alone, in the company of other like-minded men, or with a single male companion who is equally dedicated to the unsettled and unmarried life. Neither society nor domesticity holds attraction to these men; indeed, towns, cities, and an established homestead, and the routines associated with them seem to frighten such heroes more than the bandits, spies, enemy troops, malefactors of wealth, giant beasts, deadly microbes, or invaders from outer space that they must overcome. Indeed, it sometimes appears that movie-made heroes prefer cinema's modern variants of the lawless lair of the Minotaur to the safe and loving homes that their girlfriends offer to them.

Women occupy an ambiguous place in a Theseusian male's life. They need defense, deserve respect, give comfort—but expect marriage. The modern filmic Ariadne enhances her Theseus's ego and is willing to satisfy his legitimate sexual demands, but threatens his basic source of masculinity—the free, roving, and irresponsible life. The original mythic Ariadne was too good for any mortal; after Theseus deserted her, she married Bacchus, the patron saint of wine and merriment, and, when Zeus resurrected her from an untimely death, she spent immortality with her faithful and joyous god husband. In modern films, however, mortals cannot so easily be rid of their longings or their responsibilities. The Ariadne-like film women live on the earth, and their irremediable presence ensures that there will be a battle of the sexes, pitting the free and roistering male principle against the fettered and faithful female one.

Moreover, "good" cinematic women threaten men's freedom not only because they require that their men's sexual activities be confined within the bonds of matrimony, but also because they are the special agents of civilization and its attendant conventions, institutions, and discontents. In films it is women who even in time of war (Loretta Young in *China*) support the long view that education will save future generations; are committed to faith rather than fighting (Grace Kelly as the devout Quaker, Amy Kane, in *High Noon* [1952]); favor philosophy as a source of relief from men's nameless anxieties (Greer Garson, as the prototypical librarian, Emily Sears, in *Adventure*, offers the worried Harry [Clark Gable] and his deeply-troubled sea-faring pal, Mudgin [Thomas Mitchell], a classical text when they seek her help); and place courtship, marriage, and the family uppermost in their hierarchy of institutions to be defended (in *The Tender Trap* [1955] Debbie Reynolds tells devil-may-care bachelor and womanizer Frank Sinatra, "From now on, you're gonna call for me at my house, ask me where I want to spend the evening, and you're gonna meet my folks and be polite to them and bring me candy and flowers . . ."). Reynold's character represents the temporary triumph of the cinema's Ariadneac vision: For she concludes her didactic reprimand of a now abject Sinatra, "I've got to make a man out of you." In effect, Reynolds's woman asserts that mature men should willingly give up their claim to free, roistering, and all-male personal liberty in exchange for a woman's faithful love, nurturing warmth, and the security that home, a steady job, and a settled existence can provide.

Myth in Disenchantment: A Prolegomenon to Anhedonia

The skein of Ariadne began to unravel when Hollywood's *noir* films revealed that its promise of fidelity and civilization was at best deceptive, largely fraudulent, basically corrupt, and hopelessly self-deluding. Rather than being patient and loving paragons of dreamlike domesticity, women in these films are shameless schemers, who will utilize their sensual charms to lure men first into being their unwitting accomplices in crime and corruption, then to their ignominious deaths—or worse, to an awakened but irreparably anguished consciousness that neither love nor acceptance allow for an escape from a *dis-eased* civilization.

Consider three films, of uneven cinematic quality, that nevertheless typify *noir* films' vision of conventional America as the heart of darkness in which there is no haven and from which there is no exit: *Criss Cross* (1949), *Cry Danger* (1951), and *Crime of Passion* (1957).

In *Criss Cross,* Anna (Yvonne De Carlo) has already divorced Steve (Burt Lancaster), driving the heartsick armored-car driver not only to drink but to participate in a desperate attempt to regain his lost love and better his station in life. Because Anna has become engaged to the syndicate-connected gambler Dundee (Dan Duryea), Steve is willingly deceived into becoming their accomplice in robbing the armored-car company. Anna's pretense of restored fidelity—resuming her liaison with Steve and promising to leave Dundee once the crime has been successfully committed—lulls Steve into believing that there is a deviant route to restoring his lost faith in the future: Crime seems to promise the way he might obtain what he does not realize are merely shibboleths of the American dream—great wealth and a gorgeous wife. When the complex double- and triple-crosses committed by all parties to this three-cornered affair are finally exposed, revealing that no one has been honest about his or her real intentions, Anna prepares to abandon Steve and take off with the money. Dundee arrives and kills both of them. At film's end he is fleeing into the night as police sirens sound. Steve, outwardly a heroic figure, has been disappointed in love, disillusioned in his work, and dies a self-made sacrifice to his emotional obsession with Anna.

Cry Danger extenuates the criminal deceptiveness of the once-virtuous woman who waits. Rocky Molloy (Dick Powell) is suddenly released from prison where he has served five years of a life sentence for a robbery-murder he did not commit. It seems that Delong (Richard Erdman), a recently discharged marine—psychically wounded and sunk in alcoholism—has confirmed Rocky's alibi. But this apparent act of delayed justice is itself false—Delong has made up the story in the hope that Rocky will share the loot from the robbery with him. This opening deception forms an establishing leitmotiv of the screenplay and serves as a prelude to a series of unfolding revelations of bad faith. Nancy (Rhonda Fleming), once Rocky's girl, is married to the latter's best friend, Danny, who is serving out the last few months of his prison sentence as an accomplice in the same robbery. Knowing that he himself has been framed, Rocky seeks Nancy's help to clear his own and Danny's names and to prove that a gambler, Castro (William Conrad), is the real perpetrator of both the robbery and the murder. Appearing to be sympathetic and still attracted to Rocky, Nancy sounds like the postwar film's image of the "good" woman; she seeks to dissuade him from his plan, pointing out that he is free to start life anew, urging him to put his bitterness at being falsely imprisoned behind him and suggesting that he take up an honest line of work. Though she is married to his best friend, she hints that her love for Rocky is still strong. Although Rocky rejects her seemingly sensible advice, he is forced to admit that his infatuation with her has never died. However, after a series of dangerous encounters with Castro and his henchmen, Rocky discovers an utterly disillusioning truth: Nancy and Danny were partners with Castro in the original crime and the frame-up, and she has been rewarded with half of the stolen money for her silence. When, mistaken for Rocky and Nancy, Delong is seriously injured and his girlfriend, Darlene (Jill Porter), is killed, Molloy turns Nancy over to the police, and alone again, wanders into the city.

Crime of Passion shows that the woman who uses her charms to assist her husband's career advancement is not acting selflessly or out of true love, but rather is in service to her own unalloyed greed. Kathy Ferguson (Barbara Stanwyck) flees from her sexually repressed situation as a lovelorn columnist into marriage with honest but unambitious police lieutenant Bill Doyle (Sterling Hayden). Unwilling to settle for a devoted husband, a house in the suburbs, and home-cooked dinners with Bill's plain and pedestrian colleagues in law enforcement, Kathy undertakes an affair with Chief Inspector Tony Pope (Raymond Burr). Kathy convinces herself that she can use this affair to blackmail Pope into favoring Bill over his friendly rival, Captain Alidos (Royal Dano). for promotion on the detective force. Suspecting that her husband's friendship with Alidos will sap his competitive drive, Kathy goes even further, writing a series of poison pen letters that lead to Alidos's transfer. However, when Pope, about to retire, refuses to be coerced into naming Bill as his successor, Kathy shoots her illicit paramour to death. Bill, ever the persevering detective, discovers his wife's crime and, choosing duty over devotion, arrests her for murder.

In the *noir* films, women are no longer moved by the positive feelings of pure love, postprandial companionship, and practical homemaking. The society in which they live is presented as inherently corrupt. Virtually all the characters are ruthless seekers after money, power, or status, and with rare exception they will employ brute strength or brittle cunning to get them. The corrosive society finds its quintessential counterpart in the woman who can neither redeem nor be redeemed by love. Not only are the roles once essayed by Ariadneac heroines now revealed to be shabby performances of bad faith, but also the other female characters are shorn of virtues. In *Cry Danger,* for example, Darlene is not merely the good girl who befriends the lost soul ex-marine Delong; she is a pickpocket who steals his wallet even as she wins his unstinting affection.

In the two decades following her dramatic representation of one of the most long-suffering of virtuous heroines, *Stella Dallas* (1937), Barbara Stanwyck developed the preeminent persona of the homewrecking, male-destroying female. As Phyllis Dietrichson in *Double Indemnity* (1944), she is the archetypical black widow: She seduces the hitherto unassuming and honest claims agent, Walter Neff (Fred MacMurray), into violating the ethics of his profession, despoiling his deep friendship with the chief claims agent (Edward G. Robinson), committing an elaborate murder of her husband (Tom Powers) that is staged to look like the kind of accident that pays twice the insurance premium value, and, after Neff's discovery that she has used him as a foil in her secret affair with her daughter's (Jean Heather) boyfriend (Byron Barr), driving him to a murderous *Liebestod* that ends both their lives. In *The Strange Love of Martha Ivers* (1946), Stanwyck portrays the eponymous *noir* antiheroine, a woman who has inherited great wealth, the financial control of an industrial plant, and the political domination of an entire town by having murdered her aunt (Judith Anderson) and married the town's drunken and dissolute district attorney, Walter O'Neill (Kirk Douglas), who willingly assists her in keeping the crime covered up for twenty years. When a childhood sweetheart, Sam Masterson (Van Heflin), returns to Iverstown, Martha's long dormant passions for a real man are reawakened, but her fearful guilt combines with her frenetic greed to make her unwilling to surrender her ill-gotten gains for a pure and honest love. O'Neill seeks to thwart their affair by setting Masterson up with a younger and more sensual woman, Toni Marachek (Lizabeth Scott). When O'Neill's ploy fails, and Masterson uncovers the dark and tangled web of intrigue into which his own emotional involvement has drawn him, O'Neill realizes that his own life has been nothing but a sham; he shoots himself to death, but not before killing Martha. O'Neill's final words to the neurotically ambivalent Martha spell finis to the once established cinematic ethos: "It's not your fault," O'Neill points out; "it's not anybody's fault. It's just the way things are. It's just how much you want out of life and how hard it is to get it."[20] Stanwyck's eponymous character must also die in *The File on Thelma Jordan* (1950), because like Phyllis Dietrichson and Martha Ivers, Thelma has destroyed the professional and personal honor associated with enforcing the law, this time by pretending to be in love with the town's district attorney (Wendell Corey), alienating his once true affection for his quiet and unassuming wife (Joan Tetzel), and enmeshing him in her husband's (Richard Rober) scheme to rob and kill her aunt (Gertrude W. Hoffman). When Thelma drives her car over a cliff instantly killing her unrepentant criminal husband but having time to confess the whole conspiracy before she herself expires, her deathbed penitence only points up how society's norms of decency no longer hold, how Ariadne's thread has become a spiderweb to catch the unsuspecting hero unawares.

Accompanying Hollywood's transformation of alluring Ariadne into amoral arachnid was its metamorphosis of Theseus from ferocious fighter to effete fly. Such a transmutation took place literally in the science-horror film *The Fly* (1958): A well-meaning physicist (Al, later David, Hedison) falls victim to dual bimorphism when an experiment in the mobility of matter inadvertently recombines human and insect atoms, attaching his suddenly miniaturized head and right arm to the thorax of an ordinary housefly while raising his once masculine voice to one that is hysterically high-pitched. Ultimately the unfortunate scientist's piteous pleas arouse his old friend (Herbert Marshall) to action: he squashes him flat. Less fanciful films described a similar diminution in masculinity accompanying the death of the Theseusian hero. "Since men belonged at home, not on the streets or out on the prairie," Peter Biskind has noted about movies of the 1950s, "most films wanted them married, not alone or hanging out with other men."[21] War veterans had not merely to come home, marry, and settle down, but also to unbuckle. In *Sands of Iwo Jima* (1949), the tough, courageous, and steely eyed marine (John Wayne) is killed at the end, in effect shown to be fit only for a society steeped in perpetual combat, while his younger, gentler, comrade-in-arms (John Agar) survives and looks forward to the emerging type of postwar man that he hopes his son will become: "He won't have to be tough; he'll be intelligent. He'll read Shakespeare and be cultured." The new cinematic men who became masculine icons during the decade and a half immediately following World War II—for example, Montgomery Clift, Rock Hudson, James Dean, Sal Mineo, Tony Curtis, Steve McQueen, Anthony Perkins, Paul Newman—took on many of the personal qualities previously associated with emotion-laden women. They portrayed heroes who, in Biskind's words "were sensitive, in close touch with their feelings . . . ; [and who] put family ahead of career . . . [M]oderate in their ambitions, [they were] attuned to the needs of others . . . [and] not afraid . . . to ask for help . . . [M]en," he concluded, "were becoming feminized."[21]

There was both cinematic and real-life resistance to the domestication of Theseus. As Tom Dunston, in *Red River* (1948), John Wayne, who epitomized the earlier male iconography in his rugged roles on screen and his super-patriotic politics off, is pitted against Matthew Garth (Montgomery Clift) in a war over the sensibilities appropriate to a contemporary man.

Clift's sensitive portrayal of the eventually victorious Garth sounded a warning of what was to come to all those emotionally unembellished heroes who had hoped to survive the previous era unchanged. As Michael Malone put it, "the tears, the confusion, the anguished need for love, the defenselessness behind the bravura meant a rejection of the old masculinity and an assimilation of the female inside the self."[22] Wayne, however, refused to adjust on or off screen. After Kirk Douglas starred in *Lust for Life* (1956), giving a remarkably sensitive portrayal of the tortured nineteenth-century artist Vincent Van Gogh, Wayne chastised him: "Christ, Kirk! How can you play a part like that? There's so goddam few of us left. We got to play strong, tough characters. Not those weak queers."[23] Nevertheless, despite the fact that one biographer described James Dean as a "bisexual psychopath,"[24] that another sneeringly referred to Montgomery Clift's Matt Garth as "androgynous,"[25] and that James Cagney's antihero Cody Jarrett (in *White Heat* [1949]) is depicted as clearly more attached to his overbearing mother (Margaret Wycherly) than he is attracted to his oversexed moll (Virginia Mayo), the monodimensional macho men could not triumph over their soft rivals; they receded into a forgettable old age. When tough gunslinger Tom Doniphon (John Wayne) saves the town by shooting a dangerous outlaw (Lee Marvin), it is Ransom Stoddard (James Stewart), an effete schoolteacher—he wears an apron and washes dishes in the town's restaurant—who receives the accolade as *The Man Who Shot Liberty Valance* (1962), and, in this reworking of the achievement mystique, it is the fake hero Stoddard who goes on to marry the woman (Vera Miles), for whose hand he had competed with Doniphon and to rise in public estimation and election to the office of United States Senator. When old age and nagging guilt over his falsely obtained station in life at last lead Stoddard to confess the whole charade to the press, the news reporter refuses to print the story, invoking the new credo of inauthenticity that modernity seems to require: "When the legend becomes fact, print the legend." Although the bones of Theseus were eventually retrieved from their watery grave and entombed in the Acropolis, those of Tom Doniphon are left to rot in an untended plot in potter's field. Bereft of both superior strength and superpotent sexual energy, the new hero lives off his affective persona, by his calculating wits, and on the credulity of his awe-inspired public.

The Road to Anhedonia

Freud once pointed out that the essence of civilization "lies in the fact

that the members of the community restrict themselves in their possibilities of satisfaction, whereas the individual knew of no such restrictions."[26]
When the mystique surrounding Hollywood's cinematic Ariadnes was shattered by the revelations contained in the *noir* films, so also were the sacred
bonds of community broken and the individual released from his or her
confining constraints. However, this escape from conventional authority
did not find release in a supremely joyful hedonism. Rather, it pointed up
a Hobson's choice—between a free but lonesome life outside of society or
an unpromising career and unsensual marriage within it—that could only
provoke anxiety, alienation, and discontent.

Two *noir* films—*Kiss Me Deadly* (1955) and *Vertigo* (1958)—adumbrate
the theme that a world devoid of both community and a set of norms governing sex, love, and death is irretrievably meaningless—a limbo land of absurdity from which there can be no escape except in madness or death.

In *Kiss Me Deadly*, the threat of atomic holocaust provides the setting
in which neither the brains nor brawn of modern urban society's prototypical hero, a cynical private detective, can be of any help.[27] When
Christina (Cloris Leachman), an inmate escaping from an insane asylum,
is cruelly tortured and killed by unknown assailants who also injure Mike
Hammer (Ralph Meeker), a private investigator who had aided her flight
by picking her up on the highway, the detective is forced to enter into a
world of existential absurdity. Once there, he is confounded by his discovery that nothing makes any conventional sense, and that every person
involved in this labyrinthine intrigue of delusion and double-dealing is seeking the maniacal power to bring about the ultimate apocalypse. Specifically,
Hammer learns that Carl Evello (Paul Stewart), an arch criminal, has been
trying to obtain what Hammer's bored but patient and loyal secretary, Velda
(Maxine Cooper), calls "the great whatsit," radioactive material that, if
exposed to the air, will explode, causing a holocaust. Neither the FBI agents
(James Seay, Robert Cornthwaite) nor the well-meaning police detective on
the case (Wesley Addy) can ferret out the true nature of the conspiracy.
Moreover, with the exception of the poetry-loving and self-mocking
Christina, who is certifiably insane, none of the other women whom
Hammer meets in the course of his frantic attempt to get to the bottom of
the mystery is trustworthy. Friday Evello (Marian Carr) attempts to seduce
him away from her brother's crime by offering her body in exchange for his
withdrawal from the case; Gabrielle (Gaby Rodgers), Christina's only
friend, is revealed to be Lily Carver, an adventuress who has been in league
with Evello's evil scientist colleague, Dr. Soberin (Albert Dekker), all seek-

ing to get control of the atomic material. Death and deviltry are distributed to the innocent and the good. Hammer's pal Nick (Nick Dennis) uses his automotive skills to save the detective's life, but loses his own to the morbid machinations of Evello's henchmen; Velda is kidnapped and tortured by Evello; and Hammer himself is captured, beaten, and subjected to a truth drug, sodium pentothal. When he finally breaks through the maze of deception and dementia that has clouded everyone's understanding of what is going on and what is at stake, Hammer is too late. Neither knowledge nor feeling is enough to stave off the inevitable cosmic cataclysm. The deceitful Lily shoots Dr. Soberin and, unable to contain her mordant curiosity, opens the box of radioactive material, setting off a chain reaction. The horrified Hammer and Velda flee the scene as an atomic explosion reduces the absurd world that modern science has created to a pile of molten ash.

If *Kiss Me Deadly* depicts the dead end to which both cold reason and warm feelings will lead, Alfred Hitchcock's thriller *Vertigo* undermines man's faith in his power to mold a woman to his desires. In effect, this picture put an end to every man's illusory belief in his own masculine potency: if he could not possess the perfect woman—one who would combine the exotic sensuality of the "bad" temptress (e.g., Jennifer Jones as Pearl Chavez in King Vidor's classic film of lust and *Liebestod, Duel in the Sun* [1946]) with the undemanding domestic dependability of the "good" home companion (e.g., June Allyson as Mrs. Stratton in Hollywood's saccharine biography of a one-legged baseball player (played by James Stewart), *The Stratton Story* [1949])—he could create her out of the human materials available to him. The archetypical version of this illusory dream had been presented in Karl Freund's 1932 classic, *The Mummy*.[28] The Egyptian high priest Imhotep (Boris Karloff) is revived when the ancient tomb in which he was buried alive for his unholy love of Princess Anck-es-en-Amon is opened by twentieth-century archaeologists. Awakened from his slumbers, the once mummified Imhotep assumes the disguise of an Egyptian mystic, Ardath Bey, and renews his quest for the lovely princess who has eluded his amorous advances. He soon seizes upon Helen Grosvenor (Zita Johann), the daughter of the British governor of the Sudan, as the present-day incarnation of his undying love and seeks to hypnotize her into assuming the total identity—memories and sentiments as well as dress and deportment—of the dead princess. Imhotep nearly succeeds, and the audience's sympathies for his aim at the unattainable cannot help but be aroused when Helen's modern fiancé (played by the ever-pallid David Manners) rescues her from the mummy's preternatural passions, causing him to crumble into the dust from which his undead spirit had sought an erotic release.

If *The Mummy* suggested that a man should never give up his quest for the woman of his dreams, not even when death appears to kill off all possibilities, *Vertigo* called upon him to awaken from such a nightmare and, unlike Hitchcock's hopeless hero, accept stoically the fitful and restive reality that an aroused consciousness must bear. At *Vertigo's* denouement, the private detective Ferguson (James Stewart) is utterly lost. He has given up the companionate and home-loving affections of his glasses-wearing fiancée (Barbara Bel Geddes) in a rash attempt to demonstrate to himself that he is in reality the "free man" that he imagines himself to be. Hired by a man whom he remembers as an old and trustworthy friend (Tom Helmore) to shadow Madeleine (Kim Novak), supposedly his friend's suicidal wife, Ferguson's vertigo prevents him from stopping what he believes is her fatal leap from a tower. Several months later, upon release from the mental hospital where he has gone to recover from his nervous breakdown, Ferguson meets Judy (Kim Novak), a déclassé street person. He believes he has been given another chance to prove his own potency: Ferguson will transform an ordinary woman into the extraordinary object of his sensuous fantasies. He takes over the life of the dowdy Judy, seeking, like Ardath Bey with Helen Grosvenor, to make her over into the delightful Madeleine. When, at length, he realizes to his own horrifying amazement that the two personae belong in fact to a single woman, and that he has been deceived into participating in a most deadly conspiracy, he collapses altogether. His inordinate passions have led him astray, and his intelligent deductions can only lead him to a truth that shatters all illusions. Betrayed by his friend, bewitched by his desires, and bewildered by the fateful turn of events, Ferguson's fragile psyche is shaken to its foundations. At film's end he can only stare at the dead body before him and utter the two names—"Judy," "Madeleine"— representative of the twin idols of his mind, now broken forever.

The Anhedonic Family

Hollywood films had always attempted to depict those values that enjoyed widespread support in the United States. Among these were norms and sentiments that approved of honest work and cherished the family, the home, and the healing and nurturing power of love. However, by the 1960s, a sizable segment of the population no longer seemed to believe that living according to these values would prove efficacious or fulfilling. Central to the malaise that enveloped both real- and reel-life characters has been disillusion with the family. In the older formulaic endings of most films, a loving kiss sealed the matrimonial bargain between a man and a woman who loved one another and seemed to promise to continue to do so until death did them part. Their actual married life was left to the audience's imagination. However, once Hollywood introduced admirable heroines who would not accept monogamy and motherhood as a substitute for a career and a carefree existence, who refused to bask demurely in the reflected status of their husband's occupation, and who demanded every jot and tittle of equality that the law and their own individual or collective efforts might obtain, it sounded a tocsin: the troubles between the sexes were just beginning when the organ played the wedding march. Although *Klute* (1971) allowed its prostitute-heroine, Bree Daniels (Jane Fonda), to realize that her life of noncommitment to one man—Bree explains to her analyst that she prefers turning tricks with anonymous strangers because that way she remains in control—is literally tantamount to a death wish; *Kramer vs. Kramer* (1979) revealed that the typical urban middle-class American family lacked any shred of the rewards that are supposed to accrue from such a commitment. Joanna Kramer (Meryl Streep) wants out of both her marriage to her advertising executive husband, Ted (Dustin Hoffman), and her maternal duties to their toddler-son, Billy (Justin Henry). She leaves, and Ted takes over the domestic and nurturant responsibilities, proving himself to be an effective surrogate mother but at considerable cost to his career advancement. When Joanna returns, she is earning more than Ted, and having proved herself, wants both a divorce and custody of their son. As critic David Denby pointed out, "Sex and marriage have failed for the Kramers. The newly confident woman and the newly sensitized man are propelled away from each other."[29]

Ordinary People (1980) went even further in revealing the darker implications of Talcott Parsons's remark that "families . . . are 'factories' which produce personalities."[30] Mary Tyler Moore essays the role of a cold and heartless mother who presides over a despairingly anomic household. Her son (Timothy Hutton), despondent over his loveless existence, has already attempted suicide and is in therapy; her effete and feckless husband (Donald Sutherland, who, nine years earlier, as the eponymous Klute, had guided Bree Daniels to a new awareness of woman's needs) can only weep and wring his hands. The home has become the place wherein there is utter loss of hope. Ultimately, guided by the only outsider in the film, a Jewish psychiatrist whose beneficent therapies have already evoked his mother's hostile anti-Semitism, the son is helped to a semblance of emotional stability and an understanding of his father's ineffectiveness. When the mother deserts the family for good, the father and son are left to make do with one another.

Kramer vs. Kramer and *Ordinary People* sealed the fate of the nuclear family and suggested that the future portends a new ordering of the domestic and occupational verities. The all-male homestead will in the future link father and son in the only emotionally sensitized and lovingly nurturant haven in what has otherwise emerged as a heartless world; while the workplace will likely become the scene of a harsh and less than feeling competitive struggle between career-driven women and ambitious men, the battleground for a cold war of the sexes.

During the 1980s, Hollywood sought a detour around the emotional malaise suggested by its naturalistic films by cinematic escapes into fantasy. Even in this form, however, the movies could not leave off of disenchanting the mystiques that once stood sentinel over the vital moralistic center of American life. In films that are little more than celluloid comic books, celebrating the derring-do of such cardboard characters as Superman (Christopher Reeve) or Indiana Jones (Harrison Ford), the old verities that their heroes purport to serve so selflessly are discredited by a dramatically revealing tongue-in-cheek mockery. More telling is how the horror genre, once confined to the malevolence of mad scientists, militant microbes, or marauding monsters, has turned the settings of neighborly domesticity into terrifying sinkholes. Recently, these films have treated their teenage audiences to the claim that Friday the thirteenth is a date for fiendish bloodletting, that Halloween is a holiday celebrating sadistic mayhem, that sleep-away camps are places for mindless murder, and that the house on Elm Street is the residence of a child-hating monster who wreaks an unholy vengeance on what little love and security are left in the family home. Filmmakers' fantastic kitsch seems to have begun to imitate civilized life's slide into doleful discontent. In a dark comedy of despair, *Manhattan* (1970), a television writer (Woody Allen) dictates an idea for a new scenario: "People in Manhattan are constantly creating these real unnecessary neurotic problems for themselves that keep them from dealing with more terrifying unsolvable problems about the universe." But, as this film hints, the unfathomable consternations of the cosmos have now combined with the unresolvable concerns of the people, resulting in an enervation of the synapses that finds its quintessential expression in anhedonia.

One way out of the disenchanted forest of modernity is to fantasize about age-role reversal—to revolt against adulthood, turn back time itself, stop the aging process, or return grownups to a childlike state of loving credulity and uplifting hope. In *E.T.—The Extra-Terrestrial* (1982), a band of children successfully oppose the overscientized heartlessness of adults and help a being from outer space to escape from the world. In *Back to the Future* (1985), a teenager returns to the 1950s, assists his adolescent parents-to-be to mature, and shows other highschoolers how the musical future will liberate their libidos. And, in a burst of nostalgia for a wiser and simpler childhood return, Hollywood released a trio of films in 1988—*18 Again*, *Vice Versa*, and *Big*. In each, age-role reversal is put in service to the plea that childhood's sensual innocence and harmless hedonism might not only be prolonged, but that they should hold sway over a society sickened by corrosive cynicism and excessive self-regard. Yet these films too reveal the limitations of their baleful theme. *Big's* Tom Hanks must give up the grownup body and virginal sensuality that he enjoyed as a preadolescent magically transformed into a thirty-year-old; he must revert to the problematic but normal processes entailed in becoming a man; and the lovable creature from outer space, E.T., must return to his planet of origin, leaving the grade-school children to wait and hope. The world as it really is and will be awaits these children's inexorable maturation.

In 1939, modernity's disenchantment with both the affective qualities and societal functions of cinema's Ariadne and Theseus was anticipated in *The Wizard of Oz*. Dorothy (Judy Garland) and her friends, the cowardly lion (Bert Lahr), the tin woodman (Jack Haley), and the brainless scarecrow (Ray Bolger), follow the yellow brick road to the wonderful wizard (Frank Morgan), only to discover that he is a charlatan, who in response to their pitiful pleas, tells them to search their hearts and minds for the psychic strengths already resident there. *Wizard* warned us that we would have to make do with what we had within ourselves. Would that be sufficient for living? Woody Allen's sardonic schlemiel, Allen Felix, gave us one answer in *Play It Again, Sam* (1972). A woman, whom he is trying to pick up at an art gallery, tells him how a Jackson Pollock painting expresses the hopeless absurdity of modernity: "It restates the negativeness of the universe. The hideous lonely emptiness of existence. Nothingness. The predicament of Man forced to live in a barren, Godless, eternity like a tiny flame flickering in an immense void with nothing but waste, horror and degradation, forming a useless bleak straightjacket in a bleak absurd cosmos." The ever-eager Felix asks, "What're you doing Saturday night?" "Commiting suicide," comes the mordant reply. But Felix will not be defeated by the death or despair of another. For him—and for us—surviving in the face of absurdity is the only way. "What about Friday night?" he inquires.[31]

CHAPTER NINE

Without Morals or Mores: Deviance in Postmodern Social Theory

The whole history of mankind is a series of acts which are open to doubt, dispute, and criticism, as to their right and justice, but all subsequent history has been forced to take up the consequences of those acts and go on.

William Graham Sumner, Folkways: A Study of the Sociological Importance of Usages, Manners, Customs, Mores, and Morals

Postmodernism and Deviance: Introduction

Postmodernism, some of whose adumbrations deviance theorist Stephen Pfohl[1] has traced back to C. Wright Mills's foreboding commentaries[2] on how the expansion of electronic information is blurring the boundaries between "first-hand contact" and prefabricated signs,[3] has become both a promise and a prosecutor of sociological theory.[4] As a phenomenon only seemingly external to the discipline but having a profound effect on it, postmodernism has been defined by Pfohl: "the term *postmodern* ... connote[s] the historical emergence of new forms of social power—power mediated by dense and high velocity technological rituals; rituals governed by information exchange, electronic imagery, and cybernetic control mechanisms." Pfohl goes on to distinguish *postmodernity,* "a historical social form" and *postmodernism,* a term that connotes a form of epistemological or aesthetic inquiry marked by "a particular style of theoretical or poetic engagement ... giv[ing] highest value to a non-linear and decentered play of language, commentary and criticism ... , [and] suggesting a radical overturning of the 'master narratives' of white male and western claims to knowledge." Furthermore, Pfohl goes on to point out that "postmodernism must be understood as . . . a self-critical response to the political deconstruction of western white male language practices by feminists, peoples of color, postcolonial critics, gays, lesbians, and others who are marginalized in the historical organization and production of modernity."[5] Hence, it would appear to follow that postmodern sociology poses a challenge to the modernist sociologist's discourse on deviance, indeed to the very concept and ontology of deviance. In what follows, I shall examine this challenge and formulate a critique that might resolve the basic issue.

The Modernist Discourse on Deviance

A representative illustration of the late modernist conception of deviant behavior is presented in the third edition of Marshall B. Clinard's *Sociology of Deviant* Behavior: "Deviant behavior is essentially violation of certain types of group norms; a deviant act is behavior which is proscribed in a certain way. It cannot be satisfactorily defined in either statistical, pathological, or labeling terms. Societal reaction leading to labeling is an important aspect in the study of deviant behavior, but it is a contingent and unnecessary element in a definition . . . Only those deviations in which behavior is in a disapproved direction, and of sufficient degree to exceed the tolerance limit of the community, constitute deviant behavior . . ."[6]

Virtually every aspect of this definition had been challenged before the advent of sociological postmodernism. As Clinard's attempt to limit the definitional applicability of labeling theory suggests, the role of authority in deciding what kind of activity or belief is deviant and which persons are to be designated as perpetrators or adherents of deviance had done much to undermine the conceptual independence and theoretical integrity of the concept.[7] The point of this burgeoning critique is made even more clear when, in the light of the postmodern revolution in behalf of liberating some of the marginalized victims of modernist deviance theory, the conduct of the groups so labeled are listed by Clinard: Deviant behavior, he wrote in 1968, "includes . . . delinquency and crime, prostitution, homosexual behavior, drug addiction, alcoholism, mental disorders, suicide, marital and family maladjustments, discrimination against minority groups, and, to a lesser degree, role problems of old age."[8] Illustrating the change that has occurred twenty-two years after these words were written, David P. Aday Jr., attempting to develop a general understanding of deviance, devotes ten pages of his discussion of Durkheimian, Marxian, and Weberian perspectives on social order and its control mechanisms to suggesting that homosexuality is only possibly deviant.[9] But, when it comes to lengthy descriptions of other kinds of deviant behavior, he devotes four separate chapters to "heterosexual deviance," "mental illness," "violence," and "white collar crime."[10] In his discussion of methods appropriate to research on deviance, Aday emphasizes the sociologist's duty to protect his or her subjects, utilizing Laud Humphrey's participant-observer study of anonymous homosexual encounters in public bathrooms[11] as indicative of some of the ethical ambiguities that this mode of investigation entails.[12]

Even more forceful is Jack P. Gibbs's critique of what he calls the "counteraction of deviance thesis" developed by Talcott Parsons (1902–1979) in *The Social System*.[13] According to Parsons, "Every social system has, in addition to the obvious rewards for conformative and punishments for deviant behavior, a complex system of unplanned and largely unconscious mechanisms which serve to counteract deviant tendencies."[14] In support of his claim that Parsons's conception presents sociologists with "a thicket of problems,"[15] Gibbs critically appraises the convention that defines deviance by reference to what are in effect hypostatized norms that nevertheless are difficult if not impossible to conceptualize in any clear and unambiguous manner. "The problems are not solved," he observes, "by defining deviant behavior as that which is subject to social control and then defining social control by reference to deviant behavior."[16] Parsons's assertion—that the "theory of social control . . . is the analysis of those processes in the social system which tend to counteract the deviant tendencies, and of the conditions under which such processes will operate"[17]—embraces both too much and too little with respect to the scope of activities typically investigated by such a theory. Hence, Gibbs points out, to select, for example, "Hitler's efforts to further electoral support of the Nazi party" as a social control action that is a "counteraction of deviance" is to make the latter concept "unmanageably broad."[18] On the other hand, to exclude from the topics for a social control sociology the study of advertising techniques in a consumer society because they do not seek to counteract deviance would be to eliminate a plethora of processes whereby "thousands attempt to manipulate the behavior of millions." Gibbs concludes: "The general point . . . is that the counteraction-of-deviance conception of social control erroneously supposes an indisputable and empirically applicable answer to this question: What and who is deviant?"

But is it possible that Parsons has been misconstrued by Gibbs?

Parsons's theses about deviance and social control are specifically corre-
lated to behavior in and with respect to particular social systems, each of
which has its own hierarchical structure of values which in turn will define
just what and who is deviant. Thus, in discussing the directions that deviant
tendencies will take, Parsons cautions us that "it must not be forgotten that
they [i.e., the deviant tendencies] are *always* relative to a particular set of
complementary role-expectations, to a particular alter or class of alters, and
to a particular normative pattern or sub-system of them."[19] And, when treating the relationship of the theory of social control to the counteraction of
deviance, Parsons observes, "Like the theory of deviance, it must be stated
relative to a given state of equilibrium of the system or sub-system which
includes specification of the normative patterns institutionalized in that sub-
system, and the balance of motivational forces relative to conformity with
and deviance from these patterns."[20] Indeed, Parsons made his observations quite specific when, as he brought his discussion of deviance to a
conclusion, he pointed out, "Before closing this section it should be noted
that the above discussion of the social structuring of deviant behavior has
been illustrated almost entirely in terms of the American or at most the
modern Western institutional structure and value system"—adding, in
defense of his claim to have formulated a general theory with universal applications, that "There is no reason to doubt that the conceptual scheme developed here . . . is, with proper adaptation, equally applicable to the analysis
of deviance from any type of value pattern and within any type of institutional structure." It is precisely this assertion and especially its application
to the very idea of deviance, that has become a central issue in the postmodern critique of sociology.

Parsons, Hughes, and Sumner

Before turning to the postmodernists, however, a brief excursus
comparing and contrasting conceptions of deviance and social control in
the works of two of Parsons's predecessors is useful in pointing toward the
direction that postmodernist sociology would take. None of Parsons's
conceptions of America as a social system or of the patterns of variation
that it would engender is, in terms of theory, original. America's first sociologist, Henry Hughes (1829–1862), had put forth a theory of dual
American social systems, one, operant in the states above the Mason-Dixon
Line and serving to realize the values and norms of laissez-faire capitalism;
the other, in place in the South and manifesting the ideals of a seigneurial

warrantocracy.[21] Just as Parsons had seen that deviance arose out of the malfunctions or "strains" inherent in the relations of situation and social structure to individual motivation,[22] so Hughes posited a four-class hierarchy, differentiating attitudes toward the norm of work, each generating its own potential for disparate motivational responses and each requiring either internalized mechanisms or external coercion to counteract whatever deviance might occur.[23] Those most liable to innovative, alienative, or rebellious responses—for Hughes these were the African American slaves he called "warrantees," but he also cautioned his readers about women, children, and lunatics—would have to be forcibly restrained; those who were carriers of the system's values—for example, professionals, skilled craftsmen, and political leaders—would have internalized a resistance to untoward actions or beliefs on their own part.[24] Like Parsons,[25] Hughes assumed that each social system, if left to itself and not interfered with by external forces, would persevere, evolving at an orderly pace,[26] maintaining itself in what, later, the Harvard sociologist would call "dynamic equilibrium."[27] For Parsons, the bulk of whose work on this topic was done during the Second World War and Cold War eras, the threatening forces from outside the United States were Nazi Germany and the Soviet Union— each with its respective commitment to spreading the values of fascism or of Marxist communism;[28] for Hughes, the external forces were the "radicals" of the northern states with their demands for abolition throughout the Union.[29] Hughes was less and Parsons more optimistic about the future of the system.

It is William Graham Sumner's (1840–1910) particular application of his theory of the folkways and mores to the United States that differs so completely from both Hughes's and Parsons's conceptions of American social systems and, in the event, anticipates the basic theme of postmodernism. To Sumner the mores and folkways of a society constitute the infrastructure upon which meaning is based and action takes place. However, this bedrock of tradition, custom, and values is vulnerable to revolution and civil strife. "In the best case," he pointed out, "every revolution must be attended by this temporary chaos of the mores," immediately adding, "It was produced in the American colonies."[30] The Puritan folkways and mores established in the new republic had, in fact, never been secure, Sumner noted. Eventually, their doctrinal force—but not their judgmental standards[31]—had been undermined by the Civil War, a thesis he illustrated by pointing to the problems arising out of the still unresolved race question. "The civil war," he asserted, "abolished legal rights and left the two races to learn how to live together under other relations than before." But the "whites have never been converted from the old mores . . . The two races have not yet made new mores."[32] Indeed, he went on to observe, "The dislike of the colored people in the old slave states of the United States and the hostility to whites who 'associate with negroes' is to be attributed to the difference in the mores of whites and blacks."[33] Because he felt he was witnessing a widening crack in the original Puritan cake of American custom, Sumner grew even more pessimistic about the possibility of a moral reintegration. "The consequence [of Emancipation]" he wrote in 1906, "has been forty years of economic, social, and political discord."[34] Although he felt sure that "New mores will be developed which will cover the situation with customs, habits, mutual concessions, and cooperation of interests,"[35] he was equally certain that neither slavery nor tyranny had been abolished for all time. "One thing only can be affirmed with confidence; that is, that as no philosophical dogmas caused slavery to be abolished, so no philosophical dogmas can prevent its reintroduction if economic changes should make it fit and suitable again."[36] Might makes right, he insisted, a fact especially noticeable in times of moral breakdown and transition. Indeed, "might has made all the right which ever has existed or exists now."[37]

For Sumner, America in the decades after the Civil War was a society shorn of mores. Whereas, fourteen years after Sumner's birth, Hughes had perceived an antebellum America morally dichotomized by relatively stable free-market and seigneurial socialist systems, each opposed to the other and each generating its own modes of deviant responses, and four decades after Sumner's death, Parsons would hold to his thesis that America's singular universalist-achievement system would likely maintain itself in the face of its patterned forms of deviance, Sumner comes close to having foreseen the postmodern condition—one, that is, where there is no deviance because there is no normative structure against which it could react. As Sumner put it, "The mores which once were are a memory. Those which any one thinks ought to be are a dream."[38] What could either sociologist or citizen do? Look squarely into the abyss, he answered. "We are like spectators at a great natural convulsion. The results will be such as the facts and forces call for. We cannot foresee them."[39] Thus did he put an end to positivism's claim for a sociology that could predict and control—even before that claim had entered that discipline's epistemological domain.

The Postmodern Challenge

"The postmodern," observes David Lyon, ". . . refers above all to the exhaustion of modernity."[40] Modernity, in turn, is associated with the project of the eighteenth-century Enlightenment, a profound cultural meta-morphosis that had its first efflorescence in the writings of a remarkable cohort of Scottish intellectuals, among whom the principal figures were David Hume (1711–1776), Adam Smith (1723–1790), Adam Ferguson (1723–1816), William Robertson (1721–1793), James Burnett, Lord Monboddo (1714–1799), Henry Home, Lord Kames (1696–1782), and Thomas Reid (1721–1793).[41] Their works did much to displace the subjection to dependency and particularism associated with that era's theology, substituting for them the liberating themes of independence and universalism. These themes, in turn, would constitute the core value structure guiding thought and action in the Occident for the next two centuries.[42] Although it has become fashionable to date the onset[43] of the postmodern era as an accompaniment to America's use of the atom bomb to end World War II,[44] and as a response to the disillusion with the promise of the Enlightenment that emerged as both intellectuals and ordinary people gazed upon the successive havocs of the twentieth century—for example, the death camps and gulags; the genocidal policies; the wars against Jews, Gypsies, and homosexuals; the marginalization of both old and new minorities; the continuation of colonialism under a new guise; the rise of ethnocentric nationalisms in Eastern Europe, the states of the former Soviet Union, and parts of Africa, Asia, and Latin America; and a chorus of demands for liberation by spokespersons for hitherto neglected members of race, sex, and class groups[45]—some of the themes attending postmodernism are much older.[46] However, its full expression had not penetrated very far into the social sciences and moral and political philosophies in the United States until "the Cold War ended, one era of American history closed, and a new one dawned."[47] Despite the fact that such neo-Hegelian thinkers as Francis Fukuyama believe that the new era is one characterized by the triumph of the Western vision and the end of wars over opposed apocalyptic histories,[48] a different version of Hegel's cunning of reason animates the postmodernists. "Underneath the [West's] shining armor," observes Fred Dallmayr, "a certain hollowness is spreading: a suspicion that individual identity is slipping, that rationalism ignores and perhaps undermines its premises, and that progress does not necessarily yield happiness or even viable conditions of human life."[49]

For the postmodernists, the foundational wellsprings of the Enlightenment are suspect, said to be both sham and shibboleth. They are sham in the triple senses that reason has not emancipated individual identity from the prison-houses of class oppression, racism, patriarchy, or homophobia;[50] that such eufunctional passions as love[51] have been constrained by law and tradition, permitting antisocial prejudices to guide the making of public policies; and that the idea of progress is both an epistemological fallacy[52] and an ideological weapon of chauvinist-colonial oppression.[53] They are shibboleth in the sense that the entire modernist discourse—including the discursive rhetoric of sociology[54]—is said to be an unacknowledged excuse for or justification of patriarchy, hegemonism, and colonialism.[55] "Love, liberty, progress, the sovereign people, the brotherhood of man, and the oneness of spirit under a mysterious but manifest providence"—to borrow the phrasing that Jacques Barzun employs to describe the values that he believes were undermined nearly a century and a half earlier by the revolutions that swept over Europe in 1848—"these were now regarded as the vaporings of feeble minds or glib rhetoricians."[56]

As for deviance, in its modernist forms, it exists in the postmodern discourse as a feature of the all-encompassing marginalization process: Those whom the modernist elites and their collaborators—including, especially, the sociologists of deviance[57]—single out for victimization are simultaneously stigmatized. Whereas the more advanced modernist theorists of the deviance process have perceived it as a stigmatizing consequence of labeling the "Other,"[58]—that is, a product of social constructions that often have the imprimatur of criminological science,[59] the legitimacy of law,[60] or the authority of modern medicine[61] to back them up—the postmodernists wish in effect to launch an assault on the very idea of a valid modernist discourse of deviance.

As part of their project of deconstructing sociology's legacy from the Enlightenment, postmodernists cast a suspicious eye on the authenticity and sincerity of the moral, legal, and customary authority of that era's mores and folkways. True Sumnerians in spite of themselves, the postmodern opponents of deviance theory assert in effect that the whole of Enlightenment philosophy, but more especially its praxiology, works not to liberate individuals and elevate true rationality, but to privilege the Occidental adherent of the virtues that Max Weber ascribed to the Protestant ethicist, that is, the "subject" against whom the postmodern rhetoric is directed.[62] Absent the normative structure that buttresses Occidental cultural, social, and moral hegemony—an absence that is "produced" by disprivileging the "texts" that express this order of things, persons, practices, and beliefs[63]—and, it follows *logically* (though I have not yet discovered a postmodern sociologist who states this *in haec verba*),[64] that there can be no such thing as deviance. No norms, no deviance. We are looking once again into Sumner's abyss. Or into its opposite: Too many norms, each valid for its own group of adherents, none for the entire multi-cultural society.

A Paradigm Case—Homosexuality

It is instructive to select homosexuality as a paradigm case for the investigation of the impact of postmodernism on the sociology of deviance. Before, and to a considerable extent since, the advent of the gay liberation movement, homoerotic feelings and sex acts, as well as the several forms of conduct associated with them, have been said to be deviant. Indeed, perhaps none had been granted such paradigmatic consensus as such, and for so long a time, as homosexuality.[65] Because those accused of being homosexuals, or of engaging in homosexual acts, are stigmatized, social constructionist sociologists and labeling theorists have been sympathetic, but they have not found a way to release them from their misery. Homosexual advocates, on the other hand, have termed the everyday life of those who have a same-sex preference as neither sick nor criminal, but rather as a life-style deserving toleration, if not respect,—and also of equal rights to work, live, and engage in the sexually satisfying routines of life with impunity.[66]

In some academic discussions, same-sex conduct and life-style are valorized as central aspects of a "culture" that, in a truly multicultural society, would and should have equal status with that of the several racial, ethnic, and gender cultures with which it coexists and intersects.[67] However, a small but significant group of sociologists have gone even further—no longer merely calling for homosexuality to be moved from deviance to respectability,[68] but, more profoundly, demanding that the entire subdiscipline of what it insists is a fatally flawed homophobic, patriarchal, and racist sociology be dismantled.[69] In its place there is to be established an egalitarian, gynandrocentric, and multicultural social perspective organized around "queer theory."[70] As Janice M. Irvine has observed, despite the gains made by social constructionist approaches to analyses of deviance and social problems, too much of sociology has been insulated "from the interdisciplinary multi-cultural conversation concerning intersections of race, ethnicity, gender, and sexual identity."[71]

It cannot be denied that the principal texts of functionalist and psychological sociology have treated homosexuality and, indeed, same-sex intimacies, as deviant. During the Second World War, to take an example provided by Ellen Herman, "Homosexuality was a major ongoing preoccupation for clinical experts . . ."[72] Considering homosexuality a "special threat to military discipline and good morals, anyone with such proclivities was automatically rejected from the armed forces." However, because few homosexuals did, in fact, openly confess their sexual preference, any "subsequent revelation of homosexuality . . . [became] an official pretext for the psychiatric hospitalization and dishonorable discharge of thousands of soldiers and sailors." The adoption of President Clinton's "don't ask, don't tell" approach to controlling homosexuality in the American military did not lift the stigma of deviance from same-sex preferences.

However, it is as a pathology that homosexuality has proved to be an effective tool for marginalizing those so designated. As Joseph Gusfield once remarked, "[T]he American Psychiatric Association has been the owner of the problem of homosexuality, and their [*sic*] support or opposition to the definition of homosexuality as a psychiatric problem has been significant."[73] When, in 1973, at the request of the Gay Activist Alliance, the American Psychiatric Association began to reconsider the pathological status of homosexuality, Dr. Judd Marmor asserted: "Homosexuality, in itself, merely represents a variant sexual preference which our society disapproves of but which does not constitute a mental illness."[74] In the group's memorandum on the subject, the APA committee recommended demedicalization of homosexuality. But one member, Dr. Henry Brill, while seeking to shift blame for the stigmatization of homosexuals away from the mental health professionals—he insisted that it is "The public [that] assumes that all homosexuals are dangerous or sex fiends or untrustworthy or some other part of a stereotype"—would not abandon the pathological diagnosis altogether. "What are we going to do," he asked, "about the homosexual who comes to us and says he's miserable, that he doesn't like the homosexual way of life, and that he wants to change?" Apparently accepting the homosexual's choice of a psychiatrist to relieve his misery as evidence that his condition was pathological, Dr. Brill concluded that "Very often these people have very clear psychiatric problems." Nor did the APA committee discard medical rhetoric in its official memorandum. Although the psychiatrists conceded that "the 'illness' model of homosexuality is unwarranted," they justified their recommendation on the basis of "a significant body of research" that supports a contention "that a sizeable number of homosexual persons are sufficiently *well adjusted* as to be indistinguishable from a control group of heterosexuals."

Such, however, was not the conclusion that had been reached twenty-three years earlier by the authors of perhaps the single most influential study of prejudice carried out in the twentieth century—*The Authoritarian*

Personality.[75] Although that mammoth investigation was ostensibly directed at determining the psychological factors in the etiology of anti-Semitism and Negrophobia, the authors took care to point out that, "The problem of homosexual tendencies, their degree, and the subject's acceptance or rejection of them was also given consideration."[76] "The problem of homosexuality," Daniel J. Levinson believed, "relates to the different ways of failure in resolving the Oedipal conflict and the resultant regression to earlier phases."[77] In R. Nevitt Sanford's clinical discussion of "Mack," a young man identified as possessing and possessed by an authoritarian personality, the theme of homosexuality as well as homophobia looms large, a product of Mack's father complex and its attendant "authoritarian submission."[78] "One might say," Sanford concludes, "that Mack's homosexuality, repressed in childhood in a setting of sadomasochistic relations with the father, has remained on an infantile level; insufficiently sublimated, it cannot find gratification in friendly, equalitarian relations with men but, instead, it determines that most such relations have to be on a dominance-submission dimension."[79] And, in relation to the central problem that their project sought to elucidate, Else Frenkel-Brunswick pointed out that, "Again and again it became evident [that] the difference between the ethnocentric and the non-ethnocentric extremes hinges more on the rejection vs. the acceptance of such depth factors as homosexuality, or aggression, or passivity, or anality, than it does on the mere presence or absence of one or another of these tendencies."[80] Homosexuality was not only unhealthy; the failure to reject its tendencies could corrupt the personality and subvert the conscience. In contrast to the authoritarian personality who might be homosexual, "A person with a mature, integrated, and internalized conscience," Levinson suggested, "will certainly take a different stand on moral and social issues than a person with an underdeveloped, defective or overpunitive super-ego, or a person who still, as in childhood, clings to a set of rules and values only as they are reinforced by an external authority, be it public opinion or be it a leader."[81] Moreover, writing in the tradition of the authoritarian personality forty years later, one psychiatrist—while conceding, through quoting a statement by fellow psychiatrist Jonas Robitscher, namely, that "Public drunkenness, chronic alcoholism, and drug addiction were labeled as disease symptoms, as was homosexuality, in order to help the people charged with these offenses escape criminal punishment"[82]—nevertheless believes that "When someone vehemently accuses the gay community of corrupting youth and destroying the fabric of society, we can be fairly sure that he has never come to terms with his own homosexual impulses."[83]

However, it is within the systems-theoretical framework developed by

Talcott Parsons that there can be found the greatest strictures on conduct that might be interpreted as homoerotic. Steven Seidman, despite his own commitment to a postmodernist "Queer Theory," is sympathetic to Parsons's effort, holding that the fact that the Harvard sociologist "is not considered a great American social thinker . . . [is due to his inability] to articulate his social vision in a language that could speak, powerfully and compellingly, to a broad social public . . . [as well as that his] vision of a scientific sociology forced him to conceal his values, to retreat into an overdetermined theoretical language that speaks only to a narrow expert culture."[84] However, a close reading of Parsons's description of the facets of deviance to be found in a universalistic-achievement system, that is, in the normative structure of the United States of America, will show that Parsons's value commitments are not that difficult to discern,[85] and that they consist of a transvalued variant of Protestant ethicism[86] as the latter had been defined by Max Weber.[87] More to the points under discussion here are Parsons's prescriptive descriptions of the taboos surrounding expressions of intimacy among men in America—taboos that are inherent features of the system but also conducive to the generation of personal anxieties as individuals inhibit their actions in order to stave off the suspicion that they are sexually deviant. So powerful is Parsons's statement on the matter that it is worth quoting at length:

> The primary diffuse solidarities of such a society [as the United States of America] . . . are family-home, class, community, ethnic group, religious denomination, and nation. There is also room for an ecological system of diffuse affective attachments. These are exceedingly prominent in the cross-sex relationships of the "dating" period with the attendant romantic love complex, but tend to be absorbed into the kinship unit by marriage. Intrasex friendship as diffuse attachment is much less prominent, probably because it can too readily divert from the achievement complex. Among men it tends rather to be attached as a diffuse "penumbra" to occupational relationships in the form of an obligation in a mild way to treat one's occupational associate as a friend also. It is thereby spread out, and does not form a focus of major independent structuring. The very fact that affectionate bodily contact is almost completely taboo among men in American society is probably indicative of this situation since it strongly limits affective attachment . . . It is highly suggestive that normal heterosexuality is institutionalized in all known societies, hence that homosexuality is with few exceptions tabooed . . .[88]

Whether writing in accordance with Parsons's paradigm of system-generated deviance, or in terms of labeling theory, anomie orientations, or social and cultural support perspectives, later sociologists of deviance in effect amplified the status of the homosexual as that of the deviant par excellence. Becker, for example, lent support to Parsons's idea that sexual deviance would interfere with occupational achievement when he observed, in illustration of his thesis that "Treating a person as though he were generally rather than specifically deviant produces a self-fulfilling prophecy," that "while being a homosexual may not affect one's ability to do office work, . . . to be known as a homosexual in an office may make it impossible to continue working there."[89] Moreover, when, as Sykes and Matza point out, their deviance has been ratified by public opinion, common repute, self-identification, or individual or collective judgment, "Assaults on homosexuals or suspected homosexuals . . . may be [justified in the mind of the assailants as] hurts inflicted on a transgressor . . ."[90] Testing the claim that homosexuality was related to alcoholism[91] and paranoia[92] became an aspect of research on deviance in the three decades after Parsons's *Social System* was published. Perhaps the most damning estimate of the moral character of the homosexual was presented by Hervey Cleckley, who claimed that "A tendency to carry out acts that may endanger the normal development and adjustment of others is characteristic of homosexuality."[93] It is not surprising, then, that when Ronald A. Farrell and Thomas J. Morrione sought a research site on which to develop their causal model of nonnormal conduct, they chose homosexuality "because [as they explained] it represents behavior which is clearly, and with relatively little exception, defined as deviant."[94]

Homosexuality Avowed and Mitigated: Labeling Theory

As most postmodernist sociologists acknowledge, labeling theory, associated with the conceptualizations of Howard S. Becker, Edwin Lemert, Thomas J. Scheff, and Erving Goffman, has done much to challenge the stigma attached to homosexual identity and homoerotic practices. Becker, on the basis of Albert J. Reiss's study of how male juvenile delinquent hustlers disavow their putative identification as "queers,"[95] wondered "How many other varieties of homosexual behavior await discovery and description? And what effect would their discovery and description have on our theories?"[96] Although he did not disclaim the existence of a phenomenon of primary deviance, Becker asserted that, "We must see deviance, and the outsiders who personify the abstract conception, as a consequence of a process of interaction between people, some of whom in the service of their own interests make and enforce rules which catch others who, in the service of their own interests, have committed acts which are labeled deviant."[97] Lemert admonished sociologists to "be less concerned with the essential definitions of deviations . . . than with the processes by which organizations recognize or do not recognize them as moral defect or disease, make them a basis for excusing or not excusing other deviant acts, or choose to assign or not assign benefits to those to whom the deviations are attached."[98]

Among those analysts who have cast doubt on the alleged relationship of homosexuality to paranoia, Lyman and Scott, following up leads in the work of Lemert on the dynamics of exclusion,[99] have shown that the supposedly suspicion-oriented conduct of homosexuals might be a game-theoretic tactic suitable to the precarious situation in which such persons must lead their lives;[100] while Thomas J. Scheff and Suzanne M. Retzinger have claimed that "Freud's . . . analysis of the Schreber case did not show *how* the son's unconscious homosexual feelings toward his father caused paranoia. Not only is the causal chain missing, the basic elements of the theory are vague."[101] Goffman rejected the medical and legal frame of reference used conventionally to define the term "homosexual" in favor of a more restrictive one of his own devising: "I refer only to individuals who participate in a special community of understanding wherein members of one's own sex are defined as the most desirable sexual objects, and sociability is energetically organized around the pursuit and entertainment of these objects."[102] In effect responding to Becker's request for more varieties of homosexual life, he went on to distinguish among male and female homosexual communities in custodial settings[103] and "the male and female 'gay' worlds sustained in urban centers."[104] Apparently, Goffman's definition did not include the established same-sex couple domiciled as a marriage nor the individual isolate or "closeted" homosexual. but he did observe "that an individual can retain membership in the gay world and yet not engage in homosexual practices, just as he [or she] can exploit the gay [people who are sexually active] through sale of sexual favors without participating socially and spiritually in the gay community."

Clinard elaborated on Becker's invitation and concerns not only by pointing out that the "label 'homosexual,' based as it is on a person's sexual proclivities, . . . makes little sense when applied to a person; one is unlikely to speak of a nonhomosexual as a 'heterosexual' or that person's behavior as heterosexuality," but also by asserting that "Persons who engage in homosexual behavior come from all social classes, have varying degrees of education, are from a wide range of occupations and professions, have varied interests and avocations, and may be single or married."[105] But he went even further, linking a distinction (made earlier by Parsons[106]) between "variant" and "deviant" conduct to labeling practices: "Although homosexual behavior is variant behavior in itself," Clinard observed, "it need not be deviant; it becomes deviant behavior when there is societal reaction."[107] And, after quoting Michael Schofield's comment that "The social and economic value of the homosexuals in the community varies with the hostility shown them,"[108] he offered that "Some of the attitudes in parts of Western society that homosexuality is deviant behavior can be explained by certain aspects of the Christian tradition."[109] Ultimately, however, the result of the adoption of a labeling perspective by sociologists was not to obviate altogether the stigma of deviance from homosexuality or from those who felt homoerotic impulses or who engaged in same-sex practices, but rather to shift attention onto "the moral entrepreneurs" (as Becker called them),[110] or onto "the process by which degradation is translated further into denials, suspensions, and revocations of the right to follow one's livelihood" (as Lemert phrased the matter).[111]

Labeling theory has been challenged by some sociologists of deviance either for doing or promising too much or too little with respect to its supposed improvements over older perspectives.[112] Lindesmith, Strauss, and Denzin deny that the perspective designated as "labeling" is either an "approach," a "theory," or a "school"; rather, they insist, it is a specific application of the "general orientation . . . embodied in the . . . tradition of symbolic interactionist thought."[113] Deviance, they argue, arises out of conditions, situations, and processes whereby "individuals may become tainted, or spoiled interactants . . ." Homosexuals, they observe, belong to that category of the potentially stigmatized that includes "ex–mental patients, the recently divorced, unmarried parents, or former embezzlers, i.e., those whose deviance is not publicly visible." And, they concede, "for it to have interactional effects the individual must make public these hidden facts in his [sic] biography." Anticipating the risks and opportunities that might arise if "outing" were to occur, they observe: "Often it is to his [or her] advantage to do so, for a tainted past hovers over his [or her] life. If he [or she] refuses to tell, he [or she] may find that someone else will."

Quite a different challenge to labeling theory arises from those who adhere to a more comprehensive "phenomenological" perspective. Carol A. B. Warren and John M. Johnson, while recognizing the positive contributions made in the name of the labeling perspective, accuse the adherents of the latter approach of holding to an a priori belief that there are no "core values" in American society—core values, that is, against which untoward acts might be measured for their deviance.[114] Contending, quite wrongly in this author's opinion,[115] that Lemert, unlike other labeling theorists, had acknowledged that "there are certain values (or, phenomenologically, key social meanings) that come to be widely shared by most of the members of American society through their socialization experiences, and other less central values that are more diversely and pluralistically held,"[116] they insist that "From Warren's research, it appears that certain moral meanings connected with sexuality are so taken for granted by members of society that they constitute, in nonphenomenological language, a set of societal 'core values.'"[117] In addition to calling for empirical investigations into whether and to what extent core values exist in American society, Warren and Johnson object to the emphasis labelers put on what Lemert called secondary deviance,[118] that is, the responses of norm violators to being labeled deviants, responses that transform their activities into careers, communities, or stable social roles. "[B]y stressing the rule-breaking of the 'deviants' and the rule-enforcing of 'officials' who do the labeling of such actions as the central dialectic of deviance . . . , labeling theory centers its attention on acts to the exclusion of any investigation into the nature of the 'being' of the actor."[119] In contrast, again utilizing materials from Warren's field notes,[120] as well as a quotation from the pseudonymous Donald Webster Cory's autobiographical *The Homosexual in America*,[121] they claim "that among homosexuals, the 'deviant' *sex-act* is not the organizing aspect of their lives; the organizing conception is *being* homosexual, in the full sense of a condition or an identity."[122] They conclude that "homosexuality is *symbolically labeled* deviance . . . [and] that this is primarily so because, even in our immensely pluralistic society, it tends to be the one type of deviance condemned, at least rhetorically, by almost everyone."[123] Hence, it follows for Warren and Johnson that "This, in turn, gives some indication of the inadequacies of labeling theory's *implied* pluralism-of-values, and emphasis on 'acts,' deviant or labeling." Trapped between their stigmatized existence as homoerotic "beings" or as same-sex "doers," homosexuals, as well as sociologists of that phenomenon, could only acknowledge the sad praxiological truth in the argument put forward by Evelyn Hooker: "It is highly probable that it is at least as accurate to speak of the homosexual community as a 'deviant community' as to describe it as a 'community of deviants.'"[124]

Escape from Deviance: Crossing the Postmodern Divide

To postmodern sociologists concerned with the problematics of deviance theory and with the dilemmas and contradictions in the lives of those so labeled—more especially with those suffering from a lesbian or homosexual identification—the issue has been radically reformulated. The stigmas of their deviance can only be removed, so it seems to be argued, if deviance as a generalized concept, and homosexuality as deviance in particular, are withdrawn altogether from the foundational discourse of social science. The beginnings of modern social science—as well as the onset of the idea of obscenity[125]—are in the philosophy of the Enlightenment with its emphasis on reason, empiricism, and secular progress. Hence, it is through a fundamental critique of the thought and practices of the Enlightenment that this group of postmodernist sociologists hope to find their route out of deviance.

Central to the general argument is the thesis that holds that the Enlightenment, once it is subjected to a disenchanting critical analysis, will reveal itself as little more than a rhetorical mask for privilege and privileging.[126] Reason, the argument continues, finds its ultimate expression in hierarchies and dichotomies. These in turn become the representational terms for discourses on various collectivities of color, gender, lineage, culture, and praxis. Thus, to take one prominent example, Homi K. Bhabha exposes the purposes behind "colonial discourse": "The objective of colonial discourse is to construe the colonized as a population of degenerate types on the basis of racial origin, in order to justify conquest and to establish systems of administration and instruction."[127] To such post-Enlightenment critics, blacks, Asians, women, and homosexuals are the major inhabitants of that philosophy's body of warrantable excludables; or, in the language of sociology, of ostracized "deviants."[128]

The ultimate source of the marginalization of these victims of the Enlightenment is the very idea of *difference.* "The concept of difference," observes Monique Wittig, "has nothing ontological about it. It is only the way that the masters interpret a historical situation of domination."[129] But, rather than concluding in terms either of the tradition of thought that comes down to us from William James and the pragmatists, that is, the argument that differentiating categorizations are mundane but not uncriticizable necessities for sensibilizing the buzz of ubiquitous phenomena, or of reminding us of Margaret Mary Wood's admonition that although the "method of establishing categories in dealing with new phenomena . . . is itself a necessary reasoning process," its "unfortunate aspect, where people are so classified, is the frequent limitation of the categories and the nature of the emotional qualities which come to be associated with some of these,"[130] Wittig is adamant: "The function of difference is to mask at every level the conflicts of interest, including ideological ones."[131]

Lest one suppose that such hegemonically driven differences as man/woman and heterosexual/homosexual are to be retained, Wittig offers a critique of the totalizing effects of the conceptualizations of what she designates as the "straight mind"—that is, the representative carrier of the discourse at the root of modern scientific thinking, a discourse that assumes that there is a "core of nature" in modernist cultural discourse that "resists examination, a relationship excluded from the social in the analysis—a relationship whose characteristic is ineluctability in culture, as well as in nature, and which is the heterosexual relationship."[132] As Wittig sees the matter: "I can only underline the oppressive character that the straight mind is clothed in its tendency to immediately universalize its production of concepts into general laws which claim to hold true for all societies, all epochs, all individuals. Thus one speaks of *the* exchange of women, *the* difference between the sexes, *the* symbolic order, *the* Unconscious, desire, *jouissance*, culture, history, giving an absolute meaning to these concepts when they are only categories founded upon heterosexuality or thought which produces the difference between the sexes as a political and philosophical dogma."[133]

The radical character of this anti-Enlightenment discourse with respect to the recent rise of multicultural claims and controversies is indicated in Peter McLaren's demand that "Existing systems of difference which organize social life into patterns of domination and subordination must be reconstructed."[134] In the arenas where feminism, gender studies, and homosexuality carve out intellectual spaces whereon to launch their respective critiques, the debates over a liberal humanistic (and modernist) orientation and one that challenges the foundational sex-preference dichotomies illustrate contending reformist and revolutionary outlooks. Drawing upon the later works of Foucault,[135] some postmodernists have transformed the older social constructionist approaches into a political sociology emphasizing the role that sexually related labels, categories, and feelings play in "a system of discourses and practices which form part of the intensifying surveillance and control of the individual."[136] Thus, Celia Kitzinger regards the liberal humanistic position that treats "true love" as an exculpatory justification for lesbian intercourse (and which, as the dissenters to the majority perspective in *Bowers v. Hardwick,* the 1986 Supreme Court decision upholding

Georgia's antisodomy law, pointed out, treats sexual conduct among consenting adults within one's domicile as a private matter not subject to sumptuary controls)[137] as unacceptably reductionist: "In representing lesbianism as a route to perfect bliss and inner harmony, lesbianism becomes a private solution to an individual malaise."[138] In opposition to liberal humanism, Kitzinger advocates a philosophy as well as a politics of radical feminism. According to the latter outlook, the liberal-humanist perspective is to be rejected altogether because it "functions as an instrument of social control, dictating what identities are and are not appropriate for the oppressed . . . and rewarding, with a limited form of social acceptance, those members of the oppressed who present self-descriptive discourse in conformity with this ideology."[139] Perhaps the clearest statement of the kind of cultural change that the gay movement sought was given by philosopher Guy Hocquenghem (1944–1988), a charter member of the *Front Homosexuel d'Action Révolutionnaire*, and a victim of AIDS, who observed in 1972, "Revolutionary tradition maintains a clear division between the public and the private. The special characteristic of the homosexual intervention is to make what is private—sexuality's shameful little secret—intervene in public, in social organisation . . . The gay movement is . . . not seeking recognition as a new political power on a par with others; its own existence contradicts the system of political thought, because it relates to a different problematic . . . The gay movement . . . demonstrates that civilization is the trap into which desire keeps falling."[140]

To keep from falling into civilization's trap, Steven Seidman and a group of colleagues hope to inaugurate "Queer Theory" and install it as a feature of the emerging postmodern perspective.[141] Queer theory takes its point of departure not only from the epiphany that Seidman experienced upon discovering his own homosexuality,[142] but also from a more general condition—the anxieties and confusions that arose with postmodernization's problematization of the entire Western tradition.[143] For some, the separation of social theory from its modern source has led to a sense of its homelessness. As Iain Chambers puts it:

> Here culture, its presumed values and aesthetics, cannot be conceived as a timeless entity . . . Here there are no eternal values, no pure states . . . What we are now called upon to confront is the emergence of differences under the sign of "homelessness"; that is, of subjects, languages, histories, acts, texts, events . . . values that are forced to find their home in a world without guarantees . . . This idea of facing the other, of acknowledging differences, and with them the diverse inscrip-

tions that inhabit and constitute our world is . . . also a rendezvous to be found within the internal territories of our own cultures—on the "other" side of the city, culture and languages we inhabit.[144]

With respect to the sex-labeled "other," consigned to his or her less-than-respectable place under what Seidman calls the modernist, scientific, sexual and social regime—Seidman asserts "Science created heterosexuality and homosexuality as the master categories of the sexual self, and I live under this sexual regime"[145]—Donna Haraway adds "There is not even such a state as 'being' female, itself a highly complex category constructed in contested sexual scientific discourses and other social practices."[146] In effect, Queer Theory joins forces with the other postmodern assaults on Western rationality and science. Haraway concludes, "Gender, race, or class consciousness is an achievement forced on us by the terrible historical experience of the contradictory social realities of patriarchy, colonialism, racism and capitalism."[147] Queer Theory promises to participate in what Cornel West calls a "new cultural politics of difference,"[148] one that will usher in a form of multicultural life that perseveres in and through an absence of societally enforced invidious distinctions. "What we multiculturalists say," observes Tony Thomas, a self-described thirty-year-old African American inmate in the California Correctional Center at Susanville, "is that it's possible to have pluralism without hierarchy . . . [N]o one single culture can take over all the space or story—what Eurocentrism has historically done to forcibly impose or parade itself as a universal world view."[149]

The Conflict and Tragedy of Culture

For Queer theorists the strategy whereby the stigma of either primary or secondary deviance will be lifted from homoerotic beliefs and practices appears to be an unacknowledged and particularized variant of the revolution described by Simmel in his essays on the conflict and tragedy of culture.[150] Central to Simmel's depiction of a generalized dialectic of culture was his claim that there is an inherent struggle of *life* to become emancipated from all the *forms* through which it is simultaneously expressed and constrained. To illustrate his point, Simmel asserted that the cultural revolutionaries who would emerge in the twentieth century would be opposed to both marriage and prostitution because each was a form of the erotic and they would be seeking to liberate the erotic for itself.[151] According to Queer theorists Arlene Stein and Ken Plummer, one of the hallmarks of their and their colleagues' approach is to deconstruct and critique "a conceptualization of sexuality which sees sexual power embodied in different levels of social life, expressed discursively and enforced through boundaries and binary divides."[152] To these theorists such binary divides as heterosexual/homosexual are not merely dichotomies but, more significantly, discursive elements of a power-driven hierarchical division and a repressive heterosexual judgment. The strategies and tactics that would designate homosexuals as one more "minority" worthy, like African Americans or women, of civil rights are rejected, as are the corrective school's mono- or cross-cultural medical models,[153] and the constructionists'[154] depiction of homosexuality as normatively transgressive or deviant vis-a-vis a "normal" heterosexuality.[155] The liberation of the oppressed element in the dichotomy, that is, homosexuality, or the homo-erotic as such, is obtained not merely by decentering heterosexuality through an elaborated deconstructionist approach that historicizes and particularizes its emergence as an element in social as well as sociological discourse,[156] but, more profoundly, by shattering forever the dichotomous form, and indeed all dichotomous forms, thus allowing, to borrow language from the Chinese version of this dialectic, the "yang" to be liberated from its embeddedness in the "yin."[157] Simmel was prescient with respect to perceiving such a development in terms of a sociology of exhausted cultural knowledge:

> At present we are experiencing . . . a struggle of life against the form *as such*, against the *principle* of form . . . [W]hat is happening is not only a negative, passive dying out of traditional forms, but simultaneously a fully positive drive towards life which is actively repressing these forms . . . [However, since] this struggle, in extent and intensity, does not permit concentration on the creation of new forms, it makes a virtue of necessity and insists on a fight against forms simply because they are forms. This is probably only possible in an epoch where cultural forms are conceived of as an exhausted soil which has yielded all that it could grow, which, however, is still completely covered by products of its former fertility.[158]

Seidman's justification for a postmodern reinstauration of social science—one that would include Queer theory as part of its epistemology—is a striking illustration of Simmel's adumbration. Seidman points out that the "social origins of the challenge to the Enlightenment paradigm of social knowledge by Lyotard and Foucault lie in the social rebellions of the sixties and seventies."[159] For, he goes on, in "the student and labor protests, in the movement for prison and psychiatric reform, and in the feminist and gay movements, they perceive a far reaching questioning of the culture of the Enlightenment." Seidman is among those who believe that the "culture of the Enlightenment is losing its capacity to legitimate and give coherence and purpose to the lives of many of us in the west." As Seidman perceives the matter, the human and social sciences that in the seventeenth, eighteenth, and nineteenth centuries overwhelmed and replaced religion, magic, and opinion as both the forms and the sources of truth, were never able to provide foundations for themselves sufficient "to establish a line of demarcation between science and nonscience . . ." However, this epistemological critique is less important than one that points out the failure of the Enlightenment discourses to live up to their promise—that is, to contribute to human advancement. On this issue, he observes, "Whether it is feminists who view science as implicated in male domination or poststructuralists analyzing the disciplining and normalizing role of scientific-medical discourses, the claim that a scientific culture necessarily advances the progress of humanity has lost considerable plausibility." A Simmelian revolution is contemplated here. It seeks nothing less than to end the binary dialectic and free sexuality from its debilitating prison-house, and to carry out this revolution by means of a fundamental reconfiguration of the expressions of knowledge and truth.

Although Seidman and other postmodernists concede that the advent of their perspective is not a herald of the end of modernity and admit that they continue to live and work under modernist regimes of truth and power,[160] their outlook on the man/woman, heterosexual/homosexual dualisms adumbrates a scientific and cultural revolution. In this respect, Eve Kosofsky Sedgwick's *The Epistemology of the Closet,* a work that "proposes that many of the major modes of thought and knowledge in twentieth century Western culture as a whole are structured—indeed fractured—by a chronic, now endemic crisis of homo-heterosexual definition," goes on to assert "that an understanding of virtually any aspect of modern Western culture must be not merely incomplete, but damaged in its central substance to the degree that it does not incorporate a critical analysis of modern homo/heterosexual definition. . . ."[161] Seidman goes even further. Holding that the "Enlightenment tradition has organized knowledge around a series of major oppositions: science/rhetoric, science/politics, science/literature and science/narrative," he accuses that tradition of conjoining the oppositions of science/rhetoric and science/politics to "a related series of binaries" among which are "reason/affect,

disinterested/interested . . . masculine/feminine, and knowledge/power."
Moreover, "in these contrasts," he insists, "the first term is positioned as
superior."[162] When the human studies are postmodernized, he believes
"these hierarchical oppositions are marginalized or displaced" and the
"social world is fragmented into a multitude of communities, cultural traditions, and knowledges . . . [in response to which] the social analyst will abandon a legislative role in favor of an 'interpretive' role: the social analyst as a
mediator between different social worlds, as interpreter of alien cultures,
and as advocate for particular moral visions."

Stein and Plummer have put the issue more specifically: "We need to
challenge the assumption that sexuality is necessarily organized around a
binary division between homosexuality and heterosexuality."[163] And Chrys
Ingraham faults most sociologists and some feminists not only for continuing to give rhetorical support to sex- and gender-based binary
dichotomies, but also for failing to raise the same issue to macroinstitutional
proportions: "The cultural production of behaviors and expectations as
'socially learned' involves all social institutions from family, church, and
education to the Department of Defense." Indeed, she asks, "Without institutionalized heterosexuality, that is, the ideological and organizational regulation of relations between men and women—would gender even exist?"[164]

Queer Theory as a Social Movement: Sexual Life against All Its Forms

A problem for, as well as one asset that lends its support to, Queer
theory is its embeddedness in a congeries of liberating social movements.
These movements require the discipline's theoretical discourses to speak
to and in behalf of basic sociocultural changes and engaged political
action.[165] Despite the emerging Queer theorists' ambivalence about hitch-
ing their wagon-load of critiques to the fading star of sociology, there is one
point of meeting to be found. It resides in the fact that the discipline of sociology, at least in the United States, has from its inception been implicated
in what used to be called "the Social Movement." [166] "As the successor to
Protestant theology," this writer recently observed, "American sociology
has been compelled to assume the burden of providing a sociodicy equal
to or better than that of its religious predecessors . . . [Nevertheless,] it has
not yet found its own purely public philosophy."[167] Like such postmodern
approaches as Queer theory, the discipline called sociology is caught up in
the paradox of claiming to construct an authoritative social science and to

foster establishment of a rational and righteous society.[168] It is worth recalling that, in spelling out his opposition to the position taken by labeling theorists with respect to deviance, Alan F. Blum accused the latter of voiding, as well as avoiding, their moral responsibility. Sociologists, he argues, have an ethical obligation to state what conduct is properly to be designated as "wrongdoing." By transferring that decision from the sociological observer to "the labeling citizen . . . [who] then becomes the concrete ignoramus,"[169] they default on their duty both to rational science and to humanity. "To say 'deviance is an attribution' is to say that one has no desire to speak essentially about wrongdoing, that one is not interested in the Reason of wrongdoing."[170] But, Blum insists, "Sociology studies the moral life, and sociology is itself an instance of the moral life."[171] If Queer theory is to become a part of the sociological enterprise, it too will have to come to terms with this ethical conundrum.

Simmel had argued that the revolution carried on by the protagonists of *life* against all the *forms* of life would ultimately fail because there is no way that life can express itself except through or in opposition to a form of itself.[172] Seidman's and his colleagues' opposition to binary forms is revolutionary in this Simmelian sense. The forces of life are said to be found in all those second terms—especially those presented in the oppositions reason/affect, masculine/feminine, heterosexual/homosexual—that such binaries marginalize. Their liberation would occur, so the argument seems to go, only when the totalizing idea-complex that supports it—that is, the idea of binary opposition—is deconstructed.

But, should this project succeed, what would replace the totalizing idea? At this point, Seidman's and other postmodernists' arguments seem to falter and draw back. Antifoundationalism seems to call for antiformalism. As Steven Best points out, "[I]n direct opposition to modern views, postmodernists valorize incommensurability and fragmentation as liberating. They . . . emphasize difference over identity, plurality over uniformity, relativism over foundationalism."[173] And "Queer Theory," as Seidman perceives it, "wishes to challenge the regime of sexuality itself—that is, the knowledge that constructs the self as sexual and that assumes heterosexuality and homosexuality as categories marking the truth of sexual selves."[174] At present, Seidman asserts, "Sex itself is entangled in a web of dense meanings, feelings, and social and political agendas. It has become virtually impossible to forge a trail through this terrain without being forced to quickly decide whether one is a friend of choice or order."[175] Queer theorists have made a selection of sorts. Although Seidman holds that "Queer theory aspires to transform homosexual theory into a general social theory or one standpoint from which to analyze whole societies,"[176] he also is morally engaged. "My approach," he insists, "will make it much more difficult to label specific desires, acts or lifestyles as deviant or perverse."[177]

Queer Theory and Social Science

For Queer theory to be able to achieve its intended scientific and ethical objectives, it will have to become a part, if not the whole, of a reconstituted social theory. But, as Barbara L. Marshall points out, "What is unclear is how one can sustain any practical and moral intent while simultaneously eschewing such 'core modernist concepts' as 'progress, domination, liberation and humanity.'"[178] Even more threatening is that Queer theory's challenge to established science might be hoist by its own petard. Rooted as it is in an application of an elaborated version of the constructionist thesis, one that permits it to launch "a merciless war on all sociological categories,"[179] Queer theory risks having its arsenal of epistemological weaponry turned on itself. As Guy Oakes has pointed out:

> On the one hand, queer theory exhibits a peculiar loathing for binary oppositions and . . . damns them all by subjecting them to the implacable logic of radical constructionism. One the other hand, . . . queer theory is possible only on the basis of the binaries queer/straight or queer/conventional. Without these or equivalent dichotomies, queer theory would have no redoubt from which to criticize categories and transgress rules. Without some epistemically privileged distinction on the basis of which the concept of the queer can be formed, queer theory would be impossible . . . How can queer theorists avoid self contradiction? . . . Queer theorists must concede that the queer/straight binary and the concept of sexuality are merely social constructs. . . . If the constructionist logic of queer theory is followed consistently and applied to queer theory itself, then the queer project is exposed as nothing more than another arbitrary social invention . . . Queer theory is either self-contradictory or reflexively self-defeating.[179]

There are two issues here. First is what might be called the Simmelian culture paradox problem, that is, how Queer theory's version of the liberation of sexuality from all its forms is constrained by the impossibility of the project. Second is that of Oakes's challenge, that is, how Queer theory can circumvent the latter's imperative, namely, that the "theoretician must possess a conceptual apparatus that does not collapse under the weight of its own inconsistencies." In each case, the matter is not solved but only questionably resolved.

Form, Life, and the Erotic

Let us first turn to the Simmelian paradox. A close reading of Seidman's and other postmodernists' depiction of the postmodern condition does not reveal total chaos, but rather an ongoing decentering of the dominant modernist forms and their replacement occurring as a collage of forms, styles, communities, and other phenomena living symbiotically—but in an uneasy relationship with one another. The situation seems to cry out for a subliminal social contract to prevent it from becoming a Hobbesian cockpit. There are many issues entailed in this conception, but here I wish only to point to how it illustrates Simmel's conception of the "tragedy of culture."[180] In Queer theory the *idea* of form has neither been decentered altogether nor have all forms of sexuality been extinguished. For Queer theorists the postmodern situation is one wherein there is no central dominating form; rather, a multitude of forms thrive. The polymorphous erotic is no longer perverse, but neither is it unconstrained. For gay activists and self-conscious homosexuals, as well as Queer theorists, homoerotic feelings and practices are a foundational part of an individual's identity kit. Relieved from the stigma of an overarching regime of deviance labeling by the postmodernist version of deliverance, same-sex preference is not thereby relieved from every possible form of evaluative judgment. Concerning such a new order of life, K. Anthony Appiah—who makes a point of observing that he is speaking "as someone who counts in America as a gay black man"—has warned: "There will be proper ways of being black and gay, there will be expectations to be met, demands will be made." And, he concludes, "It is at this point that someone who takes autonomy seriously will ask whether we have not replaced one kind of tyranny with another."[181] Thus does Simmel's dialectic continue without promise of reaching an end.

A Phenomenological Resolution to Oakes's Challenge

Oakes's challenge can be reconceptualized—and its paradox resolved—in what must be admitted is an extratheoretical manner. The first step would be to adopt the outlook that is put forward in Maurice Natanson's analysis of history as a finite province of meaning.[182] What the postmodernists refer to as the grand historical metanarratives[183] that derive from Enlightenment thought, Natanson calls, simply, "Big history"; while those that such post-modernists as Seidman wish to privilege as "local narratives"[184] he designates as "little histories."[185] The same distinction might be made for sociological theories. "Big sociology" could be said to be exemplified by the Parsonsian perspective wherein, as Alvin Gouldner argued, "Man is hollowed out, empty, being filled with substance only by society";[186] while "little sociology" would be found in the hundreds of case studies, ethnographies, and participant-observer researches, especially those dedicated to an "emic" perspective, that is, those that "draw upon actors' interpretations and necessarily call upon local knowledge . . ."[187] Big sociology, like its sibling, Big history, tends to treat the individual as a passive receptacle for the social process to work on; little sociology, on the other hand, permits individuals and local groups to be masters of their own projects.[188]

According to the postmodern critique, modernity could be said to privilege the discourses of Big sociology and to relegate little sociologies to the underprivileged microecological corners and lowly regarded interstices of society, social thought, and social practice. Moreover, the well-established oppositional voices that are embedded within the discourses of Big sociology—Marxist critiques of capitalism are the most prominent example—might be accused of suffering from the same defects as those they oppose.[189] In this regard, Gail Dines has put the matter succinctly: "[B]y privileging class as THE major organizing feature of western society, Marxism renders other forms of oppression invisible; in a society characterized by multiple systems of inequality, this is ultimately a recipe for maintaining the status quo through failed attempts at social change."[190] Hence, it might be said to follow that, when representatives of little sociologies come to believe that they are bearers of a greater truth than that purveyed by the discourses of Big sociology, and when the latter's truth is also said to be inherently oppressive and unjust, the spokespersons for little sociologies might seek greater authority for their own outlook—they might, that is, embark on an epistemological contestation. They might seek to elevate what has been regarded as a parochial point of view to a position of universal authority.

In the case of Oakes's challenge to Queer theory, the advocates of the latter might reply by denying that they are party to a contradiction. They could agree to the central proposition of the constructionists, namely, that all paradigms of culture, social thought, and sociological conceptualizations, including their own, are arbitrary, but assert, in a manner reminiscent of Orwell's thesis about the egalitarian status of pigs in *Animal Farm,* that some constructions—that is, those that derive from the Enlightenment, itself a civilizational construction—have greater (undue) authority than others. Should Queer theorists adopt this posture, they might redesignate their perspective as a little sociology with big aspirations. That, it seems, is what Seidman means when he speaks of universalizing Queer theory. Moreover, given these aspirations, Queer theorists could be seen as having begun an intellectually instaurative social movement as well as a social theory, the former aimed at securing both academic legitimacy and epistemological hegemony for the latter. All of this, in turn, could be seen as a praxiological response to that aspect of the postmodern perspective that holds that the role of power and power struggles in both the overthrow and the legitimation of discourses is decisive.

Justice, Evil, and Deviance

The advent of the postmodern as condition and as emerging perspective has challenged both social policy and public philosophy. Whereas such modernist social thinkers as Talcott Parsons, Robert K. Merton, and Gunnar Myrdal had assumed that the dynamics of any social system, America's in particular, would inexorably push toward the comprehensive integration of its values, beliefs, and practices under conditions that would recognize deviance as consisting in norm-defying innovations, pathological maladjustments, rebellions, or revolutions, postmodernists emphasize either a Yeatsian-like belief that the normative center cannot hold and that things have fallen or will soon fall apart, or a Dadaist-like outlook that holds that the shards and shibboleths of a dying civilization herald the beginning (as well as the problematic) of a new anticultural disorder. Like many liberal and humanistic modernists, postmodernists are opponents of racism, patriarchy, hegemonism, colonialism, and environmental diffidence. But whereas the modernists regard the wrongdoings associated with each of these as deviations from the positive normative system of Reasoned thought and rational practice that grew out of the Enlightenment, postmodernists hold that these evils are representative practices of that Enlightenment. Thus, there is a revolutionary perspective on deviance in postmodernism: Stated boldly, it is that the reign of Reason and all its effects is or ought to be regarded as unprivilegeable, as in effect a regime of deviance that buttresses a deviant regime. In place of these regimes they favor a nonregime of egalitarian communities, living side by side, realizing freedoms of all sorts, and yet somehow avoiding both moral chaos and the Hobbesian cockpit.

Sociological theorists of deviance, no doubt responding to their approach's Protestant origins, have tended to emphasize one or another form of social scientific mercy rather than a rational praxis of justice. It is a conceit of some advocates of feminist theory that mercy is a female's outlook, and that it is morally superior to a male-oriented idea of justice. Thus, Carol Gilligan conceives the judicial practices of Portia—the woman judge in men's clothing in Shakespeare's *Merchant of Venice* who forces the hapless Jew Shylock to renounce his own religion, convert to Christianity, surrender his fortune, and give up his daughter to a Gentile[191]— as paradigmatic of feminist justice-as-mercy, and as standing in opposition to the masculine sense of justice that allegedly exhibits a "blind willingness to sacrifice people to truth . . . [that] has always been the danger of an ethics abstracted from life."[192] She further argues that "While an ethic of justice proceeds from the premise of equality—that everyone should be treated the same—an ethic of care rests on the premise of nonviolence—that no one should be hurt."[193] Apparently, Shylock is not a "no one."

Modernist sociological deviance theory, and especially that part of it that deals with homoerotic expressions of sexuality, despite feminist claims to the contrary, has more often called for understanding, empathy, care-giving, and mercy than it has for justice. From the time of their predecessor—Charles R. Henderson's concern to rationalize society's Christian duty to do something about "dependent," "defective," and "delinquent" classes[194]—the conventional sociologists concerned with that which is socially disapproved or jurisprudentially unlawful, whether they called theirs the study of social pathology, social disorganization, social disintegration or personal disorganization,[195] have been driven by the desire to contribute to the *cure* of souls[196] or to a beneficent social control of minds gone awry or groups gone astray.[197] The move toward labeling theory and constructionism did not so much distinguish those unjustly accused from those deserving stigmatization or punishment as it did offer both sociological understanding and a call for toleration. Thus, although Albert K. Cohen could define deviant behavior as that which evidences noncompliance with rules, or, more judgmentally, as "knavery, skulduggery, cheating, unfairness, crime, sneakiness, malingering, cutting corners, immorality, dishonesty, betrayal, graft, corruption, wickedness, and sin—in short, deviance,"[198] his analysis, insisting that "Behavior is deviant . . . only if the actor is subject to the jurisdiction of the rules that the behavior contravenes,"[199] does not offer a method or a philosophy whereby the justness of the accusation of deviance might be queried. Rather, the thrust of this representative work of modernist (functionalist) sociology is, under the guise of offering explanations for deviance, to present a variety of excuses—that is, discursive strategies wherein full responsibility for the wrongdoing is denied[200]—as mitigations for the misbehavior in question.[201]

Empathy based on explanations for homosexuality that function as excuses, rather than proposals of a theory of justice suited to a pluralistic and multicultural society, figure as the significant element in Craig B. Little's proposal that society's benevolent toleration for the diversity exhibited in the several lifeways of its minorities be extended to both male and female homosexuals, and that "Social policies . . . focus on decriminalization of homosexual activity between consenting adults . . ."[202] It is worthy of note that Seidman—in accord with the "postmodern, pragmatic standpoint [that holds that] particular sex acts and intimate arrangements carry no intrinsic moral significance,"[203] and despite the fact that his "sympathy lies with the libertarian defense of sexual pluralism" rather than a "Romanticism [that] creates a vast culture of stigmatized desires, identities, networks and even communities"—finds it necessary to propose not a theory and praxiology of justice that would focus on the rights of the unalloyed person, but, rather, an ethic of *voluntary* responsibility, rooted in the pragmatism of consequentiality. His ethic, among other things, would oppose cross-generational sex if the younger partner "is a minor or below the age of consent," but permit adult consensual sex so long as the partners to it are conscious of the consequences that might ensue. Given postmodernism's rejection of the entire culture of the Enlightenment, what theory of justice and what praxes of enforcement would institutionalize this ethic are left unanswered.

Conclusion

Rather than follow the postmodernists in their attempt to tear down the entire fabric of the classical tradition—a project designed in behalf of their claim that the "'Enlightenment' was supposed to replace the chaotic dark regions of the mythologizing psyche with sober modern reason, a project which neglected the possibility that mythic narratives might be expressions of a deeper relatedness with the powers that move humans than rational consciousness can touch"[204]—the sociologist concerned with wrongdoing and evil might better turn to a heretofore rarely considered quest: the construction of a theory of justice. As John O'Neill has pointed out, "Lyotard's debile imperative, 'Be Just!', lacks any interpretative rules. It is a commandment that will only sound out to those bewitched by a praxis without either a subject or a community that might offer any model of being true, or free, or just."[205] Although John M. Johnson has provided a signal service to the construction of a theory of justice with his comprehensive critique of both classical and modern perspectives, neither his reduction of the concept so that it embraces only "our struggle to live with virtue in our social and communal lives," nor his catalog of what he regards as the eight characteristics of justice—namely, that it is a struggle, fundamentally emotional, developmental in the course of an individual's passage through the age cycle, gendered, personal, a matter of interaction, rhetorical and language-based, and selfish in the sense that one must love oneself in order to love others[206]—gives us either an explicit or implicit sense of who the subject of justice is; moreover, his thesis restricts the operation of justice to a microecological niche.[207]

The proper subject of justice, I would suggest, is the *person,* in sociology what used to be called the *socius.*[208] In the Fourteenth Amendment to the United States Constitution the person is guaranteed the equal protection of the laws. Precisely because in its legal conception the person is unmodified, any labels legislatively attached to him or her are subject to litigation.[209] Equality of the person in the law is part of the legacy of the Enlightenment. It guarantees not that every person will be treated alike, but rather that any treatment must satisfy the judicial inquiry of whether it is reasonably related to the accomplishment of a legitimate public purpose and whether the individuals included in the categorical placement made by that treatment are in fact rightly classified.[210] A theory of justice privileging the person would do much to establish the grounds by which the powers of the labelers might be checked. It could facilitate sexual and other forms of liberation in the name of the yet unrealized promise of the Enlightenment.

Part IV

A Commencement Rather Than a Conclusion: Narrative Strategies and the Dramas of Social Reality

CHAPTER TEN

The Bequests of Twentieth-Century Sociology to the Twenty-First Century

When has anybody ever been governed by "the teachings of history"
when he was philosophizing or legislating? The teachings of history
can always be set aside, if they are a hindrance, by alleging that the
times have changed and that new conditions exist. This allegation
may be true, and the possibility that it is true must always be taken
into account.

> *William Graham Sumner,* Folkways: A Study of the
> Sociological Importance of Usages, Manners, Customs, Mores,
> and Morals

In 1933, *The Yale Review* published a long-lost essay by William
Graham Sumner entitled, "The Bequests of the Nineteenth Century to the
Twentieth."[1] Sumner's essay had in fact been written in 1901 and had been
revised a little later. Published more than two decades after his death, it
nevertheless proved to be prescient. Sumner had chosen to write about the
legacy that developments in the nineteenth century had presented to the
twentieth. His essay was uncharacteristically optimistic. Although he
predicted that a struggle would soon array the forces of plutocracy against
those of democracy, and foresaw that "the [twentieth] century will be as full
of war as the eighteenth century was and for the same reasons," he nevertheless held that:

> The nineteenth century bequeaths to the twentieth new land and new
> arts, which are the prime conditions of material welfare . . . There are
> inexhausted improvements all over the globe which the nineteenth

century undertook and paid for, the gain of which will come to the twentieth ... The population of the globe is far below the number which it could support with the present resources ... The conjuncture favors numbers. While numbers increase, the comfort per capita will increase ... The life-conditions will improve. The chances for those who inherit nothing will be good provided that they are industrious, prudent, and temperate ... So far as we can see ahead there is every reason for even rash optimism in regard to the material or economic welfare of mankind.[2]

Sumner did not concentrate his attention on the bequests of nineteenth-century sociology to the twentieth. That discipline was in its second period of incarnation at the time Sumner wrote his essay. Its first period, that had been developed by the antebellum Southern Comteans, had been cast into the historical dustbin after 1865,[3] and the science of society had been reinaugurated with Sumner's course on the subject given at Yale University in 1876.[4] There had followed developments of the discipline in newly formed departments at Columbia University, the University of Chicago, the University of Kansas, and within the Economics Department of Harvard University.[5] As a new discipline, sociology had taken as its fundamental problem what was called the "Social Question."[6] Largely influenced by Protestant endeavor and by the Social Gospel movement, the sociologists of Sumner's day (although Sumner himself was an exception to this point of view as was his arch-opponent, Lester F. Ward) undertook nothing less than forging and developing a sociodicy for America.[7] The fledgling discipline, though faced with many problems of conceptualization and application, was sufficiently optimistic about its future to require little critical analysis or self-examination at that time.[8] Sumner himself seemed to look forward to the role that quantification would play in the developing science. Thus, he observed, "Science has a mass of acquired knowledge and processes to confide to the coming generation whose power and value in the struggle for existence are beyond imagination. There are acquisitions in the higher branches of pure mathematics, which are fruitless at present but which are certain to prove of inestimable value . . ."[9]

Nearly a century after Sumner wrote, sociology cannot feel so complacent. It is a commonplace of talk and writing about the discipline to see it in *crisis*.[10] The common understanding of the crisis points to two developments. The first is a realization that two major paradigms of the discipline, structural functionalism and quantitative positivism, seem to have reached entropy, or, at least, their respective, joint and separate points of diminishing returns.[11] Although other paradigms seek to displace these two, none has achieved sufficient stature or embraced a scope wide enough to claim identification as *the* successor.[12] The second element of the crisis is said to be the decline in financial support given to the discipline of sociology by governmental agencies and private foundations.[13] These two developments have, in turn, led to a falling off in the number of enrollments in sociology,[14] a decline in the number of academic positions in sociology for newly minted Ph.D.'s,[15] and the closing down of departments of sociology in at least three important universities.[16] However, although I believe that there is a crisis in sociology—and especially that that crisis is related to concerns over sociology's mission and how sociologists are to go about their pursuit of the latter[17]—I claim that it would be better to perceive it as an opportunity. The opportunity is one that sets a new task for the discipline. Sociology must do nothing less than reinvent itself, and, in the process reestablish it raison d'être. It must, once again show why it deserves a place in both the academy and society.[18]

It used to be said that sociology's reason for existence was to answer the question, "How is society possible?" However, the term "society" is among a family of macroconcepts, including "social structure," that, as Andrew Travers has recently reminded us, are subjects of "a creeping disenchantment" and are in process of deemphasis in, if not disappearance from, the literature of the discipline.[19] "With the advent of postmodern social theory," he writes, "there is a nascent sociological inturning toward experience (of interaction), as if in response to an abrupt loss of confidence . . . in the institutional structuration of sociological studies."[20] One response to the new critique of the unwarranted hypostatization and unjustified reification of concepts has been the problematization of both ontology and epistemology, that is, of what things we can know and how we are able to know them. To the philosopher Richard Rorty, drawing on his reading of Dewey, Wittgenstein, and Heidegger, epistemology itself must be abandoned in philosophy, as philosophy rejects the very idea of a theory of representation, that is, of a correspondence between thought or language and the world.[21] Without serving as a mirror of nature, philosophy, and by extension all the human disciplines, are partakers of a "conversation." "Our certainty," Rorty writes, "will be a matter of conversation between persons, rather than a matter of interaction with nonhuman reality."[22] Moreover, that quest for a new kind of certainty entails commitment not only to continuing the conversation, but to recognizing that the hermeneutic circle on which the conversation is predicated requires "a conversation which presupposes no disciplinary matrix which unites the speakers, . . . [and] where the hope of agreement . . . is not a hope for the discovery of antecedently existing common ground, but *simply* hope of agreement, or, at least, exciting and fruitful disagreement."[23] If we follow Rorty, we are left not with the aim of developing newer and better paradigms, or general theories, but rather with proposing better story lines, ones that will keep us in the conversation, keep alive the hope of agreement and the toleration of fruitful and edifying disagreement.

Here I retell three of sociology's story lines. Of course, they are not called such in the professional literature. They are, professorially speaking, emblematic of paradigms about race and culture, social organization, and the constitutive functions of law for both. My telling is not intended as summarization, but as critique of the story line. In effect, my most general statement is that twentieth-century sociology's bequest to the twenty-first century is an imperative: Develop a more plausible story line!

The First Story: The Origin of the American Indians

The founder of sociology (or at least the person who gave the discipline its name) Auguste Comte, also presented it with a paradigm of cultural change that has proved to be simultaneously attractive and debilitating.[24] Central to this paradigm was a developmentalist theory of change that employed what came to be known as "the comparative method,"[25] and, not incidentally, held that social and cultural change proceeded in a slow, orderly, continuous, and teleological manner.[26] Despite the fact that numerous critics pointed out the defects in the latter mode of conceptualizing change, its basic argument continues to inform, and in some cases control, the orientation of our discipline to that topic.[27] However, here I wish to draw attention to the survival of Comte's "comparative method"[28] and show some anomalies that it possesses.[29] Let me take as a macrosociological instance illustrating this issue a success story that we tell to one another and to our students: how we—or, rather, anthropologists and antiquarians—solved a problem that troubled European and American ethnologists for four and one-half centuries—the question of the origin of the American Indians.

We begin with a commonplace of anthropological and historical, as well as the very few sociological, works on the subject—namely, that the history of the Americas has occurred in two distinct epochs.[30] The first epoch is labeled "pre-Columbian," and the term encapsulates all that happened on the North and South American continents before the arrival of Columbus. The disciplines to which this epoch and its terms of reference and narrative structures are assigned are anthropology and antiquarianism. By common agreement, neither history, political science, nor sociology is invited to conduct investigations or to contribute concepts or story lines to this arena of research. Precisely because the data for studies of the pre-Columbian epoch are, for the most part in the form of artifacts, pre-Columbian studies do not ordinarily employ the conventions, methods, or narrative structures of even that meagerly developed subdiscipline, historical sociology. Instead, following in the wake of a thesis that was originally developed in the fifteenth and sixteenth centuries on the basis of biblical authority—more specifically, the Book of Genesis—a secularized anthropological and antiquarian orientation insists upon the "fact" that Amerindian culture and civilization originated in and derived from extra-continental sources. Putting it plainly, what began as a conventionalized tale has become an axiomatic thesis—one that will be found in virtually every text written in the last one hundred years on the subject—that the aboriginal population of the Americas were migrants from Asia who crossed the Bering Strait in prehistoric time.[31] The cultures developed in the Americas are, hence, said to be either transplantations from that of the Asian peoples, or, adding a conjectural subplot about a cultural catastrophe that had amnesiac effects, new cultures developed by the aboriginal peoples of the Americas after they had "forgotten" their original perspectives and had begun to live life as Mircea Eliade imagines "archaic man" to have lived it, that is, *de novo*.[32]

The biblical foundation of this conventionalized but conjectural thesis—that is, the orthodoxy that required the belief that humankind had originated in the Garden of Eden, located somewhere in what is today called the Middle East, and that, hence, it must follow that the peoples and cultures found to exist in the pre-Columbian epoch outside of Eurasia must be derivative from the original population source[33]—has been forgotten by both ethnologists and other social scientists, but its acceptance has become fundamental, a kind of secular social scientific orthodoxy that is only occasionally challenged by heterodoxical scholars who have a different tale to tell, but one that employs the very same architectonic as that of the orthodox story. It is, in fact, the case that the kind of reasoning and the kind of evidence needed to establish the scientific validation of the orthodox version of this story is by no means secure; while heterodoxical theses, employing the same paradigm of diffusionist thought, are rarely, if ever, investigated for the possibility that they might be equally acceptable or even more plausible narratives.[34] Holding on to the orthodox version has had effects on the methods and the perspectives of history, political science, and sociology.

The post-Columbian epoch, although rarely labeled as such, has had its several narratives divided among three storytelling disciplines: history, political science, and sociology. At least three kinds of stories are told: one examines the development of civil society; another recites the effects that European colonialism had on the peoples and cultures of the Americas; and a third tells how, from the sixteenth through the twentieth centuries, developments in those transplanted European political, social, and economic practices and belief systems established various forms of modern and civil societies in the "New World."

Nevertheless, little has been done to connect the plot of the story in the pre-Columbian epoch with the stories of the post-Columbian period. One story that is an exception to this observation holds that the post-Columbian survivors were subjugated, made into conquered "primitives" whose ways of life are in decline but whose cultures and artifacts deserve preservation in a museum. In effect, the division point of the two epochs suggests that it marks the end-time of a historyless anthropology and the beginning-time of modern history and modern social science. The pre-Columbian narrative is a part of prehistory, nature, and naturalistic preserves; its successor, to happenings, change, and the building of social structures.

The effect on American sociology of this conventionalized story line has been latent but significant. Until recently, for example, students of race and ethnic relations, or of minorities in the United States, have been introduced to peoples whose forebears hailed from Africa, China, Japan, Southeast Asia, and the various countries of Europe. But these peoples are treated as characters in a post-Columbian dramatic narrative marked by the movement of their own respective modes of ethnocultural social organization toward dissolution in the flux of a modern civil society.[35] The aboriginal peoples, on the other hand, are to be found in a different scenario, one that is told by anthropologists, and that focuses on culture, usually confining its illustrations to items of material culture. Thus, there has developed in America's human disciplines separate narrative structures and a less-than-equal division of story lines about America's populations and about the respective outlooks that have been and that should be taken toward them. The aboriginal populations—who, until recently, were called "Indians" and are now assuming a new social representation as "Native Americans,"— seem to belong to the narrative structure of anthropology and are treated as virtually historyless peoples. The nonwhite, nonAnglo, non-aboriginal populations belong to sociology's tales of woe, deviance, and social problems, or to the newly developed narratives of ethnic and multicultural studies, claimants to a vague but powerful sense of autonomy in a societal pluralism that has not yet been fully articulated either by themselves or by sociologists. The peoples from Europe are the heroes of America's storied rise to world-power status; they are regarded either as the movers and shakers of civil society or as the peoples who have in one way or another oppressed the peoples who belong to sociology or anthropology.

One bequest of twentieth-century sociology to the twenty-first is a demand that it recognize that these narrative structures have attained their respective statuses as part of the process wherein certain discourses were granted legitimacy and elevated to a place in the commonwealth of curricular disciplines, while others went unrecognized, were subjected to rites and ceremonies of degradation, or were consigned to the ignominious status of "fictional," "magical," or "folkish" narratives.

Nor is this issue without relevance to current and past political and juridical issues involving such praxiological and public issues as civil rights. To take one example of many that might be mentioned,[36] the Supreme Court of California in 1854, basing its judgment on the chief justice's understanding of the anthropology of his day, ruled that Chinese immigrants into California had the legal status of Indians.[37] His first line of reasoning consisted in the retelling of the anthropological tale about the Bering Strait and the people who crossed it eons earlier. The immigrant Chinese, in this variation on the theme, were the descendants of the prehistoric ancestors of California's aboriginal population. It therefore followed, he claimed, that because California's legislature had enacted a law prohibiting Indians from testifying in court cases affecting whites, the eyewitness testimony of a Chinese immigrant to a murder committed by a white man in San Francisco would also be disallowed. However, the chief justice, recognizing in effect that the Bering Strait hypothesis might be a folktale invalidated by later researches, sought to buttress his ruling with an unimpeachable logic. To this end, he ruled that whether or not the Chinese immigrants were descendants of the ancestors of the California Indians, both Chinese and Indians were to be regarded as generic "blacks." He based this part of his decision on an exclusivist juridical sociologic—namely, that all persons who were not white were "black." On the basis of this decision, which in itself is an anthropo-judicial tale from the field of jurisprudence, Chinese in California were denied the right to testify in court cases involving whites for more than twenty years. Although the right to testify was restored to California's Chinese in 1873, the narrative question—that is, their relation to the story of the Amerindian aborigines and their origins—remains unresolved.

The Second Story: America—Unity in and without Diversity

Sociology in the United States encouraged belief in a future American society that would be devoid of ethnoracial diversity. Thus, in the face of the brute fact of its multiethnic and multiracial population, most of America's sociologists not only adhered to a theory of inevitable assimilation, that is, a theory that put forward a teleological promissory note about America's social organization, but also told and retold a heroic tale of how this ideal would be achieved.[38] The setting for this tale is to be found in the cities and the countryside of a developing America, in the sociological narratives about particular immigrant peoples and their progeny struggling and triumphing over adversity. In my critique of a monograph appropriately entitled *The Story of the Chinese in America*,[39] I presented a generalized précis of the plot I called "America's perpetual morality tale about its minorities."

> With but a few changes in detail, the same fable can be—and has been— told about the Japanese, Irish, Jews, Italians, Greeks, Swedes, and many more. Its form is always the same: a people beset by hardships and oppression in their own country bravely cross the seas to America, a land which promises freedom and opportunity. Once arrived, however, they encounter prejudice, oppression, and difficult times. However, they never lose faith in the dream that originally compelled them. They work hard, refuse to be discouraged by the abuses that harm their lives and hinder their progress, and eventually—usually in the second, or sometimes the third generation—succeed. The success is recognized in "contributions" made to the host country and ratified by a general social acceptance of the once despised people.[40]

Until about 1960, most sociologists regarded this fable as a mirror of social reality and the assimilative process as progressive, inevitable, and irreversible.[41] It was not only a social fact, but also a beneficent development. Once assimilation had been achieved, they argued, what was once called the race problem would be solved. For those who adhered to Marxism, the promise of assimilation, with its corollary promise of the disappearance of the races, heralded the onset of a different story and a different inevitability—the class struggle and the overthrow of capitalism.[42] For it was no less than Friedrich Engels who in 1893 had explained to his German-American correspondent that the failure of a socialist revolution to have occurred in America was due to the fact that "Immigration . . . divides the workers into two groups: the native-born and the foreigners, and the latter in turn into (1) the Irish, (2) the Germans, (3) the many small groups, each of which understands only itself: Czechs, Poles, Italians, Scandinavians, etc. And then [there are] the Negroes . . ."[43] In effect, the sociologists' prophecy of inevitable assimilation seemed to write finis to the tale that Engels had so pointedly told. Forgotten altogether, however, was another prophecy, one that foretold a hitherto unimagined denouement to the immigrant story. It had been presented in the same year by the Austrian sociologist Gustav Ratzenhofer: "In North America . . . the time will come when the population will have become dense. The struggle for existence will have to be more carefully planned. Then the people of America will be forced to stop and reflect . . . When that situation comes about, the memory of racial extraction may at last be reawakened. The different languages may become the rallying centers for the different interests. Thereupon for the first time will America confront decisively the problem of its national unity."[44] Ratzenhofer, so it now appears, proved to be the more prescient storyteller. However, his "story" is omitted from our canon.

Since 1960, the sociological commitment to assimilation as both the promise and the panacea of the race problem has receded.[45] In its place there has been revived a thesis in behalf of a multiethnic pluralism put forward as early as 1913 by the social philosopher Horace Kallen.[46] Kallen had, in fact, championed ethnoracial pluralism in America and argued that it was the duty of a democracy to preserve, protect, and rebuild itself upon the rich diversity that America's variety of cultures provided ready-to-hand. However, despite the fact that the pluralist thesis has been extant for more than seven decades, sociologists have shown themselves to have been ill prepared theoretically and conceptually (not to mention, in terms of narrative structures) to deal with its manifestation—as a veritable social movement in the United States in the 1990s.

The bequest of twentieth-century sociology to the twenty-first in this case is nothing less than an imperative that the race problem as a topic of sociological narrative be rewritten.

The Third Story: How Law Constructed Racial Identities in America

A singular error of omission with respect to sociology's concerns about race, culture, and societal organization is the discipline's disregard for and neglect of law. The law has its own narrative structures, but they impinge on the sociologist's story. What passes for a sociology of law in American sociology is all too often either study of the occupational characteristics of those engaged in the legal professions, or a conventionalized concern to understand crime, criminals, and criminal justice. Missing altogether is what I regard as crucial—a sociological narrative of American Constitutional law.[47] A focus on the Constitution, especially the Bill of Rights, and, even more specifically, on the "equal protections" clause of the Fourteenth Amendment, would give voice to a fundamental but underinvestigated character in the plot structure of sociology. That character is the socius. In the law's narrative there is no character called socius. However, there is his or her twin, the person. It is the unalloyed person who is guaranteed the equal protections of the law in the Fourteenth Amendment to the United States Constitution. It is notable that the makers of the Fourteenth Amendment put no adjective before the word *person* when they framed that addition to the Constitution. Sociologists should take note of the implications for their discipline of the fact that the Fourteenth Amendment guarantees the equal protections of the law, not to *assimilated* persons, or to persons of a certain color, creed, nativity, or outlook, but rather to *all persons* regardless of their civic, cultural, or biosocial status.[48]

Sociologists concerned with the effects that the adjudicative process has on the ethnocultural structure of American society would do well to take as their data base the stories told in hundreds of cases about the varieties of persons and their quests for the equal protections of the law. These stories are told to and critically evaluated by the justices of the Supreme Court of the United States. Since the adoption of the Fourteenth Amendment in 1868, they have been available but unread by sociologists. If they did avail themselves of these court records, sociologists would discover plots and narratives as well as a treasure trove of facts amenable to sociological interpretation. But more to the point, they would discover a fundamental difference between the outcome of judicial narrative about the equality granted by the Fourteenth Amendment and the promissory note in the theme proffered by the sociological assimilation narrative. The latter promised equality and the full panoply of civil rights only after the social process had exsanguinated the ethnic's blood-based sociocultural uniqueness. The former guaranteed it as a basic primordial right. Such a discovery ought to lead the sociologists of the twenty-first century to a reconsideration of the hiatus between the narrative structures of sociology and those of Constitutional law, as well as to a critique of that hiatus's effects on both the discipline and the characters who are subjects of the discipline's narratives.

There are other benefits that would arise from a focus on Constitutional law in sociology. One of these has to do with the construction of human typifications. The problem was presented very well in 1934 by Margaret Mary Wood in her book, *The Stranger*, when she wrote: "The method of establishing categories in dealing with new phenomena, whether they consist of human beings or of inanimate objects, is itself a necessary reasoning process. Its unfortunate aspect, where people are so classified, is the frequent limitation of the categories and the nature of the emotional qualities which come to be associated with some of these."[49]

Sociology's stories must employ categories, but practitioners must also be reflexively aware of the implications of the categories they choose to use. The law, and especially the stories that are to be found in the judicial dramas enacted to adjudicate the rights of aliens to naturalization in the United States, provide an excellent research site for investigating the problematics of human categorization.

The very categories employed to designate the races in America, and to distinguish them from one another, have, in fact, formed the plot structure of numerous court narratives. Called upon, for example, to define the word "white" in numerous cases involving challenges to the racial limitations that American law had set with respect to the naturalization of aliens, the federal district courts and the U.S. Supreme Court acted, in effect, as constitutive agents, erecting what I like to call the juridical construction of racial identity.[50] The newer sociologies that emphasize the significance of the social construction of reality would find ample opportunity to analyze an empirical instance of this process by studying the court cases in which that process was manifested.

Conclusion

Let me conclude by turning to the newest, and for some the most troublesome, development in the postfunctionalist and postpositivist era in which we now must live and work. The newest paradigm—or perhaps we should call it an antiparadigm—is postmodernism. While it is beyond the scope of the present work to elucidate all of the tenets of this newest outlook, it is sufficient here to note that one branch of this new perspective, the deconstructionist postmodernists, has asserted that all texts (and the term "text" is used in the broadest possible manner) are disprivilegeable.[51] Without an epistemology to guide us, this statement appears as a formidable challenge. Some postmodernists believe that the mere assertion of the disprivilegeability of texts will, in fact, accomplish their delegitimation in the wider world. However, this is surely not the case. One sociological question posed by the postmodernists' emphasis on disprivilegeability is, in fact, a component of the issues encompassed by the political sociology of knowledge. The postmodernist question for this subdivision of sociology is: How has it been possible for some texts to become privileged while others have not been able to do so? Looking back on what I have said in the foregoing, it can be seen that my concerns with the narrative structures attending the dichotomization of epochs in the social history of the Americas, the imagery of societal organization with or without ethnocultural diversity, and the constitutive function of Constitutional law with respect to ethnoracial identities are each instances not only of plot lines, but also and at the same time, of topics that a postmodernist political sociology of knowledge might consider. Each refers to a narrative structure, a discourse, or a "text" that has become privileged, was once so, is in process of becoming so, or is in one or another phase of disprivilege—not in the halls of academe, but in the wider world. Ultimately then, the bequest of twentieth-century sociology to the twenty-first century is a legacy of unresolved problems in narrative structures. Will we tell better and more plausible stories? Let us hope so.

CHAPTER ELEVEN

Animal Faith, Puritanism, and the Schutz-Gurwitsch Debate: A Commentary

[A] completely uniform social distribution of knowledge cannot exist . . . In any case, absolutely homogeneous knowledge is therefore unimaginable.

Alfred Schutz and Thomas Luckmann, The Structure of the Life-World

Before I begin, I should like to put before this audience the background and qualifications for making this commentary.* I joined the Department of Sociology in the Graduate Faculty of Political and Social Science at the New School for Social Research in 1972, replacing Schutz's former student, Peter Berger, who had resigned and taken a position at Rutgers University. I had already introduced a graduate seminar on Schutz's phenomenological sociology at the University of Nevada in 1970, and I continued to teach and write in that and the related pragmatic perspective while at the New

---

*Author's Note: This essay originated as an oral commentary on two papers—Steven Vaitkus's "Multiple Realities in Santayana's *Last Puritan*" and Elizabeth Suzanne Kassof's "'Paramount Reality' in Schutz and Gurwitsch"—both presented at the Alfred Schutz Memorial Symposium (November 30–December 1, 1989), commemorating the ninetieth year since his date of birth and honoring the publication of a volume of the Schutz-Gurwitsch correspondence. The invitation to present this commentary afforded me the opportunity to propose a sociohistorical resolution of the Schutz-Gurwitsch debate over the possibility of intersubjective understanding, and was the occasion for my reinterpretation of certain issues in the works of Josiah Royce, George Herbert Mead, Herbert Blumer, Erving Goffman, and Harold Garfinkel. These issues are important for understanding the relationship of modernity to postmodernity. George Pasthas, who had invited me to speak at the conference, published a slightly different version of my remarks in *Human Studies: A Journal for Philosophy and the Social Sciences.*

School. In addition, together with Arthur Vidich,[1] I began an exploration of the religious ethics affecting the spirit of American sociology. The existential and phenomenological sociology in which I have collaborated with Marvin Scott became both a resource for and a topic of the researches undertaken with Professor Vidich. All of this came together for me in a new way because of this occasion and the originality of Professors Vaitkus's and Kassab's separate studies.

It is not without relevance to recall that George Santayana was a colleague of Josiah Royce at Harvard University. I would like to suggest that there seems to be a relationship, or, at least, a possible relationship between Santayana's idea of "animal faith" and Royce's principal contribution to social philosophy, his "philosophy of loyalty."[2] Royce, who might himself have been called the last Puritan, had developed a philosophical sociology elucidating the positive functions of conflict. In so doing, he combined the ethic of Pauline theology with the idea of a metaphysical social system. The ultimate outcome of conflict, according to Royce, was the combining of hostilities at a higher level. At its zenith, this emergent would become loyalty to loyalty itself. Here was a philosophy of fidelity that seemed to promise a final, positive, and harmonious outcome—an ultimate solution to the raging social conflicts of the day.

Oliver, the central character in Santayana's novel *The Last Puritan*, appears to be on a Roycean mission. He is, as Santayana tells us, a man without "animal faith." He is engaged in a never-ending quest for the trust and fidelity of those whom he encounters. His search is always frustrated because, it will be suggested here, Oliver represents the nth point to which Puritan faith has fallen in the twentieth century. Indeed, Oliver is not only the last Puritan, but also a striking instance of the new modern individual. Oliver seems to be devoid of personality; he always expresses himself in a flat and monotonous manner. He is the quintessence of banality—the final characterology of Puritanism. Moreover, as Santayana suggests, Oliver lives in a purely perceptual world, that is, the kind of world described by Gurwitsch in his critique of Alfred Schutz.[3] What is the relationship between the last Puritan and the onset of a perceptual world? It seems to me that it is possible to advance a historical theory here, or, rather, what I should like to call a historical hermeneutic on American sociology and its relation to apprehending American social reality.

We might look at the debate between Schutz and Gurwitsch not in terms of the truth value or the logic to be discerned in either of the philosopher's points of view, but rather in terms of a recent historical development in philosophical sociology and its approach to the problem of social reality. Putting it bluntly, I would suggest that one reading of the Schutz-Gurwitsch debate is through an interpretation of Santayana, that is, through observing that both sociology and social reality have shifted from recognizing a general condition of possible and, indeed, probable intersubjective understanding to one of the extreme difficulty, if not the unlikelihood, of the latter.[4] Concomitant with that shift is the coming into interaction of the condition of perceptual vision unmediated by mutuality. The *Umwelt* of Schutz gives way to that of Gurwitsch.

Faith and Sociology in Fin de Siècle America

Professor Vaitkus tells us of the three kinds of faith that are the principal topics of Santayana's novel: bodily faith, societal faith, and loving faith. Without making these analytical distinctions, the major thinkers of American sociology in Santayana's time had come to the perilous conclusion that faith was in decline. Thus, to mention the major figures, William Graham Sumner argued that the mores that had once guided American society and ensured social order had disintegrated—a casualty of the horrors of the Civil War—and that no new mores had yet developed to replace them and to provide for some kind of consensus.[5] Sumner's American society was no longer custom-bound, nor was it guided by either the fundamental beliefs or the practical reason that followed from such beliefs. For Sumner—who was the closest thing that America ever came to having as a doom prophet—nothing could be done. "We are spectators at a great convulsion," he said. Robert Park, who much admired Sumner's thought, and who hated abstraction and metaphysics, defined the problem as the confrontation between civilization and culture.[6] By culture he meant all the faiths, customs, and folkways of Europe, Asia, and Africa that had been brought to America by immigrants, settlers, and slaves, or that had been subjected to the missions of Occidental civilization in their own colonized homelands.[7] All of these were subject to what Park believed was the secular and modern trend of civilization. He likened civilization to the locomotive of a fast-moving train and pointed out that, just like the trains of his era, so the locomotive of civilization would leave piles of "human junk" along the wayside. While some might be interested in civilization and progress and might equate the two, for Park the progress that was attendant on civilization was "a terrible thing," and he was interested in the fate and condition of the human junk that was left to cope with it.[8]

Park's greatest teacher was Georg Simmel. In the latter's book on Schopenhauer and Nietzsche he pointed to the decline of the once powerful Christian religion and noticed that with its decline there developed a quest for faith and trust in the intramundane world. Such a quest, however, would not find resolution in a Roycean philosophy of fidelity. "On one hand," Simmel writes, "we have the conviction that life is valueless, which is based on selecting from all of the diverse and nonobservable meanings only monotony, the preponderance of suffering, and failure. On the other hand, we have the belief that life is value and that every deficiency is but a step toward a new attainment, every monotony but an interplay of infinite vitality, and every pain inconsequential in light of the surge of values in the process of realization in being and action." For Simmel, such antinomies are not resolvable but instead, they are to be embraced as such. The soul, he observes, "finally embraces both the desperation and jubilation of life as the poles of its own expansion, its own power, its own plenitude of forms."[9] And, we might add, the plenitude of forms—some comprehended, some incomprehensible —becomes the basis for the agony and ecstasy of modern life.

The Decline of Animal Faith and the Rise of the Perceptual World

It might be the case that a resolution of the Schutz-Gurwitsch debate on perspective can be obtained by treating the matter in terms of the fundamental changes in the bases of morality in the civil societies of the twentieth century. I would like to suggest that Santayana's outlook in *The Last Puritan* marks a fundamental break in the modern world; we can treat the Schutz-Gurwitsch debate as emblematic of the shift after that break—the movement from a society marked by an essentially intersubjective faith in the value and truth of both self and other to one that is characterized by the delegitimation of faith altogether. In the latter society, there is an agonizing quest for trust, but it is accompanied by a deep and widespread mistrust of everyone and everything.

It seems to me that this point can be perceived by examining the fate of American pragmatic thought after Royce. Royce's most prominent student was George Herbert Mead (Mead also knew William James, but he was James's babysitter, while he was Royce's student). Mead developed his philosophical outlook—an outlook that would later be called symbolic interaction—on the basis of criticizing Royce's philosophy of loyalty.[10]

Mead held that Royce had retreated from the realities of American life and developed a purely metaphysical system that bore no relation to what actually occurred in the ordinary person's structures of consciousness.[11] From Mead's counter-Roycean perspective, there subsequently developed an elaborate sociology, led by Herbert Blumer.[12] Blumer was among the first to point out that the dialogue carried on between the self and the society might very well find its expression in the self setting itself against society.[13] The intersubjectivity that was central to Blumer's version of Mead's thought included a central place for unending conflict.[14]

In the aftermath of Blumer's thought, there developed the separate but related perspectives of Erving Goffman and Harold Garfinkel. In my judgment—and I believe I am the only one who makes this assertion— Goffman's work may be viewed from a perspective that brings together the sociology of religion and the sociology of law.[15] Goffman's sociology of religion arises in the period when God is already dead, or, in Buber's kinder outlook, has absented Himself from humankind for a while. This is also the period that comes after the death of Santayana's last Puritan. By the time that Santayana wrote, Puritanism had already begun to reach its point of no return and experience its marginal utility as praxis. In its final stage, so well personified by Oliver in Santayana's novel, Puritanism has been reduced to a characterology that, later, would be described by Talcott Parsons as one that conducts itself with and through affective neutrality.[16] For the human agent of such a character the world is flat, stale, and monotonous, existing only as a perceptual reality that is not to be trusted. Yet, at the same time, that reality is all there is.[17]

Goffman's sociology becomes relevant in and to the epoch after the last Puritan has died. In such an epoch the central problem for humankind is the locus of deification. So long as Christianity prevailed, the locus of deification and the basis of probity was God. With the death of God, by a marvelous dialectic (a dialectic that can be traced back to the dialogue between the ancient Hebrews and Yahweh),[18] the problem of the locus of deification and trust is shifted back to humanity. Each person seeks awesome charisma in his or her own self. However, since each person desires at the same time to receive acknowledgment of his or her own godlikeness but refuses to accept on face value the claimed awesomeness of the other, the deification process takes the form of strategic surveillance and tactical interaction.[19] Goffman has treated this situation in terms of the presentation of self, wherein each self-presentation seeks recognition of and acquiescence to its own self-proclaimed status while attempting to discover the reality behind, and, if necessary, to discredit the honorific claims in, the self-presentation of the other.[20]

In a society such as Goffman describes, the process of social conduct is likened to a game.[21] Therein lies embedded Goffman's—as well as Garfinkel's—sociology of law. For Goffman, life proceeds in episodes, each one of which is bounded by the rules of the game, that is, the rules of relevance and the rules of irrelevance. In the same society, communication proceeds according to certain gamelike rules of interaction. These turn out to be governed by what is described in Garfinkel's[22] orientation (and Schutz's language) as the "stock of knowledge"[23] or the "recipes for living" which everyone obeys but no one knows[24] at the liminal level.[25] The rules of relevance and irrelevance, and the conditions that govern liminal knowledge of these recipes, constitute the parameters of juridical and jurisdictional action in everyday life. Perception leads to interpretation, and the conflict of interpretation guides the welter of perceptions.

Thus it may be suggested that the polychrome perceptual world that Gurwitsch describes is the world of post-Puritan modernity, while the intersubjectively cooperative world that Schutz describes as dependent on a "reciprocity of perspectives" appears to be the core structure of the secularizing but not yet fully secularized era that preceded it.[26] From Garfinkel's experiments we learn that the recipes for living which everyone obeys but no one knows can be made known by the imposition of what Goffman calls a nasty surprise.[27] These nasty surprises correspond to what Schutz would call a crisis in the *Lebenswelt*.[28] The notion of such crises had been already perceived by the American phenomenological sociologist W. I. Thomas in his thesis about the relationship that obtains between habit, crisis, and attention.[29] In a related orientation, Frederick J. Teggart had perceived that fundamental changes in social organization were likely to occur when what he called an "intrusion" interrupted and broke down the patterns of conduct that had become habitual. With this breakdown, Teggart asserted, there occurred a crisis which in turn acted to release the human mind from its slavery to habit and convention and open it up to possibilities hitherto unimagined. But, Teggart insisted, no predictions about the released imagination and its effects could be made.[30] Garfinkel's experiments provided experimentally constructed intrusions into everyday life. What these experiments revealed, though Garfinkel may not have noticed it, is what I would like to call the principle of the conservation of society. That is to say, the principle that holds that the recipes for living form solitary cakes of custom that are difficult either to give up or to destroy. Teggart's liberating "release" might occur, but not very often. Nevertheless, unpredictability and contingency are the order of the everyday life.

By reading the Schutz-Gurwitsch debate through the prism of Santayana's novel about the last Puritan, we might formulate a hypothesis about the fundamental character of modernity, and how it is different from that of the religious age. That character is the one described in the pure perceptions that Santayana gives to Oliver's view of his *Umwelt* and is defined in the theory of the perceptual world that Gurwitsch offers up as, in effect, the successor stage to that of Schutz's intersubjectivity. It is the world both comprehended and embraced by a sociology of the absurd.[31]

CHAPTER TWELVE

The Drama in the Routine: A Prolegomenon to a Praxiological Sociology

It should be . . . kept in mind that in order to contemplate our spiritual individuality in its fullness we must free ourselves of practical life and of its routine.
    Nicolas Evreinoff, The Theatre in Life

The script of life in modern societies is more and more conceived by social scientists in a dramatistic form.[1] Of course, such an approach owes an unrepayable debt to the stimulating work on dramatism by Kenneth Burke.[2] However, much of dramatism in sociology has been constrained by the limits imposed by one of its modes—theatricality. Theatricality, especially as that concept has been elaborated by Elizabeth Burns,[3] describes, I believe, but one kind of drama. Unfortunately, that kind has been reframed into a synecdoche, the part taken for the whole, and as such it exercises an all too hegemonic sovereignty over the less flamboyant elements composing the drama of social reality. Of the latter, the drama in the routine is remarkable for its neglect,[4] since, in sociological terms, routines—habits, customs, the ongoing action that is *interrupted* by a crisis in *Lebenswelt*—constitute the praxes of everyday life, the fundamental stuff of any truly praxiological sociology. In what follows I present an elaboration of the drama in the routine; my remarks are intended as a prolegomenon, looking toward the development of such a sociology, so long promised but so far unfulfilled.

Routines: Their Origins and Persistence

In an early essay that has been much neglected, W. I. Thomas formulated a psychosocial theory of routine life and its relation to social change.[5] As Thomas conceived of the matter, most of life is carried on in accordance with habits. Habits are ways of living that have arisen as sociocultural "definitions of the situation," features of the unreflected-upon world of everyday activities. Habits go unnoticed and, for the most part, uncriticized. They are the active expression of the mores, and, if they are formalized, they appear as folk wisdom, common sense, precepts, traditions, and standardized understandings; sometimes they are coded in language, carved in stone, written out in legislation, or observed and enforced in law. "And," Thomas went on to observe, "the great part of our life is lived in the region of habit. The habits, like the instincts, are safe and serviceable. They have been tried, and they are associated with a feeling of security."[6] The habits, thence, constitute and are constituted in the routines of everyday life. In their repetitions, their carefully formulated modes of action, their characteristic rhetorics, and their moves on the stages of everyday life, they are inherently dramatic—but they are equally inherently devoid of histrionics, melodrama, or theatrics. Their drama resides precisely in their dullness. They do not stimulate the imagination; rather, they effect the unreflexive praxis.

Habitual routines are the stages from which the far more theatrical dramas of social change occur. Indeed, true, or fundamental, social changes—as opposed to those that occur in and as part of the *longue durée*—may be understood as occurring in an assault on established habits of life in the name of a proposed instauration of a new set of habits (or, to be more precise, habits-to-be). This perspective on social change offers a comprehensive dramatism, one that distinguishes the theatrical aspects of social life from those that are commonplace. The former are fewer in number, but greater in respect, and they make up the content of history and ideology. The latter are the more frequent, the less-noticed, the taken-for-granted, but, like their more remarkable counterparts, they partake of the entire panoply of the Burkean pentad: They occur as acts, in scenes, committed by persons who know how to do (or perform) them, and they serve a knowable purpose. What distinguishes them from theatrical dramas is their remarkable unremarkability.

How do routines come to be such? A dramatistic sociology of social change conceives of this as a by-no-means predetermined metamorphosis from innovatively theatrical to familiar and ordinary performances. Cultural phenomena partake of such a transformation, as the studies of Norbert Elias have documented so well.[7] Indeed, as Elias's studies seem to suggest, those elementary forms of everyday life, for example, the tie-signs that Erving

Goffman showed to be foundations of a modern civic social order,[8] had once been innovative and perhaps bizarre forms of conduct that had to overcome their original designation as strange behavior and to become legitimate ways to shore up a sagging social relationship.[9] Moreover, as the separate and independent works of W. I. Thomas,[10] Frederick J. Teggart,[11] and Victor Turner[12] have shown, what is here being called a dramatistic approach to social change stands in sharp contrast to, and in critical refutation of, the predominant developmentalist theories of sociocultural change that take their point of departure from Comte and owe their origins to Aristotle's conception of *physis*. Against the illusion that social change occurs slowly, orderly, continuously, and teleologically, the dull drama in the routine is that established obdurate reality, that body of all-too-familiar performances against which the theatrical dramas of reform, rebellion, and revolution are enacted on an irregular and surely nonlinear time track. The success of a reform, rebellion, or revolution is ultimately represented by the routinization of its once charismatic, awesome, or outlandish ideas about conduct appropriate for everyday life. The theatrical drama has then become transformed into a nontheatrical play, a feature of the taken-for-granted *Umwelt* of its practitioners.

Routines as Habits

The ethologist Konrad Lorenz believes that the formation of habits among human groups occurs as part of a process that he calls "cultural ritualization."[13] Such habitual behaviors may arise for highly specific purposes in the early history of a group—for example, the collectively enforced prohibition on eating pork among contemporary observant Jews might have originated as part of a theocratically legislated health plan designed to prevent trichinosis from debilitating the fighting strength of the ancient Hebrew settlers of Canaan—but ultimately they achieve both autonomy—that is, transcendence from the originally impelling reason for the conduct—and routinization—that is, taken-for-grantedness that is accompanied by a vague but powerful feeling that to do otherwise is fearsome, tantamount to courting danger, or unpleasant, inviting at the very least an undesirable degree of discomfort. As autonomous and routinized modes of conduct, the habits become the fundamental stuff, the "text", to use language familiar to students of society perceived in this manner, of a people's everyday life. Habits are, hence, the praxes against which, and with respect to which, deviance, is observed and measured. And deviant conduct is, in effect, would-be or potential praxis.

In effect, we may observe a theorem at work here: no praxes, no deviance; no deviance, no new praxis. And through this theorem we have part of the answer to the Hobbesian question that became the basis for sociology as a discipline. That question—how is society possible?—is answered thus: Society is possible because people have somehow come to agree upon conformity to a body of habits. As Lorenz saw the matter, cultural ritualization performs a triple function—"suppressing fighting within the group, . . . holding the group together, and . . . setting it off, as an independent entity, against other similar units . . ."[14] The very formation of the group in question, the formation of any true group (be it as small as Mead's self-reflective and internally interacting self, or as large as a nation-state or a *Gemeinschaft* of confederated states), is founded upon the establishment of such habits. As W. I. Thomas once observed, "The attitudes and values, or we may say, the attitudes toward values, which reflect the personality of the individual are the result of a process of conditioning by the influences of the cultural milieu, eventuating in a body of habits."[15]

Routines as Interaction Rituals

Routines are not only (or merely) habits. They are also rituals whose expression is manifested in rites. These rites evoke in their performers and in the audience that observes them an imperative of perfectly coordinated and precisely executed actions. As Florian Znaniecki once observed, "The attitude of a collectivity toward its moral order shows the same primary desire for integral perfection which is illustrated in all the rituals of the world. Just as magical or religious rites acquire their proper virtue only when they are perfectly performed, so moral norms sanctioned by a community or a group need to be perfectly followed to be completely valid."[16] However, if perfection were really demanded for every routine performance of an interaction ritual, the actors would suffer from inordinate amounts of stage fright.[17] In contemporary America, it appears to be sufficient for maintaining social order that, in the rituals that make up the routines of everyday life, the individual show proper deference, that is, the "appreciation an individual shows of another to that other," and an appropriate demeanor, that is, "ceremonial behavior typically conveyed through deportment, dress, and bearing which serves to express to those in his [or her] immediate presence that he [or she] is a person of certain . . . qualities."[18] Goffman lists the basic attributes of these qualities as "discretion and sincerity; modesty in claims regarding self; sportsmanship; command of speech and physical movements; self-control over his [or her] emotions, . . . appetites, and . . .

desires; poise under pressure; and so forth."[19] When a person so comports him- or herself in a manner that is taken to indicate a character that possesses these attributes, there is created in the scene wherein the conduct takes place the basic conditions of trust that undergird the social contract. These conditions correspond to those signs of probity that Max Weber noticed were taken to be signaled when, in 1904 in rural America, a person submitted to immersive baptism and to public acknowledgment that he or she was a "born-again" adherent to the Calvinist variant of the Protestant faith.[20]

The contents and qualities of performances necessary to create the conditions of confidence that permit ongoing and unaggressive human association might vary over time, place, and culture, but within the context of their own established and routinized codes, they constitute a mode of conduct that has all the qualities and confers all the qualifications of a religious ritual. Nevertheless, again within the circumscribed code, less-than-perfect performance is often tolerated. Taking note of this aspect of conduct in the context of a larger discussion of the repression of crime, Znaniecki called attention to the fact that "an objective observation of individual conduct would show at every step deviations from the standard of perfection; but communities and groups do not observe their insiders objectively. Having a fundamentally positive, lasting prejudice toward them, they either ignore or explain away their innumerable omissions and peccadillos."[21] Hence, departures from ritual perfection are not uncommon, and they usually do not shred the social fabric. And, as Znaniecki concludes on this point, "a collectivity may for a long time live under a half-voluntary illusion of the essential perfection of its moral order . . ."[22] The continued performance of routine dramas—that is, the dramas that are devoid of awesomeness, charisma, melodrama, histrionics, or theatricality—make up the everyday life process and, by their very unremarkabilty, sew together the social fabric.

The Theatricalization of Routines

A single line of thought unites the otherwise quite disparate sociologies of Thomas, Teggart, Turner, Gramsci, Schutz, Goffman, and Garfinkel. Taking notice of the significance of what they variously refer to as habits, routines, ritualized performances, behavioral presentations of self in public and private places, the *Lebenswelt*, the taken-for-granted world, and the old civilization, these students of social order and its changes correctly perceived that the routinized charisma of everyday life, that is, the drama in the routine, was protected against any easy banishment from the stage of the legitimate theater of life by the familiarity and the comfort in the familiarity of its own scenario. For Thomas, what was required to ring down the curtain on the habitual performances of everyday life was a "crisis" so great as to force the performers and their audience to come to "attention,"[23] that is, to engage in a veritable epoche of the dramas in the routine. Teggart also supposed that the onset of a crisis, in the form of an irruptive intrusion onto the fixed stage of everyday life happenings, could, if disturbing enough, bring about the release of the performers from their commitment to the text of habitual conduct.[24] Victor Turner, taking his point of departure from the studies of Van Gennep, summarized the latter's observations on the matter thus: "He insisted that in all ritualized movement there was at least a moment when those being moved in accordance with a cultural script were liberated from normative demands, when they were, indeed, betwixt and between successive lodgments in jural political systems. In this gap between ordered worlds almost anything may happen."[25] Gramsci, as interpreted by Dick Howard, perceived society to be "articulation" within a field of discursive politics. As Howard observes, "it constantly subverts itself, releasing the floating signifiers which present the possibility of new articulations." Moreover, "Articulation can—but need not—produce hegemonic practice." In Gramsci's terms, which without too much difficulty can be transposed into a dramatistic discourse, "the constitution of an 'historical bloc' . . . is possible when the old civilisation loses its coherence, setting free elements which can be recombined in a new civilisation."[26] Large-scale social change is constituted by ringing up the curtain on a new civilizational drama in the hopes that its performance will reoccur continuously on the stage of future history.

Whereas Thomas, Teggart, Turner, and Gramsci perceived these moments of disruption, liberation, and reformation of the scripts of life as macroevents, sociocultural, historical, or civilizational in scope, Goffman and Schutz noticed the microecological counterparts of similar disjunctions in the small routines of daily life. For Goffman, these are the numerous slips, gaffes, performance failures, individual or team subversions, embarrassments, and nasty surprises that threaten to bring down the props and supports of that life and to reveal the terrors of its insanity of place; however, most of these are repairable, so that the rituals of interaction persist and the conduct of daily life's dull dramaturgy goes on without suffering a destructive discreditation.[27] Schutz took special notice of those crises that disrupted the *Lebenswelten* of ordinary people, situations wherein they discovered that the recipes for living on which they had always relied no longer produced the cake of customary results for which they had in the past always been efficaciously employed. In reaction and response to such moments, individuals are in a position to perceive as it were for the first time the sense- (and the nonsense-) structures of their conscious life and to reconsider their adherence to them. The structures become visible as alterable scenarios and texts.[28] Although Garfinkel did not seem to take special note of the fact, his introduction of artificial disruptive intrusions into the daily life routines of department store shoppers, parents of college students, and participants in what appeared to be standardized psychological tests generated crises that were resolvable by forms of talk that functioned to elaborate upon, as well as to shore up, the only seemingly shaky props of modern routine dramas.[29] In all of this, however, there is a raising of the consciousness to what Turner calls "liminality," a sensory threshold.[30] That threshold bids fair to introduce theatricality into the mundane drama in the routine.

In a critique of Lyman's and Scott's *The Drama of Social Reality*, Elizabeth Burns sought to take issue with the authors' claim that the social world is inherently dramatic by pointing out that "most of life is routine, only punctuated by 'dramas.'"[31] Burns's critique fails in its intention, but it does call attention to the dialectic governing the relationship between theatrical and routine dramas. That dialectic may be described as circumscribing the transformative process by which mundane dramas in the routine are, because of a sudden burst of liminality, reconstituted as either "theatrical," that is, as those that proceed by means of exaggerated gestures and unexpected vocalizations; "histrionic," that is, as those that employ deliberately affected or overdetermined motions, movements, and tones; or "melodramatic," that is, those that rely on a heightened emotionalism and conventionally unconventional stylistics. As a hypothesis central to the validation of a dramatistic sociology of social change, it may be suggested that theatricalism (i.e., theatrics, histrionics, or melodramatics) arises in conduct when the routine dramas of everyday life are interrupted, invaded, or intruded upon by forms of action that are unexpected, unwarranted, or untoward with respect to the conventional text. The dramas-in-the-routine are performed in accordance with scripts of everyday life that place the action in unprepossessing scenes, identify the performers as uninspiring agents, employ unremarkable agencies of achievement, and accomplish expected and expectable outcomes. Theatrical dramas arise when such scenes are desublimated, their agents despoiled, their agencies deprived of efficaciousness, and the outcomes frustrated or unanticipated. The liminality that finds theatricalized expression bids fair to write a new drama of social reality, to modify but not tear up the conventional scripts toward which its exaggerated gestures, histrionics, or melodramatics are directed, or to restore and, possibly, reinvigorate the drama in the routine that is under assault. Social statics, that is, the drama in the routine, and social dynamics, that is, theatrical dramas, constitute the irregular dialectic, the warp and woof of the historic process.

The Future of the Dramas in the Routine

The characteristics of society since the advent of modernity and its successor, still so indescribable that it can only be designated "postmodern," make it possible to suggest a possible future for dramas in the routine. Such suggestions are, at best, guesses based upon the probabilities of conventionality and its survival. It was Alfred Schutz who called attention to the fact that "the social world has near and far zones: the surrounding world . . . , in which you and I experience one another in spatial and temporal immediacy, may pass over into the world of my contemporaries, who are not given to me in spatial immediacy; and in multiple transitions, [he also noted that] there are the worlds of both predecessors and successors."[32] To gauge the possibilities for routinized dramas, one must first add a corollary to Schutz's perceptive observation: Modernity is characterized, indeed, formed and reformed by the greater likelihood that interpenetrations will occur in these spatio-temporal zones. Thus, the *Umwelt* composed of my consociates is subjected to threats emanating from its unexpected collisions with the zones that contain my contemporaries as well as those that house the reconstitutable memories and histories of my predecessors and those that promise a future for my successors. Such enhanced threats in turn evoke a greater probability that theatricality will more and more overcome mundane dramas as zonal collisions and conflicts undermine established societal texts and aroused liminalities release aggressive self- and group-assertions.

Modernity finds its societal expression in the mass. Two characteristics of mass society are relevant for the dramatic modes of routine life. As Herbert Blumer has pointed out, "In a mass society, the parts are not fused into an organic whole . . . Instead, because of the overabundance of parts, many of these . . . are far removed from one another."[33] One result of this unfused conglomeration of parts is the relative autonomy of each. As autonomous units in a nonintegrated society, these units—which might be as small as a lone individual or as large as an organized collectivity—are in a position to "write" their own scripts of life, to develop what for each is its conventionalized drama in the routine. Mass society is thus something like those multiplex theaters that are increasingly found in suburban malls—a number of dramas are going on at once. The difference is that the multiplex theaters have walls to prevent the dramas from penetrating into one another. Mass society guarantees no walls to separate its autonomous scenarios of mundane life. The mutual adjustment of each to the other constitutes a problem which is resolved in a drama that overlays the discrete but interconnecting routine dramas.

A second characteristic feature of mass society is "that it is caught up in a world of constant motion."[34] Such motion is not necessarily tantamount to change, but holds out the possibility, or for some, the threat, that it might introduce an intrusion, a nasty surprise, or a contradiction that is so disturbing as to convert routine plays into theatrical dramas. More than societies founded upon castes, estates, or classes, mass societies tend to engender competition and conflicts among their parts. Such a sense of fearful disunity undermines the general conditions of trust and order, encouraging intrigues, deceptions, and interactions that are strategic rather than spontaneous. Hence, every routine drama is threatened and theatrically bids fair to become a routine in its own right.

Mass societies are not necessarily just or democratic. They entail a struggle among units—individuals and groups—for power and for the right to order the hierarchy of social status that will somehow always prevail in one form or another. These conflicts over power and status are dramas that develop their own routine dramatic forms as well as their theatrical or untheatrical cease-fires, and their histrionic, melodramatic, or unremarkable accommodations. Thus the vital order that is found in mass societies speaks not to "alienation," "anomie," "social disorganization," or imminent dissolution, but rather to an interplay of dramas in the routine and theatrical performances vying for hegemony and forming a metasocietal rhythm of macrosocial and microecological dynamics.

Notes

Introduction

1. For a spirited attempt to hold back the flood, see Stephen Eric Bronner, "The Great Divide: The Enlightenment and Its Critics," *New Politics*, n.s., 3 (summer 1995): pp. 65–86.

2. I use the Japanese term *tsunami* advisedly, for the postmodern storm has struck Asia as well. See, e.g., Charles Wei-Hsun Fu and Steven Heine, eds., *Japan in Traditional and Postmodern Perspectives* (Albany: State University of New York Press, 1995); David Y. F. Ho, "Selfhood and Identity in Confucianism, Taoism, Buddhism, and Hinduism: Contrasts with the West," *Journal for the Theory of Social Behaviour* 25:2 (June 1995): pp. 115–39; and James H. Liu and Shu-hsien Liu, "Modernism, Postmodernism, and Neo-Confucian Thinking: A Critical History of Paradigm Shifts and Values in Psychology" (paper presented at the inaugural meeting of the Asian Association of Social Psychology, Hong Kong, June 21–23, 1995).

3. John O'Neill, *The Poverty of Postmodernism* (London: Routledge, 1995), p. 3.

4. Peter Gay, *The Party of Humanity: Essays in the French Enlightenment* (New York: W. W. Norton, 1971 [1954]), p. 289.

5. Peter Gay, introduction, in idem, ed., *The Enlightenment: A Comprehensive Anthology* (New York: Simon and Schuster, 1973), pp. 13–26. Quotation from p. 17. For some positive evaluations of modernity, modernism, and the Enlightenment, see Nicholas Till, *Mozart and the Enlightenment: Truth, Virtue, and Beauty in Mozart's Operas* (New York: W. W. Norton, 1993), pp. 1–55, 117–29, 172–88; and the definitions of modernity and modernism in Elizabeth Fox-Genovese, "The Anxiety of History: The Southern Confrontation with Modernity," *Southern Cultures* Inaugural Issue (1993): pp. 65–82, at 69 and 73: "Modernity has generally been associated with three main developments: the vast acceleration of material progress that has accompanied industrial capitalism, the triumph of political democracy and the emergence of 'autonomous' individuals. These three attributes of modernity have historically, been closely intertwined—and closely associated with a general conception of progress. Taken together, they amount to a massive revolution in the conception of the nature and purpose of society, based upon a distinct conception of individualism—what I shall call bourgeois or systematic individualism—that envisions the individual as prior to society. In essential ways, modernism can be understood as the cultural articulation of modernity (although it remains debatable whether the two arose in tandem). For modernism embodies a special form of the triumph of individual subjectivity . . . Southern proslavery ideology was grounded in a repudiation of individualism as an adequate foundation for civilized society."

6.   Jean-Francois Lyotard, "The Wall, The Gulf, and The Sun: A Fable," *Political Writings*, trans. Bill Readings and Kevin Paul (Minneapolis: University of Minnesota Press, 1993), pp. 112–26. Quotation from p. 114.

7.   Lyotard, "The Grip (Mainmise)," *Political Writings*, pp. 148–62.

8.   Lyotard, "Tomb of the Intellectual (1983)" *Political Writings*, pp. 3–7. Quotation from p. 6.

9.   Jean Baudrillard, *The Transparency of Evil: Essays on Extreme Phenomena*, trans. James Benedict (London: Verso, 1993), p. 85.

10.   Ibid.

11.   Barry Smart, *Postmodernity* (London: Routledge, 1993), p. 26.

12.   Jean-Francois Lyotard, *The Postmodern Condition: A Report on Knowledge*, trans. Geoff Bennington and Brian Massumi (Minneapolis: University of Minnesota Press, 1991), p. 81.

13.   Baudrillard, *The Transparency of Evil*, pp. 81–82.

14.   Ibid., pp. 89–99.

15.   Lyotard, *The Postmodern Condition*, p. 82.

16.   In addition to the writings by Lyotard cited *supra*, see five works by the same author: *The Differend: Phrases in Dispute*, trans. G. V. D. Abbeole (Minneapolis: University of Minnesota Press, 1988); *The Lyotard Reader*, ed. Andrew Benjamin (Cambridge, Mass.: Basil Blackwell, 1989); *Phenomenology*, trans. Brian Beakley (Albany: State University of New York Press, 1991); *The Postmodern Explained: Correspondence, 1982–1985*, trans. and ed. Julian Pefanis and Morgan Thomas (Minneapolis: University of Minnesota Press, 1992); and Jean-Francois Lyotard and Jean-Loup Thebaud, *Just Gaming*, trans. Wlad Godzich (Minneapolis: University of Minnesota Press, 1989).

17.   In addition to the writings by Baudrillard cited *supra*, see ten works by the same author: *The Mirror of Production*, trans. Mark Poster (St. Louis, Mo.: Telos Press, 1975); *For a Critique of the Political Economy of the Sign*, trans. Charles Levin (St. Louis, Mo.: Telos Press, 1981); *In the Shadow of the Silent Majorities Or, The End of the Social and Other Essays*, trans. Paul Foss, John Johnston, and Paul Parron (New York: Semiotext(e), 1983); *The Ecstasy of Communication*, trans. Bernard and Caroline Schutze, ed. Slyvere Lotringer (New York: Semiotext(e), 1988); *Selected Writings*, ed. Mark Poster (Stanford, Calif.: Stanford University Press, 1988); *America*, trans. Chris Turner (London: Verso, 1988); "The Anorexic Ruins," trans. David Antal, in Dietmar Kamper and Christoph Wulf, eds., *Looking Back on the End of the World* (New York: Semiotext(e), 1989), pp. 29–48; *Cool Memories*, trans. Chris Turner (London: Verso, 1990); *Fatal Strategies*, trans. Philip Beitchman and W. G. J. Niesluchowski, ed. Jim Fleming (New York: Semiotext(e), 1990); *Seduction*, trans. Brian Singer (New York: St. Martin's Press, 1990); "Transpolitics, Transsexuality, Transaesthetics," trans. Michel Valentin, in *Jean Baudrillard: The Disappearance of Politics*, ed. William Stearns and William Chaloupka (New York: St. Martin's Press, 1992), pp. 9–26.

18.   See the following works by Jacques Derrida, *Speech and Phenomena and Other Essays on Husserl's Theory of Signs*, trans. David B. Allison (Evanston, Ill.: Northwestern University Press, 1973); *Of Grammatology*, trans. Gayatri Chakravorty Spivak (Baltimore: Johns Hopkins University Press, 1976); "Signature Event Context," in *Glyph l: Johns Hopkins Textual Studies*, ed. Samuel Weber and Henry Sussman (Baltimore: Johns Hopkins University Press, 1977), pp. 172–97; "Limited Inc. abc . . . ,"

trans. Samuel Weber, in *Glyph 2: Johns Hopkins Textual Studies,* ed. Samuel Weber and Henry Sussman (Baltimore: Johns Hopkins University Press, 1977), pp. 162–254; *Edmund Husserl's Origin of Geometry: An Introduction,* trans. John P. Leavey Jr., ed. David B. Allison (Stony Brook, N.Y.: Nicolas Hays, 1978); *Writing and Difference,* trans. Alan Bass (Chicago: University of Chicago Press, 1978); *Spurs, Nietzsche's Styles,* trans. Barbara Harlow (Chicago: University of Chicago Press, 1978) *The Archeology of the Frivolous: Reading Condillac,* trans. John P. Leavey Jr. (Pittsburgh: Duquesne University Press, 1980); *Dissemination,* trans. Barbara Johnson (Chicago: University of Chicago Press, 1981); *Positions,* trans. Alan Bass (Chicago: University of Chicago Press, 1981); *Margins of Philosophy,* trans. Alan Bass (Chicago: University of Chicago Press, 1982); "The Principle of Reason: The University in the Eyes of Its Pupils," trans. Catherine Porter and Edward P. Morris, *Diacritics,* 13:3 (fall 1983): pp. 3–20; *Signsponge,* trans. Richard Rand (New York: Columbia University Press, 1984); "Racism's Last Word" and "But, Beyond . . . (Open Letter to Anne McClintock and Rob Nixon)," in *'Race,' Writing and Difference,* ed. Henry Louis Gates Jr. (Chicago: University of Chicago Press, 1986), pp. 329–38, 354–69; *The Other Heading: Reflections on Today's Europe,* trans. Pascale-Anne Brault and Michael B. Naas (Bloomington: Indiana University Press, 1992); "Passions: 'An Oblique Offering,'" trans. David Wood in idem, ed., *Derrida: A Critical Reader* (Cambridge, Mass.: Basil Blackwell, 1992), pp. 5–35; *Aporias,* trans. Thomas Dutoit (Stanford, Calif.: Stanford University Press, 1993); and *The Gift of Death,* trans. David Willis (Chicago: University of Chicago Press, 1995).

    19.   See the following works by Michel Foucault: *Madness and Civilization: A History of Insanity in the Age of Reason,* trans. Richard Howard (New York: Random House, 1965); *The Order of Things: An Archaeology of the Human Sciences* (New York: Pantheon Books, 1970); *The Archaeology of Knowledge and the Discourse on Language,* trans. A. M. Sheridan Smith (New York: Pantheon Books, 1972); *The Birth of the Clinic: An Archaeology of Medical Perception,* trans. A. M. Sheridan Smith (New York: Pantheon Books, 1973); *I, Pierre Rivière, Having Slaughtered My Mother, My Sister, and My Brother . . . A Case of Parricide in the Nineteenth Century,* trans. Frank Jellinek, ed. Michel Foucault (New York: Pantheon, 1975); *Language, Counter-Memory, Practice: Selected Essays and Interviews,* trans. Donald F. Bouchard and Sherry Simon, ed. Donald F. Bouchard (Ithaca, N.Y.: Cornell University Press, 1977); *Discipline and Punish: The Birth of the Prison,* trans. Alan Sheridan (New York: Vintage Books, 1979); *Herculine Barbin: Being the Recently Discovered Memoirs of a Nineteenth-Century French Hermaphrodite,* trans. Richard McDougall, introduced Michel Foucault (New York: Pantheon Books, 1980); *Power/Knowledge: Selected Interviews and Other Writings, 1972–1977,* trans. Colin Gordon et al., ed. Colin Gordon (New York: Pantheon Books, 1980); *This Is Not a Pipe—With Illustrations and Letters By Rene Magritte,* trans. and ed. James Harkness (Berkeley: University of California Press, 1982); *The Foucault Reader,* ed. Paul Rabinow (New York: Pantheon, 1984); *Death and the Labyrinth: The World of Raymond Roussel,* trans. Charles Ruas (Garden City, N.Y.: Doubleday and Co., 1986); *The History of Sexuality, Vol. 1: An Introduction, Vol 2: The Use of Pleasure, Vol. III: The Care of the Self,* trans. Robert Hurley (New York: Pantheon, 1978, 1985, 1986); *Mental Illness and Psychology,* trans. Alan Sheridan (Berkeley: University of California Press, 1988); *Technologies of the Self: A Seminar with Michel Foucault,* ed. Luther H. Martin, Huck Gutman, and Patrick H. Hutton (Amherst: University of Massachusetts Press,

1988), pp. 16–49, 145–63; *Politics, Philosophy, Culture: Interviews and Other Writings, 1977–1984*, trans. Alan Sheridan et al., ed. Lawrence D. Kritzman (New York: Routledge, 1988); *The Final Foucault*, trans. J. D. Gauthier, S.J., ed. J. Bernauer and D. Rasmussen (Cambridge, Mass.: MIT Press, 1988), pp. 1–20; *The Foucault Effect: Studies in Governmentality*, ed. G. Burchell, C. Gordon, and P. Miller (Chicago: University of Chicago Press, 1991), pp. 53–104.

20.   Perry Anderson, *A Zone of Engagement* (London: Verso, 1992), esp. pp. 25–55, 130–48, 182–376.

21.   See Jonathan Turner, "The Promise of Positivism," in Steven Seidman and David G. Wagner, eds., *Postmodernism and Social Theory: The Debate over General Theory* (Cambridge, Mass.: Basil Blackwell, 1992), pp. 156–78.

22.   See Raymond Williams, "Selections from *Marxism and Literature*," in Nicholas B. Dirks, Geoff Eley, and Sherry B. Ortner, eds., *Culture/Power/History: A Reader in Contemporary Social Theory* (Princeton, N.J.: Princeton University Press, 1994), pp. 585–608.

23.   See two works Stjepan G. Mestrovic, *The Coming Fin De Siècle: An Application of Durkheim's Sociology to Modernity and Postmodernism* (London: Routledge, 1991); and *Durkheim and Postmodern Culture* (New York: Aldine de Gruyter, 1992).

24.   See Robert D'Amico, "Defending Social Science against the Postmodern Doubt," in Seidman and Wagner, *Postmodernism and Social Theory*, pp. 137–55.

25.   See, e.g., "Special Issue on Postmodernism," *Theory, Culture, and Society* 5:2–3 (June 1988): pp. 195–576; Roy Boyne and Ali Rattansi, eds., *Postmodernism and Society* (New York: St. Martin's Press, 1990); Bryan S. Turner, ed., *Theories of Modernity and Postmodernity* (London: Sage Publications, 1990).

26.   Steven Seidman, *Contested Knowledge: Social Theory in the Postmodern Era* (Oxford: Blackwell, 1994), pp. 1–17, 281–327.

27.   Walter Benjamin, "Theses on the Philosophy of History," in *Illuminations: Essays and Reflections*, trans. Harry Zohn, ed. Hannah Arendt (New York: Harcourt, Brace and World, 1968), pp. 255–66.

28.   Mike Featherstone, *Consumer Culture and Postmodernism* (London: Sage Publications, 1991), p. 3.

29.   See Laurel Richardson, "Postmodern Social Theory: Representational Practices," *Sociological Theory* 9:2 (fall 1991): pp. 173–79.

30   See Stanford M. Lyman, "The Rise and Decline of the Functionalist-Positivist Paradigm: A Chapter in the History of American Sociology: *Hyoron Shakaikagaku: Doshisha University Social Science Review* 20 (March 1982): pp. 4–19.

31.   Andreas Huyssen, "Mapping the Postmodern," in Jeffrey C. Alexander and Steven Seidman, eds., *Culture and Society: Contemporary Debates* (Cambridge, U.K.: Cambridge University Press, 1990), pp. 355–75. Quotation from p. 373.

32.   See, e.g., S. Paige Baty, *American Monroe: The Making of a Body Politic* (Berkeley: University of California Press, 1995), pp. 8, 10, whereon it is asserted that "The representative character [e.g., Marilyn Monroe] is a cultural figure through whom the character of political life is articulated . . . Remembered as product or story or some hybrid of the two, the representative character operates as a site on which American political culture is written and exchanged. Consequently, the representative character is not simply available as shared story but also for sale as product." See also Eric Lott, *Love*

and Theft: Blackface Minstrelsy and the American Working Class (New York: Oxford University Press, 1993), p. 4, wherein it is argued that "there are reasons for thinking of blackface in the years prior to the Civil War as a far more unsettled phenomenon than has been supposed . . . and . . . that in the pages of recent social history the antebellum potential for a labor abolitionism has not been adequately explored nor its failure accounted for, and that [a new analysis of] the minstrel show crucially helps address this question." I am indebted to Herbert Hill for calling my attention to Professor Lott's groundbreaking study.

33.   See, e.g., Franco Ferraroti, *Max Weber and the Destiny of Reason,* trans. John Fraser (Armonk, N.Y.: M. E. Sharpe, 1982); Lawrence A. Scaff, *Fleeing the Iron Cage: Culture, Politics and Modernity in the Thought of Max Weber* (Berkeley: University of California Press, 1989); Roslyn W. Bologh, *Love or Greatness: Max Weber and Masculine Thinking—A Feminist Inquiry* (London: Unwin Hyman, 1990); Bryan S. Turner, *Max Weber: From History to Modernity* (London: Routledge, 1993); and Asher Horowitz and Terry Maley, eds., *The Barbarism of Reason: Max Weber and the Twilight of Enlightenment* (Toronto: University of Toronto Press, 1994).

34.   See, e.g., Barry Hindess, "Rationality and Modern Society," *Sociological Theory* 9:2 (fall 1991): pp. 216–27.

35.   Pierre Clastres, *Recherches d'anthropologie politique* (Paris: Seuil, 1980).

36.   Julian Pefanis, *Heterology and the Postmodern: Bataille, Baudrillard, and Lyotard* (Durham, N.C.: Duke University Press, 1991), p. 107.

37.   Ibid.

38.   For contending analyses of what is likely to remain an unresolved issue, see Thomas B. Allen and Norman Polmar, *Code-Name Downfall: The Secret Plan to Invade Japan—and Why Truman Dropped the Bomb* (New York: Simon and Schuster, 1995); Gar Alperovitz, *The Decision to Use the Atomic Bomb and the Architecture of an American Myth* (New York: Alfred A. Knopf, 1995); Daikichi Irokawa, *The Age of Hirohito: In Search of Modern Japan,* trans. Mikiso Hane and John K. Urda (New York: Free Press, 1995), pp. 5–39; Bruce Lee, *Marching Orders: The Untold Story of World War II* (New York: Crown Publishers, 1995), pp. 457–554; Robert Jay Lifton and Greg Mitchell, *Hiroshima in America: Fifty Years of Denial* (New York: G. P. Putnam's Sons, 1995); John Prados, *Combined Fleet Decoded: The Secret History of American Intelligence and the Japanese Navy in World War II* (New York: Random House, 1995), pp. 719–35; and Ronald Takaki, *Hiroshima: Why America Dropped the Atomic Bomb* (Boston: Little, Brown and Co., 1995).

39.   In what follows I shall omit discussion of the recent works of Jürgen Habermas as a postmodernist. Habermas's emphasis on the need as well as the capability of establishing the ideal speech community is, in fact, modernist rather than postmodernist—see, e.g., Jürgen Habermas, "Social Analyses and Communicative Competence," in *Social Theory: The Multicultural and Classical Readings,* ed. Charles Lemert (Boulder, Colo.: Westview Press, 1993), pp. 416–17—as John O'Neill, *The Poverty of Postmodernism,* has shown. See also, Jürgen Habermas, "Modernity Versus Postmodernity," in Alexander and Seidman, *Culture and Society,* pp. 342–54. For my own critique of Habermas's approach, see Stanford M. Lyman, *NATO and Germany: A Study in the Sociology of Supranational Relations* (Fayetteville: University of Arkansas Press, 1995), pp. 178–81.

40.   See, e.g., Patricia Ticineto Clough, "Feminist Theory and Social Psychology," in *Studies in Symbolic Interaction: A Research Annual,* no. 8, ed. Norman K. Denzin (Greenwich, Conn.: JAI Press, 1987), pp. 3–22; Laurel Richardson, "The Collective Story: Postmodernism and the Writing of Sociology," in *Symbolic Interaction: An Introduction to Social Psychology,* ed. Nancy J. Herman and Larry T. Reynolds (Dix Hills, N.Y.: General Hall, 1994), pp. 477–86; Virginia Olesen, "Feminisms and Models of Qualitative Research," in *Handbook of Qualitative Research,* ed. Norman K. Denzin and Yvonna S. Lincoln (Thousand Oaks, Calif.: Sage Publications, 1994), pp. 158–74; Bob Hodge and Vijay Mishra, "Aboriginal Place," in *The Post-Colonial Studies Reader,* ed. Bill Ashcroft, Gareth Griffiths, and Helen Tiffin (London: Routledge, 1995), pp. 412–17.

41.   See, e.g., Jan Nederveen Pieterse and Bhiku Parekh, eds., *The Decolonization of Imagination: Culture, Knowledge, and Power* (London: Zed Books, 1995); Sidonie Smith and Julia Watson, eds., *De/colonizing the Subject: The Politics of Gender in Women's Autobiography* (Minneapolis: University of Minnesota Press, 1992); two works Trinh T. Minh-ha, *Woman, Native, Other* (Bloomington: Indiana University Press, 1989); and *When the Moon Waxes Red: Representation, Gender and Cultural Politics* (London: Routledge, 1991); Homi K. Bhabha, *The Location of Culture* (London: Routledge, 1994); Alfred Arteaga, ed., *An Other Tongue: Nation and Ethnicity in the Linguistic Borderlands* (Durham, N.C.: Duke University Press, 1994); Gayatri Chakravorty Spivak, *The Post-Colonial Critic: Interviews, Strategies, Dialogues,* ed. Sarah Harasym (New York: Routledge, 1990); Russell Ferguson, Martha Gever, Trinh T. Minh-ha and Cornel West, eds., *Out There: Marginalization and Contemporaty Cultures* (Cambridge, Mass.: MIT Press, 1990; and New York: New Museum of Contemporary Art, 1990).

42.   See, e.g., Anson D. Shupe Jr. and David G. Bromley, "Walking a Tightrope: Dilemmas of Participant Observation of Groups in Conflict," in Herman and Reynolds, *Symbolic Interaction,* pp. 139–52; Reyes Ramos, "Movidas: The Methodological and Theoretical Relevance of Interactional Strategies," in *Studies in Symbolic Interaction:* A Research Annual, no. 2, ed. Norman K. Denzin (Greenwich, Conn.: JAI Press, 1979), pp. 141–65; and Peter Reason, "Three Approaches to Participative Inquiry," in Denzin and Lincoln, *Qualitative Research,* pp. 324–39.

43.   See Maurice Punch, "Politics and Ethics in Qualitative Research," in Denzin and Lincoln, *Qualitative Research,* pp. 83–97, esp. pp. 93–95; and Leslie J. Miller, "Claims-Making from the Underside: Marginalization and Social Problems Analysis," in *Constructivist Controversies: Issues in Social Problems Theory,* ed. Gale Miller and James A. Holstein (New York: Aldine de Gruyter, 1993), pp. 153–80.

44.   See Drucilla Cornell, Michel Rosenfeld, and David Gray Carlson, eds., *Deconstruction and the Possibility of Justice* (New York: Routledge, 1992).

45.   Dorothy E. Smith, "Sociological Theory: Methods of Writing Patriarchy," in Ruth Wallace, ed., *Feminism and Sociological Theory* (Newbury Park, Calif.: Sage Publications, 1989), pp. 34–64. Quotation from p. 34.

46.   Homi K. Bhabha, "DissemiNation: Time, Narrative, and the Margins of the Modern Nation," in idem, ed., *Nation and Narration* (London: Routledge, 1990), pp. 291–322. Quotations from pp. 291 and 320.

47.   Chantal Mouffe, "Democratic Citizenship and the Political Community, in idem, ed., *Dimensions of Radical Democracy: Pluralism, Citizenship, Community* (London: Verso, 1992), pp. 225–39. Quotation from pp. 236–37.

48.   Ibid.

49.   Jean Baudrillard, *The Illusion of the End*, trans. Chris Turner (Stanford, Calif.: Stanford University Press, 1994), p. 122.

50.   Joseph A. Kotarba, "The Postmodernization of Rock and Roll Music: The Case of Metallica," in Jonathan S. Epstein, ed., *Adolescents and Their Music: If It's Too Loud, You're Too Old* (New York: Garland Publishing, 1994), pp. 141–63. Quotation from pp. 147–48.

51.   Cf. Adam B. Seligman, "Towards a Reinterpretation of Modernity in an Age of Postmodernity," in Turner, *Theories of Modernity*, pp. 117–35; with Robert J. Antonio, "Nietzsche's Antisociology: Subjectified Culture and the End of History," *American Journal of Sociology* 101:1 (July 1995): pp. 1–43; and with Horace L. Fairlamb, *Critical Conditions; Postmodernity and the Question of Foundations* (Cambridge, U.K.: Cambridge University Press, 1994).

52.   Stanford M. Lyman and Marvin B. Scott, *A Sociology of the Absurd*, 2d ed. (Dix Hills, N.Y.: General Hall, Inc., 1989).

53.   Stanford M. Lyman and Marvin B. Scott, *The Drama of Social Reality* (New York: Oxford University Press, 1975).

54.   See Peter Wagner, *A Sociology of Modernity: Liberty and Discipline* (London: Routledge, 1994).

55.   See Stanford M. Lyman, *Civilization: Contents, Discontents, Malcontents and Other Essays in Social Theory* (Fayetteville: University of Arkansas Press, 1990), pp. 22–126.

56.   See William A. Douglass, Stanford M. Lyman, and Joseba Zuleika, *Migracion, Ethnicidad y Etnonationalismo* (Bilbao, Spain: Servicio Editorial, Universidad del Pais Vasco, 1994).

57.   See Stanford M. Lyman, *Color, Culture, Civilization: Race and Minority Issues in American Society* (Urbana: University of Illinois Press, 1994); and Barbara L. Marshall, *Engendering Modernity: Feminism, Social Theory, and Social Change* (Boston: Northeastern University Press, 1994).

58.   See, e.g., John Arthur and Amy Shapiro, eds., *Campus Wars: Multiculturalism and the Politics of Difference* (Boulder, Colo.: Westview Press, 1995); Bat-Ami Bar On, ed., *Modern Engendering: Critical Feminist Readings in Modern Western Philosophy* (Albany: State University of New York Press, 1994).

59.   Cf. Michael Lind, *The Next American Nation: The New Nationalism and the Fourth American Revolution* (New York: Free Press, 1995); with Benjamin Barber, *Jihad vs. McWorld* (New York: Random House, 1995).

60.   See, e.g., Norman K. Denzin, *Symbolic Interactionism and Cultural Studies: The Politics of Interpretation* (Oxford: Blackwell, 1992), pp. 154–71; and Lester Embree, "The Problem of Representational Adequacy, or How to Evidence an Ecosystem," in S. Galt Crowell, ed., *The Prism of the Self* (Dordrecht, Netherlands: Kluwer Academic Publishers, 1995), pp. 59–70.

61.   See, e.g., J. Budziszewski, *True Tolerance: Liberalism and the Necessity of Judgment* (New Brunswick, N.J.: Transaction Publishers, 1992); and David Miller and Michael Walzer, eds., *Pluralism, Justice, and Equality* (New York: Oxford University Press, 1995).

62.   See Gerard Delanty, "The Limits and Possibilities of a European Identity: A Critique of Cultural Essentialism," *Philosophy and Social Criticism* 21:4 (July 1995): pp.

15–36; and Stjepan G. Mestrovic, *The Barbarian Temperament: Toward a Postmodern Critical Theory* (London: Routledge, 1993), pp. 119–39.

63. See Ramon G. Mendoza, *The Acentric Labyrinth: Giordano Bruno's Prelude to Contemporary Cosmology* (Shaftesbury, U.K.: Element Books, 1995), esp. pp. 215–32.

64. Mark Wardell and Anna M. Zajicek, "Social Problems: Pathways for Transcending Exclusive Sociology," *Social Problems* 42:3 (August 1995): pp. 301–17. Quotation from p. 312 encapsulating C. Wright Mills, *The Sociological Imagination* (London: Oxford University Press, 1959), p. 8.

65. See Michael Andre Bernstein, *Against Apocalyptic History* (Berkeley: University of California Press, 1994); and Kenneth Bock, *Human Nature Mythology* (Urbana: University of Illinois Press, 1994), pp. 80–116.

66. "We need to see mental life as a dynamic activity, engaged in by people, who are located in a range of interacting discourses and at certain positions in those discourses and who, from the possibilities they make available, attempt to fashion relatively integrated and coherent subjectivities for themselves." Rom Harrè and Grant Gillett, *The Discursive Mind* (Thousand Oaks, Calif.: Sage Publications, 1994), p. 180.

67. See Robert Jay Lifton, *The Protean Self: Human Resilience in an Age of Fragmentation* (New York: Basic Books, 1993).

68. See e.g., Norman K. Denzin, *Images of Postmodern Society: Social Theory and Contemporary Cinema* (London: Sage Publications, 1991), pp. 107–36, 149–57; Barry Glassner, *Bodies: Why We Look the Way We Do (and How We Feel About It)* (New York: G. P. Putnam's Sons, 1988); and Kenneth R. Dutton, *The Perfectible Body: The Western Ideal of Male Physical Development* (New York: Continuum, 1995). For an intriguing set of axioms laying a basis for an innovative sociology of sex, sexual preference, and gender, see Eve Kosofsky Sedgwick, *Epistemology of the Closet* (Berkeley: University of California Press, 1990), pp. 22–63. For a complex and illuminating analysis of gender and postmodernism, see Mary Lydon, *Skirting the Issue: Essays in Literary Theory* (Madison: University of Wisconsin Press, 1995), esp. pp. 169–230.

69. See, e.g., Robert C. Smith, *Racism in the Post–Civil Rights Era: Now You See It, Now You Don't* (Albany: State University of New York Press, 1995), pp. 141–43.

70. Thus, John M. Johnson, "In Dispraise of Justice," *Symbolic Interaction* 18:2 (summer 1995): p. 200, observes, "Our meaningful social lives are lived in the everyday worlds of family, friendship groups, neighborhoods, workgroups, churches and spiritual communities, and our other local community forms of organization. Our struggle to achieve justice in our lives is waged at this level." However, in contradiction to this recentering of the locus of justice, Todd May, *The Political Philosophy of Poststructuralist Anarchism* (University Park: Pennsylvania State University Press, 1994), pp. 99–100, writes, "If macropolitical institutions and practices are founded on micropolitical practices, this does not mean that the goals of macropolitical practices are simply those of their micropolitical constituents writ large . . . [M]icropolitics does not leave macropolitical understanding broadened but untouched in its essence."

71. See two works by Stanford M. Lyman, "Race Relations as Social Process: Sociology's Resistance to a Civil Rights Orientation," in Herbert Hill and James E. Jones, eds., *Race in America: The Struggle for Equality* (Madison: University of Wisconsin Press, 1993), pp. 370–401; and *Color, Culture, Civilization*, pp. 148–218, 326–48. On homosexuality and just laws, see Angelia R. Wilson, ed., *A Simple Matter of Justice? Theorizing Lesbian and Gay Politics* (London: Cassell, 1995).

Chapter 1: Postmodernism and a Sociology of the Absurd

1. Stanford M. Lyman and Marvin B. Scott, *A Sociology of the Absurd* (New York: Appleton-Century-Crofts, 1970).

2. Stanford M. Lyman and Marvin B. Scott, *A Sociology of the Absurd,* 2d ed. (Dix Hills, N.Y.: General Hall, 1989). Quotations in this essay will be taken from the second edition.

3. Mark Lilla, "The Legitimacy of the Liberal Age," in idem, ed., *New French Thought: Political Philosophy* (Princeton, N.J.: Princeton University Press, 1994), p. 13.

4. Steven Best and Douglas Kellner, *Postmodern Theory: Critical Interrogations* (New York: Guilford Press, 1991), p. 300.

5. E. Ann Kaplan, "Introduction," in idem, ed., *Postmodernism and Its Discontents: Theories, Practices* (London: Verso, 1988), p. 2.

6. Christopher Norris, "Introduction," in idem, *Deconstruction and the Interests of Theory* (Norman: University of Oklahoma Press, 1989), pp. 25–26.

7. Jonathan Turner, "The Promise of Positivism," in Steven Seidman and David G. Wagner, eds., *Postmodernism and Social Theory* (Cambridge, Mass.: Basil Blackwell, 1992), pp. 175–76.

8. Mike Featherstone, "In Pursuit of the Postmodern: An Introduction," *Theory, Culture, and Society* 2–3 (June 1988): pp. 195–216.

9. Charles Lemert, "General Social Theory, Irony, Postmodernism," in Seidman and Wagner, *Postmodernism and Social Theory,* p. 33.

10. Steven Seidman, "Postmodern Social Theory as Narrative with a Moral Intent," in Seidman and Wagner, *Postmodernism and Social Theory,* pp. 47–81. Quotation from p. 47.

11. Laurel Richardson, "Postmodern Social Theory: Representational Practices," *Sociological Theory* 9:2 (fall 1991): pp. 173–79. Quotations from pp. 173 and 176.

12. Zygmunt Bauman, *Postmodern Ethics* (Oxford: Blackwell, 1993). Quotation from p. 250.

13. Erving Goffman, *Relations in Public: Microstudies of the Public Order* (New York: Basic Books, 1971), pp. xiv–xv. See also Stanford M. Lyman, *Civilization: Contents, Discontents, Malcontents and Other Essays in Social Theory* (Fayetteville: University of Arkansas Press, 1990), pp. 11–21.

14. Jonathon S. Epstein and Margarete J. Epstein, "Fatal Forms: Toward a (Neo) Formal Sociological Theory of Media Culture," in Douglas Kellner, ed., *Baudrillard: A Critical Reader* (Oxford: Blackwell, 1994), pp. 135–49. Quotation from p. 136.

15. George Herbert Mead, *Mind, Self, and Society from the Standpoint of a Social Behaviorist,* ed. Charles W. Morris (Chicago: University of Chicago Press, 1952), p. 221.

16. Herbert Blumer, "George Herbert Mead," in Buford Rhea, ed., *The Future of the Sociological Classics* (London: George Allen and Unwin, 1981), pp. 136–69. Quotations from pp. 164–67.

17. Among the many works of Jacques Derrida, see especially *Speech and Phenomena and Other Essays on Husserl's Theory of Signs,* trans. David B. Allison (Evanston, Ill.: Northwestern University Press, 1973); *Of Grammatology,* trans. Gayatri Chakravorty Spivak (Baltimore: Johns Hopkins University Press, 1976); and *Writing and Difference,* trans. Alan Bass (Chicago: University of Chicago Press, 1978).

18. Madan Sarup, *An Introductory Guide to Post-Structuralism and Postmodernism* (Athens: University of Georgia Press, 1989), p. 35.

19. Lyman and Scott, *A Sociology of the Absurd*, p. 2.

20. Sarup, *Post-Structuralism and Postmodernism*, p. 38.

21. Ibid.

22. Derrida, *Speech and Phenomena*.

23. Lyman and Scott, *A Sociology of the Absurd*, pp. 112–32.

24. In addition to the works cited infra, see the following works of Jean Baudrillard, *The Mirror of Production*, trans. Mark Poster (St. Louis, Mo.: Telos Press, 1975); *For a Critique of the Political Economy of the Sign*, trans. Charles Levin (St. Louis, Mo.: Telos Press, 1981); *Selected Writings*, trans. and ed. Mark Poster (Stanford, Calif.: Stanford University Press, 1988); "The Anorexic Ruins," trans. David Antal, in Dietmar Kamper and Christoph Wulf, eds., *Looking Back on the End of the World* (New York: Semiotext(e), 1989), pp. 29–48; *Fatal Strategies: Crystal Revenge*, trans. Philip Beitchman and W. G. J. Niesluchowski, ed. Jim Fleming (New York: Semiotext(e), 1990); *Seduction*, trans. Brian Singer (New York: St. Martin's Press, 1990); and Baudrillard's three essays, "Transpolitics, Transsexuality, Transaesthetics," pp. 9–26; "Revolution and the End of Utopia," pp. 223–42; "Baudrillard Shrugs: A Seminar on Terrorism and the Media, with Sylvia Lotringer and Jean Baudrillard," pp. 283–302, in William Stearns and William Chaloupka, eds., *Jean Baudrillard: The Disappearance of Art and Politics* (New York: St. Martin's Press, 1992).

25. Jean Baudrillard, *In the Shadow of the Silent Majorities, or The End of the Social and Other Essays*, trans. Paul Foss, John Johnston, and Paul Patton (New York: Semiotext(e), 1983).

26. Jean Baudrillard, *America*, trans. Chris Turner (London: Verso, 1989).

27. Baudrillard, *In the Shadow of the Silent Majorities*, pp. 65–67.

28. The following draws on the masterful precis of Baudrillard's *oeuvre* in Edward W. Soja, "Postmodern Geographies and the Critique of Historicism," in John Paul Jones III, Wolfgang Natter, and Theodore R. Schatzki, eds., *Postmodern Contentions: Epochs, Politics, Space* (New York: Guilford Press, 1993), pp. 113–36, esp. pp. 119–20.

29. See Jean Baudrillard, *The Ecstasy of Communication*, trans. Bernard and Caroline Schutze, ed. Slyvere Lotringer (New York: Semiotext(e), 1988), pp. 29–96. See also Michel Foucault, *This Is Not a Pipe—With Illustrations and Letters René Magritte*, trans. and ed. James Harkness (Berkeley: University of California Press, 1982).

30. Jean Baudrillard, *Cool Memories*, trans. Chris Carter (London: Verso, 1990), p. 229.

31. Harold Garfinkel, *Studies in Ethnomethodology* (Englewood Cliffs, N.J.: Prentice-Hall, 1967).

32. Lyman and Scott, *A Sociology of the Absurd*, pp. 157–80.

33. Jean-Francois Lyotard, *The Postmodern Condition: A Report on Knowledge*, trans. Geoff Bennington and Brian Massumi (Minneapolis: University of Minnesota Press, 1991), p. xxiv.

34. Ibid., pp. 16–17.

35. Ibid., p. 17.

36. Charles Battershill, "Erving Goffman as a Precursor to Post-Modern Sociology," in Stephen Harold Riggins, ed., *Beyond Goffman: Studies on*

Communication, Institution, and Social Interaction (Berlin: Mouton de Gruyter, 1990), pp. 163–86.

37.   Erving Goffman, "Felicity's Condition," *American Journal of Sociology* 89:1 (July 1983): pp. 1–53.

38.   Erving Goffman, *Frame Analysis: An Essay on the Organization of Experience* (New York: Harper Colophon, 1974). The commentator is Patricia Jicineto Clough, "Reading Goffman: Toward the Deconstruction of Sociology," in Riggins, *Beyond Goffman*, pp. 187–202.

39.   Lyman and Scott, *A Sociology of the Absurd*, pp. 98–110, 157–80.

40.   Jean-Francois Lyotard and Jean-Loup Thebaud, *Just Gaming*, trans. Wlad Godzich (Minneapolis: University of Minnesota Press, 1989). The original French edition was published in 1979.

41.   Jean-Francois Lyotard, "Wittgenstein 'After,'" in *Political Writings*, trans. Bill Readings and Kevin Paul Geiman (Minneapolis: University of Minnesota Press, 1993).

42.   Lyman and Scott, *A Sociology of the Absurd*, p. 188.

43.   Sarup, *Post-Structuralism and Postmodernism*, p. 2.

44.   See the following works Michel Foucault: *Madness and Civilization: A History of Insanity in the Age of Reason,* trans. Richard Howard (New York: Pantheon Books, 1965); *The Order of Things: An Archaeology of the Human Sciences* (New York: Pantheon Books, 1970); *The Archaeology of Knowledge and the Discourse on Language,* trans. A. M. Sheridan Smith (New York: Pantheon Books, 1972); *The Birth of the Clinic: An Archaeology of Medical Perception,* trans. A. M. Sheridan Smith (New York: Pantheon Books, 1973); *Discipline and Punish: The Birth of the Prison,* trans. Alan Sheridan (New York: Vintage Books, 1979); *Death and the Labyrinth: The World of Raymond Roussel,* trans. Charles Ruas (Garden City, N.Y.: Doubleday and Co., 1986); *The History of Sexuality,* vol. 1, *An Introduction*; vol. 2, *The Use of Pleasure*; vol. 3 *The Care of the Self,* trans. Robert Hurley (New York: Pantheon Books, 1978, 1985, 1986). See also Michel Foucault, ed., *I, Pierre Rivière, Having Slaughtered My Mother, My Sister and My Brother . . . A Case of Parricide in the Nineteenth Century,* trans. Frank Jellinek, ed. Michel Foucault (New York: Pantheon Books, 1975); and *Herculine Barbine: Being the Recently Discovered Memoirs of a Nineteenth-Century French Hermaphrodite,* trans. Richard McDougall, introduced by Michel Foucault (New York: Pantheon Books, 1980). For Foucault's commentary on psychology, see his *Mental Illness and Psychology,* trans. Alan Sheridan (Berkeley: University of California Press, 1987). Among the volumes of Foucault's essays and letters that have been published, see *Language, Counter-Memory, Practice: Selected Essays and Interviews Michel Foucault,* trans. Donald F. Bouchard and Sherry Simon, ed. Donald F. Bouchard (Ithaca, N.Y.: Cornell University Press, 1977); *Power/Knowledge: Selected Interviews and Other Writings, 1972–1977,* trans. Colin Gordon, ed. Colin Gordon et al. (New York: Pantheon Books, 1980); *The Foucault Reader,* ed. Paul Rabinow (New York: Pantheon Books, 1984);and *Michel Foucault-Politics, Philosophy, Culture: Interviews and Other Writings, 1977–1984,* trans. Alan Sheridan et al., ed. Lawrence D. Kritzman (New York: Routledge, 1988).

45.   Friedrich Nietzsche, "On the Genealogy of Morals," *Basic Writings of Nietzsche,* ed. Walter Kaufmann (New York: Modern Library, 1992), pp. 437–600.

46.   Sarup, *Post-Structuralism and Postmodernism*, p. 63.

47.   Talcott Parsons, *The Evolution of Societies,* ed. Jackson Toby (Englewood Cliffs, N.J.: Prentice-Hall, 1977), pp. 24–241.

48.   See, e.g., the Foucault-inspired studies collected in Randall H. McGuire and Robert Paynter, eds., *The Archaeology of Inequality* (Oxford: Blackwell, 1991).

49.   Sarup, *Post-Structuralism and Postmodernism*, p. 64.

50.   Ibid.

51.   See Lyman and Scott, *A Sociology of the Absurd*, pp. 182–90.

52.   For my own colloquy with Burke on this matter, see Kenneth Burke, *Attitudes toward History*, 3d ed. (Berkeley: University of California Press, 1984), pp. 377–434.

53.   See Stanford M. Lyman, *Civilization*, pp. 76–126.

54.   Marvin B. Scott, "Functional Foibles and the Analysis of Social Change," *Inquiry* 9 (1966): pp. 205–14; and "Functional Analysis: A Statement of Problems," in Gregory P. Stone and Harvey A. Farberman, eds., *Social Psychology Through Symbolic Interaction* (Waltham, Mass.: Ginn-Blaisdell, 1970), pp. 21–28.

55.   See the essays collected in Stanford M. Lyman, ed., *Social Movements: Critiques, Concepts, Case Studies* (London: Macmillan; New York: New York University Press, 1995).

56.   Maurice Natanson, "History as a Finite Province of Meaning," *Literature, Philosophy and the Social Sciences: Essays in Existentialism and Phenomenology* (The Hague: Martinus Nijhoff, 1968), pp. 172–77.

57.   Cf. Jürgen Habermas, *Legitimation Crisis*, trans. Thomas McCarthy (Boston: Beacon Press, 1975).

58.   Natanson, *Literature, Phlosophy and the Social Sciences*, p. 176.

59.   Ibid.

60.   Georg Simmel, *The Problems of the Philosophy of History: An Epistemological Essay,* trans. and ed. Guy Oakes (New York: Free Press, 1977), p. 201.

61.   Ibid., p. 200.

62.   Natanson, *Literature, Philosophy and the Social Sciences*, p. 176.

63.   Michael Oakeshott, *Experience and Its Modes*, pp. 41–42. Quoted in Natanson, "History, Historicity, and the Alchemistry of Time," *Literature, Philosophy and the Social Sciences*, p. 181.

64.   Ibid.

65.   Ibid.

66.   Cf. John J. Cerullo, "The Epistemic Turn: Critical Sociology and the 'Generation of '68,'" *International Journal of Politics, Culture, and Society* 8:1 (fall 1994): pp. 169–81.

67.   The critique presented here is my own. However, Foucault's works—as well as his life—have generated a veritable cottage industry of commentaries and criticism. See, *inter alia*, Alan Sheridan, *Michel Foucault: The Will to Truth* (London: Tavistock Publications, 1980); Charles C. Lemert and Garth Gillan, *Michel Foucault: Social Theory as Transgression* (New York: Columbia University Press, 1982); Pamela Major-Poetzl, *Michel Foucault's Archaeology of Western Culture: Toward a New Science of History* (Chapel Hill: University of North Carolina Press, 1983); two works Barry Smart; *Foucault, Marxism and Critique* (London: Routledge and Kegan Paul, 1983) and *Michel Foucault* (London: Tavistock Publications, 1985); Karlis Racevskis, *Michel Foucault and the Subversion of Intellect* (Ithaca, N.Y.: Cornell University Press, 1983); Hubert L. Dreyfus and Paul Rabinow, *Michel Foucault: Beyond Structuralism and Hermeneutics*, 2d ed. (Chicago: University of Chicago Press, 1983); Mark Cousins and Athar Hussain,

Michel Foucault (New York: St. Martin's Press, 1984); J. G. Merquior, *Foucault* (Berkeley: University of California Press, 1985); John Rajchman, *Michel Foucault: The Freedom of Philosophy* (New York: Columbia University Press, 1985); Mike Gane, ed., *Towards a Critique of Foucault* (London: Routledge and Kegan Paul, 1986); James Bernauer and David Rasmussen, eds., *The Final Foucault* (Cambridge, Mass.: MIT Press, 1988); Luther H. Martin, Huck Gutman, and Patrick H. Hutton, eds., *Technologies of the Self: A Seminar with Michel Foucault* (Amherst: University of Massachusetts Press, 1988); Gary Gutting, *Michel Foucault's Archaeology of Scientific Reason* (New York: Cambridge University Press, 1989); Graham Burchell *et al.*, eds., *The Foucault Effect: Studies in Governmentality* (Chicago: University of Chicago Press, 1991); and *Michel Foucault: Philosopher*, trans. Timothy J. Armstrong (New York: Routledge, 1992). Three biographies have been published: Didier Eribon, *Michel Foucault*, trans. Betsy Wing (Cambridge, Mass.: Harvard University Press, 1991); James Miller, *The Passion of Michel Foucault* (New York: Simon and Schuster, 1993); and David Macey, *The Lives of Michel Foucault* (New York: Pantheon Books, 1993). See also "A Symposium on James Miller's *The Passion of Michel Foucault*" in *Salmagundi* 97 (winter 1993): pp. 30–99.

68.   For the distinction between a rebellion and a revolution that is used here, see Thomas Taylor Meadows, *The Chinese and Their Rebellions* (Stanford, Calif.: Academic Reprints, n.d.), pp. 24–29.

69.   Ibid., p. 25.

70.   Robert Jackall, "Re-enchanting the World: Some Reflections on Postmodernism," *International Journal of Politics, Culture, and Society* 8:1 (fall 1994): p. 186.

71.   Cerullo, "The Epistemic Turn," p. 176.

72.   Lyotard, *The Postmodern Condition*, pp. 25–40.

73.   See Martin Bernal, *Black Athena: The Afroasiatic Roots of Classical Civilization*, vol. 1, *The Fabrication of Ancient Greece*, vol. 2, *The Archaeological and Documentary Evidence* (New Brunswick, N.J.: Rutgers University Press, 1987, 1991); and three works by Molefi Kete Asante, *The Afrocentric Idea* (Philadelphia: Temple University Press, 1987); *Afrocentricity* (Trenton, N.J.: Africa World Press, 1988); and *Kemet, Afrocentricity and Knowledge* (Trenton, N.J.: Africa World Press, 1990). For an even more extreme example, see the description of Prof. Leonard Jeffries' perspective in James Traub, *City on a Hill: Testing the American Dream at City College* (Reading, Mass.: Addison-Wesley Publishing, 1994), pp. 227–72. For a critique, see Mary Lefkowitz, *Not Out of Africa: How Afrocentrism Became an Excuse to Teach Myth as History* (New York: Basic Books, 1996); and Mary R. Lefkowitz and Guy MacLean Rogers, eds., *Black Athena Revisited* (Chapel Hill: University of North Carolina Press, 1996).

74.   See, e.g., Livie Isauro Duran and H. Russell Bernard, eds., *Introduction to Chicano Studies*, 2d ed. (New York: Macmillan, 1982), pp. 1–228, 407–584.

75.   See, e.g., Aysegul Baykan, "Women Between Fundamentalism and Modernity," and Lieteke van Vucht Jijssen, "Women Between Modernity and Postmodernity," both in Bryan S. Turner, ed., *Theories of Modernity and Postmodernity* (London: Sage Publications, 1990), pp. 136–46, 147–63. See also Daphne Patai and Noretta Koertge, *Professing Feminism: Cautionary Tales From the Strange World of Women's Studies* (New York: Harper Collins–Basic Books, 1994); and Caroline Ramazanoglu, ed., *Up Against Foucault: Explorations of Some Tensions Between Foucault and Feminism* (London: Routledge, 1993).

76.   See Steven Seidman et al., "Symposium: Queer Theory/Sociology: A Dialogue," *Sociological Theory* 12:2 (July 1994): pp. 166–248. For a critique, see Stanford M. Lyman, "Without Morals or Mores: Deviance in Postmodern Social Theory," *International Journal of Politics, Culture, and Society* 9:2 (winter 1995): pp. 197–236.

77.   Cf. Garth Hallett, *Essentialism: A Wittgensteinian Critique* (Albany: State University of New York Press, 1991).

78.   Frederick J. Teggart, *Theory of History* (New Haven, Conn.: Yale University Press, 1925), pp. 71–152.

79.   See three works by Max Weber, "The Relations of the Rural Community to Other Branches of Social Science," trans. Charles W. Seidenadel. *Proceedings of the International Conference of Arts and Sciences, Universal Exposition, St. Louis*, vol. 7: *Social Sciences* (Boston: Houghton-Mifflin, 1906), pp. 725–46; "The Social Causes of the Decay of Ancient Civilization," trans. Christian Mackauer, *Journal of General Education* 5 (October 1950): pp. 75–88; and *The Agrarian Sociology of Ancient Civilization*, trans. R. I. Frank (London: NLB Books, 1976).

80.   Kenneth E. Bock, *The Acceptance of Histories: Towards a Perspective for Social Science*, University of California Publications in Sociology and Social Institutions 3 (Berkeley: University of California Press, 1956).

81.   Lyman, *Civilization*, pp. 76–84, 119–26.

82.   For a fine example, see Frederick J. Teggart, *Rome and China: A Study of Correlations in Historical Events* (Berkeley: University of California Press, 1939).

83.   Cf. Robert A. Nisbet, *Social Change and History: Aspects of the Western Theory of Development* (New York: Oxford University Press, 1969), pp. 13–136.

84.   Frederick J. Teggart, *Prolegomena to History: The Relation of History to Literature, Philosophy, and Science* (Berkeley: University of California Press, 1916).

85.   Gaetano Salvemini, *Historian and Scientist* (Cambridge, Mass.: Harvard University Press, 1939), pp. 29–33. Quoted in Bock, *The Acceptance of Histories*, p. 125.

86.   Bock, *The Acceptance of Histories*, p. 85.

87.   Recognition of the Teggart school's impact on sociology has belatedly been made in Roscoe C. Hinkle, *Developments in American Sociological Theory, 1915–1950* (Albany: State University of New York Press, 1994), pp. 65–199.

88.   Fredric Jameson, *Postmodernism, or the Cultural Logic of Late Capitalism* (Durham, N.C.: Duke University Press, 1992), pp. 26–38.

89.   Ibid., p. 26.

90.   Ibid., pp. 26–27.

91.   Here I draw on Alfred Schutz, *The Phenomenology of the Social World*, trans. George Walsh and Frederick Lehnert (Evanston, Ill.: Northwestern University Press, 1967), pp. 176–214; and David Carr, *Time, Narrative and History* (Bloomington: Indiana University Press, 1986), pp. 113–16.

92.   Kenneth E. Bock, *Human Nature Mythology* (Urbana: University of Illinois Press, 1994), p. 115.

93.   Ibid., pp. 115–16.

94.   Lyman and Scott, *A Sociology of the Absurd*, pp. 35–50.

95.   Ibid., p. 35.

96.   Ibid., p. 49.

97.   Robert E. Park, "Our Racial Frontier on the Pacific," *Survey Graphic* 56

(May 1926): pp. 192–96. For a critical discussion, see two works by Stanford M. Lyman, *The Black American in Sociological Thought: A Failure of Perspective* (New York: G. P. Putnam's Sons, 1972), pp. 27–70; and *Militarism, Imperialism and Racial Accommodation: An Analysis and Interpretation of the Early Writings of Robert E. Park* (Fayetteville: University of Arkansas Press, 1992), pp. 1–11, 41–178. For still a different view on the matter, see Vernon J. Williams Jr., *Rethinking Race: Franz Boas and His Contemporaries* (Lexington: University Press of Kentucky. 1996), pp. 86–116.

98.   Park, "Our Racial Frontier," p. 196.

99.   Ibid.

100.   Ibid.

101.   Robert E. Park, "Introduction," in Romanzo Adams, *Interracial Marriage in Hawaii: A Study of the Mutually Conditioned Processes of Acculturation and Amalgamation* (New York: Macmillan, 1937; Montclair, N J.: Patterson Smith, 1969), pp. vii–xiv.

102.   Cf. Leon Festinger, Henry W. Riecken, and Stanley Schachter, *When Prophecy Fails: A Social and Psychological Study of a Modern Group That Predicted the Destruction of the World* (New York: Harper Torchbooks, 1964); and Leon Festinger, ed., *Conflict, Decision and Dissonance* (London: Tavistock Publications, 1964).

103.   Rose Hum Lee, *The Chinese in the United States of America* (Hong Kong: Hong Kong University Press, 1960), pp. 405–30.

104.   Emory S. Bogardus, "A Race Relations Cycle," *American Journal of Sociology* 35 (January 1930): pp. 612–17; Robert H. Ross and Emory S. Bogardus, "The Second Generation Race Relations Cycle: A Study in Issei-Nisei Relationships," *Sociology and Social Research* 24 (March 1940): pp. 357–63; Emory S. Bogardus, "Current Problems of Japanese Americans," *Sociology and Social Research* 25 (September 1940): pp. 63–66.

105.   E. Franklin Frazier, "The Theoretical Structure of Sociology and Sociological Research," *British Journal of Sociology* 4 (December 1953): pp. 292–311.

106.   Tamotsu Shibutani and Kian Moon Kwan, *Ethnic Stratification: A Comparative Approach* (New York: Macmillan, 1965), pp. 116–35.

107.   James A. Geschwender, *Racial Stratification in America* (Dubuque, Iowa: Wm. C. Brown Publishers, 1978), p. 20.

108.   See Herbert Blumer and Troy Duster, "Theories of Race and Social Action," *Sociological Theories: Race and Colonialism* (Paris: UNESCO, 1980), pp. 211–38.

109.   Brewton Berry, *Race and Ethnic Relations*, 3d ed. (Boston: Houghton-Mifflin, 1965), p. 135.

110.   Thomas P. Wilson, "Normative and Interpretive Paradigms in Sociology," in Jack D. Douglas, ed., *Understanding Everyday Life: Toward the Reconstruction of Sociological Knowledge* (Chicago: Aldine Publishing, 1970), pp. 57–79. Quotation from p. 78.

111.   Pauline Marie Rosenau, *Postmodernism and the Social Sciences: Insights, Inroads, and Intrusions* (Princeton, N.J.: Princeton University Press, 1992), p. xii.

112.   Ibid., p. xiv.

113.   Ibid., pp. 69–71.

114.   Fredric Jameson, "Postmodernism, or the Cultural Logic of Late Capitalism," *New Left Review* 146 (July–August, 1984): pp. 53–92. Quotation from p. 83, quoted in Rosenau, *Postmodernism and the Social Sciences*, p. 69.

115. Cf. Arthur J. Vidich and Stanford M. Lyman, "Qualitative Methods: Their History in Sociology and Anthropology," in Norman K. Denzin and Yvonna S. Lincoln, eds., *Handbook of Qualitative Research* (Thousand Oaks, Calif.: Sage Publications, 1994), pp. 23–59.

116. Robert Nisbet, *The Quest for Community: A Study in the Ethics of Order and Freedom* (New York: Oxford University Press, 1953), and Christopher Lasch, *The Revolt of the Elites and the Betrayal of Democracy* (New York: W. W. Norton, 1995).

117. Robert Redfield, *The Little Community and Peasant Society and Culture* (Chicago: University of Chicago Press, 1960).

118. Louis Wirth, "Urbanism as a Way of Life," *American Journal of Sociology* 44 (July 1938): pp. 1–24.

119. Robert Park, "Community Organization and Juvenile Delinquency," in Robert E. Park, Ernest W. Burgess, and R. D. McKenzie, eds., *The City* (Chicago: University of Chicago Press, 1967), p. 109.

120. Rosenau, *Postmodernism and the Social Sciences*, p. 69.

121. Stanley Elkins, *Slavery: A Problem in American Institutional and Intellectual Life,* 3d ed. (Chicago: University of Chicago Press, 1976), pp. 81–139.

122. Erving Goffman, *Asylums: Essays on the Social Situation of Mental Patients and Other Inmates* (Garden City, N.Y.: Doubleday-Anchor, 1961), pp. 1–320.

123. Foucault, *Discipline and Punish*.

124. Benedict Anderson, *Imagined Communities: Reflections on the Origin and Spread of Nationalism*, rev. ed. (London: Verso, 1991).

125. Cf. Amy Kaplan and Donald E. Pease, eds., *Cultures of United States Imperialism* (Durham, N.C.: Duke University Press, 1993); and Tzevetan Todorov, *On Human Diversity: Nationalism, Racism, and Exoticism in French Thought,* trans. Catherine Porter (Cambridge. Mass.: Harvard University Press, 1993).

126. Edward W. Soja, *Postmodern Geographies: The Reassertion of Space in Critical Social Theory* (London: Verso, 1989).

127. Edward W. Soja, "History: Geography: Modernity," in Simon During, ed., *The Cultural Studies Reader* (London: Routledge, 1993), pp. 135–50. Quotation from p. 136.

128. Michel Foucault, "Questions on Geography," in Gordon, *Power/Knowledge,* pp. 63–77. Quotation from p. 70.

129. Soja, "History: Geography: Modernity," p. 137.

130. Ibid.

131. Soja, "Postmodern Geographies," pp. 113–36. Quotation from p. 133.

132. Stanford M. Lyman and Marvin B. Scott, "Territoriality: A Neglected Sociological Dimension," *Social Problems* 15:2 (fall 1967): pp. 236–49. See also Stanford M. Lyman, *NATO and Germany: A Study in the Sociology of Supranational Relations* (Fayetteville: University of Arkansas Press, 1995), pp. 1–32, 157–212.

133. Foucault, "Questions on Geography," p. 70.

134. Teggart, *Theory of History*, pp. 76–152.

135. Frederick J. Teggart, "World History," *Scientia* 69 (1941): pp. 30–35. Reprinted in Grace Dangberg, ed., *A Guide to the Life and Works of Frederick J. Teggart* (Reno, Nev.: Grace Dangberg Foundation, 1983), pp. 460–66.

136. See four essays by Kenneth E. Bock, "Evolution and Historical Process,"

American Anthropologist 54:4 (October 1952): pp. 486–96; "Cultural Differences and Race," *Commentary* 23:2 (February 1957): pp. 179–86; "Evolution, Function and Change," *American Sociological Review* 28 (April 1963): pp. 229–37; and "The Comparative Method of Anthropology," *Comparative Studies in Society and History* 8:3 (April 1966): pp. 269–80.

137.   Alexander A. Goldenweiser, *Early Civilization* (New York: Macmillan, 1922). The critique will be found in Bock, *The Acceptance of Histories,* pp. 98–99.

138.   Winifred Raushenbush, "Their Place in the Sun," *Survey Graphic* 56 (May 1926): pp. 141–45. For a critique, see Lyman, *The Black American in Sociological Thought*, pp. 30–35.

139.   See Stanford M. Lyman, "History and Sociology: Some Unresolved Epistemological Issues," *International Journal of Politics, Culture and Society* 9:1 (fall 1995): pp. 29–55.

140.   Lyman and Scott, *A Sociology of the Absurd*, pp. 22–34.

141.   Claude Lévi-Strauss, *The Raw and the Cooked,* trans. John Weightman and Doreen Weightman (New York: Harper and Row, 1969).

142.   Cf. Benita Luckmann, "The Small Life-Worlds of Modern Man," *Social Research* 37:4 (1970): pp. 580–96. Reprinted in Thomas Luckmann, ed., *Phenomenology and Sociology: Selected Readings* (New York: Penguin Books, 1978), pp. 275–90.

143.   Amitai Etzioni, "The Ghetto: A Re-Evaluation," *Social Forces* 37 (March 1959): pp. 255–62. Quotation in Lyman, *The Black American*, p. 54.

144.   Robert E. Park and Ernest W. Burgess, *Introduction to the Science of Sociology*, 3d ed. rev. (Chicago: University of Chicago Press, 1969), p. 228.

145.   Ibid., p. 229.

146.   See Gunnar Myrdal, with the assistance of Richard Sterner and Arnold Rose, *An American Dilemma: The Negro Problem and Modern Democracy* (New York: Harper and Brothers, 1944).

147.   Park and Burgess, *Science of Sociology*, p. 228.

148.   Ibid..

149.   See Stanford M. Lyman, *The Seven Deadly Sins. Society and Evil*, 2d ed. rev. (Dix Hills, N.Y.: General Hall, 1989), pp. 232–68.

150.   Park and Burgess, *Science of Sociology*, p. 557.

151.   Ibid., p. 230.

152.   Ibid., p. 556.

153.   Ibid., p. 559.

154.   Ernest W. Burgess, "The Growth of the City," in Robert E. Park et al., *The City*, p. 51.

155.   Park and Burgess, *Science of Sociology*, p. 559.

156.   Park, "Our Racial Frontier on the Pacific," op. cit., p. 196.

157.   Edward Shils, "Center and Periphery," *The Constitution of Society* (Chicago: University of Chicago Press, 1982), pp. 93–109. Quotation from p. 93.

158.   The original sentence (ibid., p. 93) reads: "The center, or central zone, is a phenomenon of the realm of values and beliefs."

159.   Ibid.

160.   Barry S. Strauss, "The Melting Pot, the Mosaic, and the Agora," in J. Peter Euben, John R. Wallach, and Joseph Ober, eds., *Athenian Political Thought and The*

Reconstruction of American Democracy (Ithaca N.Y.: Cornell University Press, 1994), pp. 252–64.

161.   Ibid., p. 254.

162.   Ibid., p. 259.

163.   Ibid., p. 260.

164.   Cf. Herbert Blumer, "Race Prejudice as a Sense of Group Position," *Pacific Sociological Review* 1 (spring 1958): pp. 3–7. Reprinted in Stanford M. Lyman and Arthur J. Vidich, *Social Order and the Public Philosophy: An Analysis and Interpretation of the Work of Herbert Blumer* (Fayetteville: University of Arkansas Press, 1988), pp. 196–207.

165.   Strauss, "The Melting Pot," p. 262.

166.   Ibid., p. 261.

167.   Ibid., p. 262.

168.   Gian Biagio Conte, *The Rhetoric of Imitation: Genre and Poetic Memory in Virgil and Other Latin Poets,* trans. Charles Segal (Ithaca, N.Y.: Cornell University Press, 1986), pp. 23–24. See the discussion of this and related concepts in Stanford M. Lyman, *Color, Culture, Civilization: Race and Minority Issues in American Society* (Urbana: University of Illinois Press, 1994), pp. 1–43, 349–84.

169.   Rosenau, *Postmodernism and the Social Sciences,* pp. 42–61.

170.   See Racevskis, *Michel Foucault,* pp. 25–40.

171.   Max Weber, *The Protestant Ethic and the Spirit of Capitalism,* trans. Talcott Parsons (New York: Charles Scribner's Sons, 1930). For one answer to the fate and promise of the self imprisoned in Weber's iron cage, see Alkis Kontos, "The World Disenchanted, and the Return of Gods and Demons," in Asher Horowitz and Terry Maley, eds., *The Barbarism of Reason: Max Weber and the Twilight of Enlightenment* (Toronto: University of Toronto Press, 1994), pp. 223–47.

172.   Rosenau, *Postmodernism and the Social Sciences,* p. 43.

173.   Ibid., p. 44.

174.   Ibid., pp. 46–49.

175.   Julian Henriques et al., *Changing the Subject: Psychology, Social Regulation, and Subjectivity* (New York: Methuen, 1984), p. 13. Quoted in Rosenau, *Postmodernism and the Social Sciences,* p. 49.

176.   See Christopher Lasch, *The Culture of Narcissism: American Life in An Age of Diminishing Expectations* (New York: W. W. Norton, 1978). For a defense of Foucaultian individualism against the charge of nihilism and moral irresponsibility, see Richard Rorty, "Moral Identity and Private Autonomy," in Timothy J. Armstrong, trans. *Michel Foucault,* pp. 328–35.

177.   See three works by Anthony Giddens, *The Constitution of Society: Outline of the Theory of Structuration* (Berkeley: University of California Press, 1984); *Modernity and Self-Identity: Self and Society in the Late Modern Age* (Stanford, Calif.: Stanford University Press, 1991); and *The Transformation of Intimacy: Sexuality, Love and Eroticism in Modern Societies* (Stanford, Calif.: Stanford University Press, 1992). See also Christopher G. A. Bryant and David Jary, eds., *Gidden's Theory of Structuration: A Critical Appreciation* (London: Routledge, 1991); and Bryan S. Turner, *Orientalism, Postmodernism, and Globalism* (London: Routledge, 1994), pp. 117–208.

178.   Pierre Bourdieu, *Distinction: A Social Critique of the Judgement of Taste,* trans. Richard Nice (Cambridge, Mass.: Harvard University Press, 1984).

179.   Richard Rorty, *Philosophy and the Mirror of Nature* (Princeton, N.J.: Princeton University Press, 1979).

180.   Ibid., p. 377.

181.   See Anthony J. Cascardi, *The Subject of Modernity* (New York: Cambridge University Press, 1992), esp. pp. 275–310.

182.   Stanford M. Lyman and Marvin B. Scott, *The Drama of Social Reality* (New York: Oxford University Press, 1975), pp. 21–42; and *A Sociology of the Absurd*, p. 17.

183.   On this point see Mas'ud Zavarzadeh and Donald Morton, *Theory as Resistance: Politics and Culture after (Post)structuralism* (New York: Guilford Press, 1994), pp. 31–54.

184.   See Luther H. Martin, et al., *Technologies of the Self*; Thomas K. Fitzgerald, *Metaphors of Identity: A Culture-Communication Dialogue* (Albany: State University of New York Press, 1993), pp. 1–22, 81–224; and Scott Lash and Jonathan Friedman, eds., *Modernity and Identity* (Oxford: Blackwell, 1992).

Chapter 2: History and Sociology

1.   Conor Cruise O'Brien, *On the Eve of the Millennium*. The Massey Lectures Series (Concord, Ontario, Canada: House of Ananse Press, Ltd., 1994).

2.   W. B. Yeats, "The Second Coming," in Richard J. Finneran, ed., *The Collected Poems of W. B. Yeats* (New York: Collier Books, 1989), p. 187.

3.   *Tanakh: The Holy Scriptures,* new JPS translation (Philadelphia: The Jewish Publication Society, 1985), pp. 382–87.

4.   See Edmund Husserl, *The Crisis of European Sciences and Transcendental Phenomenology: An Introduction to Phenomenological Philosophy,* trans. David Carr (Evanston. Ill.: Northwestern University Press, 1970), and Richard Lowenthal, *Social Change and Cultural Crisis* (New York: Columbia University Press, 1984), pp. 15–118.

5.   Quoted in Eric Hobsbawm, *The Age of Extremes: A History of the World, 1914–1991* (New York: Pantheon Books, 1994), p. 2.

6.   See Steven J. Diner, "Department and Discipline: The Department of Sociology at The University of Chicago, 1892–1920," *Minerva* 13:4 (winter 1975): pp. 514–53; and Arthur J. Vidich and Stanford M. Lyman, *American Sociology: Worldly Rejections of Religion and Their Directions* (New Haven, Conn.: Yale University Press, 1985), pp. 178–94.

7.   Albion W. Small, *The Meaning of Social Science* (Chicago: University of Chicago Press, 1910; New York: Johnson Reprint Corp., 1971), p. 6. Emphasis omitted.

8.   Ibid., p. 30.

9.   Ibid., pp. 32–54.

10.   Ibid., p. 23.

11.   Ibid., p. 27.

12.   Ibid., p. 20.

13.   Ibid., pp. 23–24.

14.   Ibid., p. 24. Emphasis omitted.

15.   Ibid., p. 29. Emphasis omitted.

16.   Ibid., p. 293.

17.   Harry H. Bash, *Social Problems and Social Movements: An Exploration into*

the Sociological Construction of Alternative Realities (Atlantic Highlands, N.J.: Humanities Press, 1995), p. 24.

18.   See Gopala Sarana, *The Methodology of Anthropological Comparisons: An Analysis of Comparative Methods in Social and Cultural Anthropology*, Viking Fund Publications in Anthropology, no. 53 (Tucson, Ariz.: Wenner-Gren Foundation for Anthropological Research, and University of Arizona Press, 1975), pp. 10–108.

19.   Bash, *Social Problems and Social Movements,* pp. 116–20.

20.   Lorenz von Stein, *The History of the Social Movement in France, 1789–1850,* trans. and ed. Kaethe Mengelberg (Totowa, N.J.: Bedminster Press, 1964 [1850]), p. 47.

21.   Ibid., p. 56. Emphasis supplied.

22.   Citations in this and the following paragraph are from Ibid., p. 62–64.

23.   See Leopold von Ranke, *The Theory and Practice of History*, trans. Wilma Iggers and Konrad von Moltke, ed. Georg J. Iggers and Konrad von Moltke (Indianapolis, Ind.: Bobbs-Merrill, 1973); and Ernst Breisach, *Historiography: Ancient, Medieval and Modern* (Chicago: University of Chicago Press, 1983), pp. 233–38 *et passim.*

24.   Lorenz von Stein, "Preface," in *Sozialismus und Kommunismus in Frankreich,* 2d ed. (1848), p. viii. Quoted in Kaethe Mengelberg, "Introduction: Lorenz von Stein, 1815–1890—His Life and Work," in Stein, *Social Movement in France,* pp. 20–21.

25.   See Frederick J. Teggart, *Prolegomena to History: The Relation of History to Literature, Philosophy, and Science,* University of California Publications in History, 4:3 (Berkeley: University of California Press, 1916; New York: Arno Press, 1974): p. 197.

26.   Ranke, *The Theory and Practice of History,* pp. 3–130.

27.   Quoted from W. M. Urban, *Valuation: Its Nature and Laws* (London: n.p., 1909), p. 8; in Teggart, *Prolegomena to History,* p. 223.

28.   Breisach, *Historiography,* p. 234.

29.   Quoted from John Caird, *University Addresses* (Glasgow: n.p., 1899), p. 255; in Teggart, *Prolegomena to History,* p. 227.

30.   For subsequent shifts in German historical thought, see Carlo Antoni, *From History to Sociology: The Transition in German Historical Thinking,* trans. Hayden V. White (London: Merlin Press, 1959). For recent shifts and a critique, see Reinhart Koselleck, *Future's Past: On the Semantics of Historical Time,* trans. Keith Tribe (Cambridge, Mass.: MIT Press, 1985).

31.   Gertrud Lenzer, ed., *Auguste Comte and Positivism: The Essential Writings* (New York: Harper Torchbooks, 1975), pp. 218–62 *et passim;* Breisach, *Historigraphy,* pp. 272–75. For Comte's influence on American social thought, see Gillis J. Harp, *Positivist Republic: Auguste Comte and the Reconstruction of American Liberalism, 1865–1920* (University Park: Pennsylvania State University Press, 1995).

32.   The writings of positivist sociologist Franklin Henry Giddings (1855–1931) are illustrative. See Franklin Henry Giddings, *The Elements of Sociology* (New York: Macmillan, 1905), pp. 231–353; *Inductive Sociology: A Syllabus of Methods, Analyses and Classifications, and Provisionally Formulated Laws* (New York: Macmillan, 1914), pp. 7–32; *Studies in the Theory of Human Society* (New York: Macmillan, 1922), pp. 66–93; *The Scientific Study of Human Society* (Chapel Hill: University of North Carolina Press, 1924; New York: Arno Press, 1974), pp. 101–3; *The Principles of Sociology: An Analysis of the Phenomena of Association and of Social Organization* (New York: Macmillan, 1926; New York: Johnson Reprint Corp. 1970), pp. 21–51.

33.   Arnold J. Toynbee, "History," in R. W. Livingstone, ed., *The Legacy of Greece* (Oxford: Oxford University Press, 1922), p. 290; Frederick J. Teggart, *Theory of History* (New Haven, Conn.: Yale University Press, 1925), pp. 42–43; Arnold J. Toynbee, "*A Study of History*: What the Book Is For; How the Book Took Shape," in M. F. Ashley Montagu, ed., *Toynbee and History: Critical Essays and Reviews* (Boston: Porter Sargent, 1956), p. 9.

34.   See the essays collected under the general title "East by West" by Robert E. Park, J. Merle Davis, Winifred Raushenbush, Elliott Grinnell Mears, R. D. McKenzie, Kazuo Kawai, William C. Smith, Emory S. Bogardus, Chester H. Rowell, William Allen White, C. Leroy Baldridge, Lewis Stiles Gannett, John Stewart Burgess, Raymond T. Rich, John Dewey and Charles and Mary Beard, in *Survey Graphic* 56:3 (May 1, 1926): pp. 135–221.

35.   See Stanford M. Lyman, *The Black American in Sociological Thought: A Failure of Perspective* (New York: G. P. Putnam's Sons, 1972), pp. 27–70.

36.   In addition to his *Prolegomena to History* and *Theory of History* cited *supra*, see Frederick J. Teggart, *Rome and China: A Study of Correlations in Historical Events* (Berkeley: University of California Press, 1939); *Theory and Processes of History* (Berkeley: University of California Press, 1941); and his many essays reprinted in Grace Dangberg, A Guide to the Life and Works of Frederick J. Teggart (Reno, Nev.: Grace Dangberg Foundation), pp. 81–562.

37.   Wilhelm Windelband, "History and Natural Science," trans. with an introductory note by Guy Oakes, *History and Theory: Studies in the Philosophy of History* 19:2 (February 1980): pp. 165–85. Quotation from p. 175.

38.   Ibid., p. 185.

39.   Guy Oakes, "Note," in ibid., p. 168.

40.   Ibid., p. 185.

41.   For the vicissitudes of the original department's struggles to avoid becoming an ahistorical department of nomothetic sociology, see Margaret Trabue Hodgen, "The Department of Social Institutions, 1919–1946" (Pasadena, Calif.: unpublished MS, 1971), a copy of which is in the University of California archives.

42.   See Stanford M. Lyman, *Civilization: Contents, Discontents, Malcontents and Other Essays in Social Theory* (Fayetteville: University of Arkansas Press, 1990), pp. 76–126, 202–21.

43.   Cf. Guy Oakes, *Weber and Rickert: Concept Formation in the Social Sciences* (Cambridge, Mass.: MIT Press, 1988), pp. 44–48.

44.   Kenneth E. Bock, "Evolution and Historical Process," *American Anthropologist* 54:4 (October–December 1952): p. 493.

45.   Franco Ferrarotti, *Max Weber and the Destiny of Reason*, trans. John Fraser (Armonk, N.Y.: M. E. Sharpe, 1982), p. 45.

46.   Gaetano Salvemini, *Historian and Scientist* (Cambridge, Mass.: Harvard University Press, 1939), pp. 29–33. Quoted in Kenneth E. Bock, *The Acceptance of Histories: Toward a Perspective for Social Science*, University of California Publications in Sociology and Social Institutions, 3:1 (Berkeley: University of California Press, 1956): p. 125. Salvemini, a historian and reform socialist, was well known in Italy for his campaigns for equality and against governmental corruption. He fled Italy in 1925 and joined the faculty at Harvard. See Richard Bellamy, *Modern Italian Social Theory: Ideology and Politics from Pareto to the Present* (Stanford, Calif.: Stanford University Press, 1987), pp. 5, 40–41, 116, 172.

47.   Piotr Sztompka, *The Sociology of Social Change* (Oxford: Blackwell, 1993), p. 320.

48.   Robert E. Park and Ernest W. Burgess, *Introduction to the Science of Sociology* (Chicago: University of Chicago Press, 1921), p. 8. Quoted in Bock, *Acceptance of Histories,* p. 122, n. 29.

49.   Bock, *Acceptance of Histories,* p. 100.

50.   Ibid., pp. 100–102.

51.   See Kenneth E. Bock, "Evolution, Function, and Change," *American Sociological Review* 28 (April 1963): pp. 229–37; and Marvin B. Scott, "Functional Analysis: A Statement of Problems," in Gregory P. Stone and Harvey A. Farberman, eds., *Social Psychology Through Symbolic Interaction* (Waltham, Mass.: Ginn-Blaisdell, 1970), pp. 21–28.

52.   Cf. two works by Talcott Parsons, *The Social System* (Glencoe, Ill.: Free Press, 1951); and *Social Systems and the Evolution of Action Theory* (New York: Free Press, 1977), pp. 145–320. The idea that society should be conceived as a system with subsystemic parts functioning to maintain its stability was put forward by America's first sociologist, Henry Hughes (1829–1862). See Henry Hughes, *A Treatise on Sociology: Theoretical and Practical* (Philadelphia: Lippincott, Grambo and Co., 1854; New York: Negro Universities Press, 1968); and Stanford M. Lyman, ed., *Selected Writings of Henry Hughes: Antebellum Southerner, Slavocrat, Sociologist* (Jackson: University Press of Mississippi, 1985).

53.   Seymour Martin Lipset, *The First New Nation: The United States in Historical and Comparative Perspective,* rev. ed. (New York: W. W. Norton, 1979), pp. 99–204.

54.   Bock, *Acceptance of Histories,* p. 113. A recent example of this kind of thinking can be found in the 1994 presidential address to the Midwest Sociological Society: The late Carl J. Couch reported that his early experiences in doing research "convinced me that social relationships, social structures, and societies only exist in process, and thus point-in-time observations cannot provide the evidence necessary for formulating generic principles about social phenomena." Carl J. Couch, "Presidential Address: Let Us Rekindle the Passion by Constructing a Robust Science of the Social," *The Sociological Quarterly* 36:1 (1995): pp. 1–14. Quotation from p. 2.

55.   Bock, *Acceptance of Histories,* p. 113.

56.   Ibid., p. 130.

57.   In addition to those cited *supra,* see the following works of Kenneth E. Bock: *The Comparative Method,* (Ph.D. diss., University of California, Berkeley, 1948); "The Social Scientist in the 'Open Society,'" *American Journal of Economics and Sociology* 10:2 (January 1951): pp. 211–19; "History and a Science of Man: An Appreciation of George Cornewall Lewis," *Journal of the History of Ideas* 12:4 (October 1951): pp. 599–608; "Discussion," *American Sociological Review* 17 (April 1952): pp. 164–66; "The Study of Social Theory," *Research Studies of the State College of Washington* 21:3 (September 1953): pp. 219–24; "Darwin and Social Theory," *Philosophy of Science* 22:2 (April 1955): pp. 123–34; "The Study of War in American Sociology," *Sociologus* 5:2 (November 1955): pp. 104–13; "Cultural Differences and Race: The History of a Problem," *Commentary* 23:2 (February 1957): pp. 179–86; "New Light on Colonialism," *Commentary* 24:1 (July 1957): pp. 86–88; review essay on Arnold J. Toynbee, *A Study of History, XII:*

Reconsideration, in *History and Theory* 2:3 (1963): pp. 301–7; "The Comparative Method of Anthropology," *Comparative Studies in Society and History* 8:3 (April 1966): pp. 269–80; "Some Basic Assumptions About Change," *Et Al.* 2:3 (1970): pp. 44–48; "Comparison of Histories: The Contribution of Henry Maine," *Comparative Studies in Society and History* 16:2 (March 1974): pp. 232–62; "Henry Sumner Maine's Moral Philosophy," *Journal of the History of Ideas* 38:1 (January–March 1976): pp. 147–54; *Human Nature and History: A Response to Sociobiology* (New York: Columbia University Press, 1980); and *Human Nature Mythology* (Urbana: University of Illinois Press, 1994).

58.　For the contention that a chastened evolutionism has exorcised from its epistemology and methods all the shortcomings that the Teggart school had complained about, see Stephen K. Sanderson, *Social Evolutionism: A Critical History* (Cambridge, Mass.: Basil Blackwell, 1990), pp. 223–28.

59.　Todd Gitlin, "The Postmodern Predicament," *The Wilson Quarterly* 13:3 (summer 1989): pp. 67–76. Quotation from p. 76.

60.　Todd Gitlin, *The Sixties: Years of Hope, Days of Rage* (New York: Bantam Books, 1987). See also Marvin B. Scott and Stanford M. Lyman, *The Revolt of the Students* (Columbus, Ohio: Charles Merrill, 1970).

61.　Gitlin, "The Postmodern Predicament," p. 76.

62.　Ibid., p. 67. Emphasis supplied.

63.　Ibid., p. 69.

64.　Ibid.

65.　Teggart, *Prolegomena to History*, pp. 276–77.

66.　See Richard Harvey Brown, *Society as Text: Essays on Rhetoric, Reason, and Reality* (Chicago: University of Chicago Press, 1987), pp. 97–117.

67.　See Richard Rorty, "Science as Solidarity," in John S. Nelson, Allan Megill, and Donald N. McCloskey, eds., *The Rhetoric of the Human Sciences: Language and Argument in Scholarship and Public Affairs* (Madison: University of Wisconsin Press, 1987), pp. 38–52.

68.　Richard Rorty, *Philosophy and the Mirror of Nature* (Princeton, N.J.: Princeton University Press, 1979).

69.　See Richard Harvey Brown, "From Suspicion to Affirmation: Postmodernism and the Challenges of Rhetorical Analysis," in idem, ed., *Writing the Social Text: Poetics and Politics in Social Science Discourse* (New York: Aldine de Gruyter, 1991), pp. 219–27.

70.　Joyce Appleby, Lynn Hunt, and Margaret Jacob, *Telling the Truth about History* (New York: W. W. Norton, 1994), p. 225.

71.　Pauline Marie Rosenau, *Post-Modernism and the Social Sciences: Insights, Inroads, and Intrusions* (Princeton, N.J.: Princeton University Press, 1992), pp. 42–61.

72.　Michel Foucault, *Discipline and Punish: The Birth of the Prison*, trans. Alan Sheridan (New York: Vintage Books, 1979).

73.　Peter Burke, *History and Social Theory* (Ithaca, N.Y.: Cornell University Press, 1993), p. 151.

74.　Teggart, *Theory of History*, pp. 148–49 *et passim*.

75.　W. I. Thomas, "Introductory," in idem, ed., *Source Book for Social Origins* (Boston: Richard G. Badger, 1909), pp. 17–19.

76.　Henry S. Pachter, "Defining an Event: Prolegomena to Any Future Philosophy of History," *Social Research* 41 (1974): pp. 443–50.

77.   Robert A. Nisbet, *Social Change and History: Aspects of the Western Theory of Development* (New York: Oxford University Press, 1969), pp. 275–83.

78.   Folke Dovring, *History as a Social Science: An Essay on the Nature and Purpose of Historical Studies* (The Hague, Netherlands: Martinus Nijhoff, 1960), p. 85.

79.   Agnes Heller and Ferenc Feher, *The Grandeur and Twilight of Radical Universalism* (New Brunswick, N.J.: Transaction Publishers, 1991), p. 537.

80.   Ibid.

81.   Steven Seidman, "The End of Sociological Theory: The Postmodern Hope," *Sociological Theory* 9:2 (Fall, 1991): pp. 131–46. Quotation from p. 132.

82.   Ibid., pp. 131, 136.

83.   Heller and Feher, *Radical Universalism*, p. 537.

84.   Seidman, *The End of Sociological Theory*, p. 139.

85.   See Richard Rorty, *Contingency, Irony, and Solidarity* (Cambridge, U.K.: Cambridge University Press, 1989), pp. 3–140.

86.   See Rorty, *Philosophy and The Mirror of Nature*, pp. 357–94.

87.   Cf. the remark of Bernard Bailyn on p. 95 of his dialogue entitled *On the Teaching and Writing of History* (Hanover, N.H.: University Press of New England, 1994): "Every generation will have its own approach and questions, since history is, in the end, an inquiry about the past. History is not an inert reconstruction of the past that gets set once and for all; it is a form of inquiry, and those inquiries will shift and renew and grow in time. Succeeding generations will write different kinds of histories—and should."

88.   See Stanford M. Lyman and Marvin B. Scott, *A Sociology of the Absurd*, 2d ed. (Dix Hills, N.Y.: General Hall, 1989).

89.   Cf. Fredric Jameson, *The Prison-House of Language: A Critical Account of Structuralism and Russian Formalism* (Princeton, N.J.: Princeton University Press, 1972).

90.   Robert A. Nisbet, "Developmentalism: A Critical Analysis," in idem, *The Making of Modern Society* (New York: New York University Press, 1986), pp. 33–69. Quotations from p. 63.

91.   See Madan Sarup, *An Introductory Guide to Post-Structuralism and Postmodernism* (Athens: University of Georgia Press, 1989), pp. 2–3 *et passim*.

92.   Unless otherwise noted, the remaining citations in this and the following paragraph are from Seidman, "The End of Sociological Theory," p. 133–42.

93.   See Steven Seidman et al., "Symposium: Queer Theory/Sociology: A Dialogue," *Sociological Theory* 12:2 (July 1994): pp. 166–248. For an incisive critique see Guy Oakes, "Straight Thinking About Queer Theory," International *Journal of Politics, Culture, and Society* 8:3 (spring 1995): p. 379–88.

94.   Fred Dallmayr, "Modernity in the Crossfire: Comments on the Postmodern Turn," in John Paul Jones III, Wolfgang Natter, and Theodore R. Schatzki, eds., *Postmodern Contentions: Epochs, Politics, Space* (New York: Guildford Press, 1993), pp. 17–38. Quotation from p. 34.

95.   See two works by Robert Heilbroner, *21st Century Capitalism* (New York: W. W. Norton, 1993), pp. 119–64; and *Visions of the Future: The Distant Past, Yesterday, Today, and Tomorrow* (New York: Oxford University Press, 1995).

96.   Quoted from p. 75 of Vladimir Smelev and Nikolai Popov, *The Turning Point* (New York: Doubleday and Co., 1989) in Heilbroner, *21st Century Capitalism*, p. 13.

97. Heilbroner, *21st Century Capitalism,* p. 154.

98. Ibid., p. 162.

99. Heilbroner, *Visions of the Future,* p. 7.

100. Ibid., p. 11.

101. Ibid., pp. 13–16, 93–120.

102. Ibid., p. vii.

103. Heller and Feher, *Radical Universalism,* pp. 539–40.

104. See, e.g., Anthony Smith, *Social Change: Social Theory and Historical Processes* (London: Longman, 1976), pp. 15–93, 122–39; and Louis Schneider, *Classical Theories of Social Change* (Morristown, N.J.: General Learning Press, 1976).

105. See Michel Foucault, *The Order of Things: An Archaeology of the Human Sciences* (New York: Pantheon Books, 1970).

106. Heller and Feher, *Radical Universalism,* pp. 537–39.

107. For discussions of Benjamin, see Terry Eagleton, *Walter Benjamin, or Towards a Revolutionary Criticism* (London: Verso, 1981); and Richard Wolin, *Walter Benjamin: An Aesthetic of Redemption* (New York: Columbia University Press, 1982).

108. Remaining citations in this paragraph are from Walter Benjamin, "Theses on the Philosophy of History," *Illuminations,* trans. Harry Zohn, ed. Hannah Arendt (New York: Harcourt, Brace and World, 1968), pp. 257–65.

109. Seidman, "The End of Sociological Theory," p. 141.

110. Ibid.

111. Admittedly, the matter is ambiguous. Seidman concedes that "Approaching identities as multiple, unstable, and regulatory may suggest to critics the undermining of gay theory and politics, but for queer theorists it presents new and productive possibilities." He asserts that "Queer theory wishes to challenge the regime of sexuality itself— that is, the knowledges that construct the self as sexual and that assume heterosexuality and homosexuality as categories marking the truth of sexual selves." And, he concludes, "As of this writing, queer theory and sociology have barely acknowledged one another." Steven Seidman, "Queer Theory/ Sociology," pp. 173–74.

112. Seidman, "The End of Sociological Theory," p. 142.

113. Cf. Maurice Natanson, "History as a Finite Province of Meaning," in *idem, Literature, Philosophy and the Social Sciences: Essays in Existentialism and Phenomenology* (The Hague: Martinus Nyhoff, 1968), pp. 172–77.

114. Carl Becker, *Everyman His Own Historian: Essays on History and Politics* (Chicago: Quadrangle Books, 1966 [1935]), p. 243.

115. Ibid.

Chapter 3: Interstate Relations and the Sociological Imagination Revisited

1. Cornelis B. Bakker and Marianne K. Bakker-Rabdau, *No Trespassing! Explorations in Human Territoriality* (San Francisco: Chandler and Sharp Publishers, 1973), pp. 11–32.

2. See Pierre Bourdieu, *Language and Symbolic Power,* trans. Gino Raymond and Matthew Adamson, ed. John B. Thompson (Cambridge. Mass.: Harvard University Press, 1991), pp. 229–51; and Zygmunt Bauman, *Postmodern Ethics* (Oxford: Blackwell, 1993), pp. 16–19, 145–250.

3.   See, e.g., Dorinda Outram, *The Body and the French Revolution* (New Haven, Conn.: Yale University Press, 1989), pp. 1–26; and Michel Feher with Ramona Naddaff and Nadia Tazi, eds., *Fragments for a History of the Human Body*, 3 vols (New York: Zone, 1989).

4.   E. Gordon Ericksen, *The Territorial Experience: Human Ecology as Symbolic Interaction* (Austin: University of Texas Press, 1980), pp. 56–78.

5.   Maurice Halbwachs, *The Collective Memory*, trans. Francis J. Ditter Jr., and Vida Yazdi Ditter (New York: Harper Colophon, 1980 [1950]), pp. 22–157; and Patrick H. Hutton, *History as an Art of Memory* (Hanover, N.H.: University Press of New England, 1993).

6.   See Benedict Anderson, *Imagined Communities: Reflections on the Origin and Spread of Nationalism*, rev. ed. (London: Verso, 1993). See also the works of Hans Kohn: *Orient and Occident* (New York: John Day, 1934); *The Age of Nationalism: The First Era of Global History* (New York: Harper Torchbooks, 1968); *Nationalism: Its Meaning in History*, rev ed. (New York: Van Nostrand Reinhold, 1971); and *The Idea of Nationalism: A Study in Its Origins and Background* (London: Collier Books, 1969).

7.   Emory S. Bogardus, "Social Distance: A Measuring Stick," *Survey Graphic* 56:3 (May 1, 1926): pp. 169–70, 206–10.

8.   See Amos H. Hawley, ed., *Roderick D. McKenzie on Human Ecology* (Chicago: University of Chicago Press, 1968); and George A. Theodorson, ed., *Studies in Human Ecology* (Evanston, Ill.: Row, Peterson and Co., 1961).

9.   Stanford M. Lyman and Marvin B. Scott, "Territoriality: A Neglected Sociological Dimension," *Social Problems* 15:2 (fall 1967): pp. 236–48. A revised version is reprinted in Stanford M. Lyman and Marvin B. Scott, *A Sociology of the Absurd* 2d ed. (Dix Hills, N.Y.: General Hall, 1989), pp. 22–34.

10.   Ericksen, *The Territorial Experience*.

11.   Edward T. Hall, *The Hidden Dimension* (Garden City, N.Y.: Doubleday and Co., 1966).

12.   Robert Sommer, *Personal Space: The Behavioral Basis of Design* (Englewood Cliffs, N.J.: Prentice-Hall, 1969); and *Tight Spaces: Hard Architecture and How to Humanize It* (Englewood Cliffs, N.J.: Prentice-Hall, 1974).

13.   Bakker and Bakker-Rabdau, *No Trespassing!*.

14.   See, e.g., the studies collected in Robert Gutman, ed., *People and Buildings* (New York: Basic Books, 1972); and in Nathan Glazer and Mark Lilla, eds., *The Public Face of Architecture: Civic Culture and Public Spaces* (New York: Free Press, 1987). See also, e.g., Cary Goodman, *Choosing Sides: Playground and Street Life on the Lower East Side* (Boston: Schocken, 1979); Charles Simpson, *Soho: The Artist in the City* (Chicago: University of Chicago Press, 1981), pp. 129–88; Witold Rybczynski, *Home: A Short History of an Idea* (New York: Viking Penguin, 1987); and Albert Mehrabian, *Public Places and Private Spaces: The Psychology of Work, Play, and Living Environments* (New York: Basic Books, 1976).

15.   Lyman and Scott, *A Sociology of the Absurd*, p. 34.

16.   Raymond Aron, *Peace and War: A Theory of International Relations*, trans. Richard Howard and Annette Baker Fox (Garden City, N.Y.: Doubleday and Co., Inc., 1966), p. 181.

17.   Herbert Blumer, "Foreword," in Ericksen, *The Territorial Experience*, p. xi.

18.   Ibid., p. xii.

19.   Ibid.

20.   See Sal Restivo, *The Sociological Worldview* (Cambridge, Mass.: Basil Blackwell, 1991), pp. 186–96; and Ericksen, *The Territorial Experience*, p. 33.

21.   Quoted in R. W. B. Lewis, *The American Adam: Innocence, Tragedy and Tradition in the Nineteenth Century* (Chicago: University of Chicago Press, 1975 [1955]), p. 42.

22.   For the definitive critique of this formulation in evolutionary biology and related fields, see Stephen Jay Gould, *Ontogeny and Phylogeny* (Cambridge, Mass.: The Belknap Press of Harvard University Press, 1977).

23.   For the concept of "home territory," see Sherri Cavan, "Interaction in Home Territories," *Berkeley Journal of Sociology* 8 (1963): pp. 17–32 and the elaborations on it in Sherri Cavan, *Liquor License: An Ethnography of Bar Behavior* (Chicago: Aldine Publishing Co., 1966), pp. 205–33; Lyman and Scott, *A Sociology of the Absurd*, pp. 24–25; Ericksen, *The Territorial Experience*, pp. 24–34.

24.   The discussion that follows draws on Celestine Bohlen, "Kaliningrad Journal: Is City Acquiring a German Accent?" *New York Times*, April 22, 1994, A4.

25.   Aron, *Peace and War*, p. 182.

26.   See Stanford M. Lyman and Marvin B. Scott, *The Drama of Social Reality* (New York: Oxford University Press, 1975).

27.   Erving Goffman, *Strategic Interaction* (Philadelphia: University of Pennsylvania Press, 1969), pp. 83–145.

28.   Lyman and Scott, *A Sociology of the Absurd*, p. 25.

29.   Quoted in Michael Lind, "In Defense of Liberal Nationalism," *Foreign Affairs* 73:3 (May–June 1994): p. 87.

30.   Walker Connor, "Ethnonationalism in the First World: The Present in Historical Perspective," in *Ethnic Conflict in the Western World*, ed. Milton J. Esman (Ithaca, N.Y.: Cornell University Press, 1977), pp. 19–45.

31.   Philippe C. Schmitter, "Dangers and Dilemmas of Democracy," *Journal of Democracy* 2 (April 1994): pp. 65–66.

32.   See Liah Greenfeld, *Nationalism: Five Roads to Modernity* (Cambridge. Mass.: Harvard University Press, 1992); and Walker Connor, "Beyond Reason: The Nature of the Ethnonational Bond," *Ethnic and Racial Studies* 16:3 (July 1993): pp. 373–89.

33.   Schmitter, "Dangers and Dilemma Democracy," p. 66.

34.   Susan Cotts Watkins, "Markets, States, Nations, and Bedrooms in Western Europe, 1870–1960," in Joan Huber, ed.. *Macro-Micro Linkages in Sociology* (Newbury Park. Calif.: Sage Publications, 1991), p. 270.

35.   See two seminal discussions: Frank J. Lechner, "Simmel on Social Space," *Theory, Culture and Society* 8:3 (August 1991): pp. 195–202; and David Frisby, *Simmel and Since: Essays on Georg Simmel's Social Theory* (London: Routledge, 1992), pp. 98–117. For an interesting critique, which despite its pointedness does not reduce the value of Simmel's work for the present discussion, see Keith Tester, *The Life and Times of Post-Modernity* (London: Routledge, 1993), pp. 6–29.

36.   Georg Simmel, "The Transcendent Character of Life," trans. Donald Levine and published in his edition of *Georg Simmel on Individuality and Social Forms* (Chicago: University of Chicago Press, 1971), p. 353.

37.   Lyman and Scott, *A Sociology of the Absurd*, pp. 27–33.

38.   Wole Soyinka, "Of Berlin and Other Walls," in *Art, Dialogue, and Outrage: Essays on Literature and Culture* (New York: Pantheon Books, 1993), pp. 199–215.

39.   Georg Simmel, "Bridge and Door," trans. Mark Ritter, *Theory, Culture and Society* 11:1 (February 1994): pp. 5–10.

40.   Henry Kissinger, *Diplomacy* (New York: Simon and Schuster, 1994): p. 276. For a detailed case study of the older style of diplomacy, see Peter Hopkirk, *The Great Game: The Struggle for Empire in Central Asia* (New York: Kodansha International, 1994).

41.   Kissinger, *Diplomacy.*

42.   James Quayle Dealey, Ph.D., *Sociology: Its Simpler Teachings and Applications* (New York: Silver, Burdett and Co., 1909), pp. 220–21.

43.   Aron, pp. 97–98.

44.   Milton J. Esman, "Perspectives on Ethnic Conflict in Industrialized Societies," in Esman, ed., *Ethnic Conflict,* pp. 371–90.

45.   Robert D. Kaplan, *Balkan Ghosts: A Journey Through History* (New York: Vintage, 1994).

46.   Kaplan, *Balkan Ghosts,* p. 39.

47.   For the idea of the body as a territory, see Lyman and Scott, *A Sociology of the Absurd,* pp. 26–27.

48.   Cf. Peter Wagner, *A Sociology of Modernity: Liberty and Discipline* (London: Routledge, 1994), pp. 48–50.

49.   Jean L. Cohen and Andrew Arato, *Civil Society and Political Theory* (Cambridge. Mass.: MIT Press, 1992, 1994), pp. 124–42.

50.   Anthony Synnott, *The Body Social: Symbolism, Self and Society* (London: Routledge, 1993), p. 262.

51.   Ibid.

52.   See Joseph S. Nye Jr., "What New World Order?" *Foreign Affairs* 71:2 (spring 1992): pp. 83–96.

53.   Cf. Roland Robertson, "Globality, Global Culture, and Images of World Order," in *Social Change and Modernity,* ed. Hans Haferkamp and Neil J. Smelser (Berkeley: University of California Press, 1992), pp. 395–411.

54.   See Peter Worsley, *The Three Worlds* (Chicago: University of Chicago Press, 1985).

55.   See Arthur J. Vidich, "Legitimation of Regimes in World Perspective," in *Conflict and Control: Challenge to Legitimacy of Modern Governments,* ed. Arthur J. Vidich and Ronald M. Glassman (Beverly Hills, Calif.: Sage Publications, 1979), pp. 286–96; Wagner, *A Sociology of Modernity,* pp. 48–51; Sally Falk Moore, *Anthropology and Africa: Changing Perspectives on a Changing Scene* (Charlottesville: University Press of Virginia, 1994), pp. 74–134.

56.   Lyman H. Legters, *Eastern Europe: Transformation and Revolution, 1945–1991: Documents and Analyses* (Lexington, Mass.: D. C. Heath and Co., 1992), pp. 63–610, 646–56; Michael Ignatieff, *Blood and Belonging: Journeys into the New Nationalism* (New York: Farrar, Straus and Giroux, 1993).

57.   See, e.g., Joe S. Sando, *Pueblo Nations: Eight Centuries of Pueblo Indian History* (Santa Fe, N.M.: Clear Light Publishers, 1992); and Arnold Krupat, *Ethnocriticism: Ethnography, History, Literature* (Berkeley: University of California Press, 1992). For a sociological analysis of the assimilation-pluralism dispute, see

Stanford M. Lyman, *Color, Culture, Civilization: Race and Minority Issues in American Society* (Urbana: University of Illinois Press, 1994), pp. 1–42, 105–384.

58.   Erving Goffman, *Relations in Public: Microstudies of the Public Order* (New York: Basic Books, 1971), pp. 28–61.

59.   Lester F. Ward, *Pure Sociology: A Treatise on the Origin and Spontaneous Development of Society,* 2d ed. (New York: Augustus M. Kelley, 1970 [1907]), pp. 205–20.

60.   Arthur J. Vidich and Stanford M. Lyman, *American Sociology: Worldly Rejections of Religion and Their Directions* (New Haven, Conn.: Yale University Press, 1985), pp. 20–35.

61.   William Graham Sumner, *Folkways: A Study of the Sociological Importance of Usages, Manners, Customs, Mores, and Morals* (Boston: Ginn and Co., 1940 [1906]), p. 78.

62.   See Lyman and Scott, "Territoriality: A Neglected Sociological Dimension," in *A Sociology of the Absurd,* pp. 22–34.

63.   See Stephen Castles and Mark J. Miller, *The Age of Migration: International Population Movements in the Modern World* (New York: The Guilford Press, 1993); and two critical works: J. M. Blaut, *The Colonizers Model of the World: Geographical Diffusionism and Eurocentric History* (New York: The Guilford Press, 1993); and Amy Kaplan and Donald R. Pease, eds., *Cultures of United States Imperialism* (Durham, N.C.: Duke University Press, 1993).

64.   Roland Robertson, "Mapping the Global Condition: Globalization as the Central Concept," in *Global Culture: Nationalism, Globalization and Modernity,* ed. Mike Featherstone (London: Sage Publications, 1991), pp. 17–18.

65.   Georg Simmel, "The Conflict in Modern Culture," in *The Conflict in Modern Culture and Other Essays,* trans. K. Peter Etzkorn (New York: Teachers College Press, 1968), p. 11. See also the discussion in Tester, *The Life and Times of Post-Modernity,* pp. 6–29.

66.   See Deena Weinstein and Michael A. Weinstein, *Postmodern(ized) Simmel* (London: Routledge, 1993), pp. 133–45.

67.   The concept of the *Lebenswelt* has been developed by Aron Gurwitsch, *Studies in Phenomenology and Psychology* (Evanston. Ill.: Northwestern University Press, 1966), pp. 120–21, 151, 163, 172, 406–47.

68.   For the concept of intrusion, see Frederick J. Teggart, *Theory of History* (New Haven, Conn.: Yale University Press, 1925), pp. 82–86, 107–49, 180–94.

69.   For the concept of crisis, see W. I. Thomas, "Introductory," *Source Book for Social Origins* (Boston: Richard G. Badger, 1909), pp. 13–26; and Alfred Schutz, "Some Structures of the Life-World," *Collected Papers III: Studies in Phenomenological Philosophy,* ed. I. Schutz (The Hague, Netherlands: Martinus Nijhoff, 1966), pp. 116–32.

70.   See Stanford M. Lyman, "The Science of History and the Theory of Social Change," *Civilization: Contents, Discontents, Malcontents, and Other Essays in Social Theory* (Fayetteville: University of Arkansas Press, 1990), pp. 76–84.

71.   Restivo, *The Sociological Worldview,* pp. 175–96.

72.   Bauman, Postmodern Ethics, p. 85.

Chapter 4: Postmodernism and the Race Question

1.   See two works by Josiah Royce, *Race Questions and Other American*

Problems (New York: Macmillan, 1908), pp. 167–226; and *The Philosophy of Loyalty* (New York: Macmillan, 1916), pp. 1–248, 349–98.

2.   See two works by Nathaniel Southgate Shaler, *The Neighbor: The Natural History of Human Contacts* (Boston: Houghton-Mifflin, 1904), pp. 21–50, 72–191, 204–338; and *The Individual: A Study of Life and Death* (New York: D. Appleton and Co., 1905), pp. 1–50, 70–97, 106–87, 286–346. See also David N. Livingstone, *Nathaniel Southgate Shaler and the Culture of American Science* (Tuscaloosa: University of Alabama Press, 1987), pp. 121–91.

3.   Robert E. Park, *Race and Culture, The Collected Papers of Robert Ezra Park,* vol. 1, ed. Everett C. Hughes et al. (Glencoe, Ill.: Free Press, 1950). See also the essays in four works by Stanford M. Lyman, *The Black American in Sociological Thought: A Failure of Perspective* (New York: G. P. Putnam's Sons, 1972), pp. 27–70; *Civilization: Contents, Discontents, Malcontents and Other Essays on Social Theory* (Fayetteville: University of Arkansas Press, 1990), pp. 127–35; *Militarism, Imperialism, and Racial Accommodation: An Analysis and Interpretation of the Early Writings of Robert E. Park* (Fayetteville: University of Arkansas Press, 1992), pp. 5–11, 41–135, 205–305; and *Color, Culture, Civilization: Race and Minority Issues in American Society* (Urbana: University of Illinois Press, 1994), pp. 1–104.

4.   See Patrick Williams and Laura Chrisman, eds., *Colonial Discourse and Post-Colonial Theory: A Reader* (New York: Columbia University Press, 1994).

5.   For a spirited attack on postmodernism (e.g., p. 131: "postmodernism is now confronting us with a far more subversive form of relativism, a relativism so radical, so absolute, as to be antithetical to both history and truth."), see Gertrude Himmelfarb, *On Looking into the Abyss: Untimely Thoughts on Culture and Society* (New York: Alfred A. Knopf, 1994), pp. 131–61.

6.   Linda Nicholson, "On the Postmodern Barricades: Feminism, Politics, and Theory," in Steven Seidman and David G. Wagner, eds., *Postmodernism and Social Theory: The Debate Over General Theory* (Cambridge, Mass.: Basil Blackwell, 1992), pp. 82–100. Quotation from p. 84.

7.   Mas'ud Zavarzadeh and Donal Morton, *Theory as Resistance: Politics and Culture after (Post)structuralism* (New York: Guilford Press, 1994), p. 56.

8.   See, e.g., Nader Saiedi, *The Birth of Social Theory: Social Thought in the Enlightenment and Romanticism* (Lanham, Md.: University Press of America, 1993), pp. 9–58, 134–60; and Reinhart Koselleck, *Critique and Crisis: Enlightenment and the Pathogenesis of Modern Society* (Cambridge, Mass.: MIT Press, 1988).

9.   See, e.g., David Spurr, *The Rhetoric of Empire: Colonial Discourse in Journalism, Travel Writing, and Imperial Administration* (Durham, N.C.: Duke University Press, 1993); and Tzvetan Todorov, *On Human Diversity: Nationalism, Racism, and Exoticism in French Thought,* trans. Catherine Porter (Cambridge, Mass.: Harvard University Press, 1993).

10.   Steven Seidman, "The End of Sociological Theory: The Postmodern Hope," *Sociological Theory* 9:2 (fall 1991): pp. 131–46, esp. pp. 132–35, 138–43.

11.   Homi K. Bhabha, "The Other Question: Difference, Discrimination, and the Discourse of Colonialism," in Russell Ferguson, Martha Gever, Trinh T. Minh-ha, and Cornel West, eds., *Out There: Marginalization and Contemporary Cultures* (Cambridge, Mass.: MIT Press, 1990), pp. 71–88. Quotation from p. 75.

12.   Robert Blauner, *Racial Oppression in America* (New York: Harper and Row, 1972), pp. 82–110.

13.   See Milton M. Gordon, *Assimilation in American Life: The Role of Race, Religion, and National Origins* (New York: Oxford University Press, 1964); and two entries in Stephan Thernstrom, ed., *Harvard Encyclopedia of American Ethnic Groups* (Cambridge, Mass.: Belknap Press of Harvard University Press, 1980): Philip Gleason, "American Identity and Americanization," pp. 31–58; and Harold H. Abramson, "Assimilation and Pluralism," pp. 150–60.

14.   See Robert E. Park, "Human Migration and the Marginal Man," in Ernest W. Burgess, ed., *Personality and the Social Group* (Chicago: University of Chicago Press, 1929; reprint., Freeport, N.Y.: Books for Libraries Press, 1969), pp. 64–77; Everett V. Stonequist, *The Marginal Man: A Study in Personality and Culture Conflict* (New York: Charles Scribner's Sons, 1937; reprint., New York: Russell and Russell, 1961).

15.   For representative case studies of marginality carried out in the modernist perspective, see H. F. Dickie-Clark, *The Marginal Situation: A Sociological Study of a Coloured Group* (London: Routledge and Kegan Paul, 1966); Noel P. Gist and Anthony Gary Dworkin, eds., *The Blending of Races: Marginality and Identity in World Perspective* (New York: Wiley-Interscience, 1972); Noel P. Gist and Roy Dean Wright, eds., *Marginality and Identity : Anglo-Indians as a Racially Mixed Minority in India* (Leiden, Netherlands: E. J. Brill, 1973); Sister Frances Jerome Woods, C.D.P., *Marginality and Identity: A Colored Creole Family Through Ten Generations* (Baton Rouge: Louisiana State University Press, 1972); Janice E. Perlman, *The Myth of Marginality: Urban Poverty and Politics in Rio de Janeiro* (Berkeley: University of California Press, 1979); Abdolmaboud Ansari, *Iranian Immigrants in the United States: A Case Study of Dual Marginality* (Millwood, N.Y.: Associated Faculty Press, 1988); John P. Meier, *A Marginal Jew: Rethinking the Historical Jesus*, vol 1: *The Roots of the Problem and the Person;* and vol. 2: *Mentor, Message, and Miracles* (New York: Doubleday and Co., 1994).

16.   George Yudice, "Marginality and the Ethic of Survival," in Andrew Ross, ed., *Universal Abandon? The Politics of Postmodernism* (Minneapolis: University of Minnesota Press, 1988), pp. 214–36. Quotation from p. 214.

17.   Julian Pefanis, *Heterology and the Postmodern: Bataille, Baudrillard, and Lyotard* (Durham, N.C.: Duke University Press, 1991), p. 5.

18.   Stanford M. Lyman and Marvin B. Scott, *A Sociology of the Absurd* (New York: Appleton-Century-Crofts, 1970; 2nd. ed., Dix Hills, N.Y.: General Hall, 1989).

19.   Cf. four essays by Zygmunt Bauman, "Sociology of the Absurd," *Jerusalem Post Magazine* (March 5, 1971): p. 13; "The Left as the Counterculture of Modernity," *Telos* no. 70 (winter 1986–87): pp. 81–93, reprinted in Stanford M. Lyman, ed. *Social Movements: Critiques, Concepts, Case-Studies* (London: Macmillan and New York: New York University Press, 1995), pp. 356–70; "Is There a Postmodern Sociology?" *Theory, Culture and Society* 5:2–3 (June 1988): pp. 217–38: and "A Sociological Theory of Postmodernity," in Peter Beilharz, Gillian Robinson, and John Rundell, eds., *Between Totalitarianism and Postmodernity* (Cambridge, Mass.: MIT Press, 1992), pp. 149–62.

20.   See Garth L. Hallett, *Essentialism: A Wittgensteinian Critique* (Albany: State University of New York Press, 1991); and Nancy Fraser and Linda Nicholson, "Social Criticism without Philosophy: An Encounter between Feminism and Postmodernism," *Theory, Culture and Society* 5:2–3 (June 1988): pp. 373–94, esp. pp. 381–91.

21. Stanford M. Lyman, "Postmodernism and a Sociology of the Absurd," in Jonathon Epstein, ed., *Wilderness of Mirrors* (New York: Garland Publishing, forthcoming).

22. Marvin B. Scott and Stanford M. Lyman, "Accounts," *American Sociological Review* 33:1 (February 1968): pp. 46–62.

23. John P. Hewitt and Randall Stokes, "Disclaimers," *American Sociological Review* 40:1 (February 1975): pp. 1–11.

24. Randall Stokes and John P. Hewitt, "Aligning Actions," *American Sociological Review* 46:3 (October 1977): pp. 838–49.

25. Lyman and Scott, *A Sociology of the Absurd*, 2d ed., pp. 182–90.

26. See, e.g., J. M. Blaut, *The Colonizer's Model of the World: Geographical Diffusionism and Eurocentric History* (New York: Guilford Press, 1993); and Trinh T. Minh-ha, *When the Moon Waxes Red: Representation, Gender and Cultural Politics* (New York: Routledge, 1991), pp. 29–52, 147–54, 185–200.

27. See Pauline Marie Rosenau, *Postmodernism and the Social Sciences: Insights, Inroads, and Intrusions* (Princeton, N.J.: Princeton University Press, 1992), pp. 42–61.

28. Walter Benjamin, "Theses on the Philosophy of History," in idem, *Illuminations: Essays and Reflections*, ed. Hannah Arendt (New York: Harcourt, Brace and World, 1968), pp. 255–66.

29. Max Weber, *The Protestant Ethic and the Spirit of Capitalism*, trans. Talcott Parsons (New York: Charles Scribner's Sons, 1930), pp. 181–83.

30. A history and critique of the idea of progress was a leitmotiv of the work of Frederick J. Teggart. See his selection of documents on the subject in *The Idea of Progress: A Collection of Readings Selected by Frederick J. Teggart*, University of California Syllabus Series, no. 223 (Berkeley: University of California Press, 1929.) See also J. B. Bury, *The Idea of Progress: An Inquiry into Its Origin and Growth* (New York: Dover Publications, 1955 [1932]); and Robert Nisbet, *History of the Idea of Progress* (New York: Basic Books, 1980).

31. Herbert Blumer, "Race Prejudice as a Sense of Group Position," *Pacific Sociological Review* 1 (spring 1958): pp. 3–7. Reprinted in Stanford M. Lyman and Arthur J. Vidich, *Social Order and the Public Philosophy: An Analysis and Interpretation of the Work of Herbert Blumer* (Fayetteville: University of Arkansas Press, 1988), pp. 196–207.

32. Herbert Blumer, "The Nature of Race Prejudice," *Social Process in Hawaii* 5 (June 1939): pp. 11–20. Reprinted in Lyman and Vidich, *Social Order*, pp. 183–95.

33. Blumer, "Race Prejudice as a Sense of Group Position," in Lyman and Vidich, *Social Order*, p. 198.

34. See Elazar Barkan, *The Retreat of Scientific Racism: Changing Concepts of Race in Britain and the United States between the World Wars* (Cambridge, U.K.: Cambridge University Press, 1992), pp. 13–276; and William H. Tucker, *The Science and Politics of Racial Research* (Urbana: University of Illinois Press, 1994).

35. See Bernard McGrane, *Beyond Anthropology: Society and the Other* (New York: Columbia University Press, 1989), pp. 77–129.

36. Richard J. Herrnstein and Charles Murray, *The Bell Curve: Intelligence and Class Structure in American Life* (New York: Free Press, 1994).

37. Thomas Sowell, *Race and Culture: A World View* (New York: Basic Books, 1994).

38. Paul Gilroy, "Cultural Studies and Ethnic Absolutism," in Lawrence

Grossberg, Cary Nelson, and Paula Treichler, eds., *Cultural Studies* (New York: Routledge, 1992), pp. 187–98. Quotation from p. 190.

39.   Donna Haraway, "The Promises of Monsters: A Regenerative Politics for Inappropriate/d Others," in Grossberg, Nelson, and Treichler, eds., *Cultural Studies,* pp. 295–337. Quotation from p. 313.

40.   Luk van Langenhove and Rom Harrè, "Cultural Stereotypes and Positioning Theory," *Journal for the Theory of Social Behaviour* 24:4 (December 1994): pp. 359–72. Quotation from p. 371.

41.   Steven Seidman, "Postmodern Social Theory as Narrative with a Moral Intent," in Steven Seidman and David G. Wagner, eds., *Postmodernism and Social Theory: The Debate over General Theory* (Cambridge, Mass.: Basil Blackwell, 1992), pp. 47–81.

42.   Richard Ashley, "The Geopolitics of Geopolitical Space: Toward a Critical Social Theory of International Politics," *Alternatives* 12:4 (1987): pp. 403–34. Quotation from pp. 409–10, as reported in Rosenau, *Postmodernism and the Social Sciences,* p. 73.

43.   Rosenau, *Postmodernism and the Social Sciences,* p. 69.

44.   Ibid.

45.   For the term "subaltern," see Gayatri Chakravorty Spivak, "Can the Subaltern Speak?" in Patrick Williams and Laura Chrisman, eds., *Colonial Discourse and Post-Colonial Theory: A Reader* (New York: Columbia University Press, 1994), pp. 66–111.

46.   See Jim Sharpe, "History from Below," in Peter Burke, ed., *New Perspectives on Historical Writing* (University Park: Pennsylvania State University Press, 1993), pp. 4–41.

47.   See Roy Porter, "History of the Body," in Burke, *New Perspectives* pp. 206–32.

48.   See Zdzislaw Mach, *Symbols, Conflict, and Identity: Essays in Political Anthropology* (Albany: State University of New York Press, 1993).

49.   Zygmunt Bauman, *Thinking Sociologically* (Cambridge, Mass.: Basil Blackwell, 1990), pp. 182–83.

50.   For the concept of "intrusion," see Frederick J. Teggart, *The Theory of History* (New Haven, Conn.: Yale University Press, 1925), pp. 82–86, 107, 116–49, 180–94.

51.   For the concept "epoche," see Alfred Schutz, *Collected Papers III: Studies in Phenomenological Philosophy,* ed. I. Schutz (The Hague, Netherlands: Martinus Nijhoff, 1966), pp. 5–7, 46–47, 57–58, 74–79, 126.

52.   See Rhoda Lois Blumberg, *Civil Rights: The 1960s Freedom Struggle,* rev. ed. (Boston: Twayne Publishers, 1991), pp. 71–90.

53.   Robert Nisbet, "Introduction: The Problem of Social Change," in idem, ed., *Social Change* (New York: Harper Torchbooks, 1972), pp. 1–45, esp. pp. 26–45.

54.   Stanford M. Lyman, *The Black American in Sociological Thought,* pp. 27–70.

55.   J. Milton Yinger, *Ethnicity: Source of Strength? Source of Conflict?* (Albany: State University of New York Press, 1994), pp. 1–198.

56.   Elliott R. Barkan, "Race, Religion, and Nationality in American Society: A Model of Ethnicity—From Contact to Assimilation," *Journal of American Ethnic History* 14:2 (winter 1995): pp. 38–75. Quotation from p. 47.

57.   Christopher A. Reichl, "Stages in the Historical Process of Ethnicity: The Japanese in Brazil, 1908–1988," *Ethnohistory* 42:1 (winter 1995): pp. 31–62. Quotation from p. 36.

58.   See Vassilis Lambropoulos, *The Rise of Eurocentrism: Anatomy of Interpretation* (Princeton, N.J.: Princeton University Press, 1993).

59.   See Ranajit Guha, "The Prose of Counter-Insurgency," in Nicholas B. Dirks, Geoff Eley, and Sherry B. Ortner, eds., *Culture/Power/History: A Reader in Contemporary Social Theory* (Princeton, N.J.: Princeton University Press, 1994), pp. 336–71.

60.   Carl Gutierrez-Jones, *Rethinking the Borderlands: Between Chicano Culture and Legal Discourse* (Berkeley: University of California Press, 1995), p. 102.

61.   Wolfgang Natter and John Paul Jones III, "Signposts toward a Poststucturalist Geography," in John Paul Jones III, Wolfgang Natter, and Theodore R. Schatzki, eds., *Postmodern Contentions: Epochs, Politics, Space* (New York: Guilford Press, 1993), pp. 165–204. Quotation from p. 169.

62.   See Stanford M. Lyman, "Territoriality as a Global Concept," *Revija za Sociologiju* 25:3–4 (Srpanj-Prosinac 1994): pp. 139–50.

63.   Barkan, "Race, Religion, and Nationality," p. 47.

64.   See Stanford M. Lyman, "Interstate Relations and the Sociological Imagination Revisited: From *Social Distance* to *Territoriality*," *Sociological Inquiry* 65:2 (May 1995): pp. 125–42, esp. pp. 135–36.

65.   See Robert E. Bieder, *Science Encounters the Indian, 1820–1880: The Early Years of American Ethnology* (Norman: University of Oklahoma Press, 1986, 1989); Curtis M. Hinsley Jr., *Savages and Scientists: The Smithsonian Institution and the Development of American Anthropology, 1846–1910* (Washington, D.C.: Smithsonian Institution Press, 1981); and two works by Francis Paul Prucha, *The Great Father: The United States Government and the American Indians*, 2 vols. (Lincoln: University of Nebraska Press, 1984); and *American Indian Treaties: The History of a Political Anomaly* (Berkeley: University of California Press, 1994), pp. 129–333.

66.   See Geoffrey Irwin, *The Prehistoric Exploration and Colonisation of the Pacific* (Cambridge, U.K.: Cambridge University Press, 1992, 1994); and G. Abeyesekere, *The Apotheosis of Captain Cook: European Mythmaking in the Pacific* (Princeton, N.J.: Princeton University Press, 1992).

67.   See Lord Lugard, *The Dual Mandate in British Tropical Africa* (Hamden, Conn.: Archon Press, 1965 [1922]); and J. S. Furnivall, *Colonial Policy and Practice: A Comparative Study of Burma and Netherlands India* (New York: New York University Press, 1956 [1948]).

68.   See the all-too-neglected study by Margaret T. Hodgen, *Early Anthropology in the Sixteenth and Seventeenth Centuries* (Philadelphia: University of Pennsylvania Press, 1964), pp. 386–516.

69.   See Arthur J. Vidich and Stanford M. Lyman, "Qualitative Methods: Their History in Sociology and Anthropology" in *Handbook of Qualitative Research*, ed. Norman K. Denzin and Yvonna S. Lincoln (Thousand Oaks, Calif.: Sage California, 1994), pp. 23–59, esp. pp. 25–31; and James L. Peacock, *The Anthropological Lens: Harsh Lights, Soft Focus* (Cambridge, U.K.: Cambridge University Press, 1986), pp. 23–47, 65–114.

70.   For an excellent example from the early nineteenth century, see J. M. Degerando, *The Observation of Savage Peoples*, trans. F. C. T. Moore (London: Routledge and Kegan Paul, 1969 [1800]).

71. Adam Kuper, *The Invention of Primitive Society: Transformations of an Illusion* (London: Routledge, 1988).

72. Stanford M. Lyman, *Chinatown and Little Tokyo: Power, Conflict, and Community among Chinese and Japanese Immigrants to America* (Millwood, N.Y.: Associated Faculty Press, 1986).

73. See Stanford M. Lyman, "The Significance of Asians in American Society" in *idem, Civilization: Contents, Discontents, Malcontents and Other Essays in Social Theory* (Fayetteville: University of Arkansas Press, 1990), pp. 149–59.

74. Talcott Parsons, "Full Citizenship for the Negro? A Sociological Problem," *Daedalus: Journal of the American Academy of Arts and Sciences* 94:4 (fall 1965): pp. 1009–54.

75. See Douglas S. Massey and Nancy A. Denton, *American Apartheid: Segregation and the Making of the Underclass* (Cambridge, Mass.: Harvard University Press, 1993).

76. Robin M. Williams Jr., *Strangers Next Door: Ethnic Relations in American Communities* (Englewood Cliffs, N.J.: Prentice-Hall, 1964).

77. Andrew Hacker, *Two Nations: Black and White, Separate, Hostile, Unequal* (New York: Charles Scribner's Sons, 1992), pp. 15–14, 219.

78. Cf. Partha Chatterjee, *The Nation and Its Fragments: Colonial and Postcolonial Histories* (Princeton, N.J.: Princeton University Press, 1993), esp. pp. 3–13, 158–240.

79. Louis Wirth, *The Ghetto* (Chicago: University of Chicago Press–Phoenix Books, 1956 [1928]).

80. W. I. Thomas and Florian Znaniecki, *The Polish Peasant in Europe and America*, vol. 2(New York: Dover Publications, 1958), pp. 1511–646; and Arthur Evans Wood, *Hamtramck: A Sociological Study of a Polish-American Community* (New Haven, Conn.: College and University Press, 1955); Helen Znaniecki Lopata, *Polish Americans: Status Competition in an Ethnic Community* (Englewood Cliffs, N.J.: Prentice-Hall, 1976); and John J. Bukowczyk, *And My Children Did Not Know Me: A History of Polish Americans* (Bloomington: Indiana University Press, 1987).

81. William Foote Whyte, *Street Corner Society: The Social Structure of an Italian Slum*, 3d ed. (Chicago: University of Chicago Press, 1981); Herbert J. Gans, *The Urban Villagers: Group and Class in the Life of Italian Americans*, exp'd. ed. (New York: Free Press, 1982); and Robert Anthony Orsi, *The Madonna of 115th Street: Faith and Community in Italian Harlem, 1880–1950* (New Haven, Conn.: Yale University Press, 1985).

82. Maxine L. Margolis, *Little Brazil: an Ethnography of Brazilian Immigrants in New York City* (Princeton, N.J.: Princeton University Press, 1994).

83. St. Clair Drake and Horace R. Cayton, *Black Metropolis: A Study of Negro Life in a Northern City*, 2 vols. rev. ed. (New York: Harper Torchbooks, 1962).

84. E. Franklin Frazier, "Negro Harlem: An Ecological Study," *American Journal of Sociology* 43 (July 1937): pp. 72–88; and Robert C. Weaver, *The Negro Ghetto* (New York: Russell and Russell, 1967 [1948]); Roi Ottley and William J. Weatherby, eds., *The Negro in New York: An Informal Social History* (New York: New York Public Library, 1967); Nathan Glazer and Daniel P. Moynihan, *Beyond the Melting Pot: The Negroes, Puerto Ricans, Jews, Italians, and Irish of New York City*, 2d ed. (Cambridge, Mass.: MIT Press, 1970), pp. 24–85, 299–316; Jervis Anderson, *This Was Harlem: A Cultural*

Portrait: 1900–1950 (New York: Farrar, Straus, and Giroux, 1982); John Henrik Clarke, ed., *Harlem, U.S.A.* (Berlin, G.D.R.: Seven Seas Books, 1967); and Kenneth B. Clark, *Dark Ghetto: Dilemmas of Social Power* (New York: Harper and Row, 1965).

85.   Ulf Hannerz, *Soulside: Inquiries into Ghetto Culture and Community* (New York: Columbia University Press, 1969); Constance McLaughlin Green, *The Secret City: A History of Race Relations in the Nation's Capital* (Princeton, N.J.: Princeton University Press, 1967); and Harry S. Jaffe and Tom Sherwood, *Dream City: Race, Power, and the Decline of Washington, D.C.* (New York: Simon and Schuster, 1994).

86.   See Michael W. Hughey and Arthur J. Vidich, "Ethnicity and Community in America," in idem, eds., *The Ethnic Quest for Community: Searching for Roots in the Lonely Crowd*, Research in Community, Vol. 3 (Greenwich, Conn.: JAI Press, 1993), pp. 3–14.

87.   Weaver, *The Negro Ghetto*, p. 7.

88.   Stephen Castles and Mark J. Miller, *The Age of Migration: International Population Movements in the Modern World* (New York: Guilford Press, 1993), p. 205.

89.   Ibid., pp. 206–8.

90.   Hughey and Vidich, *The Ethnic Quest for Community*, p. 5.

91.   Paul C. P. Siu, *The Chinese Laundryman: A Study of Social Isolation*, ed. John Kuo Wei Tchen (New York: New York University Press, 1987), p. 14.

92.   Lyman, *Chinatown and Little Tokyo*, pp. 109–224.

93.   Ibid, pp. 225–32. See also Thomas W. Chinn, *Bridging the Pacific: San Francisco Chinatown and Its People* (San Francisco: Chinese Historical Society of America, 1989), pp. 3–21, 55–295, 316–17; two works by Shih-shan Henry Tsai, *China and the Overseas Chinese in the United States, 1868–1911* (Fayetteville: University of Arkansas Press, 1983); and *The Chinese Experience in America* (Bloomington: Indiana University Press, 1986); and L. Eve Armentrout Ma, *Revolutionaries, Monarchists, and Chinatowns: Chinese Politics in the Americas and the 1911 Revolution* (Honolulu: University of Hawaii Press, 1990).

94.   See, e.g., William Toll, *The Resurgence of Race: Black Social Theory from Reconstruction to the Pan-African Conferences* (Philadelphia: Temple University Press, 1979); Thomas R. Frazier, ed., *Afro-American History: Primary Sources* (Belmont, Calif.: Wadsworth Publishing Co, 1988); and two works by Sterling Stuckey, *The Ideological Origins of Black Nationalism* (Boston: Beacon Press, 1972); and *Slave Culture: Nationalist Theory and the Foundations of Black America* (New York: Oxford University Press, 1987).

95.   William Labov, *Language in the Inner City: Studies in the Black English Vernacular* (Philadelphia: University of Pennsylvania Press, 1972); two works by J. L. Dillard, *Black English: Its History and Usage in the United States* (New York: Random House, 1972); and *Lexicon of Black English* (New York: Seabury Press, 1977); Thomas Kochman, ed., *Rappin' and Stylin' Out: Communication in Urban Black America* (Urbana: University of Illinois Press, 1972); Geneva Smitherman, *Talkin and Testifyin: The Language of Black America* (Boston: Houghton-Mifflin, 1977); Walter M. Brasch, *Black English and the Mass Media* (Amherst: University of Massachusetts Press, 1981); John Baugh, *Black Street Speech: Its History, Structure and Survival* (Austin: University of Texas Press, 1983); and three works by Roger D. Abraham, *Deep Down in the Jungle: Negro Narrative Folklore from the Streets of Philadelphia* (Hatboro, Pa.: Folklore

Associates, 1964); *Positively Black* (Englewood Cliffs, N.J.: Prentice-Hall, 1970); *Singing the Master: The Emergence of African American Culture in the Plantation South* (New York: Pantheon Books, 1992).

96.   Weaver, *The Negro Ghetto*, p. 7.

97.   Massey and Denton, *American Apartheid*, p. 217.

98.   Abrahams, *Positively Black*, p. 77.

99.   Ibid.

100.   Mitchell Duneier, *Slim's Table: Race, Respectability, and Masculinity* (Chicago: University of Chicago Press, 1992). p. 159.

101.   See Richard Majors and Janet Mancini Billson, *Cool Pose: The Dilemma of Black Manhood in America* (New York: Simon and Schuster–Touchstone, 1992).

102.   Robert Bartlett, *The Making of Europe: Conquest, Colonization, and Cultural Change, 950–1350* (Princeton, N.J.: Princeton University Press, 1993), pp. 197–242.

103.   See Peter Burke, "America and the Rewriting of World History," and David Armitage, "The New World and British Historical Thought: From Richard Hakluyt to William Robertson," in *America in European Consciousness: 1493–1750*, ed. Karen Ordahl Kupperman (Chapel Hill: University of North Carolina Press, 1995), pp. 35–51, 52–78. See also Frank M. Snowden Jr., "Before Color Prejudice: Black-White Relations in the Ancient Mediterranean World," in Genna Rae McNeil and Michael R. Winston, eds., *Historical Judgments Reconsidered: Selected Howard University Lectures in Honor of Rayford W. Logan* (Washington, D.C.: Howard University Press, 1988), pp. 193–216; and Winthrop D. Jordan, *White Over Black: American Attitudes toward the Negro 1550–1812* (Chapel Hill: University of North Carolina Press, 1968), pp. 216–68.

104.   Myra Jehlen, "Why Did the Europeans Cross the Ocean? A Seventeenth-Century Riddle," in Amy Kaplan and Donald E. Pease, eds., *Cultures of United States Imperialism* (Durham, N.C.: Duke University Press, 1993), pp. 41–58; and three works written or edited by J. H. Parry: *The Establishment of the European Hegemony, 1415–1715: Trade and Exploration in the Age of the Renaissance* (New York: Harper Torchbooks, 1966); *The European Reconnaissance: Selected Documents* (New York: Harper and Row, 1968); and *Trade and Dominion: The European Overseas Empires in the Eighteenth Century* (New York: Praeger Publishers, 1971), esp. pp. 307–28. See also J. H. Elliott, *The Old World and the New, 1492–1650* (Cambridge, U.K.: Cambridge University Press, 1970).

105.   See John R. Baker, *Race* (New York: Oxford University Press, 1974); Thomas F. Gossett, *Race: The History of an Idea in America* (Dallas, Tex.: Southern Methodist University Press, 1963), pp. 3–175; and two volumes edited by Ashley Montagu, *The Concept of Race* (London: Free Press of Glencoe, 1964); and *The Concept of the Primitive* (New York: Free Press, 1968).

106.   Sander L. Gilman, *Inscribing the Other* (Lincoln: University of Nebraska Press, 1991), pp. 36–40.

107.   Ibid., pp. 41–49.

108.   Citations in the remainder of this paragraph are from Ibid. pp. 20–23.

109.   W. E. B. DuBois, *The Souls of Black Folk* (Greenwich, Conn.: Fawcett Publications, 1961 [1903]), pp. 15–16.

110.   Barry Glassner, *Bodies: Why We Look the Way We Do (And How We Feel About It)* (New York: G. P. Putnam's Sons, 1988), p. 146.

111.   Richard M. Zaner, *The Problem of Embodiment: Some Contributions to a*

Phenomenology of the Body, 2d ed. (The Hague, Netherlands: Martinus Nijhoff, 1971), pp. 102–5.

   112.   Ibid., p. 103.

   113.   Glassner, *Bodies*, p. 146.

   114.   Quoted in Londa Schiebinger, "Skeletons in the Closet: The First Illustrations of the Female Skeleton in Eighteenth-Century Anatomy," in Catherine Gallagher and Thomas Laquer, eds., *The Making of the Modern Body: Sexuality and Society in the Nineteenth Century* (Berkeley: University of California Press, 1987), pp. 42–82. Quotation from p. 80, n. 99.

   115.   Glassner, *Bodies*, p. 149.

   116.   Ibid.

   117.   Quoted in Floya Anthias and Nira Yuval-Davis, in association with Harriet Cain, *Racialized Boundaries: Race, Nation, Gender, Colour and Class and the Anti-racist Struggle* (London: Routledge, 1992), pp. 138–39.

   118.   See Peter Burke, "History of Events and the Revival of Narrative," in Burke, ed., *New Perspectives*, pp. 233–48.

   119.   For an early study that antedates postmodernism, see Dr. J. H. Boeke, *The Interests of the Voiceless Far East: Introduction to Oriental Economics* (Leiden, Netherlands: Universitaire Pers Leiden, 1948).

   120.   See, e.g., Caryl Phillips, *The European Tribe* (Boston: Faber and Faber, 1992).

   121.   See, e.g., Frederick Krantz, ed., *History From Below: Studies in Popular Protest and Popular Ideology* (New York: Basil Blackwell, 1988).

   122.   Michael Andre Bernstein, *Foregone Conclusions: Against Apocalyptic History* (Berkeley: University of California Press, 1994).

   123.   See three works by Lyman, *Civilization*, pp. 127–35; *Militarism, Imperialism, and Racial Accommodation*, pp. 7–11, 81–135; and *Color, Culture, Civilization*, pp. 1–104.

   124.   See, e.g., Theodore W. Allen, *The Invention of the White Race*, vol. 1: *Racial Oppression and Social Control* (London: Verso, 1994); and David Roediger, *Towards the Abolition of Whiteness: Essays on Race, Politics, and Working Class History* (London: Verso, 1994).

   125.   Edward Soja, *Postmodern Geographies: The Reassertion of Space in Critical Social Theory* (London: Verso, 1989).

   126.   Edward Soja, "Postmodern Geographies and the Critique of Historicism," in Jones et al., *Postmodern Contentions*, pp. 113–36. Quotation from p. 115.

   127.   Cf. Howard Winant, *Racial Conditions: Politics, Theory, Comparisons* (Minneapolis: University of Minnesota Press, 1994), pp. 22–36, 57–129; Michael Omi and Howard Winant, *Racial Formation in the United States: From the 1960s to the 1990s*, 2d ed. (New York: Routledge, 1994). For some suggestive case studies, see Charles R. Ewen, *From Spaniard to Creole: The Archaeology of Cultural Formation at Puerto Real, Haiti* (Tuscaloosa: University of Alabama Press, 1991); and Charles F. Keyes, ed., *Ethnic Change* (Seattle: University of Washington Press, 1982), pp. 53–305.

   128.   Franklin Henry Giddings, *The Theory of Socialization: A Syllabus of Sociological Principles* (New York: Macmillan, 1897), pp. 12–20; Michael Banton, *Racial Consciousness* (London: Longman Group, 1988).

   129.   Winant, *Racial Conditions*, pp. 37–56.

   130.   For two masterful case studies carried out in accordance with the postmod-

ern approach to human geography, see Kay J. Anderson, "Constructing Geographies: 'Race,' Place and the Making of Sydney's Aboriginal Redfern," in Peter Jackson and Jan Penrose, eds., *Constructions of Race, Place and Nation* (Minneapolis: University of Minnesota Press, 1994), pp. 81–99; and by the same author, *Vancouver's Chinatown: Racial Discourse in Canada, 1875–1980* (Montreal: McGill-Queens University Press, 1991). For the social processes entailed in such adjustments, see Robin M. Williams Jr., in collaboration with Madelyn B. Rhenisch, *Mutual Accommodation: Ethnic Conflict and Cooperation* (Minneapolis: University of Minnesota Press, 1977), esp. pp. 116–408.

131.   For case studies, see Elizabeth R. Amiesen, "Exclusivity in an Ethnic Elite: Racial Prejudice as Boundary Maintenance"; Lorraine Murray, "Unique Americans: The Welsh-American Ethnic Group in the Philadelphia Area"; Erin McGauley Hebard, "Irish-Americans and Irish Dance: Self-Chosen Ethnicity"; Jennifer Krier, "Art and Indentity: Ukrainian-American Ethnicity"; and Andrew Millstein, "Ethnic Expression in a Jewish Street Person," in *Encounters with American Ethnic Cultures*, ed. Philip L. Kilbride, Jance C. Goodale, and Elizabeth R. Ameisen (Tuscaloosa: University of Alabama Press, 1990), pp. 25–76, 101–15, 116–32, 133–48, and 312–28; and Mary E. McMorrow, "An Ideological Immigrant Community: Assimilating Americans to the Germans of 1848"; Salvatorre Primeggia and Joseph A. Varacalli, "Community and Identity in Italian-American Life"; Carl Kavadlo, "World Rejecting Hedonism of the Working Classes: Irish and Italians in Queens and Brooklyn"; Mahmoud Ansari, "The Making of the Iranian Community in America"; Patricia Kolb, "The Development of the Pan-Hispanic Community in the United States"; Yolaine Armand, "Ethnic Identity of the Haitian Community"; Robert E. Millette, "Grenadians in Brooklyn: Social Ranking and Adaptation";and Tamas Tamas, "Class, Status, and Politics in an American-Hungarian Community," in Hughey and Vidich, eds., The *Ethnic Quest for Community*, pp. 17–41, 43–74, 75–96, 139–64, 165–84, 185–210, 211–24, and 225–50.

132.   Cf. J. M. Berthelot, "Sociological Discourse and the Body," in Mike Featherstone, Mike Hepworth, and Bryan S. Turner, eds., *The Body: Social Process and Cultural Theory* (London: Sage Publications, 1991), pp. 390–404; and Anthony Synott, *The Body Social: Symbolism, Self and Society* (London: Routledge, 1993).

133.   Rosenau, *Postmodernism and the Social Sciences*, pp. 42–61.

134.   Zavarzadeh and Morton, *Theory as Resistance*, pp. 55–82.

135.   Franklin Henry Giddings, *The Principles of Sociology: An Analysis of the Phenomena of Association and of Social Organization* (New York: Macmillan, 1926; reprint., New York: Johnson Reprint Corp., 1970), p. 132.

136.   George Henry Lewes, *Problems of Life and Mind: The Study of Psychology* (Boston and London: n.p., 1880), p. 165. Quoted in Giddings, *Principles of Sociology*, op. cit., p. 133.

137.   Loc. cit. Emphasis supplied.

138.   Herbert Blumer, "George Herbert Mead," in Buford Rhea, ed., *The Future of the Sociological Classics* (London: George Allen and Unwin, 1981), pp. 136–69. Quotation from p. 152.

139.   Ibid., p. 140.

140.   Zavarzadeh and Morton, *Theory as Resistance*, p. 59.

141.   See Stanford M. Lyman, "The Existential Self: Language and Silence in the Formation of Human Identity," in idem, *Civilization*, pp. 250–58.

142.   See F. James Davis, *Who is Black?: One Nation's Definition* (University Park:

Pennsylvania State University Press, 1991); William E. Cross Jr., *Shades of Black: Diversity in African American Identity* (Philadelphia: Temple University Press, 1991); Maria P. P. Root, ed., *Racially Mixed People in America* (Newbury Park, Calif.: Sage Publications, 1992); Naomi Zack, *Race and Mixed Race* (Philadelphia: Temple University Press, 1993); Lise Funderburg, *Black, White, Other: Biracial Americans Talk about Race and Identity* (New York: William Morrow and Co., 1994).

143.   See Anya Peterson Royce, *Ethnic Identity: Strategies of Diversity* (Bloomington: Indiana University Press, 1982); Mary C. Waters, *Ethnic Options: Choosing Identities in America* (Berkeley: University of California Press, 1990); Martha E. Bernal and George P. Knight, eds., *Ethnic Identity: Formation and Transmission Among Hispanics and Other Minorities* (Albany: State University of New York Press, 1993); Janet E. Helms, ed., *Black and White Racial Identity: Theory, Research and Practice* (Westport, Conn.: Praeger, 1993).

144.   Jeff Spinner, *The Boundaries of Citizenship: Race, Ethnicity, and Nationality in the Liberal State* (Baltimore, Md.: Johns Hopkins University Press, 1994).

145.   See Kwame Anthony Appiah, *In My Father's House: Africa in the Philosophy of Culture* (New York: Oxford University Press, 1992), pp. 47–84, 173–92.

146.   See Stanford M. Lyman and William A. Douglass "Ethnicity: Strategies of Collective and Individual Impression Management," *Social Research* 40:2 (summer 1973): 344–65 reprinted in Stanford M. Lyman, *The Asian in North America* (Santa Barbara, Calif.: American Bibliographic Center, Clio Press, 1977), pp. 201–14; and William A. Douglass and Stanford M. Lyman, "L'Ethnie: Structure, Processus, et Saillance," trans. Alain Kihm, *Cahiers Internationaux de Sociologie* 61 (1976): pp. 197–220.

147.   Yinger, *Ethnicity*, pp. 38–166.

148.   Stanley Elkins, *Slavery: A Problem in American Institutional and Intellectual Life*, 3d ed. (Chicago: University of Chicago Press, 1976), pp. 81–139; and George M. Fredrickson, "White Images of Black Slaves in the Old South," in idem, *The Arrogance of Race: Historical Perspectives on Slavery, Racism, and Social Inequality* (Middletown, Conn.: Wesleyan University Press, 1988), pp. 206–15.

149.   Herbert Aptheker, *American Negro Slave Revolts* (New York: International Publishers, 1963 [1943]); and Eugene D. Genovese, *From Rebellion to Revolution: Afro-American Slave Revolts and the Making of the Modern World* (Baton Rouge: Louisiana State University Press, 1979).

150.   William Still, *The Underground Railroad* (Chicago: Johnson Publishing Co., 1970 [1871]); Henrietta Buckmaster, *Let My People Go: The Story of the Underground Railroad and the Growth of the Abolition Movement* (Boston: Beacon Press, 1959 [1941]); Horatio T. Strother, *The Underground Railroad in Connecticut* (Middletown, Conn.: Wesleyan University Press, 1962);and Charles L. Blockson, *The Underground Railroad: First Person Narratives of Escapes to Freedom in the North* (Englewood Cliffs, N.J.: Prentice-Hall, 1987).

151.   See two works by Mechal Sobel, *The World They Made Together: Black and White Values in Eighteenth-Century Virginia* (Princeton, N.J.: Princeton University Press, 1987); and *Trabelin' On: The Slave Journey to an Afro-Baptist Faith* (Princeton, N.J.: Princeton University Press, 1988).

152.   Gilbert Osofsky, ed., *Puttin' on Ole Massa: The Slave Narratives of Henry Bibb, William Wells Brown, and Solomon Northrup* (New York: Harper and Row, 1969).

153.   Cf. Erving Goffman, *Strategic Interaction* (Philadelphia: University of Pennsylvania Press, 1969).

154.   See the following works of Fredric Jameson: "Imaginary and Symbolic in Lacan," in idem, *The Ideologies of Theory: Essays*, vol. 1: *Situations of Theory* (Minneapolis: University of Minnesota Press, 1988), pp. 75–118; *Late Marxism: Adorno, or The Persistence of the Dialectic* (London: Verso, 1990), pp. 15–24, 35–48, 73–122, 157–64, 202–11, 227–52; *Postmodernism: or, The Cultural Logic of Late Capitalism* (Durham, N.C.: Duke University Press, 1991), pp. 25–34 et passim; and *The Geopolitical Aesthetic: Cinema and Space in the World System* (Bloomington: Indiana University Press, 1992), pp. 9–86, 186–214.

155.   See the seminal essay by Joel Williamson, "W. E. B. DuBois as a Hegelian," in David G. Sansing, *What Was Freedom's Price?* (Jackson: University Press of Mississippi, 1978), pp. 21–50.

156.   See two essays by Stanford M. Lyman, "The Race Question and Liberalism: Casuistries in American Constitutional Law," *International Journal of Politics, Culture, and Society* 5:2 (winter 1991): pp. 183–248; and "Marginalizing the Self: A Study of Citizenship, Color, and Ethnoracial Identity in American Society," *Symbolic Interaction* 16:4 (winter 1993): pp. 379–94.

157.   See Kingsley Davis, "Intermarriage in Caste Societies," and Robert K. Merton, "Intermarriage and the Social Structure," in Rose Laub Coser, ed., *The Family: Its Structure and Functions* (New York: St. Martin's Press, 1964), pp. 105–27, 128–52.

158.   See George Eaton Simpson and J. Milton Yinger, *Racial and Cultural Minorities: An Analysis of Prejudice and Discrimination*, 3rd ed. (New York: Harper and Row, 1965), pp. 159–60, 379–80.

159.   Brewton Berry, *Almost White: A Study of Certain Racial Hybrids in the Eastern United States* (New York: Macmillan, 1963). See also Stanford M. Lyman, "The Spectrum of Color," *Social Research* 31:3 (autumn 1964): pp. 364–73.

160.   Henry Louis Gates Jr., "Introduction: Writing 'Race' and the Difference It Makes," in idem, ed., *"Race," Writing, and Difference* (Chicago: University of Chicago Press, 1986), pp. 1–20.

161.   Agnes Moreland Jackson, "To See the 'Me' in 'Thee': Challenge to All White Americans or, White Ethnicity from a Black Perspective and a Sometimes Response to Michael Novak," in Sallie TeSelle, ed., *The Rediscovery of Ethnicity: Its Implications for Culture and Politics in America* (New York: Harper Colophon, 1974), pp. 21–44. Quotation from p. 42.

162.   See Immanuel Wallerstein, "The Search for National Identity in West Africa: The New History," in Werner J. Cahnman and Alvin Boskoff, eds., *Sociology and History: Theory and Research* (London: Free Press of Glencoe, 1964), pp. 303–12; Philip D. Curtin, ed., *Africa and the West: Intellectual Responses to European Culture* (Madison: University of Wisconsin Press, 1972); and Robert H. Bates, V. Y Mudimbe, and Jean O'Barr, eds., *Africa and the Disciplines: The Contributions of Research in Africa to the Social Sciences and Humanities* (Chicago: University of Chicago Press, 1993).

163.   See Ernest Evans Kilker, "Black and White in America: The Culture and Politics of Racial Classification," *International Journal of Politics, Culture, and Society* 7:2 (winter 1993): pp. 229–58; Shirlee Taylor Haizlip, *The Sweeter the Juice: A Family Memoir in Black and White* (New York: Simon and Schuster, 1994); and Gregory

Howard Williams, *Life on the Color Line: The True Story of a White Boy Who Discovered He Was Black* (New York: Dutton, 1995).

164.   See Lyman, *Color, Culture, Civilization*, pp. 349–84.

165.   See Stanford M. Lyman, "Race Relations as Social Process: Sociology's Resistance to a Civil Rights Orientation" in Herbert Hill and James E. Jones, eds., *Race in America: The Struggle for Equality* (Madison: University of Wisconsin Press, 1993), pp. 370–401; and Milton Fisk, ed., *Justice* (Atlantic Highlands, N.J.: Humanities Press, 1993), esp. pp. 240–312.

166.   Hans-Georg Gadamer, *Truth and Method*, English trans. and ed. Garrett Barden and John Cumming (New York: Seabury Press, 1975), p. 217.

167.   Ibid., p. 269.

168.   Ibid., p. 217.

169.   Ibid., pp. 273–74, 337–38, 358.

170.   Ibid., p. 270.

171.   Ibid., p. 339.

172.   Citations in the remainder of this paragraph are from ibid., p. 273–74.

173.   See David Harvey, *The Condition of Postmodernity: An Enquiry into the Origins of Cultural Change* (Cambridge, Mass.: Blackwell, 1990), pp. 116–18; and Lambropoulos, *The Rise of Eurocentrism*, pp. 358–59, n. 118.

174.   Marina Vitkin, "The 'Fusion of Horizons' on Knowledge and Alterity: Is Inter-Traditional Understanding Attainable through Situated Transcendence?," *Philosophy and Social Criticism* 21:1 (January 1995): pp. 57–76. Quotation from p. 58.

175.   Gadamer, *Truth and Method,* p. 274.

176.   Ibid.

177.   Zygmunt Bauman, *Postmodern Ethics* (Oxford, U.K.: Blackwell, 1993), p. 85.

178.   See three works by Stanford M. Lyman, *The Seven Deadly Sins: Society and Evil*, rev. ed. (Dix Hills, N.Y.: General Hall, 1989), pp. 43–45; *Militarism, Imperialism, and Racial Accommodation*, pp. 41–80, 205–45; *Color, Culture, Civilization*, pp. 85–104.

179.   Bauman, *Postmodern Ethics*, p. 85.

Chapter 5: The Race Question and Liberalism

1.   Francis Fukuyama, "The End of History?," *The National Interest* 16 (summer 1989): pp. 3–18.

2.   Ibid., p. 3.

3.   Ibid., p. 5.

4.   Alexandre Kojeve, *Introduction to the Reading of Hegel: Lectures on the Phenomenology of Spirit,* trans. James H. Nichols, Jr., ed. Allan Bloom (Ithaca, N.Y.: Cornell University Press, 1980).

5.   Fukuyama, "The End of History?," p. 5.

6.   Ibid., p. 5, n. 3. The addendum is to be found in a footnote added to the second edition published in France in 1947 and included in the English translation. See Kojeve, *Introduction to the Reading of Hegel*, pp. 159–62 n.

7.   Fukuyama, "The End of History?," pp. 6–7.

8.   John Gray, *Liberalism* (Minneapolis: University of Minnesota Press, 1986), p. 79.

9.   John A. Hall and G. John Ikenberry, *The State* (Minneapolis: University of Minnesota Press, 1989), p. 3.

10.   Fukuyama, "The End of History?," p. 7.

11.   Max Weber, "Structure of Power," in *From Max Weber: Essays in Sociology*, trans. and ed. H. H. Gerth and C. Wright Mills (New York: Oxford University Press, 1946), p. 177.

12.   Kojeve, *Introduction to the Reading of Hegel*, p. 161 n.

13.   Fukuyama, "The End of History?," p. 9.

14.   Ibid.

15.   Gertrude Himmelfarb, "Responses to Fukuyama," *The National Interest* 16 (summer 1989): p. 26.

16.   Friedrich Engels to Friedrich A. Sorge, December 2, 1893, in Karl Marx and Friedrich Engels, *Basic Writings on Politics and Philosophy*, ed. Lewis S. Feuer (Garden City, N.Y.: Doubleday-Anchor, 1959), pp. 457–58.

17.   Robert E. Park, "The Nature of Race Relations," in Edgar T. Thompson, ed., *Race Relations and the Race Problem: A Definition and an Analysis* (Durham, N.C.: Duke University Press, 1939), p. 45.

18.   See Herbert Hill, *Black Labor and the American Legal System: Race, Work, and the Law* (Madison: University of Wisconsin Press, 1985); William B. Gould, *Black Workers in White Unions: Job Discrimination in the United States* (Ithaca, N.Y.: Cornell University Press, 1977); William H. Harris, *The Harder We Run: Black Workers since the Civil War* (New York: Oxford University Press, 1982);and David Swinton, "Economic Status of Black Americans," in Janet Dewart, ed., *The State of Black America, 1989* (New York: National Urban League, 1989), pp. 9–40. For a discussion of occupational discrimination against Asians, see Herbert Hill, "Anti-Oriental Agitation and the Rise of Working-Class Racism," *Transaction: Social Science and Modern Society* 10:2 (January–February 1973): pp. 43–54. For the situation affecting Asians, Hispanics, and Native Americans in the formative years of the United States, see Stanford M. Lyman, "The Significance of Asians in American Society," in idem, *The Asian in North America* (Santa Barbara, Calif.: ABC–Clio Press, 1977), pp. 25–38, esp. pp. 36–37, n. 88.

19.   See, e.g., Herbert Gutman, *Work, Culture and Society in Industrializing America* (New York: Alfred A. Knopf, 1976), pp. 119–208; and Herbert Hill, "Myth-Making as Labor History: Herbert Gutman and the United Mine Workers of America," *International Journal of Politics, Culture and Society* 2:2 (winter 1988): 132–200, and his "Rejoinder to Symposium on 'Myth-Making as Labor History,'" *International Journal of Politics, Culture and Society* 2:4 (summer 1989): pp. 587–95.

20.   See Stanford M. Lyman, "Interactionism and the Study of Race Relations at the Macrosociological Level: The Contribution of Herbert Blumer," *Symbolic Interaction* 7:1 (spring 1984): pp. 107–20; reprinted in idem, *Civilization: Contents, Discontents, Malcontents, and Other Essays in Social Theory* (Fayetteville: University of Arkansas Press, 1990), pp. 136–48.

21.   Thomas Sowell, *Ethnic America: A History* (New York: Basic Books, 1981), p. 187.

22.   Shelby Steele, *The Content of Our Character: A New Vision of Race in America* (New York: St. Martin's Press, 1990), p. 170.

23.   Ibid., p. 14.

24.   Ibid., pp. 10–17.

25.   Ibid., p. 16.

26.   See Jacobus tenBroek, "Thirteenth Amendment to the Constitution of the United States: Consummation to Abolition and Key to the Fourteenth Amendment," *California Law Review* 39 (June 1951): pp. 171–203.

27.   See Jacobus tenBroek, *The Anti-Slavery Origins of the Fourteenth Amendment* (Berkeley: University of California Press, 1951), esp. pp. 96–110.

28.   Justice Harlan, dissent, in *Civil Rights Cases*, 109 U.S. 3 (1883).

29.   See Stanford M. Lyman, "Asians, Blacks, Hispanics, Amerinds: Confronting Vestiges of Slavery," in *Rethinking Today's Minorities*, ed. Vincent N. Parrillo (New York: Greenwood Press, 1991), pp. 63–86.

30.   See the following works of Thomas Sowell: *Black Education: Myths and Tragedies* (New York: David McKay, 1972); *Race and Economics* (New York: David McKay, 1975); "Three Black Histories," in *Essays and Data on American Ethnic Groups*, ed. Thomas Sowell with the assistance of Lynn D. Collins (Washington, D.C.: The Urban Institute, 1978), pp. 7–64; *Knowledge and Decisions* (New York: Basic Books, 1980), *Pink and Brown People and Other Controversial Essays* (Stanford, Calif.: Hoover Institution Press, 1981), pp. 1–26, 65–67, 123–24; *Markets and Minorities* (New York: Basic Books, 1981), esp. pp. 83–102; *The Economics and Politics of Race: An International Perspective* (New York: William Morrow and Co., 1983), esp. pp. 15–20, 183–206, 243–58; *Civil Rights: Rhetoric or Reality?* (New York: William Morrow and Co., 1984); *A Conflict of Visions: Ideological Origins of Political Struggles* (New York: William Morrow and Co., 1987), esp. pp. 13–39, 67–140, 172–232; *Compassion Versus Guilt and Other Essays* (New York: William Morrow and Co., 1987); and *Preferential Policies: An International Perspective* (New York: William Morrow and Co., 1990).

31.   Thomas Sowell, *Classical Economics Reconsidered* (Princeton, N.J.: Princeton University Press, 1974), p. 13.

32.   Sowell, *Markets and Minorities,* p. 90.

33.   Ibid., pp. 83–102; and Sowell, *Classical Economics Reconsidered,* p. 13.

34.   See Alfred H. Conrad and John R. Meyer, "The Economics of Slavery in the Ante Bellum South," *Journal of Political Economy* 66 (April 1958): pp. 95–122; and Harold D. Woodman, "The Profitability of Slavery: A Historical Perennial," *Journal of Southern History* 29 (August 1963): pp. 303–325.

35.   Robert William Fogel and Stanley L. Engerman, *Time on the Cross: The Economics of American Negro Slavery* (Boston: Little, Brown and Co., 1974), pp. 263–64.

36.   See Raimondo Luraghi, *The Rise and Fall of the Plantation South* (New York: New Viewpoints, Franklin Watts, 1978).

37.   See Henry Hughes, *A Treatise on Sociology, Theoretical and Practical* (Philadelphia: Lippincott and Grambo, 1854; reprint, New York: Negro Universities Press, 1968). For a discussion of Hughes's thesis, see two essays by Stanford M. Lyman, "Henry Hughes and the Southern Foundations of American Sociology," in *Selected Writings of Henry Hughes: Antebellum Southerner, Slavocrat, Sociologist*, ed. Stanford M. Lyman (Jackson: University Press of Mississippi, 1985), pp. 1–72; and "System and Function in Antebellum Southern Sociology," *International Journal of Politics, Culture, and Society* 2:1 (fall 1988): pp. 95–108. Reprinted in Stanford M. Lyman, *Civilization*, pp. 191–201. See also Arthur J. Vidich and Stanford M. Lyman, *American Sociology: Worldly*

Rejections of Religion and Their Directions (New Haven, Conn.: Yale University Press, 1985), pp. 9–19.

38.   "Long experience," complained John Waring (c. 1716–1794), one of the "Associates of Dr. Bray," a missionary society devoted to the often-resisted task of converting and educating African slaves in the American colonies, "shows that True Religion must make the Blacks as well as whites (notwithstanding some few exceptions) better Servants; and the former have as just a claim to the Knowledge of Christianity as the latter; & Wo be unto Them who wilfully keep 'em ignorant of it." John Waring to Robert Carter Nicholas, dated at London, May 25, 1769, in John C. Van Horne, ed., *Religious Philanthropy and Colonial Slavery: The American Correspondence of the Associates of Dr. Bray, 1717–1777* (Urbana: University of Illinois Press, 1985), p. 284.

39.   Kenneth M. Stampp, *The Peculiar Institution: Slavery in the Antebellum South* (New York: Alfred A. Knopf, 1963), pp. 140–91.

40.   Herbert G. Gutman, *Slavery and the Numbers Game: A Critique of Time on the Cross* (Urbana: University of Illinois Press, 1975).

41.   See Paul A. David et. al., *Reckoning With Slavery* (New York: Oxford University Press, 1976); Kenneth M. Stampp, "Time on the Cross: A Humanistic Perspective," in *The Imperiled Union* (New York: Oxford University Press, 1980), pp. 72–104; Donald Ratcliffe, "The *Das Kapital* of American Negro Slavery? Time on the Cross After Two Years," *The Durham University Journal* 69 (1976): pp. 103–30; and Peter Parish, *Slavery: History and Historians* (New York: Harper and Row, 1989). Still another point of view has been put forward by the anthropological historian Mechal Sobel. Attending to the rise of Afro-Baptist sectarianism and to the system of production and attitudes toward work that prevailed among eighteenth-century Virginia's African and Afro-American slaves, she points to the West African cultural orientation, a civilizational complex carried across the Atlantic by enslaved victims of the Middle Passage. As a way of life for blacks in bondage, it modified how and when work was performed, shaped their religious perspective as well as the architecture of newly constructed buildings, and, in general, diffused itself among white overseers and other whites, where, among other matters, it could resonate most comfortably with similar attitudes and orientations that had come across the Atlantic with the Celts, a decidedly nonliberal populace from the hinterlands of the British Isles. See two works by Mechal Sobel, *Trabelin' On: The Slave Journey to an Afro-Baptist Faith* (Princeton, N.J.: Princeton University Press, 1988 [1979]); and *The World They Made Together: Black and White Values in Eighteenth-Century Virginia* (Princeton, N.J.: Princeton University Press, 1987). See also Grady McWhiney, *Cracker Culture: Celtic Ways in the Old South* (Tuscaloosa: University of Alabama Press, 1988) and Grady McWhiney and Perry D. Jamieson, *Attack and Die: Civil War Military Tactics and the Southern Heritage* (Tuscaloosa: University of Alabama Press, 1982), pp. 170–92; Michael Hechter, *Internal Colonialism: The Celtic Fringe in British National Development, 1536–1966* (London: Routledge and Kegan Paul, 1975); David Hackett Fischer, *Albion's Seed: Four British Folkways in America* (New York: Oxford University Press, 1989); and two works by Bernard Bailyn, *The Peopling of British North America: An Introduction* (New York: Alfred A. Knopf, 1986); and *Voyagers to the West: A Passage in the Peopling of America on the Eve of the Revolution* (New York: Alfred A. Knopf, 1986).

42.   Stanley M. Elkins, *Slavery: A Problem in American Institutional and*

Intellectual Life, 3d ed. (Chicago: University of Chicago Press, 1976), pp. 81–139.

43.   See the essays by George M. Fredrickson, Sterling Stuckey, Roy Simon Bryce-Laporte, and Eugene Genovese in *The Debate Over Slavery: Stanley Elkins and His Critics,* ed. Ann J. Lane (Urbana: University of Illinois Press, 1971), pp. 223–324. See also Herbert G. Gutman, "Enslaved Afro-Americans and the 'Protestant' Work Ethic," in *Power and Culture: Essays on the American Working Class,* ed. Ira Berlin (New York: Pantheon Books, 1987); Kenneth M. Stampp, "Rebels and Sambos: The Search for the Negro's Personality in Slavery," in *The Imperiled Union,* pp. 39–71; and Gerald Jaynes, "Plantation Factories and the Slave Work Ethic," in *The Slave's Narrative,* ed. Charles T. Davis and Henry Louis Gates Jr. (New York: Oxford University Press, 1985), pp. 98–112.

44.   The following—including the quotations—are from Robert William Fogel, *Without Consent or Contract: The Rise and Fall of American Slavery* (New York: W. W. Norton, 1989), pp. 410–11.

45.   Seymour Martin Lipset, *The First New Nation: The United States in Historical and Comparative Perspective* (New York: Basic Books, 1963), p. 333.

46.   Ibid., p. 332.

47.   Ibid. Emphasis in original.

48.   Ibid., p. 330.

49.   Ibid., pp. 99–198.

50.   Ibid., p. 330.

51.   Ibid., pp. 332, 333.

52.   Ibid., p. 343.

53.   Paul M. Sniderman and Michael Gray Hagen, *Race and Inequality: A Study in American Values* (Chatham, N.J.: Chatham House Publications, 1985), pp. 79–118.

54.   See Russell Nieli, ed., *Racial Preference and Racial Justice: The New Affirmative Action Controversy* (Washington, D.C.: Ethics and Public Policy Center, 1991). See also the op-ed essay by United States Senator from Missouri, John C. Danforth, "Stop the Brawling about Quotas," *New York Times,* June 20, 1991, p. A13.

55.   Seymour Martin Lipset, "Introduction to the Norton Edition," in *The First New Nation: The United States in Historical and Comparative Perspective* (New York: W. W. Norton, 1979), pp. xxiv–xxv. For a reanalysis and rejection of Lipset's findings about the content and distribution of black and white opinion on this issue, see Lee Sigelman and Susan Welch, *Black Americans' Views of Racial Inequality: The Dream Deferred* (Cambridge, U.K.: Cambridge University Press, 1991), pp. 132–39.

56.   See Joseph Tussman and Jacobus tenBroek, "The Equal Protection of the Laws," *California Law Review* 37:3 (September 1949): pp. 341–81.

57.   For a thoughtful reconsideration of the Supreme Court's use of laissez-faire ideology in this era, see Michael Les Benedict, "Laissez-Faire and Liberty: A Re-Evaluation of the Meaning and Origins of Laissez-Faire Constitutionalism," *Law and History Review* 3:2 (fall 1985): pp. 293–331.

58.   *Lochner v. New York,* 198 U.S. 45, 74 (1905).

59.   Sheldon M. Novick, *Honorable Justice: The Life of Oliver Wendell Holmes* (Boston: Little, Brown and Co., 1989), pp. 456–57, n. 29. See also David M. Currie, *The Constitution in the Supreme Court: The Second Century, 1888–1986* (Chicago: University of Chicago Press, 1990), pp. 41–44. See, however, Yosal Rogat, "Mr. Justice Holmes: A Dissenting Opinion," *Stanford Law Review* 15 (March 1963), pp. 254–308, for the view that Holmes was hardly the humanitarian that his admirers make him out to be and, on p.

308, that his opinions in cases on segregation in education and transportation, federal protection of political rights, rights arising under the Thirteenth Amendment, and the rights of those ordered to be sexually sterilized against their will, suggest "that the accepted image of Holmes as uniquely libertarian owes more to fantasies unloosed by the attractiveness of his personality than to the realities of his career."

60. *Barbier v. Connolly*, 113 U.S. 27, 30, 31 (1885).

61. Tussman and tenBroek, "The Equal Protection of the Laws," p. 346.

62. See, e.g. Nathan Glazer, *Affirmative Discrimination: Ethnic Inequality and Public Policy* (New York: Basic Books, 1975); Terry Eastland and William J. Bennett, *Counting by Race: Equality from the Founding Fathers to Bakke and Weber* (New York: Basic Books, 1979); Barry Gross, ed., *Reverse Discrimination* (Buffalo, N.Y.: Prometheus Books, 1977).

63. *Central Lumber Co. v. South Dakota*, 226 U.S. 157, 158 (1912).

64. See the fine discussion of this issue in Judith A. Baer, *Equality under the Constitution: Reclaiming the Fourteenth Amendment* (Ithaca, N.Y.: Cornell University Press, 1983), pp. 28–30, 80, 112–30, 183–85, 196–204, 213–15, 231–32, 251.

65. *In re Opinion of the Justices*, 207 Mass. 601, 94 NE 558, 560 (1911).

66. See tenBroek, "Thirteenth Amendment to the Constitution of the United States," 171–203.

67. *Commonwealth v. Alger*, 7 Cush. 84, quoted approvingly by Justice Brown in *Holden v. Hardy*, 169 U.S. 366, 392 (1898).

68. *In re Tiburcio Parrott*, 1 Fed. 481, 506 (1880).

69. See Carter Godwin Woodson, *The Mis-education of the Negro* (Washington, D.C.: Associated Publishers, 1933, 1969); Henry Allen Bullock, *A History of Negro Education in the South from 1619 to the Present* (Cambridge, Mass.: Harvard University Press, 1967), pp. 60–288; Horace Mann Bond, *Negro Education in Alabama: A Study in Cotton and Steel* (New York: Atheneum, 1969 [1939]).

70. Cf. Robert A. Margo, *Race and Schooling in the South, 1880–1950: An Economic History* (Chicago: University of Chicago Press, 1990), esp. pp. 129–33.

71. See Eric Foner, *Reconstruction: America's Unfinished Revolution, 1865–1877* (New York: Harper and Row. 1988); and William Gillette, *Retreat From Reconstruction, 1869–1879* (Baton Rouge: Louisiana State University Press, 1979).

72. Kenneth M. Stampp, *The Era of Reconstruction, 1865–1877* (New York: Alfred A. Knopf, 1965), pp. 186–87.

73. James H. Kettner, *The Development of American Citizenship, 1608–1870* (Chapel Hill: University of North Carolina Press, 1978), pp. 334–51.

74. For a spirited overview of the matter, see Lois B. Moreland, *White Racism and the Law* (Columbus, Ohio: Charles E. Merrill Publishing Co., 1970).

75. *Dred Scott v. Sandford*, 19 How. 393 (1856).

76. Dudley O. McGovney, "American Citizenship," *Columbia Law Review* 11:1 (January 1911): p. 248.

77. *United States v. Rhodes*, abb. U.S. 28, Fed. Cas. No. 16, 151 (1866).

78. John Hope Franklin, *Racial Equality in America*, the 1976 Jefferson Lecture in the Humanities Presented by the National Endowment for the Humanities (Chicago: University of Chicago Press, 1976), pp. 61–62.

79. Dudley O. McGovney, *American Citizenship*, p. 231.

80. *Plessy v. Ferguson*, 163 U.S. 537 (1896).

81.   See Gilbert Thomas Stephenson, *Race Distinctions in American Law* (New York: Appleton-Century-Crofts, 1910; reprint, New York: AMS Press, 1969), pp. 12–25.

82.   *Wall v. Oyster,* 36 App. D.C. 50, 31 LRA (n.s.) 180, 188 (1910).

83.   Ibid., p. 86.

84.   *Berea College v. Kentucky,* 211 U.S. 45, 67–69 (1908).

85.   See Edward F. Waite, "The Negro in the Supreme Court," *Minnesota Law Review* 30:4 (March 1946): pp. 219–304.

86.   W. E. B. DuBois, *The Souls of Black Folk* (New York: Fawcett World Library, 1961 [1903]), p. 23.

87.   Ray Stannard Baker, *Following the Color Line: American Negro Citizenship in the Progressive Era* (New York: Harper Torchbooks, 1964 [1908]).

88.   St. Clair Drake and Horace R. Cayton, *Black Metropolis: A Study of Negro Life in a Northern City,* rev., enl. ed., vol. 1 (New York: Harper Torchbooks, 1962 [1945]), pp. 99–173, 263–86.

89.   Herbert Blumer, "The Future of the Color Line," in John C. McKinney and Edgar T. Thompson, eds., *The South in Continuity and Change* (Durham, N.C.: Duke University Press, 1965), pp. 322–36.

90.   Talcott Parsons, "Full Citizenship for the Negro American? A Sociological Problem," *Daedalus: Journal of the American Academy of Arts and Sciences* 94:4 (fall 1965): pp. 1009–54.

91.   For an excellent discussion of slavery's role in fostering race and color prejudice, see George M. Fredrickson, *The Arrogance of Race: Historical Perspectives on Slavery, Racism, and Social Inequality* (Middletown, Conn.: Wesleyan University Press, 1988), pp. 189–205.

92.   *In re Ah Yup,* 1 Fed. Cas. 223 (Case No. 104), 223–24 (1878).

93.   See Elmer C. Sandmeyer, *The Anti-Chinese Movement in California* (Urbana: University of Illinois Press, 1939), pp. 40–108. For the Chinese struggle to desegregate the schools, see *Wong Him v. Callahan,* 119 Fed. Rep. 381 (1903) and the discussion in Charles Wollenberg, *All Deliberate Speed: Segregation and Exclusion in California Schools, 1855–1975* (Berkeley: University of California Press, 1978), pp. 8–81. The most comprehensive analysis of the Chinese situation in American law is Hudson N. Janisch, *The Chinese, The Courts, and the Constitution: A Study of the Legal Issues Raised by Chinese Immigration to the United States, 1850–1902,* (J.S.D. diss., University of Chicago, March 1971). See also four articles by Charles C. McClain: "The Chinese Struggle for Civil Rights in Nineteenth-Century America: The First Phase, 1850–1870," *California Law Review* 72 (1984): pp. 529–68; "The Chinese Struggle for Civil Rights in Nineteenth-Century America: The Unusual Case of *Baldwin v. Franks,*" *Law and History Review* 3:2 (fall 1985): pp. 349–73; "Of Medicine, Race, and American Law: The Bubonic Plague Outbreak of 1900," *Law and Social Inquiry* 13:3 (summer 1988): pp. 447–513; and "*In re Lee Sing:* The First Residential-Segregation Case," *Western Legal History* 3:2 (summer-fall 1990): pp. 179–96. See also Sucheng Chan, ed., *Entry Denied: Exclusion and the Chinese Community in America, 1882–1943* (Philadelphia: Temple University Press, 1991).

94.   *People v. Hall,* 4 Cal. 399 (1854); and *People v. Brady,* 40 Cal. 198 (1870).

95.   See Victor Low, *The Unimpressible Race: A Century of Educational Struggle By the Chinese in San Francisco* (San Francisco: East-West Publishing Co., 1982); and Wollenberg, *All Deliberate Speed,* pp. 8–81.

96.   Attempts to deny the Chinese the opportunity to operate laundries constituted one basis for numerous court cases in only some of which the Chinese were able to
prevail. See, e.g., *In re Quong Woo*, 13 Fed. 229 (1882); *Soon Hing v. Crowley*, 7 Sawyer
526, 113 U.S. 703 (1885); *In re Tie Loy* (The Stockton Laundry Case), 26 Fed. 611 (1886);
State ex rel. Toi v. French, 41 Pac. 1078 (1895); *State v. Camp Sing*, 18 Mont. 128 (1896);
In re Yot Sang, 75 Fed. 983 (1896); *Quong Wing v. Kirkendall*, 223 U.S. 350 (1912); and *In
re Mark*, 6 Cal. 2d (1936). One case, *Yick Wo v. Hopkins*, 118 U.S. 356 (1886), provided
the grounds for a fundamental interpretation of reasonable classification and permissible
intent. See John Gioia, "A Social, Political and Legal Study of *Yick Wo v. Hopkins*," in
*The Chinese American Experience: Papers from the Second National Conference on
Chinese American Studies (1980)* (San Francisco: Chinese Historical Society of the
United States and the Chinese Cultural Foundation of San Francisco, 1980), pp. 211–20.

97.   *Ho Ah Kow v. Nunan*, 12 Fed. Cas. 252 (Case No. 6, 546) (1879).

98.   See Theodore B. Wilson, *The Black Codes of the South* (Tuscaloosa:
University of Alabama Press, 1965).

99.   *In re Ah Quan*, 21 Fed. 182 (1884); *Chae Chan Ping v U.S.*, 130 U.S. 581
(1889); *Wan Shing v. U.S.*, 140 U.S. 424 (1890); *Fong Yue Ting v. U.S.*, 149 U.S. 698
(1893); *U.S. v. Mock Chew*, 54 Fed. 490, 7 U.S. App. 534, 4 C.C.A. 482 (1893); *Lem Moon
Sing v. U.S.*, 158 U.S. 538 (1895); *Wong Wing et al. v. U.S.*, 163 U.S. 228 (1896); *In re Li
Foon*, 80 Fed. 881, C.C.S.D., N.Y. (1897); *Ah How et al. v. U.S.*, 193 U.S. 65 (1904); and
Ng Fung Ho et al. v. White, 259 U.S. 276 (1921).

100.   *In re Gee Hop*, 71 F. 274 (Cae No. 11,200) (1895).

101.   *Chae Chan Ping v. U.S.*, 130 U.S. 581 (1889). See Sucheng Chan, ed., *Entry
Denied*.

102.   On wives, see *In re Ah Moy* (Case of the Chinese Wife), 21 F. 785 (1884); and
U.S. v. Chung Shee, 71 F. 277 (1895); *U.S. v. Mrs. Gue Lim et al.* 176 U.S. 459 (1900). On
legitimate or illegitimate offspring whether wholly or part Chinese, see *In re Knight*, 171
F. 299 (1909); *Ex Parte Wong Foo*, 230 F. 534 (1916); *Quan Hing Sun et al. v. White*, 254
F. 402 (1918); *Palo v. Weedin*, 8 F. (2d) 607 (1925); and *In re Fisher*, 21 F. (2d) 1007 (1927).
On subjects of China who volunteered and were inducted into the American military, see
Petition of Dong Chong, 287 F. 546 (1923).

103.   Children born in the United States to alien Chinese parents were also challenged, unsuccessfully, with respect to their citizenship. *U.S. v. Wong Kim Ark*, 169 U.S.
649 (1898). See also Stanford M. Lyman, *Chinese Americans* (New York: Random
House, 1974), pp. 86–92, 105–15.

104.   *Chapman et al. v. Toy Long*, 5 F. 497, 500 (Case No. 2, 611), 1876.

105.   *In re Hong Yen Chang*, 84 Cal. 163, 24 Pac. 156 (1890); *In re Gee Hop*, 71 F.
274 (Case No. 11, 200) (1895).

106.   *Louie Wah You v. Nagle*, 27 F. (2d) 573 (1928).

107.   See *Patsone v. Pennsylvania*, 232 U.S. 138 (1913); and "An Act to Repeal the
Chinese Exclusion Acts, to Establish Quotas, and for Other Purposes," United States
Senate and House of Representatives, December 17, 1943, reprinted in William L. Tung,
The Chinese in America, 1820–1973 (Dobbs Ferry. N.Y.: Oceana Publications, 1974), pp.
79–80; see also Sidney L. Weinstock and Edward D. Landels, "Right of Chinese Aliens
to Take Title to Land," *Journal of the State Bar of California* 19:1 (January–February
1944): pp. 19–34.

108.   Lucy M. Cohen, *Chinese in the Post-Civil War South: A People Without a History* (Baton Rouge: Louisiana State University Press, 1984).

109.   See *Tucker v. Blease et al.,* 97 S.C. 303, 81 SE 668 (1914). See also Brewton Berry, *Almost White* (New York: Macmillan, 1963) and Stanford M. Lyman, "The Spectrum of Color," *Social Research* 31:3 (autumn 1964): pp. 364–73.

110.   *People v. Hall,* 4 Cal. 399 (1854).

111.   *Ozawa v. U.S.,* 260 U.S. 178 (1922) and *Yamashita v. Hinkle,* 260 U.S. 199 (1922).

112.   *Rice et al. v. Gong Lum et al.,* 139 Miss. 760, 104 So. 105 (1925). The United States Supreme Court sustained this decision. *Gong Lum v. Rice,* 275 U.S. 78 (1927).

113.   An interesting mitigation of their legal status took place in Arkansas in 1927 when the supreme court of that state granted an injunction against those seeking to halt the sale of land to a Chinese resident alien. The ground, however, was a unique section of the state constitution prohibiting legal distinctions between resident aliens and citizens with respect to the possession, enjoyment, or inheritance of property. The court was careful to point out that, absent this provision, Arkansas's alien land law would have passed muster. *Applegate et al. v. Jung Luke et al.,* 173 Ark. 93, 291 SW 978 (1927). Recently a professor of law at the University of Hawaii has asserted that a form of race discrimination prevails with respect to certain vocal accents, especially those of Asian Americans and Pacific islanders. See Mari J. Matsuda, "Voices of America: Accent, Antidiscrimination Law, and a Jurisprudence for the Last Reconstruction," *Yale Law Journal* C:5 (March 1991): pp. 1329–407.

114.   *Nishimura Ekiu v. U.S.,* 142 U.S. 651 (1891).

115.   *In re Saito,* 62 Fed. 126, C.C., D. Mass. (1894).

116.   Dudley O. McGovney, "The Anti-Japanese Land Laws of California and Ten Other States," *California Law Review* 35 (1947): pp. 7–60.

117.   *Ozawa v. U.S.,* 260 U.S. 178 (1922). Quotations of Justice Sutherland are from this decision.

118.   For revival of the thesis that some Japanese might be descended from the Ainu, see John Noble Wilford, "Samurai Roots Are in Dispute: Are They Japanese?," *San Francisco Chronicle,* undated clipping in author's possession.

119.   For the details of this matter which, while outside the scope of the present study, ought to be of great interest to students of anthropology, ethnology, and sociology, see "Ozawa Case," in the consulate-general of Japan, comp., *Documental History of Law Cases Affecting Japanese in the United States, 1916–1924,* vol. 1 (San Francisco: Consulate-General of Japan, 1925; reprint, New York: Arno Press, 1978), pp. 1–121. For the background of the *Ozawa* case, see Yuji Ichioka, "The Early Japanese Quest for Citizenship: The Background of the 1922 Ozawa Case," *Amerasia Journal* 4:2 (fall 1977): pp. 1–22. For a detailed discussion of court cases affecting alien Japanese in education, marriage, occupations, deportation, etc., see Frank F. Chuman, *The Bamboo People: The Law and the Japanese Americans* (Del Mar, Calif.: Publisher's Inc., 1976), pp. 18–103.

120.   *Dred Scott v. Sandford,* 19 Howard 393, 410–424 *et passim* (1857).

121.   See Andrew D. Weinberger, "A Reappraisal of the Constitutionality of 'Miscegenation' Statutes," appendix G in Ashley Montagu, *Man's Most Dangerous Myth: The Fallacy of Race,* 4th ed. (Cleveland, Ohio: Meridian Books, World Publishing Co., 1964), pp. 402–24.

122.   *In re Takuji Yamashita*, 30 Wash. 234; 78 Pac. 482 (1902). See Milton R. Konvitz, *The Alien and Asiatic in American Law* (Ithaca, N.Y.: Cornell University Press, 1946), pp. 22–32, 80–96, 148–211; and Dr. Moritoshi Fukuda, S.J.D., *Legal Problems of Japanese Americans: Their History and Development in the United States* (Tokyo: Keio Tsushin, 1980), pp. 3–214.

123.   See, e.g., *Gordon Kiyoshi Hirabayashi v. U.S.*, 320 U.S. 81 (1943); and *Fred Toyosaburo Korematsu v. U.S.*, 323 U.S. 214 (1944).

124.   California's alien land law was finally declared unconstitutional, but it took two cases to invalidate all of its provisions. *Oyama v. California*, 332 U.S. 633 (1948); and *Sei Fujii v. State*, 217 Pac. (2d) 481 (1950). California's statute forbidding the issuance of commercial fishing licenses was declared unconstitutional in 1948: See *Takahashi v. Fish and Game Commission*, 334 U.S. 10 (1948).

125.   On the privileges and immunities, see Dudley O. McGovney, "Privileges and Immunities Clause—Fourteenth Amendment," *Iowa Law Bulletin* 4:4 (November 1918): pp. 219–44. See also Judith N. Shklar, *American Citizenship: The Quest for Inclusion* (Cambridge, Mass.: Harvard University Press, 1991).

126.   For critical discussions of the racial restrictions on naturalization in the United States, see Dudley O. McGovney, "Race Discrimination in Naturalization," *Iowa Law Bulletin* 8:3–4 (1923): pp. 129–61, 211–44; George W. Gold, "The Racial Prerequisite in the Naturalization Law," *Boston University Law Review* 15 (1935): pp. 462–506; and Charles Gordon, "The Racial Barrier to American Citizenship," *University of Pennsylvania Law Review* 93:3 (March 1945): pp. 237–58.

127.   *In re Po*, City Court of Albany—March 1894, 28 N.Y. Supp. 383 (1894).

128.   *Petition of Easurk Emsen Charr*, D.C., W.D., Mo.—1921, 273 F. 107 (1921).

129.   See *In re Buntaro Kumagai*, 163 Fed. 922, D.C., W.D., Wash., N.D. (1908); *Bessho v. U.S.*, 178 Fed. 245. 101 C.C.A. 605 (1910); *In re Zasuechi Narasaki*, 269 Fed. 643, D.C., S.D.N.Y. (1919); and *Hidemitsu Toyota v. U.S.*, 268 U.S. 402 (1925).

130.   *In re Kanaka Nian*, 6 Utah 259, 21 Pac. 993 (1889).

131.   See Alexander Saxton, *The Rise and Fall of the White Republic: Class Politics and Mass Culture in Nineteenth-Century America* (London: Verso, 1990).

132.   *In re Halladjian et al.*, 174 Fed. 834, C.C., Dist. Mass. (1909).

133.   *In re Halladjian et al.*, 174 Fed. 834, 838 (1909).

134.   *In re Halladjian et al.*, 174 Fed. 834, 845 (1909).

135.   *U.S. v. Cartozian*, 6 F (2d) 919, D.C. Dist. Ore. (1925).

136.   *U.S. v. Cartozian*, 6 F (2d) 919, 922 (1925).

137.   *In re Najour*, 174 Fed. 735, C.C., N.D. Ga. (1909).

138.   *In re Najour*, 174 Fed. 735, 736; C.C., N.D. Ga. (1909).

139.   *In re Mudarri*, 17 Fed. 465, 466; C.C., D. Mass. (1910).

140.   *In re Mudarri*, 17 Fed. 465, 467; C.C., D. Mass. (1910).

141.   See David Carliner, *The Rights of Aliens: The Basic ACLU Guide to an Alien's Rights* (New York: Avon Books, 1977), pp. 171–72.

142.   *In re Ellis*, 179 Fed. 1002; D.C., D. Ore. (1910).

143.   *Ex Parte Shahid*, 205 Fed. 812; D.C., E.D. So. Car. (1913); *Ex Parte Dow*, 211 Fed. 486; D.C., E.D. So. Car. (1914); *In re Dow*, 213 Fed. 355; D.C., E.D. So. Car. (1914); and *Dow v. U.S. et al.*, 226 Fed. 145; C.C.A.—4th Circ. (1915).

144.   *In re Dow*, 213 Fed. 355, 357; D.C., E.D. So. Car. (1914).

145.   *In re Dow,* 213 Fed. 355, 358–364; D.C., E.D. So. Car. (1914).

146.   *Dow v. U.S., et al.,* C.C.A.—4th Circ.; 226 Fed. 145, 148 (1915).

147.   *Dow v. U.S., et al.,* C.C.A.—4th Circ.; 226 Fed. 145 (1915).

148.   *Ex Parte Mohriez,* D.C., D. Mass.; 54 F. Supp. 941 (1944).

149.   *Ex Parte Mohriez,* D.C., D. Mass.; 54 F. Supp. 941, 942 (1944).

150.   *Ex Parte Mohriez,* D.C., D. Mass.; 54 F. Supp. 941, 942–43 (1944).

151.   *U.S. v. Wong Kim Ark,* 169 U.S. 649, 702–32 (1898).

152.   *Ex Parte Mohriez,* D.C., D. Mass.; 54 F. Supp. 941, 943 (1944).

153.   Ibid.

154.   *In re Ahmed Hassan,* D.C., E.D. Mich.; 48 F. Supp. 843 (1944).

155.   *In re Ahmed Hassan,* D.C., E.D. Mich.; 48 F. Supp. 843, 845–46 (1944).

156.   For a historical account of the Arabs in America, see Gregory Orfalea, *Before the Flames: A Quest for the History of Arab Americans* (Austin: University of Texas Press, 1988). See also Earle H. Waugh, Baha Abu-Laban, and Regula B. Qureshi, eds., *The Muslim Community in North America* (Edmonton, Alberta: University of Alberta Press, 1983).

157.   See Karen Leonard, "The Pahkar Singh Murder Case," *Amerasia Journal* 11:1 (spring 1984): pp. 75–88.

158.   See Joan M. Jensen, *Passage from India: Asian Indian Immigrants in North America* (New Haven, Conn.: Yale University Press, 1988), pp. 246–69; and three works by Gary R. Hess, "The 'Hindu' in America: Immigration and Naturalization Policies and India, 1917–1946," *Pacific Historical Review* 38 (February 1969): pp. 59–79; "The Forgotten Asian Americans: The East Indian Community in the United States," in *The Asian American: The Historical Experience,* ed. Norris Hundley Jr. (Santa Barbara, Calif.: Cleo Books, 1976), pp. 157–79; *America Encounters India, 1941–1947* (Baltimore: Johns Hopkins University Press, 1971). See also Ronald Takaki, *Strangers from a Different Shore: A History of Asian Americans* (New York: Penguin Books, 1989), pp. 294–314. For the saga of one American-born radical who became intimately involved with the anticolonial movement against British rule in India (and later went on to become an early supporter of the Peoples Republic of China), see Janice R. MacKinnon and Stephen R. MacKinnon, *Agnes Smedley: The Life and Times of an American Radical* (Berkeley: University of California Press, 1988), esp. pp. 69–133.

159.   Joseph C. Misrow, *East Indian Immigration on the Pacific Coast* (Stanford, Calif.: Stanford University, 1915; reprint, San Francisco: R and E Research Associates, 1971), p. 11. See also Jensen, *Passage from India,* pp. 226–45.

160.   Takaki, *Strangers from a Different Shore,* pp. 297–98.

161.   *In re Balsara,* C.C., S.D. N.Y.; 171 Fed. 294, 295 (1909).

162.   Ibid.

163.   *U.S. v. Dolla,* 177 Fed. 101 (1910); and Jensen, *Passage from India,* 250–52.

164.   *In re Ferez Din,* D.C., N.D. Calif. S.D.; 27 F. (2d) 568 (1928).

165.   *U.S. v. Balsara,* C.C.A., 2d Circ.; 180 Fed. 694, 695–6 (1910).

166.   *Wadia v. U.S.,* C.C.A., 2d Circ; 101 F. (2d) 7 (1939).

167.   *U.S. v. Bhagat Singh Thind,* 261 U.S. 204 (1923).

168.   *Wadia v. U.S.,* C.C.A., 2d Circ; 101 F. (2d) 7, 8–9 (1939).

169.   Arthur W. Helweg and Usha M. Helweg, *An Immigrant Success Story: East Indians in America* (Philadelphia: University of Pennsylvania Press, 1990), pp. 55–56; Hess, *America Encounters India, 1941–1947,* pp. 150–51, 159–60.

170.   *In re Akhay Kumar Mozumdar,* 207 Fed. 115 (1913).

171.   Jensen, *Passage from Inda*, pp. 255–69. See, e.g., *U.S. v. Akhay Kumar Mozumdar*, 296 Fed. 173 (1923); *Akhay Kumar Mozumdar v. U.S.*, 299 Fed. 240 (1924); *U.S. v. Sakharam Ganesh Pandit and Mohan Singh*, D.D., S.D. Calif.; 297 F. 529 (1924). See also Takaki, *Strangers from a Different Shore*, pp. 294–314.

172.   *In re Sadar Bhagwag Singh*, D.C., E.D. Penna.; 246 F. 496, 500 (1917).

173.   Jensen, *Passage from India*, pp. 190, 210, 237, 242.

174.   *In re Bhagat Singh Thind*, D.C., D. Ore.; 268 F. 683 (1920).

175.   *In re Bhagat Singh Thind*, D.C., D. Ore.; 268 F. 683, 685 (1920).

176.   *In re Bhagat Singh Thind*, D.C., D. Ore.; 268 F. 683, 684 (1920).

177.   *U.S. v. Bhagat Singh Thind*, 261 U.S. 204, 204–15 (1923).

178.   *Kharaiti Ram Samrao v. U.S.*, C.C.A., Ninth Circ., 12 F. (2d) 879, 880 (1942).

179.   Even after East Indians became eligible for naturalization in 1946, the plight was extraordinarily difficult for those East Indians or Pakistanis who hailed from some part of the British Commonwealth that had made citizenship for such persons difficult and who had entered the United States as students. For one instance—leading to an overthrow of the "Congressional veto" over deportation decisions—see *Immigration and Naturalization Service v. Jagdish Rai Chadha et al.*, 462 U.S. 919 (1983); and Barbara Hinkson Craig, *Chadha: The Story of an Epic Constitutional Struggle* (New York: Oxford University Press, 1988).

180.   William Graham Sumner, "The Conquest of the United States By Spain," *Yale Law Journal* 8 (1899); reprint in Albert Galloway Keller and Maurice R. Davie, eds., *Essays of William Graham Sumner*, vol. 2 (Hamden, Conn.: Archon Books, 1969), p. 300.

181.   Dudley O. McGovney, "Our Non-Citizen Nationals, Who Are They?" *California Law Review* 22:6 (September 1934): p. 606.

182.   Ibid., pp. 606–32.

183.   Ibid., pp. 608, 614.

184.   *Lucio v. Government of the Philippine Islands*, 51 Phil. Rep. 596 (1928); cited in McGovney, "Our Non-Citizen Nationals," p. 608, n. 51.

185.   See *Gonzales v. Williams*, 192 U.S. 1 (1903); *In re Giralde*, D.C., D. Md.; 226 F. 826 (1915). For a comprehensive discussion of the debate over the status of Puerto Rico and the Puerto Ricans, see Benjamin Ringer, *"We the People" and Others: Duality and America's Treatment of its Racial Minorities* (New York: Tavistock Publications, 1983), pp. 945–1097. See also Eric Williams, "Race Relations in Puerto Rico and the Virgin Islands," *Foreign Affairs* 23 (1945): pp. 308–17.

186.   *In re Alverto*, D.C., E.D. Penn; 198 Fed. 688, 699 (1912).

187.   *In re Lampitoe*, D.C., S.D. N.Y.: 232 Fed. 382 (1916).

188.   *In re Mallari*, D.C., D. Mass.; 239 Fed. 416 (1916); *In re Mascarenas*, D.C., S.D. Calif.; 271 Fed. 23 (1921).

189.   *In re Rallos*, D.C., E.D. N.Y.; 241 Fed. 686, 687 (1917).

190.   *In re Bautista*, D.C., N.D. Calif.; 245 Fed. 765, 769 (1917).

191.   *In re Bautista*, D.C., N.D. Calif.; 245 Fed. 765, 771 (1917).

192.   *U.S. v. Javier*, C.C.A., D.C.; 22 F. (2d) 879, 880 (1927).

193.   *In re Rena*, D.C., E.D. N.Y.; 50 F. (2d) 606 (1931).

194.   *Roque Espiritu De La Ysla v. U.S.*, C.C.A., Ninth Circ.; 77 F. (2d) 988 (1935).

195.   Tricia Knoll, *Becoming Americans: Asian Sojourners, Immigrants, and*

Refugees in the Western United States (Portland, Ore.: Coast to Coast Books, 1982), p. 113.

196.   Ibid., p. 105.

197.   *Alfafara v. Fross,* 26 Cal. 2d 358 (1945).

198.   Emory S. Bogardus, "Citizenship for Filipinos," *Sociology and Social Research* 29:1 (September–October 1944), pp. 51–54.

199.   Ibid., pp. 53–54.

200.   For a good example of the thesis that full citizenship would be granted to the "Asiatic" immigrant who could assimilate—coupled with proposals that immigration restriction, rather than absolute exclusion, be substituted for the then operant American policy on the matter, and that eligibility for naturalization be based on "individual ability, achievement, worth, attitudes, [and] potentiality," that is, "The test resolves itself to one of constructive assimilative ability"—see Emory Bogardus, *Essentials of Americanization,* rev. ed. (Los Angeles: University of Southern California Press, 1920), p. 213.

201.   Emory Bogardus, *Immigration and Race Attitudes* (Boston: D.C. Heath and Co., 1928), p. 9.

202.   Among studies of these mixed-bloods, see Brewton Berry, *Almost White: A Study of Certain Racial Hybrids in the Eastern United States* (New York: Macmillan, 1963); William Loren Katz, *Black Indians: A Hidden Heritage* (New York: Atheneum, 1986); and Jack D. Forbes, *Black Africans and Native Americans: Color, Race and Caste in the Evolution of Red-Black Peoples* (New York: Basil Blackwell, 1988).

203.   John Collier, "United States Indian Administration as a Laboratory of Ethnic Relations," *Social Research: An International Quarterly of Political and Social Science* 12:3 (September 1945): p. 265.

204.   *Elk v. Wilkins,* 112 U.S. 94 (1884).

205.   *Cherokee Nation v. Georgia,* 30 U.S. (5 Pet.) 1 (1831); and *Worcester v. Georgia,* 31 U.S. (6 Pet.) 515 (1832). For the effects of these decisions on the Cherokees, see William L. Anderson, ed., *Cherokee Removal: Before and After* (Athens: University of Georgia Press, 1991).

206.   *Elk v. Wilkins,* 112 U.S. 94, 109 (1884), quoting *U.S. v. Osborne,* 6 Sawy. 406, 409 (1880).

207.   *In re Burton,* 1 Alaska 111 (1900).

208.   "Indians not born in the United States and not entitled to the special privileges growing out of service in the war . . . are ineligible for citizenship." *Morrison et al. v. People of State of California,* 291 U.S. 82, 96 n. 5 (1933).

209.   Konvitz, *The Alien and Asiatic in American Law,* pp. 113–14.

210.   See Daniel McCool, "Indian Voting," in *American Indian Policy in the Twentieth Century,* ed. Vine Deloria Jr. (Norman: University of Oklahoma Press, 1985), pp. 105–34, esp. pp. 106–14.

211.   Rev. St. U.S. sec. 2079 (1871). Quoted in *In re Burton,* 1 Alaska 111, 113 (1900).

212.   *Ex Parte Green,* 123 F. (2d) 862 (1941). For the particulars of this and related cases, see Alison R. Bernstein, *American Indians and World War II: Toward a New Era in Indian Affairs* (Norman: University of Oklahoma Press, 1991), pp. 22–39.

213.   Harry A. Kersey, *The Florida Seminoles and the New Deal, 1933–1942* (Boca Raton, Fla.: Florida Atlantic University Press, 1989), p. 156.

214.   Fred B. Kniffen, Hiram F. Gregory, and George A. Stokes, *The Historic Indian Tribes of Louisiana: From 1542 to the Present* (Baton Rouge: Louisiana University Press, 1987), p. 296.

215.   Kersey, *The Florida Seminoles,* p. 155.

216.   Ibid., p. 159.

217.   Donald Culross Peattie, "Lo Takes the Warpath," *American Legion Magazine* (July 1943): p. 30. Quoted in Bernstein, *American Indians and World War II,* p. 45.

218.   *Branham v. Langley, et al.,* 139 F. (2d) 115 (1943). See the discussion in Bernstein, *American Indians and World War II,* pp. 41–42, 187 n. 7.

219.   See Joseph LeConte, *The Race Problem in the South* (New York: D. Appleton and Co., 1892; reprint, Miami: Mnemosyne Publishing, 1969), pp. 367–75.

220.   Norman Podhoretz. "My Negro Problem—and Ours," *Commentary* 35 (February 1963): pp. 93–101; reprinted in *Racial and Ethnic Relations: Selected Readings,* ed. Bernard E. Segal (New York: Thomas Y. Crowell, 1966), pp. 239–50. Recently, a sociologist examined the ambiguities, difficulties, legal issues, and international implications of the "one-drop" rule designating descendants of Negroes of any degree as "blacks." See F. James Davis, *Who is Black?: One Nation's Definition* (University Park: Pennsylvania State University Press, 1991).

221.   Ernest Porterfield, *Black and White Mixed Marriages: An Ethnographic Study of Black-White Families* (Chicago: Nelson-Hall, 1978), pp. 9–12. See also Edward Byron Reuter, *The Mulatto in the United States—Including a Study of the Role of Mixed-Blood Races Throughout the World* (New York: Negro Universities Press, 1969 [1918]), pp. 105–82.

222.   Weinberger, "Constitutionality of 'Miscegenation' Statutes," pp. 402–24.

223.   See, e.g., *Scott v. Georgia,* 39 Ga. 321 (1869); *Doc. Lonas v. The State,* 50 Tenn. (3 Heisko) 287 (1871); *Pace v. Alabama,* 106 U.S. 583 (1883); *State v. Tutty,* 41 F. 753 (1890); *Dodson v. State,* 61 Ark. 57, 31 S.W. 977 (1895); *In re Paquet's Estate,* 101 Ore. 393, 200 P. 911 (1921); *Kirby v. Kirby,* 24 Ariz. 9, 206 P. 405 (1922); *Eggers et al. v. Olson et al.,* 104 Okla. 297, 231 P. 483 (1924); *Roldan v. Los Angeles County et al.,* 29 Cal. App. 267, 18 P. (2d) 706 (1935); *In re Monk's Estate,* 48 Cal. App. 2d 603, 120 P. (2d) 167 (1941); *In re Stark's Estate,* 48 Cal. App. 2d 209, 119 P. (2d) 961 (1942); and *Jackson et al. v. City and County of Denver,* 109 Colo. 196, 124 P. (2d) 240 (1942).

224.   *Perez v. Sharp,* 32 Cal. 2d 711; 196 P. (2d) 17 (1948); *Loving v. Virginia,* 388 U.S. 1 (1967).

225.   See Robert J. Sickels, *Race, Marriage, and the Law* (Albuquerque: University of New Mexico Press, 1972); and Paul R. Spickard, *Mixed Blood: Intermarriage and Ethnic Identity in Twentieth-Century America* (Madison: University of Wisconsin Press, 1989).

226.   See the discussion in Milton M. Gordon, *Assimilation in American Life: The Role of Race, Religion, and National Origins* (New York: Oxford University Press, 1964), pp. 61–131.

227.   E.g., Robert K. Merton, "Intermarriage and the Social Structure," *Psychiatry* 4 (August 1941): pp. 361–74; and Kingsley Davis, "Intermarriage in Caste Societies," *American Anthropologist* 43 (July–September 1941): pp. 376–95.

228.   Spickard, *Mixed Blood,* pp. 23–158.

229.   Cf. Edward Byron Reuter, *Race Mixture: Studies in Intermarriage and Miscegenation* (New York: Negro Universities Press, 1969 [1931]); with Cloyte M. Larsson, ed., *Marriage Across the Color Line* (New York: Lancer Books, 1965) and with Spickard, *Mixed Blood,* pp. 233–342, and Porterfield, *Black and White Mixed Marriages,* pp. 59–172.

230.   Joel Williamson, *New People: Miscegenation and Mulattoes in the United States* (New York: Free Press, 1980), esp. pp. 187–95.

231.   See Dudley O. McGovney, "Naturalization of the Mixed Blood—A Dictum," *California Law Review* 22:4 (May 1934): pp. 376–91.

232.   *Thomas Lane v. Matthias W. Baker, Gideon Spahr, and John Ginn,* 12 Ohio 237 (1843).

233.   *In re Camille,* C.C., D. Ore.; 6 F. 256 (1880).

234.   See Everett Stonequist, *The Marginal Man: A Study in Personality and Culture Conflict* (New York: Russell and Russell, 1961 [1937]), pp. 10–53.

235.   *In re Cruz,* 23 F. Supp. 774 (1938).

236.   *Morrison et al. v. People of State of California,* 291 U.S. 82, 86 (1933).

237.   *Morrison et al. v. People of State of California,* 291 U.S. 82, 96 n. 5 (1933).

238.   *In re Cruz,* 23 F. Supp. 774, 775 (1938). An interesting problem in American law and international relations would have arisen had the illegitimate Eskimo-white and Eskimo–Afro-American offspring of Commander Robert E. Peary and Matthew A. Henson, respectively, petitioned for citizenship in the United States before 1952. Although both Kali Peary and Anaukaq Henson might have claimed jus soli citizenship because each had been born in 1906 aboard an American ship, the *USS Roosevelt,* during the Peary-Henson expedition to the North Pole, it is possible that their petitions would have been challenged. Such a challenge might have argued that Eskimos were "Mongolians," and that, in accordance with the decisions in *Camille* and *Cruz,* Kali's "white blood" and Anaukaq's "African blood" were each one percentage point short of the eligibility criterion. As it happened, Kali and Anaukaq were not discovered until 1986, when S. Allen Counter, a member of the Explorers Club and a professor of neuroscience at Harvard came upon them in Greenland and introduced them to their white and Afro-American families in the United States. See S. Allen Counter, *North Pole Legacy: Black, White and Eskimo* (Amherst: University of Massachusetts Press, 1991).

239.   Weinberger, "Constitutionality of the 'Miscegenation' Statutes".

240.   *State v. Treadaway,* 126 La. 500 (1910). See Virginia R. Dominguez, *White By Definition: Social Classification in Creole Louisiana* (New Brunswick, N.J.: Rutgers University Press, 1986), pp. 30–35.

241.   For the concept "*Herrenvolk* democracy," see Pierre van den Berghe, *Race and Racism: A Comparative Perspective* (New York: John Wiley and Sons, 1967), pp. 18, 29, 77, 88, 101, 109, 126, 147. See also Stanford M. Lyman, "The Significance of Chinese in American History," in *The Asian in North America* (Santa Barbara, Calif.: American Bibliographic Center–Clio Press, 1977), pp. 25–38.

242.   Robert E. Park, "Racial Ideologies," in *American Society in Wartime,* ed. William Fielding Ogburn (Chicago: University of Chicago Press, 1943; reprint, New York: DaCapo Press, 1972), pp. 165–84.

243.   Robert Redfield, "The Japanese-Americans," in Ogburn, ed., *American Society in Wartime,* pp. 143–64.

244.   Charles Gordon, "The Racial Barrier to American Citizenship," pp. 250–51.

245.   Ibid., p. 251.

246.   For a comprehensive description and analysis, see Mary L. Dudziak, "Desegregation as a Cold War Imperative," *Stanford Law Review* 41 (1988–89): pp. 61–120.

247.   For this military imagery of the race problem in America, see Herbert Blumer, "The Future of the Color Line," pp. 322–36.

248.   Thurgood Marshall, "Reflections on the Bicentennial of the United States Constitution," *Harvard Law Review* 101:1 (November 1987): p. 4.

249.   Recently one state governor and a president of the United States seemed to recognize this point. Governor Jim Edgar of Illinois ordered that state's Department of Human Rights to add Asian Americans and Native Americans to all affirmative action plans filed by agencies under its jurisdiction. "Illinois Governor Orders Affirmative Action Goals," *The Pacific Citizen* 113:1 (July 5–12, 1991), p. 1. On November 3, 1990, President George Bush signed the Seneca Nation Settlement Act, providing $35 million in compensation to the Native Americans of southwestern New York for the failure of the United States to fulfill its responsibilities under nineteenth-century leasing arrangements. See Laurence M. Hauptman, "Compensatory Justice: The Seneca Nation Settlement Act," *National Forum: The Phi Kappa Phi Journal* 71:2 (spring 1991): pp. 31–33.

250.   The status of women has often been compared to that of slaves. This was the case in the writings of America's first sociologist (See Stanford M. Lyman, "Henry Hughes and the Southern Foundations of American Sociology," in idem, ed., *Selected Writings of Henry Hughes: Antebellum Southerner, Slavocrat, Sociologist* [Jackson: University Press of Mississippi, 1985], pp. 40–44), and in the perspective on America's race problem provided by Gunnar Myrdal. See Gunnar Myrdal, with the assistance of Richard Sterner and Arnold Rose, "A Parallel to the Negro Problem," appendix 5 in idem, *An American Dilemma: The Negro Problem and Modern Democracy* (New York: Harper and Brothers, 1944), pp. 1073–78. See also Leslie Friedman Goldstein, *The Constitutional Rights of Women: Cases in Law and Social Change,* rev. ed. (Madison: University of Wisconsin Press, 1988); and Dorothy McBride Stetson, *Women's Rights in the U.S.A.: Policy Debates and Gender Roles* (Pacific Grove, Calif.: Brooks/Cole Publishing Co., 1991), esp. pp. 14–41.

Chapter 6: The Chinese before the Courts

1.   "Waiting for Redress," *The Toronto Star,* May 25, 1992, p. A18.

2.   The history of the "Chinese question" in Canada is, necessarily, beyond the scope of the present work. Interested parties should consult the following works and documents: *Report of the Royal Commission on Chinese Immigration* (Ottawa: Printed by Order of the Commission, 1885; reprint, New York: Arno Press, 1978); *Report of the Royal Commission on Chinese and Japanese Immigration,* sessional paper no. 54, (Ottawa: S. E. Dawson, printer to the King's most excellent majesty, 1902; reprint, New York: Arno Press, 1978), pp. 1–326; A. R. M. Lower, *Canada and the Far East—1940* (New York: Institute of Pacific Relations, 1941), pp. 3–16, 61–89; H. F. Angus, *Canada and the Far East, 1940–1953* (Toronto: University of Toronto Press, 1953), pp. 94–122; Tom MacInnes, *Oriental Occupation of British Columbia* (Vancouver: Sun Publishing Co., 1927); Stanislaw Andracki. *The Immigration of Orientals into Canada with Special Reference to Chinese,* (New York: Arno Press, 1978); Hilda Glyn-Ward, *The Writing on the Wall: Chinese and Japanese Immigration to B.C., 1920* (Vancouver: Sun Publishing Co., 1921; reprint, Toronto: University of Toronto Press, 1974); Edgar Wickberg, ed., *From China to Canada: A History of the Chinese Communities in Canada* (Toronto:

McClelland and Stewart, 1982); Anthony B. Chan, *Gold Mountain: The Chinese in the New World* (Vancouver: New Star Books, 1983); Peter S. Li, *The Chinese in Canada* (Toronto: Oxford University Press, 1988); and two works by Patricia E. Roy, "A Choice Between Evils: The Chinese and the Construction of the Canadian Pacific Railway in British Columbia," in Hugh A. Dempsey, ed., *The CPR West: The Iron Road and the Making of a Nation* (Vancouver: Douglas and McIntyre, 1984), pp. 13–34; and *A White Man's Province: British Columbia Politicians and Chinese and Japanese Immigrants, 1858–1914* (Vancouver: University of British Columbia Press, 1989). For more recent studies of Canada's Chinatowns, see Charles B. Sedgwick, "The Context of Economic Change and Continuity in an Urban Overseas Chinese Community," (master's thesis, University of Victoria, 1973); James Morton, *In the Sea of Sterile Mountains: The Chinese in British Columbia* (Vancouver: J. J. Douglas, 1974); Paul Yee, *Saltwater City: An Illustrated History of the Chinese in Vancouver* (Seattle: University of Washington Press, 1988); and David Chuenyan Lai, *Chinatowns: Towns Within Cities in Canada* (Vancouver: University of British Columbia Press, 1988). For interesting literary efforts, see Bennett Lee and Jim Wong-chu, eds., *Many-Mouthed Birds: Contemporary Writing By Chinese Canadians* (Seattle: University of Washington Press, 1991).

3.   For the Chinese situation in the labor market in the period in which union organization was beginning, see three studies by Herbert Hill, "Anti-Oriental Agitation and the Rise of Working Class Racism," *Society* 10:2 (January–February 1973): pp. 43–54; "Race, Ethnicity and Organized Labor: The Opposition to Affirmative Action," *New Politics*, n.s., 1:2 (winter 1987): pp. 31–82, esp. pp. 37–45; and "Myth-Making as Labor History: Herbert Gutman and the United Mine Workers of America," *International Journal of Politics, Culture, and Society* 2:2 (winter 1988), pp. 132–200, esp. pp. 172–83. See also two works by Alexander Saxton, *The Indispensable Enemy: Labor and the Anti-Chinese Movement in California* (Berkeley: University of California Press, 1971); and *The Rise and Fall of the White Republic: Class Politics and Mass Culture in Nineteenth-Century America* (London: Verso, 1990), pp. 215–18, 292–311; and Stewart Creighton Miller, *The Unwelcome Immigrant: The American Image of the Chinese, 1785–1882* (Berkeley: University of California Press, 1969), pp. 145–204.

4.   Ki-Taek Chun and Nadja Zalokar et al., "Civil Rights Issues Facing Asian Americans in the 1990s," *Report of the United States Commission on Civil Rights* (Washington, D.C.: U.S. Government Printing Office, February 1992), p. 200.

5.   Floya Anthias, "Race and Class Revisited—Conceptualizing Race and Racism," *The Sociological Review* 38:1 (1990): p. 21.

6.   Elaine H. Kim, "Defining Asian American Realities Through Literature," in Abdul R. Jan Mohamed and David Lloyd, eds., *The Nature and Context of Minority Discourse* (New York: Oxford University Press, 1990), p. 148.

7.   Ibid., p. 149. See also Elaine H. Kim, *Asian American Literature: An Introduction to the Writings and Their Social Context* (Philadelphia: Temple University Press, 1982), pp. 3–22.

8.   See William Purviance Fenn, *Ah Sin and His Brethren in American Literature* (Peiping [Beijing]: College of Chinese Studies cooperating with California College in China, 1933), pp. 1–44, 73–131; John Berdan Gardner, *The Image of the Chinese in the United States, 1885–1915* (Ann Arbor, Mich.: University Microfilms, 1970), pp. 1–91, 148–99; and Limin Chu, *The Images of China and the Chinese in the Overland*

Monthly, 1868–1875, 1883–1935 (Ann Arbor, Mich.: University Microfilms, 1970), pp. 305–448.

9. Frances Bret Harte, "Plain Language From Truthful James," Table Mountain, 1870. Reprinted in Fenn, *Ah Sin and His Brethren,* pp. ix–x, with a discussion on pp. 45–72. See also *Bret Harte's California: Letters to the Springfield Republican and Christian Register, 1866–67,* ed. Gary Scharnhorst (Albuquerque: University of New Mexico Press, 1990), pp. 27, 31, 113–15, 138, 154.

10. See Clarice Stasz, *American Dreamers: Charmian and Jack London* (New York: St. Martin's Press, 1988), pp. 53, 61–62, 73–74, 83–86, 129–31, 156–59, 206, 281.

11. See Earl Derr Biggers, *Charlie Chan: Five Complete Novels* (New York: Avenel Books, 1981).

12. See Cay Van Ash and Elizabeth Sax Rohmer, *Master of Villainy: A Biography of Sax Rohmer* (London: Tom Stacey, 1972).

13. See, e.g., P. W. Dooner, *Last Days of the Republic* (San Francisco: Alta California Publishing House, 1880).

14. Roscoe Pound, "Legislation as a Social Function," *American Journal of Sociology* 18 (May 1913): p. 755.

15. *Cherokee Nation v. Georgia,* 30 U.S. (5 Pet.) 1 (1831); and *Worcester v. Georgia,* 31 U.S. (6 Pet.) 515 (1832).

16. *Dred Scott v. Sandford,* 19 Howard 393 (1857).

17. See John Hope Franklin, *The Free Negro in North Carolina, 1790–1860* (New York: W. W. Norton, 1971 [1943]), pp. 58–120; Arthur Zilversmit, *The First Emancipation: The Abolition of Slavery in the North* (Chicago: University of Chicago Press, 1967), *passim;* Elbert B. Smith, *The Death of Slavery: The United States, 1837–1865* (Chicago: University of Chicago Press, 1967), *passim;* V. Jacque Voegeli, *Free But Not Equal: The Midwest and the Negro During the Civil War* (Chicago: University of Chicago Press, 1967), pp. 2, 17–18, 26–27, 77, 84–89, 166, 171; Leonard P. Curry, *The Free Black in Urban America, 1800–1850: The Shadow of the Dream* (Chicago: University of Chicago Press, 1981), pp. 88, 216–238; J. R. Pole, *The Pursuit of Equality in American History* (Berkeley: University of California Press, 1978), pp. 148–76.

18. Cf. Stanford M. Lyman. "The Significance of Asians in American Society," *Civilization: Contents, Discontents, Malcontents, and Other Essays in Social Theory* (Fayetteville: University of Arkansas Press, 1990), pp. 149–59.

19. See Janice E. Perlman, *The Myth of Marginality: Urban Poverty and Politics in Rio de Janeiro* (Berkeley: University of California Press, 1979). pp. 91–194, 242–63.

20. Robert E. Park, "Human Migration and the Marginal Man," *American Journal of Sociology* 33:6 (May 1928): pp. 881–93.

21. See two studies by Everett V. Stonequist, *The Marginal Man: A Study in Personality and Culture Conflict* (New York: Charles Scribner's Sons, 1937; reprint, New York: Russell and Russell, 1961); and "The Marginal Man: A Study in Personality and Culture Conflict," in *Contributions to Urban Sociology,* ed. Ernest W. Burgess and Donald J. Bogue (Chicago: University of Chicago Press, 1964), pp. 327–45.

22. H. F. Dickie-Clark, *The Marginal Situation: A Sociological Study of a Coloured Group* (London: Routledge and Kegan Paul, 1966).

23. Aron Gurwitsch, *Marginal Consciousness,* ed. Lester Embree (Athens: Ohio University Press, 1985).

24.   See the essays collected in Russell Ferguson, Martha Gever, Trinh T. Minh-ha, and Cornel West, eds., *Out There: Marginalization and Contemporary Cultures* (Cambridge, Mass.: MIT Press, 1991).

25.   See the editorial in *Daily Alta Californian,* May 12, 1851. The relevant portion of that editorial will be found in Stanford M. Lyman, *Chinatown and Little Tokyo: Power, Conflict, and Community Among Chinese and Japanese Immigrants in America* (Millwood, N.Y.: Associated Faculty Press, 1986), p. 235.

26.   See William Speer, D.D., *The Oldest and Newest Empire: China and the United States* (Hartford, Conn.: S. S. Scranton and Co., 1870), pp. 462–530, 554–681; Rev. Otis Gibson, A.M., *The Chinese in America* (Cincinnati, Ohio: Hitchcock and Walden, 1877; reprint, New York: Arno Press, 1978); Rev. Ira W. Condit, D.D., *The Chinaman As We See Him—and Fifty Years of Work for Him* (Chicago: Fleming H. Revell, 1900; reprint, New York: Arno Press, 1978).

27.   See, e.g., *People v. Downer et al.,* 7 Cal. 170 (1857); *Lin Sing v. Washburn,* 20 Cal. 534 (1862); *State of California v. The Steamship "Constitution" et al.,* 42 Cal. 578 (1872); *In re Ah Fong,* 3 Sawy. 144 (1874); *Chy Lung v. Freeman,* 92 U.S. 275 (1875); *Chae Chan Ping v. U.S.,* 130 U.S. 581 (1889); and *Ex Parte Ah Cue,* 101 Cal. 197 (1894).

28.   See John R. Wunder, "The Chinese and the Courts in the Pacific Northwest: Justice Denied?" *Pacific Historical Review* 52:2 (May 1983): pp. 191–211; Ralph James Mooney, "Matthew Deady and the Federal Judicial Response to Racism in the Early West," *Oregon Law Review* 63:4 (1984): pp. 561–637; Christian G. Fritz, "A Nineteenth Century 'Habeas Corpus Mill': The Chinese before the Federal Courts in California," *American Journal of Legal History* 32:4 (October 1988): pp. 347–72; and Linda C. A. Przybyszewski, "Judge Lorenzo Sawyer and the Chinese: Civil Rights in the Ninth Circuit," *Western Legal History* 1 (winter–spring 1988): pp. 23–56.

29.   See Sucheng Chan, ed., *Entry Denied: Exclusion and the Chinese Community in America, 1882–1943* (Philadelphia: Temple University Press, 1991).

30.   See Shih-shan Henry Tsai, *The Chinese Experience in America* (Bloomington: Indiana University Press, 1986), pp. 56–123, 151–66; Him Mark Lai, Joe Huang, and Don Wong, *The Chinese of America, 1785–1980* (San Francisco: Chinese Culture Foundation, 1980), pp. 46–55, 70–75, 79–83; and Peter Kwong, *The New Chinatown* (New York: Hill and Wang, 1987), pp. 3–4, 21–29, 60, 77.

31.   Jonathan D. Spence, *Chinese Roundabout: Essays in History and Culture* (New York: W. W. Norton, 1992), p. 86.

32.   Robert A. Goldwin, *Why Blacks, Women and Jews Are Not Mentioned in the Constitution, and Other Unorthodox Views* (Washington, D.C.: AEI Press, 1990), p. 20.

33.   Gary Wills, *Lincoln at Gettysburg: The Words That Remade America* (New York: Simon and Schuster, 1992), pp. 90–147.

34.   Robert H. Wiebe, *The Search For Order, 1877–1920* (New York: Hill and Wang, 1967), p. 156.

35.   Ibid., pp. 156–57.

36.   The following draws on *People v. Hall,* 4 Cal. 399 (October 1854). Unless otherwise noted, all quotations are from this report.

37.   Michael Banton, *Racial Theories* (Cambridge, U.K.: Cambridge University Press, 1987), pp. 29–30.

38.   Ibid., pp. 28–64.

39.   Indeed, forty-six years later, the curator of the Brooklyn Museum put forward

the heterodoxical thesis that aboriginal America—more specifically, the paleolithic ances-
tors of the Zuni Indians—had been carriers of their civilization to Asia. See Stanford M.
Lyman, "Asian American Contacts Before Columbus: Alternative Understandings for
Civilization, Acculturation, and Ethnic Minority Status in the United States," in
Civilization, pp. 46–75.

40.   For the most recent anthropological account of the people whom Columbus
encountered in the Caribbean, see Irving Rouse, *The Tainos: Rise and Decline of the
People Who Greeted Columbus* (New Haven, Conn.: Yale University Press, 1992). For a
fine analysis of Eurocentric imagery of the Americas in Columbus's day, see Stephen
Greenblatt, *Marvelous Possessions: The Wonder of the New World* (Chicago: University of
Chicago Press, 1991).

41.   See *Speer v. See Yup*, 13 Cal. 73 (1859); *People v. Awa*, 27 Cal. 638 (1865)—
entitling Chinese defendants to introduce Chinese witnesses in their own behalf; *People
v. Washington*, 36 Cal. 658 (1869); *People v. Brady*, 40 Cal. 198 (1870); *People v. McGuire*,
40 Cal. 56 (1872); and *In re Tiburcio Parrott*, 1 Fed. 481 (1880). For a detailed history of
the legislative, judicial, and media campaigns in this matter, see Hudson N. Janisch, *The
Chinese, The Courts, and the Constitution: A Study of the Legal Issues Raised by Chinese
Immigration to the United States, 1850–1902,* (J.S.D. diss., University of Chicago March
1971), pp. 208–28.

42.   *Dred Scott v. Sandford,* 19 How. 393 (1857). For discussions of this case, see
Vincent C. Hopkins, S.J., *Dred Scott's Case* (New York: Atheneum, 1967); Stanley I.
Kutler, *The Dred Scott Decision: Law or Politics?* (Boston: Houghton-Mifflin, 1967); Don
E. Fehrenbacher, *The Dred Scott Case: Its Significance in American Law and Politics*
(New York: Oxford University Press, 1978); Don E. Fehrenbacher, *Slavery, Law, and
Politics: The Dred Scott Case in Historical Perspective* (New York: Oxford University
Press, 1981); and Kenneth M. Stampp, *America in 1857: A Nation on the Brink* (New
York: Oxford University Press, 1990), pp. 68–109.

43.   Janisch, *The Chinese, The Courts, and the Constitution,* pp. 180–208.

44.   See Edward F. Waite, "The Negro in the Supreme Court," *Minnesota Law
Review* 30:4 (March 1946): pp. 219–304.

45.   *People v. Washington,* 36 Cal. 658 (1869).

46.   See the dissent in *People v. Washington,* 36 Cal. 658, 672–87.

47.   See, however, *People v. Naglee,* 1 Cal. 232 (1850); *Ex Parte Ah Pong,* 19 Cal.
106 (1861); and *Ah He v. Crippen,* 19 Cal. 491 (1861).

48.   Mary Roberts Coolidge, *Chinese Immigration* (New York: Henry Holt,
1909), pp. 29–38, 57, 60, 70, 431.

49.   *In re Halladjian et al.,* 174 Fed. 834 (1909).

50.   See the discussion in Jared Diamond, *The Third Chimpanzee: The Evolution
and Future of the Human Animal* (New York: Harper Collins, 1992), pp. 34–37.

51.   Richard E. Leakey and Roger Lewin, *Origins: What New Discoveries Reveal
About the Emergence of Our Species and Its Possible Future* (New York: E. P. Dutton,
1977); Richard E. Leakey and Roger Lewin, *People of the Lake: Mankind and Its
Beginnings* (Garden City, N.Y.: Anchor Press-Doubleday, 1978); and Mary Leakey,
Disclosing the Past: An Autobiography (Garden City, N.Y.: Doubleday and Co., 1984), pp.
97–184.

52.   Donald Johanson and Maitland Edey, *Lucy: The Beginnings of Humankind*
(New York: Simon and Schuster, 1981), pp. 255–376; Donald Johanson and James

Shreve, *Lucy's Child: The Discovery of a Human Ancestor* (New York: William Morrow, 1989), pp. 211–90. See also Michael H. Brown, *The Search for Eve* (New York: Harper and Row, 1990).

53.   Jia Lanpo and Huang Weiwen, *The Story of Peking Man: From Archaeology to Mystery,* trans. Yin Zhiqui (Beijing: Foreign Language Press and Oxford University Press of Hong Kong, 1990); Brown, *The Search for Eve,* pp. 19–20, 30–31, 145, 279–89.

54.   See Stephen Jay Gould, *Wonderful Life: The Burgess Shale and the Nature of History* (New York: W. W. Norton, 1989), pp. 319–23.

55.   See, e.g., Dudley O. McGovney, "Race Discrimination in Naturalization," *Iowa Law Bulletin* 8:3–4 (1923): pp. 129–61, 211–44; George W. Gold, "The Racial Prerequisite in the Naturalization Law," *Boston University Law Review* 15 (1935), pp. 462–506; and Charles Gordon, "The Racial Barrier to American Citizenship," *University of Pennsylvania Law Review* 93:3 (March 1945): pp. 237–58.

56.   *In re Ah Yup,* 1 Fed. 223 (1878).

57.   Thomas F. Gossett, *Race: The History of an Idea in America* (Dallas, Tex.: Southern Methodist University Press, 1963), pp. 37–38.

58.   See Stanford M. Lyman, "The Race Question and Liberalism: Casuistries in American Constitutional Law," *International Journal of Politics, Culture, and Society* 5:2 (winter 1991): pp. 203–32.

59.   Ralph A. Rossum, "Naturalization," *Encyclopedia of the American Constitution,* vol. 3–4 (New York: Macmillan, 1986), pp. 1300–1301; and Kenneth L. Karst, "Citizenship (Theory)," in *Encyclopedia of the American Constitution,* vol. 1–2, pp. 258–60.

60.   See Howard N. Meyer, *The Amendment That Refused to Die,* rev. ed. (Boston: Beacon Press, 1978), pp. 64–67.

61.   Judge Sawyer, together with Judge Ogden Hoffman of the United States District Court for the Northern District of California, showed both courage and judicial acumen in extending the full force of the habeas corpus principle to individual Chinese immigrants subjected to exclusion from 1882 to 1891. See Christian G. Fritz, "Due Process, Treaty Rights, and Chinese Exclusion, 1882–1891," in S. Chan, ed., *Entry Denied,* pp. 25–56.

62.   Ironically, in light of the argument being presented here, the long struggle over the so-called "incorporation doctrine" entailed the assertion that the adoption of the Fourteenth Amendment had made the provisions of the first eight amendments applicable to the states. See Judith A. Baer, *Equality Under the Constitution: Reclaiming the Fourteenth Amendment* (Ithaca, N.Y.: Cornell University Press, 1983), pp. 98–102. See also the discussion in Donald G. Nieman, *Promises To Keep: African-Americans and the Constitutional Order, 1776 to the Present* (New York: Oxford University Press, 1991), pp. 62–70.

63.   The following draws on Joseph Tussman and Jacobus tenBroek, "The Equal Protection of the Laws," *California Law Review* 37:3 (September 1949): pp. 341–81.

64.   The following is from *Ho Ah Kow v. Nunan,* 12 Fed. 252 (Case No. 6,546) (1879).

65.   E. Sandmeyer, *The Anti-Chinese Movement in California* (Urbana: University of Illinois Press, 1939), pp. 51, 63, 75.

66.   See Jonathan D. Spence, *The Search for Modern China* (New York: W. W. Norton, 1990), pp. 38–39, 48, 51, 213, 256.

67.   Stephen Johnson Field, *Personal Reminiscences of Early Days in California,* a manuscript edition of sketches taken down from Judge Field by a stenographer in San Francisco in 1877, to which other documents, commentaries and memorabilia have been attached. MS photocopy in author's possession. pp. 122–42.

68.   See Carl Brent Swisher, *Stephen J. Field, Craftsman of the Law* (Chicago: University of Chicago Press–Phoenix Books, 1969 [1930]), pp. 205–39; and Robert Green McCloskey, *American Conservatism in the Age of Enterprise, 1865–1910: A Study of William Graham Sumner, Stephen J. Field, and Andrew Carnegie* (New York: Harper Torchbooks, 1964 [1951]), pp. 72–126.

69.   Tussman and ten Broek, "The Equal Protection of the Laws," pp. 352–61, 365–68, 373–81.

70.   Ibid., p. 358.

71.   Ibid., pp. 366–67.

72.   *Yick Wo v. Hopkins,* 118 U.S. 356 (1886).

73.   See Charles W. McCurdy, "Field, Stephen J. (1816–1899)," in *Encyclopedia of the American Constitution,* vol.1–2, pp. 721–25, esp. p. 724.

74.   See the discussion and the cases cited in Janisch, *The Chinese, The Courts, and the Constitution,* pp. 233–1077; and in Lyman, "The Race Question and Liberalism," pp. 204–6.

75.   See Stanford M. Lyman, "Asians, Blacks, Hispanics, Amerinds: Confronting Vestiges of Slavery," in *Rethinking Today's Minorities,* ed. Vincent N. Parrillo (Westport, Conn.: Greenwood Press, 1991), pp. 63–86.

Chapter 7: The Assimilation-Pluralism Debate

1.   Seymour Martin Lipset, *The First New Nation: The United States in Historical and Comparative Perspective* (New York: W. W. Norton, 1979), esp. pp. v–xl, 207–348.

2.   See, e.g., Kingsley Davis, "American Society: Its Group Structure," in *Contemporary Civilization 2* (Chicago: Scott, Foresman and Co., 1961), pp. 171–86.

3.   See Leonard Broom and John Kitsuse, "The Validation of Acculturation: A Condition of Ethnic Assimilation," *American Anthropologist* 57 (February 1955): pp. 44–48.

4.   See Harold J. Abramson, "Assimilation and Pluralism," in *Harvard Encyclopedia of American Ethnic Groups,* ed. Stephan Thernstrom (Cambridge, Mass.: Belknap Press of Harvard University Press, 1980). pp. 150–60.

5.   J. Hector St. John de Crevecoeur, *Letters From an American Farmer* (New York: E. P. Dutton, 1957 [1782]), pp. 35–82.

6.   Israel Zangwill, *The Melting-Pot: Drama in Four Acts,* new and rev. ed. (New York: Macmillan, 1922 [1909]), esp. pp. 184–85.

7.   Horace Kallen, *Culture and Democracy in the United States: Studies in the Group Psychology of the American Peoples* (New York: Boni and Liveright, 1924; reprint, New York: Arno Press and the *New York Times,* 1970), pp. 67–232.

8.   Randolph S. Bourne, *War and the Intellectuals: Collected Essays, 1915–1919,* ed. Carl Resek (New York: Harper Torchbooks, 1964), pp. 107–33.

9.   See John Doyle Klier, *Russia Gathers Her Jews: The Origins of the "Jewish Question" in Russia, 1772–1825* (DeKalb: Northern Illinois University Press, 1986); and

M. J. Rosman, *The Lords' Jews: Magnate-Jewish Relations in the Polish-Lithuanian Commonwealth During the Eighteenth Century* (Cambridge, Mass.: Harvard University Press, 1990).

10.   Karl Marx, "On the Jewish Question," *Early Texts,* trans. and ed. David McLellan (Oxford: Blackwell, 1972), p. 114.

11.   Julius Carlebach, *Karl Marx and the Radical Critique of Judaism* (London: Routledge and Kegan Paul, 1978), p. 163.

12.   Ibid., p. 313. See also two works by David McLellan, *The Young Hegelians and Karl Marx* (London: Macmillan, 1969), pp. 75–81; and *Marxism and Religion: A Description and Assessment of the Marxist Critique of Christianity* (New York: Harper and Row, 1987), pp. 8, 10–13, 67–69; and Dennis Fischmann, *Political Discourse in Exile: Karl Marx and the Jewish Question* (Amherst: University of Massachusetts Press, 1991), pp. 3–120.

13.   Saul K. Padover, *Karl Marx: An Intimate Biography* (New York: McGraw-Hill, 1978), pp. 1–30. For a thoughtful discussion of Marxism as a religion in its own right, as well as its relation to Judaism and Christianity, see Robert John Ackerman, *Religion As Critique* (Amherst: University of Massachusetts Press, 1985), pp. 31–35, 43–48, 65–76, 142–52.

14.   Carlebach, *Karl Marx,* p. 314. Judaism itself underwent a divisive sectarian turn toward mystical fundamentalism in the eleventh, twelfth, and thirteenth centuries. It is the thesis of Jose Faur, *In the Shadow of History: Jews and Conversos at the Dawn of Modernity* (Albany: State University of New York Press, 1992), that mystical and fundamentalist Judaism undermined the Maimonidean legalist tradition of Andalusian Jewry, and inadvertently contributed to the vulnerability of Spain's Jews to the horrors of the Inquisition. The appearance of conversos, some of whom were secret Jews, fostered a debate over whether assimilation or pluralism would be the best way to preserve Jewish life, liberty, and property. Spinoza's heresy and its effects are regarded as a wrong and harmful move by Faur, who credits R. Solomon ibn Verga (?–c. 1520), a philosopher who abjured categories, favored historical rationality, proposed a veritable forerunner of symbolic interaction, subjectivity, and cultural and religious pluralism, as being the harbinger of postmodern society. Faur's remarkable thesis should be read in relation to such earlier commentators on the role of Spinoza's heresy for modernity, the Enlightenment, and Occidental social, cultural, and political formations as Leo Strauss, *Spinoza's Critique of Religion* (New York: Schocken Books, 1965); two works by Lewis Samuel Feuer, *Spinoza and the Rise of Liberalism* (New Brunswick, N.J.: Transaction Books, 1987); and *The Scientific Intellectual: The Psychological and Sociological Origin of Modern Science* (New Brunswick, N.J.: Transaction Books, 1992), pp. 297–318; and Yirmiyahu Yovel, *Spinoza and Other Heretics,* vol. 1: *The Marrano of Reason,* vol. 2: *The Adventures of Immanence* (Princeton, N.J.: Princeton University Press, 1989).

15.   See Jurgen Herbst, *The German Historical School in American Scholarship: A Study in the Transfer of Culture* (Port Washington, N.Y.: Kennikat Press, 1972), pp. 129–230; and Albion W. Small, "Fifty Years of Sociology in the United States (1865–1915)," *American Journal of Sociology* 21:6 (May 1916): pp. 721–864.

16.   Sarah E. Simons, "Social Assimilation," *American Journal of Sociology* 6:6 (May 1901): pp. 808–15; 7:1 (July 1901): pp. 53–79; 7:2 (September 1901): pp. 234–48; 7:3 (November 1901): pp. 386–404; 7:4 (January 1902): pp. 539–56.

17.   Gary A. Abraham, *Max Weber and the Jewish Question: A Study in the Social Outlook of his Sociology* (Urbana: University of Illinois Press, 1992), p. 8.

18.   See Werner Sombart, *The Jews and Modern Capitalism*, trans. M. Epstein (New Brunswick, N.J.: Transaction Books, 1982).

19.   Abraham, *Max Weber and the Jewish Question*, p. 231.

20.   Ibid., p. 269.

21.   See Ellsworth Faris, "If I Were a Jew," in *The Nature of Human Nature and Other Essays in Social Psychology* (New York: McGraw-Hill, 1937; reprint, Dubuque, Iowa.: Brown Reprints, 1971), pp. 350–53.

22.   Robert N. Bellah, Richard Madsen, William M. Sullivan, Ann Swidler, and Steven M. Tipton, *Habits of the Heart: Individualism and Commitment in American Life* (Berkeley: University of California Press, 1985), p. 237.

23.   Robert N. Bellah, Richard Madsen, William M. Sullivan, Ann Swidler, and Steven M. Tipton, *The Good Society* (New York: Alfred A. Knopf, 1991), p. 306.

24.   Theodor Mommsen, *Auch ein Wort ueber unser Judentum* (Berlin: Weidmannische Buchhandlung, 1880), pp. 1–16. Translated as "Another Word About Our Jewry" by J. Hessing and published in *The Jew in the Modern World: A Documentary History*, ed. Paul R. Mendes-Flohr and Jehuda Reinharz (New York: Oxford University Press, 1980), pp. 284–87. Quotation from p. 286.

25.   Max Weber, "Science as a Vocation," in *From Max Weber: Essays in Sociology*, trans. and ed. Hans H. Gerth and C. Wright Mills (New York: Oxford University Press, 1946), p. 156.

26.   See Theodor Herzl, *The Jewish State* (New York: Dover Publications, 1988), pp. 67–157. See also Ernest Pawel, *The Labyrinth of Exile: A Life of Theodor Herzl* (New York: Farrar, Straus and Giroux, 1989); and Steven Beller, *Herzl* (New York: Grove Weidenfeld, 1991), esp. pp. 35–61, 107–26. For the debate over which values—those of the "old Yishuv" in pre-Zionist Palestine, or those of the "enlightened" Zionists from fin de siècle Europe—should prevail in the Jewish homeland, see Jeff Halper, *Between Redemption and Revival: The Jewish Yishuv of Jerusalem in the Nineteenth Century* (Boulder, Colo.: Westview Press, 1991).

27.   Mommsen, *Auch ein Wort ueber unser Judentum*, p. 287.

28.   Ibid.

29.   Crevecoeur, *Letters From a American Farmer*, pp. 40, 44, 46.

30.   Zangwill, *The Melting Pot*, p. 184.

31.   Ibid., p. 199.

32.   See Gerald Sorin, *The Prophetic Minority: American Jewish Immigrant Radicals, 1880–1920* (Bloomington: Indiana University Press, 1985).

33.   See Jessa Weissman Joselit, *Our Gang: Jewish Crime and the New York Jewish Community, 1900–1940* (Bloomington: Indiana University Press, 1983); Arthur A. Goren, *New York Jews and the Quest for Community: The Kehillah Experiment, 1908–1922* (New York: Columbia University Press, 1970); Albert Fried, *The Rise and Fall of the Jewish Gangster in America* (New York: Holt, Rinehart, and Winston, 1980).

34.   See Egal Feldman, *The Dreyfus Affair and the American Conscience, 1895–1906* (Detroit, Mich.: Wayne State University Press, 1981).

35.   See Albert S. Lindemann, *The Jew Accused: Three Anti-Semitic Affairs (Dreyfus, Beilis, Frank) 1894–1915* (Cambridge, U.K.: Cambridge University Press, 1991);

and Abraham G. Duker, "Twentieth-Century Blood Libels in the United States," in *The Blood Libel Legend: A Casebook in Anti-Semitic Folklore*, ed. Alan Dundes (Madison: University of Wisconsin Press, 1991), pp. 233–60.

36.   See John Higham, *Send These To Me: Jews and Other Immigrants in Urban America* (New York: Atheneum, 1975), pp. 138–220.

37.   Ibid., p. 203.

38.   Ibid., p. 205. See also Howard M. Sachar, *A History of the Jews in America* (New York: Alfred A. Knopf, 1992), pp. 418–27.

39.   Quoted from pp. 321–22 of William James's book of 1909, *A Pluralistic Universe*, in Higham, *Send These To Me*, p. 206.

40.   Horace Kallen, "Democracy Versus the Melting Pot," *The Nation* 100 (February 18 and 25, 1915) is reprinted in Kallen, *Culture and Democracy in the United States*, pp. 67–125.

41.   Higham, *Send These To Me*, pp. 206–8.

42.   Kallen, *Culture and Democracy in the United States*, p. 124.

43.   Bourne, *War and the Intellectuals*, pp. 107–23.

44.   Ibid., p. 63.

45.   Ibid., p. 108.

46.   Ibid., p. 129.

47.   Ibid.

48.   Ibid., p. 117.

49.   Herbert Blumer, "Race Prejudice as a Sense of Group Position," *Pacific Sociological Review* 1 (spring 1958): pp. 3–7.

50.   Gunnar Myrdal with the assistance of Richard Sterner and Arnold Rose, *An American Dilemma* (New York: Harper and Brothers, 1944).

51.   Citations in this and the following paragraph are from Zangwill, *The Melting Pot*, p. 204–7.

52.   Horace M. Kallen, "Humanistic Sources of Democracy," *The Liberal Spirit: Essays on Problems of Freedom in the Modern World* (Ithaca, N.Y.: Cornell University Press, 1948), pp. 169–70.

53.   Ibid., p. 178.

54.   See Horace Meyer Kallen, *William James and Henri Bergson: A Study in Contrasting Theories of Life* (Chicago: University of Chicago Press, 1914), pp. 206–42.

55.   Bourne, *War and the Intellectuals*, p. 117.

56.   Kallen, "Humanistic Sources of Democracy," p. 190.

57.   Quoted in Edward Abrahams, *The Lyrical Left: Randolph Bourne, Alfred Stieglitz and the Origins of Cultural Radicalism in America* (Charlottesville: University Press of Virginia, 1986), p. 68.

58.   Bourne, *War and the Intellectuals*, pp. 112–13.

59.   Kallen, *Culture and Democracy in the United States*, p. 226, n. 1.

60.   Peter Kivisto, "The Transplanted Then and Now: The Reorientation of Immigration Studies from the Chicago School to the New Social History," *Ethnic and Racial Studies* 13:4 (October 1990): pp. 455–81, esp. pp. 463–68.

61.   For the details of this encounter, see Ralph E. Luker, *The Social Gospel in Black and White: American Racial Reform, 1885–1912* (Chapel Hill: University of North Carolina Press, 1991).

62.   See Lillian D. Wald, *The House on Henry Street* (New York: Henry Holt, 1915; reprint, New Brunswick, N.J.: Transaction Publishers, 1991), pp. 97–100, 216–19, 252–54, 263–66, 270–72, 302–3, 308.

63.   Residents of Hull House, *Hull House Maps and Papers: A Presentation of Nationalities and Wages in a Congested District of Chicago, Together with Comments and Essays on Problems Growing Out of the Social Conditions* (New York: Thomas Y. Crowell, 1895, reprint, New York: Arno Press and the *New York Times,* 1970), esp. pp. 91–114, 115–30, 131–42, 207–30; Arthur C. Holden, *The Settlement Idea* (New York: Macmillan, 1922; reprint, New York: Arno Press and the *New York Times,* 1970); Robert A. Woods and Albert J. Kennedy, *The Settlement Horizon* (New York: Russell Sage, 1922; reprint, New Brunswick, N.J.: Transaction Publishers, 1990), pp. 326–40.

64.   See Stanford M. Lyman, *Militarism, Imperialism, and Racial Accommodation: An Analysis and Interpretation of the Early Writings of Robert E. Park* (Fayetteville: University of Arkansas Press, 1992), pp. 41–135, 205–305.

65.   Booker T. Washington with the collaboration of Robert E. Park, *The Man Farthest Down: A Record of Observation and Study in Europe* (Garden City, N.Y.: Doubleday and Co., Page, 1912; reprint, New Brunswick, N.J.: Transaction Publishers, 1984).

66.   See, e.g., H. A. Millis, *The Japanese Problem in the United States* (New York: Macmillan, 1915); and James A. B. Scherer, *The Japanese Crisis* (New York: Frederick A. Stokes, 1916).

67.   Robert E. Park, "Racial Assimilation in Secondary Groups with Particular Reference to the Negro," in *Race and Culture, The Collected Papers of Robert Ezra Park,* vol. 1, ed. Everett C. Hughes et al. (Glencoe, Ill.: Free Press, 1950), pp. 208–9.

68.   See Stow Persons, *Ethnic Studies at Chicago, 1905–1945* (Urbana: University of Illinois Press, 1987), pp. 77–97.

69.   Judith Ann Trolander, *Settlement Houses and the Great Depression* (Detroit, Mich.: Wayne State University Press, 1975), p. 134.

70.   Ibid., p. 146.

71.   Ibid.

72.   Ibid., pp. 27–28.

73.   Aaron Berman, *Nazism, The Jews and American Zionism, 1933–1948* (Detroit, Mich.: Wayne State University Press, 1990), p. 181.

74.   See Robert G. Goldy, *The Emergence of Jewish Theology in America* (Bloomington: Indiana University Press, 1990); and Abraham J. Peck, ed., *Jews and Christians after the Holocaust* (Philadelphia: Fortress Press, 1982).

75.   See Peter Grose, *Israel in the Mind of America* (New York: Alfred A. Knopf, 1983), pp. 46–318; and Robert W. Ross, *So It Was True: The American Protestant Press and the Persecution of the Jews* (Minneapolis: University of Minnesota Press, 1980).

76.   See Edward Alexander, *The Jewish Idea and Its Enemies: Personalities, Issues, Events* (New Brunswick, N.J.: Transaction Publishers, 1991), pp. 77–96, 143–64. Alexander's work is polemical and should be read in relation to the writings of *Tikkun* editor Michael Lerner, cited in n. 90, *infra.*

77.   See Sachar, *A History of the Jews in America,* pp. 563–94; Milton Plesur, *Jewish Life in Twentieth-Century America: Challenge and Accommodation* (Chicago: Nelson-Hall, 1982), pp. 131–205; Nathan C. Belth, *A Promise to Keep: A Narrative of the*

American Encounter with Anti-Semitism (New York: Schocken Books, 1981), pp. 146–294; and Thomas A. Kolsky, *Jews against Zionism: The American Council for Judaism, 1942–1948* (Philadelphia: Temple University Press, 1990).

78. Quoted in Joseph H. Udelson, *Dreamer of the Ghetto: The Life and Works of Israel Zangwill* (Tuscaloosa: University of Alabama Press, 1990), p. 194.

79. Ibid., p. 152.

80. See Gary Dean Best, *To Free a People: American Jewish Leaders and the Jewish Problem in Eastern Europe, 1890–1914* (Westport, Conn.: Greenwood Press, 1982), pp. 218–23.

81. Ronald Sanders, *The High Walls of Jerusalem: A History of the Balfour Declaration and the Birth of the British Mandate for Palestine* (New York: Holt, Rinehart, and Winston, 1983).

82. See Herbert Blumer, "The Future of the Color Line," in Stanford M. Lyman and Arthur J. Vidich, *Social Order and the Public Philosophy: An Analysis and Interpretation of the Work of Herbert Blumer* (Fayetteville: University of Arkansas Press, 1988), pp. 208–22. For the current version of the debates among and between blacks and Jews over assimilation, culture, and pluralism, see Jack Salzman, et al., eds., *Bridges and Boundaries: African Americans and American Jews* (New York: George Braziller in association with the Jewish Museum, 1992); and the essays by Jesse Jackson, James McPherson, Cornel West, Marshall Berman, Arnold Eisen, Roger Perry and Patricia Williams, Rachel Adler, Arthur Waskow, and Jacob Neusner in *Tikkun: A Jewish Critique of Politics, Culture and Society,* ed. Michael Lerner (Oakland, Calif.: Tikkun Books, 1992).

83. David Harvey, *The Condition of Postmodernity: An Enquiry into the Origins of Cultural Change* (Cambridge, Mass.: Basil Blackwell, 1990), p. 49.

84. Warren Montag, "What Is at Stake in the Debate on Postmodernism?" in *Postmodernism and Its Discontents: Theories, Practices,* ed. E. Ann Kaplan (London: Verso, 1988), pp. 88–103.

85. Henry Louis Gates Jr., "Writing 'Race' and the Difference It Makes," in idem, ed., *"Race," Writing and Difference* (Chicago: University of Chicago Press, 1985), p. 6.

86. See Winthrop D. Jordan, *White Over Black: American Attitudes Toward the Negro, 1550–1812* (Chapel Hill: University of North Carolina Press, 1968). See also Dana D. Nelson, *The Word in Black and White: Reading "Race" in American Literature, 1638–1867* (New York: Oxford University Press, 1992). That the race question is an extension of the Jewish question, especially as that question arose in the century preceding the first voyage of Columbus and the expulsion of the Jews from Spain—both occurred in 1492—is a feature of the challenging and original thesis of Jose Faur, *In the Shadow of History,* pp. 1–27.

87. See two works by Lester F. Ward, *Applied Sociology: A Treatise on the Conscious Improvement of Society by Society* (Boston: Ginn and Co., 1906), pp. 205–38; and *Pure Sociology: A Treatise on the Origin and Spontaneous Development of Society,* 2d ed. (New York: Macmillan, 1907; reprint, New York: Augustus M. Kelley, 1970), pp. 108–10. See also the discussion of Ward's thesis in Arthur J. Vidich and Stanford M. Lyman, *American Sociology: Worldly Rejections of Religion and Their Directions* (New Haven, Conn.: Yale University Press, 1985), pp. 20–35.

88. Charles Johnson, *Being and Race: Black Writing Since 1970* (Bloomington: Indiana University Press, 1988), p. 123.

89.   See Adam Begley, "Henry Louis Gates, Jr.: Black Studies' New Star," *New York Times Magazine*, April 1, 1990, pp. 24–27, 48–50. For two of Gates's essays critically examining the depiction of blacks in earlier eras, see Henry Louis Gates Jr., "From Wheatley to Douglass: The Politics of Displacement," in *Frederick Douglass: New Literary and Historical Essays*, ed. Eric J. Sundquist (Cambridge, U.K.: Cambridge University Press, 1990), pp. 47–65; and "The Trope of the New Negro and the Reconstruction of the Image of the Black," in *The New American Studies: Essays from Representations*, ed. Philip Fisher (Berkeley: University of California Press, 1991), pp. 319–45.

90.   Henry Louis Gates Jr., *Figures in Black: Words, Signs, and the "Racial" Self* (New York: Oxford University Press, 1987), pp. xxii–xxiv.

91.   Ibid., xxvi. See also Henry Louis Gates Jr., *Loose Canons: Notes on the Culture Wars* (New York: Oxford University Press, 1992), pp. 3–42, 87–104.

92.   Henry Louis Gates Jr., "Canon-Formation, Literary History, and the Afro-American Tradition: From the Seen to the Told," in *Afro-American Literary Study in the 1990s*, ed. Houston A. Baker Jr. and Patricia Redmond (Chicago: University of Chicago Press, 1989), p. 21.

93.   Ibid., p. 20.

94.   Quoted in ibid., p. 24.

95.   Ibid., pp. 24–25.

96.   Jean Toomer, *Cane* (New York: Harper and Row, 1969 [1923]).

97.   See James Haskins, *Pinckney Benton Stewart Pinchback* (New York: Macmillan, 1973).

98.   Since the republication of *Cane* in 1969, there has been a veritable renaissance in Toomer studies. See, among many, Frank Durham, comp., *Studies in Cane* (Columbus, Ohio: Charles E. Merrill, 1971); Darwin T. Turner, *In a Minor Chord: Three Afro-American Writers and Their Search for Identity* (Carbondale: Southern Illinois University Press, 1971), pp. 1–59; Brian Joseph Benson and Mable Mayle Dillard, *Jean Toomer* (Boston: Twayne Publishers, 1980); Nellie Y. McKay, *Jean Toomer, Artist: A Study of His Literary Life and Work, 1894–1936* (Chapel Hill: University of North Carolina Press, 1984); Cynthia Earl Kerman and Richard Eldridge, *The Lives of Jean Toomer: A Hunger for Wholeness* (Baton Rouge: Louisiana State University Press, 1987); Therman B. O'Daniel, ed., *Jean Toomer: A Critical Evaluation* (Washington, D.C.: Howard University Press, 1988); Rudolph P. Byrd, *Jean Toomer's Years with Gurdjieff: Portrait of an Artist, 1923–1936* (Athens: University of Georgia Press, 1990). Republications of Toomer's works include, in addition to *Cane*, cited *supra*, *The Wayward and the Seeking: A Collection of Writings by Jean Toomer*, ed. Darwin T. Turner (Washington, D.C.: Howard University Press, 1980); and *Essentials*, ed. Rudolph P. Byrd (Athens: University of Georgia Press, 1991).

99.   Jean Toomer, "Autobiographical Sketches: The *Cane* Years," in *The Wayward and the Seeking*, op. cit., p. 121.

100.   Ibid., pp. 121–22.

101.   Citations in this paragraph are from Gates, *Figures in Black*, p. 201–2.

102.   Bernard W. Bell, *The Afro-American Novel and Its Tradition* (Amherst: University of Massachusetts Press, 1987), p. 101.

103.   The most important essays of the Frazier-Herskovitz debate will be found in "Part III: The African Diaspora and Cultural Survivals: The Frazier-Herskovitz Debate,"

in *Intergroup Relations: Sociological Perspectives,* ed. Pierre van den Berghe (New York: Basic Books, 1972), pp. 103–36.

104.   See two works by Melville J. Herskovitz, *The Myth of the Negro Past* (Boston: Beacon Press, 1958 [1941]); and *The New World Negro: Selected Papers in Afro-American Studies,* ed. Frances S. Herskovitz (Bloomington: Indiana University Press, 1966), esp. pp. 83–134, 157–98, 321–61.

105.   Melville J. Herskovitz, *The American Negro: A Study in Racial Crossing* (Bloomington: Indiana University Press, 1964 [1928]).

106.   Quoted in Arna Bontemps "Introduction" in Jean Toomer, *Cane,* op. cit., p. viii.

107.   Ibid., pp. viii–ix.

108.   Robert E. Park, "The Conflict and Fusion of Cultures with Special Reference to the Negro," *Journal of Negro History* 4:2 (April 1919): pp. 111–33. See also my discussion of Park's concept of temperament in Lyman, *Militarism, Imperialism, and Racial Accommodation,* pp. 106–12, 132. Park's essay is reprinted on pp. 290–305 of that book.

109.   See Stanford M. Lyman and William A. Douglass, "Ethnicity: Strategies of Collective and Individual Impression Management," *Social Research* 40:2 (summer 1973): pp. 344–65; William A. Douglass and Stanford M. Lyman, "L'Ethnie: Structure, Processus, et Saillance," trans. Alain Kihm, *Cahiers Internationaux de Sociologie* 61 (1976): pp. 197–220; and Stanford M. Lyman, "The Existential Self: Language and Silence in the Formation of Human Identity," in idem., *Civilization: Contents, Discontents, Malcontents and Other Essays in Social Theory* (Fayetteville: University of Arkansas Press, 1990), pp. 250–58.

110.   Toni Morrison, *Playing in the Dark: Whiteness and the Literary Imagination,* The William E. Massey, Sr., Lectures in the History of American Civilization, 1990 (Cambridge, Mass.: Harvard University Press, 1992).

111.   Ibid., pp. 32–33.

112.   See two works by Bernard Bailyn, *The Peopling of North America: An Introduction* (New York: Alfred A. Knopf, 1986); and *Voyagers to the West: A Passage in the Peopling of America on the Eve of the Revolution* (New York: Alfred A. Knopf, 1986).

113.   Jacques Derrida, *Speech and Phenomena and Other Essays on Husserl's Theory of Signs,* trans. David B. Allison (Evanston, Ill.: Northwestern University Press, 1973), pp. 82, n. 8; 129, n. 1.

114.   Citations in the remainder of this section are from Morrison, *Playing in the Dark,* p. 44–48.

115.   Derrida, *Speech and Phenomena,* p. 142. Emphasis supplied.

116.   For the concept of the time track, see Stanford M. Lyman and Marvin B. Scott, *A Sociology of the Absurd,* 2d ed. (Dix Hills, N.Y.: General Hall, 1989), pp. 35–50.

117.   Morrison, *Playing in the Dark,* p. 47.

118.   Joel Williamson, *New People: Miscegenation and Mulattoes in the United States* (New York: Free Press, 1980), p. 195.

119.   See Charles C. Lemert, "The Uses of French Structuralisms in Sociology," in *Frontiers of Social Theory: The New Syntheses,* ed. George Ritzer (New York: Columbia University Press, 1990), pp. 230–54. See also Richard Harvey Brown, *Society as Text: Essays on Rhetoric, Reason and Reality* (Chicago: University of Chicago Press, 1987), esp. pp. 97–192; and Richard Harvey Brown, ed., *Writing the Social Text: Poetics and Politics in Social Science Discourse* (New York: Aldine DeGruyter, 1992), esp. pp. 39–52, 91–116.

120.   See two works by Nathan Glazer and Daniel Patrick Moynihan, *Beyond the Melting Pot: The Negroes, Puerto Ricans, Jews, Italians, and Irish of New York City*, 2d ed. (Cambridge, Mass.: MIT Press, 1970); and with Corinne S. Schelling, eds., *Ethnicity: Theory and Experience* (Cambridge, Mass.: Harvard University Press, 1975), esp. pp. 1–266. For an earlier period see Joyce D. Goodfriend, *Before the Melting Pot: Society and Culture in Colonial New York City, 1664–1730* (Princeton, N.J.: Princeton University Press, 1992).

121.   Citations in this paragraph are from Charles Silberman, *Crisis in Black and White* (New York: Random House, 1964), p. 165.

122.   See e.g., the three essays on Frederick Douglass's narrative by Robert B. Stepto, Robert G. O'Meally, and Henry Louis Gates Jr., in *Afro-American Literature: The Reconstruction of Instruction*, ed. Dexter Fisher and Robert B. Stepto (New York: Modern Language Association of America, 1979), pp. 171–232.

123.   Roxana Robinson, "It's Not Easy Being a WASP"—a review of *False Gods* (Boston: Houghton-Mifflin, 1992), by Louis Auchincloss, *The New York Times Book Review*, March 15, 1992, p. 8.

124.   Robert E. Park, "The Nature of Race Relations," in *Race Relations and the Race Problem*, ed. Edgar T. Thompson (Durham, N.C.: Duke University Press, 1939), p. 45.

125.   Kwame Anthony Appiah, *In My Father's House: Africa in the Philosophy of Culture* (New York: Oxford University Press, 1992), p. 143.

126.   Gian Biagio Conte, *The Rhetoric of Imitation: Genre and Poetic Memory in Virgil and Other Latin Poets*, trans. Charles Segal (Ithaca, N.Y.: Cornell University Press, 1986), pp. 23–24.

Chapter 8: Anhedonia

*This chapter expands on materials presented in Stanford M. Lyman, "From Matrimony to Malaise: Men and Women in the American Film, 1930–1980," *International Journal of Politics, Culture, and Society* 1:2 (winter 1987): pp. 73–100.

1.   Thus, in films it is possible to present the symbols of emotional expressions (facial gestures, body language, vocal tones); the frames and contexts of these expressions; the lexical, prosodic, kinesic, and proxemic emotion-communicative channels; the modal dynamics (redundancy-contradiction) of lexical and nonlexical sentiments; and the modes of deniability-ambiguity within and among these channels. Martin J. Malone, "Communicating Emotion: Toward an Adequate Theory of Emotional Expression," *Sociology of Emotions Newsletter* 3:2 (July 1988): pp. 4–5.

2.   Maurice Yacowar, *Loser Take All: The Comic Art of Woody Allen* (New York: Frederick Ungar, 1979), p. 184.

3.   See Ruth Roskies Wisse, *The Schlemiel as Modern Hero* (Chicago: University of Chicago Press, 1971). For a discussion of this work, see Stanford M. Lyman's review in *Worldview* 15:5 (May 1972): pp. 55–56.

4.   A. A. Brill, "The Adjustment of the Jew to the American Environment," *Mental Hygiene* 2 (April 1918): p. 220.

5.   Yacowar, *Loser Take All*, p. 151.

6.   Brill, "The Adjustment of the Jew," p. 219.

7.   Ibid., pp. 222–23.

8.   Max Weber, *The Sociology of Religion*, trans. Ephraim Fischoff (Boston: Beacon Press, 1963), pp. 167–68.

9.   See Lary May, *Screening Out the Past: The Birth of Mass Culture and the Motion Picture Industry* (New York: Oxford University Press, 1980), pp. 167–99.

10.   Mortimer J. Adler, *Art and Prudence* (New York: Longmans, 1937). Excerpted in Gerald Mast, ed., *The Movies in Our Midst: Documents in the Cultural History of Film in America* (Chicago: University of Chicago Press, 1982), pp. 365–79. Quotation from p. 374.

11.   Edward G. Robinson, "The Movies, The Actor, and the Public Morals," in William Perlman, ed., *The Movies on Trial* (New York: Macmillan, 1936). Reprinted in Mast, *The Movies in Our Midst*, pp. 379–83. Quotation from p. 383.

12.   The following is drawn from "Motion Pictures Production Code of 1930," as reprinted in Mast, The *Movies in Our Midst*, pp. 321–33.

13.   Talcott Parsons, *The Social System* (Glencoe, Ill.: Free Press, 1951), esp. pp. 182–91.

14.   Stanford M. Lyman, "Sin and Sentiment: Toward a Sociology of the Emotions," epilogue to idem, *The Seven Deadly Sins: Society and Evil*, rev. ed. (New York: General Hall, 1988), pp. 277–98.

15.   Parsons, The *Social System*, p. 59.

16.   See William Buxton, *Talcott Parsons and the Capitalist Nation-State* (Toronto: University of Toronto Press, 1984), pp. 76–116.

17.   Clayton R. Koppes and Gregory D. Black, *Hollywood Goes to War: How Politics, Profits and Propaganda Shaped World War II Movies* (New York: Free Press, 1987).

18.   See Philip Slater, "Social Limitations on Dyadic Withdrawal," *American Journal of Sociology* 67 (November 1961): pp. 296–311; and Stanford M. Lyman, *The Seven Deadly Sins: Society and Evil* (New York: St. Martin's Press, 1978), pp. 79–81.

19.   Koppes and Black, *Hollywood Goes to War*, p. 166.

20.   Kirk Douglas, *The Ragman's Son: An Autobiography* (New York: Simon and Schuster, 1988), p. 493.

21.   Citations in this paragraph are from Peter Biskind, *Seeing is Believing: How Hollywood Taught Us to Stop Worrying and Love the Fifties* (New York: Pantheon, 1983), p. 255–57.

22.   Michael Malone, *Heroes of Eros: Male Sexuality in the Movies* (New York: E. P. Dutton, 1979), p. 140.

23.   Douglas, *The Ragman's Son*, p. 268.

24.   See Malone, "Communicating Emotion," p. 140.

25.   Robert Sklar, "Red River—Empire to the West," *Cineaste* 9 (fall 1978): pp. 14–19. Quoted in Biskind, *Seeing is Believing*, p. 281.

26.   Sigmund Freud, *Civilization and Its Discontents*, trans. and ed. James Strachey (New York: W. W. Norton, 1962), p. 24.

27.   For a fine discussion of the absurdist setting and scenario of *Kiss Me Deadly*, see Jack Shadoian, *Dreams and Dead Ends: The American Gangster/Crime Film* (Cambridge, Mass.: MIT Press, 1977), pp. 265–84.

28.   See the discussion on which I have drawn in Donald Spoto, *Camerado: Hollywood and the American Man* (New York: New American Library, 1978), pp. 126–30.

29.   Quoted in Seth Cagin and Philip Dray, *Hollywood Films of the Seventies: Sex, Drugs, Violence, Rock 'N' Roll and Politics* (New York: Harper and Row, 1984), p. 257.

30.   Talcott Parsons and Robert F. Bales, *Family, Socialization and Interaction Process* (New York: Free Press, 1955), p. 16.

31.   Quoted in Mark Shechner, "Woody Allen: The Failure of the Therapeutic," in Sarah Blacher Cohen, ed., *From Street to Hollywood: The Jewish-American Stage and Screen* (Bloomington: Indiana University Press, 1983), p. 232.

Chapter 9: Without Morals or Mores

1.   Stephen Pfohl, *Images of Deviance and Social Control: A Sociological History*, 2d ed. (New York: McGraw-Hill, 1994), pp. 495–98.

2.   C. Wright Mills, *White Collar: The American Middle Classes* (New York: Oxford University Press, 1956), pp. 332–40.

3.   Pfohl, *Images of Deviance*, p. 495.

4.   See Norman K. Denzin, *Images of Postmodern Society: Social Theory and Contemporary Cinema* (London: Sage Publications, 1991), pp. 20–64.

5.   Pfohl, *Images of Deviance*, p. 510–11, n. 96.

6.   Marshall B. Clinard, *Sociology of Deviant Behavior*, 3d ed. (New York: Holt, Rinehart, and Winston 1968), p. 28.

7.   See Kai T. Erikson, "The Sociology of Deviance," in *Social Psychology Through Symbolic Interaction*, ed. Gregory P. Stone and Harvey A. Farberman (Waltham, Mass.: Ginn-Blaisdell, 1970), pp. 709–16. For a more forceful critique, see two works by Stanley Cohen, *Visions of Social Control: Crime, Punishment, and Classification* (New York: Basil Blackwell–Polity Press, 1985); and *Against Criminology* (New Brunswick, N.J.: Transaction Books, 1988).

8.   Clinard, *Sociology of Deviant Behavior*, p. 28.

9.   David P. Aday Jr., *Social Control at the Margins: Toward a General Understanding of Deviance* (Belmont, Calif.: Wadsworth Publishing Co., 1990), pp. 21–40.

10.   Ibid., pp. 99–225.

11.   Laud Humphreys, *Tearoom Trade: Impersonal Sex in Public Places*, enl. ed. (Chicago: Aldine Publishing Co., 1975).

12.   Aday, *Social Control at the Margins*, pp. 76–77, 89–91.

13.   Jack P. Gibbs, *Control: Sociology's Central Notion* (Urbana: University of Illinois Press, 1989), pp. 56–59.

14.   Talcott Parsons, *The Social System* (Glencoe, Ill.: Free Press, 1951), p. 321.

15.   Gibbs, *Control*, p. 56.

16.   Ibid., p. 57.

17.   Parsons, *The Social System*, p. 297.

18.   Gibbs, *Control*, p. 57.

19.   Parsons, *The Social System*, p. 260.

20.   Ibid., pp. 297–98.

21.   Henry Hughes, *A Treatise on Sociology, Theoretical and Practical* (Philadelphia: Lippincott and Grambo, 1854; reprint, New York: Negro Universities Press, 1968).

22.   Parsons, *The Social System,* pp. 251–83.

23.   Hughes, *A Treatise on Sociology,* pp. 195–97, 210–13. See the discussion of this and other facets of Hughes's sociology in Stanford M. Lyman, "Henry Hughes and the Southern Foundation of American Sociology," in idem, ed., *Selected Writings of Henry Hughes: Antebellum Southerner, Slavocrat, Sociologist* (Jackson: University Press of Mississippi, 1985), pp. 1–72, esp. pp. 21–26. See also Douglas Matthew Ambrose, *"The Man for Times Coming": The Life and Thought of Henry Hughes,* (Ann Arbor, Mich.: UMI Dissertation Services, 1993).

24.   Henry Hughes, "Reopening the Slave Trade: A Series by 'St. Henry'"; "State Liberties, or the Right to African Contract Labor"; "A Report on the African Apprentice System";and "Woman in Sociology," in Lyman, *Selected Writings of Henry Hughes,* pp. 73–143, 167–88.

25.   Talcott Parsons, *Societies: Evolutionary and Comparative Perspectives* (Englewood Cliffs, N.J.: Prentice-Hall, 1966), pp. 5–29.

26.   Hughes, *A Treatise on Sociology,* pp. 47–78.

27.   Parsons, *The Social System,* pp. 272–77.

28.   Ibid., pp. 520–31; and Talcott Parsons, *The System of Modern Societies* (Englewood Cliffs, N.J.: Prentice-Hall, 1971), pp. 122–37.

29.   Hughes, *A Treatise on Sociology,* pp. 173–206.

30.   William Graham Sumner, *Folkways: A Study of the Sociological Importance of Usages, Manners, Customs, Mores, and Morals* (Boston: Ginn and Co., 1940 [1906]), p. 86.

31.   Sumner, *Folkways,* pp. 85–86, 94, writes: "The New England Puritans, in the seventeenth century, tried to build a society on the Bible, especially the books of Moses. The attempt was in every way a failure . . . The Puritan code of early New England has been almost entirely abandoned . . . The mores of New England, however, still show deep traces of the Puritan temper and world philosophy . . . The mores of New England have extended to a large immigrant population and have won large control over them . . . The extravagances in doctrine and behavior of the seventeenth-century Puritans have been thrown off and their code of morals has been shorn of its angularity, but their life policy and standards have become to a very large extent those of the civilized world."

32.   Ibid., p. 77.

33.   Ibid., p. 110.

34.   Ibid., p. 90.

35.   Ibid.

36.   Ibid., p. 266.

37.   Ibid., p. 66.

38.   Ibid., p. 78.

39.   Ibid.

40.   David Lyon, *Postmodernity* (Minneapolis: University of Minnesota Press, 1994), p. 6.

41.   James Rendell, *The Origins of the Scottish Enlightenment, 1707–1776* (New York: St. Martin's Press, 1978), pp. 28–36; and Louis Schneider, ed., *The Scottish Moralists on Human Nature and Society* (Chicago: University of Chicago Press, 1967).

42.   Charles Camic, *Experience and Enlightenment: Socialization for Cultural Change in Eighteenth-Century Scotland* (Chicago: University of Chicago Press, 1983), pp. 45–125; Marvin B. Becker, *The Emergence of Civil Society in the Eighteenth Century: A*

Privileged Moment in the History of England, Scotland, and France (Bloomington: Indiana University Press, 1994).

43. David R. Dickens and Andrea Fontana, "Postmodernism in the Social Sciences, in idem, eds., *Postmodernism and Social Inquiry* (New York: Guilford Press, 1994), p. 3.

44. Gar Alperovitz and Kai Bird, "The Centrality of the Bomb," *Foreign Policy* 94 (spring 1994): pp. 3–20; Gar Alperovitz, "Hiroshima: Historians Reassess," *Foreign Policy* 99 (summer 1995): pp. 15–34; David Harvey, *The Condition of Postmodernity: An Enquiry into the Origins of Cultural Change* (Cambridge, Mass.: Basil Blackwell, 1989), p. 13; Jean Elshtain, John Rawls, Ronald Takaki, and Michael Walzer, "Fifty Years after Hiroshima: A Symposium," *Dissent* 3d quarter (summer 1995): pp. 321–32.

45. Alan Rosenberg and Gerald E. Myers., eds., *Echoes from the Holocaust: Philosophical Reflections on a Dark Time* (Philadelphia: Temple University Press, 1988); Martin Malia, *The Soviet Tragedy: A History of Socialism in Russia, 1917–1991* (New York: Free Press, 1994); Leo Kuper, *Genocide: Its Political Use in the Twentieth Century* (New Haven, Conn.: Yale University Press, 1982); Frank Chalk and Kurt Jonassohn, *The History and Sociology of Genocide: Analyses and Case Studies* (New Haven, Conn.: Yale University Press, 1990); Trinh T. Minh-Ha, *Woman, Native, Other: Writing Post Coloniality and Feminism* (Bloomington: Indiana University Press, 1989); Partha Chatterjee, *Nationalist Thought and the Colonial World: A Derivative Discourse* (Minneapolis: University of Minnesota Press, 1993); Michael Ignatieff, *Blood and Belonging: Journeys into the New Nationalism* (New York: Farrar, Straus and Giroux, 1993); Steven Seidman, *Embattled Eros: Sexual Politics and Ethics in Contemporary America* (New York: Routledge, 1992); Berch Barberoglu, "Class, Race and Gender: The Triangle of Oppression," *Race, Sex and Class* 2:1 (fall 1994): pp. 69–78.

46. Bill Readings and Bennet Schaber, eds., *Postmodernism across the Ages: Essays for a Postmodernism That Wasn't Born Yesterday* (Syracuse, N.Y.: Syracuse University Press, 1993), pp. 1–232.

47. Daniel Deudney and G. John Ikenberry, " After the Long War," *Foreign Policy* 94 (spring 1994): pp. 21–36. Quotation from p. 21.

48. Francis Fukuyama, *The End of History and the Last Man* (New York: Free Press, 1992), pp. 39–284.

49. Fred Dallmayr, "Foreword," in Dickens and Fontana, *Postmodernism and Social Inquiry,* p. ix.

50. See, e.g., Jean Belkhir, "The 'Failure' and Revival of Marxism on Race, Gender and Class Issues," *Race, Sex and Class* 2:1 (fall 1994): pp. 79–107; and Gayatri Chakravorty Spivak, "The Politics of Translation," in Michele Barrett and Anne Phillips, eds., *Destabilizing Theory: Contemporary Feminist Debates* (Stanford, Calif.: Stanford University Press, 1992), pp. 177–200.

51. Steven Seidman, *Romantic Longings: Love in America, 1830–1980* (New York: Routledge, 1990).

52. The critique of the idea of progress antedates postmodernism. See Frederick J. Teggart, ed., *The Idea of Progress: A Collection of Readings* (Berkeley: University of California Press, 1929); and two works by Robert A. Nisbet, *History of the Idea of Progress* (New York: Basic Books, 1980); and *The Making of Modern Society* (New York: New York University Press, 1986), pp. 33–112.

53. See, e.g., Etienne Balibar and Immanuel Wallerstein, *Race, Nation, Class:*

Ambiguous Identities, trans. Chris Turner (London: Verso, 1991); J. M. Blaut, *The Colonizer's Model of the World: Geographical Diffusionism and Eurocentric History* (New York: Guilford Press, 1993); Amy Kaplan and Donald E. Pease, eds., *Cultures of United States Imperialism* (Durham, N.C.: Duke University Press, 1993).

54.   Steven Seidman, *Contested Knowledge: Social Theory in the Postmodern Era* (Oxford: Blackwell, 1994), pp. 157–320.

55.   Steven Seidman, "The End of Sociological Theory: The Postmodern Hope," *Sociological Theory* 9:2 (fall 1991): pp. 131–46.

56.   Jacques Barzun, "The Cradle of Modernism," *The American Scholar* 59 (autumn 1990): pp. 519–27. Quotation from p. 519.

57.   See, e.g., Ki Namaste, "The Politics of Inside/Out: Queer Theory, Poststructuralism, and a Sociological Approach to Sexuality," *Sociological Theory* 12:2 (July 1994): pp. 220–31, esp. pp. 226–30.

58.   Erdwin H. Pfuhl Jr., *The Deviance Process,* 2d ed. (Belmont, Calif.: Wadsworth Publishing Co., 1986), pp. 93–156.

59.   See Piers Beirne, *Inventing Criminology: Essays on the Rise of 'Homo Criminalis'* (Albany: State University of New York Press, 1993); and two works by Cohen, *Visions of Social Control;* and *Against Criminology.*

60.   Pat Lauderdale, ed., *A Political Analysis of Deviance* (Minneapolis: University of Minnesota Press, 1980); and, in a slightly different vein, M. David Ermann and Richard J. Lundman, eds., *Corporate and Governmental Deviance: Problems of Organizational Behavior in Contemporary Society,* 4th ed. (New York: Oxford University Press, 1992).

61.   Peter Conrad and Joseph W. Schneider, *Deviance and Medicalization: From Badness to Sickness* (St. Louis, Mo.: C. V. Mosby, 1980).

62.   Pauline Marie Rosenau, *Post-Modernism and the Social Sciences: Insights, Inroads, and Intrusions* (Princeton, N.J.: Princeton University Press, 1992), pp. 42–44. See also Steven Best, "Foucault, Postmodernism, and Social Theory"; and David R. Dickens, "North American Theories of Postmodern Culture," in Dickens and Fontana, *Postmodernism and Social Inquiry,* pp. 25–52, 76–100.

63.   Rosenau, *Post-Modernism and the Social Sciences,* pp. 34–41. See also Norman K. Denzin, *Symbolic Interactionism and Cultural Studies: The Politics of Interpretation* (Oxford: Blackwell, 1992), pp. 46–94, 123–71.

64.   But see Best, "Foucault, Postmodernism, and Social Theory" pp. 43–44.

65.   Laud Humphreys, *Out of the Closets: The Sociology of Homosexual Liberation* (Englewood Cliffs, N.J. Prentice Hall–Spectrum, 1972), pp. 13–100.

66.   See, e.g., John D'Emilio, *Sexual Politics, Sexual Communities: The Making of a Homosexual Minority in the United States, 1940–1970* (Chicago: University of Chicago Press, 1983); and Toby Marotta, *The Politics of Homosexuality* (Boston: Houghton-Mifflin, 1981); Conrad and Schneider, *Deviance and Medicalization,* pp. 172–214; Martin Duberman, *Cures: A Gay Man's Odyssey* (New York: E. P. Dutton, 1991), pp. 93–115; Alan P. Bell, *Homosexualities: A Study of Diversity among Men and Women* (New York: Simon and Schuster–Touchstone, 1978), pp. 180–86; William B. Rubenstein, ed., *Lesbians, Gay Men, and the Law* (New York: New Press, 1993).

67.   Jürgen Habermas, "Struggles for Recognition in the Democratic Constitutional State," trans. Shierry Weber Nicholsen, in Amy Gutman, ed., *Multiculturalism: Examining the Politics of Recognition* (Princeton, N.J.: Princeton University Press, 1994), pp. 107–48, esp. pp. 110–22.

68.   Cf. Donald W. Ball, "The Problematics of Respectability," in Jack D. Douglas, ed., *Deviance and Respectability: The Social Construction of Moral Meanings* (New York: Basic Books, 1970), pp. 326–71; and Martin Duberman, *Stonewall* (New York: Plume, 1994), pp. 213–82.

69.   Steven Seidman, "Postmodern Anxiety: The Politics of Epistemology," *Sociological Theory* 9:2 (fall 1991): pp. 180–90.

70.   Steven Epstein, "A Queer Encounter: Sociology and the Study of Sexuality," *Sociological Theory* 12:2 (July 1994): pp. 188–202.

71.   Janice M. Irvine, "A Place in the Rainbow: Theorizing Lesbian and Gay Culture," *Sociological Theory* 12:2 (July 1994): pp. 232–48. Quotation from p. 233.

72.   Quotes in this paragraph are from Ellen Herman, *The Romance of American Psychology: Political Culture in the Age of Experts* (Berkeley: University of California Press, 1995), pp. 108–9.

73.   Joseph Gusfield, *The Culture of Public Problems: Drunk-Driving and the Symbolic Order* (Chicago: University of Chicago Press, 1981), p. 10.

74.   This and remaining citations in this paragraph are from Boyce Rensenberger, "Psychiatry Reconsiders Stand on Homosexuals," *New York Times,* Feb. 9, 1973, p. 24. Emphasis supplied.

75.   T. W. Adorno, Else Frenkel-Brunswick, Daniel J. Levinson, and R. Nevitt Sanford, in collaboration with Betty Aron, Maria Hertz Levinson, and William Morrow, *The Authoritarian Personality* (New York: Harper and Row, 1950).

76.   Daniel J. Levinson, "Ethnocentrism in Relation to Intelligence and Education," in ibid., p. 316.

77.   Ibid.

78.   R. Nevitt Sanford, "Genetic Aspects of the Authoritarian Personality: Case Studies of Two Contrasting Individuals," in *The Authoritarian Personality,* pp. 787–816.

79.   Ibid. p. 798.

80.   Else Frenkel-Brunswick, "Dynamic and Cognitive Personality Organization as Seen Through the Interviews," in *The Authoritarian Personality,* p. 442.

81.   Levinson, "Ethnocentrism," p. 317.

82.   Jonas Robitscher, *The Powers of Psychiatry* (Boston: Houghton-Mifflin, 1980), pp. 151–52. Quoted in Anthony Storr, *Human Destructiveness* (New York: Grove Weidenfeld, 1991), p. 59.

83.   Storr, *Human Destructiveness,* p. 120.

84.   Seidman, *Contested Knowledge,* p. 119.

85.   See Stanford M. Lyman, *The Seven Deadly Sins: Society and Evil,* rev. ed. (Dix Hills, N.Y.: General Hall, 1989), pp. 277–98.

86.   See two works by Talcott Parsons, "The Symbolic Environment of Modern Economies," *Social Research* 46:3 (autumn 1979): pp. 436–53; and "The Marshall Lectures—The Integration of Economic and Sociological Theory," *Sociological Inquiry* 61:1 (winter 1991): pp. 10–59.

87.   See two works by Max Weber, *The Protestant Ethic and the Spirit of Capitalism,* trans. Talcott Parsons (New York: Charles Scribner's Sons, 1930); and *The Sociology of Religion,* trans. Ephraim Fischoff, introduction by Talcott Parsons (Boston: Beacon Press, 1963), esp. pp. 236–45.

88.   Parsons, *The Social System,* pp. 189, 221.

89.   Howard S. Becker, *Outsiders: Studies in the Sociology of Deviance* (London: Free Press of Glencoe, 1963), p. 34.

90.   Gresham M. Sykes and David Matza, "Techniques of Neutralization: A Theory of Delinquency," *American Sociological Review* 22 (December 1957): pp. 664–70. Quotation from p. 262 of the reprint of this essay in Ronald A. Farrell and Victoria Lynn Swigert, eds., *Social Deviance* (Philadelphia: J. B. Lippincott, 1975), pp. 255–65.

91.   Robert J. Gibbins and Richard H. Walters, "Three Preliminary Studies of a Psychoanalytic Theory of Alcohol Addiction," *Quarterly Journal of Studies on Alcohol* 21 (December 1960): pp. 618–41.

92.   Abram Kardiner, M.D., and Lionel Ovesey, M.D., *The Mark of Oppression: Explorations in the Personality of the American Negro* (Cleveland: World Publishing Co. 1951), pp. 179–90.

93.   Hervey Cleckley, "The Homosexual's Temptations and Opportunities," in William Petersen and David Matza, eds., *Social Controversy* (Belmont: Wadsworth Publishing Co., 1963), pp. 145–54. Quotation from p. 145.

94.   Ronald A. Farrell and Thomas J. Morrione, "Conforming to Deviance," in Farrell and Swigert, eds., *Social Deviance,* pp. 375–87. Quotation from p. 376.

95.   Albert J. Reiss, Jr., "The Social Integration of Peers and Queers," *Social Problems* 9 (fall 1961): pp. 102–20.

96.   Becker, *Outsiders,* pp. 167–68.

97.   Ibid., p. 163.

98.   Edwin M. Lemert, *Human Deviance, Social Problems, and Social Controls* (Englewood Cliffs, N.J.: Prentice-Hall, 1967), p. 25.

99.   Ibid., pp. 197–211.

100.   Stanford M. Lyman and Marvin B. Scott, *A Sociology of the Absurd,* 2d ed. (Dix Hills, N.Y.: General Hall, 1989), pp. 98–110.

101.   Thomas J. Scheff and Suzanne M. Retzinger, *Emotions and Violence: Shame and Rage in Destructive Conflicts* (Lexington, Mass.: D. C. Heath, Lexington Books, 1991), p. 103. Emphasis in original.

102.   Erving Goffman, *Stigma: Notes on the Management of Spoiled Identity* (Englewood Cliffs, N.J.: Prentice-Hall, 1963), pp. 143–44, n. 7. Quotation from p. 143.

103.   For empirical studies of such communities, see David A. Ward and Gene G. Kassebaum, "The Dynamics of Prison Homosexuality: The Character of the Love Affair," in Jack D. Douglas, ed., *Observations of Deviance* (New York: Random House, 1970), pp. 89–106.

104.   Goffman, *Stigma,* pp. 143–44, n. 7.

105.   Clinard, *Sociology of Deviant Behavior,* p. 353.

106.   Parsons, *The Social System,* pp. 231–33.

107.   Clinard, *Sociology of Deviant Behavior,* p. 356.

108.   Michael Schofield, *Sociological Aspects of Homosexuality: A Comparative Study of Three Types of Homosexuals* (Boston: Little, Brown and Co., 1965), p. 211. Quoted in Clinard, *Sociology of Deviant Behavior,* p. 356.

109.   Clinard, *Sociology of Deviant Behavior,* p. 357.

110.   Becker, *Outsiders,* pp. 147–64.

111.   See, e.g., Virginia Teas Gill and Douglas W. Maynard, "On 'Labeling' in Actual Interaction: Delivering and Receiving Diagnoses of Developmental Disabilities," *Social Problems* 42:1 (February 1995): pp. 11–37.

112.   Lemert, *Human Deviance*, p. 60.

113.   This and the remaining citations in this paragraph are from Alfred R. Lindesmith, Anselm L. Strauss, and Norman K. Denzin, *Social Psychology*, 4th ed. (Hinsdale, Ill.: Dryden Press, 1975), pp. 534–36.

114.   Carol A. B. Warren and John M. Johnson, "A Critique of Labeling Theory From the Phenomenological Perspective," in Robert A. Scott and Jack D. Douglas, eds., *Theoretical Perspectives on Deviance* (New York: Basic Books, 1972), pp. 69–92.

115.   In fact, Lemert, *Human Deviance*, p. 8, had written quite the opposite: "Merton's theory [of deviance] . . . deals with populations presumed to have been socialized within a common cultural tradition. However, when attention is shifted to a contemporary, urban, secular, technologically based society such as our own, the notion such a society has a common value hierarchy, either culturally transmitted or structurally induced, strains credulity."

116.   Warren and Johnson, "A Critique of Labeling Theory," p. 73.

117.   Ibid.

118.   Lemert, *Human Deviance*, pp. 17–18.

119.   Warren and Johnson, "A Critique of Labeling Theory," p. 74.

120.   Cf. Carol A. B. Warren, *Identity and Community in the Gay World* (New York: Wiley Interscience, 1974).

121.   Donald Webster Cory, *The Homosexual in America* (New York: Greenberg, 1951), p. 9. Warren and Johnson, "A Critique of Labeling Theory," p. 74, state that Donald Webster Cory is "a pseudonym for a psychiatrist-author." It is now known that Cory revealed himself as Edward Sagarin, a founder of the Mattachine Society, who held to the belief that homosexuality is an illness curable by therapy. When, in 1956, the medical model of homosexuality was rejected by the chapter to which he belonged, Cory dropped his pseudonym, withdrew from the organization, and in 1966, under the name Edward Sagarin, submitted a doctoral dissertation, *Structure and Ideology in an Association of Deviants,* to New York University. Sagarin served thereafter as a professor of sociology, with special interest in deviance theory. For an appreciation of *The Homosexual in America,* see Marotta, *The Politics of Homosexuality,* pp. 4–21, 330; and D'Emilio, *Sexual Politics,* pp. 167–69.

122.   Warren and Johnson, "A Critique of Labeling Theory," p. 74. Emphasis in original.

123.   Ibid.

124.   Evelyn Hooker, "The Homosexual Community," in Douglas, *Observations of Deviance,* pp. 115–27. Quotation from p. 127.

125.   See Lynn Hunt, "Introduction: Obscenity and the Origins of Modernity, 1500–1800," in idem, ed., *The Invention of Pornography: Obscenity and the Origins of Modernity, 1500–1800* (New York: Zone Books, 1993), pp. 9–45.

126.   See Madan Sarup, *An Introductory Guide to Post-Structuralism and Postmodernism* (Athens: University of Georgia Press, 1989), pp. 130, 167.

127.   Homi K. Bhabha, "The Other Question: Difference, Discrimination and the Discourse of Colonialism," in Russell Ferguson, Martha Gever, Trinh T. Minh-ha, and Cornel West, eds., *Out There: Marginalization and Contemporary Culture* (Cambridge, Mass.: MIT Press, 1990), pp. 71–88. Quotation from p. 75.

128.   However, among such ethnoracial minorities as Asian Americans, the turn toward valorizing hitherto unmentionable sexual preferences has opened up a painful

discussion of identity and of essentialist discourse. See Dana Y. Takagi, "Maiden Voyage: Excursion into Sexuality and Identity Politics in Asian America," *Amerasia Journal* 20:1 (1994): pp. 1–17. For sex-role inversion and drama and its consequences in Japan, see Jennifer Robertson, "Doing and Undoing 'Female' and 'Male' in Japan: The Takarazuka Revue," in Takie Sugiyama Lebra, ed., *Japanese Social Organization* (Honolulu: University of Hawaii Press, 1992), pp. 165–93. For an analysis of homoerotic feelings among Japanese, see Takeo Doi, *The Anatomy of Dependence,* trans. John Bester (Tokyo: Kodansha International, 1973), pp. 113–21.

129.   Monique Wittig, "The Straight Mind," in Ferguson et al., Out *There,* pp. 51–57. Quotation from p. 55.

130.   Margaret Mary Wood, *The Stranger: A Study in Social Relationships* (New York: Columbia University Press, 1934; reprint, New York: AMS Press, 1969), p. 266.

131.   Wittig, "The Straight Mind," p. 55.

132.   Ibid., p. 54.

133.   Ibid.

134.   Peter McLaren, "White Terror and Oppositional Agency: Towards a Critical Multiculturalism," in David Theo Goldberg, ed., *Multiculturalism: A Critical Reader* (Oxford: Blackwell, 1994), pp. 45–74. Quotation from p. 58.

135.   Michel Foucault, *The History of Sexuality,* vol. 1: *An Introduction,* vol. 2 *The Use of Pleasure,* and vol. 3 *The Care of the Self,* trans. Robert Hurley (New York: Pantheon Books, 1978, 1985,1986); *Power/Knowledge: Selected Interviews and Other Writings,* trans. Colin Gordon, Leo Marshall, John Mepham, and Kate Soper, ed. Colin Gordon, (New York: Pantheon Books, 1980), pp. 166–228.

136.   Sarup, *Post-Structuralism and Postmodernism,* p. 80.

137.   *Bowers v. Hardwick* 478 U.S. 186 (1986). Reprinted in Rubenstein, *Lesbians, Gay Men, and the Law,* pp. 132–48. See also the interesting discussion of this case in the context of the anomalous history of attempts to define and regulate sodomy in Jonathan Goldberg, *Sodometries: Renaissance Texts, Modern Sexualities* (Stanford, Calif: Stanford University Press, 1992), pp. 1–28.

138.   Celia Kitzinger, "Liberal Humanism as an Ideology of Social Control: The Regulation of Lesbian Identities," in John Shotter and Kenneth J. Gergen, eds., *Texts of Identity* (London: Sage Publications, 1989), pp. 82–98. Quotation from p. 92.

139.   Ibid., p. 95.

140.   Guy Hocquenghem, *Homosexual Desire,* trans. Daniella Dangoor (Durham, N.C.: Duke University Press, 1993 [1972]), pp. 136, 137, 138.

141.   Steve Seidman, "Symposium: Queer Theory/Sociology: A Dialogue," *Sociological Theory* 12:2 (July 1994): pp. 166–77.

142.   Seidman, "Postmodern Anxiety," pp. 180–90, esp. pp. 180–81.

143.   Steven Seidman, "The End of Sociological Theory," pp. 131–46.

144.   Iain Chambers, *Migrancy, Culture, Identity* (London: Routledge, 1994): pp. 98, 100.

145.   Seidman, "Postmodern Anxiety," p. 181.

146.   Donna Haraway, "A Manifesto for Cyborgs: Science, Technology, and Socialist Feminism in the 1980s," in Steven Seidman, ed., *The Postmodern Turn: New Perspectives on Social Theory* (Cambridge, U.K.: Cambridge University Press, 1994): pp. 82–115. Quotation from p. 91.

147.   Ibid.

148.   Cornel West, "The New Cultural Politics of Difference," in Seidman, *The Postmodern Turn*, pp. 65–81.

149.   Troy Thomas, "Know Thy Enemy, Know Thyself," in the "Your Letters" column, *Asian Week: The English Language Journal for the National Asian American Community* 16:45 (July 7, 1995): p. 3.

150.   Georg Simmel, *The Conflict in Modern Culture and Other Essays*, trans. K. Peter Etzkorn (New York: Teachers College Press, 1968), pp. 11–46.

151.   Ibid., p. 22.

152.   Arlene Stein and Ken Plummer, "'I Can't Even Think Straight': 'Queer' Theory and the Missing Sexual Revolution in Sociology," *Sociological Theory* 12:2 (July 1994): pp. 178–87. Quotation from p. 182.

153.   For a recent example of both models, see Robert J. Stoller, M.D., *Presentations of Gender* (New Haven, Conn.: Yale University Press, 1985).

154.   See Malcolm Spector and John I. Kitsuse, *Constructing Social Problems* (New York: Aldine de Gruyter, 1987), pp. 1–23.

155.   Teresa de Lauretis, "Queer Theory: Lesbian and Gay Sexualities," *Differences* 3 (1991): pp. iii–xviii. Quoted in part in Stein and Plummer, "'I Can't Even Think Straight,'" p. 182.

156.   See two works by Jonathan Ned Katz, "The Invention of Heterosexuality," *Socialist Review* 20:1 (January–March 1990): pp. 7–34; and *The Invention of Heterosexuality* (New York: E.P. Dutton, 1995).

157.   On the yin/yang dichotomy in Chinese conceptions of homosexuality, insanity, and cannibalism, see Bret Hinsch, *Passions of the Cut Sleeve: The Male Homosexual Tradition in China* (Berkeley: University of California Press, 1990), esp. pp. 90–93; Vivien W. Ng, *Madness in Late Imperial China: From Illness to Deviance* (Norman: University of Oklahoma Press, 1990), pp. 25–89; and Key Ray Chong, *Cannibalism in China* (Wakefield, N.H.: Longwood Academic–Hollowbrook Communications, Inc., 1990), pp. 43–144.

158.   Simmel, *The Conflict in Modern Culture*, pp. 12–13.

159.   Citations in this section are from Steven Seidman, "Introduction" in idem, *The Postmodern Turn*, pp. 4–8.

160.   Ibid. pp.1–2.

161.   Eve Kosofsky Sedgwick, *The Epistemology of the Closet* (Berkeley: University of California Press, 1990), p. 1. Quoted in Seidman, *Contested Knowledge*, p. 272.

162.   Seidman, "Introduction," in idem, *The Postmodern Turn*, p. 13–14.

163.   Stein and Plummer, "'I Can't Even Think Straight,'" pp. 185–86.

164.   Chrys Ingraham, "The Heterosexual Imaginary: Feminist Sociology and Theories of Gender," *Sociological Theory* 12:2 (July 1994): pp. 203–19. Quotations from p. 216.

165.   Indeed, Stein and Plummer, "'I Can't Even Think Straight,'" pp. 180, 184, while deploring the fact that most of the sociological "studies of lesbian/gay life . . . are almost exclusively within the areas of deviance, gender, or sexuality, and have barely made their mark on the discipline as a whole," worry that Queer Theory might be too academic: "There is a dangerous tendency for the new queer theorists to ignore 'real' queer life as it is materially experienced across the world, while they play with the free-floating signifiers of texts."

166.   See two works by Arthur J. Vidich and Stanford M. Lyman, *American*

Sociology: Worldly Rejections of Religion and Their Directions (New Haven, Conn.: Yale University Press, 1985); and "State, Ethics, and Public Morality in American Sociological Thought," in Mark L. Wardell and Stephen P. Turner, eds., *Sociological Theory in Transition* (Boston: Allen and Unwin, 1986), pp. 44–58. See also Cecil E. Greek, *The Religious Roots of American Sociology* (New York: Garland Publishing Co., 1992); and William Burger, *American Crime and Punishment: The Religious Origins of American Criminology* (Buchanan, Mich.: Vande Vere Publishing, 1993).

167.   Stanford M. Lyman, "Social Theory and Social Movements: Sociology as Sociodicy," in idem, ed., *Social Movements: Critiques, Concepts, Case-Studies* (New York: New York University Press, 1995), pp. 397–435. Quotation from p. 416.

168.   Cf. Peter Lassman, "Sociological Theory and Politics," in Wardell and Turner, eds., Sociological *Theory,* pp. 59–68, esp. pp. 60–66.

169.   Alan F. Blum, "Sociology, Wrongdoing, and Akrasia: An Attempt to Think Greek about the Problem of Theory and Practice," in Scott and Douglas, eds., *Theoretical Perspectives on Deviance,* pp. 342–62. Quotation from p. 356.

170.   Ibid.

171.   Ibid., p. 342.

172.   Simmel, *The Conflict in Modern Culture,* p. 25.

173.   Steven Best, "Foucault, Postmodernism, and Social Theory," in Dickens and Fontana, *Postmodernism and Social Inquiry,* pp. 25–52. Quotation from p. 29.

174.   Seidman, "Queer Theory/Sociology," op. cit. p. 174.

175.   Seidman, *Embattled Eros,* p. 8.

176.   Seidman, "Queer Theory/Sociology," p. 174.

177.   Seidman, *Embattled Eros,* p. 214.

178.   Barbara L. Marshall, *Engendering Modernity: Feminism, Social Theory and Social Change* (Boston: Northeastern University Press, 1994), p. 157.

179.   This and remaining citations in this section are from Guy Oakes, "Straight Thinking about Queer Theory," *International Journal of Politics, Culture and Society* 8:3 (spring 1995): pp. 379–88.

180.   For further aspects of the relationship of Simmel's thought to postmodernism, see Deena Weinstein and Michael A. Weinstein, *Postmodern(ized) Simmel* (London: Routledge, 1993).

181.   K. Anthony Appiah, "Identity, Authenticity, Survival: Multicultural Societies and Social Reproduction," in Amy Gutman, ed., *Multiculturalism: Examining the Politics of Recognition* (Princeton, N.J.: Princeton University Press, 1994), pp. 149–64. Quotations from p. 162.

182.   Maurice Natanson, "History as a Finite Province of Meaning," in idem, *Literature, Philosophy and the Social Sciences: Essays in Existentialism and Phenomenology* (The Hague, Netherlands: Martinus Nijhoff, 1968), pp. 172–177.

183.   Jean-Francois Lyotard, "The Postmodern Condition," in Seidman, *The Postmodern Turn,* pp. 27–38.

184.   Steven Seidman, "Postmodern Social Theory as Narrative with a Moral Intent," in Steven Seidman and David G. Wagner, eds., *Postmodernism and Social Theory: The Debate Over General Theory* (Cambridge, Mass.: Basil Blackwell, 1992), pp. 47–81, esp. pp. 70–73.

185.   Natanson, "History as a Finite Province," p. 172.

186. Alvin Gouldner, *The Coming Crisis of Western Sociology* (New York: Basic Books, 1970), p. 206.

187. Rom Harré, *Social Being: A Theory for Social Psychology* (Totowa, N.J.: Rowman and Littlefield, 1980): p. 136.

188. Cf. Natanson, "History as a Finite Province," p. 176.

189. Cf. Seidman, "The End of Sociological Theory," pp. 131–46, esp. pp. 139–41.

190. Gail Dines, "What's Left of Multiculturalism? Race, Class, and Gender in the Classroom," *Race, Sex and Class* 1:2 (spring 1994): pp. 23–34. Quotation from p. 24.

191. In light of the many ambiguities raised by Shakespeare's drama, Gilligan's interpretation (Carol Gilligan, *In a Different Voice: Psychological Theory and Women's Development* [Cambridge, Mass.: Harvard University Press, 1982, p. 105) is remarkable in missing the anti-Jewish elements involved: "[D]ramatized explicitly as a contrast between the sexes in *The Merchant of Venice*, . . . Shakespeare goes through an extraordinary complication of sexual identity, dressing a male actor as a female character who, in turn, poses as a male judge, in order to bring into the masculine citadel of justice the feminine plea for mercy. The limitation of the contractual conception of justice is illustrated through the absurdity of its literal execution, while the need to 'make exceptions all the time' is demonstrated contrapuntally in the matter of the rings. Portia, in calling for mercy, argues for that resolution in which no one is hurt, and as the men are forgiven for their failure to keep both their rings and their word, Antonio in turn forgoes his 'right' to ruin Shylock." For more considered analyses, see Benjamin Nelson, *The Idea of Usury: From Tribal Brotherhood to Universal Otherhood*, 2d ed. (Chicago: University of Chicago Press, 1969), pp. 73–165; Joseph Shatzmiller, *Shylock Reconsidered: Jews, Moneylending and Medieval Society* (Berkeley: University of California Press, 1990); John Gross, *Shylock: A Legend and Its Legacy* (New York: Simon and Schuster, 1992), esp. pp. 94–101, 122–24; and Guy Oakes, "The Problem of Women in Simmel's Theory of Culture," in idem, trans. and ed., *Georg Simmel: On Women, Sexuality, and Love* (New Haven, Conn.: Yale University Press, 1984), pp. 3–62, esp. pp. 50–55.

192. Gilligan, *In a Different Voice*, p. 104.

193. Ibid., p. 174.

194. Charles Richmond Henderson, *An Introduction to the Study of the Dependent, Defective, and Delinquent Classes* (Boston: D. C. Heath and Co., 1893).

195. Jack D. Douglas and Frances C. Waksler, *The Sociology of Deviance: An Introduction* (Boston: Little, Brown and Co., 1982), p. 8.

196. See Charles T. Holman, *The Cure of Souls: A Socio-Psychological Approach* (Chicago: University of Chicago Press, 1932), pp. 65–320.

197. See, e.g., Craig B. Little, *Deviance and Control: Theory, Research, and Social Policy* (Itasca, Ill.: F. E. Peacock Publishers, 1989).

198. Albert K. Cohen, *Deviance and Control* (Englewood Cliffs, N.J.: Prentice-Hall, 1966), p. 1.

199. Ibid., p. 13.

200. For a discussion of excuses and justifications, and their relationship to exculpatory discourses, Lyman and Scott, *A Sociology of the Absurd*, pp. 112–55.

201. Cohen, *Deviance and Control*, pp. 41–106.

202. Little, *Deviance and Control*, pp. 67–95.

203. This and the remaining citations in this section are from Seidman, *Embattled Eros*, pp. 195–207.

204.   Eugene Halton, *Bereft of Reason: On the Decline of Social Thought and Prospects for Its Renewal* (Chicago: University of Chicago Press, 1995), p. 264.

205.   John O'Neill, *The Poverty of Postmodernism* (London: Routledge, 1995), p. 195.

206.   John M. Johnson, "In Dispraise of Justice," *Symbolic Interaction* 18:2 (summer 1995): pp. 191–205. Quotation from p. 199.

207.   See the quite different view of the matter in Norman K. Denzin, *Symbolic Interactionism and Cultural Studies: The Politics of Interpretation* (Cambridge, Mass.: Basil Blackwell, 1992), pp. 164–69.

208.   See Stanford M. Lyman, "Race Relations as Social Process: Sociology's Resistance to a Civil Rights Orientation" in Herbert Hill and James E. Jones Jr., eds., *Race in America: The Struggle for Equality* (Madison: University of Wisconsin Press, 1993), pp. 370–401.

209.   Ibid., p. 397.

210.   See Joseph Tussman and Jacobus tenBroek, "The Equal Protection of the Laws," *California Law Review* 37 (September 1949): pp. 341–81. For a synthesis of this jurisprudential approach with that of symbolic interaction, see Stanford M. Lyman and Arthur J. Vidich, *Social Order and the Public Philosophy: An Analysis and Interpretation of the Work of Herbert Blumer* (Fayetteville: University of Arkansas Press, 1988), pp. 76–91.

Chapter 10: The Bequests of Twentieth-Century Sociology to the Twenty-first Century

1.   William Graham Sumner, "The Bequests of the Nineteenth Century to the Twentieth," *The Yale Review* 22 (summer 1933): pp. 732–54. Reprinted in *Essays of William Graham Sumner*, vol. 1, ed. Albert Galloway Keller and Maurice R. Davie (Hamden, Conn.: Archon Books, 1969), pp. 208–35.

2.   Ibid., pp. 208–9.

3.   See Stanford M. Lyman, "Henry Hughes and the Southern Foundations of American Sociology," in idem, ed., *Selected Writings of Henry Hughes: Antebellum Southerner, Slavocrat, Sociologist* (Jackson: University Press of Mississippi, 1985), pp. 1–72; Arthur J. Vidich and Stanford M. Lyman, *American Sociology: Worldly Rejections of Religion and Their Directions* (New Haven, Conn.: Yale University Press, 1985), pp. 9–19; and Stanford M. Lyman, "System and Function in Antebellum Southern Sociology" in idem, *Civilization: Contents, Discontents, Malcontents and Other Essays in Social Theory* (Fayetteville: University of Arkansas Press, 1990), pp. 191–201.

4.   See Roscoe C. Hinkle, *Founding Theory of American Sociology, 1881–1915* (Boston: Routledge and Kegan Paul, 1980), pp. 44–45; and Charles Page, *Class and American Sociology: From Ward to Ross* (New York: Schocken Books, 1969), pp. 73–112.

5.   Howard W. Odum, *American Sociology: The Story of Sociology in the United States through 1950* (New York: Greenwood Press, 1969), pp. 28–29; and Paul Buck, *Social Sciences at Harvard, 1860–1920* (Cambridge, Mass.: Harvard University Press, 1965), pp. 18–90.

6.   Vidich and Lyman, *American Sociology*, pp. 53–208; Cecil E. Greek, *The Religious Roots of American Sociology* (New York: Garland Publishing Co., 1992), pp.

21–192; and William Burger, *American Crime and Punishment: The Religious Origins of American Criminology* (Buchanan, Mich.: Vande Vere Publishing, 1993).

7.   Vidich and Lyman, *American Sociology*, pp. 281–309.

8.   Albion W. Small, "Fifty Years of Sociology in the United States (1865–1915)," *American Journal of Sociology* 21:6 (May 1916): pp. 721–864.

9.   Sumner, "The Bequest," pp. 208–9.

10. Alvin W. Gouldner, *The Coming Crisis of Western Sociology* (New York: Basic Books, 1970); Diana Crane and Henry Small, "American Sociology Since the Seventies: The Emerging Identity Crisis in the Discipline," in *Sociology and Its Publics: The Forms and Fates of Disciplinary Organization*, ed. Terence C. Halliday and Morris Janowitz (Chicago: University of Chicago Press, 1992), pp. 197–234; and Nicholas C. Mullins, "Sociology in America," in *What Has Sociology Achieved?*, ed. Christopher G. A. Bryant and Henk A. Becker (New York: St. Martin's Press, 1990), pp. 143–56.

11. Ted R. Vaughan, "The Crisis in Contemporary American Sociology: A Critique of the Discipline's Dominant Paradigm," in *A Critique of Contemporary American Sociology*, ed. Ted R. Vaughan, Gideon Sjoberg, and Larry J. Reynolds (Dix Hills, N.Y.: General Hall, 1993), pp. 10–52; and Niklas Luhmann, "General Theory and American Sociology," in *Sociology in America*, ed. Herbert J. Gans (Newbury Park, Calif.: Sage Publications, 1990), pp. 253–64.

12. Stanford M. Lyman, "The Rise and Decline of the Functionalist–Positivist Paradigm: A Chapter in the History of American Sociology," *Hyoron Shakaikagaku: Doshisha University Social Science Review* 20 (March 1982): pp. 4–29; and Roscoe C. Hinkle, *Developments in Sociological Theory, 1915–1950* (Albany: State University of New York Press, 1994), pp. 322–47.

13. Arthur J. Vidich, Stanford M. Lyman, and Jeffrey C. Goldfarb, "Sociology and Society: Disciplinary Tensions and Professional Compromises," *Social Research* 48:2 (summer 1981): pp. 322–61.

14. Terence C. Halliday, "Introduction: Sociology's Fragile Professionalism," in Halliday and Janowitz, eds., *Sociology and Its Publics*, pp. 3–42.

15. William V. D'Antonio, "Recruiting Sociologists in a Time of Changing Opportunities," in Halliday and Janowitz, eds., *Sociology and Its Publics*, pp. 99–136.

16. Ibid., pp. 269–88.

17. Gans, *Sociology in America*, pp. 11–18, 75–155, 169–87, 214–38, 314–33.

18. Vaughan, Sjoberg, and Reynolds, *Contemporary American Sociology*, pp. 54–251.

19. Andrew Travers, "Destigmatizing the Stigma of Self in Garfinkel's and Goffman's Accounts of Normal Appearances," *Philosophy of the Social Sciences* 24:1 (March 1994): pp. 5–40.

20. Ibid., p. 6.

21. Richard Rorty, *Philosophy and the Mirror of Nature* (Princeton, N.J.: Princeton University Press, 1979).

22. Ibid., p. 157.

23. Ibid., p. 318.

24. George Simpson, *Auguste Comte: Sire of Sociology* (New York: Thomas Y. Crowell, 1969), pp. 31–35, 42–46, 87–114; and Gertrud Lenzer, ed., *Auguste Comte and Positivism: The Essential Writings* (New York: Harper Torchbooks, 1975), pp. liii–lv, 39–49, 279–97, 424–27.

25.   Kenneth E. Bock, "The Comparative Method" (Ph.D. diss., University of California, Berkeley, 1948), p. 11–36; and Robert A. Nisbet, *Social Change and History: Aspects of the Western Theory of Development* (New York: Oxford University Press, 1969), pp. 189–208.

26.   Frederick J. Teggart, *Theory of History* (New Haven, Conn.: Yale University Press, 1925), pp. 71–152; Nisbet, *Social Change and History,* pp. 137–88, 209–304; and Hinkle, *Developments in Sociological Theory,* pp. 65–199.

27.   Robert A. Nisbet, *The Making of Modern Society* (New York: New York University Press, 1986), pp. 33–69; and Piotr Sztompka, *The Sociology of Social Change* (Cambridge, Mass.: Basil Blackwell, 1994).

28.   See three works by Kenneth E. Bock: "The Acceptance of Histories: Toward a Perspective for Social Science," *University of California Publications in Sociology and Social Institutions,* vol. 3, ed. Reinhard Bendix, Wolfram Eberhard, and Philip Selznick (Berkeley: University of California Press, 1956), pp. 43–107; *Human Nature and History: A Response to Sociobiology* (New York: Columbia University Press, 1980), pp. 41–46, 123–98; and *Human Nature Mythology* (Urbana: University of Illinois Press, 1994), pp. 1–10, 45–60, 80–100.

29.   Lyman, *Civilization,* pp. 76–126.

30.   Ibid., pp. 46–75.

31.   Stanford M. Lyman, "Stewart Culin and the Debate over Trans-Pacific Migration," *Journal for the Theory of Social Behaviour* 9 (March 1979): pp. 91–115.

32.   Mircea Eliade, *The Myth of the Eternal Return,* trans. Willard Trask (New York: Random House–Pantheon Books, 1954).

33.   Richard Popkin, "Bible Criticism and Social Science," in *Methodological and Historical Essays in the Natural and Social Sciences: Boston Studies in the Philosophy of Science,* vol. 14. ed. Robert S. Cohen and Marx W. Wartofsky (Dordrecht, Netherlands: D. Reidel Publishing Co., 1974), pp. 339–60.

34.   Lyman, *Civilization,* pp. 22–75.

35.   Stanford M. Lyman, *Color, Culture, Civilization: Race and Minority Issues in American Society* (Urbana: University of Illinois Press, 1994), pp. 1–42.

36.   See four essays by Stanford M. Lyman: "The Race Question and Liberalism: Casuistries in American Constitutional Law," *International Journal of Politics, Culture, and Society* 2 (winter 1991): pp. 183–247; "Marginalizing the Self: A Study of Citizenship, Color, and Ethnoracial Identity in American Society," *Symbolic Interaction* 16:4 (winter 1993): pp. 379–93; "The Chinese before the Courts: Ethnoracial Construction and Marginalization," *International Journal of Politics, Culture, and Society* 6:3 (spring 1993): pp. 443–62; and "Chinese Seeking Justice in the Courts of the United States: A Constitutional Interpretation," in *Origins and Destinations: 41 Essays on Chinese America,* ed. Munson Kwok et al. (Los Angeles: Chinese Historical Society of Southern California and UCLA Asian American Studies Center, 1994), pp. 41–69.

37.   *People v. Hall,* 4 Cal. 399 (October 1854).

38.   See Stephen Steinberg, *The Ethnic Myth: Race, Ethnicity, and Class in America* (New York: Atheneum, 1981), pp. 82–105.

39.   Betty Lee Sung, *The Story of the Chinese in America* (New York: Collier Books, 1971).

40.   Stanford M. Lyman, "Review of Betty Lee Sung, *The Story of the Chinese in*

America," Journal of Ethnic Studies 1:1 (spring 1973): p. 71. Reprinted in idem., *The Asian in North America* (Santa Barbara, Calif.: American Bibliographic Center, Clio Press, 1977), pp. 261–62.

41.   Vidich and Lyman, *American Sociology*, pp. 195–248; and Lyman, *Civilization*, pp. 127–59.

42.   Robert E. Park, "The Nature of Race Relations," in *Race Relations and the Race Problem: A Symposium on a Growing National Problem with Special Reference to the South*, ed. Edgar T. Thompson (Durham, N.C.: Duke University Press, 1939), p. 45.

43.   Friedrich Engels, "Letter to Friedrich Adolph Sorge, December 2, 1893," in *Marx and Engels: Basic Writings on Politics and Philosophy*, ed. Lewis S. Feuer (Garden City, N.Y.: Doubleday-Anchor, 1959), p. 458.

44.   Quoted in English translation of Gustav Ratzenhofer *Wesen und Zweck der Politik*, in Albion W. Small, *General Sociology: An Exposition of the Main Developments in Sociological Theory from Spencer to Ratzenhofer* (Chicago: University of Chicago Press, 1905; reprint, New York: Arno Press, 1974), p. 256.

45.   Harold J. Abramson, "Assimilation and Pluralism," *Harvard Encyclopedia of American Ethnic Groups*, ed. Stephen Thernstrom (Cambridge, Mass.: Belknap Press of Harvard University Press, 1980), pp. 156–60.

46.   Horace Kallen, *Culture and Democracy: Studies in the Group Psychology of the American Peoples* (New York: Boni and Liveright, 1924; reprint, New York: Arno Press and *New York Times*, 1970).

47.   See "An Interview with Stanford M. Lyman," in Lyman, *The Asian in North America*, pp. 277–91, esp. pp. 290–91.

48.   See Stanford M. Lyman, "Race Relations as Social Process: Sociology's Resistance to a Civil Rights Orientation," in *Race in America: The Struggle for Equality*, ed. Herbert Hill and James E. Jones Jr. (Madison: University of Wisconsin Press, 1993), pp. 370–401.

49.   Margaret Mary Wood, *The Stranger: A Study in Social Relationships* (New York: AMS Press, 1969), p. 266.

50.   See works cited in note 36 *supra*.

51.   Laurel Richardson, "Postmodern Social Theory: Representational Practices," *Sociological Theory* 9:2 (fall 1991): pp. 173–79.

Chapter 11: Animal Faith, Puritanism, and the Schutz-Gurwitsch Debate

1.   Arthur J. Vidich and Stanford M. Lyman, *American Sociology: Worldly Rejections of Religion and Their Directions* (New Haven, Conn.: Yale University Press, 1985.)

2.   Josiah Royce, *The Philosophy of Loyalty* (New York: Macmillan, 1916).

3.   Alfred Schutz and Aron Gurwitsch, *Philosophers in Exile: The Correspondence of Alfred Schutz and Aron Gurwitsch, 1939–1959*, trans. J. Claude Evans, ed. Richard Grathof (Bloomington: Indiana University Press, 1989).

4.   Cf. Stanford M. Lyman and Marvin. B. Scott, *A Sociology of the Absurd*, 2nd ed. (Dix Hills, N.Y.: General Hall, 1989).

5.   William Graham Sumner, *Folkways: A Study of the Sociological Importance of*

Usages, Manners, Customs, Mores and Morals (Boston: Ginn and Co., 1949 [1906]).

6.   Robert E. Park, *Race and Culture, The Collected Papers of Robert Ezra Park,* vol. 1, ed. Everett C. Hughes, (Glencoe, Ill.: The Free Press, 1950).

7.   See three essays by Robert. E. Park, "A King in Business: Leopold II of Belgium, Autocrat of the Congo and International Broker," *Everybody's Magazine* 15 (November 1906): pp. 624–33; "The Terrible Story of the Congo," *Everybody's Magazine* 15 (December 1906): pp. 763–72; "The Blood Money of the Congo," *Everybody's Magazine* 16 (January 1907): pp. 60–70.

8.   Robert E. Park, "Community Organization and Juvenile Delinquency," in Robert E. Park, Ernest. W. Burgess, and Roderick D. McKenzie, eds., *The City* (Chicago: University of Chicago Press, 1967 [1925]), pp. 108–9.

9.   Georg Simmel, *Schopenhauer and Nietzsche,* trans. Helmut Loiskandl, Deena Weinstein, and Michael Weinstein, (Amherst: University of Massachusetts Press, 1986), p. 181.

10.   George Herbert Mead, "The Philosophies of Royce, James and Dewey in Their American Setting," in Andrew J. Reck, ed., *Mead: Selected Writings* (Indianapolis, Ind.: Bobbs-Merrill, 1964), pp. 371–91.

11.   See Arthur J. Vidich and Stanford M. Lyman, "State, Ethics and Public Morality in American Sociological Thought," in Mark L. Wardell and Stephen P. Turner, eds., *Sociological Theory in Transition* (Boston: Allen and Unwin, 1986), pp. 44–56.

12.   Herbert Blumer, *Symbolic Interactionism: Perspective and Method* (Englewood Cliffs, N.J.: Prentice-Hall, 1969).

13.   Herbert Blumer, "George Herbert Mead," in Buford Rhea, ed., *The Future of the Sociological Classics* (London: George Allen and Unwin, 1981), pp. 136–69.

14.   See Stanford M. Lyman, and Arthur J. Vidich, *Social Order and the Public Philosophy: An Analysis and Interpretation of the Work of Herbert Blumer* (Fayetteville: University of Arkansas Press, 1988).

15.   See Stanford M. Lyman, *Civilization: Contents, Discontents, Malcontents and Other Essays in Social Theory* (Fayetteville: University of Arkansas Press, 1990).

16.   Talcott Parsons, *The Social System* (Glencoe: Free Press, 1951), pp. 59–61, 81–88, 103–12, 129–32, 176–90, 216–37, 262–69, 389–95, 416–27.

17.   See Stanford M. Lyman, *The Seven Deadly Sins: Society and Evil,* rev. ed. (Dix Hills, N.Y.: General Hall, 1989), pp. 277–98.

18.   See Stanford. M. Lyman, foreword to *The Existential Self in Society,* J. A. Kotarba and A. Fontana, eds. (Chicago: University of Chicago Press, 1984), pp. vii–xii.

19.   Erving Goffman, *Strategic Interaction* (Philadelphia: University of Pennsylvania Press, 1969).

20.   Erving Goffman, *The Presentation of Self in Everyday Life* (Garden City, N.Y.: Doubleday-Anchor, 1959).

21.   Erving Goffman, "Fun in Games," in idem, *Encounters: Two Studies in the Sociology of Interaction* (Indianapolis, Ind.: Bobbs-Merrill, 1961), pp. 17–84.

22.   Harold Garfinkel, "Studies of the Routine Grounds of Everyday Activities," David Sudnow, ed., *Studies in Social Interaction* (New York: Free Press, 1972), pp. 1–30.

23.   Alfred Schutz, *The Phenomenology of the Social World,* trans. George Walsh and Frederick Lehnert (Evanston, Ill.: Northwestern University Press, 1967), pp. 80–81.

24.   Alfred Schutz, "Studies in Social Theory," in Arvid Broderson, ed., *Collected*

Papers, vol. 2 (The Hague, Netherlands: Martinus Nijhoff, 1964), pp. 64–91 *et passim.*

25.   See the discussion of liminality and related concepts in several works by Victor Turner, *The Forest of Symbols: Aspects of Ndembu Ritual* (Ithaca, N.Y.: Cornell University Press, 1977), pp. 93–110; *The Ritual Process: Structure and Anti-Structure* (Ithaca, N.Y.: Cornell University Press, 1974), pp. 94–130; *Dramas, Fields, and Metaphors: Symbolic Action in Human Society* (Ithaca, N.Y.: Cornell University Press), pp. 166–271; Victor Turner and Elizabeth Turner, *Image and Pilgrimage in Christian Culture: Anthropological Perspectives* (New York: Columbia University Press, 1978), pp. 1–39, 249–50.

26.   See Aron Gurwitsch, *The Field of Consciousness* (Pittsburgh: Duquesne University Press, 1964), pp. 404–13; *Studies in Phenomenology and Psychology* (Evanston, Ill: Northwestern University Press, 1966), pp. 287–331, 390–96; *Human Encounters in the Social World* (Pittsburgh: Duquesne University Press, 1979), pp. 1–39, 50–57, 104–56; Greathoff, *Philosophers in Exile,* pp. 134–70; Alfred Schutz, "The Problem of Social Reality" in Maurice Natanson, ed., *Collected Papers,* vol. 1. (The Hague, Netherlands: Martinus Nijhoff, 1962), pp. 3–47, 61–62, 140–49, 312–29.

27.   Harold Garfinkel, *Studies in Ethnomethodology* (Englewood Cliffs, N.J.: Prentice-Hall, 1967);and Erving Goffman, *Frame Analysis: An Essay on the Organization of Experience* (New York: Harper Colophon, 1974), pp. 3–6, 201–46, 300–495.

28.   Alfred Schutz, "Studies in Phenomenological Philosophy," in I. Schutz, ed., *Collected Papers,* vol. 3 (The Hague, Netherlands: Martinus Nijhoff, 1966), pp. 116–32;Alfred Schutz and Thomas Luckmann, *The Structures of the Life-World,* trans. Richard M. Zaner and H. Tristram Engelhardt Jr. (Evanston, Ill.: Northwestern University Press,1973).

29.   W. I. Thomas, "Introductory," in *Source Book for Social Origins,* 6th ed. (Boston: Richard G. Badger, 1909), pp. 13–26.

30.   Frederick J. Teggart, *Theory and Processes of History* (Berkeley: University of California Press, 1941), pp. 149–50, 196–97, 272–96, 307–12.

31.   Lyman and Scott, *A Sociology of the Absurd.*

Chapter 12: The Drama in the Routine

1.   See, e.g., Marlis Buchmann, *The Script of Life in Modern Society: Entry into Adulthood in a Changing World* (Chicago: University of Chicago Press, 1989).

2.   This debt has been acknowledged in two recent publications: Joseph R. Gusfield, ed., *Kenneth Burke on Symbols and Society* (Chicago: University of Chicago Press, 1989); and Herbert W. Simons and Trevor Melia, eds., *The Legacy of Kenneth Burke* (Madison: University of Wisconsin Press, 1989).

3.   Elizabeth Burns, *Theatricality: A Study of Convention in the Theatre and in Social Life* (London: Longman, 1972).

4.   The phrase "drama in the routine" was introduced in Stanford M. Lyman, "Cherished Values and Civil Rights," *The Crisis: A Record of the Darker Races* 71 (December 1964): pp. 645–54, 695.

5.   W. I. Thomas, "Introductory" in idem, *Source Book for Social Origins: Ethnological Materials, Psychological Standpoint, Classified and Annotated Bibliographies for the Interpretation of Savage Societies,* 6th edition (Boston: Richard G. Badger, 1909), pp. 3–28.

6.   Ibid., p. 21.

7.   See the following works of Norbert Elias, *The Civilizing Process: The History of Manners,* trans. Edmund Jephcott (New York: Urizen Books, 1978); *Power and Civility: The Civilizing Process,* vol. 2, trans. Edmund Jephcott (New York: Pantheon Books, 1982); *The Court Society,* trans. Edmund Jephcott (New York: Pantheon Books, 1983); *Involvement and Detachment,* trans. Edmund Jephcott (New York: Basil Blackwell, 1987); *What Is Sociology?,* trans. Stephen Mennell and Grace Morrissey (New York: Columbia University Press, 1978), esp. pp. 134–74; *The Loneliness of the Dying,* trans. Edmund Jephcott (New York: Basil Blackwell, 1985); and Norbert Elias and Eric Dunning, *Quest for Excitement: Sport and Leisure in the Civilizing Process* (New York: Basil Blackwell, 1986). See also Stephen Mennell, *Norbert Elias: Civilization and the Human Self-image* (New York: Basil Blackwell, 1989), pp. 29–112.

8.   Erving Goffman, *Relations in Public: Microstudies of the Public Order* (New York: Basic Books, 1971), pp. 188–237.

9.   Cf. Stanford M. Lyman, "Civilization: Contents, Discontents, Malcontents," a review essay of Erving Goffman, *Relations in Public: Microstudies of the Public Order, Contemporary Sociology* 2:4 (July 1973): pp. 360–66.

10.   See esp. W. I. Thomas and Dorothy Swaine Thomas, *The Child in America: Behavior Problems and Programs* (New York: Alfred A. Knopf, 1928), pp. esp. 505–76; W. I. Thomas, *Primitive Behavior: An Introduction to the Social Sciences* (New York: McGraw-Hill, 1937), pp. esp. 1–48, 610–747; Edmund H. Volkhart, ed., *Social Behavior and Personality: Contributions of W. I. Thomas to Theory and Social Research* (New York: Social Science Research Council, 1951), esp. pp. 215–88; Morris Janowitz, ed., *W. I. Thomas on Social Organization and Social Personality* (Chicago: University of Chicago Press, 1966), pp. 37–56, 231–56.

11.   Frederick J. Teggart, *The Theory and Processes of History* (Berkeley: University of California Press, 1941).

12.   Victor Turner, *Dramas, Fields, and Metaphors: Symbolic Action in Human Society* (Ithaca, N.Y.: Cornell University Press, 1974).

13.   Konrad Lorenz, "Habit, Ritual, and Magic," trans. Marjorie Kenwilson, in *Ritual, Play, and Performance: Readings in the Social Sciences/Theatre,* ed. Richard Schechner and Mady Schuman (New York: Seabury Press, 1976), pp. 18–34.

14.   Ibid., p. 30.

15.   W. I. Thomas, *Primtive Behavior,* p. 1.

16.   Florian Znaniecki, *Social Actions* (New York: Farrar and Rinehart, 1936), p. 383.

17.   See Stanford M. Lyman and Marvin B. Scott, *A Sociology of the Absurd,* 2d ed. (Dix Hills, New York: General Hall, 1989), pp. 69–89.

18.   Erving Goffman, *Interaction Ritual: Essays in Face-to-Face Behavior* (Chicago: Aldine Publishing Co., 1967), p. 77.

19.   Ibid.

20.   Max Weber, "The Protestant Sects and the Spirit of Capitalism," in *From Max Weber: Essays in Sociology,* trans. and ed. H. H. Gerth and C. Wright Mills (New York: Oxford University Press, 1946), pp. 302–22.

21.   Znaniecki, *Social Actions,* p. 384.

22.   Ibid.

23.   Thomas, *Source Book for Social Origins,* pp. 16–19.

24.   Frederick J. Teggart, *Theory of History* (New Haven, Conn.: Yale University Press, 1925), pp. 71–223.

25.   Turner, *Dramas, Fields, and Metaphors,* p. 13.

26.   Dick Howard, *Defining the Political* (Minneapolis: University of Minnesota Press, 1989), p. 87.

27.   Erving Goffman, *Frame Analysis: An Essay on the Organization of Experience* (New York: Harper Colophon, 1974), pp. 300–77; *Forms of Talk* (Philadelphia: University of Pennsylvania Press, 1981), pp. 1–123.

28.   Alfred Schutz, *Collected Papers,* vol. 3, *Studies in Phenomenological Philosophy,* ed. I. Schutz (The Hague, Netherlands: Martinus Nijhoff, 1966), pp. 104–6, 116–32.

29.   Harold Garfinkel, *Studies in Ethnomethodology* (Englewood Cliffs, N.J.: Prentice-Hall, 1967).

30.   Turner, *Dramas, Fields, and Metapors,* pp. 231–70.

31.   Elizabeth Burns, review of *The Drama of Social Reality* by Stanford M. Lyman and Marvin B. Scott, in *Contemporary Sociology* 7 (March 1978): p. 158.

32.   Alfred Schutz, "The Problem of Transcendental Intersubjectivity in Husserl," in his *Collected Papers* vol. 3, p. 81.

33.   Herbert Blumer, "The Concept of Mass Society," in Stanford M. Lyman and Arthur J. Vidich, *Social Order and the Public Philosophy: An Analysis and Interpretation of the Work of Herbert Blumer* (Fayetteville: University of Arkansas Press, 1988), p. 341.

34.   Ibid., p. 343.

INDEX

AEB5157

DATE DUE

DEC - 8 1997			
DEC 1 8 2000			

DEMCO 13829810